CW00822085

Choreomania

Oxford Studies in Dance Theory

MARK FRANKO, Series Editor

CHOREOMANIA

Dance and Disorder

KÉLINA GOTMAN

OXFORD
UNIVERSITY PRESS

OXFORD
UNIVERSITY PRESS

Oxford University Press is a department of the University of Oxford. It furthers
the University's objective of excellence in research, scholarship, and education
by publishing worldwide. Oxford is a registered trade mark of Oxford University
Press in the UK and certain other countries.

Published in the United States of America by Oxford University Press
198 Madison Avenue, New York, NY 10016, United States of America.

© Oxford University Press 2018

All rights reserved. No part of this publication may be reproduced, stored in
a retrieval system, or transmitted, in any form or by any means, without the
prior permission in writing of Oxford University Press, or as expressly permitted
by law, by license, or under terms agreed with the appropriate reproduction
rights organization. Inquiries concerning reproduction outside the scope of the
above should be sent to the Rights Department, Oxford University Press, at the
address above.

You must not circulate this work in any other form
and you must impose this same condition on any acquirer.

Library of Congress Cataloging-in-Publication Data
Names: Gotman, Kélina, author.
Title: Choreomania : dance and disorder / Kélina Gotman.
Description: New York : Oxford University Press, [2018] |
Series: Oxford studies in dance theory |
Includes bibliographical references and index.
Identifiers: LCCN 2017015372 | ISBN 9780190840426 (pbk. : alk. paper) |
ISBN 9780190840419 (cloth : alk. paper) | ISBN 9780190840457 (oxford scholarship online)
Subjects: LCSH: Choreography—Social aspects. | Choreography—History. |
Dance—Philosophy.
Classification: LCC GV1782.5 .G68 2018 |
DDC 792.8/2—dc23
LC record available at https://lccn.loc.gov/2017015372

1 3 5 7 9 8 6 4 2

Paperback printed by WebCom, Inc., Canada
Hardback printed by Bridgeport National Bindery, Inc., United States of America

For Karen Ray

In the universality of the Western *ratio*, there is this division which is the Orient: the Orient, thought of as the origin, dreamt of as the vertiginous point from which nostalgia and promises of return are born, the Orient offered to the colonising reason of the Occident, but indefinitely inaccessible, for it always remains the limit: the night of the beginning, in which the Occident was formed, but in which it traced a dividing line, the Orient is for the Occident everything that it is not, while remaining the place in which its primitive truth must be sought. What is required is a history of this great divide, all along this Occidental becoming, following it in its continuity and its exchanges, while also allowing it to appear in its tragic hieratism.

Michel Foucault, *History of Madness* (1961)

And those who were seen dancing were thought to be insane by those who could not hear the music.

Friedrich Nietzsche, *Thus Spoke Zarathustra* (1883–1892)

Contents

List of Illustrations

Series Editor Foreword

KÉLINA GOTMAN'S book *Choreomania* is an interdisciplinary, or what the author terms 'a-disciplinary', investigation of dancing manias. It takes us on a journey through the vast and uncharted terrain of dance and madness, a fantastical topography that is rooted in the European imaginary of the nineteenth century. Heir to the groundbreaking works on movement, pathology, and medical discourse— Joseph R. Roach's *The Player's Passion* (1993) and Felicia McCarren's *Dance Pathologies* (1998)— Gotman's book can appear by contrast elusive in that it does not refer to particular dance works or schools of movement. In this sense, Michel Foucault's *Madness and Civilization* is its touchstone.

Gotman's project is to depart from the circumscribed realm of stage dance to engage with collective or 'popular' dancing as perceived by the medical gaze as well as colonialist attempts to suppress dances that apparently pose the threat of contagion and loss of social control. In order to assert command over such (possibly imagined) phenomena, the discourses in question must first also produce it. In this respect, the influence of Foucault on Gotman's work extends beyond his *Madness and Civilization* to encompass his less understood *Archaeology of Knowledge*. Let us recall his definition of discourse in that book: 'It is, from beginning to end, historical—a fragment of history, a unity and discontinuity in history itself'.[1] Gotman describes these unities and discontinuities as 'choreozones'. The evidence for 'choreozones' is disseminated in the texts of a wide range of disciplines from medicine and anthropology to history and biology. Gotman adds to this area a colonialist dimension, thus pairing her patron saint Michel Foucault with Edward Said.

---

[1] Michel Foucault, *The Archaeology of Knowledge and the Discourse on Language*, trans. A. M. Sheridan Smith (New York: Pantheon Books, 1972), 117.

A return to historical methodologies and even subjects is an acknowledgement that areas between the early modern and the long nineteenth century are essential to the analysis of contemporaneity. Amidst the archival turn trending in dance scholarship today, the particular originality and theoretical cachet of *Choreomania* is its focus on dance history itself as an archaeology. As the question of the archive in relation to embodied memory is being hotly debated in dance and performance studies, Gotman's book suggests the emergence of a new historical turn in contemporary dance scholarship.

Mark Franko
Series Editor

Preface

A NUMBER of significant events have transpired during the writing of this book over the past decade. Most recently and saliently, the refugee crisis in Europe, resulting from war in Syria and neighbouring countries, displacing millions, has forced nations to reckon with the porosity of their borders and questions of priority and privilege. Uprisings in the Arab world, as well as in Greece, London, and New York, have suggested waves of change and an upsurge of popular opinion against the corporate classes; we have only just begun to see the effects of this spirit of resistance on economic and government strategies. In universities, the overwhelming dominance of science, technology, engineering, and mathematics (STEM) subjects in structures of funding and reward, over the increasingly beleaguered and rapidly atrophying arts and humanities disciplines, has provoked much soul-searching among those who are still tied to the idea that the arts matter more than as instruments of public impact. All of these issues find a place in the fissures of this book, which

while dealing with nineteenth-century fantasies of medieval and colonial outbreaks of dancing and song, uncovers a whole history of thinking about the forms—the choreographies—of unrest. In particular, this book rethinks the modern formation of a nineteenth-century fantasy, 'choreomania', which emerged across scientific disciplines to designate the spontaneous and uncontrolled movements of crowds and the jerky and seemingly inelegant movements of bodies subject to fits and starts. In the concatenation of these misfirings and misformations of bodies and body politics, a whole series of prejudices against spontaneity unfolds, suggesting widespread anxieties about impulsiveness and irregularity—as well as their grotesque spectacularization—which I argue subtend contemporary biopolitical life.

At the same time, this book argues that dance as a discipline cannot be taken separately from the history of science and of the social sciences; that, on the contrary, ideas about 'dance' suffuse the modern construction of scientific disciplines. Dance, in the literature this book describes, serves discursively as the site where bodies become public, infecting audiences, including with erratic and spontaneous gestures. The 'dancing disease', choreomania, stands for this complex of medicalized, anthropologized ideas about a disorderly social body that jerks uncontrollably and in doing so unpredictably affects those around it. The flip side to this story is a story of control, the one Michel Foucault (1926–1984) has written, according to which the nineteenth century becomes a time of increasing regimentation. This book, while contributing to Foucault's discursive history—his genealogy—of the nineteenth-century scientific and political institution of madness as a site of sequestration and constraint, simultaneously opens this story out to new lines of thought around dance and the role that ideas about disorderly dance play in this process of disciplinarization. I hope this history of disciplines—what I call this *choreography*, to denote the movements and travels, the translations, of ideas across discursive grounds—will help reconfigure the 'two cultures' divide that we appear to be still entrenched in today, in spite of increasing efforts towards the institutionalization of interdisciplinarity. My aim, then, with this book is to write a history of ideas about dance, and in doing so to carve out a space of thinking about the way jaggedly moving bodies and crowds have come to signal the best and worst of modern biopolitics, construed in the broadest sense as a biopolitics of *movement*.

So is movement *good*? This book argues that movement in itself does not constitute a good or a bad thing; it is not more desirable than stillness, or more to be criticized for epitomizing the regimes of stress, hyperproductivity, overperformance—and precarity—that have led contemporary critics, including Peter Sloterdijk and Paul Virilio, to argue that speed (and uprootedness) are the characteristic traits of modern biopolitical life. Yet this book does wrestle with the relationship between movement and freedom; in particular, as I have come increasingly to understand in the development of the argument this book outlines, freedom to move signals a real privilege that reverberates across notions of bodiliness, dance, and the discourses surrounding their putative disorders. Constraints on movement—as in the current refugee crisis—signal constraints on political power and agency, on individuals' capacity to shift their standpoints and allegiances, to find more hospitable terrains. Being able to move means being able to reaggregate, to realign. Being able to move in socially unaccepted ways—here, erratically, jaggedly—similarly signals a way of bodily being that disrupts choreographies that implicitly enable the smooth and efficient functioning of social and political life. Choreic bodies that fit, startle, and jump interrupt the invisibility of bodily being in the everyday: the placid march of the metro, the line at the bus stop. *Movement* then can be understood as the capacity to move: the freedom to be still or to exercise a wider range of motions and displacements than is normally, normatively allowed. In that sense, yes, *movement* is 'good': it makes way for possibility. What we do with that possibility is an open question.

Acknowledgements

THIS BOOK, about disorderly dancing—and the language with which it has been imagined in colonial, medical, ethnographic, and other archives—has emerged across institutions, and I have many individuals to thank for travelling this journey with me. At Columbia University, Arnold Aronson, Julie Stone Peters, and Martin Puchner championed what seemed an impossible project and allowed me the freedom to roam. Bruce Robbins and Maura Spiegel received it graciously at the height of summer. Colleagues at King's College London have offered support and collegiality in various ways: thanks especially to my department chairs Mark Turner, Jo McDonagh, and Richard Kirkland, as well as to Seb Franklin, Paul Gilroy, Brian Hurwitz, Ananya Jahanara Kabir, Alan Read, Theron Schmidt, and Lara Shalson. I am particularly grateful to Richard and the School of Arts and Humanities at King's for essential research support in the final stages.

Among the many colleagues, mentors, students, and friends who have nourished this work with collegiality, conversation, and critique, published bits in progress, and offered injections of warmth, thank you especially to Michael Allan, Johannes Birringer, Melissa Blanco Borelli, Peter Boenish, Amanda Card, Broderick Chow, Nicola Conibere, Laura Cull, Thomas F. DeFrantz, Kate Elswit, Rachel Fensham, Patrick ffrench, Clare Finburgh, Tony Fisher, Avishek Ganguly, Yelena Gluzman, Sam Godin, Huw Hallam, Alvan Ikoku, Amelia Jones, Michael Jonik, Eve Katsouraki, Joe Kelleher, Anjuli Raza Kolb, Alvin Eng Hui Lim, Dejan Lukić, Jon McKenzie, Penny Newell, Clare Parfitt-Brown, Ella Parry-Davies, VK Preston, Noémie Solomon, Arabella Stanger, Shilarna Stokes, Sarah Whatley, Suzy Willson, and Alison Wood. It is often, in times of doubt, for our students that we write. I owe thanks to all those who have asked the hardest questions and followed their own improbable strands. Among the many mentors who have modelled ways of asking and offered vectors of thought, special thanks are due to Gil Anidjar, Étienne Balibar, Sylvère Lotringer, Chantal

Pontbriand, Michael Taussig, and, long ago, Ruth Harris and Miri Rubin. Unbeknownst to her, Karen Ray at Marianopolis College in Montreal set me going on dance manias in the margins of an essay I wrote for her on the Black Death, sparking the fantasy of this book. Frederick Andermann shared thoughts on the history of neurology in early stages, Lesley Sharp on Madagascar. Karl Steel and Daniel Hadas both lent a hand with the stickiest bits of Latin. For impeccable help with German, thanks to Anna Gritsch and to Matia Gotman. Ellen MacCallum helped me see that my work is all, in the end, steeped in translation.

A visiting fellowship at the Society for the Humanities at Cornell University coincided with the last stages of writing and research; I am grateful to Timothy Murray and all the fellows for their warm welcome. An Audrey and William H. Helfand fellowship at the New York Academy of Medicine enabled me to pursue vital research into the tarantella; thank you to Arlene Shaner at the NYAM Library for supporting this work from early on. Among the many librarians who have enabled this research, thanks are also due to Eleanor Fitzpatrick at the Philip Richardson Library, Royal Academy of Dance; Arlene Yu at the Dance Collection, Jerome Robbins Dance Division, New York Public Library for the Performing Arts; Mary Frances Morrow, Rodney A. Ross, and Jill Abraham at the National Archives and Records Administration, Library of Congress; Diane Richardson at the Oskar Diethelm Library, Institute for the History of Psychiatry, Cornell Weill Medical Center and New York Presbyterian Hospital; Stephen Novak at the Columbia University Health Sciences Special Collections Library; and Chris Lyons at the Osler Library for the History of Medicine, McGill University. Many thanks to all staff at the Rare Books and Music Reading Room at the British Library; the Theatre and Performance Collections, Victoria and Albert Museum; the Special Collections Reading Room, School of Oriental and African Studies, University of London; the Warburg Institute; the New York Public Library; and the Union Theological Seminary in New York.

I have shared portions of this work in progress at various seminars, conferences, and talks over the years and am grateful to all the colleagues and students who have extended a hand and indulged in the gift of conversation, including at the Society for Dance History Scholars / Congress on Research in Dance conference in Athens; the PoP Moves seedbed on dancing methodologies; the Royal Central School of Speech and Drama 'Practice (. . .) Research' conference; the Contemporary Arts Research Seminar and Chichester Festival Theatre Study Day, University of Chichester; the Research Seminar on the Theory, Practice and History of Performance at Goldsmiths, University of London; the Brunel Theatre Research Seminar Series and Artaud Forum, Brunel University; the London Theatre Seminar; the inaugural Performance Philosophy Research Seminar on 'dance(-theatre) and philosophy' and the first Performance Philosophy conference, both University of Surrey; various Theatre and Performance Research Association events at Queen Mary, University of London; Royal Holloway, University of London and King's College London; the Anglo-American Theatre, Performance and Philosophy conference at the Sorbonne; the Theatre Studies Seminar at the National University of Singapore; the Cornell Society for the Humanities; the University of Pennsylvania Graduate Humanities Forum; the Richardson History of Psychiatry Research Seminar at the Institute for the History of Psychiatry, Weill Cornell Medical College and New York Presbyterian Hospital; and the first International Congress on Epilepsy, Brain and Mind in Prague.

At Oxford University Press, Norm Hirschy and Lauralee Yeary have been keen and supportive allies. Thank you to Richa Jobin for seeing this seamlessly through production; and to Martha Ramsey for copyediting. Mark Franko's enthusiasm for the work gave me the courage to keep writing, the certainty of an audience. I am grateful to him for his trust and his vision. My anonymous reviewers provided pointed and generous feedback and suggestions for improvement without which this work would be incomparably poorer; thank you. John Doddy has offered meticulous research support.

Finally, I could not have done this work without the support of my family, who have taught me to live across languages and national lines. My parents in particular have modelled curiosity and perseverance, shown me science and art. Throughout so much of the writing, Steve Potter remained my closest critic and most trusted ear, sharing in this work with the patience of a friend and the clarity of a true reader. Dinah Gypsy has kept me laughing and awake at every conceivable hour. Thank you for your dancing and drawing, your painting and stories, your play.

Choreomania

Introduction

Choreomania, Another Orientalism

History is the concrete body of becoming; with its moments of intensity, its lapses, its extended periods of feverish agitation, its fainting spells. . . .

—Michel Foucault, 'Nietzsche, Genealogy, History' (1971)

CHOREA, CHOREOMANIA: CONCEPTS IN MOTION

This book aims to intervene into ways we think about dance; and ways we imagine dance to be embedded into the fabric of scientific ideas. Indebted to the thinking of Foucault, and to some of Foucault's successors in the postcolonial and dance and performance studies fields, notably Edward W. Said (1935–2003), this book traces a *discursive history* of ideas about dance—specifically, the dancing disease—in nineteenth- and early twentieth-century colonial medical circles. Discursive history, often likened to 'historical epistemology'—a term employed to denote histories of previous ways of knowing—takes as its primary object the way things are talked about in their time: the discourses, languages, and methods of circulation by which ideas have come to take shape and spread.[1] Importantly for the story I tell here, discursive histories do not always heed disciplinary boundaries; instead, histories of ways of thinking often take shape on interdisciplinary terrain. In the case of the

---

1. 'Historical epistemology', a term that came into vogue in the Anglo-American history of sciences in the 1990s in the wake of historian and philosopher Lorraine Daston's recuperation of the writings of Gaston Bachelard (1884–1962), Georges Canguilhem (1904–1995), Foucault, and others on the history and philosophy of ideas, suggests that knowledge can only be understood in terms of its history. Any inquiry into a way of thinking—what Foucault calls a 'discursive formation' (or discourse)—has to take into account its so-called historical context. But the context does not just frame the idea; the context suffuses, shapes, and is shaped by the idea—and adjacent ideas—in turn. Ideas and their histories are mutually imbricated fields of analysis. Yves Gingras offers a useful genealogy of the term 'historical epistemology', highlighting the spurious way it has entered the Anglo-American tradition as novelty. Yves Gingras, 'Naming without Necessity: On the Genealogy and Uses of the Label "Historical Epistemology,"' *CIRST—Note de recherche 2010-01* (January 2010), http://www.chss.uqam.ca/Portals/0/docs/articles/2010-01.pdf (last accessed 7 June 2017). For ease of navigation, every effort has been made to provide author dates where possible (except in the case of authors still living). Where it has not been possible to establish these, author names have simply been left undated.

'dancing disease', this history—what I will later refer to as a 'genealogy', after Foucault, and further, given its particularly *motional* quality, as 'choreography'—reconfigures the way we understand modern disciplines taking shape.

This approach to the history of ideas about dance and discipline is further informed by an understanding of Foucault's work articulated by his long-time friend and interlocutor, philosopher Gilles Deleuze (1925–1995). Following Deleuze's reading of Foucault's method, I argue that the formation of modern ideas about choreomania is rhizomatic: it moves, multiplies, and branches out in non-linear ways. But choreomania's genealogy may also be read according to what Deleuze describes of Foucault's method as 'topology', a description of the spaces in and through which concepts may be imagined to form. In Deleuze's account of Foucault's work, topologies emerge through both linguistic and material processes. There are thus two types of space (two sorts of topology). First is *associated space* (*espace associé*), which is characterized by meeting and cross-pollination. This sort of space is traversed by vectors or lines—trajectories—of thinking and writing, discursive 'enunciations' (phrases, words) that may become mutually entangled.[2] These entanglements may cluster, knot, and congeal into intellectual nodes, what I call discursive *zones of intensity*: conceptual formations that gather others, stiffen, and may appear to settle, but are always on the move. A discursive zone of intensity is a complex of ideas and events, a temporary holding zone in which concepts in formation overlap with one another, associating with adjacent concepts. When the zone of intensity crystallizes around movement, dance, and ideas describing the choreographic motion of bodies and bodies of thought, I call this a *choreozone*, a term that is itself on the move throughout this book. Choreozones, as moving clusters of ideas about motion, aesthetically and politically, denote a mobilizational force—a capacity continually to reassemble and transform.

Zones of intensity and choreozones further respond to Foucault's 'topological' method in what Deleuze, second, calls Foucault's notion of *correlative space*. Correlative space is a topology according to which discursive enunciations encounter material subjects and objects, as well as other concepts.[3] Correlative spaces are institutional, historical, and material. In this book, the institutional and discursive spaces of colonial medicine, psychiatry, sociology, anthropology, and related fields serve as topologies in and through which the modern idea of choreomania evolved. Disciplines in this sense may also be understood as zones of intensity, temporary clusterings of ideas, attitudes, and beliefs, which may become rigidified and canonized through institutional means. But they are also always on the move. This book in this sense describes not only a set of topologies, but what I further call the choreotopology of the dancing disease, its journey through discursive and institutional spaces, and the choreography—the movement—of this choreotopology as it clusters and transforms, revealing a sea of disciplinary changes on the way.

This book argues that fantasies of unwieldy and disruptive motion—likened to dance—saturated modern medical writing about dancing crowds; and that these ideas in turn reveal modern ways of thinking about the past as unruly and dance-like. Further at stake, then, in this book, is the history of ideas about dancing bodies in public space, and the way public space itself is imagined in the nineteenth and early twentieth centuries to be constantly threatened by a resurgence of dancing motions. This book argues that modern ideas about the dancing disease as an ancient frenzy re-emerging in present times permeate contemporary notions of the body politic: the way bodies move *in* and have the capacity to *move* public space. So whereas choreography, Susan Leigh Foster points out, 'began its life as the act of reconciling movement, place, and printed symbol', the notion of 'choreography' I work with suggests that 'printed symbol' is itself subject to movement; that place is inscribed in a bodily *trajectory*; that the history of thought is itself choreographic. Choreography then is not merely '"the art of dancing"' (the *Oxford English Dictionary* definition, as Foster points out); nor is it, more anciently, '"the art of writing dances on paper"'—nor is it even, in Foster's more expansive definition, 'a plan or orchestration of bodies in motion' (whether of office workers, troops, or traffic lights).[4] It is a manner of articulating a concept and practice of—and in—motion; of irritating the border between these; irritating the very notion of

---

2. Gilles Deleuze, *Foucault* (Paris: Les éditions de minuit, 2004), 16. All translations mine unless otherwise indicated.

3. Deleuze, *Foucault*, 16.

4. Susan Leigh Foster, *Choreographing Empathy: Kinesthesia in Performance* (London: Routledge, 2011), 15–17.

border. Choreography renders motion (gestures, attitudes, gaits, intensities, trajectories) visible, intelligible, as form. At the same time it is the very motion of bodies—books, pens, people—carrying this form, translating and further transforming it. Choreography thus shows 'planned' and 'orchestrated' or, conversely, *un*planned and *non*-orchestrated (even untraced and unrepeatable) motion occasioning the event of embodied discursivization—we might say, the practical concept—of form; specifically, the intelligibilization of order and disorder. Disorder, I submit, is the practical concept against which order comes to light; it emerges as a moving figure of thought, in the choreographic labour of articulating scenes and events.

Choreography in the sense I propose thus suggests an act of articulation, one that negotiates a border zone between order and disorder, planned and unplanned motion. Choreography may be understood as an apparatus of articulation investigating the part movement plays in structuring how we see, talk about, or embody relationships between order and disorder, historically and aesthetically. In this sense, choreography takes place between language and archive, where the archive is embodied as well as written or notated; choreography passes between systems of meaning, serving as an act of translation, at once a reinterpretation and reinscription of prior forms, returning to and moving prior systems of order along. Choreography in this sense may further be understood as the art and science of highlighting, even disrupting, practices and concepts of orderliness; and of the disciplines—bodily, artistic, and scientific—that shape and entrench or query this partition. Choreography—as a practice and zone of articulation, a choreozone—thus moves; it performs a perpetual act of reorganization. As a manner of articulating ways of moving and vectors of thought, choreography is fundamentally historical and historiographical, always going somewhere and coming from somewhere, passing through, carrying a residue. As such, choreography constitutes a manner of seeing and writing a relationship in the present to a concept of motion from the past. To write—to do—choreography is, in what follows, to articulate shifting zones of resonance (and dissonance) arising between *moving* ways of figuring order and its distempers.

This does not have anything necessarily to do with concert dance forms, such as ballet or jazz or tap—and indeed this book will deal only very fleetingly with recognized dance genres. Rather, in what follows, choreography refers to a way of organizing bodies in a discursive field, that by which concepts and practices of organization are deployed and move across disciplinary as well as geopolitical terrains. As such, choreography arbiters bodily order, and the spaces through which this 'order' moves. Significantly it is the language, genealogy, and historiography—the moving archive—of that arbitration that I rest my attention on here.

In this regard, this book also resonates with recent writing in movement and mobility studies, arising as an interdisciplinary cluster to describe the circulation of bodies and ideas in an emergent 'global' modernity. And the book questions the disciplinary foundations of performance studies and dance as fields that, in different ways, imagine themselves to arise transhistorically and transnationally from out of post-disciplinary moments paradoxically reinscribed into the disciplinary structures of their respective markets. The symposium titled 'Undisciplining Dance' at the University of Auckland and the multisite 'Fluid States' iteration of Performance Studies international testify to a new vigorous movement in these fields to rethink disciplinarity and (transnational) geographic culture. But more work remains to be done to historicize these disciplinary imaginaries and rethink the foundations of dance and performance within a global, multidisciplinary context not separated from colonial or scientific methods; and importantly founded in the same 'anecdotal' methods cultural theorist Sean Cubitt argues serve as the humanities' and some social sciences' special purview, one that distinguishes these areas of inquiry, he argues, from science. This book not only shows dance and performance long embedded in scientific and social scientific methods and imaginaries, steeped in colonial administration (and violence) but also shows that these imaginaries were articulated with writing methods just as anecdotal, rhizomatic, and cross-disciplinary as current-day performance studies and dance. The discursive history this book traces, then, compels us to rethink the cultural trenches scientific, social scientific, humanities, and arts scholars continue to build up and imagine we are able occasionally radically to trespass. At its most militant, this book argues for a reconsideration of the way dance must continue to be construed across fields; and the way the history of fields themselves must always be taken globally and relationally.

In order to articulate the notion of choreomania as a concept, a few things have to be put in place. First, what is a concept? How do concepts relate to the reality they are meant to describe? In order to answer these questions, I engage with a broadly vitalist strand of thinking articulated among others by philosopher of time and memory Henri Bergson (1859–1941) and later by Deleuze and his long-time collaborator the anti-psychiatrist and activist Félix Guattari (1930–1992), all thinkers of the transformative quality of philosophy. For Bergson, a concept is like a photographic still: it temporarily captures an aspect of reality; but reality, Bergson argues, moves more fluidly and quickly than the concept does. Choreomania, as a concept, never quite captures the reality of the events it attempts to describe. My use of 'choreomania' is indicative: whereas writers I discuss in these pages employ the term from time to time, they also speak of *epidemic chorea, chorea major*, and *demonomania*. Medical language, like other languages, moves, and whereas the history of choreomania is a history of by and large medical ideas about disorderly corporeality—spuriously linked to 'chorea' as an individual movement disorder—the broader notion of choreomania I describe here stretches to the outer reaches of psychiatric and sociological history to encompass far less clearly medical movements. This mobile nexus of ideas, this choreozone, is thus what I call choreomania: a history of ideas about an epidemic disorder, a dancing plague, as it shifts across fields of knowledge and geographic terrains.

In order further to help articulate the choreomania concept, and the notion of a concept—as well as the history of concepts—as such, I draw from Deleuze and Guattari's final joint work, *What Is Philosophy?* (1994 [orig. French ed. 1991]), in which they argue that the task of philosophy is none other than to articulate concepts. But, they argue, following Bergson, concepts have to be understood as fluid and changeable. Concepts are never fixed. Rather, concepts shift and transform as they border other concepts. The history of a concept, Deleuze and Guattari write, 'zigzags'.[5] It passes through what they call 'planes of enunciation'—areas or zones of speech, thought, and expression. Intellectual history in this view follows what I further call a choreographic trajectory, an intellectual and material zigzag, a history of bodies

and ideas moving. The history of ideas is a history that moves in fits and starts.

Choreomania, I argue, is an idea that moved quite a lot. In fact, for much of the history of 'choreomania', this term did not appear; instead, a range of associated concepts designated erratic and abrupt, as well as highly infectious, forms of corporeality, all of which looked somewhat like dance: 'chorea minor', also referred to in neurology as 'chorea', 'Sydenham's chorea', or 'Huntington's chorea', as I show further in chapter 3, describes individual jerks and tics, occasionally hereditary, often among small children. 'Chorea major' was conceived in medical history as the epidemic form of this individual neurological disorder. It was often described as 'St. Vitus's dance', a term confusingly also used by medical writers to refer to the large movement of dancers taking to streets in the late medieval post-plague world (chapter 2). These same writers used 'choreomania' more or less interchangeably with 'chorea major' and 'St. Vitus's dance'. Further terms included the 'dancing mania' or 'dance mania', *Die Tanzwuth* in German, and the *dansomanie* in French.

What arrests my attention is the complex of ideas shifting through this cluster, this choreozone in the history of ideas about movement. I use the term 'choreomania' therefore as shorthand to designate a broad spectrum of medical, historical, and anthropological approaches to collective disorderly motility, while pointing to the unstable history the term reveals. What interests me is the way this cluster of ideas formed and spread, and how in its many strands, the idea of choreomania—as an epidemic, spasmodic dancing disorder—describes thickly entangled areas of thinking about history, modernity, and the body.

ANOTHER ORIENTALISM

'Choreomania', then, designates at once the object and its critique. In this regard, I have been deeply influenced by Said's work on Orientalism, as a way of thinking about a substantial strand of intellectual and academic life—a complex of disciplines, in the case of Orientalism—and the ideological undercurrents that discursive analysis can bring to light. For Said, Orientalism suggests the idea that the Orient is a singular entity that therefore can be studied. This idea

---

5. Gilles Deleuze and Félix Guattari, *Qu'est-ce que la philosophie?* (Paris: Les éditions de minuit, 1991), 23.

is fascinating and revealing, he argues: in order for the 'Orient' to be construed, as something that the 'West' might study (and dominate), a whole complex of disparate peoples and places have to be brought together and compared. Particularities are flattened; histories romanticized, hyperbolized, and rewritten. People as far away as Egypt, Iran, and China are discussed, in the Orientalist imaginary, as one. So, too, the viewer in Orientalist discourse is largely invisible: the West, for the Orientalist, is not problematic— only the Oriental subject merits an ambivalent shower of blame and praise.[6] Although the rise of whiteness studies in the last decades has attempted to remedy this blind spot in Western intellectual history (and in many respects this book can be seen to theorize whiteness as a fantasy articulating *obscure* others), Orientalist discourse continues to pervade foreign policy and popular opinion on a proliferation of border politics and contemporary wars.[7] My aim with the analysis of choreomania is to articulate ways in which a complex of ideas about awkward and irregular movements are similarly conflated in nineteenth- and early twentieth-century scientific and social scientific fields, from the history of epilepsy and psychiatry to religious convulsions, ecstasies, and 'jerks', and from late medieval St. John's Day dancing to cargo cults. As such, this book reveals a deep suspicion against irregular motility—a preference for smooth, regular, and predictable movements over spontaneous or abrupt corporeal acts.

Choreomania, I argue, is not just *like* Orientalism, as a complex of ideas bringing disparate actions together under one discursive roof; it is saturated with Orientalist prejudices against obscurity, unintelligibility, primitiveness, and Eastern-inflected Dionysianism. In this view, unruliness, childishness, and spontaneity are described in the medical literature as simultaneously animal and ancient, historical and organic. The discursive history of choreomania, then—the history of this idea's transformation and spread—describes ways of reading bodily motion, and ways this reading itself can be construed as a conceptual act: an act of philosophy determined by the material realities of its authors' routes. This book thus continues Said's project of uncovering intellectual blind spots in the learned institutions of nineteenth-century Europe and America. But whereas *Orientalism* reveals a pervasive prejudice against Middle Eastern and African subjects and the dark, dangerous, and sexually loquacious femininity they were meant to embody first and foremost in the Orientalist academic field, this book reveals pervasive prejudice against spontaneous gestures and the suspect movement of crowds portrayed in medicine and the social sciences. The fields I describe—the history of medicine, neurology, psychiatry, psychology, sociology, anthropology, ethnography, history, and popular journalism—are all influenced by the Orientalist moment. But this book shows that the Orientalist construct can be taken further, to describe a range of nonverbal actions and the imbrication of bodily events in modern science. 'Choreomania' described everything from the moral and mental degeneration of so-called primitive people to the seemingly contagious and mechanistic behaviour of male and female bodies. As such, the node choreomania describes suggests a way of thinking about public corporeality as dark, dangerous, and ultimately unknowable, but also comedic and bizarre. The cryptic quality of 'choreomania' thus extends the Orientalist spectrum to include erratic gestures and a complex of neurological disorders that further tie the elusive other into a discourse on social politics and medicine, setting whole casts of 'marginals' apart.

Said's debt to Foucault is one I also share. In particular, this book shares an affinity with two central concerns of Foucault: the status of the outcast or 'abnormal' (often 'marginal') person

---

6. Edward W. Said, *Orientalism* (New York: Vintage Books, 1994).

7. 'Whiteness' is a complex and still not nearly often enough historicized term, in spite of the rise of critical whiteness studies since the early 1990s. On the moving borders of 'white' culture, see esp. the pioneering work of Vron Ware, *Beyond the Pale: White Women, Racism, and History* (London: Verso, 1992); Noel Ignatiev, *How the Irish Became White* (New York: Routledge, 1995); Karen Brodkin, *How Jews Became White Folks and What That Says About Race in America* (New Brunswick, NJ: Rutgers University Press, 1998). My usage best approximates what Ware, following John Hartigan Jr., describes as a 'racial situation', a basically anti-essentialist view of race that sees the construction and experience of whiteness, blackness, or what have you as being fundamentally relational; this not only historicizes the question Donna Haraway poses to Ware, as she recounts it ('When did English women first think of themselves as white?'), but also situates the fraught question of race in a changing national and international context. 'Whiteness' then becomes something not only constructed, but implicit, spectral, and shifting, as well as deeply contextual, mapped onto a host of interrelated political and social concerns, including nationalism, gender, war, etc. See Ware interviewed in Bolette B. Blaagaard, 'Workings of Whiteness: Interview with Vron Ware', *Social Identities* 17.1 (2011): 153–161, 155.

and the institution of knowledge. With Foucault, I seek to understand how discourses about otherness emerge in given historical periods, which institutional and intellectual conditions enabled their articulation, and how new fields of knowing were constituted around this stipulated 'other' as an object of understanding and eventually biopower. As Said and Deleuze point out, Foucault was interested not only in structures of power and enclosure but also in a conception of life as the excessive, the surplus lurking beyond systems of language, discourse, and idea.[8] This book seeks to understand how this surplus—this excess vitality—came to be contextualized in the nineteenth and twentieth centuries as a dancing sort of disease, a hyperbolic, feminine, and queer sort of expansive gesturality spilling beyond the individual body into public space.

What I argue, then, following the historian and philosopher of science Ian Hacking, is that choreomania is not a stable ontological or medical category. Writing about so-called multiple personality disorder, Hacking argues that today's diagnostic categories cannot be transposed onto past events; we cannot retrospectively diagnose behaviours and beliefs, because these, and the philosophical and affective systems around them, change.[9] Similarly, I do not diagnose—nor do I aim to re-diagnose—choreomania, for example to argue that it was or was not 'actually' one or another type of cultural phenomenon or disease. Instead, this book argues, there were in a sense never any 'real' choreomaniacs.

There is a vast and rich literature about something called choreomania, and a breathtaking range of events that constitute what I call the choreomania repertoire, from late medieval and early modern St. Vitus's dancers to *tarantati* in early modern Italy, eighteenth-century convulsionaries, modern Abyssinians, American religious enthusiasts, and factory workers. By the twentieth century, millennialist movements in Melanesia and Polynesia multiplied the sites for dance-like 'disorders', just as Native American Ghost Dancers were understood by at least one influential government anthropologist to be participating in a variation on the same. In twentieth-century dance halls, tango and animal dance aficionados all enjoyed a dancing 'craze' of their own, compared once again in medical and popular literature to medieval dancing epidemics. In all instances, symptomatic resemblance and loose genealogies widened the choreomania family tree, just as the concept of the dancing disease came to be so capacious as to signal almost anything or anyone that moved too much and too erratically.

This approach is slightly different from writing the concept of choreomania 'sous rature' (under erasure), the figure of speech Jacques Derrida (1930–2004) employs in *Of Grammatology* (1998 [orig. French ed. 1967]) to describe how some terms have to be written to indicate their problematic aspect as well as their unavoidability as terms for analysis. Rather than merely erase or supersede some words with

8. Edward W. Said, 'Michel Foucault, 1926–1984', in Jonathan Arac, ed., *After Foucault: Humanistic Knowledge, Postmodern Challenges* (New Brunswick, NJ: Rutgers University Press, 1991), 1–11, 5. Foucault's Nietzschean inheritance emerged most forcefully when he witnessed the Iranian revolution in 1979 and for the first time confronted, Said notes, the 'entirely collective, involuntary excessiveness which could not be herded under conventional rubrics like class contradictions or economic oppression' (9). Foucault's work on madness has been vigorously criticized by historians bent on upholding an empirical approach to the study of the past as opposed to Foucault's 'symbolist abstraction'. See H. C. Erik Midelfort, *A History of Madness in Sixteenth-Century Germany* (Stanford, CA: Stanford University Press, 1999), 7. See also H. C. Erik Midelfort, 'Madness and Civilization in Early Modern Europe: A Reappraisal of Michel Foucault', in Barbara Malament, ed., *After the Reformation: Essays in Honor of J. H. Hexter* (Philadelphia: University of Pennsylvania Press, 1980), 247–266; Arthur Still and Irving Velody, eds., *Rewriting the History of Madness: Studies in Foucault's 'Histoire de la folie'* (London: Routledge, 1992); Colin Jones and Roy Porter, eds., *Reassessing Foucault: Power, Medicine, and the Body* (London: Routledge, 1998). Whereas these studies decry the broad brushstrokes of Foucault's writing, they also underplay the philosophical and aesthetic value of the figures of thought he brought to his subjects and the labour of concept formation he contributed to the history of ideas, the only field with which he claimed any real affinity. For a cogent defence of Foucault's work against vitriolic critique by 'the historians', see esp. Colin Gordon, 'Rewriting the History of Misreading', in Still and Velody, eds., *Rewriting the History of Madness*, 167–184. Recent publication in English of Foucault's unabbreviated *History of Madness*, ed. Jean Khalfa, trans. John Murphy and Jean Khalfa (London: Routledge, 2006), replacing the long popular (and highly contested) much abbreviated version *Madness and Civilization* (London: Routledge, 1989), as well as his lectures at the Collège de France, have brought new vigour to Foucault studies, and a new appraisal of the rigour of his historiographic and philosophical thought. See e.g. Mark D. Jordan, *Convulsing Bodies: Religion and Resistance in Foucault* (Stanford, CA: Stanford University Press, 2015). Wendy Brown, in *Undoing the Demos: Neoliberalism's Stealth Revolution* (Brooklyn: Zone Books, 2015), represents a new body of writing on Foucault's interest in governmentality. On the reappraisal of Foucault's *Histoire de la folie* prior to its recent unabbreviated translation into English, see esp. Still and Velody, *Rewriting the History of Madness*.

9. Ian Hacking, *Rewriting the Soul: Multiple Personality and the Sciences of Memory* (Princeton, NJ: Princeton University Press, 1995).

others or, as anthropologist Vincent Crapanzano suggests, put them in quotation marks (a similar but equally failing strategy for ideological critique), key terms—here, 'choreomania'—can be construed to contain both ideological constructs and their critique.[10] Following Said, I do not just distance myself from choreomania by writing it under erasure or in quotation marks but posit the use of this term for describing a whole complex of desires, imaginings, and practices as well as their critique. In this book, 'choreomania' implicates historicity, antiquity, and primitivism, but also incoherence, heightened affect, and excess, to encompass nineteenth-century fantasies of historical and colonial others, and a far greater category of otherness pertinent in cultural critique today. Specifically, choreomania signals an order—and disorder—of expressive affect by which the body politic falls dramatically into disrepair.

This book thus reads the way the medical and social scientific language of the dancing disease came about: the institutional, ideological, political, and cultural worlds within which this cast of 'marginals' came to be imagined. In this regard, this book can be considered alongside works such as Lamont Lindstrom's *Cargo Cult: Strange Stories of Desire from Melanesia and Beyond* (1993), which traces the genealogy of the term 'cargo cult' within academic anthropology, particularly in the Pacific region, and its 'spread far beyond that discipline'.[11] Lindstrom, by his own account, is concerned 'with the stories we tell about cargo cult, not with their historical and ethnographic accuracy'.[12] Rather than take the notion of the cargo cult as a stable referent used to designate a coherent set of practices and beliefs, he is interested in what narratives of cargo cults say about anthropological 'desire'. As he puts it, 'Cargo cults are Melanesian, but cargo cult accounts belong to us'.[13] Similarly, this book tells us about modern scientific desires and imaginaries of dance.

Yet my emphasis is slightly different from Lindstrom's. While tracing the genealogy of ideas about choreomania in medical history first of all, this book also discovers how such a nexus of ideas moves through fields, including colonial medicine, sociology, medical anthropology, and ethnography; this book's story then is also about interdisciplinary cross-pollination and the movement of 'desires'. I also stick less closely to the singular label 'choreomania', discovering a network of fantasies having to do with incoherence, illegibility, awkward gesture, heightened movement and affect, collective seizures and trances, mass delusions, frenzy, and popular obsessions, which meet in the term 'choreomania' but also exceed it.

'Choreomania' thus comes to stand in for an interconnected set of discourses and desires articulated across fields in nineteenth- and twentieth-century intellectual life, spilling out into popular culture and sensationalizing journalism. These interconnected discourses reveal shared fantasies according to which the 'epidemic' encroachment of bodies on public space and fitful motions come to be seen as two sides of one pathological phenomenon. This book in this regard tells a prehistory of the dance and performance studies fields, excavating literature about disruptive movement imagined to emerge from ancient time to upend modern social and political life.

TORQUE

The chronological framework covered by this book coincides with what cultural theorist Hillel Schwartz has characterized as the period between 1840 and 1940 when 'movement transforms'.[14] As he writes, 'between 1840 and 1940, children and adults alike would slowly be rehearsed into a habit of gesturing and a repertoire of "streamlined" gestures'.[15] These were 'central to the new kinaesthetic—clean, fluid, curvilinear gestures moving from the center of the body outward through uninterrupted but muscularly well-controlled rhythmic impulses'.[16] This curvilinearity was what

---

10. For a pertinent discussion of Derrida and Crapanzano's notions of writing 'under erasure' and in quotation marks, respectively, see Elfriede Hermann, 'Dissolving the Self-Other Dichotomy in Western "Cargo Cult" Constructions', in Holger Jebens, ed., *Cargo, Cult, and Culture Critique* (Honolulu: University of Hawai'i Press, 2004), 36–58, 37–38.

11. Lamont Lindstrom, *Cargo Cult: Strange Stories of Desire from Melanesia and Beyond* (Honolulu: University of Hawaii Press, 1993).

12. Lindstrom, *Cargo Cult*, 12. See also Martha Kaplan, *Neither Cargo nor Cult: Ritual Politics and the Colonial Imagination in Fiji* (Durham: Duke University Press, 1995), esp. xii–xiv.

13. Lamont Lindstrom, 'Cargo Cult at the Third Millennium', in Jebens, ed., *Cargo, Cult, and Culture Critique*, 15–35, 16–17.

14. Hillel Schwartz, 'Torque: The New Kinaesthetic of the Twentieth Century', in Jonathan Crary and Sanford Kwinter, eds., *Zone 6: Incorporations* (Cambridge, MA: MIT Press, 1992), 71–127, 77.

15. Schwartz, 'Torque', 91.

16. Schwartz, 'Torque', 91.

Schwartz calls torque, the kinaesthetic torsion of the body according to an axial rotation or twist, as of a coil or spiral unwinding itself. This modern preference for clean, smooth curvilinear motion echoed through the sciences of graphology or handwriting, orature, and modern dance. Paramount in social scientific theories of motional fluidity, Schwartz argues, was the 'social intelligibility' of gesture: as a true expression of a soulful impulse, an intelligible gesture suggested trustworthiness, forthrightness, and a wholesome, honest, and expressive civic spirit.[17] This was contrary to what Schwartz notes was a concomitant 'late nineteenth-century epidemic of apparently uncontrollable gesture—an epidemic of tics, choreas, convulsions, aphasias and strangely impermanent but recurring paralyses that left so many women of all classes invalids'.[18] This book picks up this minor literature, and draws this second history of mid-nineteenth- to early twentieth-century kinaesthetic philosophy into fuller view, also edging Schwartz's chronological frame slightly further back by a decade to the 1830s, when medical historian and pioneer epidemiologist J. F. C. Hecker (1795–1850) articulated his theory of epidemic dancing and (indirectly) gestural dislocation. In 'The Dancing Mania', Hecker bridged his own historiographical interest in contagion—especially what he was first to describe as the 'Black Death'—with anecdotal accounts of religious movements in Europe, America, and the colonial world. The awkward, spasmodic, convulsive movements of dancing manias emerged with even fuller force in a fin-de-siècle discourse on hysteria, including female (and colonial) 'hysteria': these were the 'twitches, seizures and paralyses' or 'hysterical attacks' Sigmund Freud (1856–1939) would observe, eventually arguing against his teacher Jean-Martin Charcot (1825–1893) that they

'did not make any physiological sense' but were 'theatrically intelligible' as pantomime.[19]

This book thus adds to Schwartz's history of the carefully controlled and curvilinear mid- to late nineteenth and early twentieth centuries a history of the discursivization of excessive gesture at the outer edges of the bodily core: flailing arms, rolling eyes, jagged angularity, and most of all illegibility characterized circulating narratives about choreomania.

THE ARCHIVAL REPERTOIRE

In tandem with (and in counterpoint to) Schwartz's concept of torque, this book reveals a discursive history of convulsive bodies and crowds traversing the long century between 1830 and the 1940s, and founded in centuries of prior convulsive bodies and crowds imagined by medical and anthropological writers in this period. Performing what I call a brand of *exuberant comparativism*, these writers collaged and compared histories of convulsive corporeality in often slightly haphazard feats of archival recuperation. This yields what I am calling a morphing, plastic, *archival repertoire* of gestural events. As distinct from what Diana Taylor has influentially called the static and hegemonic 'archive' of written texts, opposed to a more fluid and bodily 'repertoire' of oral and performative events, the *archival repertoire* comprises a mobile, piecemeal set of archival objects, including written texts, images, and live observations travelling with their writers across the globe.[20] The archival repertoire is not fixed or hegemonic, though it is written, by and large: like bodily performances, it is subject to constant transformation, imitation, repetition, and recuperation; it is a loose and changing set of references that writers draw up and reimagine.

---

17. Schwartz, 'Torque', 92.

18. Schwartz, 'Torque', 92.

19. Schwartz, 'Torque', 92.

20. Taylor posits a 'rift' not so much 'between the written and spoken word, but between the *archive* of supposedly enduring materials (i.e., texts, documents, buildings, bones) and the so-called ephemeral *repertoire* of embodied practice/knowledge (i.e., spoken language, sports, ritual)'. See Diana Taylor, *The Archive and the Repertoire: Performing Cultural Memory in the Americas* (Durham, NC: Duke University Press, 2003), 19. William B. Worthen has retorted that an archive of written documents is as subject to changing modes of interpretation as any repertoire; it is not a privileged site for colonial power or hegemonic fixity. See William B. Worthen, 'Antigone's Bones', *TDR: The Drama Review* 52.3 [T199] (2008): 10–33. Moments of the past are constantly imbricated in present lived experience. Rebecca Schneider points out that re-enactments and reperformances blur notions of an authentic or historical real. See Rebecca Schneider, *Performing Remains: Art and War in Times of Theatrical Reenactment* (London: Routledge, 2011). Similarly, André Lepecki has argued that certain new dance practices suggest a 'will to archive' that displaces the Derridean notion of the archive as a bureaucratic site designed for storing documents and institutional history. Instead, the dancer's body presents a

At the same time, the writers I discuss here, enthusiastically collecting histories of convulsive events, remain persistently opaque in their writing with regard to the gestures themselves. It is rarely clear exactly what the 'choreomanias' looked like, or what 'choreomaniacs' were doing when they frothed, fell, and raved. But I argue, the relative illegibility of these gestures in medical and ethnographic texts reveals the very phantasmatization of this choreic movement as an epidemic disease. Indeed, the lack of careful choreographic description tells a powerful story in itself: that of the language of approximation, fictionalization, and fantasy of disorderly bodies set in motion as writers recuperated and repeated one another's narratives, spotting further instances of choreomania: awkward bodies, falling bodies, bodies prey to fits and starts. Rather than trying to rehearse their attempts to collect case studies, this book thus tells the story of the discursivization of 'dance manias': the language with which the figure of choreomania was roughly drawn.

MODERNITY

For the purposes of this book, I define 'modern' as that which posits the new in contrast to the old. In sociologist Henri Lefebvre's (1901–1991) terms, modernity is that which '[bids] for knowledge'. 'By modernity', he writes, 'we understand the beginnings of a reflective process, a more-or-less advanced attempt at critique and autocritique'.[21] Modernity can be defined as that which turns on itself, and onto the world around it, to articulate, explain, and make intelligible what is perceived to have been previously unknown or unknowable and obscure. In this respect, modernity can be understood as a process of intelligibilization; it is not just a historical period, an art movement, or a political platform, but a motion towards thought, no matter how misconstrued this thought may appear in retrospect. Indeed, modernity continues to construe thinking, in this view; to revise its understandings; to move, in a sense, intellectually forward. As I am positing

in this book, this movement 'forward' is also a movement back, as scientists and other writers in the nineteenth and early twentieth centuries sought to read bodies and movements in the present day with reference to antique lore. They gathered images and anecdotes, narratives, chronicles, and case studies, illuminating the present by way of the past. This scientific backlighting of modern corporealities with a reach to ancient history, and to the fiction of the antediluvian, automatic animality it was meant to uphold, produced an uncanny present, haunted by a felt sense of the past as boisterous other. Modern science looked forward; but as I suggest further in the next chapters, it did so, controversially, by also looking anxiously and inquisitively behind. In this regard, this book is in close conversation with Ramsay Burt's *Alien Bodies: Representations of Modernity, 'Race' and Nation in Early Modern Dance* (1998), in which he argues that modernity constructs itself in relation to 'alien' (often African) others, and that modern dance can be construed as a criss-crossing between European and African, American, and African-American forms of bodily being, all of which become uncomfortable with the rootlessness modernity brings about. 'Alien' bodies, for Burt, are uncannily other: they are not entirely at home in their own 'modern' selves: they are awkward, foreign, and yet familiar. What's more, these 'alien' bodies represent an uncanny alterity that is not only the dancer's but also the viewer's: alterity is a shared fascination, 'inscribed . . . within the most intimate interiority of the self'.[22] National and racial identity in the interwar years Burt examines (the 1920s and 1930s) are thus tensioned by a contrary motion towards foreignness, primitivism, and exoticism, embodied in Katherine Dunham's (1909–2006) African-American dance or Josephine Baker's (1906–1975) 'savage' grace. Thus 'collective identities' come to be shaped by exclusionary politics as well as the figures of exclusion against which such politics are imagined. Burt's concern, to rethink narratives of modern dance, proposes to write a history that forages at the

---

live and moving repository of information about kinetic history. See André Lepecki, 'The Body as Archive: Will to Re-enact and the Afterlives of Dances', *Dance Research Journal* 42.2 (2010): 28–48.

21. Henri Lefebvre, *Introduction to Modernity: Twelve Preludes, September 1959–May 1961*, trans. John Moore (London: Verso, 1995), 1.

22. Ramsay Burt, *Alien Bodies: Representations of Modernity, 'Race' and Nation in Early Modern Dance* (London: Routledge, 1998), 17. Burt borrows from Julia Kristeva, who suggests that we are all first of all 'foreign' to ourselves. See Julia Kristeva, *Étrangers à nous-mêmes* (Paris: Fayard, 1988).

periphery of the white European dancing subject, towards conceptual structures informed by discourses and histories of colonialism and decolonization, psychoanalysis and urbanism.[23] This book reads an earlier incarnation of this movement of cultural cross-pollination and ambivalence, of anxious doubling and phantasmatic others, emphasizing the discursive structures within which forms of embodiment are described as alien and uncannily familiar. I argue that nineteenth-century colonial modernity construes itself also in relation to 'alien' others: primarily ancient and foreign. But in doing so, this colonial scientific modernity constructs an abstract 'alien' subject against which it attempts again and again to counterpose itself. This is not only a dancing subjectivity, but a form of embodiment that spills beyond the disciplinary spaces genealogically inhabited by 'dance' practice. Figures of twisting and writhing bodies, impulsive, gregarious, and in disarray, all shape an experience of modernity structured by the repetition of narratives about the antiquity of these uncannily 'alien' forms.

Further borrowing from Paul Gilroy, I suggest that 'modernity' can thus be construed as looking uncomfortably two ways, forward and back: just as the 'Black Atlantic' suggests a trade between American and European shores, crossed by slave ships, Enlightenment ideals, and other paradoxes of the purportedly rational modern world, so too modernity in this book looks forward and back, here and elsewhere, in a dizzying zigzag, what Gilroy terms a rhizomorphic journey that slips continuously between historical regimes. Significantly, scientific modernity in the colonial age construes itself in relation to the other and the ancient in a constant to and fro as nauseating as perpetual sea voyaging.[24]

Although this book posits an intellectual history extending roughly from the 1830s to the 1940s, highlighting the chronological coincidence of 'modernity' with the rise of modern nation states and the institution of modern scientific and social scientific disciplines, 'modernity' as a feeling of difference with respect to the past also comes into play in this book as early as the early modern period. Paracelsus, born Theophrastus von Hohenheim (1493–1541), influentially set his ideas about Chorea Sancti Viti against what he saw as his contemporaries' outdated, superstitious views. In his opinion, they wrongly believed dance manias could be attributed to Satanism and witchcraft. As I show in chapter 3, Paracelsus claimed direct experimental knowledge as opposed to what he saw as his peers' backward-looking dogma. Modernity in this view is saturated with the past, and as such appositional; it posits itself in contrast to something prior, holding that apposition as fundamental to its own modernist claim. Modernity requires the past—even a highly exaggerated and fictionalized version of the past—against which to set its novelty.

Modernity in this sense also privileges a discourse of experimental reason, claiming nearly everything that came before as mere belief. Modernity, and the set of discourses I examine, privilege experimental modes of knowing, an epistemic thrust that is appetitive, that 'keeps wanting' to know. The modern epistemic appetite I describe accumulates, seeks, forages, rag-picks. But modernity also articulates its own notions of history and antiquity, against which to define itself. It is this fantasy of history—as restless, exuberant, hypermotional or hyperkinetic, and hyper*emotional*—that is the subject of this book. So whereas Sloterdijk, André Lepecki reminds us, has argued that modernity is defined by its constant motion and *busy-ness*, the version of modernity this book explores imagines its own business as rational and purposeful, opposed to the purposeless and disorganized motion of choreomania: a disease always construed as occurring in the past and on foreign shores and affecting allegedly superstitious, pre-modern, aimless subjects even in the present day.[25]

Anecdotes of dance-like happenings in factories and hospital settings—epidemics of jerks, twitches, and falls periodically described among young women—likewise reinforced the scientific discourse positing dancing manias as epidemic corporeal movements spurred on by high affect. Women, colonial subjects, and people from the

---

23. Burt, *Alien Bodies*, 5–10.

24. Paul Gilroy, *The Black Atlantic: Modernity and Double Consciousness* (London: Verso, 1993), 3–4.

25. André Lepecki, *Exhausting Dance: Performance and the Politics of Movement* (New York: Routledge, 2006), 7, 12–14. On Sloterdijk's notion that any critique of modernity is fundamentally a critical theory of movement and 'mobilization', see Peter Sloterdijk, *La mobilisation infinie: Vers une critique de la cinétique politique*, trans. Hans Hildenbrand (Paris: Christian Bourgois, 2000), esp. 42–48. Originally published as *Eurotaoismus: Zur Kritik der politischen Kinetik* (Frankfurt: Suhrkamp Verlag, 1989). See also Peter Sloterdijk, 'Mobilization of the Planet from the Spirit of Self-Intensification', *TDR: The Drama Review* 50.4 [T192] (2006): 36–43.

past all seemed, through the lens of the dancing disease, to suffer from keen sensitivity and an acute capacity for imitation. As mimics, these choreomaniacs—in effect the vast majority of human beings—performed their antiquity and alterity by being imitative, in other words, by engaging in like movements. Not only did they appear similar to one another, but as such their individuality apparently dissolved; they became a crowd, a vital, pulsating mass, a movement. And although women figure prominently in a number of the cases I describe, they were not alone in suffering from the putative dancing disease. Yet its implicit femininity, allying primitive others with ancient, infantile, and irrational bodiliness, made choreomania an Orientalist construct that extended the idea of general dissolution—and dissoluteness—to collective, spontaneous dance.

Modernity in this regard is not only simultaneously curious and haughty about the past, but—to borrow from Said, who borrows from the language of music—contrapuntal. The exile, Said writes, sees himself always 'against the memory' of another environment.[26] The scientific language of modernity sees itself always in counterpoint to ancient histories and what it construes as other, foreign (often non-European) ways of moving; and it is fascinated with disorderly figures of collectivity. This version of scientific modernity defines itself in relation to a perpetually rehearsed fantasy about the past, which it posits as unknowing, unquestioning, automatic, uncontrolled, and swarm-like. Modernity's past is not always or only that of the ancients, individual figures of authority, who may have been surpassed by modern science; rather, modernity's past from this perspective is that of the horde. And yet, as narratives about choreomania show, hordes only crystallize at particular moments, which bring the past into view, highlighting the cyclical, and occasionally wave-like, quality of history's motion.

HISTORY, GENEALOGY, METHOD

My purpose in writing this book thus has been to extend the scope of dance studies to cases of unchoreographed movement at the borderlines of dance, where it has been theorized as an epidemic disease. I show that vivid medical interest in history and alterity in the nineteenth century informed and complicate modern notions of the inchoate body politic, which 'dance manias' come to describe. My method is genealogical. In this regard, I draw from Foucault's concept of genealogy as that which seeks the 'events of history, its jolts, its surprises, its unsteady victories and unpalatable defeats'.[27] In turn drawing from Friedrich Nietzsche's (1844–1900) notion of genealogy (articulated most influentially in On the Genealogy of Morality [1887]), Foucault describes his genealogical method as being opposed to standard writings of 'history', inasmuch as, unlike history, genealogy does not search for origins or first causes. 'History is the concrete body of becoming', Foucault writes, 'with its moments of intensity, its lapses, its extended periods of feverish agitation, its fainting spells; . . . only a metaphysician would seek its soul in the distant ideality of the origin'.[28] Genealogy, for Foucault, instead signifies a radically embodied historical writing traversing various fields, contexts, and discursive regimes or modes of speech and writing. There is no supra-historical subject, no essence or transcendental object of historical analysis for Foucault; instead, the 'genealogist' considers the past by looking at discrete, interrelated elements of messy, vital, bodied life and the ways they have been described, controlled, and categorized.

But whereas Foucault's genealogical method appears to signal a philosophical interest in regimes of signification—modes of scientific, legal, and political knowledge deployed in everyday life—the vital strain in his description also highlights bodily metaphors and a bodied experience of historical events. History's fits and starts, its 'feverish agitation', suggest the uneven progress of historical events and its aleatory quality, its live processes of configuration and continual reconfiguration. History, in this view, and genealogy, as its most appropriate method of study, is not only a history of the body as it is imagined through time but also a history by the body; and, most intriguingly, a history that is performed in a bodily way: erratically, spontaneously, fitfully, spasmodically . . . in short, choreographically.

---

26. Edward W. Said, Reflections on Exile and Other Essays (Cambridge, MA: Harvard University Press, 2000), 186.

27. Michel Foucault, 'Nietzsche, Genealogy, History', in James D. Faubion, ed., Aesthetics, Method, and Epistemology: Essential Works of Foucault 1954–1984, trans. Robert Hurley, 3 vols., vol. 2 (New York: New Press, 1998), 369–391, 373.

28. Foucault, 'Nietzsche, Genealogy, History', 373.

I have taken this corporeal approach to the work of writing a genealogy to task. Shuffling through archival and government records and correspondence, medical compendia, early journals, chronicles, annals, sketches, drawings, photographs, dance manuals, missionary writings, history books, ethnographies, and other objects I hoped might reveal shreds of information about 'choreomania' as it was configured in the last couple of hundred years, I found myself performing a genealogist's dance, proceeding in fits and starts through medical history's often haphazard depictions of the strange and elusive 'dancing disease'. On some occasions, I got up to dance, as when I finally found a description of one of these intangible instances of choreomania: the Ghost Dance, genealogically linked to the paradigmatic St. Vitus's dance by its first and arguably most influential ethnographer, James Mooney (1861–1921). The Ghost Dance involved a shuffling side step to the left. This I could do. But what did the movement reveal? So little; perhaps, that dance 'manias' were also at times calm, peaceable events. What was 'manic' or excessive, as I detail in chapter 9, was the length of time the shuffling was performed; an attendant climate of fear and anger; and the concerted legal and government efforts to suppress this as a wasteful expenditure of time and energy, as fraying archives housed at the Library of Congress revealed. The Ghost Dance was a collective movement, performed by people in concert; it suggested a heightened affective state, exacerbated by an atmosphere of political tension leading to radical crisis. My own tentative embodiment of the shuffling motion prompted an experience of focus, a concentric gathering of energy, which the narratives and drawings I encountered corroborated, against the grain of official narratives and media illustrations I also read (as I detail in chapter 9). Although it is well known that the Ghost Dance was primarily an anti-colonial resistance movement, attempting to set what I read of these gestures in my body helped me better to confront the chasm between what I knew, poorly, and what I could not possibly know; between a fragile archive and a lost event. Yet in that chasm, lies another story; the story I have sought to tell. Dance history is always partial, necessarily imperfect; but narratives remain that tell of ostensibly salient events, and those can be traced.

To do that work of tracing—to perform that *choreographic* analysis—may help us grasp what histories have been told; grasp how language shapes our lives, and how it has constituted a site of (choreographic) biopower. Thus we may continue to query 'dance', reimagining its contours—including at the outermost edges of the 'dance' archive.

INTERDISCIPLINARY FORMATIONS: DANCE STUDIES ON THE EDGE

Following Foucault, I have sought to re-entangle the history of nineteenth-century thinking about disorderly bodies in public space within a broadly multidisciplinary field. My intention has been to understand how conditions for the concatenation and dissemination of knowledge about bodily alterity emerged, and how the vicissitudes of individual travels created intellectual chimeras out of ethnographic and scientific observations. At stake, then, in this book is the history of disciplines, specifically the history of interdisciplinarity as it underpins the contemporary dance studies field. The late sociologist and public arts theorist Randy Martin (1957–2015) reminds us that interdisciplinarity presents a political thrust rooted in a post-1960s multicultural moment, during which contestation, from Black Power and the feminist movements to gay pride, sought to unhinge the disciplinary finality of the old subjects and replace these with heterogeneous, volatile, often politically vulnerable fields of inquiry. Martin also reminds us that, according to political theorist Michael E. Brown, disciplines have always had interdisciplinary foundations.[29] This book seeks to take these claims further, and explore the interdisciplinary foundations to what continues to be a radically interdisciplinary field in the sense Martin proposes. So while Martin invites dance scholars to recognize dance's inherent ability to intervene in broader political (and disciplinary) arenas, as a form of action that takes mobilization as its primary thrust, this book suggests that dance studies also has to continue to destabilize itself if it is to maintain its radically interdisciplinary political potential. This resonates with Mark Franko and Annette Richards's call to dance, music, and performance studies to destabilize themselves

---

29. Randy Martin, *Critical Moves: Dance Studies in Theory and Politics* (Durham, NC: Duke University Press, 1998), 189.

by looking back at the past, troubling the seemingly axiomatic 'liveness' and 'presence' of these fields with a little bit of history.[30] This is not to say that these fields should necessarily or always 'do' history in a strictly material sense, reconstructing past performances, uncovering props and playbills, but that they should also theorize and conceptualize the very historicity they seem always to elude.

This book seeks to examine the way historicity—as the affective and intellectual experience of history, its history-*ness*—comes into play in the conceptualization of dance (and political movement) as that which returns, that which haunts the present from out of the past. Dance is not just an aesthetic form or force for mobilization, but an interdisciplinary figure, and concept, with institutional histories and schools of training that nevertheless becomes itself continually through repetition. Yet this is a repetition with difference: each reiteration and recuperation of a 'dance' cluster—a set of ideas about what constitutes dance, where it resides institutionally, and what it emerges from historically—reconfigures what dance is and might be. It is not sufficient, Martin argues, in response to Foster, to posit periods or modes of making, reading, or writing dance.[31] Instead, the discipline moves. The discipline of dance is not just constituted interdisciplinarily; it is constantly becoming interdisciplinary *again*. It must, to retain its especially *mobilizational* quality, continue to move; to falter; to start. It must continue to move jaggedly, in an organized and in an unrehearsed fashion; to reconstitute its congresses and playhouses; to go down back alleys and find dance in the furthest reaches of the social sphere. In doing so, it troubles the boundaries of 'dance' and the politico-aesthetic delineation this term inspires.

As such, this book does not showcase 'dance' exactly; readers seeking detailed descriptions of jetés, pirouettes, and entrechats may find the pickings slim. Instead, this book describes the emergence of new ideas about spontaneous fitful dancing as a figure of thought, a conceptual node at the heart of nineteenth- and early twentieth-century ways of thinking about history, politics, and corporeality. In this respect, this book performs a discursive analysis, an intellectual history; but also a theoretical intervention into ways of thinking about unruly collective and singular corporealities. This book thus allies itself with histories of thinking about dance in the margins of history and culture. More particularly, this book adds new matter to historiographical and theoretical thinking about anti-dance prejudices in modern thought. Ann Wagner has convincingly shown that the history of American popular culture is rent through with a puritanical, anti-dance (choreophobic) prejudice.[32] Similarly, Anthony Shay has argued that Islamic 'dance'—and choreophobia in Iran—can only be construed as such through a broadly Western lens, inasmuch as 'dance' only exists as a distinct social and aesthetic category in the West.[33] The writers discussed in this book do not always call what they look at 'dance', but amalgamate epilepsy, chorea, social movements, and processions in a history of epidemic disease implicitly (if not always explicitly) aligning bodily movement with a disorder disrupting the industrial West.

THE MOVEMENT OF ABSTRACTION

This book thus emphasises gestural migration, not quite the gesture of bodies on- (or off-) stage, but the migration of intellectual gestures—what I call their 'translatio'—across discursive terrains. This has meant leaving the embodied, proprioceptive, kinaesthetic experience of a dancing self behind. I have done so not without some apprehension, and of course an alternative history of the 'dancing disease' might seek to know how collective movements, upheavals, tics, and unwieldy gesticulations *felt* to those performing them. But in order to write a history of moving ideas about disorderly dance and movement, I have chosen to privilege a discursive methodology that takes the language of movement itself as its object. In doing so, I have followed a line of reasoning articulated by historian and art critic Blake Stimson as the 'gesture of abstraction'.[34]

---

30. Mark Franko and Annette Richards, 'Actualizing Absence: The Pastness of Performance', in Mark Franko and Annette Richards, eds., *Acting on the Past: Historical Performance across the Disciplines* (Hanover, NH: Wesleyan University Press, 2000), 1–9, 1–3.

31. Martin, *Critical Moves*, 201–204.

32. Ann Wagner, *Adversaries of Dance: From the Puritans to the Present* (Urbana: University of Illinois Press, 1997).

33. Anthony Shay, *Choreophobia: Solo Improvised Dance in the Iranian World* (Costa Mesa, CA: Mazda, 1999).

34. See Blake Stimson, 'Gesture and Abstraction', in Carrie Noland and Sally Ann Ness, eds., *Migrations of Gesture* (Minneapolis: University of Minnesota Press, 2008), 69–83, 70. Mark Franko has influentially argued that embodied movement and *écriture*,

Abstraction is a process of describing, categorizing, and ultimately displacing vital events onto a discursive plane. But the paradox of abstraction is that this process shifts and transforms the event itself just as it attempts to capture it. In the discourse on choreomania, dance seems to be nothing but disorganized gesture, heightened affect, irregular motility, and a theatrical predisposition to corporeal and social imitation. Yet in this articulation of inarticulacy, this conceptualization of formlessness and this abstraction from movement, a different notion of dance emerges. Bodily activity comes into the history of ideas as a site for articulation, forming, and abstraction (as gesture). Medical writing that rejects the possibility of aesthetic form in movements described conversely brings about a concept of movement wherein 'dance' emerges as the possibility of taking shape—as the incipient process of conceptualization. Without being returned to the abstract realm of the idea (as if dance had ever been separated from intellectualization in the first place), dance appears on the scene of medical history as the arguably far more productive potential for ideation. In that regard, dance contains within it the seeds of all the disciplines and discursive histories imputed to it by writers keen to take the plunge into this apparent primeval muck. In other words, the very prelapsarian, prelinguistic, and inchoate quality of the dancing manias described by medical writers and anthropologists in the nineteenth and early twentieth centuries throws up a notion of dance that positions it at the vanguard of intellectualization, and so too science.

HECKER, CHARCOT, FREUD: ANOTHER HISTORY OF HYSTERIA

Besides continuing a rich set of conversations spearheaded by Foucault, Said, Gilroy, Foster, Martin, and Burt, among others, my aim in these pages is to pursue a line of thinking on the relationship between science and dance influentially established by Felicia McCarren and

Joseph Roach. In *The Player's Passion: Studies in the Science of Acting* (1993), Roach plumbed the depths of scientific language and the history of medical theories about actors' motions and emotions decisively to show that scientific literature is inextricably bound up with theatre and dance. In doing so, he laid the ground for further explorations between philosophy, science, medicine and performance, opening up dance and performance studies to deep interdisciplinarity. McCarren further offers a groundbreaking analysis of nineteenth-century concert dance and the medical language of madness in *Dance Pathologies: Performance, Poetics, Medicine* (1998). In many respects, this book picks up where McCarren left off, offering a parallel history of the discursive links between dance and madness in modern science. But whereas McCarren focuses on stage dance, particularly ballet, this book looks at scientific literature on epidemiology and public space. This book also draws McCarren's work slightly further back in time, to consider early nineteenth-century literature on epidemic hysteria reaching back to the medieval and early modern periods. In doing so, this book resituates Charcot's experiments in conversation with earlier medical theories emphasizing not just individual disease and feminine complaints, but the epidemic disorders of nations. This book thus contributes to McCarren's work an account of collective, not always female, dance pathologies, and the movement of nineteenth-century thinking about global and transhistorical corporeality.

Charcot stands as a crowning figure in the history of modern ideas about hysteria, and this book aims to respond to a wide array of writing in this field, from Mark S. Micale's influential *Approaching Hysteria: Disease and Its Interpretations* (1995) and Elin Diamond's *Unmaking Mimesis: Essays on Feminism and Theatre* (1997) to Georges Didi-Huberman's *Invention of Hysteria: Charcot and the Photographic Iconography of the Salpêtrière* (2003 [orig. French ed. 1982]). Closer still to this book, Rae Beth Gordon's brilliant analysis of the cultural history of 'hysteroepilepsy' in relation to avantgarde (especially cabaret and film) performance in

---

gesture and trace, need not be equated, as deconstruction often seems to suggest; instead, gestures such as those performed by moving (dancing) bodies can be understood productively to occupy space and so to enable action (and thus politics). See Mark Franko, 'Mimique', republished with a new introductory note in Noland and Ness, eds., *Migrations of Gesture*, 241–258. On the concept of the gesture in dance, see also Sally Ann Ness, 'The Inscription of Gesture: Inward Migrations in Dance', in Noland and Ness, eds., *Migrations of Gesture*, 1–30. Susan Leigh Foster was instrumental in laying the groundwork for thinking about the relationship between reading and writing dance as imbricated systems of meaning, after Foucault, Hayden White, and Roland Barthes, in Susan Leigh Foster, *Reading Dancing: Bodies and Subjects in Contemporary American Dance* (Berkeley: University of California Press, 1986).

Why the French Love Jerry Lewis: From the Cabaret to Early Cinema (2001) and *Dances with Darwin, 1875–1910: Vernacular Modernity in France* (2009) sets the stage for my reading of gestural excess. In the former, Gordon offers a dazzling account of 'epileptic singers' in Parisian cabarets and the close relationship between Charcot's clinic and the artistic avant-garde. Her analysis of comic performance in the late nineteenth century attributes the awkward, jerky performance style so popular in Parisian cafés-concerts to psychiatric and physiological theories of bodily dysfunction, further linking these choreographic trends to a rising fashion for gesticulatory grimaces, tics, and automatisms in early French cinema. Analysing racialized movement, particularly the cakewalk, in *Dances with Darwin*, Gordon presents a compelling picture of complex relationships between popular entertainment, primitivism, and modernism in the sexually charged Parisian underworld in the fin de siècle. This book adds to these histories a collective slant, foregrounding epidemic dancing and genealogical relations in the medical and anthropological writings circulating at that time. What's more, this book draws the genealogy on hysteria once again slightly further back, reinscribing it into earlier concerns with national excess and popular revolution.

So whereas McCarren and Gordon concentrate their histories on Paris, the epicentre of Charcot's world, this book describes the circulation of ideas about disorderly corporeality in colonial medical circles as Charcot's ideas made their way to colonial shores. As such, this book offers a slightly different angle on the scientific study of jagged corporeality, ricocheting far beyond the French capital. I argue that the modern story of ideas about hysteria can be situated half a century earlier than it is most commonly described, and its political undercurrents can be reconsidered. So while the French surrealist poets Louis Aragon (1897–1982) and André Breton (1896–1966) famously declared hysteria to have been the nineteenth century's 'greatest poetic discovery' in an article from 1928 dating this 'discovery' to 1878,[35] earlier writing on hysteria—specifically its epidemic, dance-like form, choreomania—describes a far more ancient and collective type of gesture than even Breton allowed. Choreomania describes a distinct subtype of hysteria, convulsive and epidemic; it also presents a potent fantasy of collective disintegration far more politically grievous than the figure of the individual hysteric influential in late nineteenth-century avant-garde and scientific circles. Thus although Gordon has argued that hysteria was occasionally mentioned in the popular press as early as the 1830s as a disorder connected with hypochondria, convulsions, tetanus, and St. Vitus's dance but was far more widely discussed and therefore culturally significant by the century's close,[36] this book argues that the 1830s in fact constitute a highly significant chapter in this ancient malady's modern conceptualization. I show that hysteria went through a rarely acknowledged but highly significant conceptual phase in the 1830s, when it described a far more plural, ecosophical 'disorder' linking jerks and twitches, political movement and ecological upheaval.

MOVEMENT'S 'IMPOSSIBILITY': REARTICULATING THE FIELD

Why write about choreomania today? The history of this 'strange delusion'[37] haunts contemporary social, political, and choreographic thinking. What Lepecki has called 'choreopolitics' and 'choreopolicing' and Foster has described as 'choreographing protest' posit moving bodies in public space operating according to barely visible choreographic lines; yet the dances in these political movements are recognizable as dissensual, organized, agented events in which people wilfully come together to move history forward—or, at least, laterally (typically, in cases they describe, leftwards). For Lepecki, choreopolitics suggests the movement

---

35. Louis Aragon and André Breton, 'Le Cinquantenaire de l'Hystérie, 1878–1928', in *La Révolution surréaliste: Collection complète* (Paris: Jean-Michel Place, 1991), 22; cited in Rae Beth Gordon, *Why the French Love Jerry Lewis: From Cabaret to Early Cinema* (Stanford, CA: Stanford University Press, 2001), 2. Gordon points out that 'epileptic singers' exploded onto the café-concert scene between 1875 and 1878, while Mark S. Micale has suggested that the Salpêtrière became a household name in 1878 after a deluge of popular news coverage. In Gordon, *Why the French Love Jerry Lewis*, 3. See also Mark S. Micale, *Approaching Hysteria: Disease and Its Interpretation* (Princeton, NJ: Princeton University Press, 1995).

36. Gordon, *Why the French Love Jerry Lewis*, 2–3.

37. J. F. C. Hecker, 'The Dancing Mania', in *The Epidemics of the Middle Ages*, trans. B. G. Babington (London: Trübner & Co., 1859), 75–162, 80. All citations from this edition unless otherwise indicated.

of possibility—the 'not yet' that Hannah Arendt (1906–1975) submits defines our relationship to politics, as she observes that we have not yet learned, in Lepecki's rendition, 'how to move politically'.[38] Lepecki sees this as a challenge and an invitation to think what it might mean to marry the kinetic and the political, to see choreography as a tool for experimenting with manners of moving politically—finding structures of freedom in motion. This means confronting, even staging, the cultures of control that demarcate our daily lives—choreographies of crowd control that enforce these 'choreopolice' mechanisms—thus highlighting a practice of boundary-making and an embodied system of order which may be transgressed, trespassed, or exposed.[39] For Foster, choreographies of protest describe intelligent bodies engaging in collective action together, whether spontaneously or no; bodies reading other bodies suggest a wilful coming together that enacts grassroots activism.[40] With Lepecki and Foster, attention to the political potential of bodies moving together against structures of disempowerment presents a groundswell of opportunity for writing critical histories of movement and dance, thinking the collective shapes and distributions of order (and disorder) that surround us, and, I further highlight, the discursive histories that articulate these. Indeed, the investment of dance theory and dance history in political *movement* reaches to the heart of the discipline, where it engages bodily action and events organized (or, conversely, disorganized) to produce meaningful forms of social life. The typically hyperbolic language of *disorganization* characteristic of choreomania narratives found in the pages of medical and ethnographic journals and compendia, colonial correspondence and government archives, adds to the urgency of these analyses a murkier, messier tone. St. Vitus's dance, the tarantella, the Convulsionaries of Saint-Médard in early eighteenth-century Paris, the Abyssinian *tigretier*, the *imanenjana* in Madagascar, and other episodes of so-called choreomania perform distinct political movements and public presence. But these movements and presences come to be framed in terms that highlight a lack of organization; they appear to eschew choreographic purpose. Some are not dances at all but dance-like neurological disorders cast as instances of an epidemic dancing disease. Yet in every case, the language of disorder casts moving bodies in an act of mediation: the archival repertoire of corporeal and choreographic *disorder* reveals a complex history of stories about transgression, revealing the spectre of bodily order against which these choreic bodies trespass.

This choreomaniacal concept of movement approaches what Giorgio Agamben has described as movement's 'impossibility', its status as the 'indefiniteness and imperfection of every politics'.[41] For Agamben, the ill-defined, under-theorized, and historically ambivalent concept of movement represents all that eludes political organization. Although the political meaning of 'movement' dates to the first part of the nineteenth century—specifically the French July Revolution of 1830, which pitted the Parti du Mouvement (Movement Party) against the Parti de l'Ordre (Party of Order)[42]—and although the German political theorist Lorenz von Stein (1815–1890) posited 'movement' in opposition to the static state in *The History of Social Movements in France* (1850), movement, Agamben insists, has more recently become allied to state-sponsored fascist politics. Reading Arendt, he notes that twentieth-century appropriations of the political concept of 'movement' foregrounded demagogical and populist organizations whose totalitarian discipline moved far away from the open-ended, non-teleological flux of movement as lack, residue, and imperfection: as the 'threshold', as he puts it, 'between an excess and a deficiency that marks every politics'.[43]

In this book, 'movement' figures at once as political and as gestural excess, imperfection, and indeterminacy. Movement is that which emerges in the nineteenth-century scientific field as a node within which corporeal actions in the public sphere acquire meaning by virtue of their hermeneutic opacity, their unwillingness to signify, their aesthetic and political deficiency.

38. André Lepecki, 'Choreopolice and Choreopolitics: Or, the Task of the Dancer', *TDR: The Drama Review* 57.4 [T220] (2013): 13–27, 13. See also Hannah Arendt, *Was ist Politik? Fragmente aus dem Nachlass* (Munich: Piper, 1993), 13.

39. Lepecki, 'Choreopolice and Choreopolitics', 13–15.

40. Susan Leigh Foster, 'Choreographies of Protest', *Theatre Journal* 55.3 (2003): 395–412.

41. Giorgio Agamben, 'Movement', in André Lepecki, ed., *Dance* (Cambridge, MA: MIT Press, 2012), 142–144, 144.

42. Agamben, 'Movement', 142.

43. Agamben, 'Movement', 143–144.

While Agamben further reminds us that 'movement' was long theorized in science and philosophy, at least beginning with Aristotle (384–322 BCE), whose notion of *kinesis* represented the strategic link between power and action—specifically, power's acting qua power, its capacity to act—the new political *movements* of the nineteenth century bring a different sort of urgency to the question of movement in public space, and to what we may construe as biopower. Here, I show, movement comes to be enmeshed in a political sphere, without leaving behind the organic, the biological. Science, philosophy, and politics in the nineteenth century are entangled in a complex of ideas about human aggregates erupting into chaotic, disorderly movement, particularly during times of social revolt cast as disease.

In most of the cases I describe, these movements are not construed by their observers in the political sense, as social organization, as choreographed intercession. Rather, these movements are conceived as excrescences in the human landscape intimately accompanying historical change, as its corporeal sign and reflection. This change is not only social or political, but ecological: plagues, famines, and floods all serve as the landscapes within which 'choreomanias' erupt. Bodies, in this view, move in tandem with social, political and ecological upheaval, in what I describe, following Guattari, as an *ecosophical* conception of movement disorder (construed in a collective, political sense) and of movement disorders (to designate individual conditions). As a branch of philosophy that considers the entire ecological sphere as grounds within which concepts emerge and transform, *ecosophy* posits the radical lack of hierarchy between different aspects of mental, social, and environmental movement.[44] Bodies within this paradigm pass transversally across institutions and ideas about 'nature' in a general ecology of thought and action that co-constitutes environments within which ideas like science, politics, and dance emerge and take shape. In this regard, my work engages with a number of conversations on social and political movement (and *movements*) at the limits of dance, including Andrew Hewitt's *Social Choreography: Ideology as Performance in Dance and Everyday Movement* (2005), which emphasizes the way movement

aesthetically embodies social order, and Martin's *Critical Moves: Dance Studies in Theory and Politics* (1998), which understands dance as a social process, a means by which bodies gather, and the ends by which this gathering produces or reveals mobilization.[45] Whereas Hewitt and Martin both emphasize the broader social and cultural field within which dance emerges as the crystallization or intensification of performative movement, this book reads the discursive history of movement's disorderly exceptions: the way narratives of choreographic unrest create figures of order which they are set against. Disorder is not only positively defined; its description structures a fantasy of orderliness whose disruption choreomanias exemplify. My approach further offers a distinct view of disability within the dance and performance studies fields, and another history of alternative mobilities founding modern science. So whereas Ann Cooper Albright, Petra Kuppers, and many others have offered groundbreaking work on dance and disability foregrounding identity and social politics of difference in a normative social sphere, this book repositions the question of 'movement disorder' onto broader historical terrain to interrogate ways of thinking and writing about incoordination, disjunction, and eccentricity as crowd conditions embedded into the fabric of sociopolitical life and its imagined prehistories.

In this regard, my work engages with the emerging areas of gesture, movement, and mobility studies, cross-pollinating anthropology, history of science and medicine, performance studies, and theatre and dance, among other scientific, social scientific, and arts and humanities disciplines. These broadly interdisciplinary arenas, exemplified by recent titles including Fiona Wilkie's *Performance, Transport and Mobility: Making Passage* (2014) and Carrie Noland and Sally Ann Ness's *Migrations of Gesture* (2008), suggest the reconfiguration of disciplines in an academic landscape in which scholars continue to be intellectually restless despite increasing institutional pressures to streamline, to become ever more marketable and paradoxically, ever more disciplinary. On the contrary, the proliferation of new cross-disciplinary fields of study in the last decades suggests the continued reorganization of our ways of thinking about movement and discipline. Yet whereas Noland and Ness's

---

44. See esp. Félix Guattari, *The Three Ecologies*, trans. Ian Pindar and Paul Sutton (London: Continuum, 2008).
45. Martin, *Critical Moves*, 6.

brilliant work on gesture offers productive ways of reading barely choreographed movement at the limits of dance, their focus on the experience of the body—kinaesthetic sense—differs markedly from my own interest in the historical discourse of disorderly movement in a broadly scientific arena. Noland's emphasis on writing as a gestural act, a form of inscription and therefore movement, nonetheless prefigures what I offer here. Indeed, this book seeks to engage with the problem of writing as movement in a disciplinary, a discursive, and a material sense: this book traces the movement of ideas across centuries and disciplinary terrains, from medieval Latin chronicles to travel diaries and textbook histories of the new colonial nation states. This movement, I show, takes place as medical and other writers carry texts and concepts with them throughout the colonial world. These writers read one another, teach each other's theories, repeat examples they hear of or read about in scientific journals, operating much like Deleuze and Guattari's figure of the orchid and the wasp, cross-pollinating one another's writing, at home and overseas.

This does not mean mobility in itself is good. This book instead works through a field of thought about corporeal dislocations, and their locations and relocations in a shifting disciplinary arena. This book further responds to a recent surge of writing about dance and science, and the *scientistic* worldview with which much of this writing has been approached. Scientism understands science to constitute the greatest, most objective method and authority, and the most reliable as well as the most socially sanctioned approach to conceptualizing body, mind, disability, difference, dance, and theatre, among other things. In a climate in which the arts have had to fight bitterly for a place in elementary, high school, undergraduate, and graduate education as well as public policy, science, particularly medicine and neuroscience, have served as handy allies to help fund and legitimize otherwise precarious fields. Kinaesthetic empathy, mirror neurons, and body-mind education in particular have significantly reconfigured the way dancers, dance historians, and educators think about the dancing body in motion, allying research in experimental neuroscience with experimental dance practice. Influential writing by Glenna Batson, Dee Reynolds, Deirdre Sklar, Lena Hammergren, Bettina Bläsing, and others suggests that scientific research can productively illuminate the way we understand motion on and off the stage, including particularly the way we watch dance.[46] Without disputing the urgency or cogency of these finds, this book seeks to present a slightly different story, articulating the discursive history and genealogy of dance's broad entanglement with science, tracing very old interactions between ideas about dance, humanistic method, and scientific history. I show how a prehistory of the current 'cognitive revolution', or 'neuroturn',[47] with which artists and critics have sought to explain creative movement can productively complicate notions of priority and precedence; and thus also trouble the perceived gaps—and seemingly novel bridges—between dance and medical science posited in contemporary popular and academic discourse.

Throughout this book, I show that fantasies about dance and locomotion—particularly disruptive locomotion—suffuse scientific writing, enmeshing ideas about history, modernity,

46. See e.g. Glenna Batson with Margaret Wilson, *Body and Mind in Motion: Dance and Neuroscience in Conversation* (Bristol: Intellect Books, 2014); Dee Reynolds and Matthew Reason, eds., *Kinesthetic Empathy in Creative and Cultural Practices* (Bristol: Intellect Books, 2012); Bettina Bläsing, Martin Puttke, and Thomas Schack, eds., *The Neurocognition of Dance: Mind, Movement and Motor Skills* (Hove, East Sussex: Psychology Press, 2010). Many of these studies, and a major research initiative and conference on kinaesthetic empathy organized in 2010 by Reynolds, Reason, and others, followed on from neurologist Alain Berthoz's influential *The Brain's Sense of Movement*, trans. Giselle Weiss (Cambridge, MA: Harvard University Press, 2000). In *Choreographing Empathy*, Susan Leigh Foster puts a philosophical spin on neurophysiological approaches to watching dance. Bruce McConachie and Nicola Shaughnessy among others have been at the helm of important research in theatre and performance studies highlighting the somatic effects of body actions onstage, what has come to be known as the arts and humanities' 'cognitive revolution'. See e.g. Bruce McConachie and F. Elizabeth Hart, eds., *Performance and Cognition: Theatre Studies and the Cognitive Turn* (Abingdon, Oxon: Routledge, 2006); and Nicola Shaughnessy, ed., *Affective Performance and Cognitive Science: Body, Brain and Being* (London: Bloomsbury Methuen, 2013). In dance practice, choreographers including Wayne McGregor have productively collaborated with neuroscientists. See e.g. Kélina Gotman, 'Epilepsy, Chorea and Involuntary Movements Onstage: The Aesthetics and Politics of Alterkinetic Dance', *About Performance* 11 (2011): 159–183. Janice Ross, in 'Illness as Danced Urban Ritual', in Mark Franko, ed., *Ritual and Event: Interdisciplinary Perspectives* (London: Routledge, 2007), 138–158, offers a slightly different approach, emphasizing the therapeutic aspects of highly ritualized dance practice in Anna Halprin's choreographic work, and the alternative this poses to illness narratives.

47. For a critique of the enthusiastic appropriation of neuroscientific terminology in the contemporary arts and humanities, see Kélina Gotman, 'The Neural Metaphor', in Melissa Littlefield and Janelle Johnson, eds., *The Neuroscientific Turn: Transdisciplinarity in the Age of the Brain* (Ann Arbor: University of Michigan Press, 2012), 71–86.

culture, and politics with ideas about imitative gesture. Scientific findings are not applied to dance theory or to dance education and practice in this view, but are saturated with ideas about and images of dance and dance-like forms of corporeality. Scientific method itself appears in the pages that follow to be far less 'objective', systematic, and in this sense 'scientific' than aleatory, narrative, and in some respects quintessentially arts-like. Collage, montage, and hearsay constitute the primary methods of choreomania's articulation.[48]

A further few titles are worth mentioning, the better to provide a discursive context and critical genealogy for this work. In *Foules en délire, extases collectives* [Delirious Crowds, Collective Ecstasies] (1947) and *L'enchantement des danses, et la magie du verbe* [The Enchantment of Dance, and the Magic of the Word] (1957), the much overlooked French historian of religions Philippe de Félice (1880–1964) offers a comparative analysis of dance ecstasies around the world emphasizing spiritual rapture. His work influenced, among others, Elias Canetti's (1905–1994) now classic *Masse und Macht* [Crowds and Power] (1960). Both offer insight into histories of gregarious corporeal formations and the implicit power politics spiritual ecstasy enables. Also in the mid-twentieth century, the Swedish pharmacologist E. Louis Backman (1883–1965) compiled a broad array of narratives about religious and popular dances, many from Greek and Latin sources. His deep archival work makes this a useful and much-cited source on dance 'manias', but *Religious Dances in the Christian Church and in Popular Medicine* (1952) spuriously attributes all such dances to ergotism—a form of rye poisoning—generally over-medicalizing Latin descriptions. Drid Williams briefly mentions dance manias, including St. Vitus's dance, in *Ten Lectures on Theories of the Dance* (1991) but does not delve into the complex history of gestural events likened to St. Vitus's dance in medical literature on choreomania. And while Barbara Ehrenreich offers a celebratory account of communal dancing in her effusively upbeat *Dancing in the Streets: A History of Collective Joy* (2007), she too neglects the long and complex biomedical history of public dances and their extensive pathologization in colonial medical

and anthropological literature. More recently, Gregor Rohmann in *Tanzwut: Kosmos, Kirche und Mensch in der Bedeutungsgeschichte eines mittelalterlichen Krankheitskonzepts* [Dance Mania: Cosmos, Church and Man in the Emergence of the Idea of a Dancing Disease in the Middle Ages] (2013) and Johannes Birringer and Josephine Fenger in their edited volume *Tanz und WahnSinn/Dance and ChoreoMania* (2011) point to a rich array of events associated with the medieval 'dancing mania', from Greek concepts of enthusiasm (Rohmann) to choreographic practice (Birringer and Fenger). Both offer useful insight into the myriad ways 'dancing manias' have been figured historically and culturally, but once again largely elude the vast history of colonial representation the discursive history of 'choreomania' also occasions. From a theoretical and methodological standpoint, Stephen Muecke's short 'Choreomanias: Movements through Our Body', published in the Moving Bodies issue of *Performance Research* (2003), comes closest to sharing the critical investments I present here: with Muecke, I aim to think about the biopolitical and biophilosophical histories of dancing crowds, and discourses on abnormality attributed to fitful dancing in colonial medical culture.[49] I add to Muecke's brief study a far longer glance at the extended institutional and political genealogies by which the choreomania concept emerged and transformed. I also present Hecker as the under-acknowledged predecessor to the master of bodily fits, Charcot; and, by extension, to Charcot's most famous student, Freud. This view positions choreomania at the base of a whole field of thinking about primitivism, fitfulness, femininity, and taboo.

There are many things this book does not do. It does not go into the vast and by now extremely fraught terrain of possession, with which dance manias may be equated, though I offer alternative readings of possession culture in chapters 8 and 10 in particular, replacing this term with Agamben's in my view more productive concept of *ecstasy-belonging*, a notion he uses to describe a monarch's special status in a political system, and which I employ to read performative entanglements engaging possession culture in revolt. Similarly, I draw from Michael Taussig's notion of medicine as the *appearance* of

48. On arts and humanities methods as historically distinct from scientific (and some social scientific) methods, see esp. Sean Cubitt, 'Anecdotal Evidence', *NECSUS: European Journal of Media Studies* 2.1 (2013): 5–18.

49. Stephen Muecke, 'Choreomanias: Movements through Our Body', *Performance Research* 8.4 (2003): 6–10.

disease in medical discourse through the reification of complex social relations. This enables me to bring notions of theatricality into fuller view as I move squarely onto ethnographic terrain, in later chapters, and the choreomania concept morphs to reveal an increasingly anti-theatrical concern with feminine and colonial deceit, a concern nearly absent in earlier readings of the 'choreomaniacal' Middle Ages. Finally, this book does not attempt a comprehensive account of so-called dance manias worldwide. Instead, by performing a genealogy of the choreomania concept in the long nineteenth century, I follow the traces of particular writers as they read one another, offer new anecdotes to complement those that came before, and continue a history connected, link by link, to narrative precedent.

ROOTS AND ROUTES

Thus this book traces the fantasy of movement's surfeit across 'fields': lands and discursive encounters. Following Gilroy's and James Clifford's shared investments in the homonymous interplay between 'roots' and 'routes' in colonial politics and cultural translation,[50] I trace the 'routes' and returns to imagined 'roots' performed by scientific writers, according to the vicissitudes of their administrative appointments, affiliations, and appetites. The book proceeds at once roughly chronologically and geographically, moving from Europe through the colonial world to end up provisionally in America. Taking Hecker as the epicentre of choreomania's nineteenth- and twentieth-century formation, I ground this book in the proliferation of writings spilling out of and into his text, particularly the paradigmatic 'dance mania', the medieval St. John's (or St. Vitus's) dance, and the Orientalizing annotations offered by his English translator, Benjamin Guy Babington (1794–1866). Chapter 1 traces the institutional history of Hecker's writing in 'The Dancing Mania' through various translations, particularly its publication history in the English-speaking world. As the rest of the book shows, this history of translation and scientific dissemination decisively enabled multiple additions to and importantly the Orientalization of the choreomania figure and concept in ensuing

decades. Concerned with Hecker's interest in medical history, at a time when antiquarian feeling was widespread (and hotly contested) in science, chapter 1 considers epistemological and methodological problems associated with writing a history of epidemic dance in the literary scientific world of the nineteenth century. Chapter 2 presents the first paradigmatic case of 'choreomania', the medieval St. John's dance (retrospectively described as St. Vitus's dance), further presenting my central concern with Foucault's history of 'madness' and the way a history of 'choreomania' extends this to cases of unchoreographed dance at the edges of the social and human sciences. The chapter highlights the Eastern-inflected Dionysianism with which nineteenth-century writers, including Hecker and Nietzsche, viewed the purportedly orgiastic Middle Ages; I contrast this with my own reading of Latin chronicles and annals, to suggest that this demoniacal plague, as it was often described, actually constituted a form of social fête and, often, dancing migration. Chapter 3 moves to the early modern writings of Paracelsus on St. Vitus's dance, importantly offering the first practical and theoretical amalgamation of dancing crowds with medical theories of gestural spasms, such as would define centuries of writing on the 'dancing disease'. The chapter considers Agamben's notion of purposeless gesture, a term he employs to denote chorea's proximity to dance, specifically its non-narrative, non-teleological aspects, a 'purposelessness' that, later chapters show, would become central to the deployment of criticism against 'choreomania' as movement devoid of (in fact inhibiting) productive labour. In chapter 4, I turn further to the question of meaningless gesture, specifically as this came to describe early eighteenth-century popular religious practices among the French Convulsionnaires (Convulsionaries) of Saint-Médard, a heterodox group of enthusiasts performing acts of contortion and dissidence in the margins of the nation's capital. I argue that Convulsionaries' effusive poses, however, suggest more than a hysteroepileptic brand of acting out, as Charcot would later contend, and reveal instead a spirit of political contestation resonant with emerging theories of psychiatry emphasizing feminine and queer sorts of gestural and emotional excess. Chapter 5 takes the

50. See esp. Gilroy, *The Black Atlantic*, and James Clifford, *Routes: Travel and Translation in the Late Twentieth Century* (Cambridge, MA: Harvard University Press, 1997).

notion of excess gesture and pathological contagion further into the terrain of early sociology and the modern theorization of unruly crowds. Beginning with the dramatic upheavals of the French Revolution and their recuperation into early crowd theory, the chapter foregrounds a discursive genealogy linking revolutionary movements and the emergence of nation states with involuntary 'Jerks' among religious enthusiasts in the American South. The chapter importantly introduces the rise of crowd theory to describe (often disparagingly) the imitative gestures and mimicry particular to large, roused groups of people, a line of theorization that would become increasingly central to later theories of choreomania overseas. Chapter 6 centres on Charcot and the rise of neurology, as well as (far less often noted in studies of his work) the historiographical aspects—or 'retrospective medicine'—he and a number of his collaborators engaged in at the Salpêtrière hospital in Paris, methods that I show would decisively influence the way choreomania, as a putatively ancient disorder, would become translated and exported into medical theory overseas. The chapter argues that Charcot's recourse to ancient images, artefacts, and narratives set the stage for a significant methodological shift in scientific research from laboratory to fieldwork; and, importantly for the discursive history of choreomania I tell here, from colonial medicine to anthropology, hastening the journey of the 'dancing disease' onto colonial terrain.

Part II draws the discourse on choreomania further into colonial territory, and introduces substantial case histories. Chapter 7 turns to the southern Italian tarantella and the Orientalist exoticism imagining southern Italy as a gateway to Africa and the East. The chapter emphasizes comparative methods in medicine and anthropology and the discourse on sex, fakery, and lies that articulated choreomania as a feminine and colonial disorder of duplicity. Woman, Freud wrote, was a 'dark continent', like Africa, unknowable and other; as a disorder of colonialism and femininity, choreomania becomes a 'dark continent', obscurely ancient and also as such nearly unfathomable. Chapter 8 moves further into Africa and South America, to Madagascar and Brazil, where travelling physicians, including some of Charcot's students, meet live instances of political turmoil they read as yet another example of the dancing disease. Significantly, choreomania now comes squarely to signal the 'disorder' of anti-colonial revolt. Drawing primarily from Scottish missionary physician Andrew Davidson's (1836–1918) colonial medical writing on the disease-like protest known as the *imanenjana*, as well as from the French-trained Malagasy physician Dr. Andrianjafy's reinterpretation of the *imanenjana* as a malarial type of neuromotor disease, I argue that choreomania becomes imagined as a disorder of political contestation and regime change, displacing the polite antiquarianism of earlier nineteenth-century readings. Chapter 9 moves to the American Plains, where a further political movement, the Ghost Dance, highlights cultural contestation in response to widespread repression of Native Americans together with the rise of government-sponsored ethnographic studies. The Ghost Dance, which Mooney likened to St. Vitus's dance, provided him with a phantasmatic link between current events and earlier instances of the so-called dancing mania, positioning Native American dancers in a genealogical line with ancient ecstatics and collective delusion. Perpetuating the Orientalist trope by which antiquity and alterity meet in a convulsive, feverish display of excessive dancing by colonized subjects, the discursive history of the Ghost Dance especially highlights the politics of popular discourse on energetic waste and cultural war. In chapter 10, I turn to a further set of case histories of choreomania in the South Seas, extending the scope of the 'dancing disease' and its purported sightings to the far reaches of Antipodean life, as cargo cults and other liberation movements further complicate the genealogical relations between social bodies in distress and their (obliquely) imagined prehistories. Chapter 11 finally turns to the rise of popular dances in America—the tango, animal dances, and dance marathons—likened in medical literature to medieval dance manias, further entrenching the literature on choreomania in an Orientalist and now an increasingly racist discourse on darkness and the supposed pathological angularity of gestural disinhibition. This final chapter further inscribes the racialized body—increasingly, a black body—into the Orientalist prejudice against obscure and unknowable others. The coda ultimately brings the discussion on choreomania into the twenty-first century, to reflect on my own methodological moves in tracing this genealogical history of the dancing disease as a history of dance in an expanded field; and the implications of this extended genealogy for thinking about concepts of dance imbricated in the geo-choreopolitics of protest.

Every study is determined by its author's places and privileges. This book has been written from the standpoint of a woman long trained in classical ballet, modern and contemporary dance, and Argentine tango but also long attuned to the ambivalence and unpredictability of dancing crowds. From the centre of a mosh pit at a Nirvana concert in Montreal to a rave in the English Cotswolds, my adolescence and early adulthood were marked by moments I experienced as uninhibited dancing and the intoxication that came with what a good friend and I saw as being high on life. But with these high points came moments of anger and frustration. When a friend of mine was (as I learned subsequently) taken away by police to a psychiatric hospital because she refused to stop dancing at a protest, I was livid. This offence on the part of the local authorities epitomized to me everything that was wrong with political life: the coalescence of forces of law with the forces of capital to clamp down on a young woman taking up public space; spirited expression throttled; protest confined. This book attempts to reckon with a few of these issues, horribly incompletely. But I hope to have marked out a small area for reflecting on the meeting point between control, abnormality, and disinhibition, as well as the language of dance where it meets those of political disorder and disease. I hope this work will inspire more studies of dance, psychiatry, and colonialism, and the discourse on imitation that has branded uncontrolled movement as quaint, at best; at worst, as dangerous and unthinking.

PART I

Excavating Dance in the Archive

1

Obscuritas Antiquitatis
Institutions, Affiliations, Marginalia

I only ever wrote fictions.

—Michel Foucault, quoted in Gilles Deleuze, *Foucault* (1986)

AFFILIATIONS, AUDIENCES, AND INSTITUTIONS

'Every writer on the Orient . . . assumes some Oriental precedent', Said writes, 'some previous knowledge of the Orient, to which he refers and on which he relies'. So too, Said writes, highlighting the institutional ecologies within which such ideas take shape, 'each work on the Orient *affiliates* itself with other works, with audiences, with institutions, with the Orient itself'.[1] The Orient, as an occidental construct stretching from India to Africa and the Middle East, emerges out of pre-existing fantasies about the East assumed by Orientalist writers to be commonly shared, and extends these to produce an evolving fiction without origin or centre, even if the fiction may be concerned with both. This is a fiction that simultaneously draws on geographic regions that are real and arbitrarily connected in the Orientalist imagination; and it spins new imaginaries about this expansive terrain—the so-called Orient—by shifting and spreading the terms of its discourse rhizomatically. Orientalist works, in this sense 'affiliate' with others to construct the Orient, which they simultaneously rewrite. This chapter examines the discursive and institutional history—the affiliations and the fictions—informing Hecker's work, *Die Tanzwuth*, which I argue shapes the nineteenth-century emergence of the choreomania concept, though Hecker, I submit, is not alone 'author' of the modern notion of choreomania. Rather, Hecker

---

1. Said, *Orientalism*, 20. On the notion of *affiliation*, as a counterpart to the 'airtight' fixity or structural orthodoxy and learned homogeneity of disciplinary 'fields', see also Edward W. Said, 'Opponents, Audiences, Constituencies and Community', in Hal Foster, ed., *The Anti-Aesthetic: Essays on Postmodern Culture* (Port Townsend, WA: Bay Press, 1983), 135–159, esp. 136, 143–146.

participated in (and was in many respects at the helm of) a moment in medical science in which the very movement of modernity appeared as a discourse of experimental reason and pragmatic application, but also a literary pursuit, engaged in historiographic antiquarianism. Concepts and figures of thought among medical writers reprised ancient, often mythic tropes: in the case of choreomania, most prominently, Dionysian bacchanals.

This chapter thus foregrounds the way the choreomania concept emerged in the nineteenth century, out of other literatures and figures of thought, in tandem with a whole set of historical, material, and institutional transformations. In this regard, the chapter is about method, but also about the way method is determined by institutional configurations, audiences, and the vicissitudes of individual presses and societies, co-determining ecologies of production and circulation. What this chapter (and this book) argue is that 'choreomania' could only emerge as it did in the long nineteenth century, and that it is in this regard fundamentally reflective of the modern industrial West: the discursive history of 'choreomania' reveals an emergent set of concerns about collectivity, crowds, and disorder saturating medical and scientific thought, at a time when scientists sought to countermand an economic and political rush to the future with queries about origins, and about the human and ecological past. In this regard, I argue, 'choreomania' becomes allied with—in many respects, a variation, expansion, and transformation of—Orientalism, a force of plasticity morphing and migrating at the time, and like choreomania concerned with precedent.

In the case of choreomania, notions of irregular motion and drunken-like ecstasy already dotted medical writing; but Hecker's work put in motion a collection of scenes constituting choreomania's epidemic formulation. With Hecker, choreomania became a disorder of collective chaos increasingly mapped onto marginal bodies seeming to impede the rise of modern nation states. 'Choreomania' with Hecker and writers after him signalled all that was primeval and disruptive among groups of people apparently not *yet* moving rationally or smoothly—not yet demonstrating what Schwartz calls the modern, curvilinear quality of torque.

THE MOTION OF TRANSFORMISM

The history of choreomania thus describes what Bergson calls the biophilosophical motion of *transformism*, by which biological entities and thoughts evolve, without a first cause or origin.[2] Concepts and bodies, Bergson argues, unfold over time, displacing a moving centre through acts of invention and reduplication. Concepts thus have no 'history', no origin (even if they may be concerned with these), only present iterations that are continually displaced; in this sense, concepts perform choreographic trajectories, often weaving through discursively or institutionally marginal sites. This process, I submit, constitutes a 'marginal' function, which we may see in contraposition to Foucault's notion of the 'author' function, by which an author must be understood as an assemblage composed of many parts: editor, publishing house, social and institutional moment, and a whole discursive sphere determined to value such a thing as an 'author', and so to produce the fiction of a subject meant to inhabit that role.[3] The 'marginal' function takes into account such assemblages, and further suggests that concepts move across 'authorial' sites through repetition, recuperation, and translation: translators' footnotes, later editions, and the whole critical apparatus defining and rewriting a work in later iterations shift the site of the work's instantiation. The margin becomes the space within which works migrate and, almost imperceptibly, transform.

Writers in Hecker's wake drew fulsomely from his text, sometimes citing him, often not. He was excavating, collaging, and extrapolating from earlier scenes. Choreomania thus arises as writers pilfer from one another, splintering and redirecting vectors of information, recuperating and expanding on an ever-shifting set of archival scenes. There is no fixed 'centre' to the choreomania story; only a perpetually moving and constantly returned-to cast of illustrations, to which more were periodically added. Although Hecker's writing on St. Vitus's dance gains the consistency of a paradigm inasmuch as it is by far most often repeated and rehearsed, it does so, I venture, because his writing offers the plasticity and partiality of the example, rather than the rule. The concept of choreomania

---

2. Henri Bergson, *L'évolution créatrice* (Paris: Presses Universitaires de France, 2001), 23–44.

3. See Michel Foucault, 'What Is an Author?', in trans. Josué V. Harari, Paul Rabinow, ed., *The Foucault Reader* (New York: Pantheon Books, 1984), 101–120.

is a zone of intensity in the history of nine-teenth- and twentieth-century modernity, a clustering of cases that never quite cohere yet grow and morph across continents to describe the disorderly movements of crowds and individual disorders purported to echo and portend these. Knowledge in the story I tell here is thus not disciplined but anarchic: it borrows and steals, overhears, exaggerates, jumps between eras, and performs rash comparative acts. Knowledge of choreomania, or more often knowledge *about* choreomania, flits between neurological practice, historical speculation, exoticizing aside, and the amateur's passion for collecting outlandish tales. Choreomania, then, is constructed from discursive bits, assembled and reassembled, moving through disciplinary nodes and losing, or acquiring, new traits on the go. As an idea about bodies spilling out of bounds, choreomania itself spills out of bounds, morphing, recuperating figures of thought—about spontaneity, Dionysus, the Middle Ages, plague—across fields, without stopping for very long at any one.

In this sense, this book—rather than showing an increasingly rational scientific mind-set in nineteenth-century modernity, what Foucault calls a history of veridiction (*véridiction*), describing scientific and governmental processes of truth-making (rather than earlier regimes propounding truth or *vérité*)—offers a history of scientific literature concerned very much with neither.[4] Veridiction held little sway for writers on the dancing disease, who offered narratives as if their dramatic power alone suggested the intuitive validity and literary interest of their study. Dramatic narratives—composed of brief and loosely connected scenes of dance-like ferment—constitute this disorder's primary site of discursive instantiation, its performative coming-to-be. Choreomania became itself through discursive repetition.

SCENES AND SCENARIOS

Although I describe 'scenes' and 'scenarios', borrowing Diana Taylor's term, and the distinction between them is slight, it is nonetheless worth noting. A 'scene', in the Foucauldian sense I employ, suggests an embodied event without finality or necessarily the implication of repetition. A 'scene' is a portrait of actions and events derived from the annals of the past: people engaged in bodily activity, whether or not the exact contours of their motions, intentions, or outcomes may be clearly determined. A 'scenario', closely related to a 'scene', further denotes what Taylor describes as the quality of repeatability—what she calls the 'paradigmatic' aspect that implies 'a schematic plot, with an intended (though adaptable) end'.[5] Scenarios are social scripts which antedate the fixity of a written script, but nonetheless anchor cultural and historical realities in particular modes of narrative and performative interaction. A conquistador once again subjugating a native woman may participate in a 'scenario' that antedates a script that may later describe it, but which constitutes, by its paradigmatic status, a whole mise en scène telling performance historians of the forms of action that characterized bodily and cultural being in the past. Whereas some of the 'scenes' I describe constitute 'scenarios' of a sort—repeatable, familiar forms of action that encapsulate historical and cultural realities in a more or less paradigmatic way—I am mostly intent on describing scenes that when repeated by Hecker and others become themselves paradigmatic. The archival repertoire moves scenes along through footnotes, gossip, and asides; and becomes a 'scenario' describing medical thought in formation as it comes to be scripted into medical literature. In effect, there never is any textbook choreomania, any hegemonic fixity to the choreomania score; it is never exactly a diagnosis, but remains, through its iterations, a collection and collation of scenic events.

Choreomania in this regard was a literary and performative diagnosis: dance manias never gained a 'truer' reality than on the medical page and in its margins—margins themselves written by and large overseas, as writers continually recast choreomania as an epidemic of dancing and disrepair recurring offshore. Reconfiguring thus the terms put forward by Taylor, this genealogy—and choreography—suggests an archive of moving bodies; but also, significantly, a repertoire of archival movements and turns.

---

4. See esp. Michel Foucault, 'Leçon du 17 janvier', in *Naissance de la biopolitique: Cours au Collège de France, 1978–1979*, ed. François Ewald, Alessandro Fontana, and Michel Senellart (Paris: Éditions du Seuil/Gallimard, 2004), 29–51, 34–38.

5. Taylor, *The Archive and the Repertoire*, 13.

ARCHAEOLOGY, GENEALOGY, CHOREOGRAPHY

This book thus takes Foucault's notion of the discursive formation out of the realm of archaeology and genealogy into what I describe as choreography, a system of motion and transfer. Archaeology and genealogy are two overlapping methods Foucault presents, primarily in *Les mots et les choses: Une archéologie des sciences humaines* [The Order of Things] (1966) and *L'archéologie du savoir* [The Archaeology of Knowledge] (1969), as well as *Surveiller et Punir* [Discipline and Punish] (1975) and his essay 'Nietzsche, la généalogie, l'histoire' ['Nietzsche, Genealogy, History'] (1971) to describe his work quarrying the past as a set of layers or strata, relations and conversations, *not* moving teleologically towards increasing rationalization or better governance but comprising their own more or less coherent logics (their discourses).

Hecker's essay 'The Dancing Mania' engages such a choreographic motion. His essay appeared in multiple editions after its initial publication in Berlin in 1832, including translations into Dutch, French, and Italian.[6] Also immediately translated into English by the London-based Sydenham Society's Orientalist treasurer, B. G. Babington, Hecker's essay marked the first of the Sydenham Society's publications, distributed to all its members. A third English edition

of Hecker's text, significantly, became available for the general public in 1859, the same year as *On the Origin of Species* by Charles Darwin (1809–1882). Subtitled *Or The Preservation of Favoured Races in the Struggle for Life*, Darwin's work was also concerned, fittingly, with origins, though Darwin's iconic account posited a teleological progression which Hecker's pell-mell juxtaposition of scenes did not.[7] Translated into English as *The Epidemics of the Middle Ages*, Hecker's new volume comprised three essays, 'The Black Death', 'The Dancing Disease', and 'The Sweating Sickness', supplemented in 1859 by a short essay, 'Child-Pilgrimages', which the editors described as 'never before translated'. They deemed it especially valuable, as this volume was now 'the *first* and *only* in the English language, which contains *all* the contributions of Dr. Hecker to the History of Medicine'.[8] These editorial efforts bore fruit. Popular media quickly got wind of these tales of epidemic dancing, and from the *Penny Magazine of the Society for the Diffusion of Useful Knowledge* to *Fraser's Magazine for Town and Country*, *Chambers's Journal of Popular Literature, Science and Arts*, *Popular Science Review*, *St. James's Magazine*, and *Blackwood's Edinburgh Magazine*, Hecker's depiction of dancing manias spread nearly verbatim,[9] also informing general reference works such as the *Schaff-Herzog Encyclopedia of Religious Knowledge* (1888).[10] Choreomanias seemed to be cropping up everywhere, each revealing

---

6. The first translation of Hecker's monograph, *Die Tanzwuth, eine Volkskrankheit im Mittelalter* (Berlin: T. C. F. Enslin, 1832), was published the following year in Dutch as *De danswoede, eene volksziekte der Middeleeuwen, in de Nederlanden, Duitschland en Italië, volgens het hoogduitsch door G. J. Pool* (Amsterdam: Sülpke, 1833). It was translated the year after into French by Ferdinand Dubois as 'Mémoire sur la chorée épidémique du moyen âge', *Annales d'hygiène et de médecine légale* 12 (1834): 312–390, though an early summary account had already appeared in the *Gazette médicale de Paris* 4, 1.2, 3 January 1833, 5–6. The Italian translation was published a few years later as *La Danzimania, malattia poplare nel medio-evo* (Firenze: Ricordi, 1838). Hecker's three essays on medieval epidemics, including his essay on the dancing mania, an essay on the Black Death, and an essay on the sweating sickness, were first collected and translated in a single volume by Babington as *The Epidemics of the Middle Ages* (London: Sherwood, Gilbert and Piper, 1835) and reprised by a number of English-language publishers in London and Philadelphia, including, most prominently, the Sydenham Society, whose first publication it constituted in 1844 (at 1,750 copies). It was reprinted a second time before being released for the general public in the standard 1859 edition I refer to throughout. Hecker's trio of essays was subsequently re-edited in the German by Dr. August Hirsch and published as *Die Grossen Volkskrankheiten des mittelalters: Historisch-pathologische Untersuchungen* (Berlin: Verlag von Th. Chr. Fr. Enslin, 1865).

7. Charles Darwin, *On the Origin of Species. Or The Preservation of Favoured Races in the Struggle for Life* (London: John Murray, 1859).

8. Trübner and Co., 'Address to the Reader', in Hecker, *Epidemics of the Middle Ages*, iii.

9. See e.g. 'Dr Madden's "Phantasmata,"' *Chambers's Journal of Popular Literature, Science and Arts* 237 (1858): 34–37; 'Epidemics, Past and Present—Their Origin and Distribution', *Scottish Review* 4.13 (1865): 593–604; 'On Epidemic Delusions', *Scottish Review* 2.7 (1854): 193–208; 'Endemic and Epidemic Diseases', *Penny Magazine for the Diffusion of Useful Knowledge* 10.605 (1841): 346–348; 'A Dancing Epidemic', *Chambers's Journal of Popular Literature, Science and Arts* 20.1040 (1883): 760–762; 'General Considerations on Epidemic Diseases', *Chambers's Edinburgh Journal* 296 (1849): 132–136; and 'The Dancing Mania', *Penny Magazine of the Society for the Diffusion of Useful Knowledge* 8.488 (1839): 439–440, all of which rehearse Hecker's writing with little or no variation, except to note his work's currency and familiarity to the modern reader. 'Mental Epidemics', *Fraser's Magazine for Town and Country* 65.388 (April 1862): 490–505, further makes reference to the familiarity of the St. Vitus's name (494).

10. See e.g. Philip Schaff, ed., *A Religious Encyclopædia: Or Dictionary of Biblical, Historical, Doctrinal, and Practical Theology. Based on the Real-Encyklopädie of Herzog, Plitt and Hauck*, 3rd ed., 4 vols., vol. 1 (London: Funk and Wagnalls, 1891), 602. This encyclopedia appeared in numerous versions throughout the latter half of the nineteenth and early twentieth century, from Johann Jakob Herzog's (1805–1882) original German edition, the *Realencyklopädie für protestantische Theologie und Kirche*, published in

---

something about human life in the aggregate. For the general English reader able to procure a copy of Hecker's text in its 1859 edition or to learn about it in popular magazines, choreomanias constituted a new sort of historical curiosity, weird and wonderful. Described in nearly comical terms in popular journals, Hecker's depiction of dance maniacs emphasized physical eccentricities and emotional fervor, characteristics folded into an increasingly fashionable discourse according to which epidemic contagion was typical of modern life.

General and scientific interest in popular epidemics was growing. *Extraordinary Popular Delusions and the Madness of Crowds*, by popular historian Charles Mackay (1814–1889), published in London in 1841 and 1852, reprinted in 1856, and again in multiple further editions in the century and a half to follow, catalogued every sort of common mania for the general reader, from the 'tulip mania' to witchcraft delusions, attributing all these to human beings' apparently universal propensity for gregariousness and imitation. Although Mackay omitted dance manias in his compendium, a new foreword in 1932 by the American financier Bernard M. Baruch (1870–1965) did not fail to make the link.[11]

The cycling epidemic was a further copycat disorder alluded to with a mixture of humour and gravity in the popular press.[12] Like the dance mania, it portrayed excess locomotion among its enthusiasts, particularly worrisome when these were women. In the case of choreomania, however, epidemic dancing motions significantly *went nowhere*. They erupted as excess energy and affect rather than as the ability to escape constricted quarters and become thus independent. Choreomaniacs, unlike cyclists, seemed instead to lose their capacity for independent motion.

Movement of every sort was becoming, more than ever before, an object of study and overarching principle uniting philosophy, politics, and science. In the words of physiologist Claude Bernard (1813–1878), movement fundamentally defined behaviour. In studies conducted by Étienne-Jules Marey (1830–1904), Eadweard Muybridge (1830–1904), and others labouring in their wake to create chronotopographies that captured gestural motions frame by frame, motion could be taken as the basis for sensory as well as affective behaviour.[13] Movement, in Marey's terms, 'is the most important act, in that all other functions employ it to actualize themselves'.[14] This biological and aesthetic principle extended to the political realm. For anarchist philosopher Pierre-Joseph Proudhon (1809–1865), movement defined all of politics and economics: 'Le mouvement est; voilà tout' he proclaimed in *Philosophie du progrès* [Philosophy of Progress] (1853);[15] 'Movement is; that is all'. Life could be contained in the principle of motion.

But whereas modern concepts of movement typically emphasize forward progress (and, in Proudhon's case, political progressiveness), a

---

twenty-two volumes between 1853 and 1868, to *The New Schaff-Herzog Encyclopedia of Religious Knowledge*, published in thirteen volumes between 1908 and 1914. The English version by Philip Schaff (1819–1893), titled *A Religious Encyclopædia . . .* , based on Herzog's German editions, appeared in three editions between 1882 and 1891. Following publication of the third edition, in four volumes (the first of which is detailed above), the text became commonly known as the *Schaff-Herzog Encyclopedia*. I will refer to it as such throughout.

11. Bernard M. Baruch, 'Foreword', in Charles Mackay, *Extraordinary Popular Delusions and the Madness of Crowds* (London: L. C. Page, 1932), xiv.

12. T. Pilkington White, 'The Cycling Epidemic', *Scottish Review* 29 (1897): 56–74.

13. Étienne-Jules Marey, *Du mouvement dans les fonctions de la vie. Leçons faites au Collège de France* (Paris: Germer Baillière, 1868).

14. Marey, *Du mouvement dans les fonctions de la vie*, vi.

15. Cited in Hannah Arendt, *On Violence* (San Diego: Harcourt, Brace, 1970), 26. See Pierre-Joseph Proudhon, *Philosophie du progrès: Programme* (Brussels: Alphonse Lebègue, 1853), 39 (not 49 as in Arendt). See also Joseph Proudhon, *Œuvres complètes de P.-J. Proudhon*, 26 vols., vol. 20 (Brussels: A. Lacroix, Verboeckhoven & cie., 1850–1871), and Joseph Proudhon, *Philosophie du progrès, suivi de La justice poursuivie par l'église, nouvelle édition* (Brussels, 1868), 30. Arendt slightly misquotes Proudhon, adding an exclamation mark for emphasis, but the sentiment is accurate. Proudhon's Heraclitean anarchism takes all movement, change, transformation, 'progress' (which he opposes to 'tradition') (106), as the foundation of life and politics: 'Tout ce qui existe . . . est nécessairement en évolution; tout coule, tout change, se modifie, se transforme sans cesse: le mouvement est la condition essentielle, je dirais presque la matière de l'être et de la pensée. Il n'y a rien de fixe, de stable, d'absolu, d'invincible, que la Loi même du mouvement, c'est à dire, les *rapports* de poids, de nombre, de mesure, suivant lesquels toute existence apparaît et s'effectue' (90). Movement—manifest as relation ('*rapports*')—is the natural state and only law (30–31, 90); it is the first principle ('fait primitif') (27); throughout his work (subtitled 'programme', inviting direct action) he takes movement as 'axiomatic' (27). Elsewhere, the language of mathematics supplants biology (natural philosophy), as Proudhon argues that movement implies directionality but not end, as in a series of passages going from A → B (29, 34). Art and politics must, by the logic which proceeds from this, take place without state or nation, which perpetuate the old theological structures of immutability and eternity, thwarting movement and progress (20, 54, 71). Proudhon's logico-mathematical notion of perpetual evolution and change echoes but also subverts the Darwinian model of origins and the hierarchy of species; there is no origin (or end) for Proudhon but continuous motion and

minor literature of erratic, apparently purposeless and disorderly motions emerged as the counterpart to this brave new world's rapidly escalating and (it seemed to many) increasingly efficient pace. These moments of disturbance constituted the ripples, breaks, and surges coming up to haunt—symbolically to *disorganize or disorder*—a forward-moving present. On a technological plane, the introduction of the electromagnetic telegraph in 1833, compounded with the increasing speed and expanse of train travel and the inauguration of the underground metro system in London in 1863, meant that Europe and its allies were ever more in motion, stimulating the industrial revolution that would lead Karl Marx (1818–1883) to suggest in the *Grundrisse* (1857) that speed—time—would conquer space.[16] Marx described a capitalist regime driven to geographic expansion but even hungrier for rapid motion. Circulation, including the circulation of money and capital, defined the new era, in a system of flows connecting people and objects in relationships of power characterized by locomotion, though as I show, potentially unproductive forms of movement were typically branded as suspect.

Hecker's depiction of a dancing disease was timely. As Gilroy, Roach, and Gordon have variously pointed out, the languages of music, theatre, film, and, I add, dance—all quintessentially concerned with movement and time—underpinned the modern era, just as modern science and popular culture sidelined these as by-products, wasteful to the industrial man and woman engaged in an ethic of work, with little room left for play.[17] Yet social dance boomed at the time the choreomania diagnosis circulated. As dance historian Molly Engelhardt has shown, enthusiasm for rapid and racy ballroom dancing soared just as Victorian morality was seething from the effects of the cholera epidemics of the 1830s and 1840s. Contagion and insalubriousness seemed to threaten public life everywhere, not least among dancing groups. The medical notion of miasma, or polluted air, exacerbated already negative opinions about, and fascination for, groups of men and women rubbing shoulders in the dark and dirty dance halls of London.[18] Bodies bumping against and wriggling with one another seemed embarrassing and risqué, just as bodies moving chaotically in public space worried observers who were writing themselves, for the most part, right out of these scenes, as their somewhat disdainful hosts and raconteurs.

With the emergence of germ theory in the mid-nineteenth century, established by Louis Pasteur (1822–1895) in the 1860s, confirmed by microbiologist Robert Koch (1843–1910) in the decades following, concepts of miasma were revised, and the invisible workings of public space and interpersonal contact and communication became even more mysterious, host now to infinitesimally small creatures circulating directly between people, unknown to their carriers. In this context, crowds of people contaminating one another seemed socially disruptive. Added to this were continued colonial expansion and crisis; the explosive appearance of neurology on the medical scene; unprecedented levels of scientific exchange; renewed interest in antiquity; and the emergence of anthropology, to produce a zone of intensity within which 'choreomania' emerged.

LITERARY PROCLIVITIES: EPIDEMIOLOGY AND ANTIQUARIAN LITERATURE

Hecker's writing seized the imagination of his contemporaries not only with its urgent interest in contagiousness and disorderly public movement but also with the literary and dramatic interest it afforded readers of all sorts. A far more comprehensive work on St. Vitus's dance would appear in 1844 by the German physician Ernst Conrad Wicke, numbering nearly six hundred pages to Hecker's mere eighty, complemented by

---

horizontal affiliation. In this way, art, life, and politics are always in medias res, in the middle of things; the radical democracy this entails repudiates all religious and biological fixity or teleology. In this respect, Proudhon's work foreshadows Deleuze's anarchic mathematico-aesthetic critique of ontological and political fixity and hierarchy; see esp. Gilles Deleuze, *Différence et répétition* (Paris: Presses Universitaires de France, 1968).

16. See Karl Marx, *Grundrisse: Foundations of the Critique of Political Economy*, trans. Martin Nicolaus (London: Penguin, 1993), 539.

17. See esp. Gilroy, *The Black Atlantic*; Joseph Roach, *Cities of the Dead: Circum-Atlantic Performance* (New York: Columbia University Press, 1996); Gordon, *Why the French Love Jerry Lewis*.

18. Molly Engelhardt, *Dancing out of Line: Ballrooms, Ballets, and Mobility in Victorian Fiction and Culture* (Athens: Ohio University Press, 2009), 112–139. On miasma, see also Allan Conrad Christensen, *Nineteenth-Century Narratives of Contagion: 'Our Feverish Contact'* (London: Routledge, 2005).

clinical observations and an extensive analysis of the tarantella and the beri-beri (a dance-like degenerative neurological condition now attributed to B vitamin deficiency).[19] But Hecker's impassioned, elusive, and allusive prose left connections loose, leaping across eras and drawing historical events in sketch form, leaving his readers to imagine a landscape rife with boisterous outbursts of a dancing plague. The idea Hecker put forward was enticing: scenes of people frothing, falling, raving, jerking their bodies, twisting their faces, screaming, hallucinating, and imagining the end of the world. It was capacious enough to enable and invite new scenes to be added exuberantly to it by writers in his wake.

The objects Hecker had at his disposal to carry out his research were as motley as they were rare: ancient medical treatises, Latin chronicles, case studies culled from medical journals, and the occasional traveller's tale. In compiling his narratives, Hecker presented a compelling case of comparative medical history emphasizing dramatic forms. The anecdotal quality of his writing suggested historical progression mattered little: his scenes jumped between eras, emphasizing the Middle Ages but also drawing from classical precedent and gesturing towards early modern, Enlightenment, and modern occurrences of 'choreomania' in Germany, Italy, France, America, and Abyssinia. Human upheavals illustrated one principle: underlying modernity was a spectacularly disinhibited primeval age. He was rewriting medical science, and putting histories, crises, and epidemics at the heart of this renewed field.

In a preface to the 1888 edition of *The Epidemics of the Middle Ages*, the professor of English Literature at University College London, Henry Morley (1822–1894), one of the earliest professors of English literature in Britain, stressed Hecker and Babington's family histories in medicine, which he also shared, and their strong penchant for literary and historiographical undertakings. Hecker was the first chaired

professor of the history of medicine in Europe, a position he held in Berlin until his death in 1850. He had, in Morley's terms, a 'special genius for this form of history. It was delightful to himself, and he made it delightful to others . . . . He studied disease in relation to the history of man, made his study yield to men outside his own profession an important chapter in the history of civilisation', and stimulated scientific interest in epidemic history with his literary and historiographical flair.[20] Morley impressed on his readers Hecker's wide contribution to encyclopedias and medical journals, as well as Hecker and Babington's important roles in the medical profession. Babington had been enlisted as a physician at Guy's Hospital in London from 1840 to 1855, after serving seven years in India as a midshipman upon graduating from Cambridge University as a physician. Babington also contributed to the study of epidemics, lending his attention to the epidemic of cholera of 1832 and serving in public health administration.[21]

For Hecker, natural disasters catapulted nations into new eras. Historians of medicine had to take plagues centrally into account if they aspired to understand human life: 'Were it in any degree within the power of human research to draw up, in a vivid and connected form, an historical sketch of such mighty events [as plagues], after the manner of the historians of wars and battles, and the migrations of nations', Hecker wrote, 'we might then arrive at clear views with respect to the mental development of the human race'.[22] It 'would then be demonstrable, that the mind of nations is deeply affected by the destructive conflict of the powers of nature, and that great disasters lead to striking changes in general civilization'.[23] The German pathologist Rudolf Virchow (1821–1902), influenced by Hecker, argued that epidemics were 'nodal' points in the progress of history '[characterizing] periods of political and intellectual revolution'.[24] Disease, especially epidemic disease, suggested 'major disturbances' of individual and mass life.[25] Although

19. Ernst Conrad Wicke, *Versuch einer Monographie des grossen Veitstanzes und der unwillkürlichen Muskelbewegung, nebst Bermerkungen über den Taranteltanz und die Beriberi* (Leipzig: F. A. Brockhaus, 1844).

20. Henry Morley, 'Introduction', in J. F. C. Hecker, *The Black Death, and The Dancing Mania*, ed. Henry Morley, trans. B. G. Babington (London: Cassell & Company, 1888), 5–8, 6.

21. Morley, 'Introduction', 7–8.

22. Hecker, *The Black Death*, 1.

23. Hecker, *The Black Death*, 1–2.

24. Rudolf Virchow, *Die Einheitsbestrebungen in der wissenschaftlichen Medizin* (Berlin: G. Reimer, 1849), 46; cited in George Rosen, *Madness in Society: Chapters in the Historical Sociology of Mental Illness* (London: Routledge & Kegan Paul, 1968), 195. See also Rudolf Virchow, *Disease, Life, and Man: Selected Essays*, trans. Lelland J. Rather (Stanford, CA: Stanford University Press, 1958).

25. Virchow, *Die Einheitsbestrebungen*, 46, cited in Rosen, *Madness in Society*, 195.

Hecker was not the first physician to take interest in epidemic history—Hippocrates (460–370 BCE), Hecker noted, wrote influentially about epidemics in *Of Airs, Waters, Places,* circa 400 BCE—he sought to reinvigorate epidemiology in the present day. Medical history in general had to be restored, Hecker argued, gesturing in his inaugural 'Address to the Physicians of Germany' to the rarity of this pursuit in his time.[26]

Epidemics, for Hecker, held a vastly underestimated potential for medical research and, by extension, for human history. 'Epidemics leave no corporeal traces', he wrote, yet in them 'the whole spirit of humanity powerfully and wonderfully moves'.[27] In an extended metaphor comparing the work of historical epidemiology to intrepid world travel, Hecker described a landscape of 'barren deserts' revealing 'inexhaustible mines', in which whole portraits of 'organic collective life' lay fallow.[28] Medical history, in Hecker's exalted vision, constituted an unexplored landscape of adventure and exotic discoveries. Epidemic history revealed 'convulsions' of the 'human frame' less concrete, but more revealing, than any religious relic or geological stone.[29] With this metaphor, Hecker sought to excavate nothing less than the ancient histories of affective and corporeal life, what I am describing as the extended sphere of movement and dance history, a choreozone dissolving boundaries between movement, medicine, and social science.

Medical interest in the past was not new, as historian of medicine Nancy Siraisi has argued of antiquarian and historiographic interest among Renaissance doctors.[30] But a surge of writing in the nineteenth century heralded new spheres of scientific debate, provoking Nietzsche, by 1874, to bemoan the 'antiquarian' mode of historicization by which writers idolized the past as that which could be 'preserved' and 'revered'.[31] 'History', Nietzsche wrote, had itself become a fever.[32] Antiquarianism was in vogue, not least in medical science, though many scientists argued forcefully that they needed to look forward, not back, if they were to advance in their research. And although many scientists abjured the sort of historiography Hecker championed, popular culture in the nineteenth century was saturated with fashions in antiquarian collecting and display, aided by a rapid increase in colonial spoils and the rise of medical museums and anatomy theatres, after the physician Sir Hans Sloane (1660–1753) opened the British Museum in London with his own artefacts. Throughout the nineteenth century, new museums of every sort opened their doors to ever greater numbers of middle-class visitors,[33] and fresh efforts in archaeology revealed even more extraordinary histories than earlier generations had imagined. Medicine, Hecker thought, participated centrally in this rush to excavate the past. And the special purview of epidemic history was its reach to what was most intangible of the past: everyday bodies moving—in Hecker's view, excessively, extravagantly, noxiously—in concert.

HISTORY'S RETURNS: CONTINUING EARLIER CHOREOMANIAS BY OTHER MEANS

Hecker's account of the relationship between natural upheavals and ancient histories situated dance manias at the heart of modern medical research. History, medicine, and dance, in this formulation, formed an inalienable trio, a discursive node within which the history of humanity unfolds. But this history was as vexed as were live medical bodies. Medical writers gestured enthusiastically towards the past and the other, just as they recoiled from the same. This dual fascination and revulsion for ungainly, uncontrolled movement made choreomania a dance of captivating and suspect alterity, 'affiliating itself', to borrow Said's terms, with a complex of ideas about social aggregation in modern political life. As Said has argued of Orientalism, the

26. J. F. C. Hecker, 'Address to the Physicians of Germany', in Hecker, *Epidemics of the Middle Ages*, viii–xiv.

27. Hecker, *Epidemics of the Middle Ages*, xi.

28. Hecker, *Epidemics of the Middle Ages*, ix.

29. Hecker, *Epidemics of the Middle Ages*, 80.

30. Nancy G. Siraisi, *History, Medicine, and the Traditions of Renaissance Learning* (Ann Arbor: University of Michigan Press, 2007).

31. Friedrich Nietzsche, 'On the Uses and Disadvantages of History for Life', in Friedrich Nietzsche, *Untimely Meditations*, ed. Daniel Breazeale, trans. R. J. Hollingdale (Cambridge: Cambridge University Press, 1997), 57–123, esp. 72–77.

32. Nietzsche, 'On the Uses and Disadvantages', 60.

33. Samuel J. M. M. Alberti, *Morbid Curiosities: Medical Museums in Nineteenth-Century Britain* (Oxford: Oxford University Press, 2011).

Orient emerges in the nineteenth century as a set of ideas related to imperial practice, but also significantly as a continuation of earlier Orientalisms by other means. The Orient is not new in the nineteenth century; but the particular complex of institutional practices and ideas that emerge at that time shift the terms of its articulation. So, too, with choreomania, histories of thinking about collectivity, excess, and plague were already extant; but the terms of their recombination in Hecker's work suggested a new sort of biopolitical and ecosophical disorder that could be exported (and translated) to cases of unruly collective action overseas. With Hecker, choreomania became a disorder of epidemic proportions, ancient yet recurring in the present day.

Cases multiplied, as did the repetition of what increasingly constituted a standard set of case studies, including the late medieval St. John's and St. Vitus's dances first and foremost, the Italian tarantella, the eighteenth-century Convulsionaries of Saint-Médard, the Abyssinian *tigretier*, and more, as I detail in the coming chapters. Emphasizing spontaneous acts of convulsive imitation, Hecker depicted scene after scene in which people copied one another and supposedly tapped into corporeal exercises right out of Grecian antiquity, especially Dionysian ones. Although some cases border what we may understand as aesthetically recognizable dance, most cases were dance-like at best, constituted by an implicit fantasy of Dionysian frenzy. The Jumpers of Cornwall, a utopian religious group founded in 1760, offered Hecker a portrait of ecstatic religiosity characterized by frenetic bodily postures recalling, he thought, ancient bacchanals. Jumpers, Hecker wrote, '[worked] themselves up into a state of religious frenzy, in which they have scarcely any control over their senses'. They employed 'certain unmeaning words' and corporeal exercises, including '[jumping] with strange gestures'. They repeated these 'with all their might, until they are exhausted', collapsing into unconsciousness. 'Women who, like the Maenads, practice these religious exercises', he noted, 'are carried away from the midst of them in a state of syncope [sudden loss of consciousness], whilst the remaining members of the congregations, for miles together, on their way home, terrify those whom they meet by the sight of such demoniacal ravings'.[34]

Frenetic gesture coupled with a theatrical tendency towards imitation made religious enthusiasts into 'dance maniacs' in Hecker's view. Their state of fury was exacerbated, he argued, by imitation, an automatic, animal process provoking docile individuals pathologically—and epidemically—to mimic those who were most excited among them. 'There are never more than a few ecstatics', Hecker noted, 'who, by their example, excite the rest to jump, and these are followed by the greatest part of the meeting, so that these assemblages of Jumpers resemble, for hours together, the wildest orgies, rather than congregations met for Christian edification'.[35] The 'total loss of power over the will' Jumpers evinced produced 'an actual disease of the mind', Hecker added, conceding that its effects varied.[36] The Bacchic ecstasy that swept some Jumpers into a beatific state of rapture dragged others to despair. Jumpers, like Shakers, active in England and the United States from the late eighteenth century, and Quakers, a sectarian religious group active as early as the seventeenth century, believed in the exercise of bodily rigours (specifically music and dance) to attain spiritual states; and in the corporeal manifestation of religious ecstasy in everyday bodily acts.[37] This typically produced quaking and shaking motions—hence their evocative names—but only in the nineteenth century came systematically to be

---

34. Hecker, *Epidemics of the Middle Ages*, 140–141.

35. Hecker, *Epidemics of the Middle Ages*, 140–141. See John Evans, 'Jumpers', in John Evans, *A Sketch of the Denominations of the Christian World; to which is prefixed an outline of Atheism, Deism, Theophilanthropism, Judaism, and Mahometanism: with a chronological table of the leading events of the ecclesiastical history, from the birth of Christ to the present time*, 13th ed. (London: B. and R. Crosby and Co. Stationers, 1814), 236–240. See also Louis-Florentin Calmeil, *De la folie, considérée sous le point de vue pathologique, philosophique, historique et judiciaire, depuis la renaissance des sciences en Europe jusqu'au dix-neuvième siècle; description des grandes épidémies de délire, simple ou compliqué, qui ont atteint les Populations d'autrefois et régné dans les Monastères. Exposé des condamnations auxquelles la folie méconnue a souvent donné lieu*, 2 vols., vol. 1 (Paris: J.-B. Baillière, 1845), 168; August Hirsch, *Handbook of Geographical and Historical Pathology*, trans. from 2nd German ed. by Charles Creighton, 3 vols., vol. 3 (London: New Sydenham Society, 1886), 525; James Cornish, 'Remarkable Effects of Fanaticism on the Inhabitants of Several Towns in Cornwall', *London Medical and Physical Journal* 31 (1814): 373–379. For a contemporaneous non-medical account of the 'Jumpers', see e.g. Schaff, *A Religious Encyclopedia*, 1214–1215.

36. Hecker, *Epidemics of the Middle Ages*, 129.

37. See e.g. Clarke Garrett, *Origins of the Shakers: from the Old World to the New World* (Baltimore: Johns Hopkins University Press, 1998). Bibliography on the Shakers is vast. For an account of the central role of singing and dancing in Shaker practice, see e.g. Calvin Green and Seth Youngs Wells, 'Remarks on the Worship of God: The Origin, Practice and Reasonableness of Dancing,

described in epidemiological terms. With Hecker, all motions inspiring imitation among people could be attributed to choreomania, a condition that simultaneously epitomized and served as a paradigmatic example of this quintessentially imitative—and theatrical—pathology.

Hecker provided scenes which, when juxtaposed, added up to constituting recognizable scenarios. His genealogical method—collaging accounts alongside one another—invited writers to extend the scope of choreomania with new portrayals of pathological sympathy. Choreomania appeared not only as an epidemic occurrence of chorea, such as the French physicians Louis-Jacques Béguin (1793–1859), and others, had previously suggested in their *Dictionnaire des termes de médecine, chirurgie, art vétérinaire, pharmacie, histoire naturelle, botanique, physique, chimie, etc.* [Dictionary of medical, surgical, veterinary, pharmaceutical, natural, botanical, physical, chemical, etc., terms] (1823), after the French physician Étienne-Michel Bouteille's (1732–1816) treatise on chorea, and other chorea treatises from the early 1800s. With Hecker, choreomania became a capacious dance-like epidemic also encompassing spiritual and religious dimensions, liable to excite anyone disposed to fanaticism: particularly religious enthusiasm and, increasingly, political fervour.

Variations on the theme of dance-like epidemic contagion and imitation multiplied, largely inspired by Hecker's work. Whereas some writers tried to fold Hecker's capacious concept of choreomania into existing medical theory, others sought to leave the literary scope of the diagnosis to do the work of scientific illustration. The British physician and soon to be president of the Royal College of Physicians, Sir Thomas Watson (1792–1882), describing the 'extraordinary affections' and exalted gestures of choreomaniacs in his *Lectures on the Principles and Practice of Physic*, delivered at King's College London in 1836–1837, offered a less extravagant description than Hecker's, but an equally Grecian point of reference.[38] Watson tied choreomania into a history of instrumental music and theatrical dance, suggesting that 'when music is performed in [the choreomaniacs'] hearing, the movement becomes an actual dance'.[39] For Watson, choreomania explained and enacted classical art, specifically ancient performance and what was coming to be known as world literature. 'When crowds are collected together', Watson wrote, 'the dancing mania is apt to spread from person to person by a sort of imitative affection, realizing the fable of Orpheus, and giving origin (it may be presumed) to those romantic legends met in the literature of most ages and countries, of universal, involuntary, and unceasing saltation, at the sound of a magic pipe' to whose 'feats the term chorea is apposite enough'.[40]

At the origin of world literature, for Watson, was an incoherent, involuntary jumping motion, a dancing disease. Dance manias were an ancient disorder, he argued, at the heart of the twin sciences of medicine and art. The poetic figure of Orpheus in Watson's account illustrated and almost proved this strange disease. But it did not quite institute what Foucault called a nineteenth-century regime of veridiction, or truth-making, rather than truth. Watson was concerned with descriptive processes: like Hecker, reliance on literary and dramatic scenarios illustrated and suggested, rather than verified, medical observation. Described in nearly metaphoric terms, choreomania emerged in Watson's account as if it were not quite an actual dance but unchoreographed movement that became dance in proximity to music. This seemed strange and hardly believable to Watson, yet ancient legend, he submitted, accounted for such phenomena, enshrining them in world literature. Neither history nor popular lore explained the disease, but ancient myth helped to contextualize what appeared as a medical conundrum and to illustrate its clinical

as an Act of Divine Worship', in Calvin Green and Seth Youngs Wells, *Summary view of the Millennial Church or United Society of Believers, commonly called Shakers. Comprising the rise, progress and practical order of the society. Together with the general principles of their faith and testimony*, 2nd ed. (Albany, NY: C. Van Benthuysen, 1848), 85–97; or F. W. Evans, 'Mode of Worship', in F. W. Evans, *Shakers: compendium of the origin, history, principles, rules and regulations, government, and doctrines of the United Society of Believers in Christ's Second Appearing: with biographies of Ann Lee, William Lee, Jas. Whittaker, J. Hocknell, J. Meacham, and Lucy Wright* (New York: D. Appleton and Company, 1859), 90–93.

38. Thomas Watson, *Lectures on the principles and practice of physic; delivered at King's College, London*, 2nd ed., 2 vols., vol. 1 (London: John W. Parker, West Strand, 1848), 657–676.

39. Watson, *Lectures on the principles and practice of physic*, 669.

40. Watson, *Lectures on the principles and practice of physic*, 669. See also Jean Fogo Russell, 'Dancing Mania', in K. F. Russell, *Festschrift for Kenneth Fitzpatrick Russell; Proceedings of a Symposium Arranged by the Section of Medical History, A.M.A. (Victorian Branch)* (Carlton, Victoria: Queensberry Hill Press, 1978), 159–197, 163.

description. Watson's comparison was almost offhanded, yet it anchored his narrative in what seemed like the unshakeable truth of poetry.

THE 'TWO CULTURES': DANCE BETWEEN SCIENCE AND ART

That literature and science were closely allied in the nineteenth century is now a commonplace in studies of the period, as recent works by Engelhardt, Janice Caldwell, Laura Otis, Anne Stiles, Gowan Dawson, Nicholas Dames, Allan Conrad Christensen, Josephine McDonagh, David Amigoni, and others have shown. Otis has pointed out many writers' training in the scientific laboratory as well as in literary method.[41] Yet the use of theatrical or choreographic language to explain scientific case studies has far less frequently been addressed. Warwick Anderson points out the American Bureau of Health activities in the 1920s as a 'distant theater for the rehearsal and performance of white American male virtue' in the Philippines.[42] In *Colonial Pathologies: American Tropical Medicine, Race, and Hygiene in the Philippines* (2006), Anderson argues that twentieth-century medical and hygiene development projects sit on a continuum with earlier colonial histories, all of them concerned with asserting white (male) cleanliness against the possibility of contamination afforded travellers by variously 'differentiated', germ-ridden, and degenerate natives: Filipinos implicitly threatening to these American medical men's hardy masculinity on account of their purportedly premodern excremental practices and other forms of biosocial spillover. The uneven biopolitical and biosocial negotiation of (body) borders between Americans and Filipinos reasserted the Americans' sportiness and, implicitly, their social, scientific, and biopolitical superiority.[43] In this way, American hygiene workers exercised colonial biopower in a theatre of negotiations in which spill rather than spasm was at stake.

In Hecker's case, nearly a century earlier, dramatic narratives of contorted bodies spilling into public space did so on account not of body fluids or particles (excrement, germs) but of the choreographic process of contagious gesture and imitative behaviour. Hecker's writing, initially drawn up for a readership of medical practitioners and (he hoped) a new generation of medical historians, performed an implicit appeal to readers to understand, as if of their own capacity for intuition, the self-evidence of the scenarios depicted. This method did not only draw out literary comparisons, but employed literary flourish and dramatic tableaux to sensationalize scenes of dancing mayhem, grounding them in poetic, rather than administrative or (as in the Filipino case) 'laboratory', method and truth. Hecker's contemporaries, including Darwin, the English biologist Thomas Henry Huxley (1825–1895), and other scientific littérateurs, like Hecker typically adopted literary conventions. Gillian Beer has shown that Darwin used narrative devices in his writings—particularly plot[44]—and Caldwell has argued that pre-Darwinian writers borrowed from the Romantic materialist trope to meld self-expression and individual consciousness with natural philosophy.[45] Dawson has drawn links between Darwin's respectable persona and the complex sexual underworld with which his work was entwined.[46] And Roach has argued that acting theories fundamentally drew from physiological understandings of the body and natural philosophy to explain theatrical emotion.[47] But the spectacle of uncontrol depicted in Hecker's work gave it an especially stagy air, as if choreomania emerged on medical history's stage as a freak show lining medical curiosities up from across eras pell-mell.

41. Laura Otis, 'Introduction', in Laura Otis, ed., *Literature and Science in the Nineteenth Century: An Anthology* (Oxford: Oxford University Press, 2009), xvii–xxviii. See also Laura Otis, *Membranes: Metaphors of Invasion in Nineteenth-Century Literature, Science, and Politics* (Baltimore: Johns Hopkins University Press, 1999); Anne Stiles, *Popular Fiction and Brain Science in the Late Nineteenth Century* (Cambridge: Cambridge University Press, 2012); Nicholas Dames, *The Physiology of the Novel: Reading, Neural Science, and the Form of Victorian Fiction* (New York: Oxford University Press, 2007).

42. Warwick Anderson, *Colonial Pathologies: American Tropical Medicine, Race, and Hygiene in the Philippines* (Durham, NC: Duke University Press, 2006), 6.

43. Anderson, *Colonial Pathologies*, 7.

44. Gillian Beer, *Darwin's Plots: Evolutionary Narrative in Darwin, George Eliot and Nineteenth-Century Fiction*, 3rd ed. (Cambridge: Cambridge University Press, 2009).

45. Janice McLarren Caldwell, *Literature and Medicine in Nineteenth-Century Britain: From Mary Shelley to George Eliot* (Cambridge: Cambridge University Press, 2008).

46. Gowan Dawson, *Darwin, Literature and Victorian Respectability* (Cambridge: Cambridge University Press, 2010).

47. Joseph Roach, *The Player's Passion: Studies in the Science of Acting* (Ann Arbor: University of Michigan Press, 1993).

The volume of recent works that foreground nineteenth-century links between literature and science reveals continued anxiety among contemporary scholars to show that the division between these worlds was not always so. Indeed the notion of the 'two cultures' divide articulated by chemist, novelist, and critic C. P. Snow (1905–1980) in 1959 already gestured towards an intellectual world in which the distinctions between arts and sciences were not so strictly drawn. As cultural theorist Stefan Collini has argued in his introduction to the re-edition of Snow's pivotal text, Snow in fact sought to bring science up to the standing literature enjoyed, and even to surpass it, in the name of social and political progress. Technology in Snow's view would bring the poor of the world up to a standard of living possible only through the proper administration of natural resources honed by scientifically trained politicians. Literary intellectuals, 'Luddites', as Snow called them, were too backward, obsessed with history, nostalgic, and moored in the trappings of privilege.[48]

Although there was no room in Snow's vision for a culturally and intellectually informed scientific literature, his debate, reprised by critics F. R. Leavis (1895–1978), Lionel Trilling (1905–1975), and others, pointed to a trend towards splinterization between science and art informed by a complicated past in which scientific and literary modes of inquiry and expression were not so cut off. And indeed, if by the 1890s the president of an Oxford college could exclaim to a visiting don that 'we don't talk to *them*', that is, mathematicians, seated on either side of his unsuspecting guest, this was far less true of the fifty or hundred years prior, during which the repercussions of the *Encyclopédie* of philosopher Denis Diderot (1713–1784) and mathematician Jean le Rond d'Alembert (1717–1783) and other Enlightenment efforts at intellectual synthesis had woven the arts and sciences closer together, rather than further apart.[49] In Roach's terms, motion and emotion were twin terms characterizing human and mechanical life, doubly inflecting the theatrical and rhetorical arts and all aspects of philosophical and physiological doctrine. Writing in *The Player's Passion*, Roach argues that ideas of organism (or organicism) and vitality saturated Romantic thought, following

Enlightenment efforts to mechanize—indeed to mathematize—the 'passions', conveniently joined to the body, since René Descartes (1596–1650), in the pineal gland right in the centre of the brain. So, too, notions of spontaneity and automatism took a turn in the nineteenth century with the emergence of theories attributing spontaneous action to the *unconscious* and what Roach notes as its 'physiological counterpart', the *subconscious*, theories fundamental to Darwin and, later, Freud's work.[50] But with Hecker, spontaneous action—bodily automatism as well as uncontrollable emotion—occur as if genealogically from out of ancient time, as a biological and ecosophical force. In this sense, Hecker's concept of human vitality exceeds the individual; human bodies serve as conduits to biohistorical and geological operations which are manifest, epidemically, far beyond what Freud would later describe as 'primal urges' erupting within the strictures of human civilization.[51]

Taken in this regard, Hecker's writing on choreomania straddles a heightened period of disciplinary change, where vitalism signals not so much a concentration of spiritual and physiological forces, or yet a psychological impulse, as an ecosophical meeting of historical and corporeal intensities. Choreomanias came to be theorized with Hecker as exercises in reverberation: as a repetition of past forms, just where these broke down into formlessness *again*.

OBSCURITAS ANTIQUITATIS: ANTIQUARIAN MEDICINE AND 'HISTORICAL FEELING'

As a choreographic approach to history—and genealogy—this book emphasizes scenes of corporeal undoing, the dislocation and relocation of bodies on an imagined historical stage, and the gesture of their abstraction into medical literature. Hecker in particular captured the attention of readers at a time when the popularization of scientific ideas countermanded specialization in medicine and the arts. Likewise, a whole cast of medical men swimming upstream of the tendency towards purely practical research gravitated towards Hecker's writing in droves. If there is one institution to whose efforts the spread of

---

48. C. P. Snow, *The Two Cultures, with Introduction by Stefan Collini* (Cambridge: Cambridge University Press, 1998), 22.

49. See Stefan Collini, 'Introduction', in Snow, *The Two Cultures*, x.

50. Roach, *The Player's Passion*, 179.

51. See esp. Sigmund Freud, *Civilization and Its Discontents*, ed. and trans. James Strachey (New York: Norton, 1989).

Hecker's concept of the dancing disease may be attributed, it was the Sydenham Society, a powerhouse in disseminating medical literature in the age of empire.[52] First conceived in the 1840s in London, when 'antiquarian feeling was widespread and, as [diarist Arthur J.] Munby [1828–1910] put it, "everyone was interested in the history of *everything*,"'[53] the Sydenham Society served as a clearing house for new ideas, many translated from the ancient or the exotic. The 'historical feeling' Munby describes, evinced throughout London, provided an impetus for the founding of interest-specific societies whose purpose was 'to reprint specialized out-of-print works whose appeal was too limited for a commercial publisher'.[54] The English Historical Society and the Camden Society, both founded in 1838, and the Parker Society, created in 1841 to publish writings by founders of the English Reformed Church, were run by elected committees on behalf of an annual membership.[55] The Sydenham Society 'followed exactly the same plan[;] but on transposing that plan to a medical context', Munby remarked, it was forced to face a 'fundamental difficulty': 'for better or for worse, most medical men differ from historians in being concerned chiefly with problems of the immediate present rather than with accounts of the historical past'. This 'conflict of interest' between historical curiosity and clinical use emerged 'without ever being resolved'.[56] It was arguably the chief, though not the sole, cause of the Sydenham Society's dissolution after fourteen years,[57] though debates about 'useful' (and 'applied') science—as opposed to 'pure' science—continued to plague the Society in its

afterlife. Writing nearly half a century later in 'Science and Culture' (1880), Huxley was still lamenting the unfortunate invention of the term 'applied science', whose supposed opposition to 'pure' science was not applicable in the real world; the distinction neglected the real relationship between the two.[58]

The Sydenham Society, founded in 1843, had been designed to expand medical knowledge by looking to the past and the foreign. It declared that its mission was to meet 'certain acknowledged deficiencies in existing means for diffusing medical literature, which are not likely to be supplied by the efforts of individuals'.[59] It would publish books that were (1) rare or expensive, including standard British works whose reprint would contribute to their dissemination; (2) ancient or early modern, requiring a reprint and/or translation; (3) especially voluminous, and which could benefit from publication in digest form, whether British or by foreign authors; (4) translations of Greek and Latin authors, and works in Arabic and other Eastern languages, 'accompanied, when it is thought desirable, by the original text'; (5) translations of 'recent foreign works of merit'; and (6) 'original works of merit, which might prove valuable as books of reference' but might not otherwise be published because of their poor commercial prospects.[60] The Sydenham Society also vowed to disseminate these widely.

Hecker's collected essays on medieval epidemiology were the first such 'recent foreign works' to be published, appearing in volume 1 of the Sydenham Society publications in 1844. Babington, who was treasurer of the Society, had

52. On the emergence of publishing societies and the dissemination of scientific information in Britain and elsewhere, see esp. C. C. Booth, 'Medical Communication: The Old and the New. The Development of Medical Journals in Britain', *British Medical Journal* 285 (1982): 105–108, and David A. Kronick, 'Medical "Publishing Societies" in Eighteenth-Century Britain', *Bulletin of the Medical Library Association* 82.3 (1994): 277–282. For a history of the Sydenham Society and the debates surrounding its usefulness to the medical community, see William B. Ober, 'The Sydenham Society (1843–1857): Rise and Fall', *Mount Sinai Journal of Medicine* 41.2 (1974): 294–305, and G. G. Meynell, *The Two Sydenham Societies: A History and Bibliography of the Medical Classics Published by the Sydenham Society and the New Sydenham Society (1844–1911)* (Acrise, Kent: Winterdown Books, 1985). For a broader history, see also Geoffrey Cantor et al., *Science in the Nineteenth-Century Periodical: Reading the Magazine of Nature* (Cambridge: Cambridge University Press, 2004). For a history of the Jean-Baptiste Baillière publishing house, see J.-B. Baillière, *Histoire de nos relations avec l'académie de médecine, 1827–1871. Lettre adressée à MM. les membres de l'Académie pour servir de complément au Bulletin de l'Académie de médecine . . .* (Paris: J.-B. Baillière, 1872). See also Christian Régnier, 'J.-B. Baillière (1797–1885), The Pioneering Publisher Who Promoted French Medicine throughout the World', *Medicographia* 27.1 (2005): 87–96.
53. A. N. L. Munby, *The History and Bibliography of Science in England*, delivered at the Eighth Annual Zeitlin & Verbrugge Lecture in Bibliography, University of California, 1968, 2; cited in Meynell, *The Two Sydenham Societies*, 1.
54. Meynell, *The Two Sydenham Societies*, 1.
55. See also Ober, 'The Sydenham Society', 294.
56. Meynell, *The Two Sydenham Societies*, 1.
57. Meynell, *The Two Sydenham Societies*, 1.
58. Thomas Henry Huxley, *Science and Culture, and Other Essays* (New York: D. Appleton and Company, 1882), 26.
59. In Ober, 'The Sydenham Society', 295.
60. Ober, 'The Sydenham Society', 295.

translated Hecker's essays on the Black Death, the dancing mania, and the sweating sickness in 1832–1834 when they first appeared in German, but this 1844 re-edition enabled them to gain a new, more widespread readership among the society's members. And this membership was not inconsiderable. The Society counted over sixteen hundred medical practitioners in its first year and over two thousand the year after (among a total of about eighteen thousand medical practitioners in Great Britain at that time);[61] lending and library use increased readership further. Although by 1857 membership had declined to under seven hundred, prompting the Society's closure, already forty 'scarce and valuable medical works' and 'scarce editions of works of real value' had been reprinted or translated into English for dissemination.[62] The French were well represented in early translations, boasting works by the pioneer psychiatrist Philippe Pinel (1745–1826), among others.

Nonetheless, criticism of the Society emerged with force, suggesting that antiquity was still a contested epistemic field in medical practice. Thomas Wakley (1795–1862), editor of the influential medical journal the *Lancet*, made a number of scathing remarks with respect to the Society's scope and mission: '[antiquarians] wear eyes in their polls, in order to see backwards; but men of science require those organs forward, that whoever retrogrades they may advance. If there be one class of men to whom the ancient history of their profession is next to useless, however interesting, it is the medical'.[63] The reproduction of ancient works in particular was of little use to modern physicians, Wakley argued. As the Society's historian G. G. Meynell notes, the Society was often accused of antiquarianism, and many members considered the immediate value of ancient treatises questionable at best.

The New Sydenham Society was designed to redress this. It declared as its focus the publication of new translations of contemporary works from other European nations, and as such fostered a scientific internationalism in medical circles in the fin de siècle. Founded almost

immediately after the first Sydenham Society's dissolution, the New Sydenham Society was younger (one of its co-founders, Dr. Jonathan Hutchinson [1828–1913], was twenty-nine at the time), and strove better to respond to its membership's needs. It particularly addressed complaints that publication was delayed, funds were poorly managed, and works had 'no real value' to a readership made up mainly of practitioners: of the twenty-nine titles, or forty volumes, published between 1844 and 1857 by the Sydenham Society, only nineteen were thought to be of any practical interest. The *Lancet*'s accusations of *obscuritas antiquitatis* were answered with structural reorganization, including a more accessible annual meeting held in tandem with the annual meeting of the British Medical Association in a different town each year; this dissolved complaints that the cramped offices on Frith Street in Soho were too small to accommodate more than half a dozen members—always the same overpaid ones.[64]

In spite of these debates and challenges, the two societies effectively changed the face of medical literature and its dissemination in the nineteenth century. In the Sydenham Society's fourteen years (1844–1857) and the New Sydenham Society's fifty-three years (1858–1911), nearly 240 volumes were published, expanding the scope of medical history and medical literature in the English-speaking world considerably.[65] Medicine was now ancient and modern; its modernity was constituted by its reach to the past and to the foreign. Similar comparative and historiographical initiatives were undertaken in France, with the emergence of the J.-B. Baillière publishing house in 1821, dedicated to printing significant works of medical history as well as new medical theory reaching readers locally and internationally.

Not only was interest in the past debated; comparativism was also on the rise. With the expansion of colonial travel and new interest in comparative pathology, colonial outposts became new sites for the production of medical knowledge, just as writers repeated, rearticulated, and added to paradigmatic case studies. These writers,

61. Meynell, *The Two Sydenham Societies*, 3.

62. Dr. Ferguson Branson of Sheffield, in a statement suggesting the founding of a society of medical literature by himself and Drs. Joseph and William Bullar, of Southampton, whose letter was printed in the *Lancet*, 7 May 1842; cited in Meynell, *The Two Sydenham Societies*, 1–2.

63. Thomas Wakley, *Lancet* 2 (1841–1842): 285; cited in Meynell, *The Two Sydenham Societies*, 2.

64. Meynell, *The Two Sydenham Societies*, 3–6.

65. Meynell notes that, although the New Sydenham Society's membership rose from 1,949 in 1859 to 2,850 in 1860 and then to 3,000 in 1861, the outbreak of the U.S. Civil War saw membership drop by about a quarter. By 1862, only fourteen hundred

as Anderson points out, were 'itinerant',[66] affiliated with institutions but cross-pollinating concepts and practices—as well as affective registers (economies of feeling and prejudice) at home and overseas. 'Itinerant' writers, reprising Hecker's work, appended to it, almost imperceptibly, a gestural flourish or remark, a parenthesis; a discursive footnote. Translation and annotation constituted the marginal spaces within which other versions of choreomania arose.

The geo-choreopolitical stakes of this 'translatio'—a term denoting at once passage, transfer, and shift, as I detail in chapter 3—suggest a transformative version of scientific history, in which knowledge is not produced 'here' and then exported 'there' (as colonial baggage and discursive violence) and does not claim truth but shifts and refracts a whole host of mutually imbricated conditions and imaginaries. The discursive history of choreomania reveals a genealogical—and choreographic—process by which concept formation occurs in an expansive imaginal space and, significantly, as this plays out in relation to real places and sites. The travelling physician, confronted with new scenes, maps these onto narratives and images known to him yet in doing so shifts the discursive realm around and within which he rearticulates them, often as if mere additions to the old. The history of ideas and institutions, specifically the history of ideas about the dancing disease in this case, performs a series of translatios from one discursive realm, one field, to another, just as these translatios purport to be merely expanding the scope of scientific study, merely migrating. As I show throughout this book, choreomania moves quite radically through such processes from an antiquarian curiosity to a description of anticolonial revolt.

Choreomania thus emerges as an ancient excess of motion—and emotion—hovering on the other side of the emphatically, placidly modern. So while Foucault highlighted the disciplinarization of knowledge leading up to the nineteenth century, in *The Order of Things* and *The Archaeology of Knowledge* most influentially, I argue that disciplinarization could only occur in collusion with a contrary

motion: a rhizomatic dispersal, fragmentation, and recombination of epistemic centres. Thus, though for Foucault modern centres of power were erecting ever stricter police states characterized by institutions of corporeal and public control (the prison, the asylum, the school), medical and anthropological writers were also reading one another, as Taussig enjoins us to do, tactilely, with distraction.[67] They intuited ideas about dance and engaged in non-systematic modes of knowledge production, thumbing through fragments in annals and chronicles, chancing on anecdotes and histories. Medical and anthropological writers compared and contrasted cases of political upheaval, drew up taxonomies of fitful bodies, and in this regard produced structures of disciplinary power inasmuch as their judgments on erratic, fitful corporeality cast these as aberrant and ill. But their opaque writings were also characterized by almost Borgesian lists of seemingly unrelated events, jumbled descriptions, and hearsay. The writers I discuss in these pages collected, collaged, interpolated, and imagined choreomanias, glossing one another's observations and archival finds. Returning consistently to Hecker's essay, they repeated, with variations, what he collated in his eccentrically organized and in many respects unfinished text.

The history of choreomania, then, is a history of passages or translatios by which ideas about disorderly collectivity move across disciplines, geographies, and eras. What results is a discursive zone of intensity describing an entangled set of concepts eluding the exactness of definition. There is no definitive concept of the dancing disease, only a web of interrelated case studies. This chapter and the next argue that Hecker's narratives, however—particularly his vivid description of the St. John's or St. Vitus's dances—become paradigmatic, in the sense Agamben puts forward.[68] The paradigm, Agamben writes, is the heightened example, that to which all further examples of a particular sort refer. But the paradigm, paradoxically, becomes paradigmatic by repetition. It is, Agamben writes, reprising philosopher of science Thomas Kuhn (1922–1996), 'simply an

members were listed. Over the following years, membership fluctuated at around one thousand and more. Meynell, *The Two Sydenham Societies*, 6. See 166–169.

66. Anderson, *Colonial Pathologies*, 7.

67. Michael Taussig, *The Nervous System* (London: Routledge, 1992), 147.

68. Giorgio Agamben, *The Signature of All Things: On Method*, trans. Luca D'Isanto with Kevin Attell (New York: Zone Books, 2009).

example, a single case that by its repeatability acquires the capacity to model' further examples and attitudes.[69] Agamben writes: 'the paradigm goes from the particular to the particular'.[70] It does not describe rules or principles; it does not become more 'true' because of its adoption as a model. It only retains its status as such until it is replaced by another often repeated example or trope. In this sense choreomania is nothing more than, but also as much as, the imbricated set of examples or 'scenes' that make it up; and it transforms inasmuch as these come to be affiliated with further scenes.

In the next chapter, a closer look at Hecker's reading of the St. John's and other 'epidemic' dances reveals the fantastical incursion of Grecian bacchanals onto the medieval stage, a fantasy reprised by Nietzsche in his ambivalent discussion of the Middle Ages. Hecker's paradigmatic example then gains a genealogy of its own, linking it to earlier ideas about disorder and dissent characterizing Europe's purportedly darkest age.

---

69. Agamben, *The Signature of All Things*, 11.
70. Agamben, *The Signature of All Things*, 19.

2

Madness after Foucault
Medieval Bacchanals

... eras of greatest material and moral distress seem to be those during which people dance most....

—Philippe de Félice, *L'enchantement des danses et la magie du verbe* (1957)

FOUCAULT NEVER wrote the history of the 'Orient' that the initial preface to *History of Madness* [Folie et déraison. Histoire de la folie à l'âge classique] (1961) promised, though his work carved out a rich space of thinking about madness's discursive coming-to-be, the language and institutions that made 'madness' a thing—an object of scrutiny, language, and biopower—whereas it had been only, he argues, undifferentiated, inarticulate stuff. Madness, for Foucault, was, before the advent of self-styled 'reason', an equal player on history's stage, a set of experiences not less than any others, a series of alternative modes of being with or alongside 'truth', before 'truth' became construed and co-opted as that which reason deploys and unreason ('déraison') decries. This book, and this chapter in particular, seek with Foucault to tell the story of a madness before 'madness' came to be described; but also with Foucault to tell the history of this telling. The one cannot be conceived without the other; so, too, the telling leaves more traces for the historian—or genealogist—rendering the told a far trickier and more elusive beast. What this book also argues, however, is that dance—specifically, dancing manias—complicate the history of 'madness' Foucault outlines, and so too the history of madnesses more generally. This book, in excavating a series of proliferating narratives about the 'dancing disease', reveals a fantasy about origins such as Foucault suggests the 'Orient' represents (as in the epigraph to this book). But this fantasy also construes primitive, 'Oriental', history in plural, pre-individuated—and significantly in corporeal, dancing—terms. The choreography of this fantasy then tells of dance's origins and of dance *as origin*: that which phantasmatically constitutes the modern rational self's other, prior, beastly self—the self perpetually threatening chaotically to re-emerge as spectacle. This is spectacle as a show of origins that might engulf those watching, though they may attempt to abstract themselves, as moderns, from the rumbling horde.

NARRATIVE ENDS, MYTHIC BEGINNINGS: DANCE HISTORY

The book then is about a fantasy and paradox: dance, it seems, has no origins. But it has a history of narratives about origins. In the European tradition, Susan Leigh Foster reminds us, these narratives tell of dance's emergence from the festivities of the ancient Jews (according to Jesuit chronicler and choreographer Claude François Menestrier [1631–1705]); or, in the formulation of the French *encyclopédiste* Louis de Cahusac (1706–1759), from the primeval womb: body breathing, eyes fluttering, arms opening and closing, feet stepping.[1] The first of these origin narratives suggests a genealogical ascendance from the ancient Egyptians and the Jews to the Greeks, and from there, we may presume, to Europe and America. The second approach is physiological, describing dance as innate action of the human body, a process as essential as breath.

Choreomania narratives draw from both types of fantasy, attributing dancing plagues simultaneously to the practices of ancient revellers and to the automatic mechanisms of the human body. Hovering between culture and nature, primitive practice and bodily impulse, 'choreomania' appeared to its nineteenth-century observers to participate both in history and biology. In this regard, choreomania represents a biohistorical concept, where biohistory denotes, in Foucault's terms, 'the pressures by which the movements of life and the processes of history interfere with one another'.[2] 'Movements of life' in this view are so entangled in one another that 'life' and 'history' become indistinguishable. Biohistory further underpins the history of biopower, which Foucault understands as a morphing set of systems and ideas that govern life forms through institutions of knowledge; these institutions determine concepts of normality and normativity, as well as discursive practices: ways of seeing and saying 'truth'. This chapter argues that choreomaniacs appear in Hecker's ecosophical account not so much to deviate from but rather intensely to echo their surroundings. They do not represent a history of 'dangerous individuals' such as Foucault has described but appear and recur on history's stage as eccentric protuberances: as strange as but also as natural as a hurricane or a tornado.[3]

Hecker wrote his story of medieval dance manias in relation to another, now far better known plague, what he may have first termed the Black Death, in a trio of works titled *The Epidemics of the Middle Ages* (1859). As I showed in the last chapter, this comprised an essay titled 'The Black Death', a second titled 'The Sweating Sickness', and a third titled 'The Dancing Mania', as well as, eventually, a fourth short essay titled 'Child-Pilgrimages' (1832). In 'The Dancing Mania', Hecker posited mass dancing as a medieval phenomenon with roots in ancient Greece and Rome and echoes throughout the ages. Choreomania, Hecker thought, appeared violently around 1374, hardly a generation after the Black Death had ravaged Europe; but other, smaller dancing plagues had preceded this one, and more would follow. The fourteenth-century episode became paradigmatic, I argue, in Agamben's sense. Writing after Foucault, as well as historian and philosopher of science Georges Canguilhem (1904–1995) and Kuhn, Agamben suggests the paradigm as a sort of ur-example, the one that becomes paradigmatic retrospectively by virtue of its frequent repetition.[4] The fourteenth-century 'choreomania' becomes in this sense the paradigmatic dance mania, the example to which all others subsequently referred. Significantly, choreomania was quintessentially in Hecker's conception 'medieval': irrational, superstitious, obscure—the antithesis of the noble ballet Menestrier sought to historicize in the origin story cited above, and different from the gently organic account of dancing offered by de Cahusac. Dance manias, in Hecker's writing, were biohistorical excrescences far removed from enlightened civilization or linear historical progress. This chapter foregrounds Hecker's fantasy, but also traces, through his writings, a whole set of medieval chronicles and annals. The chapter then seeks first of all to draw out a history of late medieval European corporeality—an as yet unwritten dance history, inasmuch as the choreomaniacs' appearance in Latin chronicles and annals suggest

1. Susan Leigh Foster, 'Textual Evidances', in Ellen W. Goellner and Jacqueline Shea Murphy, eds., *Bodies of the Text: Dance as Theory, Literature as Dance* (New Brunswick, NJ: Rutgers University Press, 1995), 231–246, 231. See Claude François Menestrier, *Des ballets anciens et modernes selon les règles du théâtre* (Paris: Chez René Guignard, 1682), 8–9.

2. Michel Foucault, *Histoire de la sexualité*, vol. 1 (Paris: Éditions Gallimard, 1976), 188; cited in Jordan, *Convulsing Bodies*, 113.

3. See esp. Michel Foucault, *Le pouvoir psychiatrique: Cours au Collège de France, 1973–1974* (Paris: Seuil/Gallimard, 2003).

4. Agamben, *The Signature of All Things*, 9–32.

semi-structured choreographic formations.[5] And the chapter sets this choreopolitical history in counterpoint to Hecker's sensationalizing portrait of the dancing disease. The chapter's aim then, following Foucault, is to reconsider concepts of madness, specifically dance manias—a subject he does not treat—in the nineteenth-century medical imagination; and so to inscribe dancing manias into a longer history of thinking about plural bodies and the spectacle of corporeal intrusions into public space.

MADNESS IN FOUCAULT: UNREASONABLE FORMATIONS

Foucault articulates 'madness' in the original preface to *History of Madness* as intangible and indescribable, the primordial other against which scientific modernity construes its rational, 'reasonable' self. 'Madness', then (and *déraison* or 'unreasoning', its equally elusive other half), becomes the set of experiences categorized scientifically, legally, philosophically, in opposition to Enlightenment clarity.[6] In Foucault's work, individual madmen and madwomen appear to lack reason, but significantly their madness appears on the scene of history, scientifically, *as an abstraction*.[7] They are not individually unreasonable in this or that way but participate in a 'mad' condition: that of straying confidently from a verifiable and generally held 'truth'. As an example, Foucault offers the *Encyclopédie* entry for 'Folie' (madness), which suggests that when one strays from reason without knowing it, because one has no ideas of one's own, one is an imbecile; when one strays from reason, knowing it, because one is enslaved to a violent passion, one is weak; but when one strays from reason with confidence,

---

5. Few studies of medieval dance exist, due to the paucity of sources. Where these do exist, they tend to focus on late medieval courtly practices and music, though some recent studies have emphasized ecstatic rapture and ritual. See e.g. Karen Silen, 'Elisabeth of Spalbeek: Dancing the Passion', in Lynn Brooks, ed., *Women's Work: Making Dance in Europe before 1800* (Madison: University of Wisconsin Press, 2007), 207–227; Robert Mullally, *The Carole: A Study of Medieval Dance* (Farnham: Ashgate, 2011); Ann Buckley and Cynthia J. Cyrus, eds., *Music, Dance and Society: Medieval and Renaissance Studies in Memory of Ingrid G. Brainard* (Kalamazoo, MI: Medieval Institute, 2011); Luisa del Giudice and Nancy van Deusen, *Performing Ecstasies: Music, Dance and Ritual in the Mediterranean* (Ottawa: Institute of Medieval Music, 2005); John Stevens, *Words and Music in the Middle Ages: Song, Narrative, Dance and Drama, 1050–1350* (Cambridge: Cambridge University Press, 1986), esp. 159–198. Margit Sahlin, in *Étude sur la carole médiévale: L'origine du mot et ses rapports avec l'église* (Uppsala: Almqvist & Wiksells, 1940), offers a detailed etymological analysis of the term *carole*—widely used to denote joyous popular dancing—and a useful historiographical account of popular dance practices in relation to (often at odds with) the Christian church, including pre-Christian practices associated with St. Vitus and St. John. Frances Eustace with Pamela M. King, in 'Dances of the Living and the Dead: A Study of *Danse Macabre* Imagery within the Context of Late-Medieval Dance Culture', in Sophie Oosterwijk and Stefanie Knöll, eds., *Mixed Metaphors: The Danse Macabre in Medieval and Early Modern Europe* (Newcastle upon Tyne: Cambridge Scholars, 2011) 43–71, esp. 45–46, highlight the challenges of dance (specifically choreographic) history in the Middle Ages.

6. 'Unreason' (*déraison*), Ian Hacking points out, is an elusive but pervasive notion in Foucault's work, nearly absent in the English editions of his writing, though fundamental to his original aim. Foucault originally published *Folie et déraison. Histoire de la folie à l'âge classique* [Madness and Unreason. History of Insanity in the Classical Age] in 1961, effectively his doctoral thesis, supervised by Georges Canguilhem, and supported by philosopher Jean Hyppolite (1907–1968). A heavily abridged version soon came to be known—and widely celebrated as well as decried—in English as *Madness and Civilization: A History of Insanity in the Age of Reason*, first published in the United States by Pantheon Books in 1965, and republished in the United Kingdom by Tavistock in 1967. This in parts faulty translation by Richard Howard reprised and slightly enlarged Foucault's own radical 1964 abridgment, also published by Plon, and which, Hacking points out, not only cut almost half the original nearly seven-hundred-page text but also downplayed the term 'déraison', leaving only *Histoire de la folie* prominently visible on the cover page, with *Folie et déraison* inset as subtitle. See Michel Foucault, *Folie et déraison. Histoire de la folie à l'âge classique* (Paris: Plon, 1961) and Michel Foucault, *Folie et déraison. Histoire de la folie à l'âge classique* (Paris: Plon, 1964). Foucault's unabridged original book, republished in a newly prefaced 1972 edition (partially following bitter controversy with Jacques Derrida) as *Histoire de la folie à l'âge classique*, recently became available in English in a new translation, as *History of Madness*, ed. Jean Khalfa, trans. Jonathan Murphy and Jean Khalfa (London: Routledge, 2006). The new full English translation recovers both prefaces and ancillary material. Hacking offers a brilliantly detailed analysis of the complicated abridgments and retranslations of this work in English and French, in Ian Hacking, 'Déraison', *History of the Human Sciences* 24.4 (2011): 13–23. See also Hacking's foreword to *History of Madness* (2006), ix–xii. For further discussion of this complex history of abridgements and re-editions, see also Arthur Still and Irving Velody, 'Introduction', in Still and Velody, eds., *Rewriting the History of Madness*, 1–16; and Colin Gordon's pivotal essay '*Histoire de la folie*: An Unknown Book by Michel Foucault', first published in *History of the Human Sciences* (1990), republished in Still and Velody, eds., *Rewriting the History of Madness*, 19–42. On Foucault's prolonged dispute with Derrida, leading to the new preface, where Foucault defends his work as constituting a moment in time, an 'event' not requiring retrospective apologies or retractions, see also Michel Foucault, 'My Body, This Paper, This Fire', in *History of Madness* (2006), 550–574; Michel Foucault, 'Reply to Derrida ("Michel Foucault Derrida e no kaino")', *Paideia* 11: *Michel Foucault*, 1 February 1972, pp. 131–147', reprinted in *History of Madness* (2006), 575–590; and Gordon, '*Histoire de la folie*', 35–37. Except where otherwise indicated, I refer to Foucault's standard unabridged *Histoire de la folie* (1972).

7. Foucault writes: 'Le XVIIIe siècle perçoit le fou, mais déduit la folie'. (The eighteenth century perceives the madman, but deduces madness.) In Foucault, *Histoire de la folie*, 241.

firmly persuaded that one is being reasonable, then one is mad.[8] The mad, in the classical age (widely referred to as the 'age of reason'), are not individually so, by their own reckoning, Foucault argues; they are mad—significantly, they are perceived to be mad—in relation to a concept of reason that others hold for them. This is different from *déraison*, according to which individuals might wilfully refute concepts of 'reason'.

Madness in this sense is relational but also objective; it is determined by the purportedly rational observer, who claims, rightly or not, to possess the barometer as to what 'reason' constitutes.[9] As Foucault's work on discipline further argues, after Canguilhem's work on normality and normativity, myriad societal structures determine how the objectification of 'reason' comes to play out, largely as a complex and nearly imperceptible web of subtly coercive and normalizing measures, institutional and discursive. With choreomania, a slightly different structure of madness comes into play. In the nineteenth-century epidemiological formulation this book foregrounds, choreomania comes to denote a type of madness in which individuals neither believe themselves to be reasonable and rational (contrary to the supposedly truer perceptions of their peers), nor do they merely deviate from accepted behaviours, as 'dangerous individuals' who must be cast aside, locked up, or otherwise forcibly cured. Choreomaniacs instead appear to reverberate excessively with their age, as its pathological exaggeration. They are in this sense paradoxically truer than truth; they are *too true*, too attuned. In Hecker's ecosophical account, they amplify their era gesturally, by imitating its tremors and quakes. Dance maniacs enter their condition by proximity— what Hecker calls 'imitation—compassion— sympathy'[10]—a cluster of principles denoting multiplication, compounded with relapses over time. Choreomaniacs contagioned further choreomaniacs; but they were also significantly contagioned by a surge of historical and ecosophical factors. 'Imitation—compassion—sympathy' 'unites' human beings in what Hecker refers to as 'the general body' and, in his preface to 'The Black Death', the 'organism of the world'.[11] The dancing mania was, Hecker argued, an organic event of epic—literally of epidemic—proportions, neither individual nor social but a 'convulsion which in the most extraordinary manner infuriated the human frame'[12] according to the particular time and place at which it arose. Choreomaniacs became disorderly by surrendering to a collective impulse, spectacularizing the dissolution of individual subjectivity—a movement originating from out of a doubly primordial place: ancient history and biology, wrapped together in a general ecology unfolding over time.

As 'epidemics', choreomanias in nineteenth-century scientific literature thus further constitute a form of madness on account of their scale. Whereas individual choreomaniacs appear strange and deluded, grimacing, frothing, raving, and demonstrating what Hecker derisively called a 'disgusting spasmodic disease',[13] they were all the more noteworthy in the terms of nineteenth-century historical epidemiology on account of their capacity to multiply. Choreomanias were not isolated exceptions or deviations but magnifications in intensity as well as scale. In this respect, the history of choreomania is that of an ecosophical conception: it tells a set of ideas about epidemic madness as that which collectively exaggerates a 'primitive' form of being that is triggered by the crises biohistory brings about.

'Choreomaniacs' were thus theatrical: they represented an ecological crisis by their contorted body postures; and in doing so, they showed their era's imagined primal self to itself, as that from which it putatively boasted a slim measure of distance. As I further argue in later chapters, this conception sets the stage for Freud's notion of a (typically colonial and childlike) primitive self erupting during times of crisis, symptomatically. Choreomania thus becomes the collective disorder that theatricalizes modernity's sense of crisis. Specifically, choreomania theatricalizes the human-scale ecological crisis that returns.

In other words, I do not just with Foucault write a 'history of bodies' as opposed to a 'history of mentalities';[14] I seek also to capture

---

8. Foucault, *Histoire de la folie*, 239.
9. Foucault, *Histoire de la folie*, 240.
10. Hecker, *Epidemics of the Middle Ages*, 129.
11. Hecker, *Epidemics of the Middle Ages*, xxiii.
12. Hecker, *Epidemics of the Middle Ages*, 80.
13. Hecker, *Epidemics of the Middle Ages*, 84.
14. Foucault's claim to write a 'history of bodies' as opposed to a 'history of mentalities' is discussed, among others, by Jordan in *Convulsing Bodies*, 114. My own submission is that even this distinction maintains a spectral separation between body and thought. 'Mentalities' themselves are entangled in bodily acts.

intellectual and discursive processes by which abstraction from historical scenes produces new bodies of knowledge and truth—new fictions—which are material and mobile. Knowledge moves—it performs a *kinetic* act, where 'kinesis' denotes passage, transfer, and repetition. In the terms of Søren Kierkegaard (1813–1855), the Greek concept of χίνμσιζ (kinesis) signals the modern category of 'passage'.[15] Kinesis suggests a structure of repetition that implies priority—something happened before repetition could take place—and novelty. With repetition comes difference: the same thing is never, in this Heraclitean formulation, repeated exactly the same way. Choreomanias recur, in medical literature, with a measure of difference. So, too, the discursive formations that fashion them into fictions suggest discursive returns to prior sources and historical conceptualizations: in this chapter, a nineteenth-century return to medieval sources and specifically the imagined 'bacchantic' reality this medievalism purportedly revealed.

Choreomanias then pose a particular challenge relative to other types of 'madness' interesting for the history of ideas about dance, inasmuch as they reveal a complex node of fantasies about collective bodily movement and the public performance of disorder and distress. As temporal and spatial excrescences—public theatres of excess—choreomanias represent the choreographic embodiment of crisis. As such, the 'madness' of these events is not constitutional—it does not belong to individual bodies—but conjunctive, circumstantial. Choreomanias are the 'mad' theatricalization of a historical moment in time, a clash of temporalities and cultures. The madness in them is relative, performative: it shows a more global crisis where individuals signalling or signifying difference (as madness) do not. Significantly, as McCarren has argued of nineteenth-century dance, this madness spills out of the collective body politic as dance—in this case, disorganized and pullulating.

Choreomaniacs differ from other types of madmen and madwomen in other respects. They were not representative of the 'Danse des Fous' (the 'Madmen's Dance') Foucault mentions in his brief treatment of medieval folly in the opening chapter of *History of Madness*; or the figurative round dance Erasmus of Rotterdam (1466–1536) portrays in his playful *In Praise of Folly* (1509), in which a whole litany of professions parade their petty foibles in turn (none of them literally dancing). Nor were choreomaniacs exactly allied with later depictions of the danse macabre or Dance of Death portrayed in harrowing and occasionally humorous woodcuts by John Lydgate (1370–1451), Guyot (Guy) Marchant (active 1483–c. 1505) and Hans Holbein the Younger (1497–1543), among others, or in a 1424–1425 danse macabre mural in the Parisian cemetery of Les Saints Innocents. These slightly wry but always sobering skeletal dance-like rounds, like the medieval fools Foucault depicts, represent a particular sort of vice: foolish ignorance, individuals not knowing that their end has come.[16] Highlighting late medieval and early modern literature and portraiture in works by Jérôme (Hieronymous) Bosch (1450–1516), Sebastian Brant (1457–1521), Pieter Bruegel (or Brueghel) the Elder (1525–1569), and others, Foucault shows medieval fools travelling through everyday life in its margins: concretely but also figuratively, they travelled 'liminally', on rafts set adrift at the outskirts of society—not a suggestion that they lived a free and easy existence; but that they

15. Søren Kierkegaard, *La répétition*, trans. Jacques Privat (Paris: Éditions Payot et Rivages, 2003), 60–61.

16. On the nineteenth-century rediscovery of danse macabre prints and engravings, see e.g. Marie-Dominique Leclerc, 'Réemplois, avatars, redécouverte', in Marie-Dominique Leclerc, Danielle Quérel, and Alain Robert, *Danser avec la mort: Les danses macabres dans les manuscrits et livres imprimés du XVe au XXe siècle* (Lyon: Musée de l'imprimerie, 2004), 22. The bibliography on the danse macabre is vast. Early influential historiographies include Valentin Dufour, *Recherches sur la Dance Macabre peinte en 1425 au Cimetière des Innocents* [sic] (Paris: Bureaux du Bibliophile Français, 1873), in which the author notes that danse macabre iconography seized the early part of the century's imagination 'passionately' (i). See also Georges Kastner, *La Danse des morts: Dissertations et recherches historiques, philosophiques, littéraires et musicales* (Paris: Brandus, 1852). Eustache-Hyacinthe Langlois, in *Essai historique, philosophique et pittoresque sur les danses des morts*, 2 vols. (Rouen: Lebrument, 1851), convincingly argues that danse macabre portraiture represents actual theatrical dance practices playfully executed by living people, an observation rarely remarked on in contemporary scholarship (vol. 1, 116–160); Langlois's iconographic analysis of fifty-four visual representations of the danse macabre appears in Langlois, *Essai historique, philosophique et pittoresque*, vol. 2. Gabriel Peignot, in *Recherches historiques et littéraires sur les danses des morts et sur l'origine des cartes à jouer* (Dijon and Paris: Lagier, 1826), is widely acknowledged to have set the modern literature on danses macabres in motion. Among recent scholars noting choreographic forms, Sophie Oosterwijk suggests that danses macabres typically involved a chain of dancers, but that human life was also typically represented in a circle or semicircle depicting the ages of man, from birth to death. In Sophie Oosterwijk, 'Dance, Dialogue and Duality in the Medieval *Danse Macabre*', in Oosterwijk and Knöll, eds., *Mixed Metaphors*, 9–42, 29.

appear to have been set on a perpetually directionless course.[17] Neither are these fools fully cast out, like the Bacchic-type dancers Plato (c. 428–347 BCE) wanted expurgated from his *Republic*;[18] they are benignly and perpetually peripheral. Choreomaniacs, in contrast, tear through town. They appear mad on account of their sudden, explosive emergences, their seemingly involuntary—'organic'—outbursts on history's stage. In this regard, choreomaniacs constitute a class of people temporarily united by their folly rather than a general and terminal condition relegating them to a state of perpetual passage. In this sense, too, choreomaniacs were not engaged in the carnivalesque Mikhail Bakhtin (1895–1975) famously described in his work on François Rabelais (1494–1553): for Bakhtin, carnival signals the temporary disruption—the upturning—of everyday life, vividly reminding participants of alternative realities, opposed to official cultures.[19] Carnivals significantly take place at prescribed moments of the year yet in their chaotic, upside-down quality succeed in infiltrating popular consciousness, stimulating a revolutionary potential. The choreomanias this book describes perform a topsy-turvy world only in pockets, zones of intensity constituting a show of uncontrol potentially contagious but nearly always remote.

Choreomaniacs, furthermore, present a slightly different cast of symptoms and problems pertaining to madness from hysterics, hypochondriacs, and other types of 'maniacs', who by the eighteenth century were generally understood to suffer from excess fluids (including menstrual fluids) or a disorder of the internal spirits.[20] Although in many respects, choreomanias displayed characteristics of 'mania', including moving too much, and too spontaneously, they did so periodically rather than constitutionally. Hysterics in particular, Foucault remarks, were thought in the eighteenth and nineteenth centuries to suffer from excessive, uncontrollable motions, including especially spasms and convulsions, while melancholics were understood to suffer from a deficiency of motion, internal and externally manifest.[21] In *Dance Pathologies*, and in 'The "Symptomatic Act"' (1995), McCarren points out that madness appears in the (generally female) hysteric's body as an excess of motion, which is then translated into dance—as its quintessential sign. Concomitantly, dancers, she argues, typify madness, in nineteenth-century medicine, by symptomatizing 'madness detoured'.[22] So while dance in the nineteenth century for McCarren epitomized madness, choreomania signals a particularly nineteenth-century fantasy about madness as the collective amplification of excess gesturality: a collective hyperbole. But excessive motion translated into a mania for dance also signalled a complicated type of psychiatric

17. Controversy surrounding the correct translation and interpretation of Foucault's image of medieval madness, in terms of his employment of the well-rehearsed image of the raft, and his statement that the mad led an 'easily wandering existence', is ongoing. Foucault wrote: 'Les fous alors avaient une existence facilement errante', which I would render: 'The mad then, one might readily presume, led something of a wandering existence' (*Histoire de la folie*, 22). He was not implying that their existence was easy, only that they plausibly led a wandering one (standard critiques suggested Foucault too romantically posited that madmen and madwomen in the Middle Ages enjoyed an untroubled life). See esp. Still and Velody, 'Introduction', 1–16, 6–7; Gordon, 'Histoire de la folie', 32–33; Allan Megill, 'Foucault, Ambiguity and the Rhetoric of Historiography', in Still and Velody, eds., *Rewriting the History of Madness*, 86–104, 86–92, who emphasizes the purposeful ambiguity Foucault employs not only as a stylistic flourish but as a fundamentally philosophical stance. Dominick LaCapra, in 'Foucault, History and Madness', in Still and Velody, eds., *Rewriting the History of Madness*, 78–85, points out that historian H. C. Erik Midelfort's well-rehearsed critique of Foucault's medieval historiography. Midelfort notes that 'there is only one known instance of a madman's having been set adrift on a boat, and it is quite possible that the intention was to drown him'. In Midelfort, 'Madness and Civilization', 247–266, 254; cited in LaCapra, 'Foucault, History and Madness', 79. See also LaCapra, 'Foucault, History and Madness', 85n1; H. C. Erik Midelfort, 'Reading and Believing: On the Reappraisal of Michel Foucault', in Still and Velody eds., *Rewriting the History of Madness*, 105–109. Midelfort draws on an earlier critique of Foucault's figure of the raft scenario or *Narrenschiff* in W. B. Maher and B. Maher, 'The Ship of Fools; *Stultifera Navis* or *Ignis Fatuus*?', *American Psychologist* 37.7 (1982): 756–761. For a convincing defence of Foucault's not quite so literal use of the raft image, see esp. Gordon, 'Rewriting the History of Misreading', 173–176.

18. Plato, *Laws*, trans. E. A. Taylor, in *The Collected Dialogues of Plato, Including the Letters*, ed. Edith Hamilton and Huntington Cairns (Princeton, NJ: Princeton University Press, 2002), 1225–1503, 1385.

19. Mikhail Bakhtin, *Rabelais and His World*, trans. Hélène Iswolsky (Bloomington: Indiana University Press, 1984). Bakhtin's notion that carnival liberates revolutionary potentials has been widely refuted.

20. Excess fluids significantly 'moved' hysterics, in opposition to the heavier, more stagnant tendencies among melancholics, suggesting to Foucault that this area of medical study might be described as a 'medicine of movement' ('*médecine du mouvement*'). Foucault, *Histoire de la folie*, 357.

21. Foucault, *Histoire de la folie*, 352, 357.

22. Felicia McCarren, 'The "Symptomatic Act" circa 1900: Hysteria, Hypnosis, Electricity, Dance', *Critical Inquiry* 21.4 (Summer 1995): 748–774, 753.

disorder known in the nineteenth century as *monomania*. Choreomaniacs, who did not necessarily individually lack 'truth', or stray from it, and who were not always or necessarily 'unreasoning', became, it seemed, possessed with one thing: dancing, and the complex of hallucinatory and convulsive agitations that purportedly came with it. Thus the term applied to them: *monomaniacs*, nineteenth-century psychiatry's way of describing aberrant obsessions with singular things.[23] But whereas monomaniacs, I suggest further in chapter 4, were disorderly, inasmuch as they emoted and gesticulated too much, in excess conformity with their surroundings, medieval choreomaniacs also complied excessively with past (and foreign) forms of religiosity, clinging to practices becoming outmoded after the Black Death. As such, these dancers further represented excessive, radical resistance to change—and to modernity.

So while physicians throughout the classical age and into the nineteenth century understood mania and melancholy to be closely allied, a reflection Freud among others would further a few decades later, and while Hecker underscored the spectacularly convulsive aspect of dance manias, he also significantly sought a far more elusive etiology (or disease origin). 'Etiology' (or 'aetiology') is the science determining the source of a disease, whether its organic location (head, heart, liver, nerves, etc.) or a disruption of functional processes: in early modern medicine, for instance, an excess or deficiency of 'humours' (discussed in the next chapter). Remarkable with choreomania in Hecker's account was the basis of this hyper-motile, manic 'epidemic' not so much in bodily functions as in ancient history. The dancing disease, in Hecker's biohistorical conceptualization, emerges as if from out of the past, as a disease of archaic surfeit. Choreomaniacs appear where there is a fault line in civilization, a rupture and an opening, out of which they seem to spill. Calling the 1370s 'dancing mania' an 'extraordinary mental disorder',[24] following on the heels of the worst pandemic in human history, Hecker argued that it exacerbated an already prevailing spirit of superstitiousness made worse by the stresses plague had brought about. Dance manias in this view were organic and historical excrescences signalling the theatricalization of biohistorical crisis in bodily form.

In this sense, choreomaniacs were not just madmen or madwomen floating by on a *nef*, or raft. Their disorder was kinetic in another sense. They *passed through*, leaving spectators aghast in their wake. Reconfiguring the terms put forward by McCarren, madness in choreomania signals excess movement passing through social space as event. What's more, this is event played out as crisis: specifically, the crisis of modernity, where the past appears to emerge in and nearly to engulf modernity itself. Choreomaniacs thus swarm: they represent a disorder of teeming multitudes tapping into prior states of being, theatricalizing the sudden emergence of a disindividuated horde representing, in Hecker's words, the 'extravagances' of the past.[25] Their 'Bacchantic leaps' and 'wild dance', as they went 'screaming and foaming with fury', presented a spectacle of ancient uncontrol to contemporary eyewitnesses and later readers. As I will suggest at the end of this chapter, Nietzsche would in turn alternately celebrate and decry these archaic movements in his rarely noted remarks on St. John's and St. Vitus's dance, further linking early Christian history with the imagined excesses of a bacchanalian past.

A CONTEXT OF CRISIS: DANCING AMID FLOOD AND BONES

Historians Tison Pugh and Angela Jane Weisl argue in *Medievalisms* (2013) that every age has uses to which it puts the figure of the 'medieval', from the barbaric and the courtly to the magical and ribald.[26] Hecker portrays the medieval world as a canvas on which to project the most disorderly states of civilization not yet privy to Enlightenment rationality. Choreomaniacs, as biohistorical eruptions, were primitive and childlike: spontaneous, unpredictable, and volatile, prey to abrupt, inelegant movements that could with the hindsight of modern science and a generalist's interest in world history be described as aberrant and ill. They were quintessentially

---

23. Monomania, Foucault suggests, is an aberration even in the history of ideas about mental illness: it constitutes the exception that troubles the rule. Foucault, *History of Madness* (2006), 526–528.

24. Hecker, *Epidemics of the Middle Ages*, 91.

25. Hecker, *Epidemics of the Middle Ages*, 142.

26. Tison Pugh and Angela Jane Weisl, *Medievalisms: Making the Past Present*.(London: Routledge, 2013).

bacchantic, uncontrolled, and foreign but para-doxically also unusually responsive to the traumas and crises of their age. With vivid prose, Hecker described the first assemblages of choreomaniacs appearing in Aix-la-Chappelle (Aachen) in 1374: 'united by one common delusion', '[exhibiting] to the public both in the streets and in the churches the following strange spectacle', 'they formed circles hand in hand, and appearing to have lost all control over their senses, continued dancing, regardless of the bystanders, for hours together in wild delirium, until at length they fell to the ground in a state of exhaustion. They then com-plained of extreme oppression, and groaned as if in the agonies of death, until they were swathed in cloths bound tightly round their waists, upon which they again recovered, and remained free from complaint until the next attack'.[27] Hecker's hyperbolic language emphasized an irrational dancer caught in an uncontrollable urge to move. The cloths—and the staffs used to tie them—were employed, he surmised, to relieve the pain-ful abdominal distension that 'followed these spasmodic ravings'.[28] Bystanders coming to the choreomaniacs' aid resorted to 'thumping and trampling upon the parts affected' to relieve the dancers' discomfort, while they, 'insensible' to external stimuli, 'were haunted by visions, their fancies conjuring up spirits whose names they shrieked out'.[29] Some saw rivers of blood; oth-ers saw the heavens open up 'and the Saviour enthroned with the Virgin Mary'.[30] These hallu-cinations suggested to Hecker that 'the religious notions of the age were strangely and variously reflected in their imaginations', stimulated by the excitement that widespread death and disaster had provoked in the wake of the Black Death.[31]

The social and historical context for the dances was grim. The Black Death had devastated between half and two-thirds of the population of Europe in the mid-fourteenth century, giving rise to spectacular displays of flagellants and to what Hecker called the 'dancing malady'.[32] Grain prices had surged in the years preceding the Black Death, spurring on waves of peasant revolts in what historian Charles Briggs has described as a 'plague of insurrection' continuing into the sixteenth century, epitomized in the notorious English Peasants' Revolt of 1381, which brought festering tensions to a head.[33] But upheavals were erupting everywhere. Heightened insurrec-tions between 1355 and 1382 were exacerbated by repeat wars, including the fourteenth- and fifteenth-century Hundred Years War, and pesti-lence.[34] In this period, millions of people were displaced, without work or food, while popula-tions of entire towns and villages were slashed by more than half.[35] Gilles li Muisis (le Muisit or le Muiset) (1272–1352), an abbot at St. Martin's in the Pyrenees town of Tournay, described the countryside as gutted: 'travellers, merchants, pilgrims, and others who have passed through it declare that they have found cattle wander-ing without herdsmen in fields, town, and waste lands; that they have seen barns and wine-cellars standing wide open, houses empty, and few peo-ple to be found anywhere'.[36] 'In many different lands', li Muisis noted, 'fields are lying unculti-vated'.[37] Wolves roamed freely, entering open homes; ravens, kites, vultures, and field mice

27. Hecker, *Epidemics of the Middle Ages*, 80–81.

28. Hecker, *Epidemics of the Middle Ages*, 81.

29. Hecker, *Epidemics of the Middle Ages*, 81.

30. Hecker, *Epidemics of the Middle Ages*, 81.

31. Hecker, *Epidemics of the Middle Ages*, 81. For Hecker's essay 'The Black Death', see *Epidemics of the Middle Ages*, 1–74.

32. Hecker, *Epidemics of the Middle Ages*, 83.

33. Charles F. Briggs, *The Body Broken: Medieval Europe 1300–1520* (London: Routledge, 2011), 31. See also Samuel K. Cohn Jr., ed. and trans., *Popular Protest in Late Medieval Europe: Italy, France and Flanders* (Manchester: Manchester University Press, 2004); Michel Mollat and Philippe Wolff, *The Popular Revolutions of the Late Middle Ages*, trans. A. L. Lytton-Sells (London: Allen and Unwin, 1973); R. B. Dobson, ed., *The Peasants' Revolt of 1381*, 2nd ed. (London: Macmillan, 1983). The *Annals of Ghent* (*Annales Gandenses*) describe famine and dissent in the early fourteenth century, leading to fighting and bloodshed. Hilda Johnstone, ed., *Annales Gandenses: Annals of Ghent*, trans. Hilda Johnstone (London: Thomas Nelson, 1951), 28.

34. Briggs, *The Body Broken*, 7–36. On the biomedical history of the Black Death, see esp. Samuel K. Cohn Jr., *The Black Death Transformed: Disease and Culture in Early Renaissance Europe* (London: Oxford University Press, 2003); Samuel K. Cohn Jr., *Cultures of Plague: Medical Thinking at the End of the Renaissance* (Oxford: Oxford University Press, 2010).

35. Jacques Le Goff cites demographic analyses demonstrating a rise in the population of Europe from nearly 15 million to over 54 million in the 750 years prior to the Black Death (between c. 600 and c. 1348). Further studies showed that the population of Europe reached nearly 73 million in 1300. In Jacques Le Goff, *Medieval Civilization, 400–1500*, trans. Julia Barrow (London: Folio Society, 2011), 62.

36. Gilles le Muisit, *Chronique et annales de Gilles le Muisit, abbé de Saint-Martin de Tournai (1272–1352)* (Paris: Librairie Renouard, 1906), 85–87; cited in George Deaux, *The Black Death 1347* (New York: Weybright and Talley, 1969), 110.

37. Deaux, *The Black Death*, 110.

appeared, settling in to live with humans already starved for food and shelter.[38] Historian David Herlihy (1930–1991) has argued that in some of the more remote towns of England and Italy, up to 70 or 80 percent of the population was wiped out in the last decades of the fourteenth century.[39] According to French historian Jules Michelet (1798–1874), in his classic *Histoire de France* (1833–1841), medieval chronicles related that between five hundred and eight hundred people died daily in Paris and Saint-Denis at the height of the Black Death in 1348.[40] Ecological upheavals wreaked havoc, curbing centuries of population expansion, as new waves of floods and drought continued to demolish crops and livestock in the plague's wake. According to the *Chronicle of Liège* (1403), floodwaters overtook entire villages in 1373 and 1374. In January 1374, the waters of the Mosel ran so high they reached church altars and filled streets and market squares; villagers had to navigate through the town in rafts. The *Kölner Jarbuch* reported that on 11 February 1374, the Rhine rose so high that horses drowned in the streets, and this continued until Easter. According to a further chronicle, waters rose so high above the walls of Cologne that boats passed right over them. There, too, inhabitants had to navigate in rafts.[41]

This was the context in which the dancing upheaval arose. It had seemed that the world was coming to an end.[42] Survivors were ecstatic, and evinced a sense of urgency, gaiety, and occasionally despair. Many abandoned themselves to raucousness encouraged by municipal decree: as during plague times in Rome, when a policy of *lectisternium* mandated merriment through municipally sponsored feasts, so too in late medieval Europe, from Boccaccio and Machiavelli to Berni and Pepys, plague time was described as an occasion for dissolution.[43] Physicians had prescribed flight from plague-ridden towns to curb contamination, and a culture of countryside revelry blossomed. Gender rules shifted, as women who would not have bared their bodies to the opposite sex now, Boccaccio wryly noted, freely sought help for ailments from anyone willing to offer it. Mourning practices fell into disarray, and funerals became occasions for jauntiness rather than lament.[44]

Every sort of practice was called on to counteract the prevailing spirit of catastrophism. Historian Pierre Champion (1880–1942) in *La Galerie des Rois* [The Gallery of Kings] (1934) noted that dancing was among a regular cast of popular pastimes during periods of heightened death and disaster: 'during the plague, the *grand'mort* raged in Paris in 1348 . . . people dance and apologize: it's to chase away Death, they say. Thus, at least they may giddily forget their sorrows'.[45] The *Grandes chroniques de France* [Great Chronicles of France], compiled between the thirteenth and sixteenth centuries, similarly tells of two monks who, riding through Paris in 1348, witnessed a scene of great merriment purportedly engaged in to ward off death. They saw men and women 'dancing to the music of drums and bagpipes, and having a great celebration. So the monks asked them why they were making so merry, to which they replied: "We have seen our neighbors die and are seeing them die day after day, but since the mortality has in no way entered our town, we are not without hope that

38. Deaux, *The Black Death*, 114.

39. David Herlihy, *The Black Death and the Transformation of the West*, ed. and intro. Samuel K. Cohn, Jr. (Cambridge, MA: Harvard University Press, 1997): 17. See also Briggs, *The Body Broken*, 7–39.

40. Jules Michelet, *Histoire de France* [1833–1841], 2nd rev. ed., 16 vols., vol. 4 (Paris: C. Marpon et E. Flammarion, 1879), 218.

41. E. Louis Backman, *Religious Dances in the Christian Church and in Popular Medicine*, trans. E. Classen (London: Allen and Unwin, 1952), 215–216. See Edouard Lavallene, ed., *Histoire du Limbourg, suivie de celle des comtés de Daelhem et de Fauquemont, des Annales de l'Abbaye de Rolduc, par M. S. P. Ernst, curé d'Afden, ancien chanoine de Rolduc*, vol. 5 (Liège: Librairie de P. J. Collardin, 1840), 70; Le Goff, *Medieval Civilisation*; John Aberth, *The Black Death: The Great Mortality of 1348–1350: A Brief History with Documents* (New York: Bedford St. Martin's, 2005); John Aberth, *From the Brink of the Apocalypse: Confronting Famine, War, Plague, and Death in the Later Middle Ages*, 2nd ed. (New York: Routledge, 2010); Rosemarie Horrox, ed. and trans., *The Black Death* (Manchester: Manchester University Press, 1994); Philip Ziegler, *The Black Death* (London: Readers Union Collins, 1969).

42. The chronicler Agnolo di Tura of Siena reported: 'So many have died that everyone believes it is the end of the world'; cited in Aberth, *The Black Death*, 2. In *The Body Broken*, Briggs notes Gabriele de' Mussis's comment: 'The scale of the mortality and the form it took persuaded those who lived . . . that the last judgment had come' (20).

43. See Herlihy, *The Black Death*, 40, 63–65; Briggs, *The Body Broken*, 25–26; Deaux, *The Black Death*, 150; Peignot, *Recherches historiques et littéraires*, xxix–xxxn1.

44. See Boccaccio's account in Michelet, *Histoire de France*, vol. 4, 224; Briggs, *The Body Broken*, 25–26.

45. 'Pendant l'épidémie de peste, la "grand'mort," qui sévit à Paris en 1348 et qui fait jusqu'à huit cents victimes par jour, "les gens dansent et s'en excusent: c'est pour chasser la mort, disent-ils. Par là, du moins ils s'étourdissent."' Pierre Champion, *La Galerie des Rois* (Paris: Bernard Grasset, 1934), 118; cited in Philippe de Félice, *L'enchantement des danses et la magie du verbe: Essai sur quelques formes inférieures de la vie mystique* (Paris: Albin Michel, 1957), 10n1.

our festive mood will not allow it to come here, and this is the reason for why we are dancing."[46] Riding through town sometime later, the monks discovered that a hailstorm had killed some of the villagers and scared others into flight, suggesting that the dancing had not helped. The chronicle's editor, Jules Viard (1862–1940), posits that the chronicle may have been written by an eyewitness who would have participated in the dancing—revealing some sympathy for the dancers.[47] The German composer and folklorist Franz M. Böhme (1827–1898) further points out in his two-volume history of German dances, *Geschichte des Tanzes in Deutschland* (1886), that 'plague dances' (*Pesttänze*) in 1349 might be equated with practices among the so-called Wertheimer, who were said to dance around a forest pine tree until the Black Death left their small town; similarly, in the countryside outside Basel, there was still at the time of his writing in the late 1880s a large field called the 'witch's mat' (*Hexenmatte*) because, he notes, according to popular belief, the Walpurgis dances were held there. Remainders of 'plague dances' existed elsewhere: every seven years, Böhme recorded, in memory of those surviving the plague, the *Metzsgersprung* (or butchers' leaping) was performed by armed butchers in Munich; the *Schäfflertanz* (or barrel-makers' dance) and Echternach Spring procession (which I will treat further in chapter 6) constituted similar remainders, some dating to later plagues. In their own time, the plague dances were common enough to generate a whole repertoire of popular songs, so that by 1350 in Bern 'more than a thousand armed men' gathered in a dance of their own, mocking the masses of mad people ('Geißlerfahrten') who had passed through town

not long before with 'ridiculous dance songs' ('Geißlerlied') ('travestirenden Tanzliede').[48] One of the dance songs commonly cited is given in a late fifteenth-century Cologne chronicle as 'Here sent Johan, so so, vrisch ind vro here sent Johan', which may be translated as 'Here is Saint John, so so fresh and happy, here is Saint John!' Some confusion seems to have arisen in regard to this song. The monk Petrus de Herental (c. 1322–1390), to whom I will return, submitted in an extended poem describing the events that the dancers were calling out names of demons: 'Frisch, Friskes'. This may be a misunderstanding of 'vrisch' (suggesting lightness or joy), demonizing the dancers' worship.[49]

There was little to keep survivors from expressing vivacity. Though bouts of plague recurred for a few hundred years after the Black Death reached its peak in 1348–1350, the fourteenth-century plague signalled a shift in social mores. In the last decades of the fourteenth century, a surge of new fashions arose, emphasizing bright colours and pointed shoes: anything to signify jollity, carefreeness and, for many, a survivors' high. According to an early seventeenth-century copy of the fourteenth-century Cologne *Limburg Chronicle* (1617), 'when the deaths, the processions of flagellants, the pilgrimages to Rome and the slaughter of the Jews were at an end, the world began to live again, and to be joyful, and people put on new clothes'.[50] Taken in this light, the dance 'manias' seem rather benign.

According to cartographical analysis by the German physician Hellmuth Liebscher, dancing flocks appearing in 1373–1374 moved roughly from east to west, forking towards the north and south. These dancers first appeared in Swabia, England, and the Netherlands and then spread

46. Aberth, *The Black Death*, 164.

47. Aberth, *The Black Death*, 164.

48. Franz M. Böhme, 'Tanzwut im Mittelalter', in Franz M. Böhme, *Geschichte des Tanzes in Deutschland*, 2 vols., vol. 1 (Leipzig: Druck und Verlag von Breitkopf & Härtel, 1886), 40–44, 42–44. Samuel K. Cohn Jr. notes that in sixteenth-century Italy dancing, music, feasting, drinking, and singing brushed melancholy aside, just as dancing and other sorts of 'carnality' were accused of bringing on new bouts of plague and, in many instances, outlawed (*Cultures of Plague*, 233, 274, 292).

49. See Hecker, *Epidemics of the Middle Ages*, 143, 146; also Paul Frédéricq, 'De secten der geeselaars en der dansers in de Nederlanden tijdens de 14de eeuw', in *Mémoires de l'académie royale des sciences des lettres et des beaux-arts de Belgique*, vol. 53 (Brussels: Hayez, October 1895–June 1898), 1–62, 49; Böhme, 'Tanzwut im Mittelalter', 42.

50. 'Darnach, da das Sterben, die Geiselfarth, Römerfarth, Judenschlacht, als vorgeschrieben stehet, ein End hatte, da hub die Welt wieder an zu leben und fröhlich zu seyn, und machten die Männer neue Kleidung'. In Deaux, *The Black Death*, 216. Fashion seems to have been quite a point of contention—revelry and reviling—from at least the middle of the fourteenth century. Hecker notes that possessed dancers, among other 'enemies of fashion', showed fury against the new trend towards 'extravagant . . . love of dress'. Hecker, *Epidemics of the Middle Ages*, 82n1. The Belgian historian Paul Frédéricq (1850–1920) notes that shoemakers were temporarily forbidden to make colourful shoes following the 1370s dances ('De secten', 51). The *Limburg Chronicle*, or *Festi Limpurgenses*, is attributed to Tilemann Ehlen von Wolfhagen (c. 1348–1420), dating from the first decade of the fifteenth century; it chronicles the history of the Rhineland between 1336 and 1398; publication by Johann Friedrich Faust in 1617 was followed by various German editions in the nineteenth century, including by Arthur Wyss for the *Monumenta Germaniae historica* (1875). On

to Hainaut, Flanders, Brabant, the Lower Rhine, Cologne, Utrecht, Tongeren, and Aachen; and then south to Franconia, Metz, and Strasbourg. About a year later, they were in France, and again in Hainault and Holland.[51] By 1381, the 'dancing plague' had reached Augsburg. In 1428, a couple of isolated episodes were reported in chronicles and annals: women were seen dancing in Zurich, and a monk was said to have danced himself to death in the cloister of St. Agnes in Schaffhausen.[52] In Strasbourg, in July 1518, the dancing 'epidemic' re-emerged with force. Backman has convincingly pointed out that many dancers may have come from Bohemia, proceeding along traditional Hungarian pilgrimage routes, gathering ever-larger numbers of enthusiasts along the way. Pilgrimages typically involved dancing and song, prompted in Backman's view by the heightened excitement rippling through towns and villages in the wake of the Black Death and massive demographic upheavals that had displaced millions.[53] But every sort of petty troublemaker and free spirit seems to have joined in the throngs, as well as a motley crew of religious enthusiasts, anti-clerical revellers, and traditional feast-day celebrants, offering an ever more public appearance of revelry and debauchery to puzzled observers and peers.

FLAGELLANTS, LEPERS AND CHOREOMANIACS

Choreomaniacs were among a cast of eccentrics thus marking this period. Slightly more familiar to the contemporary reader, flagellants offered dramatic performances of penance and celebration in public space as they moved through vast swathes of Europe, like choreomaniacs often half-clothed, offering bystanders scenes of religiosity that bordered on heathenism and hereticism. Like choreomaniacs, flagellants were subject to nineteenth-century historiographic scrutiny, though little more is known of them than of so-called choreomaniacs: they appear, contrary to standard histories, to have come from all classes. As historian Samuel K. Cohn Jr. has pointed out, noblewomen cast off their jewels to join in the throngs, suggesting not only the poor were among them.[54] Writing over a century earlier, Michelet employed a biohistorical and ecosophical set of images, describing bands of flagellants in ecstatic fury moving through towns as if blown by the wind of divine wrath. Comparing flagellants to a fever, he set them in contrast to the glacial egoism of all those who locked themselves up to feast in egotistical luxury.[55] The Flemish historian J. M. B. C. Kervyn de Lettenhove (1817–1891) similarly noted catastrophic pestilence and spectacular displays among flagellants who performed their religious penance by thrusting themselves to the ground in a cross shape and rising up three times to whip themselves, while villagers gawked at the spectacle.[56] French historian Étienne Delaruelle has described this as a *rapresentazione sacra*, a theatrical representation designed to show Christ's flagellation to all those gathered to watch.[57]

In Hecker's account, flagellants carried iron-tipped scourges and beat or whipped themselves until they were bleeding, singing sacred songs and performing dramatized acts of penance in town squares—'welcomed by the ringing of the bells', as 'people flocked from all quarters, to listen to their hymns and to witness their

the midsummer dances, see Ehlen von Wolfhagen, *Die Limburger Chronik, Eingeleitet von Otto H. Brandt. Mit 17 Abbildungen und Anhang* (Jena: Eugen Diederichs, 1922), 47–48; Frédéricq, 'De secten', 41.

51. Hellmuth Liebscher, *Ein kartographischer Beitrag zur Geschichte der Tanzwut*, M. D. diss. (Leipzig University, 1931), 16; cited in Rosen, *Madness in Society*, 198.

52. See also Backman, *Religious Dances*, 235–242; Midelfort, *A History of Madness*, 33; Hecker, *Epidemics of the Middle Ages*, 90.

53. Backman, *Religious Dances*, 230–231. See Rosen, *Madness in Society*, 198–199. John Stevens notes that a collection of songs in Catalan and Latin, in the fourteenth-century *Llibre Vermell de Montserrat*, suggests in a prefatory note that 'from time to time over a long period pilgrims keeping vigil in the church of the Blessed Virgin of Montserrat have been eager to sing and dance, even in the square by broad daylight. And in that place they should not do any singing unless the songs are decent and devout'. Dancing and singing in town squares, even raucously, seems then to have been a relatively common practice, though frowned upon. In Stevens, *Words and Music in the Middle Ages*, 182. See also Eustace with King, 'Dances of the Living and the Dead', who further suggest that Perkin Revelour in Chaucer's 'The Cook's Tale', in the *Canterbury Tales*, cannot resist dancing (ll. 4370–4380) (49).

54. Samuel K. Cohn Jr., 'The Black Death and the Burning of Jews', *Past & Present* 196 (2007): 3–36, 11–12.

55. Michelet, *Histoire de France*, vol. 4, 220–221.

56. J. M. B. C. Kervyn de Lettenhove, *Histoire de Flandre, 1304–1384*, 6 vols., vol. 3 (Bruxelles: A. Vandale, 1847), 350–359. See also Kervyn de Lettenhove, *Istore et Croniques de Flandres, d'après les textes de divers manuscrits*, 2 vols. (Brussels: F. Hayez and Commission Royale d'Histoire, 1879–1880); Sahlin, *Étude sur la carole médiévale*, 125–126, 165.

57. In György Székely, 'Le mouvement des flagellants au 14e siècle, son caractère et ses causes', in Jacques Le Goff, ed., *Hérésies et sociétés dans l'Europe préindustrielle. 11e–18e siècles* (Paris: Mouton & Co. and École Pratique des Hautes Études, 1968), 229–241, 240.

penance, with devotion and tears'.[58] These were performative enactments, processions cultural historian Kathleen Ashley has suggested characterize the under-written history of medieval performance culture. Arguing that 'procession' is 'arguably the most ubiquitous and versatile public performance mode until the seventeenth century' yet 'has received so little scholarly or theoretical attention', Ashley suggests processions enabled civic negotiation of official scripts, as well as a productive 'contact zone', Mary Louise Pratt's term to describe complex, often asymmetrical encounters.[59] Ashley further argues that processions, from royal entries to carnival parades, enabled the dramatic arbitration of difference.

Choreomaniacs offered a less harmonious processional drama, a zone of contact but also of friction and disruption, an eruption into public space that grated on observers and by doing so brought out tensions already coming to a head. While often processional, choreomanias tumbled and tore through public space, theatricalizing difference—described as 'demonic'—as well as community, rearticulating the terms by which community came to be construed. Choreomanias, in temporarily joining together revellers and separating out recalcitrant witnesses and hosts, suggested temporary zones of realignment, in which social groups were not just ritually performing difference but actively, disruptively—often uninvitedly—asserting it. Choreomanias, then, suggest a medieval space of disruption and interference, for which lively foreign dances and songs serve as the choreopolitical sign.

Meanwhile, lepers had already in plague time transformed the urban landscape in what Foucault in the introduction to *History of Madness* and in his 1974–1975 lectures on the 'abnormal' at the Collège de France (*Les Anormaux: Cours au Collège de France, 1974–1975* [1999]) described as a nascent biopolitics of exclusion, whereby lepers came to be cast out of town and, more forcefully, life itself. As Foucault outlines, lepers were ceremonially deposed of their belongings, and sent to a peripheral location tantamount to social death. They were ostracized, made marginal, with no return: lepers had, for all pragmatic purposes, been made

before their actual death socially to die. Foucault describes this process as a great orgiastic fantasy of plague—a time when all laws disappear—and an occasion for the total exercise of biopower. In plague time, urban space was 'exhaustively sectioned', a practice Foucault argues determined further regimes of sequestration and marginalization well into the sixteenth, seventeenth, and eighteenth centuries, and continuing to define political practices of marginalization in the twentieth.[60]

Choreomaniacs, described in the nineteenth century as a brand of medieval 'mad', were slightly different; some, I suggest below, sequestered themselves in large encampments outside town, while also at other times conspicuously infiltrating churches and town squares. More significantly, these celebrants and carousers offered viewers a different sort of contagious spectacle. They contagioned one another and threatened to contagion viewers swept up into their enthusiastic rounds, but they also remained for the most part, like the flagellants, theatrical: they came through town and showed themselves effusively as event. Unlike flagellants, however, dance maniacs offered a portrait of hyperkinetic enthusiasm spurred on by a dubious cast of devils: they were foreign, outsiders, passing through and performing the intrusion of archaic alterity into public space.

THE TRIALS OF INTERPRETATION: MODERN MEDIEVAL IMAGINARIES

Readers from at least the seventeenth century offered a number of compelling accounts of these medieval scenes of debauchery and demonism, alternately ascribing them to psychiatric disorders and to organic illness; but also suggesting the dancers were engaging in ancient ritual practices. In his *Abrégé chronologique de l'histoire de France* [Abridged Chronology of the History of France] (1696), François Eudes de Mézeray (1610–1683) suggested dancers in the Netherlands went around naked, spinning and running, dancing and singing so vehemently they fell to the ground from exhaustion. Calling this a 'manic passion or

---

58. Hecker, *Epidemics of the Middle Ages*, 32.

59. Kathleen Ashley, 'Introduction: The Moving Subjects of Processional Performance', in Kathleen Ashley and Wim Hüsken, eds., *Moving Subjects: Processional Performance in the Middle Ages and the Renaissance* (Amsterdam: Rodopi, 2001), 7–34, 22.

60. Michel Foucault, *Les Anormaux: Cours au Collège de France, 1974–1975* (Paris: Éditions du Seuil/Gallimard, 1999), 47.

frenzy' ('passion maniaque ou phrénésie'), de Mézeray suggested they would have died from overexertion and bloating if contemporaries had not tightened their stomachs with strips of cloth. Further suggesting that bystanders watching the dancers could catch their frenzy, de Mézeray noted perfunctorily that they were generally believed to be possessed, and exorcised; their dance was also popularly ('vulgairement') known as the dance of St. John.[61] De Mézeray suggested this dancing was a sort of psychiatric disease, contemporaneous with other conditions, notably famine and the *mal des ardents* or St. Anthony's fire (also known as ergotism). But he did not equate the dancing with ergotism, as subsequent authors have done, suggesting instead that the dancers were merely exhausted by their efforts. I tend to agree with this view, but further to argue that bands of dancers travelling through towns and villages in the wake of the Black Death constituted a theatre of suspect alterity, intensifying xenophobic tendencies during this period and a heightened sense of modernity that these more ancient practices threatened to undermine. Historian Jacques Le Goff (1924–2014), articulating a well-rehearsed stance among historiographers, called the post-plague dances mental illnesses, to be classed alongside epilepsy and ergotism, noting that malnutrition and physical frailty prepared men and women's minds for spectacular hallucinations.[62] Those living at the time were not so quick to dismiss this as disease. Many eyewitnesses saw the dances as strange—often suspect—phenomena barely marginal to regular life; others saw the dancers as devil-worshippers; physicians attributed them to hot blood, but did not otherwise become involved in regimes of castigation or cure.

More convincing than accounts of mass madness and poisoning are those suggesting the dances were plausibly village rounds, made more conspicuous during this period of cultural change. As French historian Eustache-Hyacinthe Langlois (1777–1837) pointed out, in his *Essai historique, philosophique et pittoresque sur les danses des morts* [Historical, Philosophical and Pictorial Essay on the Dances of Death] (1851), the late Middle Ages were marked by regular village fêtes, ambulatory events ('fêtes balladoires') taking place on, among other occasions, the eve of the feast of St. John. As he points out, this type of popular celebration was increasingly described in heavily chastising terms as a 'procession du diable', a diabolical procession inverting Christian worship, insulting Christ according to every possible detail. The dancers' crowns of flowers (*serta*) derided his crown of thorns; their outstretched arms insulted his posture on the cross; the rouge (*belletum*) on their faces parodied the veiling of his face; and their head movements, accompanied by high-pitched cries, parodied the expiration of the divine redeemer. They performed high leaps in a circular formation, with Satan purportedly at its invisible centre. As Langlois remarks, these villagers did not dance any less on account of such inflammatory accusations—associated, I will suggest further, with witchcraft, paganism, and plausibly Jewish dances, which typically involved high leaps and rounds.[63] For Langlois, these *paroissiens* (villagers) were simply engaged in traditional forms of divertissement—the *fêtes patronales des paroisses* (village saints' day celebrations)—which for centuries had marked the Feast of Fools, of the Innocents, and of the Ass, taking place in cemeteries as well as in regular places of worship.

The clergy, Langlois notes, were no less guilty of taking part in what he wryly calls these 'infames saturnales' (infamous Saturnalia), which he notes at times degenerated into mayhem (and possibly, he implies, sexual mischief).[64] Accusations against dancing colourfully and spiritedly were designed to quell popular displays of immoral behaviour: the later development of the epidemiological, toxic, and

---

61. De Mézeray writes: 'Deux grands fléaux, . . . la famine et le mal des ardents, qui, le plus souvent, prenoit en l'aisne, tourmentèrent la France, l'Italie et l'Angleterre, cette année 1373. Il courut aussi, principalement dans les Pays-Bas, une passion maniaque ou phrénésie, inconnue à tous les siècles précédents. Ceux qui en estoient atteints, la plus part de la lie du peuple, se despouilloient tout nuds, se mettoient une couronne de fleurs sur la teste, et se tenant par les mains alloient dans les rües et dans les églises, dançant, chantant et tournoyant avec tant de roideur, qu'ils tomboient par terre hors d'haleine. Ils s'enfloient si fort par cette agitation, qu'ils eussent crevé sur l'heure, si on n'eust pris le soin de leur serrer le ventre avec de bonnes bandes. Ceux qui les regardoient trop attentivement estoient bien souvent pris du mesme mal. On crut qu'il y avoit de l'opération du diable, et que les exorcismes les soulageoient. Le vulgaire le nomma la Danse de Saint-Jean'. François Eudes de Mézeray, *Abrégé chronologique de l'histoire de France*, vol. 3, pt. 2 (Amsterdam: Abraham Wolfgang, Prés de la Bourne, 1688), 92; cited in Langlois, *Essai historique, philosophique et pittoresque*, vol. 1, 179–180. See also Frédéricq, 'De secten', 49–58.

62. Le Goff, *Medieval Civilisation*, 249–250.

63. Langlois, *Essai historique, philosophique et pittoresque*, vol. 1, 171–172.

64. Langlois, *Essai historique, philosophique et pittoresque*, vol. 1, 172–176.

psychiatric diagnosis amplified and obscured accusations initially levied on moral grounds. From this perspective, 'choreomania' signals a zone of intensity in medieval history and in the modern medieval imaginary—'modern' Europe's 'medieval' history—whereby rowdy collective dancing suggests an obscure and indescribable other surging up from suspicious indeterminate places (the East) and eras (antiquity). So while I have found no further evidence that choreomaniacs specifically danced leftwards (or stepped with the left foot), it was well-established at the time that a clockwise dance beginning with the left foot led straight to hell.[65] Jewish dances, such as the hora, typically perform a circular motion towards the right, beginning with the left foot—leading me to posit that 'choreomanias' may in some cases have constituted Jewish dances. To passing observers anxious to stamp out all signs of suspect alterity and excess archaicity, the mixture of Jewish—plausibly Bohemian—and pre-Christian traditions rendered all figures of boisterous, high-leaping rounds pestilential.

For Langlois, the involution of Christianity in these carnivalesque displays were typical 'gothic' (high medieval) expressions, not shameful, and indeed quite 'normal', if the borderline between normality and abnormality is the mark of madness. Reprising Gabriel Peignot's (1767–1849) pioneering research on danse macabre iconography, Langlois remarks that convulsive movements deriving from plague may further have given rise to strange disorderly postures.[66] As in regular expressions of chorea, in which individuals involuntarily perform dance-like movements, typical dances and celebrations may have become mixed in with plague-borne convulsive postures, resulting in the danse macabre iconography familiar at the time, and in which Death dances with Life. Death and plague had become objects of fascination in the early nineteenth

century, intensifying retrospective glances on a time when plague, life, and death were already performing gruesome rounds. Langlois suggested he first encountered a strange convulsive dance of death while riding by a 'horrible spectacle' of 'violently agitated' people offering a barely living 'portrait of death'.[67] In these accounts, convulsive dancing and death occur in the margins—under the cover of night, in footnotes, whispered as an aside.

Langlois, like Hecker, saw in these figures of corpse-like rounds in the countryside at night a reflection of his own age, choleric and plague-ridden, catapulting him into earlier centuries to seek an explanation for this theatre on the ancient scene of biohistory. But the challenges of writing such a history of inarticulacy and obscurity were great; as art historian and composer Jean-Georges Kastner (1810–1867) pointed out in Les Danses des Morts: Dissertations et Recherches historiques, philosophiques, littéraires et musicales [Dances of Death: Historical, Philosophical, Literary and Musical Dissertations and Findings] (1852), ancient chronicles juxtaposed to contemporary events hardly enlightened the reader and observer. In Alsace, Kastner remarked, a sort of St. Vitus's dance still reputedly existed at the time of his writing—hazily remembered by village elders. The movements of the body were so violent, so exaggerated, he wrote, that the dancers struck the ground with their knees and elbows. The 'analogy' between convulsive dances and diabolical rounds, Kastner suggested, produced the appearance of a connection between current events and myth. This apparent connection could be attributed, he argued, to the fact that individuals suffering from real nervous affections or psychiatric disorders causing them to perform extravagant movements were typically likened to demoniacally possessed or bewitched persons. This false attribution was not aided by

---

65. See Stevens, *Words and Music in the Middle Ages*, 161; Eustace with King, 'Dances of the Living and the Dead', 53.

66. Langlois, *Essai historique, philosophique et pittoresque*, vol. 1, 165. See also Eustache-Hyacinthe Langlois, 'Lettre de M. C. Leber à M. E.-H. Langlois sur l'origine de la danse macabre ou danse des morts', Paris, 25 July 1833, in Langlois, *Essai historique, philosophique et pittoresque*, vol. 1, 1–80, 12–13; Peignot, *Recherches historiques et littéraires*, xxviii–xxx. Peignot further tentatively highlights the relationship of the Danse des Morts (Dance of Death) to the 1347 plague epidemic and reports of dances in 1373; he suggests the first depiction of a Danse des Morts dates from the following decade, in 1383, but does not take the chronological conjecture further (xxviii). He also suggests a distinction between the generic term 'Danse des Morts' (Dance of Death) and the late medieval iconographic tradition of the danse macabre, which he posits followed the dramatic depiction of a 'Danse des Morts' in the Parisian Cimetière des Innocents (1424) (xxxii), though these categories overlap significantly. Interestingly, Kastner suggests the exact opposite—though highly correlated—causality, suggesting joy becomes illness and dance becomes death for those struck with the 'chorysantisme' of St. John and St. Vitus; with the malediction of the heavens, dances transform into convulsions, as dancers turn away from God and towards the devil: '*danser, c'est mourir!*' ('*to dance is to die!*'). In Kastner, *La Danse des morts*, 14.

67. Langlois, *Essai historique, philosophique et pittoresque*, vol. 1, 165n1.

the fact that the individuals themselves often believed that they had participated in satanic rites.[68]

Significantly for the history of ideas about disorderly movement and the choreopolitics of crowd control this book outlines, orderly dancing meant an orderly society; conversely, disorderly dancing—conceived as round dances plausibly beginning with the left foot, involving involuntary, jagged angularity—suggested that religion, state, and society were in disarray.[69] In this view, choreomaniacs' boisterous appearances suggested broader biohistorical disruptions, intensifying fourteenth-century opinion that the world was coming to an end.

OF SAINT'S DAY CABALS AND FEASTS: MEDIEVAL SCENES OF 'READING'

Contemporary accounts suggest the dancers offered strange sights to bystanders; but also that they were at the helm of a popular movement wrapping many up into an exultant dance. Some accounts suggest they amplified traditional St. John's Day practices going out of favour with the church; others imply that the dancers were strange, incomprehensible foreigners intruding into public space, but no less galvanizing on that account; others still suggested that the dancers were demonic and pestilential. In general, the dances and dance-like celebrations wrapped into the nineteenth-century choreomania repertoire seem to have constituted a motley cast of theatrical events, marginal and heretical in some cases but no less popular and certainly far from mad. Singing, feasting, and dancing were subject, in the fourteenth century, to as much praise as blame. Dancing in particular was popularly viewed as having caused the plague, by its association with licentiousness and sinfulness that had brought on God's wrath. But dancing, as I noted, was also frequently indulged in to ward

off further malignity and keep revellers' minds off the general atmosphere of bleakness and desolation. Dances in Metz seem to have provoked amusement, a welcome break in everyday life and not a particularly disorderly or diseased one. Yet according to the *Metz Chronicle*, the plight was dire: a 'sad thing happened in Metz' in 1374, the chronicler notes, when fifteen hundred people from all professions—priests, labourers, the sick, and the poor, 'danced for St. John', not stopping to eat or rest for nine or ten days. For the Metz chronicler, this round-the-clock dancing was a fate against which those struck by it were helpless. He portrays the dancers as victims, 'troubled', 'affected', and 'afflicted' by their 'strange sorrow'. Yet his narrative describes a peculiar plight: the town seems to have been bursting with life, the dancing seizing men and women from across all age ranges and classes as they set aside their everyday responsibilities and let loose for a while.[70]

The Metz chronicle suggests the dancing was primarily a local affair, but other chronicles suggest the dances at this time were noteworthy on account of the dancers' strange speech and demeanour: in particular, their high leaps, crowns of flowers, and other unusual accoutrements. In this respect, the dancers were outsiders, infiltrating local life, gathering some to their ranks, and others to watch. The monk Petrus de Herental in his life of Pope Gregory XI noted that a *mira secta*,[71] or strange, admirable, or noteworthy coterie of men and women, had appeared in Aachen from all over Germany, proceeding to Belgium and France in 1375. They were possessed by demons, he wrote, wearing wreaths in their hair, bedecked in only a towel and stave. They held each other's hands, leaped into the air, and shouted incomprehensible names throughout markets and church precincts, oblivious to the ogling of bystanders. Herental offered, as an illustration, an anonymous poem circulating at the time, which suggested the dancers begged wherever they went, and were granted some charity. The poem, which Hecker

---

68. Kastner, *La Danse des morts*, 62–63.

69. Eustace with King, 'Dances of the Living and the Dead', 43–71, 48. So, too, in the sixteenth century, dance and choreographic practices highlighted the scripted, notated—and specifically geometric—aspects of movement, Mark Franko argues, signalling to practitioners and audiences that bodies operated in space according to patterned, and thus legible, *theorizable* procedures. See Mark Franko, *Dance as Text: Ideologies of the Baroque Body*, rev. ed. (Oxford: Oxford University Press, 2015), esp. 15–30. Franko points out that 'frenetic or uncontrolled movement' in early seventeenth-century ballet also suggested unrequited love and a highly feminized state of madness (99). Similarly, popular festivity described by Bakhtin as carnivalesque occurred according to 'nongeometrical', often complex, and potentially dissonant formations (64).

70. Cited in Backman, *Religious Dances*, 211.

71. The term 'secta' designates a group in Latin, but also suggests a path, method, or principle. These dancers were viewed as constituting a tightly knit coterie, sharing a way of life and quite literally a trajectory.

reproduces in an appendix to 'The Dancing Mania', suggests the dancers enjoyed a relatively nomadic existence but were seized en route by clerics eager to exorcise their putative demons, compounding an already strange sight with the spectacle of religious exorcism. The dancers Herental's poet describes loathed the colour red and screamed, 'hating' the priests and cavorting throughout the night. But they were soon cured by the church, in a dramatic resolution that purged this modest urban crisis of its interlopers.[72]

The choreomaniacs were entertaining and outlandish but also incidental: they represented a digression from and distraction in the fabric of everyday life, even as they spectacularized a state of crisis. From a benign, festive eruption of dancing to a contorted expression of apparently genuine pain, the dancing 'plague' provoked not only awe, wonder, and bemusement but also reprobation. The dancers sorely irritated some: they had become a familiar sight, a spectacular excrescence but a grating one. The fourteenth-century chronicler Jean d'Outremeuse (Jean des Preis) (1338–1400) complained in La Geste de Liege that 'the Devil in hell was their master'. They called out loudly to St. John the Baptist, clapping their hands, leaping, striking the ground with their feet ('trippoit'), cloth tied tightly around their stomachs with a staff, provoking all who heard them to '[tremble] with fear'. 'In the churches they behaved in their usual manner, as also in towns and places round Liege and in the diocese generally. Some of them returned to Liege, shouting and bawling and making such a din that it seemed the world was coming to an end'. Like rats, 'the country was full of them'. Des Preis added that 'pregnant women and others were so distressed that they died and their bodies were carried away'. The 'attacks' were so great that 'in their homes and in secret people could not help dancing. All this I saw indeed', he wrote, underscoring his privileged eyewitness status, 'and much more also'.[73] Thankfully, he concluded, they had been driven out of town.[74] According to the Chronicle of Liège (1402), dancers in Liège jumping high before church altars terrified all those who viewed them.[75]

The stigma and metaphor of plague that colours des Preis's narrative transpires through other accounts, anticipating the epidemiological language that would come to dominate accounts of the dancers in the next centuries. As travellers—and notably, often, as foreigners—dance maniacs provoked apprehension, bringing an unwanted din to what were already difficult times. Des Preis's contemporary the fourteenth-century chronicler Johannes de Beke (Jan Beke or Beka) described in his Dutch chronicle a 'strange plague' spreading from Bohemia along the Rhine and reaching Maastricht, as men and women clad in wreaths went dancing through villages, passing in and out of churches until they fell to the ground, exhausted. They were eventually divested of their evil spirits through exorcism.[76] Another chronicler called this a 'daemoniaca

---

72. Petri de Herentals, Prioris Floreffiensis, *Vita Gregorii XI* (Paris, 1693), 483; cited in Hecker, *Epidemics of the Middle Ages*, 143–144. Frédéricq provides a detailed account of flagellants and dancers in the Netherlands in 'De secten', drawing especially from (and appending) Latin accounts provided by Petrus de Herental and Radulphus de Rivo; on the dancing 'sect', see esp. Frédéricq, 'De secten', 48–62. Frédéricq submits that the movement of dancers grew by the thousands in September and October 1374 (50); he further notes dancers in Liège, according to the Dutch chronicler Johannes a Leydis or Jan Gerbrandszoon van Leiden (d. 1504), reached three thousand; they were also banned from Ghent for fifty years 'to roam in the sunshine, unclothed'. The Dutch is ambiguous, suggesting they were 'without costumes' ('naer costuijme'), implying either mockery of their dress or that they were mandated to be naked (57). On Herental's account, see also Backman, *Religious Dances*, 192–194. On the relative normality of public nudity in the Middle Ages, see also Norbert Elias, *The Civilizing Process: Sociogenetic and Psychogenetic Investigations*, ed. E. Dunning, J. Goudsblom, and S. Mennell, trans. E. Jephcott (Oxford: Blackwell, 2000), 138–139.

73. Cited in Backman, *Religious Dances*, 212. Jean d'Outremeuse played, according to Stanislas Bormans, a somewhat legendary role in the history of Liège. His chronicle is double: on the one hand the *Myeur des histors* serves as a prose compilation of the history of the world; on the other hand *La Geste de Liege* is tens of thousands of verses (many lost) offering a poetic rendition of the history of the bishops of Tongres and Liège. Apocrypha regarding the author's birth render the mystique even greater. See Stanislas Bormans, 'Introduction et Table des Matières', in Jean des Preis (dit d'Outremeuse), *Ly Myeur des Histors, Chronique*, ed. Stanislas Bormans, 7 vols., vol. 7 (Brussels: F. Hayez, 1864–1887), i–ii, xxxiii–xxxv. On the St. John's Day dancers, see vol. 6 (1880), 697–698.

74. On dancers being banned from town, see also Frédéricq, 'De secten', 57.

75. Eugène Bacha, ed., *Chronique Liégeoise de 1402* (Brussels: Librairie Kiessling, 1900), 359. See also Alfred Cauchie and Alphonse van Hove, eds., *Documents sur la principauté de Liège (1230–1532)*, 2 vols., vol. 1 (Brussels: M. Weissenbruch, 1908). The leaping seems to have been quite ambivalent: according to Frédéricq's account, dancers alleged that Christ was watching over them from heaven, where there was a place reserved for them; that was why they jumped so high (possibly either to reach heaven, or more likely to prove their worth) ('De secten', 50).

76. Johannes de Beka, *Canonicus Ultrajectinus* (Utrecht, 1643); cited in Backman, *Religious Dances*, 198. See Johannes de Beka, *La Traduction Française de la Chronographia Johannis de Beka*, ed. Willem Noomen (The Hague: Uitgeverij Excelsior, 1954).

pestis' (demoniacal plague) of 'dansatores';[77] and yet another hypothesized that these eccentric terpsichoreans may have originally come all the way from India, suggesting some may have been Roma.[78] Others, as I have argued, may have been Jews, forced into exile from the pogroms still rampant at this time, although Jews and Roma were not the only social and religious outsiders cast out of towns and villages or subject to slander and slaughter. Lombardians, Cahorsins, and Moriscos in Spain (Muslims converted to Christianity) were among the many groups expelled or attacked for one reason or another by religious institutions increasingly attempting to account for local troubles by scapegoating.[79]

Exorcism was practiced to stun the dancers into submission. Radulphus de Rivo (d. 1403), a deacon in Tongeren in the Belgian province of Limburg, claimed in his history of the bishops of Liège that an anti-clerical dancing 'sect' (or society) had set out to murder canons, prelates, and vicars but had been stopped in its tracks when the dancers were brought before priests to be cured. He recounted a few episodes of curing by exorcism, including one at the Church of St. Mary in the convent of St. Lambert: after hearing the first words of the Gospel of St. John, the dancers were freed of the demons that tormented them and restored to a sane state of mind ('Dæmonum liberati sobriæ menti restituti fuerunt').[80]

The church was standing on shaky ground after the debacle of the Black Death, and expressions of marginal religiosity made chroniclers anxious: the dancing was dangerously close to the sort of libertinism that had reputedly spurred on the plague some decades before. And while much excitement in the wake of the Black Death had complicated the clergy's status in popular opinion—the clergy themselves were widely singled out for failing to save themselves or their constituencies from death and disaster in the plague years (thus discrediting their privileged status in the eyes of God), and many were thought to have caused the plague on account of their loose morals and 'whoring' ('Presbyteris concubinarijis'),[81] the choreomaniacs' status in popular opinion was no less ambivalent. In De Rivo's account, contemporaries attributed their wild dancing to crude ignorance of religion ('crassam ignorantiam'), countermanded, thankfully, he thought, by a new regime of divine grace that would quell the mayhem and allow the dancing chaos to be subdued.[82] Calling the choreomaniacs a 'devilish sect' ('sectæ Diabolicæ'), De Rivo suggested that many contemporaries attributed this strange dancing to the priests' immorality.[83] The priests themselves were scapegoated.

But while some priests were lax, the dancers at least were zealous. St. John the Baptist came widely to be referred to as their patron saint: dancers calling out to him were apparently relieved of their abdominal pains. It is not implausible that dancers, coming from further east into western Europe, practiced dancing associated with rituals mapped onto the figure of St. John. Saints in early Christianity served doubly to foster new and assimilate older practices; they performed focal points in the translation—what I call the 'translatio'—between pre-Christian calendrical festivities and the increasingly tentacular Christian regime.

---

77. Reference is made to a 'daemomiaca pestis' of 'dansatores' in July 1374, in Jo. Pistorii, 'De chorisantibus', *Rerum familiarumque Belgicarum Chronicon magnum* (1654); cited in Hecker, *Epidemics of the Middle Ages*, 144.

78. In de Lettenhove, *Istore et Croniques de Flandres*. See also Backman, *Religious Dances*, 212.

79. See Ram Ben-Shalom, 'Medieval Jewry in Christendom', in Martin Goodman, Jeremy Cohen, and David Sorkin, eds., *The Oxford Handbook of Jewish Studies* (Oxford: Oxford University Press, 2002), 153–192, 176. On fourteenth-century Jewish pogroms in Bohemia, including the pogrom of 1389, which might have propelled 'dancers' (in effect Jewish refugees) into flight towards Germany and the Low Countries, see esp. Miri Rubin, *Gentile Tales: The Narrative Assault on Late Medieval Jews* (New Haven: Yale University Press, 1999). On Jewish settlements prior to the mid-fourteenth-century pogroms, see also Dean Phillip Bell, *Jews in the Early Modern World* (Lanham, MD: Rowman and Littlefield, 2008). Cohn Jr. gives a detailed account of mass persecution of Jews during the 1348–1350 plague, following accusations of well poisoning, in 'The Black Death and the Burning of Jews'.

80. De Rivo's account appears in Radulphus (also Radulpho or Radulphi) de Rivo, *Decani Tongrensis, gesta pontificum Leodiensium ab anno tertio Engelberti a Marcka usque ad Joannem de Bavaria*, in Jean Chapeauville (Joannes Chapeavillus) (1551–1617), ed., *Qui gesta Pontificum Tungrensium, Traiectensium, et Leodiensium*, 3 vols., vol. 3 (Leodii: Typis C. Ouvverx iunioris, 1612–1616), 1–67, 19–23. De Rivo describes the dancers alternately throughout his account as devilish and admirable or noteworthy, first calling them an 'admirabilis hominum secta' (coterie of wondrous people) (19). See also Hecker, *Epidemics of the Middle Ages*, 91; Frédéricq, 'De secten', 51–55; Backman, *Religious Dances*, 194–196. For a brief biography of de Rivo, see Jean Chapeauville et al., *Contribution à l'historiographie liégeoise*, ed. René Hoven (Brussels: Classe des lettres, Académie royale de Belgique, 2004), 186–187.

81. De Rivo, *decani Tongrensis*, 23.

82. De Rivo, *decani Tongrensis*, 20.

83. De Rivo, *decani Tongrensis*, 20, 23.

So whereas many witnesses attributed the dancers' frenzy to demonism, suggesting these anti-clerical revellers were being punished with pain for their sins, the dancing 'sect', taking St. John at its helm, staged a choreozone in the crossfire between prior forms of religious worship and the Christian church. Dancing boisterously represented an eruption of ancient forms of ritual worship not yet fully harnessed to more modern structures of public display whereby bodies, as vessels of the soul, had to be ordered and subdued.

FESTIVAL ECONOMIES: THEATRICALITY AT THE OUTSKIRTS

Some bands of dancers, tired of being chased away from the villages they passed through, sought the privacy of peripheral sites, where they set up makeshift tents, building huts with leaves and branches from nearby forests. A grassroots market culture thrived as they were followed by crowds of enthusiasts, swelling their ranks into the thousands like a veritable pop festival. According to the *Cronica quorundam Romanorum regum ac imperatorum* [Chronicle of Early Roman Kings and Emperors], composed in the fourteenth century, a blossoming economy emerged to support the dancing 'company', gathered as if to fulfil a 'sacred vow'. As for the

Metz chronicler, this chronicler's terms were reproachful: he called the dancers' fate 'sad' and 'pestilential' ('pestilens et miseranda societas').[84] Before seeking refuge in campsites, the dancers had 'wandered about on saints' days and holy days', the chronicler notes, 'when there were large gatherings in public places, particularly in churches when Mass was being celebrated. They would be smitten by the Devil with an attack of frenzy, so that the very service was disordered'. The 'strange restlessness' that they had evinced had 'made an unseemly show for the people, for they left their homes and dwellings, their friends and parents and strolled about the streets and the markets, joining together in groups. They put wreaths and bands on their heads like crowns, and then held hands and danced mightily, like choreomaniacs, throwing their feet in the air. With arms outstretched they clapped their hands above and behind their heads'.[85] Another account suggests the dancers congregated on the steps in front of churches, at times troubling the church ceremonies, or dancing unbidden in church and town squares.[86]

As the *Cronica quorundam Romanorum regum ac imperatorum* suggests, 'when they had wearied themselves with leaping and dancing and such like exercises, they suddenly rushed wildly from place to place, screaming fearfully, raging like beasts over the land, and complaining of the most terrible internal pains'.[87] But in spite of these pains—provoked, plausibly, by famine

---

84. 'The pestilence had indeed spread far in this short time, and this sad company [societas] become numerous, for in one lonely spot in the diocese of Trier, far from the abodes of men, near the ruins of a deserted old chapel, there gathered several thousand members of this company as if to fulfil a sacred vow [vota sua]. They and others who followed to see the show amounted to some five thousand persons. There they stayed, preparing for themselves a kind of rich encampment [statio]: they built huts with leaves and branches from the nearby forest, and food was brought from towns and villages as to a market'. *Cronica quorundam Romanorum regum ac imperatorum* ('A Chronicle of Early Roman Kings and Emperors'), cited in Backman, *Religious Dances*, 207. Backman, who slightly misrenders the title as *Chronica quorundam regum et imperatorum Romanorum*, is working with a fifteenth-century copy of the manuscript held at the library of Hamburg (Hist. 31b, Pap. Fol.), remarkable, he notes, for the length and wealth of detail provided, as well as its apparent contemporaneity with the events. This is in effect the second part of two manuscripts (the first is known as *Chronica aliquorum summorum pontificum*), read together since an authoritative fifteenth-century German edition as *Die Kölner Weltchronik*, now available in reprint in *Monumenta Germaniae historica, scriptores rerum Germanicarum*, new ser., vol. 15, *Die Kölner Weltchronik 1273/88–1376*, ed. Rolf Sprandel (Munich: Monumenta Germaniae Historica, 1991). The passage on the choreomaniacs appears 116–118. The phrase 'pestilens et miseranda societas' appears 118.

85. In Backman, *Religious Dances*, 206; Frédéricq, 'De secten', 49. See Sprandel, *Die Kölner Weltchronik*, 116–117. Although Backman writes 'like choreomaniacs', the Latin is 'ad instar chorsancium', an odd construction which appears to be either a manuscript corruption of *choreancium*—from the Latin *choreare* or *chorizare*, meaning to dance or to dance a round, deriving from the Greek root 'chor-', also meaning chorus or dance; or, more plausibly, a neologism on the chronicler's part (not unusual at the time) or the chronicler's record of jargon circulating in the day. If the latter, this suggests that the dancers were novel enough to warrant their own vocabulary; more interestingly, this vocabulary did not persist in the literature of the period, also suggesting the events were seen as quite extraordinary, something nearly all chroniclers noted. I am grateful to Daniel Hadas for clarification with regard to the Latin anomaly. For more on the hazy etymological roots of 'choreomania', see also Kélina Gotman, 'Chorea Minor, Chorea Major, Choreomania: Entangled Medical and Colonial Histories', in Johannes Birringer and Josephine Fenger, eds., *Tanz und WahnSinn/Dance and ChoreoMania* (Leipzig: Henschel Verlag, 2011), 83–97.

86. Langlois, 'Lettre de M. C. Leber à M. E.-H. Langlois', 15n1.

87. Backman, *Religious Dances*, 206–207. See Sprandel, *Die Kölner Weltchronik*, 117.

and malnutrition—the dancers were engaging in what appears to have been regular folk practice. According to the *Limburg Chronicle*, 'people began to dance and rage, and they stood two against one, and they danced in one place half a day, and during the dance they fell down on the ground, and let their bellies be stamped on. They believed that thereby they would be cured [of their pains]'.[88] Dancing two against one (or, in alternate descriptions, two by two) was a common folk dance formation, suggesting the dancers were engaged in a boisterous fête, intensified to provoke its own spectacle of contest and crisis.

Theatricality played no small part in the events. As some chroniclers suggested (and as later medical historians would increasingly insist), some participants may have feigned illness in order to be granted the sort of charity normally afforded beggars and other mendicants. As outcasts, the dancers were folded into the structures of charitable tolerance that characterized late medieval Christianity, according to whose logic beggars deserved shelter and aid—though as Foucault has shown, long-standing slippages from beggar to pariah also put such characters into a social fringe, marginalized just as they were endured at arm's length.[89] The *Cronica quorundam Romanorum regum ac imperatorum* suggests some revellers displayed unusual acting talents or outright imposture: 'as among men the false is often found side by side with the true', so, too, the chronicler suggests, 'it happened that even in these terrible times many pretended to be suffering from the sickness, some to obtain the alms which Christians bestowed on the sick, and some from mere folly' ('durante commocione plurimi dictam passionem simulantes').[90] The

dancing was in this chronicler's terms an occasion for simulating other dancers' *passio*, a term denoting passion, affect, and event; it was also, when simulated, benign madness and, significantly, theatre.

Dancers did not only purportedly feign dramatic contortions for monetary gain; they also seemed, in the eyes of some, to be spreading a dissolute and parasitical lifestyle. Besides showing histrionic displays of uncertain sincerity, they reputedly engaged in rampant sexuality. The *Cronica* commentator adds that some 'joined . . . [the dancers'] company for the sake of loose living with the women and young girls who shamelessly wandered about in remote places under the cover of night'.[91] One hundred unmarried women, in one account, became pregnant as a result of these events.[92] One may wonder whether they did so wilfully—or whether 'behind the scenes' of this dancing history lies, as Jody Enders suggests of medieval theatre in this period, an unwritten history of rape.[93] The archives reveal glimpses of revelry, cast through the eyes of literate chroniclers who likely, we may presume, aligned themselves with the institutions of the Christian church. Reading against the grain of their narratives, we can only imagine scenes of mayhem noteworthy enough to have made it into the year's account. 'Normal' in this respect, the festivities were also viewed with a chastising glance from scribes sitting, sometimes bitterly, in the sidelines, irked at the image of libertinism the dances—and general climate of upheaval—appeared to represent. Magnified through the lens of nineteenth-century historiographers reading these chroniclers' lines retrospectively, the dancers come to represent the

88. Backman, *Religious Dances*, 205. Backman notes the date 1347 but is clearly referring to 1374, as confirmed in von Wolfhagen, *Die Limburger Chronik*, 47. For the full description of the midsummer 'dancing and raving', see 47–48.

89. Foucault, *Histoire de la folie*, 15–65.

90. In Backman, *Religious Dances*, 207; Latin from Sprandel, *Die Kölner Weltchronik*, 117. Interestingly, Backman renders *passio, passionati*, etc. as 'sickness', but the term *passio* denotes disease as well as strong emotion, suffering (as in Christ's suffering), and any noteworthy event, occurrence, or phenomenon, usually experienced (or submitted to) passively by the sufferer. The Latin chronicle significantly does not use the terms *morbus* or *aegritudo*, which would denote illness or sickness only, without the broader connotation of an affliction received by the person as if from an outside force. I am grateful to Daniel Hadas for this insight.

91. In Backman, *Religious Dances*, 207. See Sprandel, *Die Kölner Weltchronik*, 117. Von Wolfhagen's *Die Limburger Chronik* also notes imposture and fraud, suggesting an increasing number of (unspecified) things were done for money. See Von Wolfhagen, *Die Limburger Chronik* 47; Backman, *Religious Dances*, 205.

92. Kastner, among others, notes that one hundred unmarried women reportedly became pregnant as a result of taking part in the dancing, suggesting that open sexuality was rampant or widely imagined to have been so (*La Danse des mort*, 62). The *Limburg Chronicle* interestingly notes that women and servant girls who became pregnant by keeping shady company bound their bodies tightly so that they might appear thinner, suggesting another reading of the cloth bindings ('Und wann daβ sie tanzeten, so banden und knebelten sie sich um den Leib hart zu, daβ sie desto geringer wären'). Von Wolfhagen, *Die Limburger Chronik*, 47.

93. On the spectrality of rape in medieval chronicles and annals, see Jody Enders, 'The Spectacle of the Scaffolding: Rape and the Violent Foundations of Medieval Theatre Studies', *Theatre Journal* 56.2 (2004): 163–181.

public appearance of an orgiastic antiquity on the scene of late medieval 'modernity', as medieval writers attempt to write themselves away from the archaic excesses of their own age. The dancers are thus doubly contrapuntal: in their time, they appear foreign and inexplicable; but in the nineteenth century, they contain the strangeness of another era amplified by the orgiastic archaicity the Middle Ages had come implicitly to represent.

It is not implausible some dancers may have simulated pains in order to be granted the charity normally afforded beggars and other mendicants, employing the excuse of the feast day and charitable structures of social and religious tolerance to rush around in a state of celebratory exultation. After a day's dancing and cavorting, they may have shown admittedly strange and comical contortions to justify the public exercise. Some may also have genuinely experienced painful abdominal distension from the mixture of feasting and fasting, and heightened rapid breathing, we may surmise were involved. So while medieval physicians attributed the dances to passionate temperaments, and priests attempted to exorcise participants of their demons, to nineteenth-century observers, the *appearance* of possession made the dancers suspect as 'mad' people spreading not just the reality but also the pretence—the theatre—of this dancing madness epidemically.[94] To these later readers, the dancers swept others up into their heathen rites, stalling history's progress with

their disorderly scenes. Choreomaniacs represented the fantasy of an eruption of ancient life onto the scene of modernity to jolt and to thwart it. This fantasy, indebted to antiquarian research but also to the nineteenth-century imagination of a bacchanalian Middle Ages, posited choreomaniacs as 'mad' inasmuch as they represented the amplifications, the distortions—and in this regard, as I argue further in chapter 4—the gestural exaggerations of an earlier time.[95]

POPULAR DANCING VERSUS THE CHURCH: CONTESTED GROUNDS

Religion played no small part. Dance maniacs signalled at once the antiquity of pre-Christian practices and their (heretical) exaggeration. Yet in this regard, choreomaniacs only amplified the religious movements—and movement—of their age. The tradition of dancing boisterously on feast days, for charity or a sacred cure, was old, providing a regular occasion for entertainment. Yet the part dance played in church worship was declining in the centuries preceding the late fourteenth-century dance outburst noted by chroniclers across Europe. Dancing in churches, long a standard practice in early medieval Christianity, as well as in early Jewish and Roman traditions, had been formally outlawed at the Council of Würzburg in 1298.[96] A string of anti-dance laws dotted this period, prompting

---

94. French historian Jean-Michel-Constant Leber (1780–1859) highlights the dancers' appearance of madness ('comme s'ils eussent été fous'), and the priests' exorcism 'as if they [the dancers] had been possessed by demons', though Leber also notes contemporary physicians attributed the dances to a 'passionate' temperament, resulting in various abuses and indecencies. 'Les danseurs de Saint-Weit datent de l'année 1374. On vit avec étonnement, dans plusieurs pays allemands, sur les bords du Rhin et de la Moselle, des gens qui dansaient comme s'ils eussent été fous, pendant la moitié du jour, et deux à deux. Ils tombaient ensuite par terre; on leur marchait sur le corps, et on les regardait alors comme guéris. Ils couraient d'une ville à l'autre et s'asseyaient devant les églises. Le nombre de ces danseurs s'accrut tellement, qu'on en a vu à Cologne jusqu'à cinq cents. Les médecins attribuaient ces danses à un tempérament fougueux, d'où résultait des indécences et des abus réels; mais les prêtres les exorcisaient comme s'ils eussent été possédés du diable'. Langlois, 'Lettre de M. C. Leber à M. E.-H. Langlois', 15n1.

95. Böhme is also indicative in this regard. Calling the medieval 'dance mania' ('Tanzwut') a mass commotion, he described men and women 'appearing in bacchantic exuberance' ('bacchantischer Ausgelassenheit'), twirling and jumping wildly, and contorting their bodies shamelessly in front of their spectators; this was an outbreak of 'demonic movement' ('Ausbruch der dämonischen Bewegung') which trumped both medical and priestly attempts at intervention ('Tanzwut im Mittelalter', 40). Böhme also interestingly calls the whole string of dances running through the late fourteenth to early fifteenth centuries a 'Spuk', a nearly untranslatable term approximately rendered 'spook' or 'haunting' (or more generally a horrible episode), further suggesting the dancers were possessed, disturbingly, by a spirit from the past or otherworld ('Tanzwut im Mittelalter', 41).

96. Backman provides an exhaustive account of religious dances in the early Christian church, although as noted previously he claims rather outlandishly that these dances were all attributable to ergotism. On the Council of Würzburg, see Backman, *Religious Dances*, 9. Stevens notes church denunciations against dance and song occurred frequently between 589 (when the first Council denouncements were noted) and the seventeenth century; as Sahlin points out, the apocryphal *Acts of St John*, which antedates the year 150 CE, includes mention of a ring dance performed by Christ's disciples around him, as instructed by him (Sahlin, *Étude sur la carole mediévale*, 137–139; Stevens, *Words and Music in the Middle Ages*, 179). See also L. Gougaud, 'La danse dans les églises', *Revue d'Histoire Ecclésiastique* 15 (1914): 5–22, 229–245, who suggests that some dancers (notably in Echternach, a case I discuss in chapter 6) must have been so possessed by piety that their extravagant gestures should be understood as genuine expressions of

dance enthusiasts increasingly to resort to dancing in private or to relegate dancing to popular fêtes ever further removed from the regular exercise of religious worship. So while early medieval chronicles were littered with episodes of church dancing, suggesting that terpsichorean outbursts had long formed a central part of everyday life, by the fourteenth century, dancing had increasingly come to be associated with bawdy, insalubrious activities steeped in sexual mischief. Choreomaniacs in particular seemed to participate equally in regimes of religion and pleasure, misdemeanour and the everyday: they claimed allegiance to a saint (St. John), underscoring their religious affiliation, but danced in excess, boisterously. As such, their expression of religious enthusiasm seemed suspect to observers, and their spectacular public presence was as titillating as it was inopportune.

Choreomaniacs constituted an archaic holdover, a public eruption and interruption, and a sign of resistance to change. The midsummer St. John's Day fires had long served as an occasion for play: this was a time to engage in the Nodfyr, a pre-Christian practice of leaping through or over smoke or fire to be protected from ill health for the following year, one the church had tried anxiously to stamp out or at best to recuperate into the Christian fold.[97] The earliest 'choreomanias' suggested a battle of wills between recalcitrant celebrants and the doyens of the church. An 'oft-repeated tradition'[98] from the eleventh century suggests dancing was at the heart of battles for power. Eighteen men and women reputedly disrupted a Christmas service taking place in a church in Kolbig (or Kölbigk) near Bernburg by 'dancing and brawling in the churchyard'. The priest, Ruprecht, inflicted a curse on them in retaliation, according to which they would have to continue dancing without respite for a year. When the curse was lifted at the intercession of a couple of well-disposed bishops, the dancers, now knee-deep in the earth and nearly starved to death, reputedly fell into a deep sleep for three days. Four died, and the rest complained of tremors in the limbs for the rest of their lives. Alternative accounts suggest they wandered through the countryside and were subjected to continuing tremors.[99] This story, Hecker noted, was 'related with astonishment and horror

---

such (245); Sahlin, in *Étude sur la carole mediévale*, 137–142, further argues that the church, wary of rivals, doubly combatted and sought to assimilate dance practices and rites associated with pre-Christian worship (139, 143–186).

97. See Pierre Riché, 'Danses profanes et religieuses dans le haut Moyen Age', in Robert Mandrou, ed., *Histoire sociale, sensibilités collectives et mentalités: Mélanges Robert Mandrou* (Paris: Presses Universitaires de France, 1985), 159–167, 160; Ruth Harris, *Lourdes: Body and Spirit in the Secular Age* (New York: Viking, 1999), 102–103; Sahlin, *Étude sur la carole médiévale*, 164. Sahlin, after Böhme, further suggests that dances invoking St. Vitus derived from those performed in honour of the Slavic sun god, Swantewit (*Étude sur la carole médiévale*, 164n2), though Böhme is at pains to point out that the Slavic name Swante-wit (designating the sun god) has nothing to do with St. Vitus's dances. See Böhme, *Geschichte des Tanzes in Deutschland*, 162. Maurice Vloberg, in *Les fêtes de France: Coutumes religieuses et populaires* (Grenoble: B. Arthaud, 1936), 149–164, notes that epileptics so often called to St. John the Baptist for help that their disease came to be known as the *mal de Saint-Jean* (160). On the pre-Christian elements of increasingly Christianized village fêtes and the ambivalent role dance in particular played in these, see also Eugène Cortet, *Essai sur les fêtes religieuses et les traditions populaires qui s'y rattachent* (Paris: Ernest Thorin, 1867), 211–231; and A. Fournier, 'Vieilles coutumes, usages et traditions populaires des Vosges provenant des cultes antiques et particulièrement de celui du soleil', *Bulletin de la Société philomatique vosgienne* 16 (1890–1891): 137–205, 148–153.

98. Hecker, *Epidemics of the Middle Ages*, 90.

99. Hecker, *Epidemics of the Middle Ages*, 90–91. See also Joseph Harris, 'The Early History of European Ballads—The Legend of the Kolbigk Dance or Chorea-Famosa, Its Social Origins, Oral Tradition, and Historical Credibility. German by E. E. Metzner, 1972', *Speculum: A Journal of Medieval Studies* 50.3 (1975): 522–525. Gregor Rohmann, 'The Invention of the Dancing Mania: Frankish Christianity, Platonic Cosmology and Bodily Expressions in Sacred Space', *Medieval History Journal* 12 (2009): 13–45, argues that the dancing in the Kolbik (or Kölbigk) legend can be traced to early medieval Platonic cosmology, which proscribed dancing in sacred spaces. See also Riché, 'Danses profanes et religieuses dans le haut Moyen Age', 162–163. Stevens, in *Words and Music in the Middle Ages*, suggests the Kölbigk dancers were engaged in a round dance, specifically a *carole* (which Stevens describes as a courtly and a popular dance-song, which may or may not always have been danced in the round) (161, 164–166); see also Gougaud, 'La danse dans les églises', 229–230. Eustace and King note that the story re-emerges as a Middle English exemplum describing the 'hoppyng' dancers of 'Colbek' in Robert Mannyng's *Handlyng of Sinne* ('Dances of the Living and the Dead', 52–53). Langlois describes the same story, noting it took place outside the church of Saint-Magnus, in Saxony (also the location of Kölbigk), further suggesting this may have served as a model for later danses macabres (*Essai historique, philosophique et pittoresque*, vol. 1, 181, 183). Kastner dates this event around 1025, in Magdeburg, describing the eighteen men and fifteen women as 'larvae or ghosts insensitive to the needs of man' ('comme des larves ou des fantômes insensibles aux besoins matériels de l'homme'); they wore out neither their shoes nor their clothes, nor did they suffer from hunger or from the elements (*La Danse des morts*, 64, 64–65n5). The seventeenth-century historian Johann Christoff Beckmann (1641–1717) called this episode somewhat unusually a 'melancholischer Zufall' (melancholic occurrence or accident) and 'so zu nennende Tanz-Tollheit' (so-called dance madness), somewhat softening the language of rage and fury suggested by the slightly more truculent 'Tanzwut'. Johann Christoff Beckmann, *Gründliche Fürstellung etlicher in Hn. D.*

throughout the middle ages' so that when any 'exciting cause' for a similar type of 'delirious raving' and 'wild rage for dancing' occurred, the legend was harkened back to as precedent and warning.[100] According to musicologist John Stevens (1921–2002), these rebellious dancers may, however, simply have been engaged in a *carole*, a typically festive round dance; depictions, including the seventeenth-century woodcut by Johann Ludwig Gottfried (1584–1633), suggest moral reprobation but nothing like the frenzy Hecker suggests (fig. 2.1). Still, the legend—with its didactic message—implied that the dancers were insubordinate; they danced outside the church, not yet surrendering to the routines of a relatively more placid church service. The story intimated not only popular conflict regarding the right mode of worship but a lesson about sites and types of choreographies that should be engaged in. Choreographies across scenes of so-called choreomania varied, as did their interpretations; while leaping was a sign of indecorousness, round dances such as this one held an equally ambivalent place in the annals of the dancing disease. So, too, pilgrimages represented an occasion for rowdy display.

So just as Hecker noted the coincidence of some choreomanias with the height of midsummer, particularly St. John's Day (24 June), and some accounts suggest dancers appeared in the late summer and early autumn, or in May and June, the dancing seems by and large to have been associated with the long-entrenched midsummer festivities. Pilgrimages in particular constituted a contested ground. For Hecker, one of the earliest dance 'manias', after Kölbigk, took

place in 1237 in Erfurt, when over one hundred children reportedly danced and leaped all the way to Arnstadt, then fell to the ground, giddy with exhaustion.[101] Child pilgrimages such as this one provoked a fantasy in their own right, immortalized in the story of the Pied Piper, reprised in nineteenth-century literature by Johann Wolfgang von Goethe (1749–1832) and the Brothers Grimm (Jacob Grimm, 1785–1863, and Wilhelm Grimm, 1786–1859), among others.[102] Pilgrimages, normally associated with orderly procession, became fantasized as sites of uncontrol; movement, travel and displacement, including migration; and obsessiveness bordering on collective 'mania'.

A further so-called dancing mania took place on 17 June 1278 on the Mosel Bridge in Utrecht, involving two hundred participants ('homines chorizantes') who reputedly danced so hard the bridge fell, causing many to meet their watery deaths (fig. 2.2).[103] Hecker attributed this to 'fanaticism', pointing out that according to legend, the dancers were punished for their cavorting when a priest passed by carrying a host. But the episode occurred, significantly, on 17 June, in the lead-up to St. John's Day, when men and women would have been engaged in *tripudiae*, a well-established religious practice historian Pierre Riché suggests involved dancing while carrying relics en route to a sacred site to fête the saint and, surreptitiously, out of habit, the summer solstice.[104] Stevens further suggests *tripudiae* often involved some license, including, according to a report from a nunnery near Rouen in 1261, 'immoderate foolery and scurrilous songs'.[105] Further reports suggest the clergy

Joh. Christ. Beckmanns . . . neu ausgegangener Historia des Fürstenthums Anhalt befindlicher fürnemlich wieder das Hochfürstl, ed. Christian Knaut, pt. 3, bk. 4, chap. 4, para. 3 (Halle Im Magdeburg: zufinden in Rengerischer Bucchandlung, 1710), 467–468, 468. Beckmann describes the whole complex as indicative of an 'ungebührenen Zeit der Uppigkeit' or unseemly and impertinent time of voluptuous extravagance, suggestive of a 'malady' ('übel'), a term itself suggesting illness but also sin (468).

100. Hecker, *Epidemics of the Middle Ages*, 91.

101. On Erfurt, see Beckmann, *Gründliche Fürstellung*, 467–468; Hecker, *Epidemics of the Middle Ages*, 90; Böhme, 'Tanzwut im Mittelalter', 43.

102. Goethe's poem dates from 1803; the Brothers Grimm version from 1816. A comparative study of medieval fairy tales mapped onto the historiography of 'dance manias' presented in this book would no doubt shed much further light on the modern imagination of medieval madness and dance.

103. Martinus Minorita (Martini Minoritae), 'Flores temporum, ab hermanno janvensi continuati usque ad Carolum IV. Imp.', in Jo. Georgio Eccardo (Johann George von Eckhart), *Corpus historicum medii aevi, sive Scriptores res in orbe universo, præcipue in Germania, a temporibus maxime Caroli M. Imperatoris usque ad finem seculi post C. N. XV. gestas enarrantes aut illustrantes e variis codicibus manuscriptis* (Lipsiæ: Apud Jo. Frid. Gleditscchii, B. Fil., 1723), 1551–1640, 1632. See also Hecker, *Epidemics of the Middle Ages*, 90.

104. On the practice of dancing while carrying relics, or *tripodium*—also described as the 'translation' of relics—see Riché, 'Danses profanes et religieuses dans le haut Moyen Age', 164–167. On medieval processions more generally, see esp. Ashley and Hüsken, eds., *Moving Subjects*.

105. These took place on the occasion of the feasts of St. John, of St. Stephen, and of the Innocents. Stevens, *Words and Music in the Middle Ages*, 180. See also Sahlin, *Étude sur la carole médiévale*, 152–153.

FIGURE 2.1   Dancers of Kölbigk, in a seventeenth-century woodcut by Johann Ludwig Gottfried, from *Historische Chronica, oder Beschreibung der fürnemsten Geschichten, so sich von Anfang der Welt biß auff das Jahr Christi 1619* (also known as Gottfried's History of the World) (Frankfurt am Main: Merian, 1674), S. 505.

themselves were known to dance boisterously at times: an edict from the cathedral at Sens suggests clergy were permitted to dance at important festivals, 'provided they do not leap off the ground'.[106]

PILGRIMS AND PASSAGES

A further word remains to be said about the choreomaniacs as migrants. As choreomania was performed *in passing*, it constituted a disorder of migration. Choreomaniacs disrupted the course of everyday life, lurching through public space with leaps and songs. They were 'disorderly' inasmuch as they reconfigured the choreopolitics of public space; unlike the 'mad', who individually believed unreasonable things, sliding alongside society in its margins, choreomaniacs appeared collectively strange; they were noteworthy inasmuch as they acted disruptively in concert and

this disruption could spread. Their disorder resided in its potentially infinite intensification. Yet even in their whirling and tumbling through public space, choreomaniacs seem by and large to have constituted relatively marginal enthusiasts keeping up with ancient practices contentious in post-plague years. Circulating between western and central Europe, the dancers enacted what Clifford has called a travelling culture,[107] at once contingent on its surroundings and translational. For Clifford, pilgrimages typically perform a movement between travel (which is punctual) and nomadism (which constitutes an ongoing state), eccentrically reconstituting dwellings and encounters.[108] Pilgrims move in the margins and peripheries of sites describing zones of political inheritance or settlement. As such, pilgrims transport and translate experiences from one site to another, provoking new zones of intensity—travelling ones—along the way.

---

106. Stevens, *Words and Music in the Middle Ages*, 180. By at least the fifteenth century, leaping would become formalized as a sign of undignified dancing, contrary to the increasingly refined and courtly *basse-danse*, in which steps are executed so close to the ground as to give the dancer the appearance of gliding. Eustace with King, 'Dances of the Living and the Dead', 56.

107. Clifford, *Routes*, 39.

108. Clifford, *Routes*, 25.

FIGURE 2.2   Dancing couples, accompanied by a musician, fail to kneel before the Sacrament as it is being carried by, upon which some two hundred people fall into the river and drown. Woodcut now attributed to Albrecht Dürer. From Hartmann Schedel's *Buch der Chroniken* [*The Book of Chronicles,* or *The Nuremberg Chronicle*], printed by Anton Koberger (1493), folio CCXVII *recto.*

Choreomaniacs were disjoiners, separating themselves out from the villages through which they passed yet provoking audience participation, dividing viewers and scribes between those who greeted and those who pitied their fates. In doing so, they carved out an arena for themselves just past the edge of town in a temporarily constituted, shared social space that was parasitic yet sovereign. As visitors, passers-through, forces of 'passage' (or *kinesis*) they drew bemused audiences in and left new audiences and narratives behind, marking the rural and urban spaces that they inhabited before going off to the next dancing site. These were religious eccentrics hanging onto an outmoded and increasingly outlawed way of celebrating life and staving off ill health: gathering and dancing.

Choreomaniacs were in this sense quintessentially 'abnormal', in Foucault's sense: marginal, subject to scientific scrutiny. Like the medieval mad Foucault describes, they were in their own time by and large tolerated, albeit with some reluctance. But somewhat unlike the cases of madness Foucault describes from the annals of eighteenth- and nineteenth-century medicine, choreomania was never directly diagnosed; there were no 'choreomaniacs' actively sequestered (though some dancers in the sixteenth century were subjected to panels of medical experts and temporarily removed for relatively benign dancing cures [chapter 3]). Retrospective diagnosis performed by medical historians instead saw dance maniacs primarily as curiosities to collect and compare, relatively far removed from the castigating force of medico-penal law.[109] Individually, choreomaniacs not engaged in dancing bled into everyday life. However, individuals performing tremors and tics likened to the jagged spirit of uncontrol attributed to medieval dance manias were subject to scientific scrutiny, just as crowd movements and rowdy public behaviour were increasingly subject to municipal control. Taken from this perspective, 'choreomania' signals a zone of intensity in the modern imagination of the Middle Ages, whereby disorderly motions come to be collated and combined, suggesting a troublesome other surging

109. See esp. Foucault, *Anormaux*, 29–50.

up from uncertain places, moving—loitering, grimacing—to no particular end.

MADNESS AND REASON IN A DARK AGE

Foucault's most substantial contribution to the history of ideas (and bodies) is arguably his implicit but overarching observation that 'madness' becomes the dark hole out of which articulation occurs. From his commentary on the medieval and early modern substitution of death for madness as a prime object of anxiety to his observation that the link between madness and nothingness ('néant') would continue to be so profound as fundamentally to define experiences of madness in the 'classical' age,[110] and his reading of Victorian sexuality as that which comes to be spoken about and, as such, fashioned, Foucault speaks about that which is spoken—significantly, that which is spoken as if on top of a great void. In the initial preface to *History of Madness*, Foucault wrote that within madness lies an *'inaccessible primitive purity'* (*'inaccessible pureté primitive'*).[111] Although Hacking argues that Foucault's later revisions attempted to disentangle his work from this rather vague and obscure phrase, the notion of madness as an indefinable idea underlying contemporary biopolitics continued to inform Foucault's work. Madness, like sexuality, is one of the intellectual forms—what I am calling a discursive node or zone of intensity—that in being spoken about reveals whole provinces of silence. As Foucault argued, 'I have not tried to write the history of [psychiatric] language, but rather the archaeology of that silence'.[112] Madness emerges in Foucault's writing as a zone of intensity through which 'enlightened' modernity would construe its inarticulate self and, by extension, a cast of inarticulate others. But as Hacking points out, Foucault's aim in uncovering this silence—a

complex of experiences Foucault elsewhere refers to with a mixture of terms implicating night, darkness, and obscurity, but also dazzlement and light—suggests 'how a certain *absence* of discourse became possible'.[113] This 'absence' is the ineffable other subtending the deployment of scientific and social scientific discourse by which something opposite to 'reason' can be imagined—what I am further describing as *gesturally abstracted*. Madness, then, is paradoxically both the fiction and the truth about which things are said: it signals at once a *real* reality (an alternative way of being not aligned to 'reason') and a fabrication, a set of discourses shaping how this reality comes to be played out.

Choreomania instantiates this coming-to-be of modern thought, still in the nineteenth century entangled in the question of silence, cast as gesticulating unintelligibility. Beyond eighteenth-century reason—the era that boasted 'light' ('le siècle des lumières', denoting understanding)—nineteenth-century antiquarian epidemiology suggested a regime in which madness and reason coexisted, Bacchic echoes reverberating in the present day, liable to contagion anyone. 'Choreomania' thus represents the relatively unsystematic articulation of an imagined aggregated inarticulacy: the chaos of flailing limbs away from unreason and torque. Through readings and misreadings of ancient sources—producing whole series of persuasive fictions—choreomania became an abstraction, written in scenes of pullulating bodies out of joint with, and uncannily attuned to, their times—and purportedly also reflecting aspects of their readers' own. If, as Kate Elswit points out, reprising Franko, the task of 'reading' historical sources is also to trace contemporary resonances with them, prior sources reading sources prior to themselves similarly extract their own regimes of signification, which we can, today, attempt to trace.[114] This does not merely mean that we are only ever writing a history of the present;

---

110. Foucault, *Histoire de la folie*, 32.

111. See Hacking, 'Déraison', 16. The italics are Hacking's own. Foucault's original preface is reproduced in Michel Foucault, *Dits et écrits 1954–1988*, ed. Daniel Defert and François Ewald with Jacques Lagrange, 2 vols., vol. 1 (Paris: Gallimard, 2001), 187–195. Foucault in fact writes: 'à défaut de cette inaccessible pureté primitive', meaning given that this primitive purity is of course inaccessible, the history of madness that can be written is that of a perpetual set of decisions and exchanges separating reason from unreason, pointing towards an 'obscure common root' ('obscure commune racine') before the historical moment—the series of movements—by which the language of reason came to be separated out from the murmur of shadowy insects ('murmure d'insectes sombres') (192).

112. Michel Foucault, *Madness and Civilization: A History of Insanity in the Age of Reason*, trans. Richard Howard (London: Tavistock, 1967), 111–112; cited in Hacking, 'Déraison', 20.

113. See Hacking, 'Déraison', 17–20.

114. Franko writes that historiographical analysis seeks 'also to develop [models of the historical period under scrutiny] in the direction of relevant terms for contemporary analysis'. Mark Franko, 'Dance and the Political: States of Exception', in

but that this presentness is also constituted of fantasies about the past which were themselves—with slight variations—previously held. In tracing the relationship between past forms of historicity—past historical imaginings—we can attempt to draw out a contrapuntal, choreographic 'choreohistory'.

In the final section of this chapter, I turn to Nietzsche's concept of the bacchanalian Middle Ages as constituting alternately a sane and sick form of premodernity. Profoundly informing Foucault's work on madness and genealogy, particularly the complicated and often ironic notion of *Ursprung* ('origin') Nietzsche employs to describe the ungraspable source of Christian morality on an ever-disappearing horizon of antiquity, Nietzsche's work articulates a perpetual passage between present and past. As a genealogist, Nietzsche discovers that there is no essential thing underlying present realities but an imbricated set of prior movements, constituting a contradictory and irremediably disparate whole. There is not even a whole, but what Foucault, reading Nietzsche, calls a 'theater of procedures', in which events come to appear.[115] Significantly, Foucault remarks, these events are always and inevitably bodied; for Nietzsche, the past may be considered 'historically and physiologically'.[116] More significantly, Nietzsche foregrounds the task of genealogy as to be faithful to the movement of life rather than to a detached, critical search for fixed truths.[117] In this way, the genealogist may survey Europe's decadence once again in theatrical terms, what Foucault describes as an 'immense spectacle'; but contemporary history is not just theatrical, full of painted scenes and scenery.[118] The nineteenth century emerges with Nietzsche as an era boasting what Foucault calls a 'spontaneous historical bent',[119] a predilection for the eruptions and inconsistencies, the surprises and irregularities, of reasonably 'unreasonable' times past, which it imagines itself at its best to echo. In particular, as Dominick LaCapra is at pains to note, Foucault, borrowing implicitly from Nietzsche,

located the prehistory of the prolonged discursive rupture between 'reason' and 'unreason' not only somewhere in the Middle Ages, but more profoundly in pre-Socratic Greece. LaCapra suggests Foucault in fact rewrote Nietzsche's *The Birth of Tragedy from the Spirit of Music* (1872) in his *History of Madness*. Like Nietzsche, Foucault rearticulated the Dionysian spirit—more specifically what Nietzsche posited as an Apollonian (rational, contained) and Dionysian (ecstatic, disinhibited) duality—as a mad spirit previously enjoying an intimate and relatively uncomplicated relationship with so-called rational forms of life. But as LaCapra further notes, the on-one-level facile linear history this story seems to trace, according to which the past was freer and more accepting, belies a far greater complexity both Nietzsche and Foucault actually underscored: one in which regimes of reason and unreason have coexisted, according to varying power relations.[120] The murky space of negotiation by which one becomes written in the other was what Foucault set out to highlight. In this regard redoing Nietzsche's exuberant philological excavation of a broadly Dionysian life, Foucault sets a series of contradictory and convoluted twists and turns in so-called history's side describing the 'fits and starts', the 'fainting spells', that a complex world of madnesses represents. The contradictions in Foucault's work, like those in Nietzsche's, only highlight the always moving, 'event'-like quality of genealogical research, the writing that seeks also to be vital and, in this sense, choreographic.

NIETZSCHE'S AMBIVALENCE: A NEW HISTORY OF ENTHUSIASM

Nietzsche's depiction of the St. John's and St. Vitus's dances, indebted I surmise to Hecker, suggests modernity caught in its own complicated relation to an orgiastic past. In *The Birth of Tragedy*, as in his earlier, posthumously

Susanne Franco and Marina Nordera, eds., *Dance Discourses: Keywords in Dance Research* (London: Routledge, 2007), 11–28, 15; cited in Kate Elswit, *Watching Weimar Dance* (Oxford: Oxford University Press, 2014), xx.

115. Foucault, 'Nietzsche, Genealogy, History', 379.

116. Friedrich Nietzsche, 'Twilight of the Idols; or How to Philosophize with a Hammer', in *Twilight of the Idols and The Antichrist*, trans. R. J. Hollingdale (London: Penguin, 1999), 29–122, 108; cited in Foucault, 'Nietzsche, Genealogy, History', 382.

117. In Foucault, 'Nietzsche, Genealogy, History', 388.

118. Foucault, 'Nietzsche, Genealogy, History', 384.

119. Foucault, 'Nietzsche, Genealogy, History', 384.

120. LaCapra, 'Foucault, History and Madness', 81–82.

published 'The Dionysiac World View' (1870), Nietzsche depicted dancing hordes epitomizing a 'blissful ecstasy which arises from the innermost ground of man, indeed of nature itself'. Nietzsche saw in these hordes an ecstatic dissolution of the self that accompanied the 'breakdown of the *principium individuationis* [principle of individuation]', offering 'a glimpse of the essence of the *Dionysiac*'. Comparable to a state of 'intoxication', these forces—arising 'among all human beings and peoples who are close to the origin of things' (he writes literally 'von dem alle ursprünglichen Menschen und Völker')—erupted like 'the approach of spring when the whole of nature is pervaded by lust for life' and 'awakens' a 'Dionysiac power'. These deep-seated 'stirrings', 'as they grow in intensity, cause subjectivity to vanish to the point of complete self-forgetting'.[121] Close to the origin of all things and to nature, these dancing hordes, for Nietzsche, moreover drew from the same wells as the Bacchic dances of antiquity, uniting Europe with the Near East: 'in the German Middle Ages, too, ever-growing throngs roamed from place to place, impelled by the same Dionysiac power, singing and dancing as they went; in these St John's and St Vitus's dancers we recognize the Bacchic choruses of the Greeks, with their prehistory in Asia Minor, extending to Babylon and the orgiastic Saracea'.[122] The medieval and ancient dances to which Nietzsche referred served as a philosophical image with which to describe the ecstatic dissolution of the self in a rapturous Oriental bliss. This was an ecstasy Nietzsche deemed healthy of body and mind, although the dances were considered, he insisted, 'popular diseases' by his contemporaries. Nietzsche bemoaned this verdict, arguing that it only belied their own resentment and ill health: 'there are those who, whether from lack of experience', he wrote, 'or from dullness of spirit, turn away in scorn or pity from such phenomena, regarding them as "popular diseases" while believing in their own good health; of course, these poor creatures have not the slightest inkling of how spectral and deathly pale their "health" seems when the glowing life of Dionysiac enthusiasts storms past them'.[123]

In *Thus Spoke Zarathustra*, written over a decade later between 1883 and 1885, Nietzsche depicted a further medieval dance event: the wandering Zarathustra falls upon a chorus of celebrants indulging in the Festival of the Ass (or Feast of Fools), a medieval tradition Nietzsche had read about in an eighteenth-century account, which described the mock solemnity these thirteenth-century iconoclasts were performing in a fête whose carnivalesque overtones were generally believed to stem from the Dionysian revelries of ancient Greece.[124] Although historian Max Harris has convincingly shown that the Feast of Fools was not as rebellious or ribald as is commonly held but was in fact tightly incorporated into church liturgy,[125] the myth of these medieval merrymakers resonated with Nietzsche's anti-puritanical stance.

Yet by the late 1880s, Nietzsche found everything wrong with the dances. They—and their medicalization—now epitomized all that was amiss with the world: the medical profession and the masses spurred into contortions by an ascetic culture all signalled a world gone awry. Nietzsche described the medieval St. John's and St. Vitus's dances no longer as expressions of joy but as 'terrible epileptic epidemics' that weakened and 'emasculated' men. The dancers' convulsions mimicked those he himself witnessed and experienced in psychiatric hospitals, where individuals were forced to suffer humiliating treatments that 'shattered [the] nervous system', revealing 'terrible paralyses' and exacerbating profoundly depressive states.[126] At the cusp of his own well-known breakdown in December 1888, on the heels of a decade of poor health that had forced him to resign from his position at the University of Basel in 1879, and ushering in a further decade of institutionalization marked by debilitating paralyses, depressions, delusions, and ecstasies, Nietzsche was well-placed to poke an iron scourge into the medical establishment's side. The prevailing culture of asceticism was to

121. Friedrich Nietzsche, *The Birth of Tragedy and Other Writings*, ed. Raymond Geuss and Ronald Speirs, trans. Ronald Speirs (Cambridge: Cambridge University Press, 1999), 17; see also Friedrich Nietzsche, *Die Geburt der Tragödie aus dem Geiste der Musik* (Leipzig: Verlag von E. W. Fritzsch, 1872), 4.

122. Nietzsche, *The Birth of Tragedy*, 17.

123. Nietzsche, *The Birth of Tragedy*, 17–18.

124. Julian Young, *Friedrich Nietzsche: A Philosophical Biography* (Cambridge: Cambridge University Press, 2010), 384–385. The bibliography on Nietzsche's life and legacy is extensive. I have found Young's *Friedrich Nietzsche* to be most useful.

125. See Max Harris, *Sacred Folly: A New History of the Feast of Fools* (Ithaca, NY: Cornell University Press, 2011).

126. Friedrich Nietzsche, *On the Genealogy of Morality*, ed. Keith Ansell-Pearson, trans. Carol Diethe (Cambridge: Cambridge University Press, 1994), 112.

blame, he argued, for medieval as for modern Europe's troubles, as it forced individuals into grotesque expressions of physical and emotional pain as ugly as their Greek and Saracen antecedents had been actually wonderful and joyous. In *On the Genealogy of Morality* (1887), Nietzsche had only spite for the 'masses' as well as the priestly medicine-mongering he saw driving the St. John's and St. Vitus's dances.[127]

Yet overall, Nietzsche was excited at the prospect of the medieval dances signalling an orgiastic resurgence that could liberate men and women from the same pernicious asceticism and herd mentality he considered so destructive in his own time. Rearticulating Arthur Schopenhauer's (1788–1860) Eastern-inspired concept of the *principium individuationis*—according to which we falsely experience ourselves as individuated until the Veil of Maya falls from our eyes and we perceive other beings' suffering as our own, realizing that we are united in a common humanity—Nietzsche saw the dances as instrumental for attaining an extra-individual state. But for Nietzsche, this extra-individual state was not ascetic. Describing the blissful ecstasy of the Apollonian spirit (the spirit of the individual self) dissolving, in the dance, into a rapturous Dionysianism, Nietzsche saw collective ecstasy overtaking Schopenhauer's ascetic ideal. For Nietzsche, we had to lose the pettiness and small-mindedness of the individual self, just as Schopenhauer suggested, but also to replace it with the ecstatic joy of a life force erupting in elated dreams and inebriation. We had to choose a bacchanalian overcoming of individualism, rather than what Schopenhauer saw as a more disembodied, yogic, and abstracted conception of human mutuality. Schopenhauer had put forward an ascetic ideal that resulted in the abandonment of the will to live and of all bodily satisfaction; but in Nietzsche's terms, it was through the Dionysian principle, by which we find oblivion in extreme and jubilant corporeality, that we surpass small-mindedness and a false ego. Euripides (480–406 BCE), Nietzsche thought, had killed tragedy by turning to what he termed a Socratic, over-intellectualizing dramatic mode and away from the impulsiveness of the ancient ecstasies that characterized the earlier Attic tragedians, Aeschylus (c. 523–c. 456 BCE) and Sophocles (c. 497–c. 406 BCE) in particular. Although himself indebted to Euripides's *Bacchae* in *The Birth of Tragedy*, as he described Dionysian revelries at one with nature much as Euripides described them in the *parodos* (or opening choral segment) of his late play, Nietzsche found the true tragic spirit to constitute an ecstatic overcoming of rational life.[128]

The St. John's and St. Vitus's dances were at once symbolic of a fantasy of the dissolution of the individuated self—and corresponding return to an idyllic Dionysianism—and proof of the tortured results of ascetic ideals championed by a European civilization caught in the throes of a self-destructive Christianity. Although both perspectives claimed disinhibited dancing and movement as good and corporeal repression as bad, Nietzsche saw in the frantic gesticulations of the St. John's Day dancers a particularly contemporary sign of misery and despair. It is highly likely that he had encountered Hecker's work, given the wide currency of Hecker's writing in the decades preceding Nietzsche's career, and its recuperation by scientific celebrities such as Charcot, whose writings Nietzsche had encountered.[129] But Nietzsche was also tapping into widespread uneasiness about collective exuberance and the movements of crowds current at the time of his writing. His own apprehensions about the St. John's Day dances—which in his view were not just primitive and good but modern and ugly too—suggest that in these poorly understood figures of singing, writhing, and wreathed dancing throngs, a host of legends and symbols could be read casting them as wonderfully disinhibited and free but, just as easily, disturbed.

Nietzsche's interest in ancient Greece was not new. A century of German writing on antiquity had preceded his iconoclastic account, but he set new terms for the interpretation of Greek culture highlighting the admittedly ambivalent exaltation of Bacchanalian joy. The German art historian and archaeologist Johann Joachim Wincklemann (1717–1768) had set the grounds for an exaltation of Greek temperance in his influential essay 'Reflections on the Imitation of Greek Works in Painting and Sculpture' (1755),

---

127. Nietzsche, *On the Genealogy of Morality*, 112.

128. See Albert Henrichs, 'The Last of the Detractors: Friedrich Nietzsche's Condemnation of Euripides', *Greek, Roman and Byzantine Studies* 27.4 (1986): 369–397.

129. On Nietzsche's familiarity with Charcot's work at the Salpêtrière, see Gregory Moore, *Nietzsche, Biology and Metaphor* (Cambridge: Cambridge University Press, 2004), 144–145.

reprised in various celebrations of Greek moderation and harmony by Gotthold Ephraim Lessing (1729–1781), Johann Gottfried von Herder (1744–1803), Wilhelm von Humboldt (1767–1835), Friedrich Schlegel (1772–1829), Christoph Martin Wieland (1733–1813), and Goethe, among others.[130] Further debates about the Greek character emerged in the wake of Friedrich Hölderlin's (1770–1843) suggestion that the Apollonian spirit served as a Grecian counterpoint to what he called the Junonian spirit of sobriety and self-restraint.[131] But Nietzsche's version of the Dionysian underscored ecstasy and enthusiasm, excess, rapture, and a life force so great it spilled into the world beyond the individual, constituting what he would eventually term the 'will to life' or 'will to power', a 'superabundance' of vitality and 'overflowing of energy pregnant with future' manifesting as the 'eternal joy of becoming' and the 'eternal joy of creation' given to the woman in the agonies of labour, and to all those who trounced pain.[132]

For Nietzsche, this healthy biopower welcomed and overcame the pessimism and self-destructiveness of the small man, whose experience of pleasure was undercut by his own perpetual sense of defeat. As I have been suggesting, Foucault borrowed from Nietzsche's work a vacillating style and effusive mode of inquiry that also sought philosophically to draw out the affect driving bodily being. The emphasis both writers placed on life forms—and illness—suggested not just a desire to recuperate looser, lighter ways projected at times fervently into the past, but more urgently to think in embodied ways about what it means to be embodied, to move, to pass between states of consciousness and experience—to trespass. Nietzsche's figure for this was 'dance', fantasized as a space of pure being away from the heaviness of everyday life. For Foucault, 'madness', like unreason, served as the perpetually murmuring zone within which alternative truths are imagined. I suggest the intensity with which modern figures of medieval Dionysianism appear in the nineteenth century also points towards another Dionysianism in the age of torque: a fantasy of disorderly gestural

excess, the phantasmatic counterpart to the ever more efficient rhythms of the industrial age.

The challenges of the convulsive body, and of the convulsive *body politic*, a concept I will return to at greater length in chapter 5, thus come more fully into view: as Mark D. Jordan points out in *Convulsing Bodies: Religion and Resistance in Foucault* (2015), convulsive bodies are also those that resist the strictures of power.[133] They squirm and twist in ungainly ways, troubling the suaveness of torque; their very being appears anaesthetic and uncontainable. It seeks to relieve pain and to pervert exhortations to beauty, as well as to still, quiet, or controlled motion. These warped and unruly bodies suggest a zone of contestation between pre- and early Christian forms of religiosity and the orderly state represented by the rising institutions of the Christian church. Choreomania thus appears on history's stage as a marker of religious dissent.

In the next chapter, I turn to Paracelsus's sixteenth-century theories of chorea and St. Vitus's dance, and to a different sort of contested space of illegibility: the illegibility of choreic gesture, an individual movement disorder he and further authors likened to the group dances of the Middle Ages and of his own time. As the next chapter argues, chorea posed particular problems to the early modern medical theorist: apparently similar to epilepsy and other falling and trembling movements, chorea baffled all those steeped in centuries of theology, supernaturalism, and demonism. But Paracelsus's iconoclastic approach, emphasizing direct observation and fieldwork, shook the medical establishment in his day, laying the groundwork for a legacy of treatises on chorea still dubiously linking all sorts of trembling and falling movements with medieval and early modern religious and popular fêtes. Significantly, with Paracelsus, the conflation of choreic and choreomaniacal movements catalysed a surge of writing on purposeless, meaningless motion. Choreomania became a disorder of gestural aimlessness: no longer the medieval fools' ship's passage but meaningless gesture reproducing itself apparently without origin or cause.

---

130. A useful discussion of the Greek imaginary in German and English literature is offered by Kenneth Haynes, *English Literature and Ancient Languages* (Oxford: Oxford University Press, 2003), 138–173.

131. Haynes, *English Literature and Ancient Languages*, 140.

132. Young, *Friedrich Nietzsche*, 446–447, 502.

133. See esp. Jordan, *Convulsing Bodies*, 86–91.

3

Translatio

St. Vitus's Dance, Demonism, and the Early Modern

Madness cannot be defined, any more than reason.

—Louis-Florentin Calmeil, *De la folie* (1845)

STATES OF EMERGENCE: PURPOSELESS GESTURE

Describing Gilles de la Tourette's (1857–1904) writing on spasms, tics, and jerks in *Étude sur une affection nerveuse caractérisée par de l'incoordination accompagnée d'écholalie et de coprolalie* [Study on a Nervous Condition Characterized by Lack of Motor Coordination Accompanied by Echolalia and Coprolalia] (1885), later known as Tourette's syndrome, a condition since then understood to be closely allied to—often indistinguishable from—chorea, Agamben highlights a 'catastrophic' 'proliferation' of gestures. Writing in 'Notes on Gesture' (1992), Agamben highlights de la Tourette's 'description of an amazing proliferation of tics, spasmodic jerks, and mannerisms—a proliferation that cannot be defined in any way other than as a generalized catastrophe of the sphere

of gestures. Patients can neither start nor complete the simplest of gestures. If they are able to start a movement', he adds, 'this is interrupted and broken up by shocks lacking any coordination and by tremors that give the impression that the whole musculature is engaged in a dance (*chorea*) that is completely independent of any ambulatory end'.[1] The 'catastrophe' Agamben highlights is purposeless gesture, gesture without end; gesture that is going nowhere, that cannot complete itself. Significantly, this catastrophe looks like dance—in his terms, *chorea*: a particular sort of spasmodic, tic-like dance ('*chorea*') that has no destination.

Choreomania, a broad category of dyskinetic gestures and movement disorders allied, in medical literature, to Tourette's syndrome and chorea, appears shocking to observers because it seems to lack precision, control, and purpose. It erupts, seemingly epidemically, onto the scene of

---

1. Giorgio Agamben, 'Notes on Gesture', in *Means without End: Notes on Politics*, trans. Vincenzo Binetti and Cesare Casarino (Minneapolis: University of Minnesota Press, 2000), 48–59, 50.

modernity as a series of purposeless fits: attacks of the uncontrolled body in a rationalized public space in which bodies are meant to be doing something, going somewhere. In Agamben's formulation, non-catastrophic (non-choreic) bodies complete their gestures; they do not leave them half-finished, interrupted, or broken off. Chorea, in contrast, stutters, stumbles, collapses, falls. It is a gesture that does not move towards a goal or complete a circuit. This chapter argues that within the associated spaces of chorea, Tourette's syndrome, epilepsy, rheumatism, and an increasing constellation of narratives—after the medieval dances described in the last chapter, an outbreak of dancing in Strasbourg in 1518, and a whole host of Italian cases of tarantism (a condition medically associated with melancholy, and the dance of the tarantella)—'choreomania' became so capacious as to encompass nearly any seemingly purposeless motion.

The translatio from a humoral to an ecosophical and eventually a neurophysiological terrain of diagnosis, however, does not suggest a linear progression towards greater scientific understanding, proof, or verification but physicians' continued bafflement as to what the erratic gestures of the 'dancing disease' meant or how they should be categorized; and these same physicians' increasing recourse to cultural history for explanation. Imagined genealogies took the place of taxonomy. Yet in this double move, at once to observe and to compare with past (and increasingly, later chapters show, foreign) cases, the conflation of gestural disorder in the present and social upheaval in the past further entangled chorea (*chorea minor*), as an individual neuromotor disorder involving spasms and tics, and choreomania, the morphing complex of desires and fantasies according to which all spontaneous and irregular movement is 'mad'.

TRANSLATIO: ECOSOPHIES AND VITAL SPIRITS

This chapter then hinges on early modern formulations of the dancing disease, mapped decisively onto the figure of St. Vitus, and their lasting imprint in nineteenth-century medical treatises. With the renegade physician Paracelsus, an ambivalent nexus of concepts comes into play in the early modern period: 'St. Vitus's dance', at once medical, historical, ecosophical, and

physiological (as opposed to demonic), denoting since Paracelsus a type of falling sickness and simultaneously a type of insanity, begins to signal a complex and, as I show by the end of this chapter, lasting interpenetration of falling, spasming, and jerking forms.

Paracelsus, in the early sixteenth century, ventured an anti-establishmentarian view: what he called chorea merely echoed nature's ripples, tremors, and falls. Thus wresting otherwise unexplained gestures from a history of religious and scientific writings on witchcraft—a trope that, for centuries, had seemingly accounted for unwanted intrusions into everyday life—Paracelsus claimed that the natural world was the sole cause of trembling movements. Witchcraft, this chapter argues, was thus the prime discursive space within (and against) which the medical language of chorea would arise, though abrupt and unstructured gestures would remain marked with the spectre of a dark and unknowable force. Significantly, Paracelsus performed a political move in designing to make choreic gestures appear meaningless; to make them appear to go nowhere, to be caused by nothing exogenous, and as such to become 'merely' medical (rather than demonic). In replacing the invisible world of spirits by what he contended was a verifiable world of natural correspondences and vital locomotion, Paracelsus described chorea corresponding to the gestures of a natural world saturated with a whole range of smooth but also sudden and uncontrolled movements; I have elsewhere called this mixture *alterkinetic*.[2]

Concerned with directly observable reality, Paracelsus submitted that chorea, epilepsy, and other involuntary movements offered formal evidence of diseases far removed from the invisible forces (and institutional politics) of armchair academicism. But he still needed to account for bodily movements somehow. 'Vital spirits', or *spiritus vitae* (also occasionally translated as 'spirit of life'), Paracelsus posited, were neutral forces that moved through (and moved) all matter. They constituted an underlying principle of locomotion that did away with exogenous means and ends—particularly, with the supernatural, witchy interference his academic peers expounded upon. Presaging Bergson's theories of vitalism by a few hundred years, and what Bergson would call the *élan vital* or vital thrust (also denoting a life force without origin or end), Paracelsus thrived on a method of

---

2. Gotman, 'Epilepsy, Chorea and Involuntary Movements Onstage'.

experimental discovery, seeing chorea in every-day life; and seeing, as Bergson would, processes of nearly continuous transformation.

Paracelsus's vitalist philosophy catapulted chorea, and what he was the first systematically to describe as St. Vitus's dance, onto the modern medical scene. Brushing away the cobwebs of theologically and academically entrenched theories attributing epilepsy, chorea, and other forms of dyskinetic gestures to demonism and witchcraft, Paracelsus instituted a shift, almost a bifurcation, in the emerging choreomania story, constituting what I refer to as a trans-latio, a transfer or passage from one regime of knowledge and power to another. I borrow the medieval concept of translatio to describe pas-sages between aesthetic and disciplinary con-figurations; in Medieval Latin, *translatio* was employed alternately to signify *translatio imperii* (denoting transfer of power or rule, generally from East to West, as from Athens to Rome and Rome to Paris) and *translatio studii* (denot-ing transfer of culture, study, or knowledge, for example between fields).[3] 'Translatio' in this sense describes a passage or shift—literally, *kinesis*, movement, route—between political and intellectual modalities that the narrower concept of 'translation' does not quite capture. So whereas the notion of translatio is gener-ally acknowledged in literature on medieval and early modern history, and more recently in com-parative literature, it is absent from dance and performance studies, in spite of these fields' marked investments in discourses of disciplin-ary power and institutional history, and in the politics and practices of movement. I use this term throughout this book to describe the pas-sage and transformation of the choreomania concept across nations and modes of knowledge, from Germany and other parts of Europe to the far reaches of the colonial empires, and from medical history and colonial medicine to anthro-pology. But the translatio is never total or exact; there is never a complete consummation (or, in Roach's terms, *surrogation*) of one field of know-ledge by another, nor is there ever a conclusive passage from one to another shore. Rather, the perpetual sea-voyaging Gilroy describes of the Black Atlantic imprints the story of choreoma-nia with an equally ambivalent (and multiva-lent) set of trajectories: voyages and returns. So whereas the previous chapter (chapter 2) and this chapter emphasize a translatio from bois-terous village dance spurred on by foreign pil-grims and local merrymakers to organic events suggesting individual disorders of the nervous system, choreic tremblings continued to repre-sent a cacophony of movements that remained to their observers illegible, incoherent, and, as I show by the end of this chapter, obdurate in their failure to conform to new medical forms.

'SABBATH, SABBATH': PARACELSUS, CHRISTIANITY, AND THE WITCH

While St. John reigned as patron saint of the medieval dance manias I described in the pre-vious chapter, St. Vitus emerges in the early modern period to represent the jerky gestural vocabulary and odd mixture of comic move-ment and theatricality that came to define the dancing disease. Vitus (c. 284–305) was an early Christian zealot, whose unlikely story gained prominence in the wake of the Black Death and ensuing dancing upheavals, as late fourteenth- and early fifteenth-century European folklore

---

3. In a slight twist on the formulation I suggest above, literary critic Ernst Robert Curtius influentially described *translatio studii* specifically as the transfer of learning from Athens to Rome and Rome to France, and *translatio imperii* as the transfer of power from one empire to another, often provoked by poor stewardship. Arguably, the transfer of learning and power also often go hand in hand. See Ernst Robert Curtius, *European Literature and the Latin Middle Ages*, trans. Willard R. Trask (Princeton, NJ: Princeton University Press, 1991), 29, 384. In Elise Bartosik-Vélez's terms, 'translatio' describes the 'transfer of empire, according to which occidental empire and Western civilization itself was believed to have moved progressively from east to west, first from Asia to Greece and then to Rome (and sometimes to Germany)'. Elise Bartosik-Vélez, 'Translatio Imperii: Virgil and Peter Martyr's Columbus', *Comparative Literature Studies* 46.4 (2009): 559–588, 560. On the concept of translatio in a discourse of power, sov-ereignty, and legitimacy, given practices of translation and grammar in nineteenth-century Colombia, see Rosé María Rodríguez-García, 'The Regime of Translation in Miguel Antonio Caro's Colombia', *diacritics* 34.3 (2004): 143–175. For David A. Boruchoff, the early modern recuperation of the translatio figure is linked to George Hakewill's seventeenth-century notion of *circular progresse*, or that which passes 'from place to place, and from nation to nation'. David A. Boruchoff, 'New Spain, New England, and the New Jerusalem: The "Translation" of Empire, Faith and Learning (*Translatio Imperii, Fidei ac Scientiae*) in the Colonial Missionary Project', *Early American Literature* 43.1 (2008): 5–34, 18. On translatio, see also Le Goff, *Medieval Civilisation*; Douglas Robinson, *Translation and Empire: Postcolonial Theories Explained* (London: Routledge, 2014), 50–55; and Emily Apter, *The Translation Zone: A New Comparative Literature* (Princeton, NJ: Princeton University Press, 2006). See also Kélina Gotman, 'Translatio', *Performance Research* 21.5 (2016): 17–20.

increasingly associated uncontrollable dancing with epilepsy. Though Vitus had reputedly cured the son of the Roman emperor Diocletian (244–311) of epilepsy (widely attributed to demonic possession), he was a Christian and as such was considered an apostate and fed to lions—or dumped into a cauldron of boiling oil, according to alternate accounts—and miraculously, it was thought, escaped unscathed. By the early ninth century, his relics had been transferred to Saxony, and the story of his miraculous delivery gave rise to a host of further cures reported on and around his sepulchre. His cult proliferated. Eventually legend emerged in Germany according to which Vitus had prayed to God while he had his neck to the sword such that all those suffering from the dancing mania would be protected for a year if they solemnized the day of his commemoration (15 June) and fasted on the evening before.[4] Vitus became, by extension, the patron saint not only of epileptics but also of dancers, actors, and comedians, as well as lightning and rabid dog bites—simultaneously thus representing comical contortions, jagged angularity, sudden movements, virulence, and theatrical deceit.

This translatio, from St. John to St. Vitus, emerged in a late medieval context in which unruly dances were increasingly integrated into civic discourse, in collusion with clerical authority. Intermingled with clerical and civic debate, medical discourse gained ground, and the transition from St. John to St. Vitus solidified: although both saints continued to be employed almost interchangeably in reference to collective bouts of unruly dancing, the St. Vitus myth linking collective dances to nervous complaints emerged in the early modern period in full force.

A range of medical and religious hypotheses had emerged between the fourteenth and sixteenth centuries to account for the dancers' contortions—half dance and half leaping, grimacing performances of real agony. Late medieval physicians steeped in the classical theory of humours—according to which disease comes from an imbalance in one of the four bodily elements, either blood, yellow bile, black bile, or phlegm—typically thought the dancers suffered from hot blood. The *Cronica quorundam Romanorum regum ac imperatorum* suggested that many contemporaries considered the dances a 'mania' arising from 'natural causes', 'for the sufferers seemed to be crazed, uttering confused sounds, with strange movements of their bodies, as if mad'.[5] Young women were most prone to this sort of dancing, the *Cronica* noted, although young and old, women and men, were equally liable to catching the disease.[6]

Other writers thought this was the work of demons, a hypothesis that remained strong through the early modern religious wars and the Reformation. The notorious *Malleus maleficarum* [Hammer of Witches] (1487), written by the inquisitors Heinrich Krämer (1430–1505) (also known as Henricus Institoris) and Jacob Sprenger (c. 1436–1495), appeared at a time when witchcraft trials were all the rage in parts of Germany and the continent, peaking in the period between about 1450 and 1700.[7] The sixteenth-century *De la démonomanie des sorciers* [Of the Demon-Mania of Witches], by French writer Jean Bodin (d. 1596), published in French in 1580 and almost simultaneously translated into German, Italian, and Latin, was one of the most widely disseminated works on demonism, appearing in over twenty-three editions. It offered one of the most systematic treatments of the witches' nightly sabbaths, articulating fears that had run rampant in the European imagination since at least the Middle Ages. But Bodin's analysis now also comprised references to madness and the civic treatment of dancing manias, linked in his view to witchcraft, inasmuch as both could be cured with the exercise of slow, heavy movement. He claimed: 'there is no [witches'] assembly carried on where they do

4. See F. G. Holweck, *A Biographical Dictionary of the Saints, with a General Introduction on Hagiography* (Saint Louis: Herder, 1924), 1027–1028; Alban Butler, *Butler's Lives of the Saints*, rev. Kathleen Jones, ed. Paul Burns, 12 vols., vol. 6 (Collegeville, MN: Liturgical Press, 1997), 109–110; David Hugh Farmer, *The Oxford Dictionary of Saints*, 5th ed. (Oxford: Oxford University Press, 2003), 528; John J. Delaney, *Dictionary of Saints* (Garden City, NJ: Doubleday, 1980), 578; Dom Basil Watkins, ed., *The Book of Saints: A Comprehensive Biographical Dictionary*, 7th ed. (New York: Continuum, 2002), 592; and Hecker, *Epidemics of the Middle Ages*, 86.

5. Cited in Backman, *Religious Dances*, 205–206.

6. Backman, *Religious Dances*, 205–206. See Sprandel, *Die Kölner Weltchronik*, 116.

7. Jonathan L. Pearl, 'Introduction', in Jean Bodin, *On the Demon-Mania of Witches*, trans. Randy A. Scott (Toronto: Centre for Reformation and Renaissance Studies, 1995), 14; originally published as *De la démonomanie des sorciers* (Paris: Jacques du Puys Libraire Juré, 1580). According to Pearl's introduction, the 'witchcraft crisis reached its peak in Western Europe between 1550 and 1650', and 'during this century, witches were actively prosecuted in the law courts and could be punished with death' (14).

not dance', adding that these dances made men frenzied and women abort.[8] He argued that 'all raving and frenzied [furieux, & forcenez] people perform such dancing and violent leaping' but could be cured with the enforcement of calm, heavy rhythmic movements [posément, & en cadence pesante], such as those imposed on 'the mad [insensez] people in Germany struck with the illness [maladie] known as St. Vitus and St. Modestus'.[9] More intriguingly, Bodin notes that dances were engaged in on feast days, as dancers raised their hands in the air, shouting 'sabbath, sabbath', to show their joy ('allégresse'), a practice he compared to ancient Hebrew dances and oblations at the Temple, including those performed by David, who danced and played his harp as a sign of joy.[10] Bodin was quick to add that ancient prophetic dances, unlike these demonic ones, engaged the body in movement that had 'nothing offensive' ('rien d'insolent'), praising heaven and God rather than the Devil.[11] This would, however, suggest that the 'dancing manias' were in some cases plausibly Jewish dances, reinterpreted as witchcraft and subsequently disease.[12]

In all cases, the concept of the demonic was radically polysemic, referring as much to the uncontrolled as to the obscure. It also, significantly, described a fear of shape-shifting; these dancers, whose contorted bodies distorted them beyond recognition, had in that respect 'demonic' sympathies. Yet their status perplexed many: were they devil-worshipping and demonic outright? Were they suffering from naturally explainable pains?

While some charity was granted the dancers in previous centuries, as Herental's account, described in the previous chapter, suggests, no sustained medical discussion had yet emerged, and no real medical theories were propounded besides recourse to the humoral notion that they suffered from hot blood. Plenty of medical debate had emerged surrounding the Black Death, arguing that it was caused by astrological conjunctions, mixed with bad air that exacerbated a form of *contagium*, as Siraisi, Cohn, Vivian Nutton, and others have shown.[13] But the dances were 'plague-like' in image only. Now, one firebrand physician keen to understand the roots of these agitated gestures argued against prevailing theories of the day according to which the dancers suffered from demonic influence, substituting what he saw as politically motivated religious prejudice with hard fact based on empirical research.

Paracelsus wrote his treatise *Diseases That Deprive Man of His Reason, Such as St. Vitus' Dance, Falling Sickness, Melancholy, and Insanity, and Their Correct Treatment* in the 1520s, nearly a century and a half after the medieval dancing mania's zenith in 1374–1375, when new waves of religious reform and theories of malicious demonism were holding sway.[14] He discovered that he could observe people suffering from tics,

---

8. Bodin, *De la démonomanie des sorciers*, 87–89. See also Bodin, *On the Demon-Mania of Witches*, 9, 120.

9. Bodin, *De la démonomanie des sorciers*, 88–89. See also Bodin, *On the Demon-Mania of Witches*, 120–121. Unsurprisingly perhaps, Scott and Pearl reprise the usual conflation between neuromotor disorder and popular dance to explain St. Vitus's dance as a 'special form of rheumatic fever (Sydenham's chorea) which caused involuntary twitching or writhing movements' in their English edition, adding that the 'term is also commonly applied to a range of neurological disorders'. Bodin, *On the Demon-Mania of Witches*, 121n70.

10. Bodin remarks on the ancient Hebrew term *haga* (חגב), meaning simultaneously festival or celebration and dance ('feste, & danse'). Bodin, *De la démonomanie des sorciers*, 88.

11. Bodin, *De la démonomanie des sorciers*, 88.

12. I have found only scanty evidence of this hypothesis, but Bodin's remark suggests more work may yield important insight on the connection between Jewish dances and what was coming to be known as the dancing disease. Either way, it seems highly unlikely that the dancing mania would be an exclusively Jewish phenomenon, only that certain Jewish dances would be wrapped up into the dancing mania lore.

13. These theories have long been well documented. See Nancy G. Siraisi, *Medieval and Renaissance Medicine: An Introduction to Knowledge and Practice* (Chicago: University of Chicago Press, 1990), 128–129; Vivian Nutton, 'The Seeds of Disease: An Explanation of Contagion and Infection from the Greeks to the Renaissance', *Medical History* 27 (1983): 1–34.

14. Paracelsus, 'The Diseases That Deprive Man of His Reason, Such As St. Vitus' Dance, Falling Sickness, Melancholy, and Insanity, and Their Correct Treatment', trans. Gregory Zilboorg, in Paracelsus, *Four Treatises of Theophrastus von Hohenheim called Paracelsus*, ed. Henry E. Sigerist (Baltimore: Johns Hopkins University Press, 1996), 127–212. See also Paracelsus, *Paracelsus (Theophrastus Bombastus von Hohenheim, 1493–1541): Essential Theoretical Writings*, ed. and trans. Andrew Weeks (Leiden: Brill, 2008), 778–793, on St. Vitus's dance; Walter Pagel, *Paracelsus: An Introduction to Philosophical Medicine in the Era of the Renaissance*, 2nd rev. ed. (Basel: Karger, 1982), 55–56; Andrew Weeks, *Paracelsus: Speculative Theory and the Crisis of the Early Reformation* (Albany: State University of New York Press, 1997); Allen G. Debus, *The Chemical Philosophy: Paracelsian Science and Medicine in the Sixteenth and Seventeenth Centuries*, 2 vols. (Mineola, NY: Dover, 2002). See also Geneviève Aubert, 'Charcot Revisited: The Case of Bruegel's Chorea', *Archives of Neurology* 62 (2005): 155–161, 155; L. J. Donaldson, J. Cavanagh, and J. Rankin, 'The Dancing Plague: A Public Health Conundrum', *Public Health* 111 (1997): 201–204, 201.

convulsions, and epilepsy directly, substituting abstract theorization for his own hands-on, investigative methodology: wandering in the countryside to discover the causes of natural disturbances through direct observation. He rallied students along the way and wrote, subversively, in the vernacular. Paracelsus was reputed to have lived like a slob, drunken and dishevelled, but to have claimed more effective remedies than any academic physician.[15]

Drawing up a manifesto that set out his plans for accessible daily lectures based on experience, he burned a handbook by the widely regarded eleventh-century Persian author Avicenna (980–1037), who represented the canon of academic medicine at the time, fittingly enough in a St. John's Day fire, further establishing his own reputation as an iconoclast and garnering him a cast of devotees and enemies alike.[16] Paracelsus's new approach did away, he claimed, with the complacent theorization popular among prominent humanists, including Andreas Vesalius (1514–1564), Otto Brunfels (1488–1534), Leonhart Fuchs (1501–1566), Konrad Gessner (1516–1565), and Georgius Agricola (1494–1555); and with the religious superstition rampant in what he saw as a corrupt clerical establishment. 'We must not forget to explain the origin of the diseases which deprive man of reason', he wrote, 'as we know from experience that they develop out of man's disposition. The present-day clergy of Europe attribute such diseases to ghostly beings and threefold spirits; we are not inclined to believe them'. Instead, he argued, 'nature is the sole origin of diseases'.[17] By positing a type of sympathy between parts of the individual and the whole, underscoring analogical relationships across swathes of the natural world, he was overturning the humoral approach to medicine according to which disorders were caused by constitutional imbalances exacerbated by demonic influence. The church and the academic establishment were swept away in one stroke.

Paracelsus's natural philosophy complemented his political convictions. As a radical reformer living at a pivotal time in the history of the Christian church, when Lutheran and Protestant reforms were on the rise, Paracelsus operated alongside a small coterie of religious nonconformists whose attitudes garnered them sympathy from townspeople and peasants agitating against the Catholic authorities, who were in turn clamping down on rabble-rousers of all stripes. Although his spiritualist and mystical leanings and Kabbalistic activities caused him to be accused of heresy and black magic by some of his humanist peers,[18] Paracelsus maintained an active and successful medical practice, boasting patients across the lower and upper classes. His theories were bewilderingly complex, and decidedly cartographic, emphasizing relationships between microcosm and macrocosm and the rhizomatic journeys disease could take. As he described it, disease located in the roots of a tree at one point spread to the animal or human's liver or heart at another, and passed from that to the limbs, echoing environmental modulations and climatic changes. The substance of the disease was the same; only its locus and intensity shifted. Even St. Vitus's dance was caused by atmospheric disturbances, which disturbed the dancer's 'vital spirits'; the clergy had simply used these tremors to preach against demonic possession and instill fear in the people.[19]

Comparing what he called St. Vitus's dance to epilepsy, he argued that dancers were moved by 'imagination' and 'sympathy' as they imitated images (or 'mental impressions') and sounds that affected them, as a child might be affected when seeing an object and imagining something else—a ghost, a boogeyman—as a result. This phantasm, he thought, provoked the movement of the imagination and so, too, the movements of the limbs, not by the work of any outside agent but by virtue of the patient's mind alone. This was not a figurative imitation but ecosophical and kinetic: the 'imitation' operated at the level of a tremor, a shake. Paracelsus used the terms *chorea* (from the Latin, 'dance')

---

15. Paracelsus said in his own defence: 'Whence have I all my secrets, out of what writers and authors? Ask rather how the beasts have learned their arts. If nature can instruct irrational animals, can it not much more men?' Cited in Deaux, *The Black Death*, 212. On Paracelsus's dishevelled ways and general notoriety, see also Charles Webster, *Paracelsus: Medicine, Magic and Mission at the End of Time* (New Haven, CT: Yale University Press, 2008); Pagel, *Paracelsus*; and Weeks, *Paracelsus*.

16. Pagel, *Paracelsus*, 20. Webster suggests that this may have been a student textbook summarizing classical ideas, in *Paracelsus*, 13.

17. Paracelsus, 'The Diseases', 142. See also Pagel, *Paracelsus*, 55–56.

18. Webster, *Paracelsus*, 22, 158–159.

19. Paracelsus, 'The Diseases', 145–146

and *chorea lasciva* (meaning playful, mischievous, or immodest dance) to describe this movement, arguing that the dancing was an 'opinion' or 'idea' conjured in the imagination of persons predisposed to act on mental impressions which caused them to jerk and twist their bodies.[20] Paracelsus attributed this movement to the 'laughing veins', which caused, as he put it, a 'ticklish feeling' in the limbs. This feeling, significantly, could originate in the heart and rise to the head, depriving persons of their reason.[21] Thus, Paracelsus accounted for the apparent madness of those swept up in the dance. Just as the occultist and demonologist Johann Weyer (1515–1588) would argue in *De praestigiis daemonum* [On the Deceits of Demons] (1563) that witchcraft only amounted to readily observable hallucinatory melancholy caused by organic dysfunction rather than demonic intervention,[22] Paracelsus's rationalist attention to corporeal motion found cause and consequence for dancing and twitching alike in the mundane movements of the natural world.

This was the first theory significantly to attend to the purportedly demonic provenance of the dancers' motions, finding echoes for these motions in the observable natural world. Paracelsus argued that disturbances of the vital fluids or *spiritus vitae* mirrored disturbances in nature, which had actually provoked the dancing; this was an ecosophical conception, positing that human bodies and their environments work inseparably. It was also an aesthetic conception, as metaphor and metonymy enabled him to draw links between individual and ecological realms, and between parts of the body and the whole: 'Just as the earthquake takes place in one part but shakes everything within its reach', he wrote, so too a disease located in the head 'afflicts all that it touches'. The same was true of the liver, whose 'brewing' vapours 'creep into the *spiritus vitae*' and 'reached the head and the whole body like a wind blowing along the roads'. The motions of the heart similarly affected the whole body, like an earthquake that shakes the world but 'is unable to cause poisoning unless the upper parts be broken by the shaking and trembling'. As Paracelsus put it, 'just like an earthquake is wrecking a house, this breaking-up . . . is not due to the poison of the *spiritus vitae* but to its motion'.[23] The repetition of 'just as', 'just like', and 'the same as' suggested parallels between phenomena in the natural world and more specifically correspondences between them defined by principles of locomotion.[24] Similarly, correspondences between earthquake, head, liver, heart, intestines, abdomen; herb; house; and, above all, root, suggested relations between human, animal, plant, and mineral worlds, connected to one another through fundamental laws of similarity. The principle ensuring their connection was the ubiquitous *spiritus vitae* running through all of nature, affecting humans, animals, and plants in analogous ways. Paracelsus's rhizomatic theories conceptualized all parts of the natural world as moving through one another, connected by contiguity and resonance.

This early kinaesthetic conceptualization of the dancing disease privileged movement. As a vitalist philosophy, Paracelsus's vision integrated observations across spiritual and material planes, combining empiricism and pragmatism, progressive politics and medical analysis, privileging a conception of the body that was open, porous, and polysemic. Still radical to the contemporary ear, Paracelsus's early formulation of choreomania presents an affiliational view of human, animal, and plant species that draws out intensities of motion and affect, as well as resonances, hiccups and breaks, and their dramatic effects. Paracelsus argued that shaking—and the characteristic tremor of the limbs found in St. Vitus's dance—was often latent and 'sometimes . . . appears after a shock'. But the shock was not the cause of the disease; the disease was 'merely inflamed by the shock, which causes the *spiritus vitae* to swell and boil'. Joy could also cause shaking, by affecting the *spiritus vitae* that have an 'inclination' towards it.[25] Thus, 'trembling, falling, foaming, and spasms of the limbs are caused because the living spirits [spiritus vitae] of the patients are ill, and therefore the patients too are suffering'.[26] This

20. Paracelsus, 'The Diseases', 158.
21. Paracelsus, 'The Diseases', 159–160.
22. See Midelfort, *A History of Madness*, 196–217.
23. Paracelsus, 'The Diseases', 145.
24. Paracelsus, 'The Diseases', 142.
25. Paracelsus, 'The Diseases', 146–147.
26. Paracelsus, 'The Diseases', 145.

unified theory—which he employed to explain epilepsy, the 'falling sickness', as well as St. Vitus's dance—accounted for patent similarities between paroxysms, including epileptic and epileptiform seizures and other sudden involuntary falls (including ones provoked by dancing).

Paradoxically, the paroxysmal gestures of choreics and epileptics rendered them more like dance understood in a contemporary aesthetic sense: as movement without signing, abstract rhythm foregrounding structure and form but not necessarily 'ends'. As a sort of purposeless movement, dance in this sense calls forth objects and spaces but is shorn of the sort of ostensive signification of drama. In Agamben's terms, gesture 'communicates communicability' but does not communicate a particular object or thing. Gesture is the pure 'mediality' of language: for Agamben, gesture *gestures*.[27] It gestures its ability to signify, to mean, point to, stand in for. As a metonymic conception, this sense of gesture differs from gesture conceived as nonteleological movement: movement that does not require an end. For Paracelsus, the gestures of choreics' limbs, torsos, and faces have no symbolic signification. Yet aesthetically they are linked, inasmuch as they formally resemble one another: Paracelsus's theory of choreic movement thus links chorea to earthquakes and other natural cataclysms by virtue of their formal and rhythmic similarities: in all cases, bodies tremble, quake, and quiver. With Paracelsus, the interrelation of ecological movements across the natural world represents a different sort of catastrophe than what Agamben would note of chorea: not the catastrophe of purposeless gesture but the catastrophic emergence of gestural upheaval, rhythmic resonance, and a brand of mutual imitation without beginning or end. For Paracelsus, the tremor of the limbs equals the tremor of a tree and of the earth; these are equivalent movements in the eruption of vital forces onto the world stage.

As medical historian Walter Pagel (1898–1983) has pointed out, however, Paracelsus was not entirely immune from belief in supernaturalism or witchcraft himself, and some of his psychiatric theories suggested burning as a means to keep patients from becoming instruments of the devil;[28] but by and large, Paracelsus's philosophical medicine, rent through with arcane deliberations, sought to go beyond what he saw as the sclerotic academicism of his day. As literary critic and historian Andrew Weeks has further suggested, ambiguity played a pivotal role in Paracelsus's thinking and style: wordplay, rhetorical riddles, paradox, and complex allusions deliberately reconfigured the fields he was seeking to redefine.[29]

Paracelsus's later writings, from around 1530, rearticulated St. Vitus's dance as an 'invisible disease', which he nonetheless observed in the first instance in a woman who, he argues, affected illness and danced herself to exhaustion purportedly to annoy her husband; he linked this to what he saw as questionable Anabaptist practices that abused faith for the sake of 'imagined ceremony'.[30] In this sense, the discourse on St. Vitus's dance served as a thinly veiled criticism of superstition once more. Although Paracelsus himself only barely escaped the threats of imprisonment and death suffered by some of his radical compatriots,[31] his vitalist conceptions paved the way for a new era of medical debate, shifting the discourse on the dancing disease: no longer primarily demonic, foreign, or strange, it had natural and human causes and, as such, should be wrested from clerical control. This conception set the grounds for a new legacy of writings linking St. John's·and St. Vitus's dance as popular practices to epilepsy, religious heresy, dissent, and thinly veiled feminine revolt now cast as disease.

THE STRASBOURG MANIA: MUNICIPAL STAKES

Paracelsus's visionary contributions to natural science initially remained marginal. But throughout the sixteenth century, practical

---

27. Agamben, 'Notes on Gesture', 58.

28. In Pagel, *Paracelsus*, 152.

29. Paracelsus, *Paracelsus*, 24–25.

30. The 'invisible', as opposed to the 'visible' diseases, all related to perversions of the human faith, and included St. Valentine's disease (St. Valentine was one of many saints besides St. Vitus associated among other conditions with epilepsy), St. Anthony's fire (most closely associated with ergotism), and St. Vitus's dance. Paracelsus's relative Gnosticism meant that he saw humans at the centre of the world, composed of two natures, visible and invisible. See Paracelsus, *Paracelsus*, 720–937. For the anecdote on 'Lady Troffea', who 'adopted strange moods' and 'turned stubborn against her husband', '[affecting] a manner as if she were ill and [concocting] a disease that would suit her purposes', hopping and jumping, singing and eventually collapsing 'in order to offend her husband', see Paracelsus, *Paracelsus*, 778–781. For the link to Anabaptism and bad faith see Paracelsus, *Paracelsus*, esp. 782–783.

31. Webster, *Paracelsus*, 247.

solutions to the so-called dancing disease mul-tiplied as municipal authorities keen to keep disorderly expressions of kinetic enthusiasm in check increasingly siphoned troublemakers off to the church. Tensions had come to a head in Strasbourg in 1518, in a second outbreak of the dancing 'plague' smaller in scope to the large-scale, travelling dance mania of the 1370s described in chapter 2 but more complexly theo-rized and documented by its contemporaries. In this case, the city's methods for dealing with the outbreak were at first pragmatic: dancers were encouraged—even mandated—to dance themselves to exhaustion in prescribed areas. Exorcism was practiced as a last resort, and standard medical opinion called on to legitimize it: the church, city, and medical establishment worked in concert to assuage, even to contain, though never fully to punish, the dancing.

Meanwhile, medical discussions attempt-ing to account for the events proliferated. The *Strasbourg Chronicle* described the dancing in terms of its potential fatality: 'A remarkable disease spread / At this time among the people. / . . . many in their madness / Began to dance, / Which they did day and night / And with-out interruption / Until they fell down uncon-scious. / Many died in consequence'.[32] Another Strasbourg chronicle reported that hundreds of men and women began 'To dance and hop . . . / In the public market, in alleys and streets / Day and night; and many of them ate nothing / Until at last the sickness left them. / This afflic-tion was called St Vitus' dance'.[33] Legend had it that the dancing was triggered by one woman; within four days, she was joined in dancing by thirty-four men and women, and soon enough two hundred people were dancing. Within four

weeks, more than four hundred people of all ages were dancing in the streets and in the private homes of Strasbourg.[34]

With increasing recourse to St. Vitus as patron saint of these dances, theories concerning the dancing frenzies gained a new lease of life, and casual bystander observations of the St. John's dances of the previous centuries gave way to a new era of medical and municipal debate. Exorcism was used to great effect: on the chief magistrate's orders, dancers were taken in wagons to the nearby chapel of St. Vitus by Zabern, in Alsace. They reportedly continued to dance along the way; then fell to their knees before the image of St. Vitus and promptly recovered their senses.[35] The proximity of the St. Vitus chapel to the Strasbourg 'mania' may have inspired the shift towards St. Vitus as patron saint, gradually occluding the earlier village kermesses and fêtes celebrated in the name of St. John (though these continued for many centuries independently to take place).

The sixteenth-century architect Daniel Specklin (1536–1589) noted in his Strasbourg chronicle that platforms for dancing were set up in the horse and grain markets, and two guild-halls were reserved for the dancers. These were provided with hired guards specially brought in to contain the dancing and keep dancers from harming themselves, as well as moderat-ing the influence they might have on others.[36] According to another eyewitness and chroni-cler, Hieronymous Gebwiler (1473–1545), the hired guards 'danced day and night with those poor people, but toward evening they tied them all onto wagons and took them to St. Vitus of Hohenstein. And after their pilgrimage there was finished and they were danced all out, they took them home again'.[37] This was a disorder

32. In Backman, *Religious Dances*, 238. See also Arlene Epp Pearsall, 'Johannes Pauli and the Strasbourg Dancers', *Franciscan Studies* 52.1 (1992): 203–214. John Waller gives a popular account of the Strasbourg 'epidemic' in *A Time to Dance, a Time to Die: The Extraordinary Story of the Dancing Plague of 1518* (London: Icon Books, 2009) and in John Waller, 'In a Spin: The Mysterious Dancing Epidemic of 1518', *Endeavour* 32.3 (2008): 117–121.

33. In Backman, *Religious Dances*, 237.

34. See Alfred Martin, 'Geschichte der Tanzkrankheit in Deutschland', *Zeitschrift des Vereins für Volkskunde* 24 (1914): 113–134, 225–239, 116, 119; cited in Midelfort, *A History of Madness*, 33. Daniel Specklin and Jean Wencker both note that 'young and old' ('iungen [or yungen] und alten') were dancing in Daniel Specklin, *Les collectanées de Daniel Specklin, chronique strasbourgeoise du seizième siècle. Fragments recueillis par Rodolphe Reuss*, in L. Dacheux, ed., *Fragments des anciennes chroniques d'Alsace*, 4 vols., vol. 2 (Strasbourg: Librairie J. Noiriel, 1890), 488; and Jean Wencker, 'La chronique strasbourgeoise de Jean Wencker', in L. Dacheux, *Les chroniques strasbourgeoises de Jacques Trausch et de Jean Wencker. Les annales de Sébastien Brant. Fragments recueillis par l'abbé Dacheux*, in *Fragments des anciennes chroniques strasbourgeoises*, 4 vols., vol. 3 (Strasbourg: Imprimerie Strasbourgeoise, 1892), 75–207, 148.

35. See R. H. R. Park and M. P. Park, 'Saint Vitus' Dance: Vital Misconceptions by Sydenham and Bruegel', *Journal of the Royal Society of Medicine* 83.8 (1990): 512–515.

36. Specklin, *Les collectanées de Daniel Specklin*, 488–489; cited in Midelfort, *A History of Madness*, 35.

37. Karl Stenzel, ed., *Die Straßburger Chronik des elsässischen Humanisten Hieronymus Gebwiler* (Berlin, 1926), 74–75; cited in Midelfort, *A History of Madness*, 33–34. Böhme notes that a century later, in 1615, a servant girl in Basel was 'overtaken by such a horrifying dance mania [Tanzwut], she danced herself sick for over a month and danced the soles of her feet off. She slept and ate

of excessive movement; but as in the medieval rounds described in chapter 2, its prescribed cure came in the form of movement as well: like purportedly cured like. Dancing, mandated by the municipal authorities, would expunge itself. Too exhausted to resist, dancers were susceptible to the emotional charge of the saint's intercession and—in the case of some—found satiety for a while.

For Gebwiler, the event offered a lesson from God that one should practice moderation in all things, including dancing. Dancing should never be lewd or shameful, he wrote; and one should never dance with 'inappropriate persons' such as monks or nuns, or 'in the wrong places' such as in cloisters or nunneries. Otherwise, God would punish them as he had the Egyptians, 'and for our obstinacy He will let us sink in a Red Sea of sins'.[38]

Some dancers appear to have actually died in the process of dancing, as reported, among others, by Specklin.[39] Those who went to church were greeted with a special mass and given small crosses and red shoes,[40] an observation echoed for the year 1517 in the Strasbourg chronicle of public official Jean Wencker (1590–1659).[41] Music seems to have played no small part in the affair: Specklin noted that besides hired guards, a cast of musicians was brought in to accompany the dancers with flutes and drum. But although music was initially prescribed by the city to help assuage these zealous dancers, it was soon outlawed, as it seemed to have the opposite effect: drums in particular increased the dancers' excitement. On 3 August 1518, municipal authorities declared that all dancing should be suspended until the end of September, since 'sadly' the 'horrible episode' that had '[arisen] with the sick, dancing persons', and which had 'not yet stopped' was not aided by dances organized for this or any other purpose, which '[took] away the recovery of such persons'. The 'only exception' noted was 'that if honorable persons wish to dance at weddings or celebrations of first Mass in their houses, they may do so using stringed instruments, but they are on their conscience not to use tambourines or drums'. Festive clothing and jewellery were also banned, and 'loose persons' cast out of the city until the excitement subsided.[42]

Whereas the Franciscan friar Johannes Pauli's (1450–1520) Strasbourg sermons suggest that the dancing may have derived from the *ballo in Christo*—what historian Arlene Epp Pearsall has described as an ecstatic religious exercise performed by worshippers known as *chorisanten* or *dansatores*, loosely related to the flagellants, and pronounced heretical a century earlier[43]—the dancing seems also to have become a fashion flaunting excess. Women and men of all ages mixed, cavorting on Sundays and other feast days, disrupting the pious exercise of religious worship. As noted, many dancers may have come from the labouring classes, but records suggest the wealthy indulged liberally as well. Johann Schenck von Grafenberg (1530–1598), a physician in Freiburg im Breisgau, noted that well-to-do dancers hired help on their own account to guide these communal fêtes:

---

little, but kept dancing in one spot, until she was completely devoid of energy'. She was eventually brought to a hospital and 'cured'. But while she was dancing, municipal authorities 'assigned two strong men to the dancer, dressed in red, with white feathers on their hats and one after the other they had to dance with the dance maniac [Tanzwüthigen]'. In this case, concerted attempts at wearing her out failed; the hospital cure is more perplexing, suggesting she either suffered a neuromotor disease that looked like dance which they were somehow able to treat or, more likely, that the hospital setting itself sobered her. The detail of the red dress and white feathers is also unusual, indicative of official dress. In Böhme, 'Tanzwut im Mittelalter', 43. See also, for the same story, Beckmann, *Gründliche Fürstellung*, 467.

38. Stenzel, ed., *Die Straßburger Chronik*, 74–75; cited in Midelfort, *A History of Madness*, 33–34.
39. Specklin writes: 'Viel tantzten [sic] sich zu tode'. *Les collectanées de Daniel Specklin*, 489.
40. Backman, *Religious Dances*, 237. See also Specklin, *Les collectanées de Daniel Specklin*, 489.
41. Wencker, 'La chronique strasbourgeoise de Jean Wencker', 148. These are the same red shoes that reappear in Hans Christian Anderson's (1805–1875) fairy tale of *The Red Shoes* (1845), in which a young girl is so possessed by her dancing shoes that she cannot stop dancing, until eventually her feet are cut off, and her shoes go off dancing on their own into the distance. Further nineteenth-century accounts of women dancing themselves to death with red shoes appear in the Brothers Grimm's *Snow White* (1812), in which the jealous stepmother is compelled to wear red-hot iron dancing shoes and dance until she dies. So, too, Giselle is compelled by the spirit-world Wilis to dance herself to death. These nineteenth-century tales of obsession, vengeance, and despair emphasized the involuntary aspects of the dance, overlooking the collective, civic aspects of the dances in the sixteenth century. Dancing shoes, particularly red ones, merit a study of their own. For a useful overview of the symbolic power of red shoes over the centuries, see e.g. Hilary Davidson, 'Sex and Sin: The Magic of Red Shoes', in Peter McNeil and Giorgio Riello, eds., *Shoes: A History from Sandals to Sneakers* (London: Bloomsbury, 2006), 272–289.
42. Midelfort, *A History of Madness*, 35–36. See also Specklin, *Les collectanées de Daniel Specklin*, 239.
43. Pearsall, 'Johannes Pauli and the Strasbourg Dancers', 209.

'those who were looking after [the dancers] used to carry around benches and high chairs with which they would ring them in if they still lived when the dancing was over. In this way their madness was assuaged'.[44] Does this comment belie a hint of irony? Were the dancers actually risking their lives? Many may have been intoxicated or behaved as if they were, showing little reserve, letting loose for a while. Those who could afford such fêtes may have died from the efforts in rare cases; as in any extreme physical activity, excess can prompt unintentionally grave results. But the dancers appeared to be all the more morally suspect on this account, even if Schenck's portrayal suggests only gentle chastisement. He was bemused by the phenomenon, describing St. Vitus's dance in his *Observationes medicae de capite humano* [Medical Observations] (1584) as an 'enthusiasm' or 'amazing kind of madness [insania] that has corrupted many of [our] ancestors especially in Germany'.[45] It was interesting, extraordinary, and novel in its incarnation but old in its genealogy: this was, for Schenck, the same phenomenon that had beset dancers in the 1370s. It was a recurring disease in Germany and yet, as far as he was concerned, still a surprising and enigmatic one.

According to municipal accounts, physicians were brought in to testify before the guild-led Council of Twenty-One in Strasbourg in the summer of 1518. As Erik Midelfort has remarked, physicians still typically agreed that the dancing was 'a natural sickness that came from hot blood',[46] a diagnosis offered among other physicians by Wencker in his Strasbourg chronicle.[47] But a new body of theories emphasizing individual insanity was also emerging, giving the dancers a stamp of frenetic but, once again, medically justified lack of control. Melancholy, it was thought, prompted delusions, to which the dancers were especially

prey. Felix Platter (Platerus) (1536–1614), a physician at the University of Basel, described the dancing frenzy as a kind of insanity, noting in his *Observations* (1614) that one woman had reportedly danced compulsively for a month; and others, falling in exhaustion to the ground, realized, when recovering, he surmised, that they had succumbed to folly.[48]

In 1625, Gregor Horst (Horstius) (1578–c. 1635), a professor of medicine in Giessen and the city physician of Ulm, ventured a rare early neuromotor diagnosis: for him, *saltatio sancti viti* (St. Vitus's dance) was a physical disorder provoked by organic dysfunction. Convulsive movements, tense pains in the limbs, growing fatigue, and heavy-headedness causing confusion provoked the afflicted person to dance.[49] But his theory gained little ground as far more popular theories of melancholy and insanity proliferated in the hundred years following the Strasbourg outburst. Philippus Camerarius (1537–1624) retrospectively attributed the fourteenth-century dance mania to the disorder of melancholy, noting: 'if [the dancing mania] is to be classed as an illness, the only category into which it seems to me to fit is a delirium of melancholia, which has of course quite a wide range. In such cases the mind is entirely disordered'.[50] The Oxford polymath Robert Burton (1577–1640), writing in 1628, argued in his widely influential *The Anatomy of Melancholy* that St. Vitus's dance was attributable to a subtype of madness—a fury stronger than, though allied to, melancholy, also involving a disordered state of mind. This madness was similar to ecstasy, he argued, and was characterized by a variety of behaviours and beliefs, including enthusiasm, revelations, and visions, as well as obsessions with, or a belief in, possession by devils and sibylline prophecy. It also suggested symptoms characteristic of the

44. 'Those who were rich kept paid attendants to see that they did not hurt themselves or others, and to act as leaders who would guide the crazy band'; cited in Backman, *Religious Dances*, 214. See Hecker, *Epidemics of the Middle Ages*, 97.

45. See Johannes Schenck von Grafenberg, 'Praefatio ad lectorem', in *Observationes medicae de capite humano: hoc est, exempla capitis morborum, causarum, signorum, eventuum, curationum, ut singularia, sic abdita et monstrosa. Ex claris. medicorum, veterum simul & recentriorum scriptis* (Basel: Ex Officina Frobeniana, 1584), n.p. Also in Midelfort, *A History of Madness*, 170.

46. Midelfort, *A History of Madness*, 34.

47. 'In mehreren Sitzungen wurde von Veitstänzern gesprochen: die Aerzte erklärten es für eine natürliche krankheit, die von hitzigem geblüt herkomme'. In Jean Wencker, ed., 'Annales de Sébastien Brant: Suite et fin', in L. Dacheux, *Fragments des anciennes chroniques d'alsace*, 4 vols., vol. 3 (Strasbourg: Imprimerie Strasbourgeoise, 1901), 243–470, 252.

48. In Robert Burton, *The Anatomy of Melancholy*, ed. Floyd Dell and Paul Jordan-Smith (New York: Tudor, 1927), 124, and Backman, *Religious Dances*, 215. On Platter, see also Midelfort, *A History of Madness*, 174–179. Beckmann describes another case reported by Platter, according to which a young prelate began having countless convulsions, after which he fell into a steady insanity; his body moved 'as if in a dance' (Beckmann, *Gründliche Fürstellung*, 467).

49. Martin, 'Geschichte der Tanzkrankheit in Deutschland', 122–123; cited in Midelfort, *A History of Madness*, 39–40.

50. Cited in Backman, *Religious Dances*, 214. On theories of melancholy (and mania) in early academic psychiatry see also Midelfort, *A History of Madness*, 141–157.

consumption of noxious herbs and spider bites, although he insisted that the dancing should not be reduced to a poisonous etiology; more was at play than toxicity. The most common manifestations of this type of mad fury, Burton thought, were *lycanthropia* (belief that one has turned into a wolf), *hydrophobia*, and Chorea Sti Viti. The latter, he remarked, had been discussed in prior medical literature by Paracelsus, who 'bragged' about the number of persons he cured of it, and by Schenck von Grafenberg. The Arabs, Burton added, gesturing towards a comparative medical nosography, called it a type of palsy.[51]

As the term 'chorea' came increasingly in the sixteenth and seventeenth centuries to be disengaged from the clerical stronghold and integrated into medical debate, discussions of the affliction shifted: from an emphasis on demons, followed by a nosography describing earthquakes, plagues, famines, paroxysms, and the 'vital spirits' in the work of Paracelsus, and claims to melancholy and insanity among others, a new scene emerged for the medical interpretation of this affliction. 'Chorea' was now being described as a nervous and psychomotor condition afflicting individuals as well as larger groups. Not only did *chorea*, *chorea lasciva*, and Chorea Sancti Viti describe the medieval dancing mania, with its swarms of people dancing and disrupting public order, these terms now came to describe all sorts of convulsions, motor spasms, and tics. The popular and semi-religious dancing 'plague' was conjoined with a wide range of physiological symptoms to make boisterous dance and sudden movements a common kinetic event, now a neurological disease as vague as it was seemingly widespread.

BACCHEGGIAVA: POISONOUS WINDS AND FERTILE MINDS

Choreomania's *translatio* into the realm of neurological and physiological theory endured. The idea that choreomania was provoked by a combination of organic factors and cultural habit, and was thus curable by the same, prevailed throughout much of the seventeenth century. Theories of tarantism (the medical disorder

and cultural practices associated with the tarantella), which I discuss further in chapter 7, amalgamated popular dancing, music, and falls, along with various other symptoms, including hallucination, melancholy, insanity, and poison. Medical approaches to tarantism in the seventeenth century typically argued that poisonous spider bites provoking spasmodic motions, lethargy, dancing, and melancholic fits of despair were cured through music and dancing. The dancing, as in Strasbourg, was at once a symptom of disease and its cure. Although medical views in Italy differed as to the causes and forms of the tarantula disease (tarantism) and the specific operations of its accompanying music and dances (tarantellas), a proliferation of theories in the fifteenth, sixteenth, and seventeenth centuries set popular dance practices into the pages of medical lore. From *De venenis* [Of Venom] (Venice, 1492) by Santes de Ardoynis (dates unknown) to *Cornucopiae latinae linguae* [Cornucopia of the Latin Language] (Basle, 1536) by Niccolò Perotti (1429–1480), *Genialum dierum* [Genial Days] (Paris, 1539) by Alexander ab Alexandro (1461–1523), *Commentarii secundo aucti, in libros sex pedacii dioscoridis* [Second, Expanded Commentary, in Six Books] (Venice, 1560) by Petrus Andreas Mattioli (1501–1577), *De venenis et morbis venenosis tractatus locupletissimi* [Of the Treatment of Venom and Poisonous Substances] (Venice, 1584) by Hieronymus Mercurialis (1530–1606), and *Centum historiae* [A Hundred Historical Observations and Medical Cases] (Venice, 1621) by Epifanio Ferdinando (1569–1638), authors proffered toxic etiologies, according to which the dancing stemmed directly from the physiological effects of the spider's venom on a person's humours and vital or animal spirits; and psychic etiologies, citing lonely people's abuse of the so-called tarantula dances to dance and wear bright colours, feigning that they had been bitten. Most authors offered a combined approach, by which the spider's venom created a disturbance in the person's animal spirits, which were also cured by music and dancing. By inciting people to dance and thus to sweat, the music helped dispel noxious substances through glands activated by vigorous motion in the summer heat.[52] Ferdinando called this vigorous

51. Burton, *The Anatomy of Melancholy*, 121–125.

52. See Santes de Ardoynis, *De venenis* (Venice: Bernardinus Rizus, 1492); Niccolò Perotti, *Cornucopiae latinae linguae* (Basle: J. Walder, 1536 [first published 1521]); Alexander ab Alexandro, *Genialum dierum* (Paris: Riogny, 1539); Petrus Andreas Mattioli, *Commentarii secundo aucti, in libros sex pedacii dioscoridis* (Venice: Valgrisiana, 1560); and Hieronymus Mercurialis, *De venenis et morbis venenosis tractatus locupletissimi* (Venice: Paulum Meietum, 1584).

dancing *baccheggiava*, after the Bacchic frenzy from which he thought it derived.[53] Alternative popular accounts, highlighted by dance historian Karen Lüdtke, suggest Satan was at the origin of the tarantellas, prompting witchy women to catch tarantulas and set them off to bite unsuspecting hosts.[54]

The Renaissance polymath Athanasius Kircher (1602–1680), in *Magnes, sive, De Arte Magnetica* [On the Art of Magnetic Phenomena] (1643), like Paracelsus, underscored the importance of music's ability to echo natural processes in the person's body. For Kircher, music aroused the afflicted persons to dance by creating a motion in the air, compelling them—by the pleasurable sensation this produced—to replicate the movement of the music through their bodies. Eventually, the movement and dancing caused the victim to sweat the venom right out and be restored to health. Kircher argued, in line with Paracelsus's theory of natural correspondences, that this process was achieved through a series of magnetic effects: stringed instruments moved the air, which was in turn moved. The air then penetrated the body through the faculties of reason and emotion, which were stirred in turn; they then stirred the vital spirits, compelling the person to dance. Dancing was thus neither a purely emotional nor a natural, animal, or even physiological function but the result of complex operations involving magnetic correspondences between music, air, mind, and vital spirits. The heat produced in the body led to the opening of the 'air holes' (or pores) through which poisonous winds and humours were exhaled. Dancing thus corresponded at once to the disorder and its cure; movements in spiders, in the air, and in musical instruments echoed one another. The world, in this view, was an ecological machine composed of parts, each of which, when

disturbed, affected another. Dance was naturally cause and consequence of other ecological phenomena; studies of science and dancing, poison and music, were completely enmeshed.

For the professor of medicine and anatomy at the University of Rome, Giorgio Baglivi (1668–1707), writing in his widely influential medical textbook *De praxi medica* [Of Medical Practice] (1699), the medical history of tarantism was part of the general history of poisons, connected to the history of music and dance.[55] He put forward a unified, 'mechanical doctrine of music, poison and dancing',[56] arguing that these were intimately related, and comparable to other animal sources of psychomotor disease such as those produced by rabid dog bites, which also caused an 'exaltation of the humors' and agitation.[57] But tarantism had a particularly close relation to music, which stimulated dancing, purging patients of the venom infiltrating their 'animal spirits' because of the tarantula's own tendency to dance to music by wiggling its furry legs.[58] The tarantula was thought mimetically to transfer its propensity to dance to the animals it stung.[59] Baglivi recommended dancing to relieve patients of tarantula bites, citing numerous case histories to prove this practice.

He also noted the way this practice gave rise to cultural traditions, enshrining the dancing in local lore and in the yearly festive calendar. Because of the mimetic relationship between humans and animals, the tarantula's poison, Baglivi argued, continued to act well after the first bite, perpetuating the affected person's need for dancing. Once attacked by a tarantula, in other words, one was infected more or less for life: symptoms re-emerged every year at harvest time, when the summer heat was most intense, aggravating the poisonous winds. This occasioned what Baglivi described as 'a long series

53. See e.g. Ernesto de Martino, *La terra del rimorso: Contributo a una storia religiosa del Sud* (Milan: Il Saggiatore, 1961), 140, English translation in Ernesto de Martino, *The Land of Remorse: A Study of Southern Italian Tarantism*, ed. and trans. Dorothy Louise Zinn (London: Free Association Books, 2005), 97n; Jerri Daboo, *Ritual, Rapture and Remorse: A Study of Tarantism and Pizzica in Salento* (Bern: Peter Lang, 2010), 134.

54. Karen Lüdtke, *Dances with Spiders: Crisis, Celebrity and Celebration in Southern Italy* (Oxford: Berghahn Books, 2009), 55–56. The literature on tarantism is vast. Especially pertinent here, the medieval origins of tarantism in the cult of St. Paul—adopted as protector saint of all those bitten by spiders—reaching back to ancient Greek (typically Dionysian) cults, is widely referenced in standard histories. See e.g. Lüdtke, *Dances with Spiders*, 55–64, and de Martino, *La terra del rimorso*, 228–241.

55. In Giorgio Baglivi, *The practice of physick, reduc'd to the ancient way of observations containing a just parallel between the wisdom and experience of the ancients, and the hypothesis's of modern physicians . . . Together with several new and curious dissertations; particularly of the tarantula and the nature of its poison: of the use and abuse of blistering plasters: of epidemical apoplexies, &c. . . . ,* 2nd ed. (London: D. Midwinter, B. Lintot, G. Strahan, J. Round, W. Taylor, J. Osborn and J. Clark, 1723), 334.

56. Baglivi, *The practice of physick*, 313.

57. Baglivi, *The practice of physick*, 315.

58. Baglivi, *The practice of physick*, 348–349.

59. Baglivi, *The practice of physick*, 349–350.

of evils, which would be very annoying to the patients, if they did not take due care of their health by dancing and balls'.[60] He cited the case of one woman who was stung by a tarantula and suffered the typical symptoms of tarantism—lethargy, listlessness—'but by dancing according to the Custom of the Country, turn'd them off, and was very well that Year. But every Year after, about the wonted Revival of the Poison, her Toes were seiz'd with a most violent Pain . . . . The lady being oblig'd to dance, after the Exercise was over, found her self presently cur'd of the foremention'd Symptoms of her Toes and whole Body'.[61]

The poison's effects recalled the symptoms of melancholy, what Baglivi called the 'green sickness', and other diseases, echoing Burton's attribution of St. Vitus's dance to melancholy. 'Many of these persons are never well but among graves, and in solitary places', Baglivi wrote; 'and they'll lay themselves along on a bier, as if they were really dead; they'll throw themselves into a pit, as if they were in despair. Maids and women, otherwise chaste enough, without any regard to modesty, fall a sighing, howling, and into very indecent motions, discovering their nakedness: they love to be tossed to and again in the air, and the like. There are some', he added, 'that will rowl themselves in the dirt like swine . . . . And there are some that take a great pleasure in running'.[62] Baglivi noted that the symptoms of tarantism also resembled malignant fever, with pains in the heart, difficulty breathing, strange irregularity and disorder of the pulse, and a 'sudden and almost fatal failure of the animal and vital actions'. This meant that doctors often misdiagnosed patients (as his father had frequently done), until the patient's relations sent for musicians. When the patients then started to dance—one 'fairly danced himself off the stage'[63]—the diagnosis was revised. From then on, only music and dance would be employed to cure them.

Women's tendency to engage in the tarantella, particularly when they were suffering from heartbreak or otherwise lacking in the 'Benefit of free Converse with Men', should not, however, Baglivi added, lead one to believe that all cases of tarantism were feigned.[64] Nevertheless, some were. 'Here it must not be conceal'd', he wrote, 'that tho' in our Country there is really such a Thing as the Poison of the Tarantula, and Persons infected with it; yet Women, that make up a great Part of that Number, very frequently counterfeit it under the Mask of its usual Symptoms'. They did this when they were suffering from loneliness and seeking respite from the mundanity, trials, and tribulations of daily life: 'whether they be under the Power of Love, or have lost their Fortunes, or meet with any of those Evils that are peculiar to Women, they never leave poring upon the mournful Object, till they run into Despair, or downright Melancholy, or at least are upon the Borders of it. And then they are also under a Disadvantage of living a solitary Sort of Life, like that of Nuns'.[65] Because, moreover, these women were young and excitable, liable to bouts of 'mopishness', they were particularly well disposed to seek this form of dancing, Baglivi thought, since it was normally reserved only for those stung by the tarantula. 'The Climate is sultry, their Constitution is of the same Nature, their Food hot and very nourishing, and their Life early', Baglivi wrote. 'Partly from the former, and partly from the latter of these Causes, 'tis no rare thing with them to turn mopish and melancholy: No wonder then, if they be mightily delighted with Variety of Musick and Dancing; whence they feign themselves to be stung by the Tarantula, on purpose to enjoy the agreeable Diversion of Musick, which is only allow'd to such Persons; and then the Sham passes the better, for that the Pretext is accompany'd with a real Paleness of Face, Sadness, Difficulty of Breathing, Sorrow of Heart, a depraved Imagination, and the other Symptoms of the pretended, rather than true Poison of the Tarantula'.[66] This conjunction of factors, predisposing women to fake poisoning in order to be able to dance and enjoy the 'musical Entertainment' which was 'so very

---

60. Baglivi, *The practice of physick*, 314.

61. Baglivi, *The practice of physick*, 355.

62. Baglivi, *The practice of physick*, 331.

63. Baglivi, *The practice of physick*, 332

64. Baglivi, *The practice of physick*, 334–335. 'There are some Persons', he notes, 'otherwise both Learned and Religious, who not being satisfied of this upon the Credit of Persons that were stung, have made the Experiment upon themselves, . . . [and] have confessed, [that] unless the Musick had been ready at hand, their Lives would have gone for't' (335).

65. Baglivi, *The practice of physick*, 334.

66. Baglivi, *The practice of physick*, 334–335.

agreeable' to them, granted the merrymaking rites a local name, "Il' Carnevaletto delle Donne" (The Women's Little Carnival).[67] Shamming was at the heart of medical and popular imaginations of the tarantella.

'EVERYTHING IS EXTRAORDINARY IN THIS DISEASE'

Chorea and tarantism increasingly came to be understood in the ensuing centuries as cultural practices masking an underlying physiological condition suggesting the duplicity of theatre. Chorea and tarantism were worrisome on account of their spontaneity and, paradoxically, the way this spontaneity seemed, in the eyes of their observers, to be shammed. This section turns to the translatio from early modern medical theories of chorea (and tarantism) in the sixteenth and seventeenth centuries to the growing amalgamation of physiological and cultural histories in eighteenth- and nineteenth-century medicine, describing the associated spaces within which chorea and choreomania became discursively allied. So whereas Italian theories of tarantism offer a somewhat parallel history (and genealogy) of the 'dancing disease' (and a somewhat separate correlative or institutional space), nineteenth-century narratives in northern Europe did not fail to make the link between these 'dancing' forms. I will return to the Orientalist appropriation of southern Italian dance histories in chapter 7.

Paracelsus's observations ultimately set the discourse on St. Vitus's dance squarely in line with a growing body of literature on organic disorders of the nervous system. Now a reference not only to the medieval dancing mania, 'chorea' came to refer to every sort of spasm as well. In 1686, Thomas Sydenham (1624–1689), known as the 'English Hippocrates', reprised Paracelsus's Chorea Sancti Viti to designate two things: first, *chorea minor*, which Sydenham used to describe a neurological affection now also often referred to as Sydenham's chorea (or simply chorea). This described an involuntary, spasmodic motion of the limbs, typically among young children. The condition, for Sydenham, had to be distinguished from *chorea major*, the historical event—the mass dances—popularly also known as St. Vitus's dance. Yet the similarity of the terms *chorea minor* and *chorea major*—and the shorthand for both, 'chorea', typically shortened from Chorea Sancti Viti (St. Vitus's dance)—prompted continued comparisons between the 'major' and 'minor' forms, as well as persistent medical attempts to link these historically as well as biologically.

Sustained medical interest in all types of chorea waned in the eighteenth century, appearing in only a few accounts reliant, for the most part, on historical lore. John Harris (c. 1666–1719), a scientist and theologian endeavouring to make scientific advances at the Royal Society public, put forward a definition of Chorea Sancti Viti in his *Lexicon technicum, or an universal English dictionary of arts and sciences* (1704–1710) that largely overlooked Sydenham's still relatively rare clinical usage of the St. Vitus term but recuperated earlier eyewitness accounts. Borrowing from the early seventeenth-century physician Gregor Horst, discussed earlier, Harris described Chorea Sancti Viti as a nebulous mental disorder compounded by a general 'restlessness' of the limbs. Chorea Sancti Viti, Harris wrote, was 'a sort of Madness, . . . wherein the Person affected . . . ran hither and thither dancing to the last gasp if they were not forcibly hindred'. Horst, Harris reported,

spoke with some Women, who paying a yearly Visit to the Chapel of Saint

67. Baglivi, *The practice of physick*, 335. More recent theories of tarantism and the tarantella suggest they should be set alongside other forms of ecstatic trance and possession, following the pioneering work of I. M. Lewis (1930–2014), among others; and as a potent form of music therapy, following Gilbert Rouget's influential *La musique et la transe* (1980). Rouget, writing in a long line of cultural ethnographers and ethnopsychiatrists from the 1950s and 1960s onwards, including András Zempléni, Mircea Eliade (1907–1986), and others, saw tarantism—and possession more generally—as a therapeutic phenomenon, an institutionalized form of hysteria, and its socialization. In this view, the hysteric person (the tarantulee) can perform her hysteria in public, 'coming out' with her inner misfortunes and, although not curing these, expressing them socially. See e.g. Gilbert Rouget, *Music and Trance: A Theory of the Relations between Music and Possession*, trans. and rev. Brunhilde Biebuyck in collaboration with the author (Chicago: University of Chicago Press, 1985), 164–165; de Martino, *La terra del rimorso*; Fabrizio Manco, 'Bodied Experiences of Madness: A *Tarantato*'s Perception', in Birringer and Fenger, eds., *Tanz und WahnSinn/Dance and ChoreoMania*, 264–283. Manco adopts an ethnographic and auto-ethnographic approach following Rouget and de Martino, calling his analysis a 'shamanistic interpretation' emphasizing anthropomorphic transformation (274), and tarantism a 'living archive', 'transgressive' and transformative, 'between madness and grace, between mortification and bliss': *tarantati* in his view are not so much possessed and healed as 'dis-possessed' (281–282). For a broad but useful overview of music therapy in the Mediterranean and elsewhere, see e.g. Peregrine Horden, ed., *Music as Medicine: The History of Music Therapy since Antiquity* (Aldershot, Hants: Ashgate, 2000).

Vitus, . . . near the City Ulme in Swedeland, have been taken with such a *violent fit of dancing Night and Day*, together with a sort of *Frantickness in the Mind*, that they fall together like so many People in Extasies; and are sensible of little or nothing for a Year together till next May, about which time they perceive themselves so tormented with a *Restlessness in their Limbs*, that they are forced to repair to the same place again about the Feast of Saint Vitus to dance.[68]

St. Vitus's dance in Harris's view was a psychiatric disorder compounded by physical symptoms wrapped up into popular lore. It was curious but benefited from the direct observation of earlier authors. So, too, the French physician François Boissier Sauvages de la Croix (1706–1767), in *Nosologie méthodique* [Methodical Nosology] (1772), offered a then relatively rare account of St. John's Day dancers suffering from what he described as 'epidemic madness', as they ran through streets, wreathed, singing and leaping to the point of exhaustion.[69]

But in the early nineteenth century, a surge of new writings on chorea appeared, as emerging interest in nervous diseases brought a new currency to the term *chorea*, and so, too, to its curious prehistory. From *An essay on chorea Sancti Viti*, the 1805 thesis of Felix Robertson (1781–1865) at the College of Physicians and Surgeons at the University of Pennsylvania, to Étienne-Michel Bouteille's *Traité de la chorée, ou, Danse de St. Guy* [Treatise on Chorea, or, Dance of St. Vitus] (1810),[70] Henri Bouvier's (1799–1877) *De la chorée ou danse de Saint-Guy* [On Chorea or the Dance of St. Vitus] (1859), and *On Chorea and Choreiform Affections* (1894) by the Canadian physician Sir William Osler (1849–1919), drawn from his observations at the Infirmary for Diseases of the Nervous System in Philadelphia,

chorea was emerging as a disease of choice for medical study. In France alone, over fifty medical treatises on chorea appeared between 1810 and 1889, further confusing disorders of muscular locomotion with popular dance histories.

Yet, as Osler wrote, chorea was still poorly understood and hardly constituted a recognizable category of medical disease. It characterized, instead, any number of vague spasmodic conditions. Details varied in the descriptions offered by medical writers, he wrote: 'there have been scores of specific designations, indicating the quality of the movement, the locality involved, &c'. But chorea continued to baffle. 'In the gradual growth of our knowledge of spasmodic affections this confusion has perhaps been inevitable', Osler argued. But 'even to-day it is not possible to make a satisfactory etiological classification, and the best we can do is to separate certain well-defined clinical forms, to which we may attempt to limit the use of the term chorea'.[71] Osler noted that confusion arose from Sydenham's unfortunate terminological choice, which centuries of usage had perpetuated and magnified. Although for Osler the 'epidemic disorder of motion' that Paracelsus had first described as Chorea Sancti Viti had a 'sort of prescriptive right to the name', Sydenham had muddled the issue by applying this same set of names—chorea and St. Vitus's dance—to 'an affection of a totally different nature . . . so that to these two forms, known respectively as chorea major and chorea minor, and each as St. Vitus's Dance, the name will doubtless cling'.[72]

As Osler bemoaned, attached to St. Vitus's dance 'comes a long series of motor disorders in which the term has been freely used—the habit spasms and the various forms of tic so often confounded with chorea minor, the so-called symptomatic choreas, the chronic, the hereditary, the congenital, and the spastic forms, and the

68. John Harris, 'Chorea Sancti Viti', in *Lexicon technicum: or, an universal English dictionary of arts and sciences: explaining not only the terms of art, but the arts themselves*, 2 vols., vol. 1 (London: D. Brown, et al., 1704), n.p. Emphasis mine. See Gregor Horst (1578–1636), *Observationum medicinalium singularium*, 4 vols. (Ulm: Typis Saurianis, 1628).

69. François Boissier Sauvages de la Croix, *Nosologie méthodique, ou distribution des maladies en classes, en genres, et en espèces, suivant l'esprit de Sydenham, & la méthode des botanistes . . .* , 10 vols., vol. 2 (Lyon: Chez Jean-Marie Bruyset, Imprimeur-Libraire, 1772), 735.

70. For Bouteille, 'tout est extraordinaire dans cette Maladie; son nom est ridicule, ses symptômes singuliers, son caractère univoque, sa cause inconnue, son traitement problématique. De graves auteurs ont douté de son existence; d'autres l'ont cru simulée, quelques-uns l'ont réputée surnaturelle ou magique; le célèbre [William] *Cullen* semble incliner à penser que l'imagination y joue un grand rôle, et [Joseph] *Lieutaud* pour ne l'avoir jamais observée, s'est permis de la nier'. He adds that the seventeenth-century physicians Platter, Hortius, and Sennert are the first really to have accounted for it. In Étienne-Michel Bouteille, 'Préface', in *Traité de la chorée, ou, Danse de St. Guy* (Paris: Vincard, 1810), n.p.

71. Sir William Osler, *On Chorea and Choreiform Affections* (Philadelphia: P. Blakiston, Son & Co, 1894), 1.

72. Osler, *On Chorea*, 1.

pre- and post-hemiplegic disorders of motion'.[73] Sydenham's chorea, or *chorea minor*, referred to 'an acute disease of childhood . . . characterized by irregular, involuntary movements' and a 'variable amount of psychical disturbance'. It was often associated with arthritis and endocarditis (an infection of the heart valve) and usually considered as a kind of neurosis, although more severe cases involving heart and joint complications suggested that it may have been caused by a 'specific poison'.[74] But *chorea major* was the St. Vitus's dance of the past, known from chronicles dating back hundreds of years. In it, Osler noted, 'psychical impressions, emotional disturbances, and imitation play the most important *role*'. A third kind of chorea, Osler remarked, included 'choreiform affections' and 'pseudo-choreas', referring to 'various forms of habit spasm or tic'. These were minor movement disorders, generally, like hysteroepilepsy, which I will describe further in chapter 6, only partly involuntary. Finally, 'symptomatic' or 'secondary' choreas constituted 'chronic disorders of motion, which depend upon degenerative and irritative lesions of the motor cortex or path'. These included pre- and post-hemiplegic disorders of movement (disorders preceding or following paralysis of one side of the body), 'the so-called spastic choreas', 'and many of the cases of congenital and chronic chorea'. These were complex disorders, accompanying and often provoked by other degenerative conditions. 'One malady alone in this group may be separated as an independent affection', he added, 'the chronic progressive form, so-called Huntington's chorea'.[75] But Huntington's chorea, too, continued in popular terminology to be called 'St. Vitus's dance' or '*that* disorder' well into the nineteenth and twentieth centuries; and it continued to be stigmatized. As historian Alice Wexler has shown, sufferers have until recently continued to be hidden away by their families for fear of ostracization.[76] As with many neurodegenerative and psychiatric conditions, the unfamiliarity of the sufferer's irregular gestures and apparent lack of control provoked

mistrust. And while physicians generally agreed that this was neither the work of the devil nor of the vital spirits, bodily agitation worried all those still unsure just what this was.

Definitions and classifications proliferated. In some cases, chorea remained a mostly psychiatric disorder, taking on different hues variously emphasizing the relationship between mind and matter, action and the imagination. In *Des névroses* (1864), the French-educated Russian psychiatrist Alexandre Axenfeld (1825–1876) argued that chorea tended to be complicated by manic delirium.[77] He was referring to Sydenham's chorea, what he called the 'real chorea' (*chorée légitime* or *chorée vulgaire*, also *petite danse de Saint Guy, danse, cadence,* etc.), though manic delirium also appeared in *chorea major* (choreomania) (alternatively the *dansomanie* or *danse de Saint-Guy, Saint-Whyt,* or *Saint-Modeste*).[78] For others, chorea was primarily mechanical. The Scottish physician William Aitken (1825–1892) listed 'St. Vitus's dance—chorea' in his widely read medical handbook, *The Science and Practice of Medicine* (1857), among half a dozen 'cephalic diseases, characterized by exalted, perverted, or suspended functional activity'. These included hysteria, catalepsy, epilepsy, cerebral dropsy (hydrocephalus), sunstroke, and insanity. But Aitken also referred St. Vitus's dance to its historical precedent, as if it boasted roots in the dancing mania that had swept through medieval Europe and now occurred in only rare and isolated cases. 'The history of this disease is a sad picture of superstition', he wrote. 'As late as the close of the fifteenth century it does not appear to have been studied by physicians, but was supposed to depend on supernatural causes or "demoniacal possession." In Germany it was said for two centuries to have been epidemic, and the patients, probably many of them maniacs, were wont to join in frantic dances'. Aitken's account underscored the psychosomatic quality of the events, arguing that masses and hymns may have 'cured' the dancers 'simply by the influence of the intense moral impression'.[79] The 'effects' of the religious 'performances' were on their own sufficient to quiet the dancers for a while.[80]

73. Osler, *On Chorea*, 1.

74. Osler, *On Chorea*, 2.

75. On the distinctions between Huntington's chorea, Sydenham's chorea, and chorea major, see also Aubert, 'Charcot Revisited', 155.

76. Alice R. Wexler, 'Chorea and Community in a Nineteenth-Century Town', *Bulletin of the History of Medicine* 76.3 (2002): 495–527.

77. Alexandre Axenfeld, *Des névroses* (Paris: Germer Baillière Libraire-Éditeur, 1864), 504.

78. Axenfeld, *Des névroses*, 498–499.

79. William Aitken, *The Science and Practice of Medicine*, 2 vols., vol. 1 (London: Charles Griffin and Company, 1864), 333.

80. Aitken, *The Science and Practice of Medicine*, 333.

Aitken's story of historical precedent bolstered the increasingly popular idea that the medieval dancing manias were but poorly understood episodes of neurological disease. The German comparative pathologist August Hirsh (1817–1894) offered one of the most succinct accounts of this discursive genealogy, while perpetuating the rapprochement between neuropathological and psychiatric diagnosis. In his article 'Chorea', in the third volume of his *Handbook of Geographical and Historical Pathology* (1883–1886), he notes in a chapter titled 'Neuroses' the tortuous paths the name 'St. Vitus' has taken:

> The name of St. Vitus' dance (Chorea Sancti Viti) was originally given to a hysterical psychopathy which appeared in the fourteenth and fifteenth centuries in some parts of western Germany in the form of the dancing mania (*Tanzwuth*, choreomania); it is still commemorated in the grotesque 'procession of the jumping saints' which is held every Whitsuntide at Echternach (Luxemburg). The same word (chorea) was subsequently used by Sydenham to designate the spasmodic malady which is now universally known under that name; and from that time a distinction began to be made between a 'chorea Germanorum' (the 'greater' St. Vitus' dance, or choreomania) and a 'chorea Anglorum' (the 'lesser' St. Vitus' dance, or neurosis of the central organs characterised by incoherent action of the muscles). Great as are the merits of Sydenham's classical description of this disease, . . . still his choice of a name for the malady he described has had a confusing effect on the views of his successors.[81]

Physicians such as Hirsh were well aware that St. Vitus's dance was not at once the medieval processions and the jerks and tics described by Sydenham. Yet, as he and Osler, among others, complained, the continued conflation of these irregular gestures tied them together in

an increasingly thorny complex, what I am calling choreomania, an entangled set of discourses linking irregular gesture and unruly popular fête. Awareness of the faulty conflation between phenomena did not lessen the concept's pull in the popular and medical imaginations; on the contrary, throughout the nineteenth century, the continued imbrication of tics, spasms, falling, frothing, music and dance, boisterous eruptions, heightened emotion, theatricality, and fêtes further gelled into a complex of ideas about irregular and unpredictable movement in public space.

PROLIFERATING DIAGNOSES: ANOTHER HISTORY OF AMBIGUITY

Collective movements and individual movement disorders involving spasms and tics bewildered and frustrated medical historians and neurologists confronted with what appeared to be sheer hermeneutic impenetrability. Spasms did not just denote unbidden motion, but a zone of indiscernibility and indetermination; spasms provoked observation but resisted closure. Osler, like many of his contemporaries, wrote almost exclusively about *chorea minor*, casting aside any serious study of *chorea major*, its reputedly epidemic, collective form, as the interest of *chorea major* in relation to *chorea minor* was, Osler thought, historiographical at best and impossible to grasp in retrospect.[82] But the problematic relation between the two types of event continued to plague medical discourse. Andrew Davidson lamented the unhelpful analogy between *chorea minor* and *chorea major* in his 1867 article on choreomania in Madagascar, arguing that 'this disease, which we shall name Choreomania, was . . . originally called chorea, or Saint Vitus's dance; but these terms are now inseparably, though inaptly, applied to another and perfectly distinct nervous affection. From this change in name, along with the disappearance of the original chorea from Europe,

81. Hirsch, *Handbook of Geographical and Historical Pathology*, vol. 3, 531.

82. Although confusion between Sydenham's chorea, rheumatic fever, and the so-called epidemic chorea of the Middle Ages has subsided, scholars and medical practitioners who continue to bemoan (and discuss) this confusion include, among others, A. C. Eftychiadis and T. S. N. Chen, 'Historical Note: Saint Vitus and His Dance', *Journal of Neurology, Neurosurgery and Psychiatry* 70 (2001): 14; and, previously, David Chas. Schechter, 'St. Vitus' Dance and Rheumatic Disease', *New York State Journal of Medicine* 75 (1975): 1091–1102. Schechter wrote: 'the connotation of St. Vitus with rheumatic disease by both the laity and medical profession is so commonplace that its incongruity is hardly noticed'. He goes on to discuss 'the origins of that bizarre and ill-begotten eponymic relationship', citing Hecker extensively (1091).

considerable confusion has arisen'.[83] Davidson cited as an example of this terminological confusion *Study of Medicine* (1822), by physician John Mason Good (1764–1827), adding that 'some authors have classed with choreomania many anomalous forms of nervous manifestation, some of which are evidently the result of organic disease of the nervous centres'.[84] The real chorea, Davidson said, was—except in furthest Africa (as he claimed to observe [chapter 8]) and other non-European locations—extinct.

Ergotism was also often highlighted as a possible cause: a form of rye poisoning, ergotism can provoke severe hallucinations and convulsions, as well as a gangrenous blackening of the limbs. Yet virtually none of the dances described as choreomanias involved such severe degenerative symptoms. Only one case, the one discussed in chapter 2 involving a small group of men and women dancing in a churchyard in c. 1021 in Kölbigk, may plausibly have involved some ergotism. As reported by the German physician Daniel Sennert (1572–1637), one of the dancers' arms purportedly fell off when another one tried to pull on it.[85] This could have been caused by ergotism, given the severe decomposition of the limbs that occurs when ergot poisoning is advanced.[86] But to suggest that ergotism alone successfully spurred on dozens, hundreds, or occasionally even thousands of people to shake their bodies in all or even most so-called dancing manias seems misguided at best. If occasional dancers suffered from ergotism or epilepsy, and others danced alongside them, these were not causes but accidents; at most, catalysts. Yet the ergot hypothesis remains strong, and since about the sixteenth century dancing manias of every sort have been attributed to ergot poisoning. Occasional studies, after Paracelsus, have also compared dancing manias to epilepsy, which, however, like chorea, does not occur epidemically.[87]

Rheumatic fever, which Sydenham discussed but had not considered a form of chorea, was eventually also associated with choreiform affections, in the wake of the work of English physician Richard Bright (1789–1858) on chorea and rheumatism, *Reports of Medical Cases* (1831), adding one more elusive condition to the already extensive chorea family. Bright claimed that 'the instances of the combination and alteration of rheumatism and chorea are very numerous' and suggested that the 'irritation' that caused both was communicated to the spine via the pericardium (the sac enclosing the heart) when it was inflamed.[88] This organic lesion accounted for chorea and rheumatism's similarity and apparent interchangeability: one condition not infrequently morphed into the other, and vice versa. Bright also thought that the cerebrospinal mass might be involved in this transmutation but that that was less likely.[89]

As Bouteille wrote in *Traité de la Chorée, ou Danse de Saint Guy* [Treatise on Chorea, or St. Vitus's dance] (1810), chorea baffled: 'everything is extraordinary in this disease', he grumbled. 'Its name is ridiculous, its symptoms odd, its cause unknown, its treatment problematic'.[90]

83. Andrew Davidson, 'Choreomania: An Historical Sketch, with Some Account of an Epidemic Observed in Madagascar', *Edinburgh Medical Journal* 13.2 (1867): 124–136, 124.

84. Davidson, 'Choreomania', 125.

85. On Sennert, see Backman, *Religious Dances*, 307.

86. On ergotism, see e.g. S. Wright, 'An Experimental Inquiry into the Physiological Action of Ergot of Rye', *Edinburgh Medical and Surgical Journal* 52 (1839): 293–334, and 52 (1840): 1–35; Donaldson et al., 'The Dancing Plague', 203; Caroline De Costa, 'St Anthony's Fire and Living Ligatures: A Short History of Ergometrine', *Lancet* 359 (2002): 1768–1770; Mervyn J. Eadie, 'Convulsive Ergotism: Epidemics of Serotonin Syndrome?' *Lancet Neurology* 2.7 (2003): 429–434; J. M. Massey and E. W. Massey, 'Ergot, the "Jerks", and Revivals', *Clinical Neuropharmacology* 7.1 (1984): 99–105.

87. Donaldson et al. cite this hypothesis in 'The Dancing Plague', 202. On epilepsy, see also the standard history by Oswei Temkin, *The Falling Sickness: A History of Epilepsy from the Greeks to the Beginnings of Modern Neurology*, 2nd rev. ed. (Baltimore: Johns Hopkins University Press, 1994).

88. In Eftychiadis and Chen, 'Saint Vitus and His Dance', 4; see Schechter, 'St. Vitus' Dance', 1091–1102, esp. 1097–1099. See Richard Bright, *Reports of Medical Cases, selected with a view to illustrating symptoms and cures of diseases by reference to morbid anatomy* (London: Longman, 1831), n.p. On chorea and rheumatism, see also Alfred Muhry and Edward G. Davis, *Observations on the comparative state of medicine in France, England, and Germany, during a journey into these countries in the year 1835* (Philadelphia: A. Waldie, 1838), 334; Germain Sée, *De la chorée. Rapports du rhumatisme et des maladies du cœur avec les affections nerveuses convulsives* (Paris: Baillère, 1850); Henri Roger, *Recherches cliniques sur la chorée, sur le rhumatisme et sur les maladies du cœur chez les enfants* (Paris: Asselin, 1866).

89. As Eftychiadis and Chen note in 'Saint Vitus and His Dance', Bright could not have known that rheumatism is caused by infection, something only discovered in the 1930s (14).

90. See n70 here. See also Schechter, 'St. Vitus' Dance', 1099.

Persistent terminological confusion plagued physicians trying to understand, much less treat, this disease. As the American professor of cardiovascular and thoracic surgery David Charles Schechter wrote in 'St. Vitus' Dance and Rheumatic Disease' (1975), 'although it did not take long to find out that Sydenham's selection of the St. Vitus cognomen was inappropriate to the clinical state which he had described, countless publications continued to bear that title'. The usage of 'St. Vitus' was condoned partly out of deference to Sydenham, partly from force of habit, but chiefly because the terminology sank deeper and deeper into a morass of synonyms, including, most notably, 'the dance', 'chorea', 'saltus', 'saltatio', and 'morbus of St. Vitus', also referred to as St. Guy in France and St. John or St. Modestus elsewhere. 'In their sincere desire to abandon the names of saints, as Paracelsus had tried to do', Schechter wrote, 'diverse authors instead muddied the waters even more by interjecting the terms *tanzsucht, morbus sacer, morbus gesticularius, morbus mentaphora, morbus germanorum, orchestromania, ballismus, tanzplatz, epilepsia saltatoria, epilepsia procursiva, epilepsia mira, jactatio epileptica, gesticulatio spastica, synclonus chorea, synclonus saltans, convulsiones rhythmicae, tripudatio spastica*, and so forth',[91] a testament to the power of Sydenham's use of the chorea trope—which played not the sole but arguably a significant role in the birth and miscegenation of the extended chorea family.

In Sir Thomas Watson's terms, chorea was composed of a motley array of variations. Each offered 'points of resemblance, like . . . the different members of a large family, in which the individuals have the same general cast of features, and yet preserve each his particular identity'.[92] This genealogical metaphor enabled not a few further comparisons, extending the scope of chorea further still in a translatio from collective to individual disorder and back; and from a demonic and psychiatric as well as neurological plane to an epidemiological one. The dancing disease in this sense comes into the nineteenth century from late medieval and early modern histories of medical iconoclasm at the edges of academic practice, revealing an archive in motion, an archival repertoire passing through discursive fields, reconstituting itself and them along the way. 'Chorea' came to denote not just a conflation of individual and ecological tremors and tics but the opacity of movement, gesture eluding resolution. Chorea became the disorder of volatility par excellence: a disorder whose definition, emerging between observation and hearsay, defied the closure of representation. Chorea, if anything, gestured only obscurity.

In the next chapter, convulsions take on a theatricality all their own, with the so-called Convulsionaries of Saint-Médard in the 1730s, passing between their preferred gravesite in the suburbs of Paris and the theatrical stage, where they are mocked for their exaggerated and at times patently feigned religious enthusiasm doubling as popular revolt. With the Convulsionaries and other enthusiasts, monomania also appears on the scene of psychiatric history, describing a highly theatrical, heightened enthusiasm, including one for national dance forms. The next chapter thus suggests a translatio between religious theatre and modern psychiatry, as medical authors map convulsive expressions of high affect onto the emergent disorders of nation. From the comic dramatizations of buffoonish anti-establishmentarians to vaudeville representations of exaggerated zeal, choreomania arises as a disorder of excess enthusiasm reaching beyond its subjects' bodies into politically contested public space.

91. Schechter, 'St. Vitus' Dance', 1098–1099.
92. Watson, *Lectures on the principles and practice of physic*, 645.

4

The Convulsionaries
Antics on the French Revolutionary Stage

The mark or signature of possession . . . will have a fundamental importance in Western medical and religious history: [it is] the convulsion.

—Foucault, *Abnormal: Lectures at the Collège de France 1974–1975* (2003)

CONVULSIONS APPEAR on the scene of modern science as quintessentially illegible signs yet, as such, paradoxically, also as prime markers of science's capacity to 'read' and to decipher. In Foucault's analysis, convulsions represent an 'immense spider-notion' spanning seventeenth- and eighteenth-century religion and mysticism, medicine and psychiatry, reason and unreason, and modern disciplinary reforms.[1] But convulsions also typically succeeded in generating a few laughs; there was no better place, this chapter argues, to poke fun at these uncertain markers of religious and scientific 'truth' than at the theatre. Histrionic performances of convulsionary activity in Parisian cemeteries and on the vaudeville stage prefigure the popular dances of the Parisian cabarets, all signs of a popular culture thriving on the dramatic potential of comic contortions and public display. For themselves and for their audiences, convulsionary carousers produced outrageous scenes of spontaneous ferment, 'acting out' a politics of volatility and contagious enthusiasm indicating the potential for political change.

At stake, then, in this chapter, is the show of gestural excess in the public sphere, as it comes to be mapped onto political moments of contestation. These scenes constitute choreographies of protest in the sense Foster describes—self-organizing bodies acting (and *acting out*) in public space, at times with the aim of achieving distinct political ends. But these scenes also reveal shows of exaggeration and gestural surplus that fall just short of the direct mobilization of collective energy Foster imagines. The gestural theatre expressed in the following scenes is indirect, often ambiguous, and indubitably zany in its exaggeration; these are bodies that perform too much, hyperbolically, and so remain unconvincing. They are not smoothly persuasive—torque-like—but buffoonish, amateurish, and distorted. As Jana Braziel and Kathleen LeBesco argue in

---

1. Foucault, *Les anormaux*, 198 and 202–211.

their introduction to a special issue of *Women & Performance* (2005), Bakhtin, Georges Bataille (1897–1962), and others have theorized excess as a politically subversive force of cultural resistance; but excess is also, they argue, characteristic of particularly female and queer subjectivities.[2] The 'too muchness' of the feminine (and queer) conceit reveals a marginal status that keeps women and queers both to the side of and always protruding into public space.

Choreomania, in this respect a feminine and queer sort of excess, performs exuberant intrusion, 'too muchness' in the public sphere: not quite the calendrical upheaval of Bakhtinian carnival but everyday instances of gestural and affective extension, zones of intensity in which enthusiasts throw out their limbs at discomfiting angles and overperform their passions at the risk of falling into public ridicule. Unrestrained and highly demonstrative enthusiasm comes onto the discursive scene of scientific modernity implicitly in contrast to the grace and control of torque: a way of speaking and moving in public space that persuades without deceit, and inspires trust by the purposefulness and eloquence of measured and elegant gestures. The public sphere in this chapter thus becomes a space of pathological imitation as individuals and groups appear effusively to gesture their exuberant desire to exceed the bounds of the emergent nation by identifying with it 'too much'.

ENTHUSIASM, EXCESS, AND EXAGGERATION: LESSONS FROM ROUSSEAU AND KANT

In this respect feminine and queer, choreomania can be understood as a disorder not only of theatre but of exaggerated theatricality. As such, it is subversive, and marginal; choreomania plays out—*acts* out—in the peripheries of national becoming, surplus spaces represented by suburban cemeteries, by scientific illustration and footnotes. Choreomania represents a bifurcation in the long history of philosophical thought about enthusiasm, a concept that passes—translatios—into the sphere of neurological and psychiatric disorder by the mid-nineteenth century. Significantly, the scenes of enthusiasm this chapter foregrounds dramatize the theatricality of religious enthusiasm imagined as a disorder one spectates and, in spectating, can catch. This situates the modern discourse on choreomania in a long line of anti-theatrical thought counterposing the duplicity of theatre with the natural spontaneity of dance. Choreomania thus straddles two prejudices: anti-theatrical and choreophobic. Whereas dance, as I will show, appears (in Romantic discourse) natural, opposed to the fakery of theatre, excessive dance is equally pernicious. It becomes entangled in the anti-theatrical language of popular revolt.

In a long footnote to his notoriously anti-theatrical *Lettre à d'Alembert sur son article Genève* [Letter to d'Alembert] (1758), philosopher Jean-Jacques Rousseau (1712–1778) sets the stage for this comparison, indexed in the margins of his text. Rousseau draws the portrait of a 'simple' village dance, which he sets against the morally devastating effects of the theatres of Geneva. In the scene he offhandedly draws out, staged as a casual reminiscence, a few hundred soldiers and their officers have just returned from their military exercise and, after a meal, begin to dance around the local fountain. They perform a serpentine motion, in cadence, holding hands to the sound of fifes and drums. Soon, their wives, who had gone to sleep, open their windows and, drawn to the dancing and spirit of celebration, join in, along with their children, who are now also awake. A temporary suspension of the dancing ensues, as all and sundry embrace in this happy reunion. Rousseau's father, watching the event from his window with his son, turns to him and, embracing him, says: 'Jean-Jacques, love your country. See these good Genevese; they are all friends; they are all brothers; joy and concord rule among them'. Rousseau's father adds that one day Jean-Jacques will encounter other peoples, in other places, where such camaraderie does not exist. Rousseau, retrospectively meditating on the event, reflects on this expression of joy, which he sees as spontaneous and governed by the 'sentiments of Nature'. For Rousseau, paradoxically removed from the scene, this was quintessentially a 'public' joy. 'The only pure joy is public', he writes, 'warmed' 'in his heart' and 'through his eyes' at the sights and sounds, as well as the emotions, the spectacle of this spontaneous dance produces in him.[3]

---

2. Jana Evans Braziel and Kathleen LeBesco, 'Performing Excess', *Women & Performance: A Journal of Feminist Theory* 15.2 (2005): 9–13, 9.

3. Jean-Jacques Rousseau, *Lettre à d'Alembert sur son article Genève*, ed. Micheal Launay (Paris: Garnier-Flammarion, 1967), 248–249n1.

The concept of 'sublime enthusiasm' of Immanuel Kant (1724–1804), Rousseau's contemporary, sounds a greater note of caution. Kant described 'sublime enthusiasm' as an extreme form of the sublime, not a public but a highly private experience. Whereas the 'sublime' for Kant denotes the affective and philosophical experience of pleasure in one's own individual mastery over nature, 'sublime enthusiasm' suggests the heightened exaggeration of this experience. In the scenario Kant depicts, sublime enthusiasm comes to be epitomized in the heightened emotion experienced by remote spectators of the French Revolution. Carried away by the political possibilities afforded their neighbours, the spectators' sublimely enthusiastic bliss risks tipping them into blind pathological dementia and madness ('Wahnsinn'), excited by their unfettered imaginations.[4] They experience an extreme—pathological—form of spectatorship, in which their projected participation in a faraway show of enthusiastic revolution exists, Kant suggests, too enthusiastically in their minds. As such, they experience theatre; not the spontaneous, natural village theatre Rousseau depicts—so natural it is not theatre but artless common dance—but a theatre of enthusiastic imitation in which they have excessively imagined themselves to partake.

Kant's politically inflected concept of sublime enthusiasm informed the critique of religious enthusiasm of the English philosopher Isaac Taylor (1787–1865). In Taylor's estimation, such enthusiasm coincided with a surge of religious fanaticism similarly spurred on by high affect and performed through excessively and hypocritically demonstrative gestures. In *The Natural History of Enthusiasm*, which enjoyed eleven editions from its first publication in 1829 until 1868, and in his follow-up volume, *Fanaticism* (1833), Taylor sought to dissociate what he saw as true, reasonable, and rational religious piety from the shallow, exploitative, and feigned religiosity of an overzealous and increasingly missionary Christianity characterized by what he saw as illusoriness and 'vain exaggerations'.[5] This critique echoed earlier critiques of effusive religiosity put forward by, among others, the poet and priest John Langhorne (1735–1779),

in his *Letters on Religious Retirement, Melancholy, and Enthusiasm* (1762), in which he describes 'modern enthusiasm' as luxurious indulgence in religious passions leading to 'irregular and intemperate raptures' also occasionally bordering on insanity. The inconstant bodily demonstrativeness of religious enthusiasts that Langhorne described was at odds with the rational and discreet exercise of 'right devotion'.[6] Earlier still, the Earl of Shaftesbury had argued in 'A letter concerning enthusiasm to my Lord . . .' (1707) that critiques of folly and extravagance were more in vogue at the time of his writing than ever before. Enthusiasm, it seems, was subject to its own brand of enthusiastic rebuke.

The scientific literature on choreomania suggests that enthusiasm and theatre were two sides of a coin signalling a manic 'too muchness' quickly tipping into untrustworthiness and lunacy. But, as this chapter argues, the senseless 'too muchness' of religious and political enthusiasts also mapped onto a particular sort of national over-identification by the mid-nineteenth century, so that one could be too much a French or a Polish national or too much a dance lover. Choreomania, theorized by the early to mid-nineteenth century not only as an epidemic but also as a psychiatric disorder, suggests too much dancing and zeal of a national sort. Choreomania becomes, in the terms of pioneer psychiatrist Étienne Esquirol (1772–1840), a 'disease of civilizations', queering nationalism and religion alike. Shifting Foucault's analysis of modern discipline and psychiatry slightly away from a well-rehearsed focus on the 'great confinement'—characterized by punitive institutions and systems of surveillance and containment—and towards the theatrical acting-out of choreomaniacs and other so-called monomaniacs, this chapter highlights a history of madness as public enthusiasm.

Although as Deleuze reminds us, Foucault suggested that the 'containment' ('renfermement') of deviant individuals in the nineteenth century also implied their unwanted protrusion into public space—their public presence and indeed their *appearance* as 'mad' people to be interned—this chapter underscores the more boisterous other side to this dark history.[7] From

---

4. See Jean-François Lyotard, *L'enthousiasme: La critique kantienne de l'histoire* (Paris: Éditions Galilée, 1986), 57–77.

5. Isaac Taylor, *Natural History of Enthusiasm*, 4th ed. (London: Holdsworth and Ball, 1830), 33. See also Isaac Taylor, *Fanaticism* (London: Holdsworth and Ball, 1833).

6. John Langhorne, *Letters on Religious Retirement, Melancholy, and Enthusiasm* (London: H. Payne and W. Cropley, 1762), 6–8.

7. On the interplay of enclosure and visibility in Foucault's work, see e.g. Deleuze, *Foucault*, 55.

the early eighteenth century, Convulsionaries were acting out their differences by over-identifying with a politically recalcitrant saint. Their gestures, alternately understood to be real and feigned, became increasingly theatricalized, recuperated into the medical and psychiatric history of the dancing disease: a disease of quintessentially theatrical excess.

THE CONVULSIONARIES OF SAINT-MÉDARD IN 1730s PARIS: A JANSENIST ST. VITUS'S DANCE

Early eighteenth-century convulsionary antics, read through the lens of late nineteenth-century neurology, epitomized extreme religious states in a public sphere within which political and religious authority were highly contested. What came to be known as the Convulsionary movement swept through Paris in the 1730s, in the crossfire between church and state politics. A papal bull, *Unigenitus*, had been passed in September 1713 by Pope Clement XI (1649–1721) as an attack on the heterodox Jansenist movement, in particular Father Pasquier Quesnel (1634–1719), whose devotional handbook, *Les Paroles de la Parole incarnée, Jésus-Christ, Notre Seigneur, tirées du Nouveau Testament* [The Words of the Word Incarnate, Jesus Christ, Our Lord, Drawn from the New Testament] (1668), had provoked a storm of controversy: it was written in French and intended for laypeople.[8] Quesnel's success had prompted him to write more popular religious tracts, such as *Le Nouveau Testament en français, avec des réflexions morales sur chaque verset, pour en rendre la lecture plus utile et la méditation plus aisée* (1692), a French-language translation of the New Testament with commentary provided to readers to aid understanding. Pope Clement XI declared Quesnel a false prophet and

charlatan, dangerous to the moral well-being of Christians who would be led astray by his and other Jansenist teachings. But the politics that resulted from this proclamation, and from the favourable reception of the papal bull by the French king, Louis XIV (1638–1715), mobilized a wider contingency, tapping into broader currents of discontent already running through the nation.[9]

The French were divided into 'Acceptants', who supported the pope and king, and 'Appellants', who challenged the papal bull. By 1719, a compromise was reached known as the *accommodement* (concession), written in a *corps de doctrine*, leading to the creation of a third group, the 'Accommodants', which nominally backed both Appellants and Acceptants but was favourable to the bull overall (with minor provisions). By 1722, a royal decree had sanctioned the bull, under the pretext that the bishops of France had agreed to sign it. This created an even greater rupture between Gallicans and Papists, but did not stop the most committed *anti-constitutionnaire* bishops from continuing to attempt reformation. When Philippe II, Duke of Orléans (1674–1723), regent since the death of Louis XIV, died in his turn, André-Hercule de Fleury (1653–1743), a Jesuit and former preceptor to the king, called on the young Louis XV (1710–1774) to reinforce *Unigenitus*, declaring the recalcitrant bishops' stance to be misled. Fleury was proclaimed cardinal, and the Appellants lost all further right of appeal. As de Félice wrote in *Foules en délire, extases collectives* [Delirious Crowds, Collective Ecstasies] (1947), only a 'miracle' could save them.[10]

This miracle emerged in the form of François de Pâris (1690–1727), a famous Appellant and fervent Jansenist deacon, whose funeral on 3 May 1727, in the small working-class neighbourhood of Saint-Médard, then in the outskirts of Paris, immediately gave rise to prodigious cures. These cures were soon verified by doctors, priests, family,

8. B. Robert Kreiser, *Miracles, Convulsions, and Ecclesiastical Politics in Early Eighteenth-Century Paris* (Princeton, NJ: Princeton University Press, 1978), 8. See also Catherine-Laurence Maire, *De la cause de Dieu à la cause de la Nation: Le jansénisme au XVIIIe siècle* (Paris: Éditions Gallimard, 1998); Catherine-Laurence Maire, ed., *Les convulsionnaires de Saint-Médard: Miracles, convulsions et prophéties à Paris au XVIIIe siècle* (Paris: Gallimard/Julliard, 1985); Daniel Vidal, *Miracles et convulsions jansénistes au XVIIIe siècle: Le mal et sa connaissance* (Paris: Presses Universitaires de France, 1987); Brian E. Strayer, *Suffering Saints: Jansenists and Convulsionnaires in France, 1640–1799* (Eastbourne: Sussex Academic Press, 2008); Michèle Bokobza Kahan, 'Ethos in Testimony: The Case of Carré de Montgeron, a Jansenist and a Convulsionary in the Century of Enlightenment', *Eighteenth-Century Studies* 43.4 (2010): 419–433; Lindsay Wilson, *Women and Medicine in the French Enlightenment: The Debate over Maladies des Femmes* (Baltimore: Johns Hopkins University Press, 1993), i.

9. See Kreiser, *Miracles, Convulsions, and Ecclesiastical Politics*, 14–15.

10. Philippe de Félice, *Foules en délire, extases collectives: Essai sur quelques formes inférieures de la mystique* (Paris: Éditions Albin Michel, 1947), 243.

and friends and, once notarized, described in clandestinely published tracts widely disseminated to convince sceptics of the efficacy of posthumous intercession by a figure whose public opposition to the bull was well known.[11] The miracles described were wide-ranging. Convulsions produced at mere contact with Pâris's funeral stone, chunks of earth taken from the tomb area, and relics from Pâris himself were all believed to allow people to recover their health. The most dramatic of these cures were kinetic, involving the sudden recovery of movement by individuals who had been previously paralysed. Some *miraculés* performed acrobatic feats of prowess upon being cured, further proof of the deacon's miraculous intercession. The first known miracle described a young parishioner who suffered from paralysis in her left arm. She introduced herself into the deacon's premises while he was being prepared for burial, kissing his foot through the shroud and rubbing her arm against the bier. She then went home to spin silk and had now recovered the use of both her arms. News of this miracle spread, and throngs began fighting over the deacon's relics. As word of these cures reached beyond the Saint-Médard neighbourhood, Pâris's tomb became a destination of choice for Jansenist sympathizers, aristocrats, artisans, priests, magistrates, and an increasing number of new recruits, many of whom sought healing for lifelong infirmities. Others sought social validation for political grievances through Pâris's new status as martyr. Many gathered to watch.[12]

The legal problems caused by the massive congregation of individuals led the government to enact severe, though not often heeded, legislation. Louis XV promulgated a law on 27 January 1732 forbidding public congregation around the deacon's tomb. He was compelled to issue another one on 17 February 1733, as the first had been ignored. Both laws were issued in defence of public order and included stipulations against the performance of convulsions in private homes as well as at the deacon's gravesite.[13] The site had been turning into a hotbed of street theatre and a source of regular entertainment; it was now, as the king protested, a circus.[14] Reading Kant's concept of enthusiasm as an 'effect', Jean-François Lyotard (1924–1998) suggests that enthusiasm implies both the deceit of theatre and performative action. Enthusiasm in this sense propels men and women into choreographies of heightened affect, enacted in effusive bodily poses which, uncontained and potentially uncontainable in public space, succeed also in acting on it. The heightened theatricality of enthusiasm, translated into the gestural sphere, thrusts itself performatively into the world. Enthusiasm's affective surplus, 'effective' in this regard, spills into the public arena to overwhelm and transform it.

Choreomania, taken in this sense, implies affect and effect, as well as a (feminine, queer) theatricality that simultaneously performs its own 'too muchness' and in doing so threatens to affect—to contagion—its spectators. The Convulsionaries of Saint-Médard were a case in point: convulsions themselves were theatrical. In Foucault's terms, the possessed person's body (usually that of a woman) 'is the site of a theatre'.[15] It is, significantly, as Jordan points out in *Convulsing Bodies*, the site where the medieval *supplice*, or torture spectacle, becomes powerful again.[16] With the possessed nuns of Loudun, made famous in Michel de Certeau's (1925–1986) *La possession de Loudun* (1970) and reprised in numerous fictional and cinematic works since then, the pornographic theatre of naked bodies the nuns' convulsions represented suggests a renewed regime of biopower. The young nuns move according to the dictates—quite literally, the theatrical directing—of the pastorate, and

11. De Félice, *Foules en délire*, 244. On Pâris's famously short and pious life, see also Christian Bernadac and Sylvain Fourcassié, eds., *Les possédés de Chaillot* (Paris: Jean-Claude Lattès, 1983), 15–17.

12. Bernadac and Fourcassié, eds., *Les possédés*, 17–18. See also Paul Regnard, *Les maladies épidémiques de l'esprit: Sorcellerie, magnétisme, morphinisme, délire des grandeurs* (Paris: E. Plon, Nourrit et Cie, 1887), 116–118. Regnard situates this narrative in a line of spontaneous recoveries from partial paralysis among hysterics at the Salpêtrière and across the ages. I will return to this history in chapter 6.

13. For the full text of these edicts, see Pierre-François Mathieu, *Histoire des miraculés et des convulsionnaires de Saint-Médard* (Paris: Didier et Cie, 1864), 217–219 and 227–228.

14. See Kreiser, *Miracles, Convulsions, and Ecclesiastical Politics*, 175–180. Bernadac and Fourcassié describe the authorities' vigorous handling of the affair, arguing that the events at Saint-Médard recalled the seventeenth-century insurrection known as the Fronde, considering that scenes of collective hysteria at the gravesite could become a hotbed of contagious effervescence (*Les possédés*, 29). De Félice suggests the Convulsionaries' collective ecstasy recalled the origins of dramatic art, when spectators and actors alike were presumably transported outside of themselves and, thus 'subtracted from reality', shared in a 'common fiction' (*Foules en délire*, 241–258, 247).

15. Foucault, *Les anormaux*, 197.

16. Jordan, *Convulsing Bodies*, 87–91.

so become at once abstracted and alienated, even while they might be expressing a brand of discontentment in these performances of real pain.[17] In contrast, the convulsions performed by the eighteenth-century Convulsionaries suggest a theatrical acting-out that posits 'abnormality' in a theatre of effusive *self*-travesty: the Convulsionaries, while for the most part entirely serious about their miracles and political difference, also played *out* and played *at* this difference, choreographing a site of resistance in Paris's margins without a notable directorate—without the intercession of a conductor of souls.[18]

As Hecker noted in his discussion of the Convulsionaries, wrapping them into the broader history of dance manias and epidemic disorders, the spectacles performed by these enthusiasts were enthralling: novel and comical at once. But they were also too novel, too comical, disrupting Parisian life with their theatrical pull. Nonetheless calling the Convulsionaries of Saint-Médard 'patients', Hecker underlined their outlandish circus-like acts: they 'bounded from the ground, impelled by the convulsions, like fish out of water'. 'Some spun around on their feet with incredible rapidity, as is related of the dervishes', he noted; 'others ran their heads against walls, or curved their bodies like rope-dancers, so that their heels touched their shoulders'.[19] Others showed more typical signs of motor disease: these 'patients were seized with convulsions and tetanic spasms, rolled upon the ground like persons possessed, thrown into violent contortions of their heads and limbs, and suffered the greatest oppression, accompanied by quickness and irregularity of pulse'. But the spectacle of their contortions prompted its own furore. This 'novel occurrence excited the greatest sensation all over Paris, and an immense concourse of people resorted daily to the above-named cemetery, in order to see so wonderful a spectacle'.[20] The scene, Hecker remarked, eventually

'degenerated' into 'decided insanity'.[21] The cemetery had given rise to a fusion of psychiatric, neuromotor, and social madness: convulsions were spectacular, and though resembling acrobatic antics in their mere gestural extravagance and their accidental comic resemblance to fish or rope dancers, they gave way, in Hecker's account, to a real epidemic of enthusiastic spectatorship. The Convulsionaries excited one another, and in doing so excited their all too readily enthused compatriots.

Charcot and Paul Richer (1849–1933), following Hecker's lead, argued in *Les démoniaques dans l'art* [Demoniacs in Art] (1887) that the convulsionary spectacle resembled St. Vitus's dance and tarantism,[22] a reflection earlier articulated by the pharmacologist, chemist, physicist, and popular science writer Louis Figuier (1819–1894), who in his *Histoire du merveilleux dans les temps modernes* [History of the Marvellous in Modern Times] (1859–1862), described convulsions performed by one woman, Marie-Anne Vassereau, as a kind of St. Vitus's dance. For Figuier, her convulsions triggered a modern dancing epidemic that swept through Enlightenment France:

Marie-Anne [Vassereau]'s convulsions were the spark that set the new St. Vitus's dance off, tearing through eighteenth-century Paris with infinite variations, each more miserable or comic [bouffonnes] than the next. People converged on the Saint-Médard cemetery from everywhere to participate in the shaking and quivering [frissonnements], the stiffenings [crispations] and the trembling. Whether they were ill or not, each endeavoured to convulse in his or her own way. It was a universal dance, a veritable tarantella. Soon the countryside, jealous of the favours the Saint [Pâris] was bestowing upon his city,

17. De Certeau writes that the physician's task, in attempting to determine whether a 'possessed' woman is actually possessed or merely feigning, is to 'see and to visit' ('voir et visiter') as at a theatre. Although physicians might be caught up in the emotion of the spectacle of her contorted body, verification of the truth of her possession would be assured statistically: the more such physicians performed the work of observation, the more certain their agreed readings were presumed to be. Michel de Certeau, *La possession de Loudun* (Paris: Éditions Gallimard, 1990): 216–217.

18. Foucault describes the medieval pastorate's role of 'conducting souls' in Michel Foucault, *Security, Territory, Population: Lectures at the Collège de France 1977–1978*, ed. Arnold I. Davidson, trans. Graham Burchell (London: Palgrave Macmillan, 2007).

19. Hecker, *Epidemics of the Middle Ages*, 137–138.

20. Hecker, *Epidemics of the Middle Ages*, 136–137.

21. Hecker, *Epidemics of the Middle Ages*, 138. The image of the cemetery becoming a 'theatre' as well as a spectacle, a fairground, a tribunal, etc. is reprised in Kreiser, *Miracles, Convulsions, and Ecclesiastical Politics*, 179, 243–244; Maire, ed., *Les convulsionnaires*, 13; Wilson, *Women and Medicine in the French Enlightenment*, 18.

22. See Jean-Martin Charcot and Paul Richer, *Les démoniaques dans l'art* (Paris: A. Delahaye et E. Lecrosnier, 1887), 78–90.

and claiming a place of its own, contributed tastes of local colour to the show.[23]

To the medically attuned eye, the tetanic spasms, tympany, falling and rolling on the ground, contortions of the limbs, and irregular pulse all appeared to correspond to the choreomania of the Middle Ages, to the extent legible through visual archives and anecdote. While Charcot and Richer had imagined the convulsionary performances as instances of hysterical acting-out—a theatre of suffering entirely fabricated by its players—Hecker insisted that political and religious excitement served as a general ecology within which such outbreaks appeared. Like the medieval dance manias, Hecker ventured, these convulsions were provoked by social crisis and widespread superstition, revealing an uneven progression towards modernity. The French state of mind was still 'medieval', Hecker contended, in spite of French claims to Enlightenment.[24] Although the revolution of 1789 'shook the structure of this pernicious mysticism', it was not stamped out entirely: 'even during the period of greatest excitement, . . . secret meetings were still kept up; prophetic books, by Convulsionnaires of various denominations, . . . appeared even in the most recent times'. They had done so as recently as 1828, Hecker noted, only four years before he wrote 'The Dancing Mania', proving that choreomanias not only recurred, but lingered. The fanatical 'sect' of Convulsionaries was still active, he lamented, 'although without the convulsions and extraordinarily rude aid of brethren of the faith, which, amidst the boasted pre eminence of French intellectual advancement, remind us most forcibly of the dark ages of the St. John's dancers'.[25]

Convulsionaries offered a popular theatre of aberration, characterized by contractions, paralyses, and ecstatic deliverance. In its time, it was decried as medical theatre: not just charlatanism, but a low-level comedy of cures that bedazzled the public, in the words of one disgruntled critic who complained of the scandalous performance of circus-like feats and the imposture the Convulsionaries presented under the guise of religion. In a desperate letter denouncing their most histrionic performer, the notorious Father Bescherand (or Bécherand) de la Motte, the anonymous critic bemoaned the ridicule convulsionary theatrics brought on the institution of the church, theatrics flaunting excess and mesmerizing a fickle audience.[26]

THEATRICAL CHOREA AND CONVULSIONARY FAKERY

The Convulsionaries' spasms and contortions were ostentatious; but they were also allegorical and, as such, instrumental in furthering the Convulsionary movement. In etchings provided by the Convulsionary apologist Carré de Montgeron (1686–1754), reproduced in *Les maladies épidémiques de l'esprit: Sorcellerie, magnétisme, morphinisme, délire des grandeurs* [Epidemic Mental Illnesses] (1887), by Charcot's student and collaborator Paul Regnard (1850–1927), a cast of characters is shown 'before' and 'after' their cure. 'La demoiselle Thibaut' (Miss Thibaut) (figs. 4.1 and 4.2) is one character, presented first in a position suggesting lethargy, as she lies on the ground, bloated, with her eyes cast upward, while a desperate friend or family member prays for her in the background. In the next image, she has seemingly regained a slimmer size and prays thankfully in turn. Marie Anne Couronneau, another Convulsionary, shown with crutches, leans back in an awkward, arched position, almost a typical *arc de cercle* (a back drawn like a bow) such as Charcot and his colleagues observed among so many of their 'hysteroepileptic' patients, as I discuss further in chapter 6. Again, in the next image, she is shown freely walking up stairs with her

---

23. Cited in Mathieu, *Histoire des miraculés*, 214–215. Reprised in Regnard, *Les maladies épidémiques*, 171.

24. Hecker, *Epidemics of the Middle Ages*, 138.

25. Hecker, *Epidemics of the Middle Ages*, 136, 139.

26. In a letter titled 'Au sujet des choses singulieres & surprenantes qui arrivent en la Personne de Monsieur l'Abbé Bescherant à Saint Médard', Paris, 18 October 1731, in *Dissertation sur les miracles, Et en particulier sur ceux qui ont été operés au Tombeau de Mr. de Pâris, en l'Eglise de S. Medard de Paris, avec la Relation & les preuves de celui qui s'est fait le 3e Novembre 1730 en la personne d'Anne le Franc de la Paroisse de S. Barthelemy* (Paris, 1731), n.p. See also Charles-Gaspard-Guillaume de Vintimille Du Luc, *Mandement de Mgr l'archevêque de Paris au sujet d'un écrit qui a pour titre: Dissertation sur les miracles, et en particulier sur ceux qui ont été opérez au tombeau de M. de Paris en l'église de S. Médard de Paris; avec la Relation & les preuves de celui qui s'est fait le 3e Novembre 1730 en la personne d'Anne le Franc, de la Paroisse de S. Barthelemy* (Paris: Chez Pierre Simon, 1731), n.p.

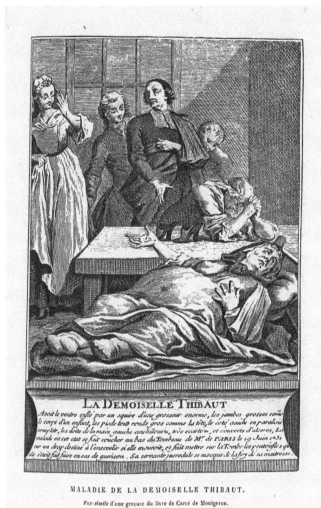

LA DEMOISELLE THIBAUT

Avoit le ventre enflé par un squire d'une grosseur enorme, les jambes grosses comme le corps d'un enfant, les pieds tout ronds gros comme la tête, le coté gauche en paralysie complète, les doits de la main gauche anchilosés, très ecartés, et couverts d'ulceres. La malade en cet etat se fait coucher au bas du Tombeau de Mr de PARIS le 19 Juin 1731 sur un drap destiné à l'ensevelir si elle mouroit, et fait mettre sur le Tombe les rentrûtes qu'elle s'etoit fait faire en cas de querison. Sa servante incredule se mocque de la foy de sa maitresse.

MALADIE DE LA DEMOISELLE THIBAUT.

Fac-simile d'une gravure du livre de Carré de Montgeron.

FIGURE 4.1 'Ms. Thibaut's Disease' [enormous distension of the abdomen, legs, paralysis, etc.]. Courtesy the New York Academy of Medicine Library.

crutches propped up high, as if triumphantly to demonstrate that she does not require them any longer.[27] These 'before and after' portraits, foreshadowing contemporary dieting advertisements, iconographically perform the passage from distemper and disorder to deliverance. The images show that cures happened and invite more. Captions narrate the miraculous transitions in pithy prose, suggesting quick snapshots encapsulating the benefits of convulsionary practice, just as Charcot and his team would later reappropriate these images as proof that convulsionary disorders partook of the broader category of hysteroepilepsy. The

27. Reproduced in Regnard, *Les maladies épidémiques*, 121–130. Regnard notes that Mlle. Thibaut's case was attributed to hydropia by Carré de Montgeron but would in his own time be described as meteorism with hysterical contracture (125). He provides further similarly illustrated case studies culled primarily from Montgeron and Mathieu (see esp. 118–171), noting that by 1732 the Saint-Médard cemetery was a rendezvous for all the hysterics of Paris ('le rendez-vous de tout ce qu'il y avait d'hystériques à Paris'), and the site of a 'whole new Saint Vitus's dance, resuscitated in the eighteenth century in the very heart of Paris' (171).

LA DEMOISELLE THIBAUT

Est guerie sur le champ le 9.ᵉ jour 19 Juin 1731; Tous ses membres hidropiques
se desinflent a la veue des spectateurs, elle se leve, s'assied sur le Tombeau, et fait
voir en joignant les mains que son bras gauche et devant paralitique, et ses doits et de
vant anchilosés et couverts d'ulceres, sont gueris; Sa servante, qui luy met ses pantoufles,
est frappé d'étonnement de voir ses pieds si fort et si subitement desenflets .

GUÉRISON DE LA DEMOISELLE THIBAUT.

Fac-simile d'une gravure du livre de Carré de Montgeron.

FIGURE 4.2 'Ms. Thibaut's Cure' [she is cured on the spot on June 19, 1731, when all her hydropic limbs are deflated before the spectators' very eyes . . . and to her servant girl's amazement]. Courtesy the New York Academy of Medicine Library.

images suggested the shaky 'truth' of art and scientific validation.

Charcot and his colleagues argued the images from convulsionary activities revealed a host of epileptiform attacks that suggested imitative poses rather than strictly neurodegenerative disease; in this respect, the Convulsionaries, they argued, suffered from a disorder of the imagination. Hysteroepileptics were too theatrical: their effusive poses and jagged gestures revealed a disorganization of the mind moving a theatrical body. In Les démoniaques, Charcot and Richer discuss an engraving of a crowd scene around Pâris's tomb, noting that one person sprawled on the floor, as if in an epileptic seizure, is not actually frothing at the mouth or rolling the eyes; this person has fallen but is not actually suffering from epilepsy (fig. 4.3).[28] Other characters, in this and similar images, displayed further stages of so-called miraculous intercession,

---

28. Charcot and Richer, Les démoniaques, 88–89n1.

LES GRANDS SECOURS

Fac simile d'une gravure de B. Picart extraite des *Cérémonies et coutumes de tous les peuples*, etc.

FIGURE 4.3   'The *grands secours*'. From Charcot and Richer, *Les démoniaques dans l'art* (1887). Courtesy the New York Academy of Medicine Library.

presenting an overview of convulsionary events uncannily resembling and ostensibly prefiguring the poses Charcot's patients would take.[29] While recognizing arched backs and upward-roving eyes among the subjects depicted in these engravings, Charcot also noted the same among his patients, further cementing the link between past and present corporeal forms and so, too, the backward reach of modern clinical neurology. He and Richer concluded that from the most ancient forms of ritual possession to present-day clinical hysteria, the 'exaltation of the emotions has not changed'.[30] Their task was to parse this anatomically, morphologically, and dramaturgically and so to recuperate past disorders into the contemporary scientific fold.

Yet with this scientific method, ambiguity played a fair part, as did fiction: these were attitudes, poses, tableaux, theatrics, 'representations' that performed just as they enacted a rigid sequence of events.[31] They were also not always entirely involuntary: Regnard quotes a long account provided by the nineteenth-century historian Pierre-François Mathieu (1808–1864) in his *Histoire des miraculés et des convulsionnaires de Saint-Médard* [History of the Miraculously Cured and the Convulsionaries of Saint-Médard] (1864) which suggests that some of the Convulsionaries performed deliberate actions, often together, so as to imitate or represent moments of Pâris's life. These actions were strung together with a set of further theatrical tableaux, involving spectators

29. In Charcot and Richer, *Les démoniaques*, 82.

30. In Charcot and Richer, *Les démoniaques*, 85.

31. The term 'representation' appears in various passages. See e.g. Jean-Martin Charcot, *Œuvres complètes* [hereafter Charcot, *Œuvres complètes*], ed. Désiré Magloire Bourneville et al., 9 vols., vol. 3 (Paris: Bureaux du progrès médical, 1886–1890), 219–220.

in a mini-drama that he called 'comedy' ('le comique'). Other 'actresses' engaged in tragic or tragicomic performances of ecstasy, representing Christ's passion, which they 'expressed through their movements and gestures', embodying every detail that might supplement the scene; Mathieu termed these movements 'figurative' ('figuratives'). Another brand of theatrical Convulsionary Mathieu classed as visionaries or 'apocalyptiques': they saw angels. The *thaumaturges* performed, or imagined that they performed, miracles themselves. Priestesses and prophetesses were among the—in his account—predominantly female cast of theatrical convulsionary artists, all of whom, often scantily clad, allowed themselves to be pressed and trampled upon when they were not leaping and pirouetting about.[32]

Notwithstanding the dismissive tone with which Mathieu taxonomizes these convulsionary performers, the choreography of pain and cure that they enacted suggests a public display of religious autonomy away from the disciplinary sphere of church and state. As collective expressions of pious enthusiasm, the Convulsionaries offered playful and also arguably powerful portraits of women (and men) taking religion into their own hands. This was a choreopolitics of revolt through corporeal acts of mimicry and representation. But for Charcot and his nineteenth-century audience, paralyses and contractures presented a different set of problems. Convulsionaries were not only acting out; they displayed a cast of specific, recognizable bodily deformities and falls. What are now typically described as non-epileptic seizures or pseudo-seizures, with no special brain wave activity (no EEG abnormality), account for nearly a quarter of hospital admittances for epilepsy today.[33] In Charcot's time, these were described as convulsions with a semi-conscious intent, translated into the language of hysteria, imposture, or

forgery. Freud, who kept a lithograph of the famous painting by Pierre Aristide André Brouillet (1857–1914), 'Une leçon clinique à la Salpêtrière' [A Clinical Lesson at the Salpêtrière] (1887) of his teacher Charcot's famous Leçons du mardi [Tuesday Lessons] in his studies in Vienna and London, attempted to dig at the root of these pseudo-performances, taking Charcot's *Leçons sur les maladies du système nerveux* [Lessons on the Diseases of the Nervous System] (1875–1887)—whose authorized translation he offered to a German readership in 1886 as *Neue Vorlesungen über die Krankheiten des Nervensystems, insbesondere über Hysterie*—into the realm of psychology. But these were complex psychosomatic events, whose designation as a disease and as theatre did not sufficiently explain, let alone diagnose, the knot of goings-on.

Ambiguity concerning cases of 'real' and 'hysterical' epilepsy was hotly debated, among others by the English neurologist and contemporary of Charcot William Gowers (1845–1915), who wrote that 'the convulsions that are called "hysterical"' are normally characterized by 'spasmodic movements of a more or less coordinated character'. These muscular contractions are, Gowers noted, 'in the main, such as may be produced by the will. Hence', he added, 'the spasm has a somewhat purposive aspect'.[34] This 'purposive aspect' often lent hysteroepileptic patients the allure of theatrical performers. The French physicians Louis Jacques Bégin (1793–1859), François-Gabriel Boisseau (1791–1836), and others defined 'Convulsionaries' in their *Dictionnaire des termes de médecine, chirurgie, art vétérinaire, pharmacie, histoire naturelle, botanique, physique, chimie, etc.* [Dictionary of Medical, Surgical, Veterinary, Pharmaceutical, Natural History, Botany, Physics, Chemistry, etc., Terms] (1823) as feigned *or* actual invalids. The ambivalence of the definition was fundamental.

---

32. In Regnard, *Les maladies épidémiques*, 186–191.

33. The literature on non-epileptic seizures is vast, with hundreds of articles published in the past few years on the still fraught subject of what are typically referred to as psychogenic non-epileptic seizures. A slightly lower estimate (10–22 percent) appears in Selim R. Benbadis and W. Allen Hauser, 'An Estimate of the Prevalence of Psychogenic Non-epileptic Seizures', *Seizure: European Journal of Epilepsy* 9.4 (2000): 280–281, 280. For a recent overview of literature and estimates, see Hannah Wiseman and Markus Reuber, 'New Insights into Psychogenic Non-epileptic Seizures 2011–2014)', *Seizure: European Journal of Epilepsy* 29 (2015): 69–80. Gaston Baslet, Ashok Seshadri, Adriana Bermeo-Ovalle, Ken Willment, and Lorna Myers suggest 'up to 30% of admissions to epilepsy monitoring units are diagnosed with PNES [psychogenic non-epileptic seizures] at discharge', with the total incidence of PNESs per year estimated at between 1.4 and 4.9 per 100,000. Gaston Baslet et al., 'Psychogenic Non-epileptic Seizures: An Updated Primer', *Psychosomatics* 57.1 (2016): 1–17, doi: 10.1016/j.psym.2015.10.004, accessed 3 March 2016. See the recently much-expanded standard text by A. James Rowan and John R. Gates, in Steven C. Schachter and W. Curt LaFrance Jr., eds., *Gates and Rowan's Nonepileptic Seizures*, 3rd ed. (Cambridge: Cambridge University Press, 2010).

34. Cited in Don W. King et al., 'Convulsive Non-epileptic Seizures', in A. James Rowan and John R. Gates, eds., *Non-epileptic Seizures* (Boston: Butterworth-Heinemann, 1993), 31–37, 31. See W. Gowers, *Epilepsy and Other Chronic Convulsive Disorders: Their Causes, Symptoms and Treatment* (London: J. A. Churchill, 1881).

The term 'Convulsionnaire' was used 'in the past', they noted, to describe 'people in whom religious ideas *or* the hope of a dishonest wage provoked real convulsions *or*, alternately, voluntary contortions'.[35] Convulsionaries were by definition either real or fake, either actors or agents. What mattered was that their contortions had all the appearance of theatre. It was increasingly this very theatricality that neurologists and psychiatrists sought (indirectly) to diagnose.

Enlightenment philosophers had long ago jumped on the anti-theatrical bandwagon, declaring these convulsionary events to be—offensively—like theatre: the encyclopedist Jean Le Rond d'Alembert (1717–1837), who attended some convulsionary activities clandestinely with Charles Marie de La Condamine (1701–1774), a French geographer and explorer, proposed that the convulsionaries gained their public appeal through secrecy, enhancing the notorious drama of the whole affair. The Enlightenment philosopher Voltaire (1694–1778) argued that this convulsionary theatre was extreme and dangerous; in his view, it enacted the public performance of resistance to the papal bull.

As historian Lindsay Wilson has argued, by the later part of the eighteenth century, the term 'Convulsionary' itself had become equated not just with shamming but with fanaticism.[36] For some authors, including the literary critic Charles-Augustin Sainte-Beuve (1804–1869) and the abbé Paul Gagnol (1850–1928), writing in 1911, this fanaticism marked a period of decline: Jansenism, as the stalwart, rational retort to absolutism, put forward by philosophers and dramatists from Blaise Pascal (1623–1662) and Jean Racine (1639–1699) to Nicolas Boileau-Despréaux (1636–1711), had degenerated into sheer idolatry in the figure of the convulsions, signs made to stand for divine intercession. The convulsions suggested a

shallow and merely theatrical extravaganza far removed from the Jansenist movement's original rigour and noblesse.[37]

Convulsions were undeniably in vogue: increasingly represented by gestures suggesting the work of God, as its supposedly visible proof, they gradually eluded and surpassed the movement's initial *anti-constitutionnaire* thrust. The ridicule prompted by the Convulsionaries' feats soon came to inspire countless satires further dramatizing what were already patently theatrical games. From a semi-haphazard performance of miraculous cures and resistance to regal and papal authority, new dramas emerged, flung gaily into the arms of a Parisian public all too avid to judge and laugh at—as well as with—the agents of this overenthusiastic performance of pain; but not before the performers themselves were driven underground, further adding to the mystery and mystique, the inscrutability and the opacity, of the Convulsionaries' collective acts.

GUILLAUME-HYACINTHE BOUGEANT AND THE JANSENIST COMIC PÈRE BESCHERAND

Once the deacon's tomb had become outlawed as a site for Convulsionaries' activities, convulsionary enthusiasts had to find new sites for the performance of their pain.[38] But they had already made a lasting impression on Parisian society: satires emerged, most notably by the Jesuit playwright Guillaume-Hyacinthe Bougeant (1690–1743) in his trio of works *Apologie des miracles faits ou à faire au tombeau de M. de Pâris* [Apology for Miracles Performed or To Be Performed at Mr. Pâris's Tomb] (1732), *Le Saint déniché, ou la Banqueroute des marchands de miracles* [The Saint Exposed, or, Bankruptcy of the Miracle Peddlers]

---

35. In Louis Jacques Bégin, *Dictionnaire des termes de médecine, chirurgie, art vétérinaire, pharmacie, histoire naturelle, botanique, physique, chimie, etc.* (Paris: Baillière, Crevot, Béchet, 1823), 178. Emphasis mine.

36. In Wilson, *Women and Medicine in the French Enlightenment*, 33. See also Voltaire, 'Convulsions', in *Dictionnaire philosophique portatif, Nouvelle Édition, revue, corrigée & augmentée de divers Articles par l'auteur* (London: J. B. H. Leclerc, 1765), 142–143; 'Convulsionnaires', in Denis Diderot and Jean le Rond d'Alembert, eds., *L'Encyclopédie ou Dictionnaire raisonné des sciences, des arts et des métiers*, 3rd ed., 28 vols., vol. 9 (Geneva: Chez Jean-Léonard Pellet, 1779), 368. Regnard reproduces a humorous poem by Voltaire decrying the relative idiocy of the Saint-Médard proceedings, which, as depicted in Voltaire's poem, after attracting the blind, the lame, and the deaf, drew all sorts of people to its creed. In Regnard, *Les maladies épidémiques*, 175.

37. In L'abbé Gagnol, *Le jansénisme convulsionnaire et l'affaire de la planchette, d'après les archives de la Bastille* (Paris: Librairie générale catholique, 1911), 7–8.

38. A royal decree required the Paris police to close the cemetery on 29 January 1732. Kreiser, *Miracles, Convulsions, and Ecclesiastical Politics*, 243. On the proliferation of new makeshift sites of worship, see Kreiser, *Miracles, Convulsions, and Ecclesiastical Politics*, 250.

(1732), and *Les Quakres françois, ou les Nouvelles trembleurs, comédie* [The French Quakers, or the New Tremblers, Comedy] (1732).[39] In these plays, Bougeant casts the Convulsionaries as actors in a ridiculous drama meant for the diversion of an equally ridiculous audience, entertained by improbable theatrics sustained by individuals most of whom were believed to be totally out of their senses. The events at Pâris's tomb were cast as histrionics prompted by the audience's insatiable thirst for amusement, the 'great troupe'[40] of acrobats and trapezists giving its regular show twice daily for the public's benefit. The dangerous feats the convulsionary performers executed only added to an already titillating experience, coloured by its marginal urban location and *anti-constitutionnaire* hue.

The most famous of the Convulsionaries was Father Bescherand, known for his 'sauts de la carpe', wild carp-like leaps performed in spite of a famously bad limp. In *Les Quakres Francois ou les nouveaux trembleurs*, Bougeant satirizes Father Bescherand as a complex plot unfolds to grace this virtuosic Convulsionary with a troupe of men and women paid to jump and leap with him so that he does not look so absurd performing his antics alone. In the play, M. du Sault (homonymously suggesting Mr. Jump) is a thinly veiled portrait of Bescherand. Bougeant claimed in his preface that the real man had made such a spectacle of himself to the city of Paris and to all of France already that it was only fitting his performance should find a new life in the theatre.[41] At first persuaded by M. Hablador (Mr. Smooth-talking), a Molière-type doctor, and M. de Bonnefoy (Mr. Good Faith), a not-so-pious Jansenist priest, to leap about the deacon's tomb until the blood flowed through his bad leg, pumping and extending it by a few inches, M. du Sault eventually tires of this. He complains that he understands the principle—though he argues that if the blood extends his bad leg, it could extend and bloat the rest of his body as well—but all he has gained in the process is exhaustion. Even the spectators were starting to tire of this performance. 'If you want me to continue', M. du Sault tells M. de Bonnefoy, 'you need to find me a partner, or two or three,

to imitate my movements. It is absurd, and scandalous, that out of so many people who come to pray at the deacon's tomb, I should be the only one to have convulsions, which, I have noted, are anyway starting to wear on the spectators'.[42] Du Sault would serve as a model for a small group of adepts, all of whom were to help him create a drama of pain more plausible because of the number of people performing it.

This scenario poked fun at the supposed fakeries of the Convulsionaries, as well as the behind-the-scenes work of local doctors, cast as charlatans. The play also suggested that these leaps and bounds offered a performance of disorder and distress to an audience growing in intensity; but these convulsionary antics, as theatre, were displacing the religious and revolutionary cause. Bougeant's satire hardly exaggerated public opinion. A notice had not long before been posted at the entrance to the Saint-Médard cemetery, proclaiming that the Convulsionaries' pious exercises had devolved into a regular acrobatic show:

PUBLIC NOTICE, LADIES AND GENTLE-MEN, THE GREAT TROUPE OF JUMPERS AND ACROBATS OF SR. PÂRIS, which has until now sought only the pleasure and edification of those who do it the honor of coming to watch it, will give its regular performance evening and morning for the convenience of the public. Mr. Bécheran the Lame, who here has the honor of entertaining the princes and princesses, lords and ladies of the Court with success and applause will continue his regular exercises until the extinction of his strength, and for the satisfaction of the curious will perform many times the new and dangerous leap, holding himself only on his own two feet and with the help of only three people . . . . The rest of the troupe will forget nothing to merit the esteem and goodwill of those who will honor its performance.[43]

Although cast as an epidemic disease and hysterical disorder by neurologists and historians looking back on these events a century later, religious

---

39. See Kreiser, *Miracles, Convulsions, and Ecclesiastical Politics*, 176n106.

40. Kreiser, *Miracles, Convulsions, and Ecclesiastical Politics*, 176n106.

41. Kreiser, *Miracles, Convulsions, and Ecclesiastical Politics*, 176 n106.

42. 'Au moins si vous voulez que je continuë, il faut necessairement que vous me trouviez quelque compagnon, & s'il se peut, plusieurs, qui sachent imiter mes mouvemens. De tant de gens qui viennent prier au saint Tombeau, il est ridicule, & même scandaleux, que je sois le seul à avoir des Convulsions, dont entre nous je m'apperçois qu'on se lasse, pour ne rien dire de plus'. Guillaume-Hyacinthe Bougeant, *Les Quakres françois ou les nouveaux trembleurs. Comédie* (Utrecht: H. Khyrks le Jeune, 1732), 12.

43. Cited in Kreiser, *Miracles, Convulsions, and Ecclesiastical Politics*, 176n106.

zealots and opportunists of every stripe were not duped at the time: this was popular enter-tainment, and it was a popular religious exercise. Some miracles may have taken place at the start; but now the convulsionary happenings pre-sented an occasion for play. Amateur actors and acrobats joined in with the rest. As Bougeant's theatre rehearsed the Convulsionaries' popular leaps and bounds, performers and devotees alike occupied the parish cemetery with an ever evolv-ing set of stunts and pranks.

In *Le saint déniché ou la banqueroute des march-ands de miracles*, Bougeant exploits comic antics derived from the performance of a supposed convulsive attack. He stages a character named M. Gautier, a Jansenist convert and fervent believer in the convulsionary miracles, suffer-ing an episode of convulsions upon donning a fake relic wig (supposedly belonging to Father Quesnel) purchased at an exorbitant price and 'delivered' to him by his mischievous servant, Mathurin.[44] M. Gautier, resembling a warlock on his way home from a sabbath, in Mathurin's insubordinate view (the wig is tangled, render-ing it all the more 'real'), comes to be overtaken with emotion: 'Wait. What do I feel? All my blood, I think, is shaken by some extraordin-ary motion. Mathurin, quick, quick, a chair'. Mathurin, bringing a chair to his master, asks him what is wrong. 'A chair, I tell you, a chair', replies M. Gautier who, sitting, then sighing in relief, tells him: '*Ouf . . .* I think I am having convulsions'. Mathurin replies, 'confusions?' to which M. Gautier responds, indignantly: 'Shut up, you idiot, it's a miracle'.[45] Bougeant's mock-ery of these supposed miracles unfolds as a whole cast of paralytic and otherwise misshapen characters are summoned to become subjects of miraculous cures. M. Caffart, another Jansenist Molière-type doctor, intent on proving the real-ity of the miracles occurring at the deacon's tomb, explains to M. Gautier that a paralytic man has recovered his mobility, as was certified by a doc-tor, a surgeon, and a local priest. Yet when this man is made to demonstrate his recovery, the sceptic M. Germain, M. Gautier's cousin, points out that although he was previously paralysed

in his left arm, he is now paralysed in the right. M. Caffart's sole response to this—and to other accusations that his host of paralytic and other-wise physically challenged characters are fakes—is that Saint Pâris does not perform perfect miracles: 'that time has passed'. What's more, he was still in his apprenticeship stage.[46]

This theatrical mockery by a Jesuit critic was arguably proffered in a spirit of play as well as opportunist exploitation of the convulsions' comic potential. But the plays emerged against a backdrop of virulent anti-theatrical and anti-Convulsionary pamphleteering, equally viru-lently countered by tracts written in defence of the Convulsionaries. These included writing by Jansenist converts and the most outspoken and prolific of all, Montgeron, for whom con-vulsionary feats were acts of God.[47] Yet the leg-acy of ridicule was set: a proliferation of tracts, etchings, and other visual sources amplified the popular appeal of this phenomenon—not quite a dance but a form of agitated gesticulation and collective theatre of motion that drew com-parisons to dancing manias and other psychic and hysteroepileptic epidemics for some time. As the physician and hypnotist Anton Mesmer (1734–1815), father of 'mesmerism', saw it, the Convulsionaries' gesticulations theatricalized the complex imbrication of cause, symptom, and cure, informing his and his followers' own stud-ies of animal magnetism.[48] As with Charcot's hysteroepileptic patients, the Convulsionaries' gestures appeared to stem from tantalizingly invisible sources, useful in articulating psycho-logical theories of illusion.

A 'TRANSPORT CHARACTERISTIC OF DELIRIUM': *DANSOMANIES* ON THE VAUDEVILLE STAGE

Choreomania epitomized corporeal and affective overzealousness. As a potentially revolutionary affect and 'effect', which could be experienced by

44. Guillaume-Hyacinthe Bougeant, *Le saint déniché ou la banqueroute des marchands de miracles. Comédie* (La Haye: Pierre Oiseau, à la Cycongne, 1732), 93–96.

45. Bougeant, *Le saint déniché*, 93.

46. Bougeant, *Le saint déniché*, 102–111.

47. See debates collected in *Dissertation sur les miracles*. See also Louis-Basile Carré de Montgeron, *La vérité des miracles opérés par l'intercession de M. de Paris, Démontrée contre M. l'Archevêque de Sens. Ouvrage dédié au Roy. Par M. de Montgeron, conseiller au parle-ment* (Utrecht: Libraires de la Compagnie, 1737).

48. See Maire, *Les convulsionnaires*, 238–240; Wilson, *Women and Medicine in the French Enlightenment*, esp. 10–16, 104–124.

those engaging in it and by those watching from near or far away, spontaneous and excessive gesture signalled the possibility of a social body falling into disarray and reconstituting itself along different lines. Choreomania represented marginality, insignificance, and 'too muchness', derided in the public sphere; but also the slightly worrying energetic excess of social revolt. Dance manias afforded vaudeville entertainers opportunities for a spoof not only on overzealous acts of national or religious emotion but also on the medical gaze that overzealously in its turn saw this excess nationalism and religiosity as a disorder in its own right.

In *La dansomanie, folie-pantomime, en deux actes* [The Dancing Mania, Folie-Pantomime, in Two Acts], a comic ballet that premiered at the Théâtre de la République et des Arts (precursor to the Opéra de Paris) in June 1800, the long-standing opera choreographer Pierre Gardel (1758–1840) prefaced the text of his ballet with an apology to the reader for the 'audacity' ('hardiesse') of his coinage: he could not, he claims, find a better word to describe the particular sort of madness ('folie') suffered by his protagonist than to call him a 'dansomane', a choreomaniac: a person literally crazy about dancing.[49] Gardel might have been describing himself: as head of ballet at the Paris Opéra from 1787 to 1829, he was a balletomane and ballet master who would have seen the introduction of as many new popular dance forms as French political regimes. The waltz was introduced for the first time on this stage, and as dance historian John Chapman has suggested, Gardel's own proclivities had him side against Jean-Georges Noverre's (1727–1810) influential theory of the *ballet d'action*, a type of ballet designed almost entirely to showcase drama, in favour of ballet that showcased dance and drove plot through movement.[50] Gardel's revolutionary sympathies in particular had prompted him to become involved in choreographing patriotic fêtes and anarchist theatre in the years following the French Revolution. With *La dansomanie*, he showcased the common man and woman in a comic spoof that prefigured an emergent national discourse on monomania in psychiatric analysis.[51]

Gardel did this with a satirically light touch. The sort of madness his protagonist suffers is benign: M. Duléger (Mr. Lightfoot) is so obsessed with dancing that he refuses to allow his daughter to marry a man who cannot perform sufficiently skilful *ronds de jambe, entrechats*, and *jetés-battus*, until the girl's mother conspires with her vassals and her husband's dance teacher to trick him into awarding their daughter to the best dancer at a mock competition they stage at a masquerade ball. M. Duléger falls for the trick, and his daughter happily marries her intended. Besides offering a pretext for executing virtuosic steps on the stage, this comic play of dancing prowess brings into view a portrait of the protagonist that pokes fun at his obsessiveness. So, while dance historians Lisa Arkin and Marian Smith have suggested that national character dances occupied as much space on the Romantic stage as the ethereal portraits of sylphs that have predominated in contemporary imaginings of the period, the playful exaggeration of national traits also aligned itself with a new psychiatric language of excess.[52]

M. Duléger suffers from a 'transport characteristic of delirium' ('transport qui tient du délire') and a 'dancing religion'. He is described as 'ridiculous' and single-minded.[53] Although arguably a spoof on Molière's (1622–1673) *Le malade imaginaire* [The Imaginary Invalid] (1673) and other pre-revolutionary works staging the decadent bourgeoisie and laughable doctor class, Gardel's operatic ballet spoof was also taking a far more serious leap into the comic world of national disorder. Nation was increasingly a site for the contestation of normalcy: personal obsessions aligning themselves with new national characteristics provided occasions for the theatrical display of comic deviance. These deviants identified too much with the new nation; they were overly enthusiastic, effusive, and prone to spontaneous displays, including singing, dancing, and gambolling in public. Whereas certain instances of deviant

---

49. 'Je pressens les reproches que l'on peut m'adresser sur ma hardiesse à me servir d'un terme qui n'est point reconnu en français; mais comme il est le *seul* qui exprime juste l'idée de cette folie, j'ai cru pouvoir m'en servir, sans tirer à conséquence'. Pierre Gardel, *La dansomanie, folie-pantomime, en deux actes* (Paris: De l'Imprimerie de Ballard, 1800), 1n1.

50. See John V. Chapman, 'Forgotten Giant: Pierre Gardel', *Dance Research* 5.1 (1987): 3–20, 4.

51. Chapman, 'Forgotten Giant', 7–8.

52. Lisa C. Arkin and Marian Smith, 'National Dance in the Romantic Ballet', in Lynn Garafola, ed., *Rethinking the Sylph: New Perspectives on the Romantic Ballet* (Middletown, CT: Wesleyan University Press, 1997), 11–68.

53. Gardel, *La dansomanie*, 9, 11.

behaviour accompanied radical agitation, others merely performed gestural impetuosity in a public show of slightly disruptive disinhibition. This slightly reconfigures the notion of 'partial madness' Foucault argues predominated until about 1850; from then on, he suggests, there were no halfway measures with the mad: they were either entirely insane or they were not so. They had to be either entirely culpable when committing a crime or misdemeanour or not culpable on account of madness.[54] With the integration of juridical and medical power in the second half of the nineteenth century, madness became a condition different from *déraison*; one could not consciously 'act out', inasmuch as one could not simultaneously and knowingly hold, let alone perform, a fictitious and a real identity, one of which would be revealed in the theatricalization of the other.[55] This was where, as I will detail later, a new brand of neuropsychiatric and neurological research would take over the work of decoding convulsive and other bodily signs, through historiographic and performative fieldwork in the clinic and beyond. These signs came to stand for the significantly involuntary actions of a body not able to express itself through other means. The cavernous depths of psychic disturbance in the nether reaches of primitive impulse paved the way for excavators like Charcot, Mesmer, and later Freud to activate and 'read' what seemed like a subtextual message. Yet early nineteenth-century psychiatry, and the monomaniacal fixations its subjects seemingly expressed, suggested a surface order of reality in which bodily signs such as convulsions held far less weight as a cipher. These were merely accidents in a general regime of accidents, for which there were multiple sites of performance and power. Monomania, in the genealogy this chapter tells, constituted not only a troubling form of partial madness but, more dramatically, a hyperbolic sameness, an overidentification with national and other often comical types.

REVOLUTIONARY SCENES OF EXCESS: THE NEW NATION

At the cusp of a century of new nationalisms, marked by the Congress of Vienna in 1814–1815 and the revolutions of 1848, leading to the unifications of Germany and Italy and uprisings throughout the Habsburg Empire, geopolitical territories around the world were defining new borders, ushering in a shift towards state autonomy and patriotic discourse. Concomitant with this was increasing attention to nations themselves as receptacles for the production and performance of collective affect; in turn, I argue, heightened instances of nationally tinged affective display were recast as a medical conundrum and psychiatric disease. So although Foucault has convincingly argued that the eighteenth and nineteenth centuries were times of acute medicalization when nearly everything began to fall into the purview of police and state discipline, enabled by a castigating, judicially allied medical gaze, and although he has decisively shown that medical authority increasingly rationalized forms of deviance along political lines the better to sideline marginals (what he called, after Canguilhem, 'abnormals'),[56] another look at nineteenth-century medical and psychiatric writings suggests that physicians were also interested in collective figures representing—often performing—slightly exaggerated national politics. More specifically, the theatricalization of national affect played out on stages and in the pages of medical compendia suggests that individual dispositions to act out according to exaggerated national types provoked as much interest and controversy as did individual attempts to deviate from a supposed political norm. Slavoj Žižek has described strategies of over-identification as subversive means to critique political regimes through subtle acts

---

54. See esp. Foucault, *Les anormaux*, 145.

55. Foucault argues that in the mid-nineteenth century, 'psychiatry becomes [the power of] medical jurisdiction over every sort of behaviour'. He attributes this specifically to a shift around 1845–1847 from the approach taken by Esquirol—whom Foucault considers the last of France's *aliénistes*—which emphasized the question of madness ('folie'), as of a relation to truth ('rapport à la vérité'), as opposed to that taken by Jules Baillarger (1809–1890)—whom Foucault calls the first of France's psychiatrists—which emphasized instead the distinction between voluntary and involuntary, instinctive and automatic, processes at the heart of 'mental illness'. Foucault, *Les anormaux*, 147–148. On Foucault's ongoing analysis of the interpenetration of juridical and psychiatric reason in the nineteenth century, see also Michel Foucault, ed., *Moi, Pierre Rivière, ayant égorgé ma mère, ma sœur et mon frère . . . Un cas de parricide au XIXe siècle* (Paris: Gallimard, 1973).

56. See esp. Foucault, *Les anormaux*; Georges Canguilhem, *The Normal and the Pathological, with an Introduction by Michel Foucault*, trans. Carolyn R. Fawcett with Robert S. Cohen (New York: Zone Books, 1991).

of performative exaggeration,[57] but portraits of national enthusiasts in the pages of early nineteenth-century psychiatric literature suggest that few boasted such clear agendas. On the contrary, expressions of comically exaggerated national character showcased a different sort of transgressive excess and zeal. These enthusiasts drew their contemporaries' medical attention and social mockery on account of their indulgence in pleasure and close sympathy with others: they were too French or too Spanish, too much into dancing or too morbid. Enthusiasm—particularly for other people's cultures as well as one's own—seemed liable to become as hazardous as any display of the 'dangerous individuality' Foucault has described.

While elsewhere concerned with displays of individual difference, early psychiatrists were also intent on describing how enthusiasm could spread within groups and transpire across them, provoking instances of social porosity that might stimulate broader—genuinely grievous—social or political revolts. The lessons of the French Revolution were still being learned, and the heights of agitation that had led throngs of people violently to occupy public space and dispossess the aristocracy had physicians and early social commentators busily scratching their heads.

In the shadow of Napoleon's invasion of Spain in 1808, *Le procès du Fandango ou la fandangomanie, comédie-vaudeville, en un acte* [The Trial of the Fandango or Fandangomania, Vaudeville Comedy in One Act], by Jean-Baptiste Radet (1752–1830), Pierre-Yvon Barré (1749–1832), and François-Georges Fouques Desfontaines (1733–1825), first performed at the Théâtre du Vaudeville in Paris in 1809, theatricalizes the ambivalence and threats of excessive identification with other nations—suddenly and confusingly now also one's own. In this play, a legal battle is staged to determine whether residents of the small village of Saint-Jean de Luz, on the Spanish border, should be permitted to indulge in a new Spanish dance fashion: the fandango, introduced by a Spanish dance teacher and

posing, as its detractors argued, a grave threat to the upright men of the town left in the dust by the lively widows and other young people getting wind of this seductive and 'extravagant' new dance.[58] The supposed dangers presented by the dance's lead critic, M. Clopineau (Mr. Hobble), draw on the irrational excesses to which such dancing purportedly led its enthusiasts: Mme. Folignac (Mrs. Crazymer, a love-struck widow), like M. Duléger in *La dansomanie*, was a self-avowed 'dansomane', a choreomaniac, because she was 'crazy about dancing'.[59] Although she owned her choreomania proudly, arguing that it was 'delicious' and 'fabulous' to experience such a happy and 'tender delirium',[60] the tribunal of husbands and jealous men led by M. Clopineau complained that this type of dancing—very different from the composed, stately, supposedly honest (and emphatically French) minuet—disturbed the public peace, as the enthusiasts' feet got the better of their minds.[61] The problem was not simply that they danced too much; they danced too fervently and, one is led to understand, in a passionate manner that was locally alien. Yet at the end of the play, the audience is asked to weigh in on the debate and tacitly give their approval to the new dance form in a spirited call to arms: women should not be locked up in the home, the tribunal's supporters claimed, but allowed to dance freely and gaily wherever they please. The dance enthusiasts win their case, and an example of the fandango is executed onstage with flourish by M. Gavotino, the Spanish dance teacher, and his avid dance student. Dancing, equated with libertinism and a Spanish-inflected—as well as a patently feminine—passion, is targeted for threatening to disrupt the masculine moral order, on gendered as well as on national grounds. M. Gavotino is unmistakably Spanish, just as M. Duléger, although French, was instructed by a dance teacher who disguised himself and his co-conspirators in national dress (Turkish, Chinese, and Basque) to enact the mock dance competition in *La dansomanie*. In both cases, dancing is depicted through the performance of national traits, enabling the comic portrayal of talent

57. See e.g. Slavoj Žižek, *The Plague of Fantasies* (London: Verso, 1997), 21, 74; also *Predictions of Fire*, dir. Michael Benson (Kinetikon Pictures, 1996).

58. Jean-Baptiste Radet, Pierre-Yvon Barré, and François-Georges Fouques Desfontaines, *Le procès du Fandango ou la fandangomanie, comédie-vaudeville, en un acte*, 2nd ed. (Paris: Fages, libraire du théatre du Vaudeville, 1810), 23.

59. Radet et al., *Le procès du Fandango*, 4.

60. Radet et al., *Le procès du Fandango*, 8.

61. Radet et al., *Le procès du Fandango*, 24.

and effusive corporeal as well as affective excess among others. The dances were exotic and, in both cases, flamboyant. Accusations of madness amounted to accusations of national extravagance, displaced onto other nations and, just as humorously, onto one's own. While enjoying the spectacle of his daughter's dance master's nationally themed dancing display, M. Duléger also ultimately suffered too much enthusiasm for his own national form: ballet.

In this regard, choreomania was a disease not of excess movement only but of overindulgence in national pastimes. It was idle and zealous; feminine and (usually) foreign; and, most of all, it performed an energetic surfeit at odds with modern nations' celebration of what Marx in 1867 would describe as measured physiological expenditure, necessary for the efficient accumulation of capital in a labour economy.[62] Men and women frolicking about in a public show of kinetic zeal were liberated but ridiculous, failing properly to harness the sort of national enthusiasm necessary for them to perform an industrious model citizenry. Yet in their zeal, they were rehearsing the sort of leisure—and pleasure—economy that would cement nations to their imagined histories and cultural inheritances in the incipient discourse on national culture Benedict Anderson (1936–2015) describes,[63] all while covertly exercising their right to public corporeal jouissance. Modern nations, while explicitly celebrating traditions of social display largely invented, in Anderson's terms, for the sake of social cohesion, paradoxically tended to overlook just the sort of collective corporeal ebullience that nurturing and transforming these cultural conventions requires.

MONOMANIA: A 'DISEASE OF CIVILIZATION'

The nineteenth-century choreography of national affect was reflected in a host of psychiatric theories accounting for a mood of heightened public theatricality. So, too, dance, according to McCarren, represented the pathological expression of heightened affect. As McCarren shows, the Romantic heroine Giselle, in Théophile Gautier's (1811–1872)

eponymous 1841 ballet, suffers from an excess of emotion in the most famous mad scene of the nineteenth century, epitomizing the notion that dance represents madness as such; and that madness, in this view, is bodily, unspeaking, and so quintessentially feminine. Yet the libretto, which depicts a young peasant woman in the medieval countryside who dances herself to death, plausibly also drew from stories of medieval dance manias beginning to circulate at the time; with this in mind, Giselle's dance depicts a complex of medical stories: not only chorea or syphilis, but choreomania, a dancing mania, individualized. That Giselle should have danced herself to death suggests a form of monomaniacal obsessiveness with dancing that was intently theorized in the nineteenth century and was dramatically portrayed in Andersen's nearly contemporaneous story, *The Red Shoes* (1845), in which the hapless heroine dances herself to death as a result of wanting to dance too much. As with the story of Giselle, the significance of the red shoes reprises widely circulating tales of medieval dance manias, tales in which dancers react violently to the colour red. Figures of the medieval danse macabre or Dance of Death were also by the nineteenth century well known (chapter 2), but the frisson provided by tales of St. Vitus's dance as a deadly epidemic also reflected the new psychiatric discourse on obsessive fixation. As such, stories of dancing diseases provoked a new phantasm: the idea that people could dance themselves to death was itself in the nineteenth century a puzzle and an obsession. That one could do anything obsessively, to the point of death, signalled a form of affective excess that if left unchecked, moralists suggested, could lead to class and national transgressions, among other things. Overidentifying with others meant one could lose a sense of one's own rank.

Prosper Lucas (1808–1885), in his doctoral thesis at the Faculté de Médecine in Paris, offered one of the earliest studies of imitative 'monomanias' or obsessive fixations, arguing in *De l'imitation contagieuse, ou de la propagation sympathique des névroses et des monomanies* [Of Contagious Imitation, or, Of the Sympathetic Propagation of Neuroses and Monomanias] (1833) that popular movements had become

---

62. Karl Marx, *Capital*, vol. 1, trans. Ben Fowkes (London: Penguin Books, 1990), 137.

63. Benedict Anderson, *Imagined Communities: Reflections on the Origin and Spread of Nationalism*, rev. ed. (London: Verso, 2006).

increasingly political, and so too had imitative monomanias, so that government reforms, for good or ill, while sometimes resulting in social alienation, also provoked agitation of the body politic, which could lead to disturbing acts of social revolt and collective madness.[64] Esquirol, one of the founders of modern psychiatry, argued that all manic disorders had national or historical conditions at their root. All manias, Esquirol thought, should be seen as 'monomanias', including the monomania for dancing. In his monumental *Des Maladies Mentales* [Of Mental Illness] (1838) Esquirol wrote: 'monomania . . . borrows its character . . . from the various ages of the societies in which it is found'. In more 'advanced' societies, it is characterized by pride, faithlessness, ambition, gaming, despair, and suicide. Monomania, Esquirol argued, was thus the disease of civilization par excellence ('la maladie de la civilisation').[65]

Although this characterization was considered true of madness ('folie') in general, for Esquirol monomania offered more insight into the intense expressions of passionate affect that marked societies at all times. Monomania, he argued, ought to be considered not only mere obsession but also an extreme heightening of the characteristics of a given culture. In France, he argued, a new form of monomania had emerged with the disintegration of the old system of religious belief and the rise of the police force: this was paranoia, a new type of persecution delirium, which filled the halls of mental asylums. During the French Revolution and ensuing periods, various forms of monomania had emerged, he noted, each characterized by circumstantial factors: in 1791 in Versailles, a prodigious number of suicides were reported by Pinel, who attributed these to widespread imitation of the French revolutionary figure Georges Jacques Danton (1759–1794). Similarly, 'superstitious' monomanias had re-emerged after the pope's visit to France; and in the age of empire, many monomaniacs believed they were emperors or kings. The war against Spain had produced

its own monomanias, spurred on by terror. In ancient history, Stoics had killed themselves out of pride, and the Japanese killed themselves out of excess virtue. These were all culturally specific forms of national delirium.

For Esquirol, 'the state of a society exercises a considerable influence on the production and character of monomania. The study of this form of disease', he argued, 'thus requires knowledge of the customs and habits of each people'.[66] He was putting forward a concept of psychiatry founded in the description of cultural characteristics whose excesses presented cases of mental alienation. Nation, in this view, constituted one of the main categories for taxonomizing disease. As I show further in chapter 7, comparison was emerging as a method of choice for scientific analysis, emphasizing variations across nations and eras, occasionally complicated by the intensity of the similarities between them. One such similarity in particular troubled Esquirol: 'convulsions have occurred in all eras, because they depend as much on the organism as on the imagination', he wrote, 'complicating all forms of mental alienation'.[67] Unlike national behaviours and beliefs, convulsions were symptomatic of various disorders all over the world. This complicated the view that psychiatric diseases were determined by national characteristics.

For Esquirol's student the psychiatrist Louis-Florentin Calmeil (1798–1895), quoted in the epigraph to chapter 3, the mind alone was at fault. Choreomania, in Calmeil's terms, was a type of monomania in which the patient evinced an overzealous passion for dance, in contrast to other forms of monomania, such as vampirism or somnambulism.[68] And although religious deliria and other types of madness typically produced spasmodic muscular convulsions and hallucinatory phenomena, choreomania, Calmeil thought, should not be defined solely in psychomotor terms. It was, like other monomanias, a product of extreme single-mindedness only.[69] This was ostensibly what M. Duléger and Mme. Folignac suffered from in *La dansomanie* and *La*

64. Prosper Lucas, *De l'imitation contagieuse, ou de la propagation sympathique des névroses et des monomanies* (Paris: Didot le Jeune, 1833), 69–70.

65. Étienne Esquirol, *Des maladies mentales considérées sous le rapport médical, hygiénique et médico-légal*, 2 vols., vol. 1 (Paris: J.-B. Baillière, 1838), 400.

66. Esquirol, *Des maladies mentales*, vol. 1, 400–401.

67. Esquirol, *Des maladies mentales*, vol. 1, 516.

68. Calmeil, *De la folie*, vol. 1, 81.

69. 'Assez souvent', he writes, 'on voit . . . la lésion des sentiments religieux s'associer à la lésion des sens et à la perversion des mouvements volontaires. Les hallucinations qui font croire à l'obsession diabolique, les tressaillements spasmodiques, les

fandangomanie, although both were eventually acquitted of their obsessions in narratives that promised audiences their own merriment to come. At the close of the tribunal staged in *La fandangomanie*, the audience is invited to celebrate the dancing duo and implicitly to take its side, on the promise that in doing so they too will have a chance to dance after the show is over. This was a far cry from the inflated language of social plague that would set medical writers off to the four corners of the colonial world and into the trenches of national archives to find extravagant examples of dancing manias with which to bewilder their polite readers. In Calmeil's account, choreomania seems rather unthreatening. Although he describes it in terms of collective folly and epidemic madness, it frequently adds up to little more than a highly spirited fête. Describing a case of choreomania in Apulia in the seventeenth century in *De la folie, considérée sous le point de vue pathologique, philosophique, historique et judiciaire, depuis la renaissance des sciences en Europe jusqu'au dix-neuvième siècle* [On Madness, Considered from a Pathological, Philosophical, Historical, and Legal Point of View, from the Renaissance of the Sciences in Europe to the Nineteenth Century] (1845), Calmeil wrote: 'youth . . . has a passion for balls, flying, as if compelled by some secret instinct, to every party [fête] in sight as long as some glimmer of hope for happiness [bonheur] is to be found there. Some care only to dance, and deliver themselves to this with an ardour that appears to partake of a sort of frenzy'.[70] Music served as a powerful stimulant, so that, Calmeil wrote, 'the impulse transmitted to the sensory nervous system via the musical instruments acts on the choreomaniacs by producing an irresistible transport, translated externally into a succession of rhythmically cadenced movements'.[71] Calmeil's philosophico-psychiatric diagnosis explained the dancing by recourse to a theory of musical impulses converted in the body into musically cadenced rhythmical steps, a variation on Baglivi's theories of tarantism, discussed in chapter 3. But unlike Baglivi's tarantists or Plato's Bacchic dancers, whose rhythms, Plato thought, should be outlawed on account of their irregularity, Calmeil's censure emphasized the intensity with which dancers carried out their movements. For Calmeil, youthful festivity invited psychiatric concern because the boys and girls enjoyed themselves too much: they suffered excess zeal.

This emphasis on excess pleasure and joy revealed a curious shift in concepts of health and disease, holding onto older, humoral ideas about imbalance but seeing 'frenzy' as the mechanical appearance of overzealousness only, stimulated by mental impressions. Calmeil and his contemporaries, it seems, were baffled by every sign of ebullient movement and powerful emotion. Religious enthusiasm, which Calmeil described as 'theomania' or 'theo-choreomania', provoked zealous excitement by disturbing the 'faculty of reason', causing hallucinations and obsessions with the devil, as well as spasms and convulsions, and the 'incessant need to dance'.[72]

Dancing was a sign and a symptom of excess passion, troublesome for the impulses that bodily movements could provoke. The catchiness of a tune was worrying because of its propensity kinetically to enthuse entire groups: for Calmeil, 'this bizarre form of monomania' (choreomania) was 'susceptible to rapid propagation: it easily becomes contagious'.[73] A further example he describes is telling in this respect: a band of excited audience members reportedly exiting a production of Euripides's *Andromeda* was seized with what Calmeil called contagious enthusiasm, resulting in what he describes as 'epidemic madness' ('folie épidémique'), as they went singing and dancing down the street, in imitation of Perseus, all the way home.[74] Like the young Italian revellers, these theatregoers from

---

contractions musculaires disharmoniques, les convulsions générales momentanées, forment quelquefois encore aujourd'hui le cortège de l'aliénation religieuse affective'. He adds: 'La folie peut succéder à une affection aigüe du cerveau, à un délire fébrile, à une apoplexie avec lésion du mouvement, à des convulsions générales, à une attaque d'épilepsie; l'aliénation mentale peut se compliquer, dès son invasion ou pendant le cours de sa durée, avec une affection spasmodique, avec un état de paralysie plus ou moins complet, avec l'épilepsie, la catalepsie, l'extase, les phénomènes de l'hystérie'. Calmeil, *De la folie*, vol. 1, 58, 66–67.

70. Calmeil, *De la folie*, vol. 2, 159.
71. Calmeil, *De la folie*, vol. 2, 159.
72. Calmeil, *De la folie*, vol. 2, 159–160.
73. Calmeil, *De la folie*, vol. 2, 160.
74. Calmeil, *De la folie*, vol. 2, 161–162. The case is also reported in Lucas, *De l'imitation contagieuse*, who notes, drawing on Sauvages's *Nosologie*, that the story was reported by Lucian and constituted one of the sole cases related to nervous epidemics in antiquity, although it was not an epidemic outright (37).

Abdère—first reported as a medical case linked to the Italian tarantella by Boissier Sauvages de la Croix—were hardly suffering in any usual medical sense; they certainly didn't seek medical help. But they displayed contagious zeal, excitement that warranted a place in the ranks of psychiatric disorders considered, as Calmeil put it, from every point of view: historical, legal, philosophical, and medical. Psychiatry was not just a science of physiological disorders; it also described movements occurring at every level of the social and cultural sphere.[75]

Although early psychiatrists were not typically involved in implementing punitive measures against such dancers, the slightly bewildered tone of caution articulated by Calmeil reflected concerns also voiced in the political arena: crowds whose energies proliferated quickly were potentially hazardous. As Jacques Rancière has suggested, theatregoers and patrons of the new cafés-concerts in Paris in the 1830s and 1840s risked, in the police prefecture's eyes, being roused to political action by the songs, dances, and dramatic acts that put them 'outside the simple role of spectator'.[76] They risked erupting into a revolutionary crowd, spurred on by the 'mass theatricality' that served as a 'conduit' '[complementing] the reverie of mobile minorities'.[77] Not only were workers indulging in bourgeois pastimes—pleasures that exceeded the requirements of hard labour—but also, by passing over class barriers in this way, they risked dreaming themselves out of their present existence. They would, in this event, adopt alien characteristics—middle-class ones—and so destabilize a fragile post-revolutionary regime.

But Rancière points out the workers' own derision of displays of carnival spectatorship. Bourgeois decadents who came in swarms to gawk at working-class fêtes held at the Champs-Elysées or elsewhere spoiled, they thought, the zone of safety such revelries provided.

Detractors argued that privacy was necessary to help workers avoid slipping continuously—in their observers' eyes—back into the stereotype of the lazy, sloppy, and uncouth brute. The workers, in Rancière's terms, were in this respect puritanical: just as they held fast to the privileged space of the fête, so, too, they resisted the label of drunken depravity that justified paternalistic intervention on the bourgeois' part.[78] The performance of pleasure in public was at stake, and its disinhibited show was discomfiting for all the constituencies sitting, revelling, or strolling on either side. Dance and the public fête served as a battleground not only for the liberation of unspent energies and collective jouissance, but for the right to occupy public space free from the tyranny of judgmental observation, in a social theatre vexed with class distinction. The public fête was a site of contestation for the right temporarily to unleash passion and emotion in the paradoxical privacy of socially delimited public space.

The increasingly porous and open sociality of public space and the contested territories within which these roving parties moved made the dancing festivities a fraught affair, a zone of intensity at the heart of the nation's new radical politics. Spontaneous acts in particular were problematic, as they threatened to contagion any passerby. As Clare Parfitt-Brown has shown, spontaneity was employed in the early nineteenth century as a measure of impropriety, particularly with regard to bodily display and dance. Cancan dancers on trial in Paris in the 1830s and 1840s were questioned about whether their performances had been improvised: wilder, 'indecent' forms known as the *chahut* were more suspect than the choreographed and thus more predictable movements of dance routines overseen by dance masters. Likewise, Parfitt-Brown argues, dancing that subverted classical norms of grace, energy, poise, and bodily contact was considered suspect.[79] Like the choreomanias described by Esquirol

---

75. Although it went out of favour for nearly a century, the notion of excessive emotion—including joyous emotion—returned in the 1920s with Pierre Janet (1859–1947), professor of psychology at the Collège de France, who argued that excess, rather than deviance, troubled everyday life. Joy, he wrote, provokes agitation, resulting in a type of delirium characterized by its intensity: patients who are too happy show this corporeally too much; they intrude into the public sphere with their extravagance, slipping outside the boundaries of a normally, and normatively, more contained individual self. Pierre Janet, *De l'angoisse à l'extase: Études sur les croyances et les sentiments*, 2 vols., vol. 2 (Paris: Félix Alcan, 1926–1927).

76. Jacques Rancière, *Staging the People: The Proletarian and His Double*, trans. David Fernbach (London: Verso, 2011), 185.

77. Rancière, *Staging the People*, 188.

78. Rancière, *Staging the People*, 198–205.

79. Clare Parfitt-Brown, 'The Problem of Popularity: The Cancan between the French and Digital Revolutions', in Sherrill Dodds and Susan C. Cook, eds., *Bodies of Sound: Studies across Popular Music and Dance* (Surrey: Ashgate, 2013), 9–24.

and Calmeil, the *chahut* suggested uncontrolled gestures stimulating collective contagion, provoking a potential for sharing ideas and emotions that could get socially and politically out of hand. Whereas earlier dance prohibitions had typically been enforced on religious grounds that high leaps and some rounds were 'demonic' (chapter 2), the nineteenth-century injunction against singing, dancing, and revelling bodies comparatively emphasized the dangers of mutual sympathy that overt enthusiasm stoked.

In the next chapter, crowd theory emerges out of sociological writing indebted to neurology, French revolutionary history, and social psychiatry, all grappling with the changes that revolutionary and post-revolutionary crowd and popular movements occasioned. Significantly, religious enthusiasms—including the 'jerks' in Kentucky and Tennessee—became grounds for theorizing mimetic impulses as a social psychiatric problem, an epidemic reflecting the particular sorts of boredom and restlessness besetting the modern working class.

5

Mobiles, Mobs, and Monads
Nineteenth-Century Crowd Forms

Whether Foucault is discussing biopower or discipline, law or sovereign edict, subjects are governed or resist being governed *as* individual subjects or as disciplinary bodies. There is no *political* body, no demos acting in concert (even episodically) or expressing aspirational sovereignty; there are few social forces from below and no shared powers of rule or shared struggles for freedom.

—Wendy Brown, *Undoing the Demos: Neoliberalism's Stealth Revolution* (2015)

The present generation is born exhausted; it is the product of a century of convulsions.

—Philippe Tissié, *La fatigue et l'entraînement physique* [Fatigue and Physical Sport] (1897)

CROWDS AFTER FOUCAULT

Witnessing the Iranian revolution in 1979, Foucault confronted for the first time, Said notes, the 'entirely collective, involuntary excessiveness which could not be herded under conventional rubrics like class contradictions or economic oppression'.[1] The affective and energetic surplus of history, spilling out into crowd movements, constituted an entirely different order of collective being and becoming; a scene of ferment characterized not by structures of oppression, surveillance, and control but by the apparently involuntary amplification of emotions and energies surging up during moments of communal anguish and hope. This chapter plunges deeper into the discursive history of crowd movements, mass upheavals, and gestural spontaneities that theatricalize national becoming in the revolutionary era, roughly the eighteenth to the late nineteenth century. But rather than suggest a 'history' of increasing nationalism, or the rationalization and disciplinarization of modes of thinking about histories, nations, and crowds, this chapter offers a discursive history of bodily turmoil, scenes within which the public spectacle of excessiveness plays out, ultimately to argue that crowds serve in the nineteenth century as a privileged site of theorization about spectacular spontaneity. The chapter further moves the study of crowds into the sphere of 'dance' broadly construed, with Hewitt, as social choreography: the movement of bodies forming social space, at the edge of the 'aesthetic continuum' he describes as constitutive of modern art and social life.[2] Crowds do not constitute aesthetic formations—orderly objects of contemplation—but the

---

1. Said, 'Michel Foucault', 9.

2. Andrew Hewitt, *Social Choreography: Ideology as Performance in Dance and Everyday Movement* (Durham, NC: Duke University Press, 2005), 35; see also 19–20.

dissolution of orderly aesthetics into its converse, what I am calling an *anaesthetic* regime of ungainly, disorganized moves. But the figure of this disorderly crowd significantly forms political imaginaries in the nineteenth century: imaginaries that emerge discursively against the grain of the putative primordial herd.

In this respect, the chapter carves out a further scene of thinking choreomania conceived in the nineteenth century as an unruly crowd condition, a surge of ungoverned and nearly ungovernable life. This extends Foucault's analysis of biopower to include movements subject to the 'involuntary excessiveness' he alludes to in the anecdote offered by Said—a sphere of inquiry otherwise conspicuously absent from Foucault's writing. Even Foucault's analysis of biopolitics as a mode of government exercised on individual subjects through regimes of social and corporeal regulation implicating scientific research, statistics, and population control eludes direct engagement, Wendy Brown further notes, with the 'demos', the 'people'.[3] For Brown, Foucault's work suffers from an oversight as far as group life is concerned: his lens focuses on the individual, subject to pressures exercised discursively and politically through regimes of thought and discipline (concerning sexuality and madness, criminality and deviance) constituting the subtle workings of biopower. Foucault fails, Brown argues, to consider the 'people' as a biopolitical unit, an entity rising up and organizing itself from below, to form an alternative, plural, and autonomous politics. But even in Brown's rereading of Foucault's work, the demos appears on the page as an already formed discursive ideal. Her analysis does not engage with the performative, spontaneous crowd out of and through which the demos arises as a politically cogent force and against which the demos is discursively constituted.

The volatile and improvisatory body of the crowd appears, I argue, in nineteenth-century social science at a time of proliferating uprisings, drawing attention to themselves and to the history with which they appear to resonate. As with Foucault's observation of the revolution in Iran, they emerge as fantasy objects of social science, revealing and forming nineteenth-century ideas of rational subjecthood indirectly. Cast in nineteenth-century literature as disorderly, excessive, and uncontrolled but also, significantly, as diseased, crowds emerge as a force of nature against which the liberal subject Foucault outlines would appear.[4] Imagined as indefinite and temporary, improvisatory and artless, but also vulnerable to contagion, gatherings of individuals in crowds become subject to discursive inquiry and medicalization, a problem Foucault and Brown pass over. So whereas the individual subject, like the demos, arises in post-Enlightenment philosophy as an organized constellation of forces moving history forward into modernity, the disorganized mass of moving bodies pullulating on the scene of revolutionary political life comes to light in nineteenth-century social science as a subject of biomedical and biohistorical writing against the grain of historical progress. Significantly for dance studies, crowds come to be construed in social scientific literature as bodily beings shifting the course of historical progress by virtue of their tendency, in times of crisis, chaotically to appear. As Judith Butler and Athena Athanasiou note in *Dispossession: The Performative in the Political* (2013), crowds are performative inasmuch as they *appear* in public space and in doing so show themselves as political constituencies. They demonstrate their presence and, as such, become political bodies publicly.[5] Significantly, crowds appear in nineteenth-century medical and social scientific literature as an involuntary, bodily, automatic return to a prior state of group life—one of unthinking imitation and aggregation, herd- and hound-like. They serve discursively to illustrate the flip side of scientific modernity's obsession with another sort of automatism: that of the machine. Their automatism signals the prehistorical within modernity; as such, dance—appearing as the swarm-like movement of plural bodies in public space—constitutes modernity's

---

3. Brown, *Undoing the Demos*, 85–87.

4. Foucault describes the late twentieth-century crisis of liberalism as a crisis of the economic and political mechanisms set up in the early decades of the twentieth century specifically to counter communist, socialist, and national socialist movements—what I am reading here as movements, and their detractors, that had their roots in eighteenth- and nineteenth-century insurgencies and in the fear of these insurgent crowds articulated in nineteenth- and early twentieth-century social scientific literature. In the view I am articulating, the nearly systematic—almost always scientifically validated—disparagement of collective movements led to the emergence of 'liberal' state protection of the 'individual', almost always contrasted to the quasi mythical threat of the horde. See esp. Michel Foucault, *Naissance de la biopolitique: Cours au Collège de France 1978–1979* (Paris: Éditions du Seuil/Gallimard, 2004), 70.

5. Judith Butler and Athena Athanasiou, *Dispossession: The Performative in the Political* (Cambridge: Polity Press, 2013).

unscientific, irrational, antimodern other half, that out of which it arises. Crowds thus represent a choreopolitical state of emergence and its discursivization, the impetuous movement of bodies cast as a primal force disrupting the smooth forward march of modernity into an efficient industrial age. Crowds in nineteenth-century social theory appear to gather, like a storm, against the productive machinism of rational economic life. The organic metaphor prominent in medically inflected social theory posited crowds as biological beings, violent and unpredictable like nature. As such, moving crowds in the nineteenth century epitomize the disorder of a pre-industrial age overwhelming the modern moment with its own brand of biopower. This suggests not only what Jeffrey T. Schnapp highlights as Freud's concept of the 'oceanic', a beatific collective feeling overwhelming individuals with a liberatory sense of disindividuation,[6] but crowds as swarms performing unpredictable gestures—in choreographic terms, flowing and starting, liquid and angular, explosive and resonant—bodies tumbling awkwardly into modernity from another age. Crowds, this chapter shows, signal in the nineteenth century the intensification of all bodily potential for disorder and turmoil as well as their converse, a choreopolitics of control.

So whereas literature on crowd theory has witnessed a boom since the social and political movements of the 1960s, from Canetti's *Masse und Macht* [Crowds and Power] (1960) to R. A. Nye's *The Origins of Crowd Psychology* (1975), Salvador Giner's *Mass Society* (1976), Susanne Barrows's *Distorting Mirrors: Visions of the Crowd in Late Nineteenth-Century France* (1981), Serge Moscovici's *L'âge des foules* [The Age of the Crowd] (1981), J. S. McClelland's *The Crowd and the Mob* (1989), Jaap van Ginneken's *Crowds, Psychology, and Politics 1871–1899* (1993),

Étienne Balibar's *La crainte des foules* [Fear of Crowds] (1997), Howard Rheingold's upbeat *Smart Mobs* (2003), Schnapp and Matthew Ties's *Crowds* (2006), and Christian Borch's *The Politics of Crowds: An Alternative History of Sociology* (2013), among others, the relationship between crowds, choreopolitics, and biopower remains overlooked. Crowd theory's little-acknowledged prehistory in de Félice's writing on ecstatic dances, which decisively influenced Canetti's foundational work on group life, merits a further look, not only to clarify the extended genealogy of these intellectual movements in what one may construe as a prehistory of dance and performance studies but also better to distinguish the dancing crowd and dramaturgies of collective, imitative, and gesturally 'showy' assemblies from others. My aim in this chapter, then, is to outline a history of abrupt and fitful gestures in religious and neurological literature where these intersect with nineteenth-century discourses on collective pathology; and to think through the pathological 'showiness' of fitful gestures and their converse, play. This approach highlights the choreopolitics of early crowd theory as an animal, automatic, and comedic genre. The chapter thus places crowds at the basis of dance history, considered as the study of bodies moving in (and moving) social space, in this case just past the outer edges of torque-like grace.

This chapter thus furthers the previous chapter's thinking about the queer space of popular religion where it overlaps with public instances of political protest, what Foster has called the choreographies of protest and Lepecki describes with regard to choreopolicing. Here, with the emergence of sociology and neurology, society at large appears periodically excessive, effusive, and uncontrolled. Its eruption onto the scene of urban modernity in the nineteenth century suggests a general 'convulsion', as one of its

---

6. Jeffrey T. Schnapp, 'Mob Porn', in Jeffrey T. Schnapp and Matthew Tiews, eds., *Crowds* (Stanford, CA: Stanford University Press, 2006), 1–45, esp. 3–7. Schnapp notes that 'the "oceanic crowd" is . . . traceable at least as far back as the long-standing conflation in Greco-Roman culture of *turbulence*, whether maritime, meteorological, or political, with the *turba* (τυρβε), which is to say, the mob' (4). On recent crowd theory in the broader social and historical sciences, see also esp. Christian Borch, *The Politics of Crowds: An Alternative History of Sociology* (Cambridge: Cambridge University Press, 2013). Michael Hardt and Antonio Negri differentiate what they term the (politically agential) 'multitudes' from the crowd, mass, or mob, which they consider passive and not politically efficacious; see esp. Michael Hardt and Antonio Negri, *Multitude: War and Democracy in the Age of Empire* (London: Penguin, 2004); Michael Hardt, 'Bathing in the Multitude', in Schnapp and Tiews, eds., *Crowds*, 35–40. On Edmund Burke's (1729–1797) introduction of the notion of 'masses' and 'mobs' to describe the purportedly volatile and violent lower classes (in *Reflections on the Revolution in France* [1790])—and eventually the ambivalent power of a democracy ruled by numbers—see Stefan Jonsson, 'The Invention of the Masses: The Crowd in French Culture from the Revolution to the Commune', in Schnapp and Tiews, eds., *Crowds*, 47–75, esp. 51–53, 74. Jonsson further discusses the ambivalent notion of a 'people' (as sovereign nation, or as social force, and eventually as event), 55–59. I follow Borch's contention that to distinguish e.g. crowds from masses is to eschew the 'politics of definition' by which such terms continue to change over time (Borch, *The Politics of Crowds*, 13). A discursive genealogy of the language of masses, mobs, crowds, multitudes, and people would constitute another study in its own right.

historians put it, which had the potential to upend political life.[7] The analysis of choreomania as a disorderly crowd condition therefore moves the discursive history of jagged movement to the street, and to the choreopolitics of large-scale revolution and revolt. Central to the discussion on choreomania as a disorderly crowd condition is the emergence of sociology as a science that would, following modern history, in its turn following the language of medicine, return to the French Revolution as a primal scene of dangerous and contagious politicality epitomizing the disruptive choreopolitics of public protest. With the French Revolution, crowds retrospectively came to be described as unthinking, animal, organic, even ecological movements performing their excessive presence as a giant nervous spasm traversing political life. Further drawing the literature on the animalization of crowd movements into a new body of neurological literature on jerks, twitches, and tics in large crowds of religious enthusiasts in the American South, I argue that choreomania appears in the nineteenth century as a disease of disruptive sociality. The social body comes to be described in terms of its potential to erupt.

Publicness thus comes to the fore in the discursive history of the dancing disease. Public space, as a contested sphere within which nineteenth-century nation states were defining themselves, required what Foucault called 'docile bodies': pliant, submissive bodies that did not draw attention to themselves. Bodies that were emphatically not theatrical: docile bodies hide, conform.[8] Discourse on the unwelcome appearance of eruptive, restless corporeal formations suggests the articulation of publicness as an arena within which fitful movement has no place.

ORGANIC METAPHORS: TAINE AND THE ORIGINS OF FRENCH BIOHISTORY

Organic metaphors suffused the nineteenth-century language of social contagion. While the revolution of 1848 and Paris Commune of 1871 swept France into a fury of political protest in the latter part of the nineteenth century, interest in crowds in Germany was spurred on by the epidemics of cholera that swept away thousands of men and women in 1832, 1848–1849, and 1854, sensitizing physicians to human vulnerability in the new urban centres and awakening a new interest in social and medical history, revealing precedents for prevailing bouts of contagion in the popular movements of the past. The French historian Hippolyte Taine (1828–1893), in his six-volume *Les origines de la France contemporaine* [The Origins of Contemporary France] (1876–1894), following Hecker's work in medical history, set the stage for a biohistorical analysis of crowd movements in France, depicting dramatic acts of popular dissolution in terms likening them to cataclysmic geological events. Writing a century after the height of the French Revolution, Taine looked back at the revolutionary outbursts of the previous century with disapproval: crowds had behaved like wild animals or children, he wrote, wreaking havoc as a beast of burden might when suddenly taking cognizance of its situation and shaking the shackles off its back, throwing its rider overboard.[9] Taine took his disparaging organic metaphors further: rowdy crowds of revolutionaries, overtaking cafés, armed with pamphlets, standing on tables and chairs, seizing moderates by the collar and trampling them in the mud,[10] reached ecological proportions as their movements became, he put it disapprovingly, like a 'human torrent'.[11] These same crowds further reached mythopoeic stature: following an exegetic tradition depicting Liberty as a sympathetic, fulsome, and galvanizing woman maternally and seductively leading men and women into revolutionary action, Taine personified the revolution as a monstrous, barking Liberty, a Miltonian woman girdled in Cerberean hounds, a figure of Night as 'terrible as Hell', advancing with giant steps, shaking a dagger and wreathed in a poor semblance of a royal crown. Like ten Furies, she deployed a destructive power at the head of an unrelenting and irresistible herd: tens of thousands of judges and executioners joined in a chaotic surge of motion behind her.[12] This revolutionary figure was fearsome—an ancient goddess terrifying for

---

7. See Maxime Du Camp, *Les Convulsions de Paris*, 4 vols., vol. 1 (Paris: Librairie Hachette, 1878).

8. Michel Foucault, *Surveiller et punir: Naissance de la Prison* (Paris: Éditions Gallimard, 1975).

9. Hippolyte Taine, *Les origines de la France contemporaine*, 6 vols, vol. 2 (Paris: Librairie Hachette, 1878); see esp. 'L'anarchie spontanée', 3–106.

10. Taine, *Les origines*, vol. 2, 42–45, 44.

11. Taine, *Les origines*, vol. 2, 56.

12. Taine, *Les origines*, vol. 2, 66–67.

her pre-civilized barbarity. This led Taine to political indictment. He wrote that crowds needed governments as animals needed heads: to think and to control with; to see and to domesticate with; and to be refined, intelligent, and moderate—in other words, fit to rule.[13] Though modern nation states had reached back to Greek figures of democratic self-governance, they had first, according to Taine's depiction, to conquer their own primal forces, lurking within themselves. The new nation had not yet quelled its own revolutionary hounds; nor had it fully outgrown its potential for stupid herd-like life. By all accounts, the French people in Taine's depiction were brutal, animal: even at their most docile, they were too beast-like to turn away from the more violent leaders among them.

Coinciding with centenary celebrations marking the uprisings of the French Revolution, Taine's chilling narrative set a hostile tone for discussions on crowd behaviour at the close of the Second Empire, when a new set of uprisings and the widespread fires of the Paris Commune of 1871 were fresh in the minds of readers and writers alike. Unprecedented access to the Archives Nationales, which were enjoying greater support than ever before by a government keen to inscribe national history into the collective curriculum, allowed Taine to draw vivid scenes of men and women taken up in the fury of a revolutionary herd. This was an organically inflected history of collective motion, taking the cataclysmic movements of groups as its formidable object, prompting Nietzsche to call Taine 'the *foremost* historian now living', although, Nietzsche complained, the intellectual life Taine represented still suffered from a pessimistic and vulgar Germanic sentiment indebted to Hegel, progressing, as its proponents thought, towards a predetermined, static, and despondent futurity. This did not, for Nietzsche, yet herald an intellectual disposition living up to the surges of collective life that Taine's history evoked.[14]

The organic metaphors Taine deployed nevertheless proved catchy. The notion of crowd movements as biological events similar to individual bodily spasms in particular inscribed political life into a social scientific discourse emphasizing individual and social crisis. In his contemporaneous four-volume history of the Paris Commune, *Les convulsions de Paris* [The Convulsions of Paris] (1878–1880), Maxime Du Camp (1822–1894) described a 'wind' of 'revolutionary madness' 'paralysing' and corrupting the urban machine.[15] In his earlier six-volume *Paris: Ses organes, ses fonctions et sa vie dans la seconde moitié de XIXe siècle* [Paris: Its Organs, Functions, and Life in the Second Half of the Nineteenth Century] (1869–1876), arguably anticipating Foucault's biopolitical analyses of institutional structures of power, Du Camp claimed the danse macabre as a furious passion that struck men and women in Germany, France, Holland, Italy, America, and the Islamic Orient like a frantic scourge that threw exhausted populations into motoric frenzy.[16] Du Camp, like Taine, drew from broadly medical language, which with Hecker had already begun to characterize crowd movements in terms likening them to giant spasms and convulsive plagues. For the physician Jean Baptiste Vincent Laborde (1830–1903), writing in the heat of the insurrection of 1871, the 'terrible events' of the Paris Commune offered a 'sad and simultaneously a strange spectacle' to their contemporaries, a 'wind of madness' revealing a society so 'sick in spirit and body' it could only signal a 'mental illness', a 'collective madness'. The entire mechanism of the social body was broken.[17]

In Laborde's view, this state of crisis played out mechanistically through the exercise of tics and gestures, 'spasmodic contractions' representing 'involuntary motor impulses', which showed the organism's state of (often hereditary) disrepair.[18] As the expressive 'play' of a pathologically disturbed 'moral physiognomy',[19] this degenerative theatre made public the 'absolute

---

13. Taine, *Les origines*, vol. 2, 68.

14. Nietzsche bitterly notes the 'tyrannical influence' of Hegel through Taine and the spirit of pessimism to which French intellectual culture as a whole was succumbing. Friedrich Nietzsche, *Beyond Good and Evil: Prelude to a Philosophy of the Future*, trans. Walter Kaufmann (New York: Vintage Books, 1989), 193.

15. Du Camp, *Les Convulsions de Paris*, vol. 1, i.

16. Maxime Du Camp, *Paris: Ses organes, ses fonctions et sa vie dans la seconde moitié de XIXe siècle*, 6 vols., vol. 4 (Paris: Hachette, 1873), 376.

17. J. V. Laborde, *Les hommes et les actes de l'insurrection de Paris devant la psychologie morbide: Lettres à M. le docteur Moreau* (Paris: Baillière, 1872), i, iii, 3.

18. Laborde, *Les hommes*, 12.

19. Laborde, *Les hommes*, 13.

perversion' of the individual's dysfunctional, psychomorbid state. The individual assimilated tics, copied these, and in doing so revealed intergenerational transmissibility and influence. Violent revolutionary excitement, similarly 'monstrous' and hereditary (as well as often, in his view, bohemian and atheistic), showed the same sort of 'organopathological' dysfunction.[20] Human weakness, wrote Laborde, quoting Rousseau, impelled men to seek association, gathering like herds and eventually arriving at politics. But for Laborde, this form of political association was not just a 'human weakness', as Rousseau had suggested; it more forcefully indicated psychological disease.[21] Proof was in the portrait, and the annals of psychopathology and crowd psychology revelled in scenes each more outrageous and each demonstrative of a more passionate and instinctive,[22] as well as a more theatricalized affect, than the next. One revolutionary character—a Girondin, or republican, 'of the most *common* sort'—whose case Laborde describes fluctuated between emotions and opinions with an alarming degree of 'mobility', carried himself nervously, and trembled, suggesting the exact 'portrait' ('peinture') of a madman ('halluciné').[23] Others, similarly affected by alcoholism exacerbating what Laborde saw as hereditary predispositions to insanity, showed no fear in the face of danger. A friend of his, venturing out into the 'orgiastic' underside of Paris's guarded battle zones, performed an 'unforgettable' 'peregrination'. In one street, this friend and his guide encountered an energetic and savage dance, a vertiginous, unbridled round, replete with hurrahs, while bullets flew overhead. A number of revellers, 'bacchant-men', were lying in pools of blood on the ground, singing raucously, contagiously insensitive to danger or pain. The scenes reminded Laborde's friend of the 'joyous and insane indifference' given to men stung by tarantulas. The friend's guide, in order to cross an especially perilous street, got down on his hands and knees, crawling through a chaotic brawl, though Laborde's friend notes

he himself had been able to conserve his dignity and walked across the street—though not quite holding his head high—at least without 'for a minute, descending to the rank of the quadruped'. He eventually succeeded in escaping this 'Bacchic' 'Hell', 'without looking once behind'. Laborde reflects that his friend, and he himself, at a remove, thus were able to 'witness, with a shudder, these impulsive events' ('On assiste, en frémissant, à ces manifestations impulsives').[24] In Laborde's analysis, these men not only suffered from an alcoholic disposition, but also showed symptoms of 'violent and total excitement', involuntary manifestations suggestive of a 'truly *insane* gaiety' ('une gaieté véritablement *folle*').[25] They suffered, Laborde thought, from too much enthusiasm, translated into a Bacchic frenzy. Even at their most spectacular, men and women caught in the throes of social disease, Laborde argued, contagioned one another gesturally without going anywhere, without exercising rational, purposeful action. 'Passions', in nineteenth-century medical terminology, were also referred to as 'mobiles', as Laborde's writing makes clear: volatile energies, bodily and mental movements spurring individual and collective action and affect, generally, his depictions underlined, to no good.[26]

The social choreography of these outbursts, to reprise Hewitt's language, suggests mobility on the 'aesthetic continuum' of social and political life at the jagged edge, where disorderly bodies reveal society falling apart. For Hewitt, the 'aesthetic continuum of bodily articulation' suggests the extension of bodily life across art and political forms: bodies shape social being in the public sphere by indicating ways of holding oneself singly and in relation to others: ways of moving and aggregating.[27] The forms bodies take make, reflect, and disrupt the choreographic forms—the choreopolitics—of social life. In cases described here, bodies gather to disrupt political life and simultaneously to constitute it anew as a popular force: not yet a demos, but a potential for communal rule.

20. Laborde, *Les hommes*, 29, 48, 75.

21. Laborde, *Les hommes*, 69.

22. Laborde, *Les hommes*, 37.

23. Laborde, *Les hommes*, 97–99.

24. Laborde, *Les hommes*, 109–124.

25. Laborde, *Les hommes*, 123.

26. Laborde is borrowing terminology put forward by the psychiatrist Louis Delasiauve (1804–1893), in Laborde, *Les hommes*, 72. See also E. A. Ross, *Social Psychology: An Outline and Source Book* (New York: Macmillan, 1908), 54.

27. Hewitt, *Social Choreography*, 35; see also 19–20.

SOCIAL THEORY AFTER TAINE

Taine's writing influenced a wave of social theorists, all contributing to the new literature on social disease. Writers including Gustave Le Bon (1841–1931), Gabriel Tarde (1843–1904), Émile Durkheim (1858–1917), and Henri Fournial (1866–1932) in France, Scipio Sighele (1868–1913) in Italy, and William McDougall (1871–1938) in Britain, contributed to an emerging discourse on crowds in social scientific and legal terms. Amply cited, among others, by Fournial, Tarde, Sighele, and Le Bon, whose writing on the psychology of revolutions was littered with references to his work,[28] Taine spurred on a wave of new writing on crowd movements that typically derided the little man and feared the worst from the mob.[29] May Day riots, strikes, and demonstrations were erupting throughout Europe, stimulating analysis. The new social theories, generally conservative in tone, reacting against the rapid industrialization and urbanization also mobilizing a socialist Left, and based on distrust of aggregation, drew from studies of epidemics and neuromotor disorder, psychiatry and criminology, to depict scenes of deviant behaviour. The pathologization of crowd and social movements linked natural eruptions, spasms, and antisocial behaviour in a disciplinary node ultimately to show that all bodily and social eruptions were pathological.

In choreographic terms, the social body in distress emerged on the scene of industrial modernity as a weak (undisciplined) animal capable of sudden rage, tearing through the fabric of social life, just as biologically conceived society was becoming socially and politically constituted. Crowds, in nineteenth-century criminology, law, and psychology, were fantasized as the eruption of a radical force moving against otherwise rational and efficient progress. Crowds were thought to represent what was most mobile and unpredictable in the past and, as such, what was most mobile and unpredictable in the present, an antediluvian force emerging onto the scene of contemporary life to upturn it. Crowds in this sense were imagined to stand outside time; and they represented the present moment's most dramatic disruption, its uncontrolled and inevitable coming-to-be. Characterized as a force of nature that could at best be described and hardly prevented or cured, this seemingly pernicious aggregate vitality suggested a state of organic disrepair, the dramatic point of convergence between history and nature: crowd movements, in early social science, appeared to echo and amplify one another. They transformed social space by engaging a primal state of collective corporeality, a horde-like impulse actualized in moments during which individuals came into the closest possible proximity.

Crowds were choreopolitical in the sense I have been outlining, inasmuch as they represented the spectacular *disorganization* of bodies in social space. If choreography articulates not just the organization (as Lepecki contends) but also the disorganization of bodies, their spectacular undoing, then crowds, including and especially the riotous crowds described in nineteenth-century social science, represented a choreopolitics in disarray. Crowds invite a choreographic reading inasmuch as they constitute the aggregation of bodies in space according to regular and irregular, patterned and unpatterned, arrangements. Choreography is in this sense informed not only by the positive concept of compelling (or inviting) a body to do or to perform an action or to engage in an individual or plural configuration in space, a rhythm or presence, but also by its converse: choreography also represents the negative fantasy of dispersal or undoing against which orderly being is construed, revealing a contemporary politics of form. This approach to choreography brings to light the modern social choreographic (or choreopolitical) preference for smoothness, predictability, and 'torque' that Schwartz outlines against the impulsive excess of choreomania. Significantly, this suggests the concept of 'torque' shadowed by the imagined threat of its disruption—the ever-looming presence of its choreopolitical underside.

Thus, whereas 'social choreography' may be employed to denote processes of 'social order', as Hewitt notes, movement that 'derives its ideal from the aesthetic realm and seeks to instill that order directly at the level of the body',[30]

---

28. See Jaap van Ginneken, *Crowds, Psychology, and Politics 1871–1899* (Cambridge: Cambridge University Press, 1992), 48, and Dominique Cochart, 'Les foules et la commune, analyse des premiers écrits de psychologie des foules', *Recherches de psychologie sociale* 4 (1982): 49–60.

29. Hecker, *Epidemics of the Middle Ages*, 85.

30. Hewitt, *Social Choreography*, 3.

I am proposing a concept of social choreography that foregrounds processes of choreographic dissolution. This writing of social order through figures of disorder was deployed in the nineteenth century for conceptualizing the emergent nation *against* acts of bodily dissolution: individual undoings, as in neuromotor disorders, including spasms, jerks, and tics, and the precipitate movements of crowds. Nineteenth-century crowd theory thus, I argue, imagines the upright social body as that which emerges in counterpart to and *around* the pulsating, pullulating crowd as its more refined and arguably abstracted other part. In this respect, I draw again from Hewitt's analysis of mid-nineteenth to early twentieth-century social choreography as an aesthetic (or in this case what I call an anaesthetic) formation. Writing of the emergent paradigm of everyday labour and of art as work in a broadly transatlantic modernity, Hewitt argues that moving bodies not only reflect but also shape ideologies; from walking, ballet, and body culture to chorus lines, bodies regulate political, biological, and aesthetic life by organizing (giving figure to) social form. Hewitt argues that while such formal abstraction is 'a sort of refusal to represent—or simply an incomprehension', it also 'more positively . . . mark[s] the attempt to distill the essence of a social formation from out of its contingent and confusing manifestations'.[31] Abstraction is the rarefication of imagined disorder into an orderly form. Abstraction, I add, thus also signals the movement of writing a social body out of its imagined negative—out of the figure of *dissolution*, which implies social *solution*, a social body that has resolved the inherent contradictions and tensions rumbling within it. The fascistic connotations of the Final Solution deployed in Nazi Germany are not unintended; as a form of social cleansing, fascistic body politics seeks to drain a political body of its supposedly messy, dark, heterogeneous elements; those jutting out too angularly or excessively into public space—typically imagined as being represented in the bodies of blacks, queers, women, and Jews.

As in Foucault's analysis of liberalism in *The Birth of Biopolitics*, social being emerges discursively in the nineteenth century as that which organizes itself and is organized in counterpoint to a purportedly uncontrollable and socially or racially inferior core, transposed onto Hewitt's 'aesthetic continuum' as ugly, angular, and dark. This self-organizing, discursively disciplined constituency performs itself as an aggregate body temporarily engaged in a state of emergence into public space; but it is also significantly made to emerge by the discursive literature deployed around it—that which draws attention to jagged gestures as being indicative of disease. For Foucault, liberalism, like madness and sexuality, comes with Enlightenment modernity to signal an empty middle, that about (and around) which talking, writing, and organizing happens. With liberalism, economics emerges as the social force around which governments operate; the work of governance comes to be, rather than regulation—the economic counterpart, arguably, to aestheticization (the organization of bodies)—*not to touch* market processes, to leave them alone (this is the concept of laissez-faire).[32] Modern liberalism signals the emergence of a system of governance that deliberately fails to organize bodies in space; it fails to choreograph, and in doing so writes into being the concept of a social body that represents another order, that of disorder: a state of perpetual crisis and undoing or disaggregation. In my analysis of crowd theory, sociology emerges to think society organizing itself around, and in a sense away from, self-organizing aggregates, what could be construed as an emergent radical politics. Anarchically moving bodies come to figure as society's anaesthetic other: its ugly other half—not in this view organized, beautiful, or economically rational or good but fundamental to scientific modernity's self-description as that which abstracts itself from the putatively unmanageable horde, the animal being, quivering at the heart of modern biopolitical life.

Political and religious movements offered scenes of spectacular epidemic madness that social theorists likened to plague. For Sighele, religious movements propagating like wildfire on the arid prairies of America drew social bodies into line with natural disasters. Crowds were natural eruptions, transcending eras and cultural worlds. For these social scientists, all eras were prone to spectacular bouts of disruptive insanity. Citing Nietzsche, for whom insanity was the rule among religious sectarians, Sighele argued that political parties, like religious sects,

---

31. Hewitt, *Social Choreography*, 5.
32. See esp. Foucault, *Naissance de la biopolitique*, 3–51.

were rife with epidemic psychoses. Arab and Indian dervishes, medieval demonomaniacs and their Italian heirs (dancers of the tarantella), Shakers and Christian Perfectionists in America, Russian nihilists, communitarians and ecstatics, as well as early followers of Christ and even Sturm und Drang enthusiasts in Germany, were all in Sighele's view indicative of moral epidemics pathologically constituted by spontaneous suggestion.[33] According to Sighele, the 'spectacle' of a single 'irritated individual' triggered the whole movement of a crowd, by virtue of the suggestive influence this individual's gesture provided to those who were its witness, and who were by virtue of this representation animalistically impelled to follow.[34] In this view, individuals were at least as prone to imitate pathological behaviour as to imitate pacific gestures and moods. Yet in a rare concession to the calm energy that can be displayed by crowds, Sighele also suggested that on some occasions crowds may turn gay or generous, bursting into laughter or sparing a vulnerable life.[35] But the vast majority of his depictions, like those of his peers, showed aggregates of people as dangerously animalistic, as well as fickle, volatile, and unmistakably feminine.[36]

Social imitation and 'contagion' were increasingly considered to be politically hazardous. In a lecture on criminal anthropology titled 'Psicosi epidemica' [Epidemic Psychoses] (1888), given at the cusp of massive demonstrations among unemployed workers and students in Rome and Milan, Giuseppe Sergi (1841–1936) argued that 'epidemic psychoses' could further spur on epidemic criminal activity, a thesis that gained currency among penal and crowd theorists in the ensuing decades.[37] Philosopher and sociologist Georg Simmel (1858–1918) argued that negative affect—a feeling of revulsion for crowds—was necessary for maintaining individual mental health. This view downplayed positive imitative factors, substituting them for the alien and alienating figure of a magnetic force by which negative undercurrents sweep up to a group's surface in the spontaneous act of imitation, the impulsive moment of collectivity. This concept of human beings as intensely mobile—vulnerable to reversals—revealed a pessimistic approach to social life that was shared by many during the long nineteenth and twentieth centuries.

With Le Bon, social theory moved to the heart of state power. One of the most influential and socially conservative of the crowd theorists—indebted (though he rarely acknowledged it) to the Italian school spearheaded by Sighele and Enrico Ferri (1856–1929)—Le Bon argued that a magnetic impulse generated in a crowd exercised a hypnotic effect on individuals such that their conscious personalities vanished. This made crowds primitive mental units (what he termed 'l'unité mentale des foules'), in which individuals' actions were reduced to 'the unconscious activities of the spinal cord'.[38] This enabled him to explain why crowds were often dangerous: collective life, when frenzied, was entirely autonomic. Individuals surrendering to the impulsive activity of their spinal cords, regressing to an infant state of mind, suggested a depersonalized and pre-civilized state of being—barbaric,

33. Scipio Sighele, *La foule criminelle: Essai de psychologie collective* (Paris: Félix Alcan, 1901), 46–47.

34. Sighele, *La foule criminelle*, 54–55.

35. Sighele, *La foule criminelle*, 108.

36. On the 'feminine' nature of the crowd, prone to exaggerating emotions and passing quickly to affective extremes, see for example Gustave Le Bon, *Psychologie des foules* (Paris: Félix Alcan, 1895), 27, 38.

37. 'Everybody knows that there are mental illnesses, and also that there are special institutions for the mentally ill. But maybe very few believe in the existence of the possibility of collective disturbances—a psychological disease propagating and spreading itself like harmful epidemics. Observations on various historical periods and on contemporary events among peoples, have clearly demonstrated to me [the existence of] such collective psychological diseases, which behave in their propagation just like any other epidemic; therefore I have named them *epidemic psychoses*'. Giuseppe Sergi, 'Psicosi Epidemica', *Rivista di Filosofia Scientifica*, ser. 2a, 8 (1889): 151–172, 151; cited in Van Ginneken, *Crowds*, 72.

38. Le Bon, *Psychologie des foules*, 12, 14, 19; also in William McDougall, *The Group Mind, a Sketch of the Principles of Collective Psychology, with Some Attempt to Apply Them to the Interpretation of National Life and Character* (Cambridge: Cambridge University Press, 1920), 40. On Sighele's bitter attempt to redress Le Bon's usurpation of the role of founder of crowd psychology, and more specifically Le Bon's unacknowledged use of Sighele's work, see the preface to the second French edition of Sighele's *La foule criminelle*, i–ii. Sighele also engaged in a protracted debate with Tarde, among others, arguing that whereas sociology compared individuals to droplets of water in a vast, tranquil, and immobile sea, collective psychology saw the sea as stormy, tempestuous, unpredictable, and perilous (22). Continuing with the geological metaphors, Le Bon saw individuals in crowds as grains of sand lifted indiscriminately by the wind (Le Bon, *Psychologie des foules*, 20). Opinions, likewise, were comparable to sand, 'mobile' and 'changing', blowing on the surface of a rock—representing, in his extended metaphor, the underlying beliefs and principles of a 'people' or 'race' (129).

instinctive, spontaneous, violent, and ferocious, as well as occasionally heroic and enthusiastic in the manner of 'primitive beings'. This theory helped Le Bon justify the superiority of individual, rational activity (and elite leadership) over all other forms of social organization.[39] The organic simile enabled him effectively to abstract crowd movements from democratic politics and to depict what seemed like a natural, scientifically grounded alternative: crowds were not democratic but merely animal mechanisms. For Le Bon, the human motor was not only unintelligent but inefficient; it triggered uncontrollable chain reactions that had to be directed—in Foucault's terms, governed.

Le Bon's recourse to organic metaphors (inspired by Taine) rendered governmental structures implicitly necessary for curbing a merely animal, unthinking social body, protecting it from harm: 'The psychological group is a provisional being formed of heterogeneous elements', he wrote, 'which for a moment are combined, exactly as the cells which constitute a living body form by their reunion a new being which displays characteristics very different from those possessed by each of the cells singly'.[40] This figure of speech, configuring the social body negatively as an organic whole, compared individuals to the cells that make it up. This reduced individual agents to biological units as interdependent as they were purportedly separable from one another at the outset. Elsewhere, Le Bon argued that ideas, affects, emotions, and beliefs are as powerfully and nefariously contagious in crowds as is the effect of microbes.[41] Notoriously influencing a generation of politicians across the political spectrum, from Theodore Roosevelt (1858–1919) and Charles de Gaulle (1890–1970) to Adolf Hitler (1889–1945) and Benito Mussolini (1883–1945), Le Bon styled himself a consultant to the political elite. His vituperative views on crowd behaviour enabled these state leaders better to understand and ultimately to shape rising tides of political discontentment and, ultimately, biopower.[42]

Crowd scenes offered case after case of the apparently spectacular dissolution of individuality, constituting the modern subject by virtue of his or her capacity to withstand the herd. Individual subjectivity, as social psychology and later psychoanalysis would increasingly put forward, stemmed from the successful suppression of base, animal drives. Freud, whose theories I return to later, was particularly influenced by crowd psychology and its foundational writing in the myth of a savage Dionysianism pulsating at the heart of social life, liable to erupt and overpower it at any time. Freud was particularly influenced by McDougall, for whom 'the individual, in becoming one of a crowd, loses in some degree his self-consciousness, his awareness of himself as a distinct personality, and with it . . . consciousness of his specifically personal relations; he becomes to a certain extent depersonalized'.[43] McDougall argued that individuals regain an animal or childlike state when they are among crowds: their willpower dissolves in an overwhelming current of energy. McDougall's language was dramatic, emphasizing the primordial power of collective irrationality over the rational individual, who otherwise stands, his portrayal implies, staunchly in isolation: 'the individual', he writes, 'feels himself enveloped and overshadowed and carried away by the forces which he is powerless to control; he . . . does not feel called upon to maintain the attitude of self-criticism and self-restraint which under ordinary circumstances are habitual to him'.[44]

Freud, reprising McDougall's concept of the 'group mind' in *Group Psychology and the Analysis of the Ego* (1921), saw this overpowering force as an occasion for religiously inflected 'oceanic bliss'. Individuals were not only subject to a suppression or repression of their base animality (as well as their tragic Greek inheritance); they also occasionally transcended themselves in rare moments of collectivity. 'Men's emotions are stirred in a group to a pitch that they seldom or never attain under other conditions', McDougall wrote; 'and it is a pleasurable experience for those who are concerned, to surrender themselves so unreservedly to their passions and

39. Le Bon, *Psychologie des foules*, 20.

40. I quote Le Bon here from a passage highlighted by Sigmund Freud in *Group Psychology and the Analysis of the Ego*, ed. and trans. James Strachey (New York: Norton, 1959), 7. See Gustave Le Bon, *The Crowd: A Study of the Popular Mind* (London: Benn, 1920), 29; Le Bon, *Psychologie des foules*, 15.

41. Le Bon, *Psychologie des foules*, 113.

42. Van Ginneken, *Crowds*, 171, 185–187.

43. McDougall, *The Group Mind*, 57.

44. McDougall, *The Group Mind*, 57.

thus to become merged in the group and to lose the sense of the limits of their individuality'.[45] As Freud saw it, this surrendering of the self in a crowd offered a rare occasion for collective bliss—significantly, for Freud, teetering at the edge of the ecstatic dissolution of the ego. But Freud's recuperation of the collective power of crowds articulated by McDougall into a psychological discourse on animal pleasure and prohibition was more frequently countermanded by his concern that loss of individuality spelled danger and pernicious excess.[46]

Conservative sociology's concept of spontaneous psychophysical degeneration contrasted with earlier medical theories put forward by, among others, the physician Prosper Despine (1812–1892), for whom individuals were not fundamentally transformed in crowds; their natural behaviours were intensified in crowd situations only. In *De la contagion morale; faits démontrant son existence, son explication scientifique; du danger que présente pour la moralité et la sécurité publiques la relation des crimes données par les journaux* [Of Moral Contagion; Facts Demonstrating Its Existence and Scientific Explanation; of the Danger for Morality and Public Security Presented by the Relation of Crimes Given in Newspapers] (1870), Despine argued that 'moral contagion' stems from individuals' predispositions instinctively to reproduce actions or feelings they witness in others (such as— most perniciously—those spread through news reports). But Despine insisted that such contagion occurs only inasmuch as individuals already have a tendency towards particular actions or feelings within themselves.[47] The crowd does not reverse the individual's psychological being, only catalyses and intensifies it. Crowds do not create new monsters out of women and men; but crowds nonetheless had to be curbed, Despine argued, because of their capacity to stimulate already existing positive as well as negative impulses. Thus Despine pleaded for moral apologists to labour with him in an effort to thwart the social 'poison' spread by unruly popular opinion, spurred on in particular by the press.[48]

Not all theorists emphasized the pernicious effects of plural bodies or even the existence of such metaphorical (or organic) entities. The legal philosopher Hans Kelsen (1881–1973) wrote: 'it is incorrect to talk of a bond "between" individuals'.[49] Society is imagined by every individual, insofar as the whole concept of society is a 'psychic phenomenon'.[50] With Kelsen, individuality comes to the fore as an object of political analysis, in which 'society' is a fiction only. Individuals, for Kelsen, are responsible as legal agents; their actions have no bearing on others. But Sighele, Fournial, and others, not content with this premise of individuality, pored over problems of legal responsibility in groups—groups moreover embedded in ecosystems. One response was to argue that crowds were led by *meneurs*, leaders, whose example served as a catalyst to action in others, even if those others were operating on the basis of automatic impulses (or, as Fournial ventured, on account of a full moon).[51] Still, someone in the mob had to be held accountable before an increasingly codified justice system. Legal analysis and organic cellularity meshed poorly. This left a gap in biosocial analyses of governmentality, according to which economic (and ecological) imperatives also moved the sociopolitical body along. This left little room for accident. In Foucault's analysis of biopolitical power, the legal determines the economic and is determined by it.[52] Rational actions—performed by efficient bodies, not subject to 'involuntary excessiveness'—move modernity along without the biosocial disruptions that catapult groups into temporary states of archaic surplus or impulsive animality.

45. Cited in Freud, *Group Psychology*, 22.

46. Laborde spells this out in *Les hommes*, 66.

47. Prosper Despine, *De la contagion morale; faits démontrant son existence, son explication scientifique; du danger que présente pour la moralité et la sécurité publiques la relation des crimes données par les journaux* (Marseille: E. Camoin, 1870), 4.

48. Despine, *De la contagion morale*, 21.

49. H. Kelsen, 'The Conception of the State and Social Psychology with Special Reference to Freud's Group Theory', *International Journal of Psycho-Analysis* 5 (1924): 1–38, 5.

50. Kelsen, 'The Conception of the State', 5.

51. Sighele, *La foule criminelle*, 120–164; on *meneurs* and *menés* (leaders and led), see esp. 146–151. Henri Fournial cites the French Revolution in particular as exemplary of the sorts of criminal acts, gestures, emotions, and attitudes that may be propagated contagiously in a crowd, in Henri Fournial, *Essai sur la psychologie des foules. Considérations médico-judiciaires sur les responsabilités collectives* (Lyon: A. Storck; and Paris: G. Masson, 1899), 81. Fournial also interestingly considers meteorological events among other ecological factors influencing crowd behaviour; he notes that of 125 noteworthy incidents recorded of the French Revolution, 48 fell on a full moon, further underscoring the crowd as an uncontrollable and feminine natural force (33).

52. Foucault, *Naissance de la biopolitique*, 168.

So while animals may behave according to perfectly docile and controlled systems of mutual interdependence, the fiction and fantasy of animal spontaneity—operating at the base of the spinal cord, in Le Bon's terms—situated unruly social life in a lesser plane on the increasingly interdependent scales (and spaces) of biopower. Men and women, conceived increasingly, with liberalism, according to Foucault, as homo economicus, economic agents first and foremost, emerged as such inasmuch as they did so against the grain of a mythically animal and irrational, collective and chaotic—indeed lawless—plural being, whose anarchism would threaten liberalism with the truly democratic rule the demos nominally aspires to.

PUBLICS AND PUBLIC OPINION: THE DREYFUS AFFAIR

Crowds, mobs, masses, and multitudes were forming discursively in the pages of social scientific theory, often interchangeably. Occasionally, terms emerged to describe a unique type of social or collective formation. So whereas I use the term 'crowd' generally to depict the movements of groups (following Borch's contention that any etymological or epistemological delineation of such terms belies their historical imbrication in social scientific literature),[53] the notion of the 'public' also came in the late nineteenth century to signal a particularly theatrical and cohesive form of social choreography and a relatively more organized social formation. By the time of the infamous Dreyfus affair in the mid-1890s, discourse on the 'public' emerged to complement literature on the crowd. Publicness with the Dreyfus affair became the crowd's politically representative face, the discursive interpellation of the demos. Staunchly defended in an open letter, 'J'accuse' ['I Accuse'] (1898) by the realist novelist and radical sympathizer Émile Zola (1840–1902), whose vivid depictions of crowd uprisings virtually sparked a new literary genre, the Jewish military officer Alfred Dreyfus (1859–1935) came to the forefront of intellectual opinion. Dreyfus, Zola intoned, had been unjustly subjected to a government-backed smear campaign, imprisoned for allegedly communicating state secrets to German officials. Zola's manifesto was supported by a wide circle of Parisian intellectual and artistic luminaries, including Tarde, mobilizing against increasingly aggressive anti-Semitic and xenophobic popular opinion. The repercussions of this case would divide French opinion for years to come. The city streets and pages of local newspapers simmered with debate on the Dreyfus affair, accompanied by a host of further scandals, revealing a new social scientific interest in national bodies and the ways they banded together, divided, and organized. Publicness, conceived as a gathering together of opinions rather than bodies, suggested a discursive social choreography abstracted from its messy and corporeal counterpart. Social choreography—understood in this case, I submit, as the shaping of ideas through their movement across social space—emerged in this case in the motion towards a consolidation of ideas about social bodies and the concerted, generally written, public defense of public life. Social choreography in this regard contributed to forming what I call the archival repertoire of public life, a discursive force that shapes as much as it reflects ongoing public and social scientific debate. Social bodies do not just organize or move through space; they move the language that defines and forms it, aesthetically, politically, and choreographically.

Paris and other European capitals were in motion, and the emergence of the intellectual class through the activities of the press was countermanded by an equally powerful and often virulent discourse on the dangers and triumphs of political association. Sighele argued that the term 'publics' encompassed individuals with common literary, artistic, and intellectual interests, even when they were physically dispersed; but the term 'publics' also referred to popular groupings that shared political opinions.[54] In Tarde's analysis, the public was more liberal than the crowd, inasmuch as one could participate in a few publics at once, just as one read various newspapers. In this view, publics were expansive and diverse; and they could overlap, unlike crowds, which were physically proximate and could intensify emotions to the point of violence or insanity.[55] Not all social theorists considered individuals, taken together, to form base or at worst dangerous social bodies. Many took individuals to constitute the basic units

53. See n6 here.
54. Sighele, La foule criminelle, 218–249.
55. See esp. Gabriel Tarde, L'opinion et la foule, ed. Dominique Reynié (Paris: Presses Universitaires de France, 1989).

of society, not dissolvable into others, though individual moments and views might be shared (and transformed). Crowds, like opinions, gathered but did not always create new, more stupid, or more volatile social beings. Society was also conceived of as a positive force for aggregation: a vital capacity for the expansion and transformation of public life.

TARDE: INTER-INDIVIDUALISM AND COLLECTIVE ACTION AS ART

In a rare homage to the positive vital politics of group being, Tarde offered a counterpoint to his contemporaries' alarmist readings of plural formations. As a social motor, groups, in Tarde's analysis, also afforded the occasion for the positive transcendence of individuality and herd mentality. In a relatively exceptional deployment of socially progressive philosophy in the emerging sociological field, Tarde offered a view of groups and individuals positively and creatively engaging in imitative behaviour. A crowd is able to multiply itself and so becomes, in his terms, molecular. Tarde argued in *Les lois de l'imitation* [The Laws of Imitation] (1890) that imitation is a prime social and historical mover, often positively shaping social activity and political, artistic, and intellectual life, accounting for acts of creative and scientific invention.[56] Although he also acknowledged, like his contemporaries, the temporary insanity that could lead reasonable individuals to perpetuate base, criminal acts in crowds, he was most interested in the minute instances of imitation that also brought about positive social and intellectual change.[57] For Tarde, imitations, oppositions, repetitions, and innovations constituted a world of vital activities operating inter-individually. Objects and relations were never static in a given moment but morphed slightly and continuously. Tarde's theory of inter-psychology suggested that human actions, taken at the level of their most incremental associations, offered

an ever-evolving landscape of social, intellectual, and artistic movement. Rehabilitated in Deleuze and Guattari's *Capitalisme et schizophrénie 2: Mille plateaux* [A Thousand Plateaus: Capitalism and Schizophrenia] (1980), Tarde's interest in micro modulations paved the way for a new, though quickly marginalized, discussion on groups—social aggregates—and what he described, after Gottfried Wilhelm Leibniz (1646–1716), as 'monadology', in 'Monadologie et sociologie' ['Monadology and Sociology'] (1893), a world of radical differentiations connecting the universe and all its motions together.[58] This world of dynamic differences reconceived the body as an energetic composite made up of infinitely varying '"creatures," "worlds," or "monads,"' yielding a collective subject, and the collective constitution of the biophysical (and metaphysical) universe.[59] For Leibniz, the monad was a vital and a material principle, a force of organic clustering according to which all beings moving through the world were made up of infinitesimally small and dynamic parts that could be shared across bodies and recombine. Tarde saw in this a model for inter- and intra-corporeal association: a way of reconceptualizing the social sphere as being made up of minute movements, continually reorganizing people and things—imbricating them dynamically in one another.

Tarde was putting forward a theory of imitation foregrounding mutuality. The consequences for politics were significant: for Tarde, every world is social, just as every thing is a social thing—a society—vitally co-constituting inter-individual beings and publics in perpetual flux. These pluralities or interrelations tend towards gatherings ('rassemblements')[60] and relationships of inter-possession that have the potential to undo social hierarchy and the fixity of political roles. As a radically progressive social philosophy fundamentally at odds with his contemporary Durkheim's positivist theories of static and universal social structures, Tarde's affective biopolitics transcended individual and social formations in favour of diversity, difference, and change. Dancing, in this regard, like

56. Gabriel Tarde, *Les lois de l'imitation*, ed. Bruno Karsenti (Paris: Éditions Kimé, 1993), 77.

57. Gabriel Tarde, *Études pénales et sociales* (Lyon: A. Storck; and Paris: G. Masson, 1892), 303.

58. Gabriel Tarde, *Monadologie et sociologie*, ed. Éric Alliez (Le Plessis-Robinson: Institut synthélabo pour le progrès de la connaissance, 1999). See also Gilles Deleuze and Félix Guattari, *Capitalisme et schizophrénie 2: Mille plateaux* (Paris: Les Éditions de Minuit, 1980), 267. Deleuze notes Tarde's influence on Foucault in *Foucault*, 81n6.

59. See Éric Alliez, 'Présentation: Tarde et le problème de la constitution', in Tarde, *Monadologie et sociologie*, 9–32, see esp. 12, 20–25.

60. Tarde, *Les lois de l'imitation*, 212–213.

other forms of art, can occur collectively; so, too, new movements might be invented by individuals, then imitated, and thus incrementally transformed. Movement—moving bodies, in particular—served as modern science's litmus test for understanding crowds and, by extension, the transformations of social life.

Metaphorically and materially, movement, dance, and the figure of dancing—particularly 'Bacchic'-type ecstasies—operated as lenses through which to view the forms and misformations of social aggregation. This way of seeing social formations by attending to the movements and mutual influence of bodies in space emerged in fuller force with the aestheticized, popular dance cultures of chorus lines represented (in Britain) by the famous precision-engineered Tiller Girls, discussed by Hewitt, Burt, and others; but may have emerged in the late nineteenth century in discourse on the far more ambivalently choreographic (and choreo-political) movements of bodies spilling through streets.[61]

Positive theories of imitation were not entirely new. As with the incendiary depictions of crowds as impulsive, beastly forces, earlier nineteenth-century medical theory provided the organic language and an alternative political ground for theorizing group life. Prosper Lucas, sixty years before Tarde, had set forward a theory of imitation foregrounding genius and art. In *De l'imitation contagieuse* [Of Contagious Imitation] (1833), Lucas posited that voluntary or 'mimic' imitation ('imitation mimique')—which he set in opposition to involuntary, 'sympathetic' imitation—constituted an art form in its own right, when employed intelligently, through the exercise of the passions, by persons of genius.[62] Even voluntary imitation of pathological phenomena—most frequently madness, chorea, epilepsy, and hysteria—contained a portion of artistry, derision, or simply interest, he argued, which could turn mimic or feigned symptoms real if performed with too much conviction (and art).[63] This view emphasized casual, recreational imitation, simulating slight convulsive movements or 'nervous attacks' and suspended at will.[64]

SOCIAL BODIES

The 'social body' in nineteenth-century literature on choreomania is disruptive, spastic, jagged, and queer; dark, animal, and feminine; but also, significantly, aggregate. As a disorder of aggregate bodies, choreomania comes onto the modern social scientific scene as uncontrolled movement, signalling a choreopolitics of corporeal upheaval, implicating bodies forming (and deforming) an emergent sense of public space. Purposeful corporeal movement, positively allied with modern factories and modern,

---

61. Though the Tiller Girls were most famously described in the late 1920s by Siegfried Kracauer (1889–1966), they were active in Manchester as early as the 1890s (having formed as a group in 1889). Masterminded by music hall director John Tiller to counter the chaotic chorus lines of the day and offer instead a model of corporeal efficiency and precision, they quickly became emblems of the new, Taylorized, rationalized industrial West. See esp. Ramsay Burt, *Alien Bodies*, 72–85; Hewitt, *Social Choreography*, 177–212; Mark Franko, *The Work of Dance: Labor, Movement, and Identity in the 1930s* (Middletown, CT: Wesleyan University Press, 2002), 31–37; Felicia McCarren, *Dancing Machines: Choreographies of the Age of Mechanical Reproduction* (Stanford, CA: Stanford University Press, 2003), 142–144. See also Siegfried Kracauer, 'The Mass Ornament', in *The Mass Ornament: Weimer Essays*, ed. and trans. Thomas Y. Levin (Cambridge, MA: Harvard University Press, 1995), 75–86.

62. Lucas, *De l'imitation contagieuse*, 4–6. Drawing from Hecker's work on choreomania, recently summarized in French by Émile Littré in the *Gazette médicale de Paris* [Paris Medical Gazette] (1833), as well as the article on chorea by French physician Jean-Baptiste Bouillaud (1796–1881) in the *Dictionnaire de médecine et chirurgie pratique* [Dictionary of Medicine and Surgical Practice] (1829–1836), Lucas emphasized the intensity, 'strange colour' ('étrange couleur'), and 'most bizarre force of contagious propagation' ('la force la plus bizarre de propagation contagieuse') characterizing cases of 'sympathetic imitation' in the 'vast' epidemics of choreomania as well as in the chorea of his day. Further describing cases of epidemic convulsions among nuns in Germany, in Holland, and at Loudun, as well as among the Convulsionaries of Saint-Médard, Lucas suggested that these were variously marked by epilepsy, insanity, catalepsy, trembling, bleating like sheep or making other animal cries, and ecstasy. In *De l'imitation contagieuse*, 33–43. Noting that these cases had first been described by, among others, Pinel and Kaaw Boerhaave (1705–1753), Lucas turned his attention to the nuns' barking, nosebleeds, coughing, and other types of 'neurotic motility' and 'extreme sensitivity' situating these phenomena in a diagnostic line with choreas and choreomanias (8–21). Lucas argued that the nuns' acts of imitation constituted sympathetic—involuntary—imitations of complex neuroses, whose symptoms could be observed even if underlying physiological processes could not be (32–33). See J. Bouillaud, 'chorée', in G. Andral et al., *Dictionnaire de médecine et de chirurgie pratiques*, 15 vols., vol. 5 (Paris: Gabon, Méquignon-Marvis, J.-B. Baillière, Crochard, 1829–1836), 262–272; and *Gazette médicale de Paris* 4, 1.2, 3 January 1833, 5–6.

63. Lucas, *De l'imitation contagieuse*, 7–8.

64. Lucas, *De l'imitation contagieuse*, 8.

streamlined, efficient regimes of work—what Anson Rabinbach describes as an industrial regime of *productivism*[65]—thus comes into contrast with an entire regime of collective corporeal activity understood in medical literature to be fitful, erratic, spontaneous, unnecessary, excessive, and uncontrolled—in short, unproductive. Associated with women, children, and 'primitives', this regime of corporeal activity was further likened in the nineteenth century to a host of neurological disorders, psychiatric conditions, and epidemic outbursts. At its most forceful, this fitful regime of corporeality was likened to plague.

In this view, choreomania was a disorder of imitative crowds; specifically, choreomania erupted among groups of people imitating one another's gestures, attitudes, and moods pathologically, as it seemed to those who viewed and attempted to diagnose them. With this medical theatre, the concept of the social body as something that could be ill and tended to violence came more fully into view. In Mary Poovey's analysis, the 'social body' in early nineteenth-century Britain signalled at once the mass of poor people to be disciplined and cared for by generally well-meaning individuals who classed themselves as their social superiors; and the larger organic whole into which these poorer people were folded. The notion of a 'social body' suggested at once separation and sequestration; tending-towards (or caring for) and keeping at bay. The social body thus came to signify a space of cultivation, hovering between the unkempt organic state in which the sick and poor were understood normally to reside and the charitable structures of uplifting which new social policies and institutions increasingly engaged.[66] Describing this modern set of practices as a process of 'disaggregation', Poovey argues that the social body emerged discursively in the nineteenth century as a sphere separate from politics and economics; this set in motion a range of ideas designed to cultivate society as an organic entity abstracted from political or economic pressures.[67] The emergence of sociology in the early decades of the nineteenth century

thus configured itself in terms of social disorder and care; with this, neurology, the new science of motion, described pathological movements among disorderly groups and individuals in isolation. The 'social body' emerged in the nineteenth century as a body liable to be diseased on account of its excess movements, which multiplied and intensified through processes of imitation exacerbated in groups.

In less politically incendiary cases, the social choreography of disrepair revealed a regime of machinic efficiency against which bodies and minds reacted: individuals engaging in inane kinetic sport, either semi-involuntarily mimicking one another through the corporeal play of jerks and twitches or finding ludic routes of escape from otherwise boring or oppressive living and working conditions. In some cases, eccentric bouts of religious enthusiasm served as a playground for kinetic agitation in gatherings as large and popular as their participants were corporeally—and affectively—transfixed. In America, where new utopianisms were seizing religious groups in what appeared to be a wave of religious frenzy, eruptive movements— including all sorts of spasmodic individual corporeality—passed ever more into the scientific limelight, articulated in crowd psychology, neurology, and epidemiology as nervous disorders.

'ALL THE COUNTRY WAS IN COMMOTION': THE 'JERKS' IN KENTUCKY AND TENNESSEE

The 'jerks' in Kentucky and Tennessee were a far cry from the psychopathological, criminal crowd behaviour described in early social psychology, according to which idle men and women—those not engaged in productive labour—were most liable to gather, agitate, and revolt, provoking no less, in Fournial's terms, than civilization's degenerate collapse.[68] Yet as in the case of the medieval and early modern dancers described in previous chapters, religious enthusiasts' spectacular

---

65. Anson Rabinbach, *The Human Motor: Energy, Fatigue, and the Origins of Modernity* (Berkeley: University of California Press, 1992), 3.

66. Poovey notes that the 'social body' is a nineteenth-century variation on the medieval concept of the body politic, transformed by early modern times into the body of councillors extending the king's own body and eventually in the eighteenth and nineteenth centuries into the mass of urban poor. Mary Poovey, *Making a Social Body: British Cultural Formation, 1830–1864* (Chicago: University of Chicago Press, 1995), 7–8.

67. Poovey, *Making a Social Body*, 13.

68. In Fournial, *Essai sur la psychologie des foules*, 37.

displays of gregarious behaviour came to be folded into medical literature on nervous disease and nervous imitation, further extending epidemiological analyses of crowds and theatrical gesture. Felix Robertson wrote his M.D. thesis, *An Essay on Chorea Sti Viti*, at the College of Physicians of Philadelphia in 1805, capitalizing on his native knowledge of the American South to contribute a new case study to the European literature on chorea, which was becoming one of the most fashionable fields of medical study. His work on the 'jerks' in Kentucky, Virginia, and his home state, Tennessee, brought a new etiological perspective to Chorea Sancti Viti, emphasizing the brain and nerves' susceptibility to the influence of 'external bodies'. Stimuli exercised on one person's brain and nerves provoked muscular reactions characterized by a 'sympathy of motion', accounting for the epidemic spread of choreic affections.[69]

The mere presence of kinetic agitation in the public sphere increased the likelihood of further agitation, as people imitated other people's movements. The impressions left on their nervous systems provoked a motor response causing the spectators, as he called them, to reproduce any movements they observed, yielding a result not unlike, he mused, 'the resemblance that often takes place between man and wife, a resemblance which, before their marriage, did not exist'.[70] To avoid the pernicious effects of this 'sympathy

of motion' when the movements performed were excessive or violent, as in the case of the 'jerks' at Methodist camp meetings, Robertson exhorted physicians to isolate patients as much as possible. Physicians should keep patients' minds 'occupied on new and agreeable subjects . . . which would best be done by travelling with an agreeable companion through a highly cultivated or wild romantic country', and 'visiting natural and artificial curiosities, particularly of the more sublime kind. By these means', he added, 'new trains of associate motions would be produced, which from their novelty, &c. might at length overcome those which produced the disease, and the excitability of the brain would thus be expended'.[71] Simple exposure to fresh landscapes provided stimulus enough for patients to encounter new—far more wholesome—objects and actions to emulate.

The case study that formed the core of Robertson's dissertation, enabling him to examine this 'sympathy of motion' in some detail, was an outbreak of imitative movement that swept through the United States from Ohio to Kentucky, Tennessee, and parts of Virginia in 1799–1805, presenting, as he put it, an 'unparalleled blaze of enthusiastic religion'.[72] Hundreds, and soon thousands, of men, women, and children had started to participate in camp meetings, outdoor religious services that lasted from four days to three or four weeks. Participants travelled

---

69. Robertson prefaces his essay with a note that 'the subject of the following pages is an inquiry into the affection denominated CHOREA ST. VITI, or the dance of St. Vitus; and although my principle design is to give a history of the epidemic Chorea, at present prevailing in the states of Kentucky, Tennessee and Virginia, I shall also transcribe the substance of what has heretofore been written on the subject', thus situating his work in a historical line with—and as an extension of—treatises on chorea. Felix Robertson, *An Essay on Chorea Sancti Viti* (Philadelphia: Joseph Rakestraw, 1805), 5. Babington includes a long passage from Robertson's essay in appendix 5 to 'The Dancing Mania', in Hecker, *Epidemics of the Middle Ages*, 151–153. See also the Canadian physician Thomas B. Futcher (1871–1938), *An account of the dancing mania of Europe and of epidemic convulsions in Kentucky* (Baltimore, 1905).

70. Robertson, *An Essay on Chorea Sancti Viti*, 19.

71. Robertson, *An Essay on Chorea Sancti Viti*, 14. See also Léon Babonneix on isolation: '*isolation* imposes itself in all cases. Not only does it prevent the patient's neighbours from seeking, more or less unconsciously, to reproduce his or her involuntary movements, it also cuts short unfortunate epidemics of chorea, hitherto so fashionable in children's hospitals, and places the patient in the best conditions for curing his or her chorea. It is convenient both for the acute period and, perhaps even more so, the period of decline, when so many small choreics seek, so to say, their path, and ask only to teeter into some neurotic manifestation: tic, electric chorea, etc.'. Léon Babonneix, *Les chorées: Avec 34 figures dans le texte* (Paris: Ernest Flammarion, 1924), 210.

72. Robertson, *An Essay on Chorea Sancti Viti*, 9. As Peter Cartwright wrote, in his *Autobiography of Peter Cartwright* (New York: Abingdon Press, 1956), 'all the country was in commotion' (47). 'Thousands heard of the mighty work, and came on foot, on horseback, in carriages and wagons. It was supposed that there were in attendance at times during the meeting from twelve to twenty-five thousand people. Hundreds fell prostrate under the mighty power of God, as men slain in battle . . . . It was said, by truthful witness, that at times more than one thousand persons broke out into loud shouting all at once, and that the shouts could be heard for miles around' (33–34). See also Richard M'Nemar, *The Kentucky Revival, or, a short history of the late extraordinary outpouring of the spirit of God in the western states of America, agreeably to scripture promises and prophecies concerning the latter day: with a brief account of the entrance and progress of what the world call shakerism among the subjects of the late revival in Ohio and Kentucky. Presented to the true Zion traveler as a memorial of the wilderness journey* (New York: Edward O. Jenkins, 1846). See also e.g. J. B. McMaster, *A History of the People of the United States: From the Revolution to the Civil War*, 8 vols., vol. 2 (New York: D. Appleton, 1883–1913), 578–582; Ross, *Social Psychology*, 50–53; Catherine C. Cleveland, *The Great Revival in the West, 1797–1805* (Chicago: University of Chicago Press, 1916); Charles A. Johnson, *The Frontier Camp Meeting: Religion's Harvest Time* (Dallas: Southern Methodist University Press, 1955); Rosen, *Madness in Society*, 214–217.

as many as forty, fifty, even one hundred miles to attend them, setting up makeshift camps in surrounding areas, increasing the potential for the direct communication of their motoric enthusiasm.[73] In his *History of the Presbyterian Church in the state of Kentucky* (1847), Rev. Robert Davidson (1808–1876) noted that attendance at these meetings was widespread, as 'the labourer quitted his task; age snatched his crutch; youth forgot his pastimes; the plough was left in the furrow; the deer enjoyed a respite from the mountains; business of all kinds was suspended; dwellinghouses were deserted; whole neighbourhoods were emptied; bold hunters, and sober matrons, young men, maidens, and little children, flocked to the common centre of attraction; every difficulty was surmounted, every risk ventured'.[74] The enthusiasm appeared so violently and wholly to possess participants' bodies and minds as to constitute in Robertson's view a religious epidemic: 'The disease no sooner appeared than it spread, with rapidity, through the medium of the principle of imitation: thus it was not uncommon for an affected person to communicate it to a greater part of the crowd, who, from curiosity or other motives, had collected around him'.[75] Though at the time of Robertson's writing the excitement was present in 'almost every part of Tennessee and Kentucky, and in various parts of Virginia', it had died down and was thought 'not to be so contagious (or readily communicated) as at its commencement'. This suggested to him that predisposition to religious enthusiasm was a prerequisite for the contagiousness to take effect. As it had abated, so too had the camp meetings.[76] But the contagiousness that had been reported, and the violence of the gestures performed, spawned a host of medical theories linking imitation, contagion, and acute scenes of enthusiastic motility constituting a whole literature on choreomania as social affect. David W. Yandell (1826–1898), professor of surgery at the University of Louisville, Kentucky, emphasized the gestures' communicability. Writing in *Brain* in 1881, he remarked that 'the movement proved highly contagious and spread in all directions'.[77] In his view, this was, again following Robertson, a form of chorea, though in some cases it bore a strong resemblance to epilepsy and, in the majority of cases, hysteria, not least on account of its contagious aspect. It 'was eminently sympathetic in its nature', Yandell wrote, 'as has been so often remarked of these affections. The convulsions once started in a congregation spread quickly through it, until all the fit subjects were convulsed'. He added that 'repetition greatly increased the proneness to the disorder, which was invited by the masses on the supposition that it was a true religious exercise'.[78]

Clinical descriptions offered by Robertson and Yandell suggest a paroxysmic event, invariably involving a spiritual leader whose magnanimous oration and ostentatious demonstrations of his own states of excitement provoked followers into similar states. This was markedly different from previous clinical descriptions of epidemic choreas and other epidemic events, in which whole groups seemed spontaneously to rise up as if of their own accord, without a leader. 'After a rousing appeal to the feelings of the listeners', wrote Yandell, 'and especially during spirited singing, one and another in the audience would fall suddenly to the ground and swoon away. . . . Some fell suddenly as if struck by lightning, while others were seized with a universal tremor before they fell shrieking'. Only a few excited individuals were needed to get the whole assembly going.[79]

Involuntary arm and leg gestures constituted the disorder's dramatic other half, setting this

73. See David W. Yandell, 'Epidemic Convulsions', *Brain* 4.3 (1881): 339–350, 340–341. He writes that at a religious meeting in the courthouse in Knoxville, 150 people were reported by an eyewitness to have been 'jerking' at one time. But elsewhere 'the frenzy reached a greater height', so that 'at a religious meeting in Kentucky, not less than three thousand persons fell in convulsions to the ground'. He also notes one concourse at which twenty thousand people were said to have been in attendance (340), although Peter Cartwright cites as many as twenty-five thousand in his *Autobiography*. Cartwright also estimates that some camp meetings lasted for a few weeks at a time, with up to thirty or forty ministers from different denominations preaching in different parts of the camp simultaneously (43). 'And here', writes Yandell, 'were united all the elements best suited to stir the emotional nature of man, and to derange his nervous system' (341).

74. Cited in Yandell, 'Epidemic Convulsions', 340–341.

75. Robertson, *An Essay on Chorea Sancti Viti*, 10. See also 17, where Robertson concludes that 'the disease thus produced in some, was excited in others by the principle of imitation'.

76. Robertson, *An Essay on Chorea Sancti Viti*, 9.

77. Yandell, 'Epidemic Convulsions', 344.

78. Yandell, 'Epidemic Convulsions', 349.

79. 'A few shrieks never failed to put the assembly in motion, and set men and women to falling all around'. Yandell, 'Epidemic Convulsions', 344.

'epidemic' of insanity alongside dancing disorders and crowd movements characterized by their spectacular showiness, the 'involuntary excessiveness' with which they appeared in public space. Further symptoms included 'a sense of "pins and needles,"' 'numbness of body', and '[loss] of all volitional control of [the] muscles'. Some symptoms seem to have provoked habituation, causing participants to 'fall again under circumstances by no means exciting'. Narration alone provoked paroxysms in the most unlikely (and often comical) circumstances: 'women who had suffered repeat attacks sometimes fell from their horses' while relating their experiences and exercises to friends on their way to or from meeting-houses.[80] Some suffered from catalepsy—a suddenly rigid bodily state—lasting from a few minutes to two or three hours or, in extreme cases, up to a few days. As Yandell observed, drawing from eyewitness accounts, 'others were violently convulsed as in hysteria or epilepsy, "wrought hard in fitful nervous agonies, the eyes rolling wildly". . . The extremities were cold; the face was pale or flushed, the breathing hard. Sensibility was annulled'.[81]

Extreme motion and extreme absence of motion equally characterized this apparently epidemic dancing disease. Strangest of all, eyewitnesses wrote, was when voluntary motion turned involuntary, so that actions commenced by choice came to be repeated as if automatically, producing an awkward sense of purposelessness and thus also of sheer theatre among those engaging in as well as viewing them. In Robertson's terms, participants 'found themselves unable by voluntary efforts to suppress the contraction of their muscles, and to their own astonishment, and the diversion of many of the spectators, they continued to act from *necessity* the curious character which they had commenced from *choice*'.[82] Contractions occurring primarily in the trunk and upper part of the body moreover made for a ridiculous countenance, resembling, Robertson put it, more a 'live fish, when thrown on land, than any thing else to which I can compare them'.[83] To counter this mimetic return to an animal-like state, 'bodily exercises' were generated to discipline

the participants, regularizing the wild and frantic gestures their enthusiasm compelled them to perform. This theatricalization of initially spontaneous exercises made for a ritual of imitation and counter-imitation and a codified set of games that gained the popularity of a new sport, viewed with a frisson from the medical trenches.

W. L. Sutton (1797–1862), in his 'Report on the Medical Topography and the Epidemic Diseases of Kentucky', published in *Transactions of the American Medical Association* (1858), described the 'jerks', 'or, as it has been called, epidemic epilepsy', in some detail.[84] He noted that the 'Jerking Exercise' was the 'most common' and 'most remarkable form of these remarkable manifestations', first appearing in East Tennessee, 'where several hundred of both sexes were seized with this strange affection'. It 'soon became so common, and marked by such strongly-marked motions, as to give the generic name to all these extravagances'. Their 'first and most simple appearance consisted in quick and violent motions of the forearms', '[agitating] the whole body violently'. Alternately, muscles of the neck were affected, so that the head 'jerked right and left, with a force and velocity perfectly inconceivable; no feature could be distinguished'. His account suggests familiarity with Robertson's dissertation and reliance on direct observation, coloured by his amazement at the spectacularity of the whole affair:

At the first twitch, the headdresses and combs of females would be thrown to a distance, and when the hair was long, it would snap and crack like a whip. This may seem to some incredible, but numbers, now alive, were old enough then to mark and remember the fact. At times, the muscles of the back would be affected, and then the subject would be thrown violently to the ground, and suffer the most violent contortions, graphically compared to the fluttering of a fish when thrown upon the ground. Again, the muscles of the whole body would be affected, and the person would be jerked to and fro, in all directions. All control of the muscles was lost, and he must

80. Yandell, 'Epidemic Convulsions', 344.
81. Yandell, 'Epidemic Convulsions', 344.
82. Robertson, *An Essay on Chorea Sancti Viti*, 10.
83. Robertson, *An Essay on Chorea Sancti Viti*, 11.
84. W. L. Sutton, 'Report on the Medical Topography and the Epidemic Diseases of Kentucky', *Transactions of the American Medical Association* 11 (1858): 74–165, 110.

necessarily go as he was driven, whether it was in a violent dash to the ground, or to hop round with the head, limbs, and trunk jerking in every direction, as if they must inevitably fly asunder. The bosom would heave violently, and the countenance become disgustingly distorted.[85]

His revulsion was patent. Rev. Richard M'Nemar (1770–1839), an eyewitness and participant in the camp meetings, provided a further account in *The Kentucky Revival* (1807), emphasizing the jerkers' rapid head movements and radical disfiguration: they appeared to be inebriated, possessed by a violent movement that threw them uncontrollably to the ground and propelled them in every direction. This was a dramatic performance of dangerous sport: 'nothing in nature could better represent this strange and unaccountable operation', he wrote, 'than for one to goad another, alternately on every side, with a piece of red-hot iron'.[86] Engaging with increasingly frenetic enthusiasm in hopping, running, twitching, and tossing objects and bodies about, they 'bounced from place to place like a football', losing all motor control. It was 'no small wonder to spectators', he added, that they might 'escape without injury'.[87]

Rev. Peter Cartwright (1785–1872) noted in his *Autobiography* (1856) that 'persons taken with the jerks, to obtain relief . . . would rise up and dance. Some would run, but could not get away'. Those who resisted usually suffered from the jerks even more.[88] Variations proliferated. The Rolling Exercise 'consisted in becoming violently prostrated and doubled, with the head and feet together, rolling over and over, like a wheel; or turning over and over sidewise, like a log'. It required intense physical exertion: 'the subject took a sudden start, and felt impelled to run at his greatest speed, as if engaged in a race, leaping over obstacles in his way, with surprising agility. This was continued until his strength was completely exhausted, when he fell down in a syncope'.[89] Finally, the Dancing Exercise emerged.

Although it was not one of the original forms of 'bodily exercise', it had become a regular practice among Kentucky revivalists by the winter of 1805. Following the lead of a Mr. Thomson, they would 'go to dancing', as Sutton noted. Thomson was reported at the close of a camp meeting at Turtle Creek in 1804 to have 'gone to dancing, . . . [continuing] this movement around the stand, in a regular manner for an hour or more, repeating in a low voice, all the time, "This is the Holy Ghost! Glory!" '[90]

Offering writers a puzzling picture of kinetic prostration, delusion, and collective insanity, these religious enthusiasts appeared nonetheless to be having a raucous good time just as they were transfixed by the motions—and emotions—of their collective games. Like the Dancing Exercise, the Barking Exercise was a latecomer to the fad, consisting 'in the subject getting down on his hands and feet, and barking, snapping, and growling in a degree so natural as to deceive the unwary, unless they had their eyes directed to the spot whence the sounds proceeded. It may be difficult in ordinary times', wrote Sutton, 'to conceive how decent, respectable men could be induced to go through these extravagances'.[91] Their mimetic return to animality was so genuine it 'looked strangely enough to see it done with the utmost solemnity'. But, Sutton argued, 'it would seem that no man could command his countenance, when he would hear these ejaculations interspersed with texts of Scripture: as, "Every knee shall bow—wow—wow; and every tongue shall confess." '[92] The Barking Exercise served as a culmination of all the others, so that even members of high society were possessed by this 'mortifying' fervour and barked.[93] Barking might also lead to dancing, and vice versa, so that once a 'paroxysm had come on, and the will was powerless to arrest it', subjects could 'substitute other actions for the form with which he had been seized. Thus those who were invaded by the *'barking exercise'* were usually able to change it into *'dancing!'*[94]

---

85. Sutton, 'Report on the Medical Topography', 119–120.
86. Cited in Yandell, 'Epidemic Convulsions', 346.
87. Cited in Yandell, 'Epidemic Convulsions', 346.
88. Cartwright, *Autobiography*, 45. M'Nemar also remarks that 'the quickest method to find releasement from the jerks and barks, was to engage in the voluntary dance' (*The Kentucky Revival*, 66).
89. Sutton, 'Report on the Medical Topography', 120.
90. Sutton, 'Report on the Medical Topography', 120–121.
91. Sutton, 'Report on the Medical Topography', 121.
92. Sutton, 'Report on the Medical Topography', 121.
93. Sutton, 'Report on the Medical Topography', 121.
94. Sutton, 'Report on the Medical Topography', 122.

Yandell argued that 'some of the actors in these strange scenes' bordered on insanity. One participant related that 'while under conviction on account of his sins he went about the woods for two years, through rain and snow, "roaring, howling, praying, day and night." '[95] Millennialist visions and trances seized thousands,[96] exacerbating the excitement already produced by this festival atmosphere, recalling for some observers, such as Robertson, the St. Vitus's dancers whose apocalyptic hallucinations and fits of syncope caused them to jerk and twitch, leaping over imagined rivers of blood (chapter 2). But to physicians reading the eyewitness reports, the fits of agitation and visions provided a theatre of observation in its own right: viewed from afar, these contorted figures had the appearance of persons possessed by a strange delirium doubling as a neuropathological condition foregrounding involuntary movement, and presenting all the difficulties of interpretation that any piece of theatre or literature might.

In Sutton's terms, all had one thing in common: extravagance. These were reckless exercises performed without reason or restraint. The theatricality and baroqueness of the movements constituted their status as disease: they appeared superfluous, wasteful, luxurious, and irrational. Those engaging in them did so without reserve. This was why they were, he thought, potentially dangerous: together, these people exacerbated one another's motoric impulses, stimulated by sympathy and a kinetic contagiousness that spread uncurbed. Appropriately, the most commonly prescribed remedy against these fits of dancing, barking, jerking, falling, visions, and trances—besides Robertson's exhortation to isolation and sublime walks in the woods—was the exercise of moral discipline and fear. At a few of the congregations, including one led by Rev. Joseph Lyle in a sermon titled 'Order' in July 1803, threats to turn convulsive members out of doors succeeded in dampening down some of the frenetic activity, until it abated entirely.[97]

This proved to observers figuratively offstage that the movements were not literally contagious, not in a bacteriological sense, although members of the congregations excited one another so as to feel—and, significantly, look— as if these movements were spontaneous, automatic, and out of control. In Foucault's terms, a regime of discipline had gradually emerged over the course of the eighteenth and nineteenth centuries aligning the individual, the subject and 'somatic singularity'; the individual was controlled through institutional mechanisms of punishment and an insidious system of normalizing checks and balances.[98] But the medical literature on epidemic disorders of the nervous system also suggests a process of disindividuation that called for corporeal control just as it set aside the idea of the juridical or the individual subject—those Foucault claimed constituted 'Man' in the nineteenth and twentieth centuries.[99] Instead, epidemic madness and collective group behaviours suggested to writers a gregarious impulse at the heart of religious and social movements that warranted medical attention in its own right. The individual was not the only or even the prime subject of modern scientific debate; groups, and the many forms they could take, swarmed at the heart of modern concepts of energetic expenditure, affective belonging, and states of body and mind co-constituting the political subject, as well as its amorphous underclass, the 'social body'. The movements of groups, and the choreographies defining these movements—triggered by leaders, and abated by sermons—revealed a disciplinary node conjoining medical, political, religious, social, and aesthetic figures in a modern state of being (and collective association) that enveloped the past into its folds. This collective figure appeared in social scientific literature as primitive and contemporary, animal and modern: moving groups offered insight into the workings of social life and the mechanisms of spontaneous human activity that were apparently moving its cogs.

95. Yandell, 'Epidemic Convulsions', 342. Yandell also notes, however, that the exercises did not usually cause insanity: 'it is remarkable that, notwithstanding the intensity and duration of this nervous disorder', he wrote, 'no instance is recorded in which permanent insanity resulted from it' (349).

96. At a camp meeting at Cane Ridge three thousand persons were said to have 'fallen' in the Falling Exercise, while at Paint Creek and Pleasant Point, two hundred and three hundred persons, respectively, fell to the ground in fits of syncope. Trances and visions were common, so that 'those who had been subject to syncope or swooning, would, upon recovering, detail visions which they had seen, and sing "in the strains of heaven," and discourse and exhort in a style far beyond what was supposed to be their ability' (Sutton, 'Report on the Medical Topography', 119–121). See also Cartwright, Autobiography, 46.

97. Yandell, 'Epidemic Convulsions', 349.

98. See esp. Foucault, Le pouvoir psychiatrique, 56–60.

99. Foucault, Le pouvoir psychiatrique, 60.

EPIDEMIC CONVULSIONS IN HOSPITALS, SCHOOLS, CONVENTS, AND FACTORIES

Factories, convents, and schools proved key sites for the observation of pathological acts of sympathetic imitation, prompting a further explosion of medical literature drawing attention to the mechanistic responses of bodies to institutional settings. As Robertson and others noted, the human propensity to imitate motor behaviours sympathetically was not confined to large religious or political groups, although emotions were at a peak in those settings. A range of further cases offered opportunities for direct observation in confined spaces, where sympathy was even more liable to spread. 'In the Pennsylvania Hospital', Robertson wrote, 'there occurred a few years since a . . . remarkable instance of . . . [sympathy of motion]; an epileptic patient was brought into the house and was seized in the long room with a fit; and a number of convalescents having collected around him, several of them were in like manner, seized with convulsions'.[100] In an episode reported from the Shetland Islands, a single epileptic seizure catalysed a cluster of fits resembling it in form though not in substance: the imitators were not epileptic but seemed to have reproduced the epileptic seizure almost perfectly. Not only was the capacity for imitation noteworthy, but the convulsive nature of these gestures arrested physicians' attention as well.[101]

One case, born, in its observers' terms, from physically and morally oppressive working conditions, emerged in the context of a cotton manufactory at Hodden Bridge, Lancashire, reported in a 1787 issue of *Gentleman's Magazine*. One young woman had—in jest—slipped a mouse into another one's shirt, knowing that the girl was terrified of mice. The latter

'was immediately thrown into a fit, and continued in it, with the most violent convulsions, for twenty-four hours'. The next day, three more girls were 'seized' in this way, and the next day six more. According to Hecker, who saw this as a case of morbid sympathy, the women were not predisposed to nervous disorders—they had not suffered any in the past—but the instinct of imitation provoked them to react to the first girl's convulsions with more of the same. News spread, and now the sole idea that the cotton might be infected provoked yet more convulsions, among people not all of whom worked at this factory. The mere idea that the cotton might have been infected sufficed to set up to twenty-four people, mostly young women, into seizures, characterized by fits of anxiety, strangulation, and convulsions 'so violent as to last without any intermission from a quarter of an hour to twenty-four hours, and to require four or five persons to prevent the patients from tearing their hair and dashing their heads against the floor or walls'.[102]

The initial reports had caused such alarm that the cotton mill was shut down, on the grounds that a disease might have been introduced into a bag of cotton.[103] A doctor was sent for, who administered electric shocks by way of a 'portable electric machine', which 'universally relieved' the patients, who were then enjoined to 'take a cheerful glass and join in a dance'; they returned to work the next day, with the exception of two or three, who were 'much weakened by their fits'. In a rare moment of sympathy with the plight of these women—working women, in this case—Hecker attributed this episode to their 'miserable and confined life in the workrooms of a spinning manufactory',[104] although he also mused that this sort of situation was far less likely to produce convulsions than it was religious enthusiasm. The girls may have been bored

100. Robertson, *An Essay on Chorea Sancti Viti*, 19.

101. See Hecker, *Epidemics of the Middle Ages*, 135; Samuel Hibbert, *A description of the Shetland Islands, comprising an account of their geology, scenery, antiquities, and superstitions* (Edinburgh: A. Constable & Co., 1822), 399–401. Further accounts of church grounds in Shetland from the same period, including *The History and Description of the Shetland Islands* (1838) by Rev. James Catton (1823–1863), suggest that as in many very remote areas, churchgoing was an occasion for villagers to meet socially, travelling often many miles. James Catton, *The History and Description of the Shetland Islands; with an account of the manners, customs, circumstances, superstitions and religion of the inhabitants* (Wainfleet: P. I. Tuxford, 1838). See also Anon., *A Walk in Shetland by Two Eccentrics* (Edinburgh: Stillies, Brothers; and Aberdeen: Lewis Smith, 1831). Eliza Edmondston (1802–1869), in *Sketches and Tales of the Shetland Islands* (1856), points out the Shetlanders' quite ambivalent relationship to religion. Shetland was, she wrote, 'a wild and primitive district'; it presented 'pictures' of 'a state of society rapidly disappearing under the influence of modern advancement'. In Eliza Edmondston, *Sketches and Tales of the Shetland Islands* (Edinburgh: Sutherland & Knox; and London: Simpkin, Marshall & Co., 1856), 3, 16.

102. Hecker, *Epidemics of the Middle Ages*, 130.

103. Hecker, *Epidemics of the Middle Ages*, 130.

104. Hecker, *Epidemics of the Middle Ages*, 131.

and suffered from exhaustion caused by the strenuous and repetitive nature of their work. This sparked an upheaval on the workroom floor, quickly abated by the use of the electric shocks and, paradoxically, a socially sanctioned, medically prescribed dance.

Scenes of imitation frequently involved young women, who in medical literature epitomized an automatic and animal tendency to spontaneous and uncontrolled movement. In January 1801, a young woman visited a patient being treated for tetanic spasms at the Charité hospital in Berlin. Upon entering the ward, the woman suddenly 'fell down in strong convulsions', at the sight of which 'six other female patients immediately became affected in the same way, and by degrees eight more were in like manner attacked with strong convulsions'.[105] Hecker argued that the women's behaviour was comparable to that of a 'flock of sheep' and suggested that convulsions were signs of strong emotion: 'every species of enthusiasm', he wrote, 'every strong affection, every violent passion, may lead to convulsions— to mental disorders—to a concussion of the nerves, from the sensorium to the very finest extremities of the spinal cord. The whole world is full of examples of this afflicting state of turmoil, which, when the mind is carried away by the force of a sensual impression that destroys its freedom, is irresistibly propagated by imitation. Those who are thus infected do not spare even their own lives, but, as a hunted flock of sheep will follow their leader'.[106] Women were at the helm of a new feminized social sphere catalysing volatile tendencies among bodies in public to move without the supposedly rational benefit of foresight. Imitation, widely construed in medical literature as an elemental component of social interaction and social life, also described a type of pathological contagion on the rise as urban centres and industrial labour were increasingly putting women (and men) in proximity with one another. Paris, in Laborde's terms, was the first true capital of the world, but it was also an agitated den teeming with perversions, ambitions, and madness.[107] Durkheim argued in De la division du travail social [On the Division of Social Labor] (1893) that social solidarity however was also on the rise as well following the Industrial Revolution, as was individual autonomy—and both were rising in tandem with broader negative and positive transformations of social relations resulting from the new division of social labour.[108] This set of changes resulted in increased contact among strangers as well as a sense of social alienation, what Durkheim called anomie, a feeling of lawlessness which provoked crises and depressions among workers for whom the order of the world had become overturned.[109] In this context, the seeming rise of epidemic hysteria and convulsions revealed a rift: individual and collective bodies were rebelling, and the subjects' minds and bodies appeared disengaged.

As a metaphor, the motor impulse coincided with a rise in mechanistic approaches to labour—allied with productivism—rendering women especially vulnerable. For the French polymath Émile Littré (1801–1891), St. Vitus's dance (which he equated with chorea) was a mental epidemic disorder propagated by motoric imitation.[110] August Hirsch (1817–1894), in his Handbook of Geographical and Historical Pathology (1886), described a hysterical outbreak 'of a religious kind' in Haute-Savoie in 1857, intimating that women, whom he considered more subject to imitation, were at once more animal, more

---

105. Hecker, Epidemics of the Middle Ages, 131.

106. Hecker, Epidemics of the Middle Ages, 132. Félix Bricheteau reports a similar episode in 'Relation d'une épidémie de chorée observée à l'Hôpital Necker', Archives générales de médecine 1 (1863): 433–447 and 532–549.

107. Laborde, Les hommes, 38.

108. Émile Durkheim, De la division du travail social, 8th ed. (Paris: Presses Universitaires de France, 1967), xliii–xliv.

109. See also Durkheim's study of anomie, specifically 'anomic suicide', in Le suicide (Paris: Presses Universitaires de France, 2002), 264–311. For his indictment of Tarde's concept of imitation as 'contagion', see esp. 108–117.

110. Sighele, La foule criminelle, 42. See Émile Littré, 'Des grandes épidémies', Revue des Deux-Mondes, 15 January 1836, reprinted in Émile Littré, Médecine et médecins (Paris: Didier, 1872), 1–40. Littré borrows liberally from Hecker's recently translated writing on the dancing mania and the Black Death, which he summarized in a book review published in the Gazette médicale de Paris (see chapter 1 here). See also Littré's detailed account in his Dictionnaire de médecine, de chirurgie, de pharmacie et des sciences qui s'y rapportent [Dictionary of Medicine, Surgery, Pharmacy, and Related Sciences]. Émile Littré, 'Chorée', Dictionnaire de médecine, de chirurgie, de pharmacie et des sciences qui s'y rattachent, 21st ed., ed. Gilbert Augustin (Paris: J.-B. Baillière, 1905–1908), 313–315. Under the entry for 'Chorémanie', Littré refers the reader to 'Chorée', which he designates as its synonym (315). In the foundational Dictionnaire de la langue française [Dictionary of the French Language], Littré offers brief entries for 'Chorée' and 'Chorémanie', though he notes them as synonyms only. Both designate an 'illness, also referred to as St. Vitus's dance [danse de St-Guy], consisting of continuous, irregular, and involuntary movements'. In Émile Littré, Dictionnaire de la langue française, 4 vols. (Paris: Hachette, 1873), vol. 1, 612.

machinic, and less well adapted to the strictures of a new mechanistic workplace, which favoured individualism just as it sought to break labour down into its component parts. Imitation was at the opposite end of individualism, dissolving it, reaggregating men and women into a social horde. The horde was in this sense understood as feminine and impulsive. Yet sympathetic behaviours also revealed states of social solidarity and mutuality, discursively tied back in Hirsch's writing, as in his contemporaries', to a pre-civilized state. Modernity and sociality seemed at once inextricably tied together and fundamentally incompatible. Attempts in the new social scientific fields to come to terms with motor impulses in groups and individuals persisted in describing restless states as ancient, feminine, and organic, revealing a pervasive prejudice according to which purportedly premodern beings sit closer on the biosocial scale to an automatic animal core.

'WORKING THE BODY LIKE A MACHINE': COMIC ANTICS IN THE BACKWOODS

What theorists of the 'mirror neuron' have observed, in dance and performance studies, as a propensity towards imitation constitutive of the kinaesthetic experience of watching dance (articulated in Foster's work among others) corresponds in late nineteenth-century neurology with a slightly more awkward formulation according to which imitation of pathological behaviour produced a comic game of mockery and horseplay. In this view, reversions to automatic behaviours were described in medical literature as laughably theatrical, excrescences into the public sphere from out of a premodern age. For Rabinbach, social medicine and reform emerged in the last quarter of the nineteenth century to remedy new regimes of

hyperproductivity entangled in a physiological discourse on energetic fatigue signalling the converse of play.[111] Workers engaged in too much work became sick with exhaustion and loss of vitality. Indeed, alongside the scientization of worker productivity (productivism), moments of idleness, boredom, and play arose as instances of archaic excess, a premodern vitality that had no more place in the normative sphere of overwork, whose disorder and disease paradoxically appeared as an excess of imitative gesture. Imitation thus worked doubly hard in the nineteenth century as a metaphor suggesting at once the breakdown of individuality and the human spectacle of mutuality in shared gestures that mechanically jolted workers out of their monotonous everyday—eruptions of premodern idle life onto the industrial stage. Imitation in this sense was experienced as pathological and entertaining, science and art. But most humorous was individual men and women's bodies' awkwardly attempting to mimic the jagged angularity and automatisms of the machine. Amply theorized with regard to the cinematic representation of it by Charlie Chaplin (1889–1977) in *Modern Times* (1936), as Gordon has shown, automatic angularity had a far earlier start as a neurological disease allying boredom, monotony, involuntary gesture, and work.

The neurologist George Beard (1839–1883), in an article published in the *Journal of Nervous and Mental Disease* in 1878, described a lumberjack community in the Moosehead Lake area of northern Maine, some of whose members, in response to a loud noise, sharp command, or 'startle', jumped suddenly and engaged in echolalia (the immediate and apparently meaningless repetition of someone else's words) and automatic obedience, performing actions such as hitting a close friend upon command or placing their hands in a fire. They could repeat lines from Virgil and jump off the ground, 'the height of the jump [being] proportional to the degree of unexpectedness of a startle'.[112] Sighele called this 'psychic mimeticism', a neurosis

---

111. Rabinbach, *The Human Motor*.

112. In R. Howard and R. Ford, 'From the Jumping Frenchmen of Maine to Post-Traumatic Stress Disorder: The Startle Response in Neuropsychiatry', *Psychological Medicine* 22.3 (1992): 695–707, 700. See George Beard, 'Remarks upon Jumpers or Jumping Frenchmen', *Journal of Nervous and Mental Disease* 5 (1878): 623–640, and George Beard, 'Experiments with the Jumpers of Maine', *Popular Science Monthly* 18 (1880): 170–178. On Beard's work, see esp. F. Andermann and E. Andermann, 'Startle Disorders of Man: Hyperekplexia, Jumping and Startle Epilepsy', *Brain & Development* 10.4 (1988): 213–222, 216–217; and F. Andermann and E. Andermann, 'Hyperekplexia and Other Disorders of Startle: Differential Diagnosis with Epilepsy', in Peter W. Kaplan and Robert S. Fisher, eds., *Imitators of Epilepsy*, 2nd ed. (New York: Demos Medical, 2005), 185–190; Ronald C. Simons, *Boo! Culture, Experience, and the Startle Reflex* (Oxford: Oxford University Press, 1996). On the neurophysiological triggering of various automatic behaviours including startle, see also Devereux, 'Normal et anormal', 58–62.

that compels people to imitate the words and gestures of others.[113] Such cases were reported again as recently as the 1960s and, according to neurologists M.-H. and J.-M. Saint-Hilaire and L. Granger, 'related to the historically boring nature of life for lumberjacks in the forests of Québec and Maine, where jumpers provided a welcome distraction'.[114] Neurologists Frederick and Eva Andermann further note that the jumpers themselves, and those watching them, laugh after being startled; 'jumping provided a ready source of amusement in the lumber camps'.[115] Beard was aware of the hereditary nature of the disease but, Andermann and Andermannn add, 'did not believe that the condition represented a "pathological nervous disease"; instead he considered it to be a "fixed psychological state" and "a remarkable illustration of the involuntary life."' A long day's work in the logging camps prompted loggers to engage in 'mutual tickling, punching, and startling of the fearful', so that 'this repeated horseplay' led to jumping as '"probably an evolution of tickling."'[116]

Acts of automatic imitation offered participants a source of release from the boredom of everyday life. As Mary Merryweather (c. 1813–1880) noted in *Experience of Factory Life* (1862), she and her co-workers were often bored and sought socially sanctioned forms of relief: 'when no other [excitement] was provided, religious

enthusiasm would occasionally take its place'.[117] Osler further argued that 'the habit of working the body like a machine', which was a product of the Industrial Revolution, led to a new concept of energy, including 'energy depletion' and fatigue,[118] and concepts of stress. Yet jerking and 'startle' behaviours and acts of kinetically comical and excessive religious enthusiasm offered social solidarity as well as an occasion for recreation, often at the protagonist's expense. De la Tourette, who translated Beard's writing on startle disorders, argued in 'Étude sur une affection nerveuse caractérisée par l'incoordination motrice accompagnée d'écholalie et de coprolalie' [Study on a Nervous Affection Characterized by Motor Incoordination Accompanied by Echolalia and Coprolalia], in the *Archives of Neurology* (1884), that startle disorders, including miryachit (in Siberia) and latah (in Southeast Asia), presented a theatrical performance of motor actions and role play.[119] Coprolalia (involuntary swearing) added a verbal dimension to these bodily acts. Transculturally and transhistorically, bodies in states of boredom performing automatic jumps and startles provided a spectacle to peers apparently suffering from a dearth of productivity—idleness understood in these terms to be pathological. Rabinbach suggests 'idleness and savagery' were widely viewed in the nineteenth century together, both equally

113. Sighele, *La foule criminelle*, 68.

114. See M.-H. Saint-Hilaire, J.-M. Saint-Hilaire, and L. Granger, 'Jumping Frenchmen of Maine', *Neurology* 36 (1986): 1269–1271; also M.-H. Saint-Hilaire and J.-M. Saint-Hilaire, 'Jumping Frenchmen of Maine, Videotape Documentary', *Movement Disorders* 16.3 (2001): 530, and M.-H. Saint-Hilaire and J.-M. Saint-Hilaire, 'The "Ragin' Cajuns," Videotape Documentary', *Movement Disorders* 16.3 (2001): 531–532. The term 'startle neurosis' was given by F. C. Thorne to a syndrome characterized by hyperaesthesias (extreme, especially haptic, sensibility), excessive startle reactions, and associated personality reactions in 1944, found in about one in two thousand men screened for induction into military service in the United States. Howard and Ford argued that as with the jumping Frenchmen, this condition provoked ill-willed mockery among servicemen, so that although the condition was not degenerative, its sufferers' psychosocial states became so: 'repeated startling of affected individuals, for the entertainment of their companions, led to seclusiveness and aggressiveness, and eventually "neurotic invalidism" in sufferers' (Howard and Ford, 'From the Jumping Frenchmen of Maine', 700). F. C. Thorne, 'Startle Neurosis', *American Journal of Psychiatry* 101 (1944): 105–109. The gradual disappearance of the jumping Frenchmen has been attributed to the reduction of boredom and isolation among modern lumberjacks (Howard and Ford, 'From the Jumping Frenchmen of Maine', 704); also Saint-Hilaire et al., 'Jumping Frenchmen of Maine', 1269–1271. J. Hardison described a similarity to 'gooseyness' in 'Are the Jumping Frenchmen of Maine Goosey?', *Journal of the American Medical Association* 244 (1980): 70.

115. Andermann and Andermann, 'Startle Disorders of Man', 219. George Rosen argues that psychic epidemics, including the Kentucky revival, are caused largely by their geographic location, when it causes social isolation due to remoteness. 'Under such conditions', he writes, 'there were few sources of recreation to relieve the monotony of daily life'. In Rosen, *Madness in Society*, 217.

116. Andermann and Andermann, 'Startle Disorders of Man', 217.

117. Mary Merryweather, *Experience of Factory Life, being a record of fourteen years' work at Mr. Courtauld's silk mill at Halstead, in Essex*, 3rd ed. (London: E. Faithfull, 1862), 18. See Rosen, *Madness in Society*, 220.

118. In L. J. Kirmayer and D. Groleau, 'Affective Disorders in Cultural Context', *Psychiatric Clinics of North America* 24.3 (2001): 465–478, 469.

119. Gilles de la Tourette, 'Étude sur une affection nerveuse caractérisée par l'incoordination motrice accompagnée d'écholalie et de coprolalie', *Archives of Neurology* 9 (1884): 19–42; 158–200. Andermann and Andermann, in 'Startle Disorders of Man', draw comparisons between latah and jumping, underscoring the performative value of what neurologist R. C. Simons calls 'Role Latah', the last of three phases of latah: the three phases, Andermann and Andermann write, include 'first, the immediate response, corresponding to excessive startle; second, the attention capture which corresponds

applicable to the degenerate, primitives, and the working classes.[120]

Role play was not new and suggested the comedic interchangeability of individuals via the interplay of their gestures. Sydenham had noted the pantomimic—highly entertaining—quality of St. Vitus's dance in *Schedula Monitoria* (1686), in which he described involuntary actions resulting in an uncannily automatic performance, and thus comedy. 'St. Vitus's dance shows itself by a halting, or rather an unsteady movement of one of the legs, which the patient *drags*', he wrote. 'Then it is seen in the hand of the same side. The patient cannot keep it a moment in its place, whether he lay it upon his breast or any other part of his body. Do what he may it will be jerked elsewhere convulsively'. This provoked entertainment for onlookers: 'if any vessel filled with drink be put into his hand, before it reaches his mouth he will exhibit a thousand gesticulations like a mountebank. He holds the cup out straight, as if to move it to his mouth, but has his hand carried elsewhere by sudden jerks. Then, perhaps, he contrives to bring it to his mouth. If so, he will drink the liquid off at a gulp; just as if he were trying to amuse the spectators by his antics'.[121] The pantomimic aspect of the jerks and convulsions, further remarked upon by Dr. Alexander Tweedie (1794–1884) in *A System of Practical Medicine* (1840) and Hirsch in his *Handbook of Geographical and Historical Pathology*, helped these authors explain the tendency towards imitation observed among the disorder's spectators, so engrossed in the performance that they responded in kind. This automatic mimesis accounted for the gestures' tendency to 'spread by contagion' or 'sympathy',[122] through the involuntary movement of the sympathetic nervous system. This was a social theatre of jerks, convulsions, and twitches, translated into medical terms; it defined the new field of social epidemiology, in which ambivalent forms of motor contagion and ostensibly benign social play were described as pathological events.

From a social and affective standpoint, the lumberjacks' horseplay may have troubled some of those suffering from startle, who would have been ostracized; so, too, those performing sharp, involuntary gestures may have unwillingly amused their witnesses, in the cases of St. Vitus's dance that Sydenham describes. Involuntary gestures were comical to spectators, belying a fear of social contagiousness, motor dysfunction, and loss of control. Bergson, Tarde's successor at the Collège de France in 1904, wrote that broken, awkward bodies, subject to mishaps—trips, falls, burps, and farts—are humorous, comic bodies, as opposed to nearly abstract the body of the tragic actor, who does not sit, for fear of drawing attention to corporeal vulnerabilities. The humour involved in comedy is that which draws attention to the mechanical, even mechanistic quality of a body that can fall apart.[123] Taken in this light, choreomania appeared to signal the subversively comic

to expletive, echopraxia and automatic obedience'. The third component, according to Simons, they write, is ' "Role Latah", consisting of an elaboration of some of the responses into intentionally amusing performances. This may be an important component of this disorder in Imu, the Ainu equivalent of latah, where affected individuals attend special functions expecting to "perform." ' But, they add that this 'willingness to perform is not a feature of jumping, which is considered a handicap and a disability in North American society' (219). See R. C. Simons, 'The Resolution of the *Latah* Paradox', *Journal of Nervous and Mental Disease* 168.4 (1980): 195–206. *Miryachit*, or 'Arctic hysteria' (also known as 'olonism'), from the Siberian Tungus word meaning ' "doing something stupid and useless because of a sudden fear" ', is a startle disorder with a 'social function', Howard and Ford note reprising Russian anthropologist Sergei M. Shirokogoroff, 'in that it provides a spectacle and entertainment for the Tungus, "without which Tungus life would be impoverished" ' (Howard and Ford, 'From the Jumping Frenchmen of Maine', 700). See Sergei M. Shirokogoroff, *The Psychomental Complex of the Tungus* (London: Kegan Paul, 1935), and David F. Aberle, 'Arctic Hysteria and Latah in Malaysia', *New York Academy of Sciences* 14 (1952): 291–297. Howard and Ford note that 'Gilles de la Tourette (1884), who translated Beard's writings, was the first to suggest that miryachit and latah were the same condition (as were, he believed, "jumping," and the convulsive tic that bears his name)' ('From the Jumping Frenchmen of Maine', 700). William A. Hammond describes an account of a journey from the Pacific Ocean through Asia to the United States by two navy men who witness a disorder 'known to Russians by the Name of Miryachit'; Hammond compares this to Beard's description of the jumping Frenchmen, as well as to a sleep disorder ('sleep-drunkenness') resulting in sudden acts of violence. In William A. Hammond, 'Miryachit: A Newly Discovered Disease of the Nervous System and Its Analogues', *British Medical Journal* 1.1216 (1884): 758–759.

120. Rabinbach, *The Human Motor*, 29.

121. Cited in Osler, *On Chorea*, 3 (emphasis mine). See Thomas Sydenham, *Processus integri in Morbis fere omnibus Curandis* (London, 1692).

122. See Hirsch, *Handbook of Geographical and Historical Pathology*, vol. 3, 525, where he describes the Kentucky revivalists as engaging in 'a pantomime performance called "the jerks." ' Dr. Alexander Tweedie writes that 'the patient . . . moves irregularly from side to side, or proceeds by jumps or starts; one foot is rather dragged than lifted, and the movements of the arms resemble the gesticulations of players'. Alexander Tweedie, *A System of Practical Medicine* (Philadelphia: Lea & Blanchard, 1840), 327.

123. Henri Bergson, *Le rire: Essai sur la signification du comique* (Paris: PUF Quadrige, 1999).

potential of clumsily moving bodies to contagion one another and thus to assail the social whole.

PRIMITIVISM, FASCISM, AND THE 'BIOLOGIC CORE'

Increasing distinctions at the turn of the twentieth century between contagion, suggestion, and imitation revealed the continued growth of scientific interest in these fields as ideas about—and practices harnessing—social bodies became ever more powerfully aligned with the efficient workings of nation states. As the chief physician at the Asiles de la Seine, Dr. Auguste Vigouroux (1866–1918), and Dr. Paul Juquelier (1876–1921), professor of clinical medicine at the Faculté de Médecine in Paris, wrote in *La contagion mentale* [Mental Contagion] (1905), experimental psychology in the early twentieth century used 'contagion' metaphorically to discuss cases of mental contamination or infection not literally caused by germs. But this type of contagion was a variant of (and to be differentiated from) 'imitation', inasmuch as 'mental contagion' was involuntary. It also differed from 'suggestion' (in the old sense of Mesmerism, or hypnosis), whose effects may emerge over time. Mental contagion was, in contrast, they argued, always spontaneous.[124] As they put it, it was the pathological transmission of an element or agent—not exactly microbial—whose effects on the person 'contagioned' by the 'contagioner' were immediate, involuntary, and irresistible. 'Mental' (or 'psychic') qualities were a function of the cerebrospinal axis, so that 'contagioners' could affect the physical reflexes, voluntary movements, and emotional states, as well as the ideas and beliefs, of others.[125]

But although the metaphorical use of contagion, suggestion, imitation, and sympathy to describe crowd movements was becoming popular among some psychologists, sociologists, and other medical and social scientific writers by the early twentieth century, others still used these terms to denote physical or biological hierarchies across cultures, setting those who were purportedly lowest on the evolutionary scale as those most prone to various types of mimesis. F. M. Davenport (1866–1956), in his work of religious and social anthropology *Primitive Traits in Religious Revivals* (1905), argued that 'nervous instability' was 'a normal characteristic of primitive man', appearing among northern Siberian tribes, North American Indians, and others.[126] 'Likeminded people are those whose mental and nervous organizations respond in like ways to the same stimuli', Davenport argued. 'They might conceivably respond *unconsciously* to the same stimuli, as animals do', in which case 'we should . . . call them instinctively likeminded'. But, such a 'low scale of human development' being unlikely, '*sympathetic* likemindedness' more accurately described the mental characteristics of people acting under the influence of suggestibility, imitativeness, imagination, and heightened emotion. These traits, which he deemed 'exceedingly primitive' and 'probably universal', were responsible for 'impulsive social action' exercised primarily among people 'who have least inhibitory control'. A population 'under control' was, conversely, one in which these tendencies were in check; and in which 'we have deliberation and public opinion and social evolution rather than revolution'.[127] Supposedly, primitive people—not only in the past but in the present as well—were not only more prone to impulses leading to acts of sympathetic contagion but also on that account more liable to engage in spontaneous acts of social rebellion and political revolt.

As theories of crowds and mobs, masses and publics, came to be developed more systematically in the 1910s and 1920s in works of social psychology by E. A. Ross (1866–1951) and others linking democratic and social democratic movements to biologically conceived public life, so too interest in crazes, fads, fashions, and the aesthetic structures of nation states gained greater sway.[128] Psychoanalyst and

---

124. Auguste Vigouroux and Paul Juquelier, *La contagion mentale* (Paris: Octave Dion, Éditeur, 1905), 2–3.

125. Vigouroux and Juquelier, *La contagion mentale*, 1. On contagion and state politics, see also Peter Baldwin, *Contagion and the State in Europe, 1830–1930* (Cambridge: Cambridge University Press, 1999); Andrew Robert Aisenberg, *Contagion: Disease, Government, and the 'Social Question' in Nineteenth-Century France* (Stanford, CA: Stanford University Press, 1999); and Alison Bashford and Claire Hooker, eds., *Contagion: Historical and Cultural Studies* (London: Routledge, 2001).

126. F. M. Davenport, *Primitive Traits in Religious Revivals: A Study in Mental and Social Evolution* (New York: Macmillan, 1905), ix–x.

127. Davenport, *Primitive Traits*, 2–3.

128. See Ross, *Social Psychology*; and Wilfred Trotter, *Instincts of the Herd in Peace and War* (London: T. Fisher Unwin, 1916), influenced by Le Bon. The frequent reprinting of Mackay's *Extraordinary Popular Delusions and the Madness of Crowds* at the start of the twentieth century suggests its continued influence in those years.

social theorist Wilhelm Reich (1897–1957) took this further: fascism, which his 'medical experiences [as a physician] with men and women of various classes, races, nations, religious beliefs, etc.' taught him penetrates the 'biologic core', 'relies . . . on the mystical thinking and sentiments of the masses'.[129] It could be fought 'only if . . . the *mystical contagion* of the masses is tackled through education and hygiene'.[130] The social-psychological disease he was describing, a disease of 'all the *irrational* reactions of the average human character',[131] took physical and mental order, contagion, imitation, and sympathy to the 1930s world of over-mechanization and 'biologic rigidity'. People engaged in mundane, mechanical work, detached from their natural, biological needs, including sexual health and gratification (what he called the 'function of orgasm'), yielded a 'sick society'. Depersonalization and dissociation from the biologic core resulted not only in fascism but the inhibited, miserable, and angry mysticism of the masses. A renewed sex-economy, for Reich, would liberate society from this enclosure.

By the time of Canetti's writing in the 1960s, a renewed taxonomy of crowds included the *masse de fête*, a celebratory gathering marked by joy and vitality, movement and gregariousness, for the sake of release rather than collective strain. The *masse de fête* was also marked by repetition, linking pastness and futurity, bringing individuals together in a celebration that promised further fêtes to come. These were the fêtes that implicated a positive vital politics, one whose emphasis on the public performance of play, and the corporeal show of solidarity, served as grounds for the constitution of a living political arena allowing for insubordination and vivacity in equal parts.

The next chapter turns to the emergence of neurology as a science of movement recuperating ancient figures into a modern clinical setting. Practicing what they termed 'retrospective medicine', informed by visual and narrative montage, Charcot and his collaborators read scenes from the past as scenes of hysteroepilepsy and hysteria, chorea and choreomania. As the chapter further shows, this comparative exercise spurred at least one student, Henri Meige, to pursue his comparative work outside hospital walls, seeking modern-day remains of choreomania in neighbouring Luxembourg. With Meige, the shift to an ethnographic method gives way to a flurry of further sightings of 'choreomania' in the colonial world.

---

129. Wilhelm Reich, *The Mass Psychology of Fascism*, ed. Mary Higgins and Chester M. Raphael, trans. Vincent R. Carfagno (New York: Farrar, Strauss and Giroux, 1970), xiii, 121; see also esp. xi–xxvii and 115–142.

130. Reich, *The Mass Psychology*, 121.

131. Reich, *The Mass Psychology*, xiv.

6

Médecine Rétrospective

Hysteria's Archival Drag

Hysteria marks the eruption of the lower, the animal, signifying a sexuality that is anti-social, even criminal, and— worst of all— inexplicable.

—Elin Diamond, *Unmaking Mimesis* (1997)

To understand history . . . one has to be a physician.

—Lucien Nass, *Les névrosés de l'histoire* (1908)

Hysteria . . . requires an audience

—Georges Devereux, 'Normal et anormal' (1956)

HYSTEROEPILEPTIC REPERFORMANCE AND ARCHIVAL DRAG

Hysteria, Diamond points out, is fundamentally illegible.[1] Yet physicians have persisted in trying to 'read' hysteria in their patients' bodies for over a century. Symptoms including tremors, falls, hallucinations, and a cast of melodramatic bodily gestures taxonomized by Charcot betray the hysteric's psychosomatic disintegration and, simultaneously, her unwitting participation in a knowable, codifiable language of sexual and emotional repression and excess. Often female, the hysteric is conceived as a mad woman, barely more than a girl, whose affliction is not just organic but also fantastical. She imagines her ills and performs her distress according to a repeatable, even learnable language composed of sexually suggestive *arcs de cercles* (arched backs); hammering and other 'labouring' motions; religious poses, including crucifixions; and whole-body actions reminiscent of popular dances. As Janet Beizer suggests, the hysteric has typically been considered in twentieth- and twenty-first century feminist and cultural criticism heroically to express the inexpressible, rallied to a feminist cause influentially articulated by Hélène Cixous and Catherine Clément (in *La Jeune Née* [1975]).[2]

---

1. Elin Diamond, *Unmaking Mimesis: Essays on Feminism and Gender* (Abingdon: Routledge, 1997), 9. See also Ludmilla Jordanova, *Sexual Visions: Images of Gender in Science and Medicine between the Eighteenth and Twentieth Centuries* (Madison: University of Wisconsin Press, 1989). Jordanova suggests that 'during the eighteenth and nineteenth centuries it was taken for granted that the human body was legible, even if there was no consensus on exactly how it could and should be "read"'; she cites phrenology and physiognomy as two sciences dedicated to 'decoding' bodily signs (51).

2. Janet Beizer, *Ventriloquized Bodies: Narratives of Hysteria in Nineteenth-Century France* (Ithaca, NY: Cornell University Press, 1994), 1–2. See Hélène Cixous and Catherine Clément, *La Jeune Née* (Paris: Éditions 10/18, 1975). See also Elaine Showalter, 'Hysteria, Feminism and Gender', in Sander L. Gilman, Helen King, Roy Porter, G. S. Rousseau, and Elaine Showalter, *Hysteria beyond Freud* (Berkeley: University of California Press, 1993), 286–335. Micale, in *Approaching Hysteria*, argues that the 1970s saw a

But the 'hysteric' also, this chapter argues, gains scientific currency from her ability paradoxically to reperform the past. She not only corporealizes what is linguistically inexpressible; she is imagined also to tap into an otherwise inaccessible, ancient type of corporeality. Her jagged gestures supposedly reproduce ecstatic, 'demonic', movements first performed in premodern times, reactualized through her body, operating as a transhistorical—even ahistorical—conduit.

This chapter considers 'hysteria' as a concept suffusing modern scientific writing on the dancing disease, considered in this respect as a disorder of illegibility and concomitantly of scientific articulation. Scientists—neurologists, in this chapter, in particular—explain the inexplicably gesticulating body by recourse to comparison and historical artefact, which illustrate the contemporary body in distress by juxtaposing it to past and foreign forms. Without ever being entirely explained, the 'hysterical' body becomes science's site of greatest articulation: the fitful body serves as a litmus test for modern science's capacity to account for hermeneutically impenetrable figures and events. And this occurs through a process of stylized, dramatic, and richly illustrated narration. Neurology, as modern science's arguably most interdisciplinary discipline to emerge in the nineteenth century, draws from history and art history, illustration, psychiatry, epidemiology, and other fields to inscribe erratic gestures into new systems of thought in which these gestures achieve a recognizable, patterned status. Irregular gestures and poses become recognizably abnormal forms that can be treated; and they do so inasmuch as they are convincingly mapped onto historical precedent. Repetition—repeatability—and, in this sense, theatre become the mode by which neurology enters scientific modernity. Hysterical gestures are understood inasmuch as they reproduce poses culled from the annals of the past. History becomes a measure of universality; and science becomes itself, in its purported universalism, through the (semi-choreographed) bodily representation of past forms.

This chapter then moves chronologically through modern neurology's imaginaries—its ways of seeing antiquity first in ancient artefacts

then more recent but still past cultural narratives; and finally in the clinic, and further afield, outside hospital walls. In all these instances, neurology construes itself as a science paradoxically finding, remembering, and knowing the present by way of an excavated past. This variation on the old Platonic principle—by which knowledge is remembrance—imagines modern science as an art of repetition, in short as theatre. Modern neurology, from the late nineteenth century, emerges as a science steeped in humanistic methods foregrounding narrative, anecdote, ekphrasis (the description of images and scenes), performance, and reperformance. Neurology *sees* and *does* gestural reprise.

Scientificity, then, appears in the nineteenth century as a method connecting contemporary corporealities and past expressions of these corporealities, in short, as a way of reading bodily history through choreographic congruences. These congruences emerge in the neurology clinic in terms of patients' apparent echoing ways of moving their limbs with visual and narrative depictions of motion and gesture highlighted in literature and visual arts by Charcot and his team. This slightly recasts what Lepecki has described as dance's special way of archiving movement through choreographic redos and reenactments, which remember and preserve—but also transform—dance and bodily practices in and through dancers' bodies. So whereas Lepecki sees current dance practice's 'will to archive' as a method for understanding dance history through dancers' bodies in choreographic reprises and homages, neurologists in this chapter read patients' movements and subtly instruct their bodies. This instruction maps patient gestures onto an excavated corporeal and choreographic history folded retrospectively into a neurological core.[3] Neurology patients, in other words, seemingly involuntarily repeat choreic, hysteric, or epileptic movements without an origin; they appear to reveal a phantasmatic meeting point between their own supposed disorders and the visual or historical depictions of similar movements their physician directors endeavour to replicate in their patients. These congruences, echoes, and repetitions provide a false sense of evidence of

---

rise in studies of hysteria across disciplines—what he semi-jokingly terms New Hystericism (3–18). Micale offers a useful review of scholarly literature in *Approaching Hysteria*, 33–107, arguing that the 'first attempts to set down in a systematic fashion the intellectual history of hysteria' date from between 1890 and 1910, with the work of Charcot's students, Gilles de la Tourette in particular (33–34).

3. Lepecki, 'The Body as Archive'.

the universality and scientific validity of these gestures—the arched back, the cross shape—which come to appear dramatically as neurological diseases, though the gestures themselves are neither entirely confirmed nor newly created in this exercise of juxtaposition. As Foucault argues of madness, discourse creates something out of a chasm, an absence, an unarticulated complex of experiences; makes a concept and singularity out of and around myriad things. Neurology produces an imagined relationship between current and older movements, finding resonances, but also finally revealing an empty middle, a fantastical conjuration—rather than a 'will to archive', what we might call a 'will merely to repeat'.

Modern neurology in this sense approximates what Rebecca Schneider has influentially described as 're-enactment', whereby present performances of seemingly authentic actions do not just copy something prior but become entangled in a thick knot of doublings, false originals, and their equally (un)original reproductions.[4] The 'temporal tangle'[5] that results from this perpetual redoing suggests a porous relationship between the present and the past, in which neither is quite separated from the other: the present does not sit outside of and return to the past, nor is the past entirely separated from the present. Rather, what Schneider, following Elizabeth Freeman, calls 'temporal drag' suggests 'pastness—. . . on the move': pastness that does not stay fixed but enacts what Freeman describes as 'temporal transitivity', a sort of constant becoming-other that requires the flitting and fleeting motion of a temporal to and fro.[6] Temporal ambiguity, including as regards 'origins', suggests a choreographic motion that does not just reveal history's fits and fainting spells, moments of (historical) intensity that gather and dissipate, but the hopping, skipping, and jumping motion—the lateral, diagonal, or zigzag move—of ideas and bodies across time revealing that 'history' is never linear; nor is it ever entirely 'past'. 'History', Schneider writes, 'remains before us'.[7] In Charcot's clinic, history remains in the hysteric's body, whose forms

Charcot takes it upon himself to describe, rechoreograph, and recode.

Hysteroepilepsy, in Charcot's formulation, serves as a privileged site for tapping into past somatic manifestations: figures and scenes of antiquity remerging in present-day hospital settings. The past, in this view, is saturated with hysteroepileptic events, represented in and re-enacted by modern hysteroepileptic bodies. The past emerges as an antediluvian force rippling through the archaeological layers of urban civility and modern bourgeois life. The past operates contrapuntally in the present as 'archival drag'—performance theorist David Román's term, after Freeman, reprised by Schneider, to describe the process of 'dragging' images, myths, statues, into the present in tableaux vivants that enact 'stillness': a quality of being still here—or still there;[8] still in a 'temporal drag' between archive and performance. This chapter then draws a number of strands together, performing a hinge function in the narrative of this book, centred on Charcot and the journeys (the choreography) of his ideas through various roots and routes—which subsequent chapters will explore in Madagascar and beyond. Framed by Charcot and his collaborators' historiographic and iconographic experiments at the Salpêtrière, particularly their exercises in visual and historiographic montage, the chapter also returns to the Convulsionaries of Saint-Médard, who for Charcot represented a prior order of bodily fits and starts that prefigured those of his patients. The chapter shows that Charcot's comparison of the Convulsionaries' *attitudes* with *attitudes* he observed firsthand among his patients at the Salpêtrière inspired at least one student, Meige, to seek further evidence of hysteroepilepsy outside the hospital's walls. The passage (or translatio) from historiographic and clinical exercise to fieldwork thus, with Meige's itinerant adventure, comes into fuller view, articulating the move this book highlights from a broadly medical to an anthropological field of observation, whereby the dancing disease becomes, by the early twentieth century, a disorder of (predominantly racialized) national and ethnographic 'culture'.

---

4. Schneider, *Performing Remains*, 9–10.
5. Schneider, *Performing Remains*, 10.
6. Schneider, *Performing Remains*, 14–15.
7. Schneider, *Performing Remains*, 23.
8. Schneider, *Performing Remains*, 75.

RETROSPECTIVE MEDICINE: ST. VITUS'S DANCE AS HISTORICAL ANTECEDENT

In his *Études sur l'hystéro-épilepsie, ou Grande Hystérie* (1881), Richer, the French neurologist and visual artist and a former student of Charcot, offered a hundred-page addendum to his study, titled 'Historical Notes', in which he performed a review of the medical and non-medical literature on hysteria. He was practicing what he called 'retrospective medicine' ('médecine rétrospective'), drawing from artefacts, images, and historical narratives to demonstrate the historicity of contemporary clinical events. In doing so, he revealed the burgeoning field of neurology as a product of nineteenth-century historicism—travelling across eras—and comparativism, travelling across geographic sites and disciplines, to forge new ways of seeing bodily fits. Referring to works ranging from Calmeil's *De la folie* (1845) to Littré's 'Un fragment de médecine rétrospective' [A Fragment of Retrospective Medicine] in *La philosophie positive* (1869), 'Des rapports entre l'hystérie et les affections convulsives épidémiques liées à la folie religieuse, comme la possession, les manifestations des convulsionnaires' [Of the Relationships between Hysteria and Epidemic Convulsive Affections Linked to Religious Madness, Such as Possession and Convulsionary Manifestations] by Theodor Valentiner (1854–1913), in *Le mouvement médical* (1872), and Charcot's own *Leçons sur les maladies du système nerveux* [Lectures on the Diseases of the Nervous System] (1872–1883) delivered at the Salpêtrière in the 1870s and 1880s, Richer outlined historical precedents of clinical cases that were defining the new neurological field of hysteroepilepsy: a type of hysteria resembling epilepsy in its choreography (its bodily attitudes) only.[9] Richer's approach, informed by Charcot's studies, reconsidered broadly held notions that dance maniacs were in some cases actually epileptic. Hecker had written: 'where the disease was completely developed, the attack commenced with epileptic convulsions': 'those affected fell to the ground senseless, panting and labouring for breath. They foamed at the mouth, and suddenly springing up began their dance amidst strange contortions'.[10] Epilepsy, like many other neurological conditions, was still poorly understood; and the retrospective comparisons that Richer and Charcot outlined between hysteria, epilepsy and chorea sought not only to lift prior bodily forms and mental states out of religious art into medicine but also to attempt to clarify the complex space of interchange between imagination and fitful bodily movement.

This 'retrospective' gesture reinscribed the extended history of fitful movement disorders into a new drama of hysteroepileptic diagnosis, a disease category broadly described by Charcot in terms of epileptiform movements provoked not by organic but by 'hysterical' (non-organic) causes.[11] The range of conditions Charcot considered hysterogenic was enormous. In his work with Richer, Charcot described hysteroepileptic phenomena including religious ecstasies; demonic possession, satanism, and witchcraft; psychic contagion; catatonic states, spasms, paralyses, and contractions; and benign popular traditions. In drawing together this dizzying array of somatic behaviours, Charcot and Richer were effectively claiming nearly all of human

---

9. Paul Richer, *Études sur l'hystéro-épilepsie, ou Grande Hystérie* (Paris: Adrien Delahaye et Émile Lecrosnier, 1881), 615–726. Richer was a professor of artistic anatomy at the École des Beaux-Arts. On Charcot's use of visual art in his research, see esp. Christopher G. Goetz, 'Visual Art in the Neurologic Career of Jean-Martin Charcot', *Archives of Neurology* 48.4 (1991): 421–425. Goetz argues that 'art . . . misguided Charcot's career when he relied heavily on artwork in his attempt to convince critics that disorders seen at the Salpêtrière Hospital, Paris, France, were independent of his suggestive influence' (421). Goetz also notes Charcot's lifelong attraction to art and early dream of becoming a visual artist before deciding on a medical career; this led him to seek to 'justify scientific credibility through art', earning him a reputation as a 'multitalented and culturally sophisticated man' and drawing to him an audience of artists and philosophers. See also Christopher G. Goetz, 'Shakespeare in Charcot's Neurologic Teaching', *Archives of Neurology* 45.8 (1988): 920–921; Christopher G. Goetz, Michel Bonduelle, and Toby Gelfand, *Charcot: Constructing Neurology* (New York: Oxford University Press, 1995); Rhona Justice-Malloy, 'Charcot and the Theatre of Hysteria', *Journal of Popular Culture* 28.4 (1995): 133–138; Sigrid Schade, 'Charcot and the Spectacle of the Hysterical Body: The "Pathos Formula" as an Aesthetic Staging of Psychiatric Discourse: A Blind Spot in the Reception of Warburg', *Art History* 18.4 (1995): 499–517; Sander L. Gilman, 'The Image of the Hysteric', in Gilman et al., *Hysteria beyond Freud*, 345–436; and Sander L. Gilman, *Seeing the Insane: A Cultural History of Madness and Art in the Western World* (New York: Wiley, 1982).

10. Hecker, *Epidemics of the Middle Ages*, 81.

11. See Jean-Martin Charcot, 'Treizième Leçon: De l'hystéro-épilepsie', in *Œuvres complètes*, vol. 1, 367–385. Charcot notes that hysteroepilepsy is not a new term or idea but was first outlined by Jean-Baptiste Louyer-Villermay (1776–1838) and amply described by others (369–370).

history as precedent for hysteroepilepsy. The new field of neurology was construing itself as a brazenly all-encompassing answer to religious and spiritual paroxysms from across historical eras, transcending historicism to arrive at a universal scientific field. As Richer wrote, 'why should it be a cause for surprise that in periods of great exaltation, religious excitement provoked reactions of the nervous system which, in the end, resulted in the *grande hystérie!*'[12] In their view, these reactions had simply not been recognized or diagnosed properly before.

Paroxysmic types of religious enthusiasm were, for Charcot, Richer, de la Tourette, Regnard, Désiré-Magloire Bourneville (1840–1909), and others, actually nervous conditions triggered by hysteria. In effect, these bodily attitudes were, they thought, hysteriform phenomena (phenomena taking the form of hysteria) only now diagnosed but ancient in their expression. The possibilities afforded neurologists' historiographic studies were nearly boundless: from prehistoric figurines and Greek vase paintings to friezes, caricatures, ivory plates, tapestries, engravings, miniatures, and the authors' own photographic service at the Salpêtrière, the world seemed to be filled with precedents for hysteroepilepsy. Greek ecstasies and choreas all fit the hysteroepileptic bill. As the caption below an image of a maenad 'having a fit' ('en état de crise'), in Richer's *L'art et la médecine* [Art and Medicine] (1903), reads: 'the demoniacs had as their ancestors . . . Bacchic orgies, zealous divination ceremonies, the rites of the cult of Dionysus with their noisy cortege of Maenads and Satyrs . . . the dancing mania ['dansomanie'] also called St. Vitus's dance ['danse de Saint Guy'] in Germany and tarantism in Italy, etc.' (fig. 6.1).[13] The 'etc.' is significant: the list presupposes continuity between these phenomena as well as the self-evidence of their similarity. This was a list to which readers might, the 'etc.' implicitly suggested, add. The contours of demoniacal complaints appeared in Richer's depiction as received knowledge—denoted by the list of cases inviting further additions and comparisons—yet this was also modern science at the cutting edge of a new field. Those who had been possessed could be wrapped into the relatively—it seemed to Richer—self-explanatory purview of historical cases now cast as 'pure pathology'.[14]

Comparison between eras enabled Richer to extend the scope of his visual project and situate the newly named hysteroepilepsy within the broader framework of human history. As he noted, 'the analogies . . . between ancient convulsive epidemics and the *grande hystérie* that we observe sporadically today are founded in the same type of nervous contagion that we have demonstrated among hysterics, and on comparable symptomatic manifestations'.[15] The analogy between 'ancient convulsive epidemics' and clinical studies enabled him to abstract from each on the basis of apparent visual and morphological similarity: proof was in the image and choreography of bodies on the page. This is not to say that there were not also movement disorders in the past—seizures, contractions, paralyses, falls—but that the overwhelming concatenation of all these gestures into a neurological fold pathologized a far greater range of events than merited it. Richer's recuperation of ancient figures into modern diagnoses allowed him to map out an expansive neurological terrain according to which nearly every ecstatic dance or village fête was an expression of an organic (neurological) disorder. This exuberant comparativism arguably over-recuperated the complex corporeal and spiritual past into the domain of modern medical science, a field far more expansive, heterogeneous, and humanistic in its reliance on visual art, theatre, and anecdote than the myth of scientific objectivism—and ahistoricism—allows. Neurology was, Richer claimed, engaging in a historiographic method, retrospective medicine, looking back to the past and drawing from its iconographic sources to explain and supplement phenomena witnessed presently in the neurology clinic. The method was enabled by Richer's own visual arts training in human anatomy, which allowed him to depict and describe graphic and postural similarities between subjects: among them, the famous *attitudes passionnelles*, the dramatic postures Charcot described as gracing the crowning stage of a hysteroepileptic seizure, including the hysterical *arc de cercle*.[16]

But as Hacking notes, retrospective diagnosis frequently misconstrues personalities, events,

---

12. Richer, *Études sur l'hystéro-épilepsie*, 615–616.

13. Paul Richer, *L'art et la médecine* (Paris: Gaultier, Magnier, et cie., 1903), 161.

14. Charcot and Richer, *Les démoniaques dans l'art*, vii.

15. Richer, *Études sur l'hystéro-épilepsie*, 615–616.

16. See esp. Richer, *L'art et la médecine*; Charcot and Richer, *Les démoniaques*; and Jean-Martin Charcot and Paul Richer, *Les difformes et les malades dans l'art, avec 87 figures intercalées dans le texte* (Paris: Lecrosnier et Babé, 1889).

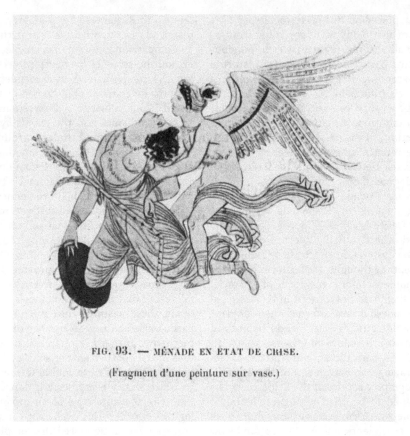

FIG. 93. — MÉNADE EN ÉTAT DE CRISE.

(Fragment d'une peinture sur vase.)

FIGURE 6.1   'Maenad having a seizure'. From Paul Richer, *L'art et la médecine* (1903). Courtesy the New York Academy of Medicine Library.

and bodily or mental formations found in literature and the visual arts, reading into these only what modern paradigms imagine. Knowledge of past experiences cannot be drawn from visual or narrative juxtaposition only; a whole discursive network and concepts of suffering or spirituality, disease or health, underlie these images, construing them retrospectively as depictions of one or another state. Disease, which we may understand as an abnormal state of bodily or mental suffering and even, with Canguilhem, organic degeneration tending to an abnormally rapid movement towards death, is historically and socially constituted. Canguilhem notes that disease refers to that which comes to be construed as abnormal, non-normative, in a given culture; and this can include something as basic and in many respects natural and normal as dying.[17] Neurology, as a modern science, deliberately takes as its subject forms of life which in earlier times may not have constituted diseased states but which neurologists recast as such: epileptic seizures, long associated with shamanic visions, only come to be seen and lived as forms of suffering to be treated (even eliminated) inasmuch as individuals come socially and culturally to be unable to participate in the everyday structures of economic and political life, rendering their conditions widely experienced as undesirable. This is not to say that all disease is only socially or historically constructed, or that there are no transhistorical and transcultural events that can be recognized to be similar (even identical); but that states of being have histories *as disorders*—ways of moving, speaking, or feeling that run counter to current cultural norms. Dancing manias similarly emerge in the nineteenth century as diseases because present bodily forms

17. See esp. Canguilhem, *The Normal and the Pathological*.

are compared to ancient ones, in a juxtaposition that reads both in pathological terms.

For Richer, the grounds for comparison across cases of 'hysteroepilepsy' were various. Choreomania in the Middle Ages, epidemics of 'demoniacal possession', the Convulsionaries of Saint-Médard, and ecstatics were among the myriad hysteroepileptics he depicted. In *Les démoniaques dans l'art*, he and Charcot began their graphic journey with an image of Jesus curing a possessed man in a fifth-century mosaic in Ravenna, before passing to further images of Jesus and a cast of saints, including Saint Catherine of Sienna delivering a possessed woman, in a late sixteenth- or early seventeenth-century fresco by Francesco Vanni (1563–1610). Saint Ignacio likewise delivered a swarming cast of demoniacs of their possession in a painting by Peter Paul Rubens (1577–1640). Nearly all the images involved a saint's intercession and the performance of a cure, to which Charcot as healer would inevitably be compared—by visual analogy, though never by explicit reference. Charcot himself was first struck by the visual similarity between these depictions and the gestures and contortions of his own patients in a visit to the church of Saint-Ambroise in Gènes. As Richer, who was his intern at the time and on the visit with him, reports, Charcot was struck by the 'spectacle' ('spectacle'), literally the theatre that a possessed woman presented, in a painting by Rubens he saw at the church. For Charcot, this painting presented a scene, a 'tableau' 'crying out with truth and, it seemed, borrowing brushstroke by brushstroke from the convulsive scenes occurring daily in his practice at the Salpêtrière'.[18]

Thus began their odyssey, dedicated, in Richer's words, to Apollo, god of medicine and art.[19] Soon enough, their adventure would encompass multiple volumes of large-format depictions of various ecstasies culled from the past. Charcot and Richer did not rely on visual comparison only; narrative histories further grounded their case studies in an appeal to antiquity, reconfigured through the lens of modern medicine. Their recuperation of ancient historical sources was nearly boundless. Significantly, their use of prior medical literature included not only Calmeil's psychiatric studies, but Hecker's writings on St. Vitus's dance and on the Convulsionaries of Saint-Médard. Hecker's essay 'The Dancing Mania', translated into French by Dubois in the *Annales d'hygiène et de médecine légale* in 1834, provided vivid narrative precedents to the sorts of convulsive events Charcot and Richer saw in early European history. In a way, Charcot and Richer thought, these characters were all demoniacs: jerking, twisting, and bending their bodies, performing obscure spasms and re-enacting ancient convulsive postures; often, they thought, these 'demoniacs' merely indulged in theatrical posturing.[20] In that sense, Charcot and Richer argued, the 'demoniacs' were hysterical: possessed by overly active imaginations. Contemporary histories of the pilgrimage to Echternach and word of mouth on the part of a contemporary judge helped Charcot and Richer complete the cursory picture of medieval 'possession' to which contemporary hysteroepileptics were still, in their view, subjected.[21] Further visual sources serving as evidence of these recuperations of the past in present hysteroepileptic forms were suggested to them by a Florentine colleague, Dr. Tommaso-Tommasi, to whom they give thanks throughout the pages of *Les démoniaques dans l'art*, as well as by various other writers who joined in this grand project of iconographic and historiographical collage.[22]

As an exercise in amateur art historiography, Charcot and Richer's full-colour, large-format compilations presented a baffling array of bodily contortions, ecstasies, and exorcisms, each performing a theatre of transport and distress. Page after page, each event seemed at once more extraordinary and more banal than the next. In *Les*

---

18. Richer, *L'art et la médecine*, 3–4.

19. Richer, *L'art et la médecine*, 3.

20. Hecker, 'Mémoire sur la chorée épidémique du moyen âge'. See Richer, *Études sur l'hystéro-épilepsie*, 617–621; and Jean-Martin Charcot, *Œuvres complètes: 1, Leçons sur les maladies du système nerveux*, ed. Désiré Magloire Bourneville, 1 vol. (Paris: Bureaux du progrès médical, 1892), 336–337. In Calmeil's words, Convulsionaries were prone to 'ecstato-convulsive theomania', not quite a hysteroepileptic diagnosis but a psychiatric descriptor that roughly fit the bill. See Calmeil, *De la folie*, vol. 2, 314. Also in Maire, ed., *Les convulsionnaires de Saint-Médard*, 241.

21. In a long footnote to the brief section on the St. Vitus's dancers, Charcot and Richer give thanks to M. Majerus, a judge in Luxembourg, for his firsthand account of the dancing procession, which involved thousands of pilgrims gathering outside Echternach, before proceeding into town, according to a well-defined and rhythmically regulated hopping pattern: three hops forward and one back; or five hops forward and two back. In Charcot and Richer, *Les démoniaques*, 36n1.

22. In Charcot and Richer, *Les démoniaques*, 12.

difformes et les malades dans l'art [The Misshapen and Diseased in Art] (1889), Charcot and Richer compiled images of lepers, syphilitics, idiots, dwarves, and other 'grotesque' characters—including the dead—depicted in sumptuary, religious, and lay iconography, echoing case studies in the Salpêtrière clinic.[23] Implicitly performing a comparative analysis, they juxtaposed visual images from the annals of art and church history, only slightly glossed—a paragraph or two for each—enough to draw each back, 'again and again', as Schneider suggests theatrical re-enactment and archival drag do,[24] to the *grande attaque hystérique*, the great hysterical attack. The *grande attaque*'s contours would then become apparent to readers through this exercise of repetition and juxtaposition. Repetition—and here recuperation—would make the *grande attaque* emerge as a distinct figure encompassing nearly all of the body's paroxysmal and convulsive movements. Charcot and Richer's iconographic collage and clinical re-enactments (staged 'again and again'), offered a choreographic spectacle of the body in distress, stage-managed by a small group of scientific mages.

As Charcot and Richer wrote of the 'epidemic of convulsions' at Saint-Médard, convulsions constituted a 'theatre' exhorting all in attendance to recognize the power and proof—the evidence—of religion,[25] just as Charcot and Richer would, implicitly, through their works, exhort their own readers to recognize the new neurological science's historicity: its place in the annals of saintly exorcism, now sanctioned and verified by experimental research. Didi-Huberman has argued that the photographic work of image-making at the Salpêtrière provided a theatre of hysteria in which patients staged themselves for their master, Charcot.[26] But Charcot and Richer's encyclopedic exploration of figures of contortion and pain also reveals a historiographical methodology casting the new in light of continual returns to the old. This was a theatre of transformation, a mystical exercise infusing contemporary models with ancient art. The theatrical

method forged, as much as it observed, hysteria and specifically hysteroepilepsy as an exercise in repetition with a slight measure of difference. This was science not as novelty but as theatre—performing a return, with difference ('again and again'), to the past.

THE EVIDENCE OF IMAGES: HYSTEROEPILEPSY AND ICONOGRAPHIC ILLUSTRATION

In *Les démoniaques dans l'art* (1887), Charcot and Richer collected visual and historical materials pertaining to 'demoniacal possession' to showcase examples of hysteroepilepsy in history. These episodes, which involved convulsions and often tympany were, they argued, forms of hysteria, a broadly psychosomatic condition whose contours they were seeking to describe. Unlike previous definitions of hysteria, such as those articulated by Hecker, theirs emphasized individual predispositions to act out according to highly patterned and predictable corporeal forms, rather than the excited, often religiously stimulated life of groups. Hysteroepilepsy resembled epilepsy inasmuch as it involved falls or swooning. As Charcot and Richer noted of an image depicting a procession of dancers in Echternach, 'it is quite easy immediately to recognize the role hysteria and hysteroepilepsy play in this case, as in the epidemics themselves'.[27] They were referring to what may be the most often reproduced visual 'evidence' of dance manias, an image also frequently cast as an example of what may be an epileptic procession, furthering the confusion between epilepsy, hysteroepilepsy, and dancing manias.

This was an illustration now attributed to Pieter Bruegel the Younger (c. 1564–1637),[28] reproduced in a nineteenth-century woodcut by Jean-Nicholas Huyot (1780–1840), depicting what is plausibly a procession of persons

23. Charcot and Richer, *Les difformes et les malades dans l'art*, i.

24. Schneider, *Performing Remains*, 6, 18–19.

25. In Charcot and Richer, *Les démoniaques*, 85.

26. Georges Didi-Huberman, *Invention of Hysteria: Charcot and the photographic iconography of the Salpêtrière*, trans. Alisa Hartz (Cambridge, MA: MIT Press, 2003).

27. 'Il est facile, en effet, d'y reconnaître à première vue que l'hystérie et l'hystéro-épilepsie jouaient là, comme elles l'ont fait dans les épidémies proprement dites, un rôle prédominant'. Charcot and Richer, *Les démoniaques*, 35.

28. This is by far the image most widely, if not the only one, used to represent St. Vitus's dance. Although it was long attributed to Pieter Bruegel the Elder, it is now considered to be the work of his son. See Park and Park, 'Saint Vitus' Dance', 514.

DANSEURS DE SAINT-GUY CONDUITS EN PÈLERINAGE A L'ÉGLISE DE SAINT-WILLIBROD, A EPTERNACH, PRÈS DE LUXEMBOURG¹

D'après un dessin de P. Breughel, à la galerie de l'archiduc Albert, à Vienne.

FIGURE 6.2 'Saint Vitus' dancers driven as pilgrims to the church of Saint-Willibrord, in Epternach [sic], near Luxembourg. After a drawing by P. Breughel, in the gallery of the archduc Albert, in Vienna'. From Charcot and Richer, *Les démoniaques dans l'art* (1887). Courtesy the New York Academy of Medicine Library.

suffering from chorea or other movement disorders on a pilgrimage to a cure (fig. 6.2). Copper plates of Bruegel's artwork were made by Henricus Hondius the Younger (1597–1651) in 1642 (fig. 6.3). Charcot and Richer employ both the Bruegel and Hondius images in *Les démoniaques dans l'art* and the *Leçons sur les maladies du système nerveux* to illustrate St. Vitus's dance (the *danse de Saint-Guy*), only somewhat convincingly. In both pictures, a small group of women, apparently ill at ease, are lifted off the ground and each one carried firmly by two strong men; the procession is accompanied by musicians playing bagpipes.[29] As neurologist Geneviève Aubert has suggested, the original Bruegel drawing exists in at least three versions, at the Albertina Museum in Vienna, the Rijksmuseum in Amsterdam, and the Staatliche Museen in Berlin. The Vienna and Amsterdam versions are known as 'Die Epileptikerinnen von Meulebeeck' (The Epileptic Women of Meulebeke) and 'Pelgrimage naar Meulebeke' (Pilgrimage near Meulebeke), respectively, and bear inscriptions in Old Dutch that read: 'Those are the pilgrims who on St John's day, outside Brussels in Molenbeek, must dance, and when they have danced or jumped over a bridge, then they are cured for a whole year of St John's sickness'.[30] The inscription accompanying the Berlin version notes the word

---

29. Charcot and Richer, *Les démoniaques*, 34–38. See also Charcot, *Œuvres complètes*, vol. 1, 459–461. Reprised in Richer, *L'art et la medicine*, 128–132. For a discussion of Charcot's use of this image, see esp. Aubert, 'Charcot Revisited', 155–161.

30. The inscription accompanying the seventeenth-century version of Bruegel's drawing, transferred to copper plate by Hondius, in a version constituted by a set of three engravings, each depicting one third of the original scene, reads: 'How the pilgrims, on St John's day, must dance to Molenbeek outside Brussels. And when they have danced over the bridge, or have been forced to do so, then they seemed to be cured for a year of the falling sickness. Ahead go the musicians or bagpipers, then follow the pilgrims held by strong servants, reluctantly against their will (as shown in the following second and third figures), sometimes shouting and vociferating; but when they come near the bridge, then they turn around, using great resistance; however, they are promptly overcome and carried and lifted over the bridge; once crossed, they sit down on the ground, as if exhausted: and then come the servants of the place quenching their thirst and giving them something warm: and so is the work accomplished. / Nicely

UN GROUPE DE DANSEURS DE SAINT-GUY
Fac-simile d'une gravure de Hondius.

FIGURE 6.3 'A Group of St. Vitus' Dancers. Facsimile of an engraving by Hondius [1642]'. From Charcot and Richer, *Les démoniaques dans l'art* (1887). Courtesy the New York Academy of Medicine Library.

'pilgrims' only.[31] What is surprising, Aubert suggests, is that neither inscription mentions Echternach or St. Vitus. Charcot seems to have drawn the conclusion that these were St. Vitus's dancers from a spurious caption inscribed under Bruegel's drawing in a posthumous publication by the French collector Paul Lacroix (1806–1884) in 1873, which reads: 'Sufferers from St Vitus' Dance going on a pilgrimage to the church of St Willibrord, Epternach [*sic*], near Luxembourg. After a drawing by P. Breughel (Sixteenth Century), in the gallery of Archduke

depicted by the excellent and skillful painter Pieter Breugel. Engraved and published by Henricus Hondius' house, in The Hague, 1642'. In Aubert, 'Charcot Revisited', 158.

31. Aubert, 'Charcot Revisited', 157–158.

Albert, at Vienna'.[32] That the Echternach dancing procession was not, in spite of this depiction, particularly choreographically legible was overlooked by Charcot and Richer, as these figures all indistinguishably came to designate what they considered to be epileptiform movement disorders.

More interesting yet, a descriptor provided to me by the Rijksmuseum suggested in parentheses that the image of these St. Vitus's 'dancers' (or, confusingly, epileptics) is alternately titled 'Landscape with Four Drunken Men and Two Drunken Women'.[33] Molenbeek, named after a creek in what is now greater Brussels, boasted a sacred well dedicated to Saint Gertrude, known for its miraculous cures. It attracted thousands of pilgrims, including epileptics. Some pilgrims may have been drunk on their way to the wells. Others may have performed seizure-like motions, even though it is unlikely all would have been undergoing epileptic (or even non-epileptic) seizures at once. One woman's open mouth and the others' awkwardly turned heads suggest they are in states of relative discomfort, perhaps undertaking the pilgrimage against their will. But the prominence of the women in this image—all the central characters are women—and the presence of male companions or attendants with them gives pause. The women, judging by their dress, are likely of a lower class, as Charcot and Richer point out, and would not necessarily have been able to afford hired help. Charcot and Richer's gloss suggests that the men were companions, also on the pilgrimage, and that servants in the background were gathering water from the stream for its curative properties or perhaps to quench the pilgrims' thirst.[34] But two of the women are also quite large-bellied. Are they merely corpulent, or are they pregnant, performing a pilgrimage for an unborn child? The other

two women appear to be lifted almost off the ground as the men grasp their armpits to hold them up. This may have been a way to help them jump, mimetically to enact the cure.

The description noted on the Hondius engraving reads: 'Two epileptic women walk, each supported by two men, on a country road, near the right. The first woman is screaming'. The second reads: 'Two epileptic women walk, each supported by two men, over a country road. In the background, a third woman, also supported by two men. A fourth woman sits by the side of the road under a tree'.[35] These images, taken together, represent a scene, in which, plausibly, a cast of female pilgrims to the waters in Molenbeek are being held—and helped—so that they can 'dance' (or leap), in the belief that this motion will help protect them or their unborn children from motor disorders—including epilepsy or chorea—at least for the following year.

Read as a performative *pre*-enactment, this scene depicts the pre-emptive representation of choreic distress, designed to quell further paroxysms. As pilgrims perform the jump or struggle with a bodily fit that might occur outside the heightened time of the pilgrimage, they use the intensity of the pilgrimage to ward off further attacks. This medical theatre represents and significantly *pre*-presents physical distress to its sufferers (and their deferred audiences) in a cyclical structure of yearly returns that tries to break that very cycle in the performative event. As deferred viewers, we retrospectively grapple with the discursive claims presented by the captions accompanying these images and the choreography captured as a still. Trumped only by the deceptive half legibility of the gestures, our reading is necessarily partial: considered on their own, these women seem to be prone to emotional paroxysms, organic or mechanical falling,

32. Aubert, 'Charcot Revisited', 159. See P. Lacroix, *Vie militaire et religieuse au Moyen Age et à l'époque de la Renaissance* (Paris: Librairie Didot, 1873). On the dancing procession at Echternach and its connection to St. Willibrord, see also Backman, *Religious Dances*, 116–126.

33. The title indicated reads 'De pelgrimstocht van epileptici naar de kerk van Meulenbeke (Landschap met 4 dronken mannen en twee dronken vrouwen. Pieter Breugel inv)'. Identification provided by email from Susan van Gelderen, information specialist, Collection Information Department, Rijksmuseum, 'RE: Brueghel—Pelgrimage naar Meulebeke', to the author, 9 November 2012. The description has since been modified to read: 'Twee epileptische vrouwen worden door hun begeleiders meegenomen op de pelgrimstocht van epileptici naar Molenbeek bij Brussel op Sint Jansdag. De voorste vrouw protesteert luid'. This eliminates mention of drunkenness but emphasizes the first pilgrim's loud protestation, still suggesting significant contestation regarding the event of the scene, as well as the increasing inscription of this image into the annals of the history of epilepsy, associated by art historians and curators with St. John's Day, though it is still not clear why the first pilgrim is ostensibly distressed; https://www.rijksmuseum.nl/en/search/objects?q=RP-P-1904-525&p=1&ps=12&ii=0#/RP-P-1904-525,0, accessed 17 March 2016.

34. In Charcot and Richer, *Les démoniaques*, 35–36.

35. In Dutch, 'Twee epileptische vrouwen lopen, elk ondersteund door twee mannen, over een landweg, naar rechts. De voorste vrouw loopt te schreeuwen' and 'Twee epileptische vrouwen lopen, elk ondersteund door twee mannen, over een landweg. Op de achtergrond komt een derde vrouw aan, eveneens ondersteund door twee mannen. Een vierde vrouw zit langs de kant van de weg

or fits. They are clearly struggling, though it is uncertain whether they are struggling against their companions; and there is a group of them, winding their way through the countryside as if on a cacophonous parade. But the men's bodies are contorted as well, as they hold the women up. It may be that they are also performing the pilgrimage or that they are merely struggling under the women's weight. The women are disproportionately large in the image, which may explain why they required two men, one at either side. Their disproportionate size may also suggest their importance as focal points in the image, though (unless my hypothesis that they are pregnant stands) it is not certain why the women are foregrounded in this event. The musicians appear to cower, suggesting the whole affair may have been trying: this is not quite a jubilant, boisterous fête.

Charcot and Richer's reading of these pilgrims moving through the countryside reveals at once a retrospective neurological reading and the faintness of a pageant gone by, recuperated into the choreomania repertoire. Repeated again and again by neurologists in the last century, this image has become the quintessential—often the only—representation of choreomania. As such, the image comes to epitomize a collective fantasy, shot through with layers of artefactual readings. Charcot and Richer saw the form St. Vitus's dance, confirmed in their eyes by a caption, enveloping this pilgrimage into the hysteroepileptic fold: a collection of disparate images and scenes made to support, and evidence, what they encountered in Charcot's clinic.

As McCarren has pointed out, hysteria and the myriad neurological disorders associated with it—including chorea or St. Vitus's dance—pose the problem of visuality inasmuch as they resemble dances and, resembling one another, suggest sameness where there may be none. But this privilege accorded to dance and movement as a site of seeing—Charcot's realm of greatest expertise (as opposed to his student Freud's preference for the aural)—and thus to dance, movement, and theatrical gesturality as the art forms of the unsayable, misses a crucial point. While dance may be 'the ability to represent itself in images, through movement', as McCarren suggests,[36] and thus to express femininity, for instance, in a semiotic system in which women, like children, are to be seen and not heard, dance and femininity in Charcot's iconographic system also point to other systems—other histories—which moved. Juxtaposed to one another, the images Charcot and Richer stage in their work perform a class of intertextual movement that situates dance-like gesturality, leaping performances, and hysteria on a continuum with the historical relic, and thus too with the antiquarian past. These figures all participated in the grand iconographic repertoire of religiosity and the expressive language of visual art. Rather than signifying silence, these images signalled bodies whose choreographies Charcot and Richer, as neurological mavens, took it as their task to interpret and to collate. The bodies, rather than appearing silent, appeared to be gesturing through the ages, constellations now finally read in collusion with science. In recognizing these scenes as hysteroepileptic, choreic, and choreomaniacal, Charcot and Richer grounded their findings in a fantasy of premodernity.

Few images of choreomania exist. While the Bruegel image has come to epitomize visual 'proof' of choreomania as a serious medical condition associated with popular lore, caricatures depicting the ridiculousness of the so-called St. Vitus's dance highlight the difficulty of diagnostic legibility and the condition's comic potential as movement gone awry. A medical caricature published in L'album comique de pathologie pittoresque, recueil de vingt caricatures médicales dessinées par Aubry, et al. [Comic Album of Picturesque Pathology, Collection of Twenty Medical Caricatures Drawn by Aubry, et al.] (1823) depicted buffoonish sufferers of St. Vitus's dance (the danse de Saint Guy) performing a comical and pathetic village round with floppy hats and soft faces, their legs bent in a seemingly haphazard fashion (fig. 6.4). Charcot reproduced this image in his Nouvelle

onder een boom'. Identification provided by email from Susan van Gelderen to the author, 9 November 2012. The description has since been modified to emphasize St. John's Day and epilepsy once again, and the context provided by the larger image according to which these pilgrims (carried by their male companions) have to jump over the bridge to stave off epilepsy for the following year: 'Twee epileptische vrouwen worden door hun mannelijke begeleiders meegenomen op de pelgrimstocht van epileptici naar Molenbeek bij Brussel op Sint Jansdag. Daar moeten zij over de brug dansen om voor een jaar te worden genezen van hun epilepsie. Op de achtergrond wordt een vrouw over de brug gedragen. Aan de overkant rust een vrouw uit'; https://www.rijksmuseum.nl/en/search/objects?q=brueghel+pelgrimmage&p=11&ps=12&ii=1#/RP-P-1904-526,121, accessed 17 March 2016.

36. McCarren, Dance Pathologies, 13, 16–17.

LA DANSE DE SAINT GUY

D'après une lithographie coloriée de l'*Album Comique*.

Phototypie Berthaud, Paris

FIGURE 6.4   Saint Vitus's dance. Lithograph from *Album comique* (1823). Reproduced in *Nouvelle iconographie de la Salpêtrière* (1904). Courtesy the New York Academy of Medicine Library.

iconographie de la Salpêtrière [New Iconography of the Salpêtrière] (1904) as yet another illustration of the dancing disease from the uncertain annals of choreic history.

Actual motor disorders characterized by incoordination and involuntary movement could, it seemed, be covered up by popular dances, just as popular dances, in the caricaturist's depiction, presented a choreic potential: all popular dances had the potential to appear odd and ridiculous. But I have also been arguing that these awkward gestures became archival 'stills', 'dragged' into live clinical scenes apparently demonstrating the recursion of ancient gestures in the present. The archival repertoire of choreic movements became live *again* in Charcot's patients' theatrical illustrations. In the next sections, I turn to Charcot's experimentation with scenes of chorea and hysteroepilepsy among patients who were reproducing, as it seemed to him, figures from the archival past.

SPONTANEOUS CRUCIFIXIONS AND HYSTEROEPILEPSY: CONVULSIONARY REMAINS

In order to link ancient iconographic scenes and his own patients' gestures, Charcot and his colleagues studied an intermediary medical theatre, offered by neurology 'patients' whom they read retrospectively as suffering from neurological disorders in the more recent past. In order to do this, Charcot drew from a repertoire of case studies depicting individuals steeped in scenes of highly theatrical religiosity and popular lore. The Convulsionaries of Saint-Médard offered an ideal case in point. They were contorted, excited, and histrionic; and they showed particular gestures that captured Charcot and his colleagues' attention in terms of their potential for neurological study. In his *Leçons sur les maladies du système nerveux*, Charcot described the Convulsionaries as a case study in hysteroepilepsy, particularly showcasing what he described as hysterical hemianaesthesia (anaesthesia in half of the body). He argued that if the Convulsionaries were reported not to have experienced pain on the penetration of a sharp object—such as a sword—into their skin and if contact with such an object did not produce any hemorrhaging, this was because they were not actually experiencing physical pain. They were engaging in a theatre of pain; their heightened emotion presented a case of 'acute hysteria'.[37] The whole spectacle was a charade but a no less medically diagnosable one. Although specific forms of religious gesture appeared in epileptic, hysteric, and hysteroepileptic fits, their exact character could be attributed, Charcot thought, to the range of symbols and signs available to them in a given culture. Christianity offered a fountain of iconographic gestures, in the cases of the Convulsionaries. Many Convulsionaries, he wrote, 'operated veritable crucifixions among themselves, placing those among them on crosses and fixing them there with nails going right through their hands and feet. These "saints," who more or less allowed themselves to be crucified, were hysterics'.[38]

Proof included testimony by La Condamine, who wrote that the Convulsionaries suffered and shed blood only when they were pierced on the right sides of their bodies. This corroborated what was observed at the Salpêtrière: hysteria was often characterized by hemi-anaesthesia.[39] Charcot observed 'spontaneous' crucifixions among his own patients at the Salpêtrière, documented among others by Regnard. In *Les maladies épidémiques de l'esprit*, Regnard depicts a figure of a young woman performing a crucifixion

(fig. 6.5) juxtaposed to identical images drawn from Charcot's clinical practice (fig. 6.6). These crucifixions constituted one of the primary *attitudes passionnelles* and characterized any number of mental (or spiritual) epidemics. But, significantly, such *attitudes* were involuntary and spontaneous, Charcot and Regnard noted. Although the *attitudes* mimicked Christ's passion on the cross, they differed from 'artificial' crucifixions, poses performed by Convulsionaries, among others, with intention—as theatre. Artificial poses involved an elaborate mise en scène on the part of performers and bystanders, who collected hammers and nails as props for these convulsionary performances. The border between theatre and 'real' neurological disease was thin in Charcot's practice; significantly, his recuperation of popular theatre into the domain of neurology made of this new science a retrospective historiographic exercise in medical choreography. Neurology recuperated and reperformed gestures from the past recast as disease.

Yet what Charcot called hysterical convulsions—those not entirely acted out but in his view genuine symptoms of organic dysfunction—represented in his view real instances of heightened emotion affecting the neurological core. For Charcot, this diagnosis helped dispel eighteenth-century medical opinions, such as the opinion the physician Philippe Hecquet (1661–1737) influentially expressed in *Du naturalisme des convulsions dans les maladies de l'épidémie convulsionnaire* [Of the Naturalism of Convulsions in the Diseases of the Convulsionary Epidemic] (1733) that crucifixion was provoked by insanity ('aliénation d'esprit').[40] Charcot countered this with the view that crucifixions instead constituted a neurological disorder: they were partially imagined (and so psychiatric) but played out in

---

37. Charcot writes: 'in the Saint-Médard epidemic, for example, the *sword thrusts given* to the Convulsionaries did not, it is said, produce any hemorrhaging. The reality of this cannot be disclaimed without examination; if it is true that many of these *Convulsionaries* were guilty of sleight of hand [jonglerie], we are nonetheless obliged to recognize, after careful consideration of the question, that most of the phenomena presented, whose history has been transmitted to us via naïve description, were not all simulated, but amplified, exaggerated. It was almost always a case, the critics have demonstrated this, of hysteria taken to the highest level; and so, for these women struck by anaesthesia not to shed blood when pierced by a sharp instrument such as a sword, it was sufficient . . . that the instrument should not be pushed in too deeply'. Charcot, *Œuvres complètes*, vol. 1, 303–304.

38. Désiré-Magloire Bourneville and Paul Regnard, *Iconographie photographique de la Salpêtrière (Service de M. Charcot)*, 3 vols., vol. 1 (Paris: Aux bureaux du Progrès Médical, 1876–1880), 45.

39. Bourneville and Regnard, *Iconographie photographique*, vol. 1, 45–46.

40. Bourneville and Regnard, *Iconographie photographique*, vol. 1, 46–47. Lindsay Wilson provides a useful discussion of Hecquet's beliefs and practices as a physician, such that he was too frail to attend the events firsthand but retorted that he had seen and studied convulsions all his life; his detractors on the other hand should go see the events for themselves. He argued for the 'naturalism' of the convulsions, i.e., their status as physiological, rather than supernatural, events, a stance that contradicts Charcot's retort. But Hecquet's naturalism was determined largely by the 'imagination', as he attributed the convulsions to a disturbance of the vapours, among men occasionally and nearly universally among women, when the passions were ignited. In Wilson, *Women and Medicine in the French Enlightenment*, 26–30.

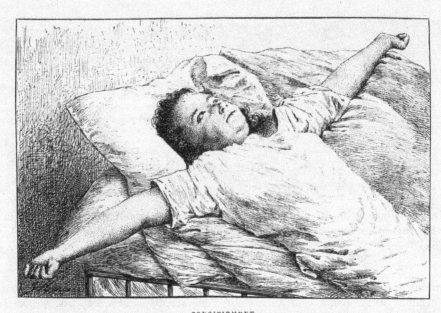

CRUCIFIEMENT

D'après l'Iconographie photographique de la Salpêtrière, par Bourneville et P. Regnard.

FIGURE 6.5 'Crucifixion. From the Iconographie photographique de la Salpêtrière'. From Paul Regnard, *Les maladies épidémiques de l'esprit* (1887). Courtesy the New York Academy of Medicine Library.

the nervous system. In that regard the convulsionary theatre presented a form of neurological hysteria: the body disordered without the direct action of the will. Neurology in this view captured mind and matter, history and biology. This was a science at the forefront of medical research, recuperating all the most invisible and nearly illegible gestures into its fold; neurology in this sense performed the ultimate 'reading' of all the subtlest and most dramatic gestures from the annals of religion, spirituality, and culture, and its proponents were the new spiritual and hermeneutic elite, the new interpreters of movement across the cultural and historical spectrum. Charcot considered that the particular quality and form of apparently involuntary gestures, including crucifixions, reflected cultural and historical scenarios—representations possible only at the time and place at which they arose—as well as biological fact. The gestures he observed were not general biosocial responses to environmental stress, as Hecker had argued, or universal, autonomic actions of the nervous system, but represented events and gestural

codes reflecting the cultural imagination of his patients as it directed their limbs—often with his aid. The science of neurology then was born as a choreographic process, engaged at once in reading gestures as historical artefacts and in representing and reproducing these gestures in clinical, controlled settings, before audiences, for the purposes of potentially infinite repetition and recuperation.

TYMPANY, *SECOURS*, AND OVARIAN COMPRESSION

The Convulsionaries of Saint-Médard offered neurologists vast grounds for retrospective diagnosis, their practices full of potential for dramaturgical readings that could translate into and inform case studies in the clinic. The Convulsionaries were subject to apparently intense tympanic pains and subjected one another to abdominal binding. As with St. John's Day dancers, bystanders often also administered relief. This resulted in a

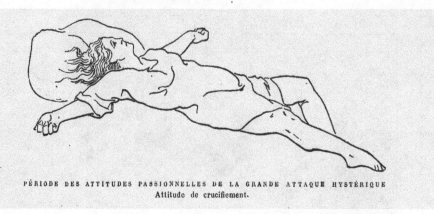

PÉRIODE DES ATTITUDES PASSIONNELLES DE LA GRANDE ATTAQUE HYSTÉRIQUE
Attitude de crucifiement.

FIGURE 6.6 'Stage of the *attitudes passionnelles* of the great hysterical attack: attitude of crucifixion'. From Charcot and Richer, *Les démoniaques dans l'art* (1887). Courtesy the New York Academy of Medicine Library.

dramatic mise en scène, complete with theatrical props including 'stones, hammers, swords, clubs, &co'.[41] But whereas St. John's Day dancers may have suffered severe nutritional deficiency, provoking pain and intestinal bloating (chapter 2), the Convulsionaries would have suffered far less severe nutritional deprivation. Charcot's theory was to link this epigastral discomfort to a long line of thinking associating abdominal troubles and hysteria. Writing as early as 1746, the physician John Andree (c. 1699–1785) associated hysteric fits with 'a Working in the *Abdomen*', followed by 'Distention and Rumbling of the Hypochondria [upper abdomen], with a Swelling at the Stomach'.[42] Although hysteric fits resembled epileptic seizures, Andree wrote that their 'seat' was in the abdomen, not the cerebellum.[43] But hysteric and epileptic seizures might occur simultaneously, he added, if the nervous system was so weakened as to admit the two disorders at once.[44] Tweedie, in *A System of Practical Medicine* (1840), also noted that 'a tympanic state of the abdomen was a frequent symptom' in St. John's and St. Vitus's dances.[45]

But as Charcot and Richer noted, convulsionary activities did not always include abdominal distension or tympanic pain. At first, miracles had occurred without convulsions; then, they thought, epileptics made their way to the Saint-Médard cemetery to seek help for their own convulsive movements, initiating a second phase, characterized by some miracles accompanied by real convulsions. Finally, a third (the longest and most satirized) phase, lasting over a century, was characterized by convulsions without miraculous cures.[46] Those who imitated real epileptics in the second phase now outnumbered those who had actually suffered from neurological disease. It was during the second and third phases that tympanic binding emerged as a routine (theatricalized) practice; and the administration of *secours* (or help), performed by *secouristes* (or helpers), provided a gripping show to all who gathered to watch.[47]

Although noting the high proportion of 'imagination' playing out in these scenes, Charcot was convinced that their purpose was not primarily entertainment—or lewd entertainment,

41. Hecker, *Epidemics of the Middle Ages*, 137.

42. In John Andree, *Cases of the Epilepsy, Hysteric fits, and St. Vitus Dance, with the Process of Cure: Interpreted with Practical Observations . . .* (London: W. Meadows and J. Clarke, 1746), 26–27.

43. Andree, *Cases of the Epilepsy*, 26–27.

44. Andree, *Cases of the Epilepsy*, 26–27.

45. Tweedie, ed., *A System of Practical Medicine*, 329.

46. Charcot and Richer, *Les démoniaques*, 79–80. See also Bernadac and Fourcassié, eds., *Les possédés*, 24. For the story of the young Marie-Elizabeth Giroust, an epileptic woman discovered one night by her father clutching a relic from the deacon Pâris's tomb, apparently performing non-epileptic convulsions, see Bernadac and Fourcassié, eds., *Les possédés*, 25–28.

47. According to one eyewitness, *secours* were divisible into five categories: (1) kicking or trampling on the Convulsionary; (2) exercising pressure by heavy weights, or squeezing with tongs; (3) beating with clubs; (4) pricking with swords, spits, etc.; and

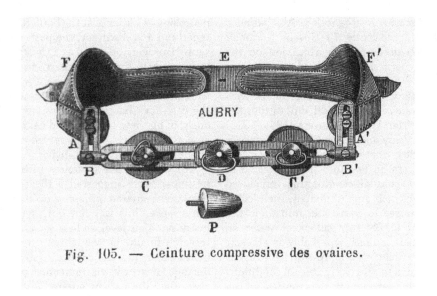

Fig. 105. — Ceinture compressive des ovaires.

FIGURE 6.7 'Ovarian Compression Belt'. From Paul Richer, *L'hystéro-épilepsie, ou grande hystérie* (1881). Courtesy the New York Academy of Medicine Library.

as Hecquet had disapprovingly argued. 'I don't see', wrote Charcot, 'what lewdness could have to do with these *andiron and pestle blows* administered with such violence, although I am capable of recognizing that a depraved mind will engender practices such as this. But I think it is much simpler and more legitimate to admit that the *secours* . . . were administered in response to a very pragmatic and empirical concern, whose sole result was to produce a real improvement upon the torments suffered in a hysterical attack.'[48] Charcot sought his own means to relieve hysteria's tympanic symptoms. 'Ovarian compression', a technique he sought to perfect, enabled those wearing an apparatus he devised to benefit from continuous compression of the ovaries (fig. 6.7). In Regnard's wry note, ovarian compression successfully administered might have curbed many a witch's demons, sparing much of the violence of the Inquisition; unfortunately, compression had only emerged as a regular practice at Saint-Médard.[49] Ovarian compression, acting on the body, cured apparently demonic disorders of mind. This cure was particularly dramatic because hysteria left no

material traces: 'at the autopsy of a hysteric one finds nothing', wrote Regnard, 'neither in the brain, nor in any other organ'.[50] Hysteria was a condition of excess fancy, he and Charcot thought. It was the imagination that provoked bodily fits. Only these could be observed, compared, and decoded.

Charcot did not claim to have invented ovarian compression, although his new ovarian implement facilitated its exercise. Thomas Willis (1621–1675), he remarked, practiced compression of the abdomen to suspend convulsive spasms thought to originate in the abdomen. This kept spasms from progressing to the patient's head and neck. Compression was performed either by embracing the patient strongly around the waist or using tightly bound sheets. The Spanish physician Luiz de Mercado (1525–1611) also used abdominal friction as early as the sixteenth century, Charcot noted, with the aim of containing the uterus, which Mercado believed travelled, 'according to the ancient doctrine'. One of Mercado's compatriots, Nicholas Monardes (1493–1588), similarly used this method to attempt to keep the uterus from

---

(5) crucifixion. In Ronald A. Knox, *Enthusiasm: A Chapter in the History of Religion, with special reference to the XVII and XVIII centuries* (New York: Oxford University Press, 1950), 383. For a detailed account of the *secours*, see Regnard, *Les maladies épidémiques de l'esprit*, 191–199.

48. Charcot, *Œuvres complètes*, vol. 1, 337.

49. Regnard, *Les maladies épidémiques de l'esprit*, 110.

50. Regnard, *Les maladies épidémiques de l'esprit*, 110.

'rising', by placing a large rock on the patient's stomach. More recently, Dr. Joseph Récamier (1774–1852) used to place a cushion on the patient's stomach, requiring a medical attendant to sit on it.[51] But in spite of Charcot's success, and this litany of historical precedents with which he framed his practical innovation, the British physician William Gowers (1845–1915) noted in *Epilepsy and Other Chronic Convulsive Diseases* (1881) that ovarian compression was rarely successful in England. This suggested to Gowers that cultural conditioning influenced patients' behaviour and, ultimately, their 'cure'. Gowers preferred to administer iron tonic and pour one or ideally two gallons of water on patients' heads, a remedy probably as efficient in context as Charcot's compression belt. Just as fantasy seemed to provoke hysterical conditions that translated into kinetic deformities, so too their treatment depended on equally powerful fantasies, practiced on the part of physician and patient alike.[52]

CLINICAL THEATRES: FROM MOTOR DELIRIUM TO THE GREAT LABOURING, OR 'HAMMERING', CHOREA

Charcot directed, or choreographed, many scenes of hysteroepilepsy reproducing and confirming what he and his colleagues saw in history and the visual arts. Case studies in his clinic abounded, corroborating ancient scenes of corporeal disarray with everyday medical practice. This section turns to Charcot's clinic, in which images and archives appear 'live'. This is not to suggest that archival research held precedence for Charcot and that his patients in all cases mimicked what he read or saw in galleries and picture books; but that the translatio between archival and iconographic research and performative practice in Charcot's clinic constituted

neurology as a science at the borderline between repetition and discovery, the past and the present. Neurology operated as a theatre of repetition, in which the past appeared in the present in neurological form. The present was saturated with the persistence of ancient gesture, just as the past, for Charcot, appeared rife with previously, in his view, undiagnosed neurological disease. Contemporary bodies served as his canvas and testing ground for this hypothesis.

For Charcot, live instances of hysteria and hysteroepilepsy suggested a theatre in which the patient entered the 'scene' or 'stage' of modern science. This was not only symbolic on a historiographic level, as hysteria came with his research finally, he thought, to be diagnosed; but in a more mundane sense, hysteria occurred onstage presently, via individual performance every day. The patient entered onto the scene of science in Charcot's clinic dramatically, at the culmination of a prolonged, but repeatable and increasingly, through observation, predictable set of acts—a rechoreographable dance. Charcot and his colleagues marked out stages of a hysteroepileptic attack, rendering it more narratable and its stages transposable onto ancient figures and scenes. The patient's seizure presented a dramaturgical arc, from onset to crisis and resolution. The first, epileptiform stage of a hysteroepileptic attack appeared, Charcot and his collaborators noted, to some extent like epilepsy but was not actually epileptic. (It did not involve insuppressible neuromotor abnormality.) The second phase, which they thought was characterized by contortions and 'large' or 'great movements' ('grands movements'), represented a period of 'clownisme' ('clowning'), involving 'illogical', 'strange', 'unexpected', 'implausible', and 'fantastical' attitudes or poses; these were 'invraisemblables', implausible, not true to life.[53] The third stage, that of the *attitudes passionnelles*, worked like a tableau vivant involving 'passionate' or highly affective gestures and often hallucinations in which 'the patient enters

---

51. Charcot's chronology seems to be skewed. He dates Mercado's use of ovarian compression to 1513, effectively before Mercado was born. Charcot, *Œuvres complètes*, vol. 1, 334–335.

52. Hydrotherapy, hydropathy, and gymnastics were commonly prescribed in the eighteenth and nineteenth centuries to treat what was seen as nervous exhaustion. William Aitken, in *The Science and Practice of Medicine* (1864), cited the medicinal use of cold baths and cold showers, as well as various plant and mineral remedies, including *Cannabis indica* (Indian hemp), nitrate of silver, and spirit of nitrous ether, often used in combination with camphor, to relieve tension. The use of electricity also appears in a few compendia, as do herbs such as valerian, still commonly employed today by herbalists to induce calm. By the twentieth century, psychotherapy was being employed to treat a variety of choreic affections—with mixed results—as were new chemical and biological medicines such as cerebrine extracts and arsenic. See William Aitken, *The Science and Practice of Medicine*, 2 vols., vol. 2 (London: Charles Griffin and Company, 1864), 341–342; Babonneix, *Les chorées*, 241, 187–215.

53. In Charcot and Richer, *Les démoniaques*, 97. See also Charcot, *Œuvres complètes*, vol. 3, 437–438.

himself into the scene' and simultaneously (the French enables this double entendre) 'makes of himself a mise en scène' ('entre lui-même en scène') so that 'by the expressive and animated mimicry in which he engages, and the fragmentary phrases which he lets loose, it is easy to follow all the incidents of the drama which he believes he attends and in which he plays the principal role'.[54] The fourth stage of an epileptiform seizure involves the gradual resumption of normalcy: consciousness returns choppily, cut in with leftover hallucinations and brusque gestures, contractions, and cramps. The patient is exhausted and somewhat distressed.[55] These illustrations resonated, Charcot and his colleagues argued, with the ecstasies depicted by artists in the past, though these artists had sought primarily to portray a religious feeling, prayer or passion, rather than a violent contraction or convulsion, thus distorting the true character of hysteroepilepsy—a medical condition which enjoyed, they wrote, 'all the constancy and inflexibility of scientific law'.[56]

Yet this apparently inflexible law found incarnations in various, at times, they wrote, 'implausible' and nearly illegible contemporary scenes. Near illegibility rendered Charcot's readings all the more magisterial, priest-like. The script he interpreted was obscure, difficult, yet he read it as an expert in decoding unpredictable gestures and cracking gestural codes. Choreomania, like hysteroepilepsy, was essentially an Orientalist fantasy, at once other and governable, unwieldy and tamable, undisciplined and disciplinarizable. Choreomaniacal gesture represented the final frontier of modern science's capacity to capture in language what eluded it—the body in a state of anarchic disarray. The patient Geneviève B. presented an especially vivid case study of what Charcot called hysteroepileptic chorea. In March 1872, when she was twenty-nine years old, she demonstrated symptoms Charcot classed as acute hysteria accompanied by hallucinations, tympany, and jumping (or leaping) chorea. She first showed a period of delirium, in which she began to perform 'a bizarre sort of dance' ('une espèce de danse singulière'). She would leap into the air and throw her head alternately backwards and forwards.

This 'motoric delirium' ('délire moteur'), which was caused, according to Charcot, by her hallucinations, persisted as long as she was not lying in bed. Her fits continued until he discovered that compression of her left ovary allowed them to subside. He further noted acute tympany, a sure sign that her case was attributable to hysteroepilepsy.[57] Geneviève was not performing—or, with his guidance, reperforming—tableaux from the art historical past but showcased gestures that appeared in this case to borrow from everyday dance and popular practice. As with patients whose cases I further outline later, Geneviève engaged in partly strange but also very common movements, seemingly automatically. The 'bizarre sort of dance' she performed suggested to Charcot that she was suffering from chorea, a recognizable and yet to his mind still largely unspecific motor disease, indicated, with some frustration on his part, by the vague 'sort of'.

Yet neurologists were working hard to describe these irregular movements and to ascribe to them names and regular and predictable forms. In April 1873, Charcot suggested that Geneviève suffered from a seizure characterized by an incessant need to move; she jumped and danced around, holding herself up at the foot of her bed, raising her skirt, endeavouring to embrace everyone around her, and showing 'extreme lewdness'. By September, she was agitated ('secousses') and restless, running around the garden, threatening to break everything, while emitting sharp cries, which seemed, however, momentarily to relieve her distress. Again, she complained of sharp pains in her left ovary. Her tympany by then, Charcot noted, was enormous. As before, compression in the left ovarian region calmed her fits. But the cure was not conclusive. By the following April, after an epileptiform seizure, she was seized again by a 'leaping' or 'dancing' delirium ('délire saltatoire'). She began to hallucinate, seeing ravens and speaking to them; she jumped, cried, and pulled her skirt alternately between her legs and over her head, 'as if to chase snakes away'.[58]

This chorée saltatoire (or leaping chorea) seemed 'to be co-ordinated on a definite plan', Charcot wrote, imitating, for example, specific dances or professional activities. This mimetic aspect led

54. In Charcot and Richer, Les démoniaques, 102. See also Charcot, Œuvres complètes, vol. 3, 438–439.
55. Charcot and Richer, Les démoniaques, 102. See also Charcot, Œuvres complètes, vol. 3, 439.
56. Charcot and Richer, Les démoniaques, 109.
57. In Bourneville and Regnard, Iconographie photographique, vol. 1, 57–58.
58. Bourneville and Regnard, Iconographie photographique, vol. 1, 60.

him to argue that chorea was suggestible, explaining why so many hysteroepileptics performed specific poses, lying in some cases prostrate with both arms outstretched as in imitation of the cross, or piercing themselves with swords without drawing blood. They were succumbing to extreme states of emotion leading to a specific, automatically triggered set of motions. In the case of the leaping chorea, patients engaged in expressive movements 'such as those of the dance, and particularly character dances'. But another, nearly interchangeable sort of chorea presented a similar set of recognizable everyday activities: in the hammering chorea ('chorée malléatoire'), patients completed '*professional actions*, such as the movements performed by an oarsman or a blacksmith'.[59] The leaping and hammering chorea in Charcot's writing appear almost interchangeably: dancing and working offered similar gestural models that his patients appeared to imitate. It is not always clear from his descriptions, however, whether the patients deliberately performed these or whether he saw in his patients' movements professional or leisure activities that he then made reference to in describing them, plausibly in so doing further influencing his patients' actions. But that was also the point. For Charcot, susceptibility to influence was a major trait of hysteroepilepsy. He sought for his patients to be suggestible, just as he noticed that they were so. Saying that the patients were performing an action like beating eggs or dancing a mazurka helpfully, to him and his colleagues, described the gestures and simultaneously further influenced the patients' repetition of them *as if* they had been voluntarily and deliberately doing these specific things at the outset. The measure of cause and effect was often blurry, confirming the extent to which Charcot was studying a special subset of hysteria, in which involuntary gestures and heightened emotional states produced the semblance of a voluntary action, which was in effect, he argued, performed somewhere between a voluntary and an involuntary state—what Freud

would later further articulate as the subconscious. The gesture then could be traced through the ages as corresponding to and also revealing specific cultural forms, simultaneously universal and culturally specific. In this way, Charcot believed he was mapping contemporary neurological disorders onto cultural history, carving out new scientific territory and folding into it nearly all gestural culture from the past.

In his lecture on 'rhythmic hysteric chorea' ('chorée rythmique hystérique'), Charcot described the case of a young woman who typically performed a rhythmic swaying motion on the right side of her body, which she swung backwards and forwards. She would do this, he wrote, systematically, to a distinct rhythm which—according to those knowledgeable in these things, he wrote—was reminiscent of popular dances known as 'mazurkas'.[60] This did not mean she was performing one, only that the comparison to the mazurka enabled his scientific description. Elsewhere, Charcot described the case of Flor—, who performed 'rapid rhythmical movements', in which, he wrote, she '[seemed] to be whipping eggs'. Flor—would also '[bend] her fingers, applying their tips to the thumb; and raising her arm, [make] the gesticulation of an orator who is demonstrating', or '[dance] alternately on each foot, very nearly imitating a jig or dance of the Tsiganes, or of the Zingari of Andalusia'.[61] He characterized her chorea as 'hammering' ('chorée malléatoire'), although it suggested dances as well as professional activities. Most important for Charcot was that Flor—'s chorea was distinct from what he called the 'vulgar' choreas (chorea minors) described by Sydenham, in which there was no voluntary action or repetition, only a general, slightly disorganized, non-patterned tremor of the limbs.[62] Charcot's innovation was to see specific patterns and gestures in his patients' motions and to attempt to describe these in terms of their paradoxically involuntary imitation of specific

59. Jean-Martin Charcot, *Clinical lectures on diseases of the nervous system*, ed. with an introduction by Ruth Harris, trans. Thomas Savill (London: Tavistock/Routledge, 1991), 189–190.

60. Charcot, *Œuvres complètes*, vol. 1, 391–392.

61. Charcot, *Clinical Lectures*, 192. See also Charcot, *Œuvres complètes*, vol. 3, 217–221.

62. Charcot, *Œuvres complètes*, vol. 1, 393. Tweedie, like Charcot, described a hammering motion he called 'malleatio': it 'consists in an apparently irresistible disposition to beat the knees with the hands as with a hammer. The action is regular but involuntary', Tweedie remarked, 'and occurs in paroxysms. Instances have occasionally occurred of involuntary rotatory motion of the whole or part of the body . . . . Propulsion, either forwards, backwards, or in zigzags, has occasionally occurred'. One case was recorded of 'a man who sometimes went out and walked forwards till he was exhausted and obliged to be carried home in a litter'. The physician Mr. Kinder Wood, Tweedie noted, had also earlier described a woman whose 'nervous susceptibility' provoked her to suffer 'pains in the face', succeeded by a 'twinkling of the eye, motions of the legs, and rotation of the arms'. She beat the palms of

things. In other words, Charcot was diagnosing instances of neurological disorder as a sort of dance theatre: movements that could be described by their repeatability and their participation in a spectrum of gestures from ancient history and everyday life.

'Labouring' actions seemed paradoxically purposeful yet automatic and involuntary, and in this sense they resemble what Hewitt has described after Agamben as dance. 'Dance', Hewitt writes, reprising Agamben, 'as movement "independent of any motor purpose"—might be taken as paradigmatic of a Kantian aesthetic of "purposiveness without purpose."'[63] Charcot's patients' actions were 'purposive without purpose', gestural movements imitating specific activities yet involuntary. Taken on a large scale, dance manias and other seemingly epidemic instances of 'purposive'-seeming—yet in this sense purposeless—gesture constituted a 'dancing' disease in the nineteenth century: a disease of involuntary gesture imitating other gestures, including those representing specific activities or past times. For Charcot, the dancing mania and other epileptiform convulsions all represented or appeared to represent gestures previously performed by others, typically elsewhere. Patients were thus first and foremost interpreters, mimes; they did not initiate, but reproduced what was suggested to them. St. John's or St. Vitus's dance, epidemic possession in Loudun, the tarantella and the Convulsionaries of Saint-Médard, thus could all be attributed, Charcot argued, to participants' susceptible imaginations—to their capacity for automatic and involuntary imitation. But in this capacity, they also, he thought, were able to access and represent for him and his amphitheatre audiences a bodily portrait of past forms: they served as contemporary keys to the corporeal past. Hysteria, Charcot's work submitted, encompassed nearly all the mind and body might conjure and theatricalize in a public show of distress. His patients' gestures abstracted movements from everyday life, revealing a theatre of hysteria in which an aspect of everyday reality entered onstage, *en scène*—specifically onto the scientific stage—performed by the patient, who could not, however, in her depictions, entirely master it. The patients seemed always to be at the edge of uncontrol and of the inexpressible, showing in their gestures a side of reality they seemed unable fully to hold. If many patients willingly helped Charcot's theatrical show by complying, consciously or unconsciously, performing gestures he argued they would show if he suggested them, they may have done this as a way to exercise their own theatrical proclivities, or in order to gain the favour of a powerful man whose influence on scientific and cultural life in Paris was immense. Significantly, however, they did so at the borderline between apparently voluntary and involuntary gesture—that which marks choreomania as a 'modern' disease of repetition, a hiccupping, hesitant entrance into modernity.

This does not mean patients did not also suffer. As Asti Hustvedt has compellingly argued, many of Charcot's patients may have suffered real psychogenic disorders, some of which may also have been lastingly relieved over the course of their stay at the Salpêtrière.[64] The theatrical flourishes that their choreas involved, often triggered and manipulated by Charcot—although many patients themselves were arguably adept at triggering theatrical choreic gestures—won them substantial accolades from a Parisian public dazzled by their convulsive moves. As Gordon has convincingly argued of epileptic cabarets inspired by Charcot's clinic, Charcot's fame increased just as his patients' did through these performative scenarios: all were performers on a Parisian stage where distinctions between patient and pundit, science and art, blurred. But the not so subtle sexualization of these patients'

---

her hands on her thighs and beat her feet on the ground, as if to produce a rhythmic cadence. 'On some occasions', Wood added, 'she would move up and down, or from side to side on her chair, and then springing on her feet, leap and jump, or be propelled forwards'. At other times, 'she would go into every corner of the room, striking the furniture'. But her movements were not always violent: Wood noted that she would also 'frequently dance on one leg, holding the other in the hand'. This way, her beating and tapping gestures gained 'musical time': 'In the course of the complaint it was observed, that the blows on the furniture were in musical time, and the involuntary actions, as they were considered, changed to a measured step. Although ordinarily an inexpert dancer', he added, 'she would on these occasions move about elegantly as in a minuet. It was ascertained', Wood further remarked, 'that there was always a tune in her mind impelling her to these movements. When this tune was performed on the drum, she ran up to the instrument and danced with great activity and apparent delight, but the movements were always stopped by the rolling of the drum. Although yielding, as it seemed, unavoidably to the desire of dancing', she nonetheless 'always wished for the rolling of the drum, that the muscular excitement might be checked'. In Tweedie, ed., *A System of Practical Medicine*, 330–332.

63. Hewitt, *Social Choreography*, 83.

64. See Asti Hustvedt, *Medical Muses: Hysteria in Nineteenth-Century Paris* (London: Bloomsbury, 2012).

movements—in spite of Charcot's claims to the contrary—also allied dancing, working, involuntary convulsions, and heightened hallucinations and fantasy in a discomfitingly subterranean world of implicit desires for power and control, in which the work of observation abstracted and governed impulsive movements.

As Freud would note, lurking beneath the involuntary movements he himself observed in Charcot's clinic was the spectre of an obscure other side—a 'dark continent', unknowable and ungraspable except through opaque signs that came up to the surface like sylphs.[65]

HYSTEROEPILEPSY, GENDER, AND ANTIQUITY: THE POETIC REDISCOVERY OF THE NINETEENTH CENTURY

Not all hysterics were women. Charcot and Richer made a point of this in the concluding section to *Les démoniaques dans l'art*, although younger women figure prominently in their hand-drawn illustrations.[66] But the confusion between St. Vitus's dance and epilepsy and, in Charcot and Richer's terms, the new catchall diagnosis, hysteroepilepsy, drew on an increasingly feminized conception of disorderly gesturality—gestures queering public space by virtue of being 'too much'. Femininity, characterized by Freud as a 'dark continent', was to him unknown and nearly unknowable. The dancing disease thus became feminine and 'dark' largely through its association with premodern (ancient and medieval) corporealities in distress, hardly legible, but read again and again nonetheless, through the annals and images that nineteenth-century medical writers increasingly relied on to perform their diagnoses. Choreomania became in this way a disorder of the nineteenth-century imagination,

at once articulating a present scene of scientific historiography and, in doing so, exposing—excavating—scenes of corporeal mayhem.

As an ancient yet strikingly 'modern' disorder ('modern' inasmuch as it was articulated in a contrapuntal relationship to the past), hysteroepilepsy came to signal scientific modernity's capacity to read the past in present bodies, implicitly understood to be attuned to the subtle undercurrents still rumbling through them. Hysteria, Breton famously declared, was the nineteenth century's 'greatest poetic discovery'.[67] But in Charcot's clinic, hysteria signalled poetic rediscovery, a method for rereading ancient gestures in present terms, as a disorder of involuntary recurrence. The late nineteenth century, through hysterical and hysteroepileptic, fitting bodies, tapped into—or believed it tapped into—an ancient, highly feminine past. Yet many hysteroepileptics were also men, feminized through their involuntary gestures, which marked them as not quite modern, not entirely up to the modern-day work culture of hyperproductivity, purposiveness, and speed. As Micale has pointed out, the overlooked prominence of men in Charcot's service suggests that hysteria was not just feminine but also described a general weakening of the nervous system—including weakening from work-related strain—observed at the time. Micale notes that Charcot published more than sixty case histories of male hysterics in the 1880s, and between a quarter and a third of the case studies he described overall related to children and men.[68] All hysteroepileptics were curable by ovarian—or, for men, testicular—compression, as well as other forms of blows and bindings such as were depicted in earlier medical literature. Significantly, Charcot's theatrical mise en scène of hysteric patients on his lecture-hall stage complemented a cast of iconographic sources and visual collage that allied contemporary and ancient forms of convulsive theatricality. In this sense, we may argue that

---

65. See esp. Ranjana Khanna, *Dark Continents: Psychoanalysis and Colonialism* (Durham, NC: Duke University Press, 2003).

66. Charcot and Richer outline various ways in which male and female convulsions and *attitudes* differ, in *Les démoniaques*, 91–106.

67. Louis Aragon and André Breton, 'Le Cinquantenaire de l'Hystérie, 1878–1928', in *La Révolution surréaliste*, 22; cited in Gordon, *Why the French Love Jerry Lewis*, 2.

68. Mark S. Micale, 'Charcot and the Idea of Hysteria in the Male: Gender, Mental Science, and Medical Diagnosis in Late Nineteenth-Century France', *Medical History* 34.4 (1990): 363–411, 365. Micale points to the explosion of feminist and Freudian psychoanalytic literature on hysteria since the 1980s, virtually eclipsing the history of male hysterics in Charcot's work (364); Mark S. Micale, 'Hysteria and Its Historiography: A Review of Past and Present Writings', *History of Science* 27 (1989): 223–261 and 317–351; Mark S. Micale, 'Hysteria and Its Historiography: Future Perspectives', *History of Psychiatry* 1 (1990): 33–124. See also Mark S. Micale, *Hysterical Men: The Hidden History of Male Nervous Illness* (Cambridge, MA: Harvard University Press, 2008). Although Micale suggests that robust workers were as liable to succumb to hysteria in Charcot's analysis as effeminate types, Jan Goldstein describes the hysterical diagnosis as an occasion for gender subversion among men, including Gustave Flaubert. In Jan Goldstein,

modern neurology was the nineteenth century's greatest poetic creation: it operated as poesis, as making—in this case, making and remaking the fantasy of a just barely graspable origin—an ever-receding primal core—which Freud would, at the cusp of the twentieth century, take into the realm of psychoanalysis. Scientific knowing was, paradoxically, for these poet-mages a work of collage and bricolage, pilfering methods from across art history and anatomy, historiography, and clinical observation in an attempt to go up history's stream, reaching ancient times, as if history and biology met in the uncertain space of the spontaneously fitting body. This gesture of abstraction performed a return, to articulate a sense that present diseases have always been here, buried in the detritus of pre-revolutionary France or ancient Greece, imperfectly preserved through images forecasting disorders now observable in hospital settings.

Characters from the past peopled Charcot and his colleagues' analyses, appearing to corroborate clinical trials with precedent. Yet nothing would enable Charcot and his students better to grasp the past's afterlife than fieldwork in places where choreas were reputedly still present. This sideways movement from the archive to the field signals a translatio from a historiographic to an ethnographic plane, prompting the expansion and transformation of the choreomania repertoire into the realm of anthropology, and ever further into colonial lands: yet another repository of fantasies about the past and primal 'other', ever more racially marked. I will turn to this racially marked, colonial history in part II.

ARCHIVAL RETURNS: THE DANCING PROCESSION AT ECHTERNACH

Meige, a student of Charcot, visited the site of a reputedly still active medieval dancing procession to see what traces of the hysteroepileptic past might be found there, outside hospital walls.[69] In an article published in the 1904 issue of *Nouvelle iconographie de la Salpêtrière*, 'La procession dansante d'Echternach' [The Dancing Procession of Echternach], Meige suggested that he was disappointed to find the remains scanty. The great medieval leaping procession he had expected to witness firsthand, in its more or less 'still' active state, had been by 1900 almost unrecognizably transformed. Although more well-attended than ever, it was comparatively staid, even controlled—not at all the grimacing expression of spontaneous hysteroepileptic unleashing that he had imagined. There were,

'The Uses of Male Hysteria: Medical and Literary Discourse in Nineteenth-Century France', *Representations* 34 (1991): 134–165. Feminist readings emphasizing the male construction of a 'female malady' were spurred on most influentially by Elaine Showalter. See Elaine Showalter, *The Female Malady: Women, Madness and English Culture, 1830–1980* (New York: Pantheon Books, 1986). See also Showalter's return to questions of gender, masculinity, and homosexuality in esp. Elaine Showalter, *Sexual Anarchy: Gender and Culture at the Fin de Siècle*, new ed. (London: Virago Press, 1992); and Showalter, 'Hysteria, Feminism and Gender'.

69. See Henri Meige, 'La procession dansante d'Echternach', *Nouvelle iconographie de la Salpêtrière* 17 (1904): 248–264 and 320–336. For a further discussion, see Paul Krack, 'Relicts of Dancing Mania: The Dancing Procession of Echternach', *Neurology* 53.9 (1999): 2169–2172, 2169–2170. Krack notes that this site for 'people struck with dancing disease' is not cited by Hecker. Yet it does bear a striking resemblance to episodes Hecker discusses, and the first outbreak that Hecker cites, at Aachen, or Aix la Chappelle, was not far from Echternach. Krack describes the Echternach story as follows: 'the oldest legend about a group of people struck with dancing disease as a punishment from God for disturbing the Christian mass goes back to an anonymous manuscript from the Echternach scriptorium in the 11th century. A contemporary painting from the Echternach scriptorium shows a group of dancers in a Biblical scene, which is likely to have been inspired by the Dancing Procession. In 1227, the provincial synod of Trier issued a ban on dances and similar secular games (*tripudia et choreas et huismodi ludos saeculares*) in graveyards and inside churches. Trier, the oldest Roman city in Germany, is situated near the small town of Echternach, and the intervention of the local Christian authorities probably was aimed at the pagan dances at Willibrord's grave'. He adds that 'around 1100, the abbot Thiofried reported an important annual pilgrimage to the grave of Saint Willibrord during the week after Pentecost each year, with pilgrims coming from all of the Gallic and Teutonic provinces (*ab universa Galliae et Germaniae provincia*)'. See also J. Schroeder, 'Zur Frage frühmittelalterlicher Kulttänze am Grabe Willibrords in Echternach', in G. Kiesel and J. Schroeder, eds., *Willibrord: Apostel der Niederlande, Gründer der Abtei Echternach* (Luxembourg: Editions Saint-Paul, 1989), 186–193. Significantly, the line formation, made up of rows of people connected to one another by holding a handkerchief, appears in an illustration of an early fourteenth-century manuscript of the *Roman de la Rose* in the Royal Library, The Hague. Eustace and King point out that this image, and an alternative illustration, in which dancers hold one another by the sleeves, reprises the familiar medieval trope according to which Death holds onto his partners by their sleeves or other parts of their garments ('Dances of the Living and the Dead', 55). On the Echternach procession, see also Sahlin, *Étude sur la carole médiévale*, 160–164; A. Neyen, 'De l'origine et du but véritable de la procession dansante d'Echternach', *Bulletin de l'Institut archéologique liégeois* 15 (1880): 223–297; also H. Gaidoz, 'Le Grand-Duché de Luxembourg', *Nouvelle Revue* 66 (1890): 800–817; M. Tresch, *La chanson populaire luxembourgeoise* (Luxembourg: Victor Buck, 1929): 80–90; H. Attwell, 'The Echternach Whitsuntide Dancers', *Notes and Queries* 7.9 (1890): 381–382; Gougaud, 'La danse dans les églises', 240–242.

he moaned, 'at best two choreic little girls and a man with a tic; nothing, nothing of the great hysterical leaping chorea'.[70]

According to legend, Saint Willibrord (c. 658–739), also known as Saint Witt (or Saint Vitus) in Germany and Saint Guy in France, still held a special status in this small town, dramatized in the annual recurrence of a procession in his honour on Whit Tuesday, the Tuesday after Pentecost. Meige had hoped to see specimens of the *chorea major* he knew from Charcot's lectures, which may, they surmised, have represented a holdover from medieval days. But, as Meige wrote in 'La procession dansante d'Echternach', most of the men and women in attendance appeared quite unspectacular. He hypothesized that this may have been due to the presence of policemen lining the procession, ordered to carry anyone away who was suffering from a real epileptic or hysterical seizure. In addition, some participants now sent relatives or hired the services of professional dancers to replace them in the procession. For Meige, who admitted that he still 'felt some emotion', the sight was not unimpressive. But the annual dancing procession first mentioned in the Echternach city archives in 1497 and reported to have begun as early as the eighth century, after Willibrord's death, when his tomb became a site for miraculous occurrences, had diminished, Meige thought, to a mere shadow of its former self. As the neurologist Paul Krack has pointed out, previous iterations of the procession seem to have offered more spectacular body postures for the interested observer. A seventeenth-century depiction of the procession shows a pilgrim performing an *arc de cercle* in front of Willibrord's tomb; and a legend written down in 1858, probably of medieval origin, suggests that an Echternach citizen named Veit (Vitus) had provoked a dancing madness by playing his fiddle; Willibrord had had to intervene against the disease, and pilgrims processed annually in his honour so as to be protected from the dancing madness for a year.[71] St. Vitus was at once protector and provoker of the dancing disease.

But the event Meige encountered resembled more of a military march, with men and women lined up in neat rows, flanked at the front and the back by musicians, who were also interspersed between them, forming their own tightly choreographed group. Spectators lined the event in neat rows, perhaps mildly amused by the hops the processing participants performed in tune with a brass band (fig. 6.8). The few ecstatic faces, abrupt gestures, and expressions of enthusiasm Meige did observe were not caused, he thought, by any particular pathology—although he did witness hysterical and epileptic crises after the procession was over, attributable he surmised to exhaustion and to the excess of emotion experienced by some participants.[72] Rather, singing, dancing, and laughing, he argued, influence our motor behaviours, especially if we are 'suggestible'. Because religious enthusiasm increases individual susceptibility to impulsive behaviours, provoking imitation, impulsive behaviours and fits may occur in and around a procession, in an attenuated form.[73] Religious faith is particularly contagious, he argued; this explained why religious dances were often characterized by zealous motor activity.[74]

In Meige's journey, a new figure of the dancing disease emerges, revealing a will to archive and 're-cognize' choreomania through a methodological process of live returns. With Meige, the modern scientific body encounters a living archive by becoming co-present, experiencing the frisson of what appears to be *still past* at an ethnographic site that seems to have preserved history better than a modern clinical setting. Luxembourg was hardly a primitive place in the French imagination, compared to the European imagination of colonial worlds I will discuss in later chapters. But the town of Echternach's apparent preservation of an ancient tradition promised to reveal kinaesthetic histories elsewhere unavailable to the modern neuroscientist. As an effort to recapture the past and re-encounter an original cast of gestural events, this scientific journey was

---

70. 'C'est à peine si j'ai pu entrevoir deux petites choréiques et peut-être un tiqueur; . . . de la grande chorée, de la chorée hystérique, saltatoire, pas le moindre spécimen'. Meige, 'La procession dansante d'Echternach', 260.

71. Krack, 'Relicts of Dancing Mania', 2170. For more on the modern legend of Saint Willibrord and dance procession at Echternach, see also Pierre Kauthen, 'La procession dansante dans la 1re moitié du 20e siècle', in Kiesel and Schroeder, eds., *Willibrord*, 251–263. Kauthen argues that the nineteenth century represents a high point for dancing processions and for the Echternach procession in particular, as clergy now seized the opportunity to encourage the mass expression of spiritual devotion, after having condemned it in the past as unorthodox (251).

72. In Krack, 'Relicts of Dancing Mania', 2170. See Meige, 'La procession dansante d'Echternach', 248–264 and 320–336.

73. In Krack, 'Relicts of Dancing Mania', 2171.

74. In Krack, 'Relicts of Dancing Mania', 2171–2172.

LA PROCESSION DANSANTE D'ECHTERNACH
(Henry Meige.)

FIGURE 6.8 'The Dancing Procession of Echternach'. From *Nouvelle iconographie de la Salpêtrière* (1904). Courtesy the New York Academy of Medicine Library.

set to fail; yet it dramatized a modern attempt to find the corporeal past *over there*, in a place that can still be reached. While this arguably genealogical method did not purport to seek an 'origin' for the dancing disease, it sought to find a more ancient, better preserved, and more original copy of present-day variations. The journey to a corporeal past that Meige performed revealed a hope to encounter what Roach has called a 'mnemonic reserve': a set of gestures, dances, and imaginaries contained not in written records but in the bodies and movements of people.[75] The mnemonic reserve—what we may further think of as a repertoire of cultural histories—also reveals a cluster of fictions about the past, articulating a narrative recombining the contortions of earlier generations with present-day scientific imaginaries to constitute

75. 'Performance genealogies', writes Roach, describe 'expressive movements as mnemonic reserves, including patterned movements made and remembered by bodies, residual movements retained implicitly in images or words . . . and imaginary movements

an archival repertoire, living and in 'drag', inasmuch as events are translated—dragged—across discursive and geographic planes.

Although Meige's archival return left little trace of the event, other contemporary narratives enable us to see what it was that he saw and thus to reconstruct the social choreography of the dancing procession as an actually very orderly, deliberate, and planned affair—not at all the scene of mayhem that Charcot's 'demoniacs' suggest. As in previous narratives describing Bruegel's pilgrims, local traditions in Echternach claimed that the dancing procession was preventative: it constituted a popular theatre of movements engaged in at a designated time of the year to protect participants—even through the intermediary of hired dancers—from suffering choreiform and other movement disorders, as well as epilepsy, for the following year. The *Irish Jesuit Province*, in a short article titled 'The Leaping Procession at Echternach', published in 1886, barely more than a decade before Meige's participatory return, suggested that the 'dancing saints' ('saints dansants') making their pilgrimage to Echternach every year did so in the hope of being 'cured or spared by imposing on themselves as a penance, the convulsive movements and contortions accompanying the dreaded illness'.[76] 'One of the most curious relics of the Middle Ages', the author of this short article noted, 'existing in its primitive form to the present day, is the annual procession in honour of St. Willibrord, held at Echternach, in Luxembourg, and popularly known as "The Leaping Procession."' The village of Echternach had been a 'famous place of pilgrimage', and though 'the origin of this strange devotion is doubtful', was still 'crowded at Pentecost by sufferers from St. Vitus' dance, epilepsy, and similar disorders, accompanied by their friends and relations'. Most pilgrims, coming from Eifel, Upper Moselle, Saar, or further yet, arrived in bands of thirty, forty, or more, 'headed by their parish priest and a banner-bearer' as well as their own bands of musicians, 'march[ing] the whole way, singing hymns and litanies'. Others arrived by train and were 'conducted to the places prepared for their reception—great barn-like rooms, roughly fitted as dormitories, with beds of straw'. 'Curious sight-seers of a better class are few', the author noted, 'and consequently, have no difficulty in getting accommodation at the inns or in the houses of well-to-do villagers'.[77]

The image offered in this account suggests a significant concourse of people and a dramatic city-wide affair. One correspondent at the *Cologne Gazette* remarked in 1880 that nine thousand pilgrims took part in the procession, 'without counting the large body unable, through age or infirmity, to leap with the others';[78] spectators swelled the ranks further. The whole procession was orderly, as the Echternach priests had 'thoroughly organised the smallest details' so as to provoke 'no disturbance nor noisy mirth',[79] so that the 'exercise' might not 'degenerate into a frolic, and have to be suppressed'.[80]

The dancing procession was a carefully choreographed event: early on Whit Tuesday, the town was 'astir' as pilgrims followed a precisely delineated route through the streets.[81] Young villagers, 'lads and lasses, sixteen years of age and under', took part as hired dancers, agreeing to 'leap and jump not for themselves but for others, being *hired* by pilgrims who are unable themselves to take part in such vigorous exertions'. They accosted strangers, asking 'Wolt Ihr mich dangen für zu sprangen?' ('Will you hire me to jump for you?'),'' and danced for a few pennies, all the more vigorously if they had been hired by a few pilgrims at once.[82] By the time Meige visited, expecting dramatic contortions, the procession had become even more orderly and imposing. A few years after that, Willibrord's tomb was relocated to the Echternach basilica, providing further space for participants and watchers to gather. By 1920, at the height of the dancing procession, over twenty-four thousand people made the pilgrimage to this small town.[83] But the procession was still comparatively tame,

dreamed in minds, not prior to language but constitutive of it, a psychic rehearsal for physical actions drawn from a repertoire that culture provides'. In Roach, *Cities of the Dead*, 26.

76. C. O'C. E., 'The Leaping Procession at Echternach', *Irish Jesuit Province* 14.155 (May 1886): 257–260, 259.

77. C. O'C. E., 'The Leaping Procession', 257–258.

78. C. O'C. E., 'The Leaping Procession', 257.

79. C. O'C. E., 'The Leaping Procession', 257.

80. C. O'C. E., 'The Leaping Procession', 260.

81. C. O'C. E., 'The Leaping Procession', 257–258.

82. C. O'C. E., 'The Leaping Procession', 259.

83. Kauthen, 'La procession dansante', 251.

including fewer and fewer choreics and other visible sufferers of movement disorders than may have been present at the start. In the coda, I briefly outline my own return to Echternach to perform Meige's journey in archival drag.

NEW GENEALOGIES: MEDICAL PRACTICE AND EARLY ANTHROPOLOGISTS MOVING OUT TO THE 'FIELD'

Fieldwork was becoming a prime site for diagnostic observation, prompting what I argue constitutes a shift—a translatio—in the discursive history of the dancing disease. The journey from a broadly medical to an ethnographic field was fittingly fitful, wayward—what I am calling 'choreographic', denoting the sideways movements that fields perform and the rhizomatic routes they travel. Scientific articulation of the dancing disease in the last decades of the nineteenth century passes from an ekphrastic and historiographic to an ethnographic mode, criss-crossing (zigzagging across) geographic areas—mostly colonial ones—to become ever more 'illegibly' not just feminine but also African. Anthropology is typically understood to have emerged in the nineteenth century out of the older fields of natural science and natural history, as well as archaeology, marked by the rise of museums; anthropology also arose with the increasing burden on administration in the imperial colonies,[84] and was as such often complicit with colonial rule.[85] But anthropology and ethnography were also, I argue, steeped in medicine's own fascination for antiquity. Colonial medicine and medical history in particular provided an antiquarian pull, setting the stage—providing 'scenes'—for the new ethnographic study of exotic behaviours and beliefs. Physicians, like anthropologists, stationed all over the world, had a privileged perspective on human movement, positioned to view, as from upon a hill, like a monarch, as Pratt suggests, the plains of what they saw as scientific history stretching out before them.[86]

Anthropology and ethnography emerged out of colonial medicine as sites—literally, fields—for observing the dancing disease. This is significant on a few accounts. The concatenation of historiographic and ethnographic methodologies—reaching to the past and the other—continued to embed modern scientific imaginations of choreomania in an elusive field of writing in which ancient history re-emerges as repetition taking place elsewhere. Choreomania in the late nineteenth century became a disorder of historical alterities just as these alterities seemed to erupt not only on ancient and modern European but American and, even more markedly, colonial land. Choreomania appeared antediluvian, primeval—not just historical and superstitious but prehistorical, inarticulate, animal, and prediscursive. Choreomaniacal bodies festered and erupted, like boils, wherever 'modernity' was not—as its imagined other.

Anthropology was the science of exotic body politics; but so, too, it perpetuated the study of human movement. Jean Christian Marc Boudin (1806–1867), one of many under-acknowledged nineteenth-century writers who straddled medicine and anthropology, suggested that movement and travel ('déplacement') are at the heart of human history.[87] The relatively untranslatable notion of 'déplacement' is suggestive, denoting at once displacement—a usually undesirable sense of being no longer in one's home territory—and the far more neutral choreographic sense of merely moving aside. 'Déplacement' suggests a transfer of people, objects, and ideas between sites (or fields). This provokes a shift: what I am calling translatio. The process of déplacement suggests not only a movement away from one place and towards another but a residual carrying over, a remainder—the drag and dragging—of memories and habits from one location, or field, to another. Boudin calls this sense of movement 'irresistible'.[88] But it also suggests a passage—a discursive choreography—between

---

84. The Aborigines Protection Society was founded in Britain in 1837, with the motto 'Out of one blood'. See Henrika Kuklick, 'The British Tradition', in Henrika Kuklick, ed., A New History of Anthropology (Malden, MA: Blackwell, 2008), 52–78, 52.

85. Talal Asad, ed., Anthropology and the Colonial Encounter (Amherst, NY: Prometheus Books, 1995).

86. See Mary Louise Pratt, Imperial Eyes: Travel Writing and Transculturation, 2nd ed. (London: Routledge, 2008), 201–223.

87. J. C. M. Boudin, 'Sur les Chorées épidémiques de Madagascar, d'Italie et d'Abyssinie', Bulletin de la Société d'Anthropologie de Paris 6 (1865): 441–454; cited in Andrianjafy, La Ramanenjana à Madagascar (Chorémanie d'origine palustre) (Montpellier: Imprimerie Delord-Boehm et Martial, 1902), 13.

88. Boudin, 'Chorées épidémiques de Madagascar', 441; cited in Andrianjafy, La Ramanenjana à Madagascar, 13.

areas of knowing, determined not only by geographies but by methods of reading and knowing. Boudin, who foregrounded travel and movement in his concept of human history, was heavily involved in the early days of the Société d'Anthropologie de Paris, a body initially composed mainly of medical professionals. Founded in 1859 and formally established in 1864 by the government of France for the 'scientific study of the human races', the Société d'Anthropologie translated early medical comparativism into the increasingly systematic study of human populations in colonial outposts overseas. Other founding members of the Société besides Boudin likewise came from medical and psychiatric ranks.[89] Further professions listed among those practiced by the Société's founding members included geography, history, geology, public administration, Orientalism, linguistics, law, art, archaeology, and literature. But the majority of listed affiliates were from the medical world, from pharmacists and anatomists to military physicians. The ubiquity of physicians affiliated with the military and imperial orders in particular multiplied the number of medical professionals having access to exotic behaviours and disease, accounting for the vast majority of early publications on the new anthropological scene. In 1865, a year after the French anthropological society's founding, over a third of the titulary members residing in Paris were primarily active in medicine; two thirds of the members outside Paris (including the British physician Thomas Aitken) were also medical professionals. Among national correspondents, half listed medical affiliations. By 1895, with the gradual institutionalization and professionalization of the new anthropological field, medical affiliations waned: out of roughly 550 members, only about 90 (less than one-sixth) were primarily active in medicine and related sciences.[90]

Similarly, in England, the Anthropological Society of London, founded in 1863 by James Hunt (1833–1869) of the Ethnological Society of London (with which significant rivalry would ensue), claimed an affinity with the natural and medical sciences.[91] The German Anthropological Society and the Berlin Society for Anthropology, Ethnology, and Prehistory, founded by Virchow, himself a writer on movement and dancing epidemics, likewise boasted interests in the intersection between medicine, culture, and society. Although the development of anthropology in Germany, which had virtually no colonial presence, revolved around the concept of *Völksgeit*, national character, articulated by Johann Gottfried von Herder among others, and *Bildung*, learning for self-edification, believed to foster a spirit of curiosity about the world's people and to inspire novel approaches to culture, it similarly boasted a foundation in biological science and travel. Alexander von Humboldt (1769–1859), who wrote a preface to Hecker's essay 'The Dancing Mania' and whose voluminous

---

89. A glance at the list of members included at the start of the society's annual publications reveals that the early anthropologist Paul Broca (1824–1880) was professor at the Faculté de Médecine and a surgeon at the Saint-Antoine Hospital, while Henri de Castelnau (1814–1890) was the former associate inspector general of the prisons and insane asylums of France; Isidore Geoffroy Saint-Hilaire (1772–1844), also a founding member, was a medically trained zoologist and professor at the National Museum of Natural History in Paris, specializing in organic anomalies and the science of monstrosity (or teratology); and Littré, famous for his *Dictionnaire de la langue française* [Dictionary of the French Language] (1859–1872), was an honorary member affiliated with the Institut de France and the Imperial Academy of Medicine. Among national correspondents—members resident abroad—many were also medical professionals. D. M. P. Faure was a colonial physician in Cheraga, Algeria; Lautré was a missionary physician in New Caledonia; Touchard was a navy surgeon in Gabon; Pierre-Émile Barthélémy-Benoît (b. 1822), also an imperial navy surgeon, was stationed in Senegal; Adolphe Bourgarel was a surgeon in the imperial marine; D. M. P. Chanot was the former imperial marines surgeon of the Ile de la Réunion. See *Bulletin de la société d'anthropologie de Paris* 1865, 1880, and 1895.

90. See *Bulletin de la société d'anthropologie de Paris* 1865, 1880, and 1895.

91. On the early history of anthropology in Britain, see Alfred C. Haddon, *History of Anthropology* (London: Watts, 1910). For a comprehensive review, see especially Kuklick, ed., *A New History of Anthropology*, 52–78. Haddon (1855–1940) noted in his preface to a collection of essays edited by E. E. Evans-Pritchard (1902–1973), Raymond Firth (1901–2002), Bronisław Malinowski (1884–1942), and Isaac Schapera (1905–2003) that the pioneer ethnologist C. G. Seligman (1873–1940) himself had come to anthropology from medical pathology, having earned his M.D. in London on pathological research conducted in New Guinea. The famous Cambridge Anthropological Expedition to Torres Straits in 1898–1899, which Haddon had organized, introduced him and a small cast of other medical practitioners—among them, W. H. R. Rivers (1864–1922)—to the new discipline and methodology and the questions and investigations characterizing the anthropological field. Rivers, celebrated as a physiologist, similarly experimented with ethnology and psychology after his participation in the Torres Straits expedition and his fieldwork there. See Alfred C. Haddon, 'Appreciation', in E. E. Evans-Pritchard, Raymond Firth, Bronisław Malinowski, and Isaac Schapera, eds., *Essays Presented to C. G. Seligman* (London: K. Paul, Trench, Tübner, 1934), 1–4. See also Alfred C. Haddon, ed., *Reports of the Cambridge Anthropological Expedition to Torres Straits* (Cambridge: Cambridge University Press, 1901).

writings were collected in the influential five-volume *Kosmos* (1845–1862), covered nearly every field of scientific inquiry in his research, from zoology and botany to plant and physical geography, minerology, chemistry, anatomy, and political economy, largely inspired by his journeying through Central America.[92]

These anthropological and ethnographic endeavours represented a seismic shift in disciplinary understandings of corporeality and movement, as writers translated colonial and missionary medical observations to a new discursive plane, foregrounding what Clifford has called a 'travelling culture', which involved research increasingly performed 'in the field'.[93] Moving bodies in anthropology were being described in cultural terms, at once grounded in and abstracted from the places where they were observed. And whereas these anthropologists were engaging in the increasingly professionalized world of medium-term travel and in the 'circulatory system' Gilroy has described as characterizing the modern transatlantic (and modernism more generally), they were also methodologically entrenched in a collecting culture. From this perspective, non-European natives seemed to reach back to—to re-enact—pre-European time. As such they were representational, artefactual: history's excess and residue, its remainders. Foucault noted that the early ethnographic sciences imagined non-European cultures to exist outside of what they imagined as modern, linear (European) time; non-European cultures were considered to be ahistorical.[94] Choreomania, conceived as an ancient and non-European disease, was also thus 'ornamental': a disorder of superfluous gesture,

baroque in its iconography and peripheral to the European core. Choreomania was fantasized as ahistorical in its tendency to re-emerge and repeat; it did not belong to (linear, European) time but offered, through European bodies, a theatrical re-enactment of pre-civilized other states.

Choreomania thus represents movement at the limits of modern, imperial Europe and the migration and circulation—the choreography—of ideas about these limits across fields. In the next chapter, comparativism comes to the fore as a methodological force that further meshes ideas about chorea and choreomania in the obscure otherworld of colonial medical fantasy. The tarantella, long described in early modern medical literature by writers as a popular practice designed to expel a spider's noxious poison, emerges on the nineteenth-century medical scene as a site of bacchanalian revelry. The next chapter moves not only to southern Italy, imagined as Europe's gateway to Africa, but also to the African 'dancing disease', the *tigretier*, described by the British explorer and travel writer Nathaniel Pearce (1779–1820) as a tradition that, like tarantism, primarily implicated unhappy women. Further excavating the genealogical links between fantasies of African tarantellas and colonial others, the chapter moves to a modern case of an African 'dancing disease', imagined as a tarantella by government officers worried that it was performed, deceitfully, to mock them. Lies, sex, and dance form the trio that set choreomania apart in the Italian south as a holdover dubiously connecting northern Europe to a 'dark' and—to many of its observers'—inscrutable African past.

92. See H. G. Penny and M. Bunzl, eds., *Worldly Provincialism: German Anthropology in the Age of Empire* (Ann Arbor: University of Michigan Press, 2003).

93. See esp. James Clifford, 'Spatial Practices: Fieldwork, Travel, and the Disciplining of Anthropology', in Clifford, *Routes*, 52–91.

94. Michel Foucault, *Les mots et les choses: Une archéologie des sciences humaines* (Paris: Éditions Gallimard, 1966), 388.

PART II

Colonial and Postcolonial Stages

Scenes of Ferment in the Field

7

'Sicily Implies Asia and Africa'
Tarantellas and Comparative Method

At the end of Naples, begins Africa.

—Traditional Italian saying, in Jerri Daboo,
Ritual, Rapture and Remorse (2010)

Each work on the Orient *affiliates* itself with other works, with audiences, with institutions, with the Orient itself.

—Edward W. Said, *Orientalism* (1978)

TRAVELLING CULTURES: POSTCOLONIALISMS AND DARK CONTINENTS

Part II delves deeper into the colonial and postcolonial spheres within which choreomania moved. No longer only a European fantasy of prior disorderly movements—among post-plague dancers, the Convulsionaries of Saint-Médard, and 'hysterics', as well as French revolutionary hordes—coming up to haunt a figure of modernity imagined contrapuntally against these prior 'disorders', the concept of choreomania now comes to signal a whole new amalgamation of bacchanalian fantasies, with uprisings in Africa, the Americas, and the South Seas. As I will show in the ensuing chapters, 'choreomania' travels with its translations in and out of colonial outposts and missionary, medical, and government archives—coming out always slightly transformed. From Orientalizing marginalia to eyewitness accounts, new archival repertoires emerge, contributing to moving the discourse on choreomania along to new shores. These discursive choreographies—always linked genealogically by scientific writers to discursive precedent—transform the language of choreomania from a slightly awkward medieval hold-over into a dark, feminine, and archaic return. If Europe was moving forward, the rest of the world, it seemed, was dancing impulsively far behind. Choreomaniacs in the literature surveyed in the following chapters, however, do not just move too much or display too much enthusiasm, as in previous cases; they increasingly epitomize an antediluvian force of duplicity, an ungovernable propensity to shamming as well as to insurrection. Still jagged and erratic, apparently purposeless and unpredictable, the gestures of choreomania come with the new fieldwork to signal an ever more thrilling—and dangerous—Dionysian proximity to ancient times, suggesting foreign bodies served as imaginary access points to an ever-receding past: Europe met its own (dancing) history of misrule in the exotic 'East'.

Not all writers in this genealogy were European, though many were European-trained; thus while many bodies and narratives I consider moved from west to east and north to south, some travelling researchers offered observations far outside Europe, contributing to an increasingly transnational set of scientific narratives cross-pollinating between regions, systems of practice, and thought. Choreomania's discursive history thus further zigzags, picking up an ever more indiscriminate array of case histories to add to and to confound its paradigmatic scenario, its ur-example—the St. John's or St. Vitus's dances of the European Middle Ages.

Underpinning this travelling history of ideas about the dancing disease is a persistent cluster of myths about unintelligible others. In order to think through the fantasy of colonial and postcolonial unknowability, and its imbrication in discourses about disorderly bodies moving through the new scientific disciplines, I borrow from postcolonial feminist theorist Ranjana Khanna, who describes, after Said, Foucault, and Frantz Fanon (1925–1961), the colonial legacies underpinning the 'dark continent' of psychoanalysis. Reprising Freud's claim that woman is a 'dark continent'—mysterious, obscure, and other, like Africa—Khanna traces psychoanalysis's lineage back to colonial anthropology and archaeology, situating modern psychoanalysis at the heart of the colonial enterprise and, significantly, in a melancholic longing to return to a primeval womb-like state of comfort and unknowing. But modernity cannot unknow what it knows, and so the trauma of colonialism serves as a powerful 'specter', she writes, haunting postcolonial legacies and aspirations.[1] So, too, spectres of alterity and prehistory haunt choreomania, as disruptive others emerge onto the scene of scientific modernity as figures of the alluringly unknowable past. Choreomaniacs appear abstruse and uncannily familiar, perpetually erupting in a cacophonous display of vitality on history's stage. Modernity thus construes itself in relation to a past and an other conceived as dark, odd, and inchoate. This chapter situates colonial modernity's 'dark' other—African and feminine—in southern Italy and the African continent seen to lie at its door. It argues that nineteenth-century medical and ethnographic literature on tarantism crafts an Orientalist fantasy by which tarantellas, and their imagined African variants, notably the *tigretier*, signify ancient practices that could be observed and reconstructed over the course of colonial travel and fieldwork, by which 'primitive' bodies could be 'excavated' for the benefit of scientific and artistic reproduction in the present.

Continuing thus the previous chapter's reflection on reperformance, historiography, and visuality, this chapter shows a new brand of comparativism emerging in the nineteenth century as a choreographic process multiplying sites for comparison: across discursive fields (*translatio studii*) and geographic ones (*translatio imperii*), in the construction of an ever more disjointed modern body, subject to proliferating origins and recentrings. The history of colonial-era comparativism concerning 'dance' and disease thus moves Said's contention, via Foucault, that the West construes the East through Orientalist structures of knowledge and power familiar from traditional learning and government structures—including the classics, the Bible, philology; public institutions, trading companies, geographical societies, and universities; writing in travel books, exotic literature, and so on[2]—and towards a concept of comparativism taking place transversally, across fields and geographies. My argument is that comparativism in the age of torque emerges motionally, choreographically, as a perpetual *decentring*, rather than as the paradoxical transposition of 'new' spheres of knowledge gained from colonial administration in Africa and the East onto older structures of knowledge acquisition and power. The relative novelty of colonial modernity as an emergent globalism performs a slightly different paradoxical motion: that of the semi-haphazard collection of comparatives.

Rather than suggest a structure of *accumulation* of knowledge about others, which are fitted into pre-existing categories, modern structures of knowing comparatively emerge through series of proliferating encounters, each of which maps only somewhat onto a pre-existing scheme. The paradigmatic quality of prior models (St. Vitus's dance, or the Italian tarantella, also described in nineteenth-century medicine as a form of St. Vitus's dance) thus shifts, perpetually displaced and replaced—in Roach's terms, *surrogated*—by new models that nonetheless reach back to the

---

1. Khanna, *Dark Continents*, 30.
2. Said, *Orientalism*, 202.

old. Surrogation, unlike repetition, or imitation, suggests the imperfect mapping of a present onto a displaced, lost, or abandoned past; with surrogation, the novel copy of the old removes what came before by merely setting it to one side rather than eliminating it completely.[3] So whereas the 'old' structure (St. Vitus's dancing, or classical philology) remains, formally—if only in name—its coordinates also shift in the process. 'St. Vitus's dance' or the 'tarantella' comes to signal something quite different with repetition and does so by virtue of the series of encounters and translatios performed through it. This suggests a vital model of concept formation by which terms, figures, and forms coalesce into conceptual or discursive nodes, things about which a certain collection of things are said.

In this chapter, the 'tarantella' becomes paradigmatic of a whole subset of concerns about the dancing disease, namely fakery, forgery, and deceit (generally but not always among women), as well as a particular sort of 'madness': colonial depression, to use a term anachronistically in order to designate a whole complex of affects and conditions, including fatigue, listlessness, and a (right) sense of oppression. Following Foucault's contention that the history of madness, and of the human sciences more broadly, is a 'history of the Other'—simultaneously construed as internal and foreign—as well as of the order imposed on things, that is, as a creation of sameness where there may be none, the chapter proposes a look at the tarantella as a concept that moves between orders of otherness and sameness without ever revealing a stable or unchanging core— an origin.[4] The tarantella rather comes to be construed in nineteenth-century colonial medical and anthropological literature as a disorder broadly signalling modernity's alienation from a supposedly prior, carefree, classical dancing self that it tries to recapture; modern colonial travellers attempt to find the remains of what they read in classical literature in colonial backyards and are disappointed not to find it matching up. But in the differential relation between the imagination and the encounter lies a space of transfer, a translatio, the movement of the concept from classical reproduction to a different sort of theatre—the theatre of forgery and lies, according to which colonized and lower classes

seemingly represent the classical past but fail to do so properly in their execution. 'Choreomania' then comes to signal the impoverishment of the classical past in a present too gauche, too poor (for most), to match up to it.

Thus furthering Burt's contention that the 'alien' body of early twentieth-century modernity sought roots in faraway places to empower a rootless and disenfranchised modern self— Katherine Dunham, for instance, travelling to Haiti to bolster her African-American community in the present[5]—this chapter shows broadly Western (mostly European) scientists and anthropologists, travellers, and administrators marking modernity out as a space between sameness and difference, self and other, also with respect to the imagined other contained within the supposed modern self. Writers, artists, and scientists found people and events in other places that could, they thought, deepen and enrich their present with an order many felt had been lost. This suggests the experience of modernity in the age of torque as diminished, materially and spiritually, yet seeking to augment itself with less alienated, more natural, and more authentic other places (in Foucault's terms, heterotopias), which nevertheless revealed themselves to be frustratingly (to their observers) never quite right. Thus the rhizomatic history of an emergent global modernity suggests travellers imagining themselves in an 'uncanny' relationship to faraway places and other histories: neither at home nor quite not at home in them. Conversely, colonial subjects encountering travelling physicians we may surmise doubled themselves in an attempt to remember what was asked of them to reperform, discovering an uneasy mismatch in their own concepts of self and other and their own situation as objects of desire and distrust.

Increasingly in the nineteenth and twentieth centuries, otherness became 'uncanny', Burt argues, inasmuch as modern bodies—those experiencing themselves in relation to and yet as being different from a past nonetheless still accessible, many thought, in other lands— sensed that the divide was not so great. And so the experience of modernity became that of reconciling differential relations—what Said has described in terms of contrapuntal negotiations

---

3. Roach, *Cities of the Dead*, 2–4.

4. See Michel Foucault, *The Order of Things: An Archaeology of the Human Sciences*, trans. Alan Sheridan (London: Routledge Classics, 2002), xxvi.

5. Burt, *Alien Bodies*, 1–2.

between master narratives and *other* narratives (colonial or otherwise marginal narratives with regard to a dominant West) running through them[6]—slippages complicating experiences of self and other, here and elsewhere, and their mutual entanglements. The discourse surrounding these encounters and misconstruals produces modernity as a contrapuntal movement, a choreography or choreotopology of tos and fros, a set of meeting points and discursive nodes decentring themselves, including those at the height of empire: the late nineteenth and early twentieth centuries, when colonial powers, Said reminds us, dominated up to 85 percent of the inhabitable world.[7] Following Gilroy, a new politics of authenticity emerges in the (terrifying) recursion of supposedly purer, prior, 'unsayable' forms of culture (in the cases he describes, music; in cases here, movement bordering on dance) in a version of modernity that is at once obsessed with and fearful of these other expressions. Gilroy writes: 'the anti-modernity of these [black musical] forms, like their anteriority, appears in the (dis)guise of a premodernity that is both actively reimagined in the present and transmitted intermittently in eloquent pulses from the past'.[8] The contrapuntal movement, then, is double: simultaneously an insuppressible re-emergence, even eruption, of (typically darker and more ancient) alterities in a present never quite able to contain them and the wilful recuperation, even restoration or (violent) repossession, of these alterities in a self-styled upright present that is perpetually anxious nevertheless to know (and to master) them.

Beginning with a discussion of the emergence of comparativism as a method of choice in the nineteenth century, first in medical geography and then in comparative literature, the chapter goes on to discuss Orientalist fantasies about the Italian South, widely perceived to be more ancient and dark than the North, closer to Africa and Greece, and thus ideal for comparative analyses and recuperations. The chapter then discusses travellers' encounters with the tarantella there, and Nora's tarantella in *A Doll's House* (1879), by Henrik Ibsen (1828–1906), as well as Pearce's encounter in colonial Abyssinia (present-day Ethiopia) with a dance, the *tigretier*, he thought reminiscent of the tarantella. Attentive to the Orientalist marginalia in Babington's translation of Hecker's writing, the chapter traces the expansive and transformative movement of 'choreomania' on North African and 'Arabian' terrrains. Finally I consider more recent ethnographic recuperations of the 'tarantella' in Nigeria, similarly cast as forgeries and fakes. Medical and anthropological literature, all these cases show, increasingly associated the reperformance of popular dances with feminine and colonial deceit, marking a new turn in the literature on the dancing disease as a disorder of colonial duplicity and ultimately resistance to rule.

COMPARATIVISM AND COLONIAL RULE

Said points out the origins of comparative literature in a period of high imperialism, specifically the nationalisms emergent across Europe in the period between 1795 and 1830.[9] But far less salient in contemporary literature on comparativism is another history situating these cross-cultural interests in medical research. Thus, although comparativism had become by the end of the nineteenth century the de facto method of choice for literary and cultural analysis, this chapter shows that comparativism also began in medicine, specifically in medical geography and medical history, two fields that I argue sit at the heart of concerns now prominent in cultural, performance, and especially dance history and theory: concepts of movement and archiving first and foremost. The translatio from a broadly medical to an anthropological and now a 'performative' and dance field suggests not only (certainly not primarily) a continuity between these areas of research, methods, and conceptual problems; but, more saliently, a fundamental mobility between discursive fields of analysis and therefore an important historicization and destabilization of the disciplinarity of our disciplines. Rereading the history of dance in medicine allows us to rethink both—as well as a host of affiliated—fields' myths of origins, including any notion suggesting that these fields have as

---

6. See e.g. Said, *Culture and Imperialism*, 66–67. Said offers a further account of the 'contrapuntal' in Edward W. Said, *Freud and the Non-European* (London: Verso, 2003), 23–24.

7. Said, *Orientalism*, 41.

8. Gilroy, *The Black Atlantic*, 74.

9. Said, *Culture and Imperialism*, 43.

their primary task anything other than to read bodily movement and forms. In this sense, dance and medicine share a common heritage, and participate in a shared sphere of cultural prejudice, including suspicion concerning (and attempts to smooth out) jerky and uncontrolled movements, such as those that characterize what are now commonly referred to as movement disorders: conditions marked by tics, jerks, spasms, contractions, paralyses, and sudden, unbidden falls. So although some contemporary dance practice embraces such alterkinetic aesthetics, and the whole domain of hip-hop, krumping, and popping relies on quick contractions and highly controlled, virtuosic muscular spasms as well as improvisation, the relative marginalization of these movements socially coheres with what I describe as choreomania, a pervasive prejudice against sudden, irregular gesture.[10]

Hecker saw choreomania as a 'disease of nations', one that arose out of specific times and places—often cataclysmic ecologies—but nonetheless shared traits across histories and cultures. This comparativism set the stage for further analyses and a new fashion for finding examples around the colonial world. Hirsch, who edited Hecker's essay on the dancing mania in an 1865 German edition, declared the need among the scientific class to study what he called 'public' or 'national' diseases from a comparative standpoint. He wrote in the preface to his *Handbook of Geographical and Historical Pathology* (1881–1886) that medical geography and medical history were gaining a new currency among his peers as commerce with colonial peoples was enabling physicians to grasp entirely new realms of research. In particular, his English-language translator noted: 'the English-speaking race are most directly interested in the subject of this book, and their observations in various parts of the world have supplied a large part of the materials for it'.[11] Indeed, although Germany had long engaged in worldwide exploration, and travel narratives gained a new currency in the wake of Humboldt's journeys through equatorial America between 1799 and 1804, the absence of any widespread colonial presence had typically oriented German scientific interests towards what was thought of as learning for its own sake (*Bildung*). Still, Humboldt was interested in what Hecker had to say, and provided the 1832 German edition of *Die Tanzwuth* with a short foreword that extolled the virtues of comparative medical research.[12] By 1879, the German psychiatrist Ludwig Witkowski (1849–1927) argued that all dance frenzies should be studied from a comparative standpoint. Borrowing liberally from Hecker, Witkowski called St. Vitus's dance a 'psychic infection' 'analogous' to earlier cases of mental or spiritual illness (*Geisteskranke*) and 'melancholic delirium', from the Sufi brothers to the Jumpers in England.[13]

Thus, Hirsch noted, English and American but also French physicians contributed to the publication of monographs, official reports, and journals, aiding in construing the expanding field of medical geography. The Health Reports of the War Offices of England and the United States and the *Archives de médecine navale* in France, among other state-run publications, offered medical professionals new platforms for acquiring and disseminating information on the medical anthropology of parts of the globe 'formerly unknown in these respects, or known imperfectly'.[14] New research in epidemiology offered comprehensive coverage of diseases previously unheard of in Europe, through reports issued by the English Health Department, the *Transactions of the Epidemiological Society* of London, and the Official Sanitary Reports of Sweden. 'All such labours have not only added on the grand scale to our knowledge of the distribution of diseases

---

10. On the recent history of hip-hop in relation to postcolonial *displacements* in France, see esp. Felicia McCarren, *French Moves: The Cultural Politics of Le Hip Hop* (Oxford: Oxford University Press, 2013).

11. Charles Creighton, translator's note, in Hirsch, *Handbook of Geographical and Historical Pathology*, vol. 1, xi. I discuss the Sydenham Society's considerable (though not undebated) investment in publishing medical cases from around the world in chapter 1. Although similar initiatives were undertaken in France, with the emergence of the publishing house J.-B. Baillière in 1821, none matched the scope of the English societies. In 1895 and 1897 alone, volumes on leprosy in the New Sydenham Society collections included chapters on Iceland, South Africa, Australia, China, Indo-China, Malaya, the Archipelago, Oceania, and Hong Kong. See Baillière, *Histoire de nos relations avec l'académie de médecine, 1827–1871*; Régnier, 'J.-B. Baillière'.

12. Alexander von Humboldt, 'Foreword', in Hecker, *Die Tanzwuth, eine Volkskrankheit im Mittelalter*, v–vi.

13. Ludwig Witkowski, 'Einige Bemerkungen über den Veitstanz des Mitelalters und über psychische Infection', *Allgemeine Zeitschrift für Psychiatrie und Psychisch-Gerichtliche Medizin* 35 (1879): 591–598. See Rosen, *Madness*, 205.

14. Hirsch, *Handbook of Geographical and Historical Pathology*, vol. 1, v–ix.

in time and place, and of the causal connexion between them and the human environment', wrote Hirsch, 'but, moreover, these researches have been invested with a scientific value such as pertained to only a small part of the earlier writings in the field of Medical Geography'.[15]

Modern increase in world travel prompted comparisons of climate, diet, and disease. By the end of the nineteenth century, comparison was arising as a method of choice for literary and scientific endeavours, so that 'the comparative method of acquiring or communicating knowledge' that Hutcheson Macaulay Posnett (1855–1927) described in his landmark *Comparative Literature* (1892) was 'in one sense as old as thought itself, in another the peculiar glory of our nineteenth century'.[16] Although the Greeks had reached an admirable state of civilization, Posnett wrote, they were in no position to perform the comparative analyses that the 'new European civilisation' could enjoy, as the discovery of the New World had 'awakened' men to every species of contrast. Commerce aided, 'giving a greater degree of personal freedom to the townsmen of the West than they had ever possessed before'.[17] More important for Posnett, the comparative mode enabled enquiry into aspects of the material world free from religious dogma; it could encompass philological comparisons popular among scholars of classical literature and surpass these with forms of empirical study facilitated by technological progress. 'Many new influences have combined to make the mind of Europe more ready to compare and to contrast than it ever was before', Posnett argued. 'The steam-engine, telegraph, daily press, now bring the local and central, the popular and the cultured, life of each European country and the general actions of the entire world face to face; and habits of comparison have arisen such as never

before prevailed so widely and so vigorously'.[18] Comparative thinking heralded a paradigmatic shift in the way people and nations related to and interpreted one another, particularly for those with the financial and technological means to do so: northern Europeans travelling, for the most part, south.

Orientalism provided ideal grounds for pursuing this comparativism, linking sameness and alterity, Greece and the East. In Said's terms, Orientalism was founded on series of comparisons, ways in which, to the westerner, 'the Oriental was always *like* some aspect of the West'.[19] Orientalists, Said notes, make it their business to '[convert] the Orient from something into something else':[20] something strange into something familiar and then, one may add, back into something strange again, as the imagined negative of the imagined self. Orientals are created as objects of discursive interest, imagined by way of mimetic doublings: the other's alterity is annulled, rendered same, and yet their alterity is highlighted as being *like* the self but, to reprise Homi K. Bhabha, '*not quite*'.[21] All this phantasmatic projection occurs through the mechanisms of professional and amateur societies and associations, presses, vocabularies, and the like. These mechanisms yield what Said sees as a process of 'schematization', though as I show of choreomania, this process also comes with a concomitant *ambiguation*, as choreomania passes through various associated and correlative spaces—spaces of recombination—encountering new material and disciplinary topologies within which it continues to move.[22] Put in other terms, choreomania continues to be reconstituted through various encounters between disciplinary zones of intensity (colonial medicine, medical geography, etc.) just as it is inscribed in new scenes. Choreomania is always reconstituted;

15. Hirsch, *Handbook of Geographical and Historical Pathology*, vol. 1, vi. See also an early account in Muhry and Davis, *Observations on the Comparative State of Medicine in France, England, and Germany*, who note that they are interested in 'the conditions under which diseases are distributed over the world, or are confined to certain districts', suggesting that 'when the laws which regulate health and disease among the human family began to be elucidated by the facts of *physical geography*, combined with those of *vital statistics*', a 'new branch of medical etiology opened up', 'variously named medical geography or noso-geography' (897–898).

16. Hutcheson Macaulay Posnett, *Comparative Literature* (New York: D. Appleton, 1892), 73.

17. Posnett, *Comparative Literature*, 75.

18. Posnett, *Comparative Literature*, 76.

19. Said, *Orientalism*, 67.

20. Said, *Orientalism*, 67.

21. In Bhabha's by now iconic formulation, 'colonial mimicry is the desire for a reformed, recognizable Other, *as a subject of a difference that is almost the same, but not quite*. Which is to say, that the discourse of mimicry is constructed around an *ambivalence*; in order to be effective, mimicry must continually produce its slippage, its excess, its difference'. Homi K. Bhabha, *The Location of Culture* (London: Routlege, 1994), 122.

22. Said, *Orientalism*, 67–68.

just as writers travelled across Italy and Africa, the means by which choreomania came to signal a particular sort of colonial and feminine dancing disease depended on the anecdotal evidence they juggled and rewrote relationally. Choreomania, as a disorder fantasized contrapuntally, emerged through narratives that writers replayed; and, significantly, through the narratives they told about these narratives' relations to other ones.

In this sense, the history of choreomania, as of virtually any other concept, I submit, is a history of *transfers* and associations, a variation on the notion of '*displacements* and *transformations*' that Foucault, borrowing from Canguilhem, employs to describe the history of a concept as a history in motion.[23] I call this movement a choreographic process: a movement of ideas in relation to other ideas, bodies, and geographies constituting an always shifting network or node, a zone of intensity according to which concepts do not just become displaced onto other fields but also become associated with new sites and other indigeneities. In this sense, concepts—including the 'tarantella', as a notion associated with St. Vitus's dance in medical history and geography—transform through repetition and association across what Foucault calls the 'order of things', categories of sameness and difference, which I construe as perpetually shifting, not only according to deep-seated (archaeological) a prioris but also by virtue of myriad aporias and black holes, a near infinite string of readings, rereadings, and misreadings that constitute the choreomania concept 'again and again' on the fly.

BABINGTON'S MARGINALIA: GEOGRAPHIC THRILLS AND COLONIAL EXOTICA

Addition, annotation, and marginalia constituted some of the most fecund means by which choreomania expanded and moved. Babington in particular offered a growing cast of narratives freely appended to Hecker's own, opening the floodgates to further tales emphasizing Oriental others. Freshly back from his travels in India, as interest in colonial administration was buzzing in the medical halls of London, Babington, a widely read polyglot who dabbled in poetry,

published a volume of sonnets, stanzas, and songs and translated folktales from the Tamil, as well as a Tamil grammar translated from the Latin. He integrated into Hecker's compendium a range of anecdotes and asides from England's imperial realm, adding a flavour of exoticism and thrill to Hecker's already outlandish mix.

Hecker himself had set the stage for such comparisons, employing a number of foreign sources to compile his study, notably Pearce's autobiography and travelogue *The Life and Adventures of Nathaniel Pearce, written by himself, during a residence in Abyssinia, from the year 1810 to 1819* (1831), published fortuitously as Hecker was composing his essay. Hecker used Pearce's story as 'testimonial', an 'eye-witness' account of the African 'dancing mania', the *tigretier*.[24] Quoting from Pearce at length, Hecker employs the example of the *tigretier* to reinforce the notion that dance manias occurred everywhere: one had only to reach to the nearest edition of the local newspaper or the nearest reprint of a traveller's tale to find studies of wild and disinhibited dancing. In this respect, Hecker drew from the past, but also the exotic present, inviting more such exoticizing asides.

Babington was zealous in his use of footnotes and appendices, employing his status as translator to advance what had become an increasingly global comparative project. Besides adding bibliographic references and details—such as mention of wax figures ('*peri cunculas*') believed to have been used by witches at the time of Paracelsus's writing on St. Vitus's dance[25]—Babington provided entire case studies of the condition. An eleven-year-old girl in Renfrewshire in 1696, whose account he has learned of from the Glaswegian physician Robert Watt (1774–1819), 'had violent fits of leaping, dancing, running, crying, fainting, &c'. But, as Watt put it, because 'the whole narrative is mixed up with so much credulity and superstition . . . it is "impossible"', he lamented, 'to separate truth from fiction'. Watt's account, published in Edinburgh in 1698 as 'A true Narrative of the Sufferings of a Young Girl, who was strangely molested by evil spirits, and their instruments, in the West, collected from authentic testimonies', attributed this episode to witchcraft. A Privy Council held on 19 January 1697 had issued a warrant, Babington

23. Michel Foucault, *L'archéologie du savoir* (Paris: Éditions Gallimard, 1969), 11.

24. Nathaniel Pearce, *The Life and Adventures of Nathaniel Pearce, written by himself, during a residence in Abyssinia, from the year 1810 to 1819*, ed. J. J. Halls, Esq., 2 vols., vol. 1 (London: Henry Colburn and Richard Bentley, 1831).

25. Babington, translator's note, in Hecker, *Epidemics of the Middle Ages*, 94n1.

notes, on the 'grounds of suspicion of witch-craft in Renfrewshire'; the commission, signed by eleven privy councillors, issued a further warrant on 5 April 1697 'to try the persons accused of witchcraft, and to sentence the guilty to be burned, or otherwise executed to death'.[26] This historical footnote, indebted to Watt's article, 'Cases of Periodical Jactitation, or Chorea', published in *Medico-Chirurgical Transactions* (1814), recuperated Watt's story of witchcraft and delusions into a comparatively new biomedical and biohistorical sphere, between dance, disease, and the history of 'superstition'. The girl's fits of leaping, dancing, running, and crying—erroneously, Babington reasoned after Watt, attributed to witchcraft—could now be folded into the arena of neurological science and the renewed science of epidemic disease: specifically, the dancing mania.

Babington's examples, like Hecker's, appeared pell-mell. This story was followed immediately by another lengthy example, which Babington appended to Hecker's mention of 'Lycanthropy', a phenomenon discussed, Babington suggests, by Burton in his *Anatomy of Melancholy*, as well as by Avicenna (980–1037), Pliny (23–79), and a wide range of other classical authors.[27] In the example Babington puts forward, a group of nuns reportedly began mewing like cats; one nun had begun this trend, and was followed by her peers. In Germany a similar case of so-called zoanthropy occurred in which a nun 'fell to biting all her companions'; soon 'all the nuns of this convent began biting each other'. As 'the

news of this infatuation among the nuns soon spread', it 'passed from convent to convent throughout a great part of Germany', reaching Holland and Rome.[28] Babington saw this as a case furthering the scope of Hecker's interest in lycanthropy (belief that one has turned into a wolf), which had served as a particular example of pathological imitation not necessarily involving dance.

Babington's comparative transcultural approach to events analogous to St. Vitus's dance extended Hecker's transcultural and transhistorical study to form a second history of the 'dancing mania' in the margins of Hecker's essay, providing readers with a taste of Orientalist exoticism largely absent from the original. In a footnote appended to Hecker's general comment about the existence of 'similar fanatical sects [exhibiting] among all nations of ancient and modern times the same [dancing] phenomena'—an implicit invitation to further Hecker's narrative with new case studies—Babington offered yet another example of his own. He described a case of 'religious fanaticism' in Cairo, narrated in *Recollections of Egypt, by the Baroness Von Minutoli* (1827). The narrative, which he reproduced verbatim, described a monk 'singing, or more properly crying . . . while *dancing* on his heels, the name of Allah, till, completely exhausted, he sank down insensible'. Wolfardine Auguste Luise von Minutoli (1794–1868), Babington noted, wrote that 'these unhappy visionaries . . . often expire at the end of this holy *dance*', prompting Babington to add, again

---

26. Babington, translator's note, in Hecker, *Epidemics of the Middle Ages*, 99–100n2.

27. Babington, translator's note, in Hecker, *Epidemics of the Middle Ages*, 101n1. The article is by Robert Watt, president of the Faculty of Physicians and Surgeons at Glasgow, physician to the Royal Infirmary, and lecturer on the theory and practice of physic at Glasgow, in *Medico-Chirurgical Transactions* 5 (1814): 1–23. Watt opens his essay with a brief story of dancing at St. Vitus's chapel, near Ulm, adding that although this tradition and 'the convulsive disease to which children are liable' may be 'considerably different' phenomena, 'yet the two affections are perhaps nothing more than different species or varieties of the same disease'. He proceeds to note that he had the opportunity to see 'one of these restless people', an account of which he submits to the Medical and Chirurgical Society of London, adding that this disease, which seems to have a range of subspecies and varieties, is always characterized by an 'ungovernable propensity to motion' and is always relieved by 'muscular exertion' (1).

28. Babington, translator's note, in Hecker, *Epidemics of the Middle Ages*, 117–118n4. Further species of pathological contagion were noted by Hecker in cases describing the human imitation of wolves (lycanthropy). He wrote that it is 'an extraordinary species of insanity, which, having existed in Greece, before our era, spread, in process of time, over Europe, so that it was communicated not only to the Romaic, but also to the German and Sarmatian nations, and descended from the ancients, as a legacy of affliction to posterity'. Calmeil, *De la folie*, describes cases of lycanthropy from the annals of French history, 87–88, 279–283, 310, and 416–427. Esquirol cites cases of lycanthropy and cynanthropy (belief that one has turned into a dog) in *Des maladies mentales* (1838). For Esquirol, this behaviour was attributable to 'demonomania', a form of monomania descended from pagan cults in which animal sacrifice was a socially sanctioned way to give thanks to the gods. Esquirol, *Des maladies mentales*, 521–522. See also Jules Bernard Luys, *Études de physiologie et de pathologie cérébrales* (Paris: Baillière, 1874); T. K. Osterreich, *Possession, Demoniacal and Other, among Primitive Races, in Antiquity, the Middle Ages, and Modern Times*, trans. D. Ibberson (New York: Richard R. Smith, 1930), 191–192. Georges Devereux, in 'Le diagnostic en psychiatrie primitive: Théorie générale du diagnostic' (1963), describes the 'chien fou' (mad dog) syndrome, a term used to designate behaviour accepted in Crow culture as a means to express anger. Georges Devereux, *Essais d'ethnopsychiatrie générale* (Paris: Gallimard, 1970), 286–316, 310.

for the sake of comparison, that 'the same fanatical zeal' exists in Arabia.[29]

Babington culls the Arabian case from an anonymous history of the Wahabis published in Paris in 1810, according to which sheiks cried a prayer out to Allah for hours until they were forced at length to be silenced. Exhausted and sweating profusely, they fell down in the middle of a crowd of pious onlookers, who gathered around them, quickly lifting them back to their feet. The ecstasies were dangerous, Babington wrote, for happenstance Christian onlookers, who were forced to witness these events because of their unhappy public location.[30] But Babington was not too concerned with the Christians' moral sanity, simply noting the discomfort this enforced proximity produced in them; his stated concern was to depict cases of dancing manias and similar events around the world and thus to extend Hecker's already comparative project with illustrations further proving its global range.

In his 'Translator's Preface', Babington warned his readers that he had taken the liberty of adding footnotes to Hecker's text that he trusted would be 'not inapplicable' to his readers' interests and might shed further light on the cases described. His footnotes and appendices consisted 'chiefly of parallel accounts in illustration of what is set forth in the text'.[31] An appendix, consisting of a detailed account of 'fits of dancing' from the Edinburgh Medical and Surgical Journal, excerpts from Felix Robertson's medical thesis (chapter 5 here), an article by Mr. Kinder Wood (1785–1830) published in Medico-Chirurgical Transactions, and other contemporary sources, completed his substantive contribution to Hecker's study. But Babington was also not impervious to the entertaining quality of his stories for the curious modern reader. He remarked in his preface that the purpose of the compilation—by which 'the physician may enlarge his knowledge of disease, and the moralist may gather a hint for the intellectual improvement of his fellow-men'—also resided in 'leisure', a term he used repeatedly

to characterize the activity that consisted of reading these accounts and the danger among those doing so to succumb to the 'disorders' the narrations described. 'There is no class', wrote Babington, 'even in this age of boasted reason, wholly exempt from the baneful influence of fanaticism. . . . And instances are not wanting, in our own days, and in this very capital, to prove, that disorders (how can we more charitably designate them?) much resembling some of those described in the following pages, may make their appearance among people who have had all the advantages of an enlightened education, and every opportunity of enlarging their minds by a free intercourse with refined society'.[32] This medical history served doubly to enlighten and to entertain—as well as to counsel—his readership, constituted, in Babington's view, as much by physicians as by 'moralists'.[33] His project was to caution as well as to please. Building on the legacy of 'polite' leisure that the eighteenth-century reader of geography had enjoyed, Babington noted that his own modern reader suffered a new sort of pleasure, a real frisson in the face of dangers—each more exotic than the next—looming on every page. Fifty years earlier, in the New and complete system of geography, containing a full, accurate, authentic and interesting account and description of Europe, Asia, Africa, and America, etc. (1778–1779), Charles Theodore Middleton, Esq., had described the experience of reading about foreign parts of the world 'by the most polite . . . persons of both sexes' as procuring a delightful form of leisure as well as self-edification. 'Next to the knowledge of ourselves', Middleton wrote, 'the knowledge of the world is essentially necessary, which can be acquired only by the pleasing study of Geography. This interesting science . . . [is] at once instructive and entertaining, by conveying the most useful information in the delightfullest manner, and giving to precepts of the utmost importance all the captivating graces of a refined amusement'.[34] Geography presented its readers with the spectacle of faraway lands peopled by extraordinary creatures, customs, and landscapes.

29. Babington, translator's note, in Hecker, Epidemics of the Middle Ages, 139n5. See Baroness von Minutoli, Recollections of Egypt, by the Baroness von Minutoli, trans. S. L. H. (London: Treutell & Würtz, Treuttel, Jun. & Richter, 1827), 69.

30. Babington, translator's note, in Hecker, Epidemics of the Middle Ages, 139–140n5.

31. B. G. Babington, 'Translator's Preface' ['The Dancing Mania'], in Hecker, Epidemics of the Middle Ages, 76–78, 78.

32. Babington, 'Translator's Preface' ['The Dancing Mania'], in Hecker, Epidemics of the Middle Ages, 77.

33. Babington, 'Translator's Preface' ['The Dancing Mania'], in Hecker, Epidemics of the Middle Ages, 77.

34. Charles Theodore Middleton, 'Preface', in A new and complete system of geography. Containing a full, accurate, authentic and interesting account and description of Europe, Asia, Africa, and America . . . , 2 vols., vol. 1 (London: J. Cooke, 1778–1779), n.p.

It was a tool for exercising the imagination, 'by contrasting the manners of savage and civilized nations together . . . insensibly [to] [benefit] by the bright side of the comparison'.[35] But as Middleton writes, this sort of comparativism 'fed' and 'grew rich' on 'captivating speculations' born from the 'polite' contemplation of climates and revolutions, political and commercial interests of state, and the rise and fall of empires. It concerned the historian, the politician, the philosopher, the naturalist, the antiquarian, the merchant, and the literatus, as well as the 'simply curious' person. By the nineteenth century, a far more sensationalizing approach to world geographies had gained ground as extensive colonial administration prompted physicians to disseminate their findings to audiences worldwide. Babington, after Hecker, was at the helm of this boat, which travelled on what appeared to be far rockier waters.

Babington's most sensationalizing contribution to Hecker's work may be an extensive footnote to a passing comment Hecker makes regarding the tarantella. Hecker describes the Persian habit of counteracting the ingestion of venomous substances—such as the tarantula's poison—by drenching the wounded person in milk 'and then, by violent rotary motion in a suspended box, [compelling] him to vomit'.[36] Babington argues in his footnote that among the Psylli of Egypt, 'another illustration' tells of a sect that, 'according to the testimony of modern writers', 'continues to exhibit the same strange spectacles as the ancient serpent-eaters of Cyrene'. 'A band of these seeming madmen', Babington writes, 'with bare arms and wild demeanour, held enormous serpents in their hands which writhed round their bodies and endeavoured to make their escape. These Psylli, grasping them by the neck, tore them with their teeth and ate them up alive, the blood streaming down from their polluted mouths. Others . . . striving to wrest their prey from them' struggled 'mightily', offering the 'populace' (which 'followed them with amazement') performances 'believed . . . to be miraculous'. These serpent-eaters passed 'for

persons inspired' and possessed by a spirit who destroyed the serpent's effect.[37] Although the example otherwise bore little resemblance to the tarantella, the public spectacle of poison extraction warranted a lengthy comparison.

Examples proliferated in Babington's version of Hecker's text. Serpent-eating, associated with dramatic performances of poison ingestion, constituted a marginal form of choreomania in Babington's view. A recent explorer's narrative provided by the French naturalist Charles-Nicolas-Sigisbert Sonnini de Manoncourt (Sonnini) (1751–1812) and published in *Hunter's Translation of Sonnini's Travels* (1799) offered a further eyewitness account, enabling Hecker's scenes to resonate with contemporary history and once again offering medical practitioners and the general public a stimulating read. Although Babington did not add any further gloss to Sonnini's tale and merely integrated it into his marginalia verbatim, his decision to append it to the word 'imposture', which Hecker employed to describe tarantism, underscored the analogy of these events with reported practices in the Orient. Sonnini's account, recuperated by Babington, likened the practices of an Egyptian sect and a late medieval Italian form of a so-called dancing mania exhibiting similar types of venomous ingestion and imposture. The tale underscored three variables: poison; convulsions and frenzy; and the theatrical imposture governing the whole affair, staged as a public event putatively to inspire terror and awe. There was notably little dancing involved. But for Babington, the mise en scène of the expulsion of poison presented an occasion to describe what looked like contemporary remnants of an early modern phenomenon, especially dramatized in the flamboyant East. Sonnini was 'not so fortunate as to witness a public exhibition of such performances', Babington noted, but his account of a private encounter with members of the sect offered him 'a remarkable specimen of the extravagance of man', albeit orchestrated by himself.[38] Every year, Sonnini noted, the Saadi (serpent-eaters) 'walk in procession through

35. Middleton, 'Preface', n.p.

36. Hecker, *Epidemics of the Middle Ages*, 119–120.

37. Babington, translator's note, in Hecker, *Epidemics of the Middle Ages*, 120–121n4. Von Minutoli describes the Psylli as a 'separate class, descended from the ancient Psylli, mentioned by Pliny, Celsus, and other writers of antiquity', further linking, as Babington and others would do, modern Egyptians to a broadly Mediterranean antiquity recuperated into the history of the modern (often northern) European West (in *Recollections of Egypt*, 67).

38. Babington, translator's note, in Hecker, *Epidemics of the Middle Ages*, 121n4. See Charles-Nicolas-Sigisbert Sonnini de Manoncourt, *Travels in Upper and Lower Egypt, undertaken by order of the old government of France, by C. S. Sonnini, engineer in the French navy, and member of several scientific and literary societies. Illustrated with forty engravings; consisting of portraits, views, plans, a*

the streets, each holding in his hand a living serpent, which he bites, gnaws, and swallows piecemeal, with frightful grimaces and contortions'. Sonnini then 'contrived to procure [himself] . . . in [his] own house [such] a spectacle'.[39] As Babington recounts it, Sonnini tells of a Saadi coming to his apartment with a priest of the sect. This entailed the performance of a sort of snake-dance, in which the Saadi bit the snake's head off, ingesting its poison, which caused him to writhe and convulse. Sonnini's words, translated by Rev. Henry Hunter (1741–1802), were reprised by Babington in the same footnote:

> With a vigorous hand the *Saadi* seized the serpent. . . . He began to appear agitated; his countenance was discomposed; his eyes rolled; he uttered terrible cries, bit the animal in the head, and tore off a morsel, which we saw him chew and swallow. On this his agitation became convulsive; his howlings were redoubled, his limbs writhed, his countenance assumed the features of madness, and his mouth, extended by terrible grimaces, was all in foam . . . . Three men endeavoured to hold him, but he dragged them all three round the chamber. His arms were thrown about with violence on all sides, and struck everything within their reach.[40]

As the priest took hold of the 'madman' and 'recited some prayers', his 'agitation diminished, and subsided into a state of complete lassitude'. Sonnini went on to note that the Turks who were present at this 'ridiculous and disgusting ceremony' firmly believed in the reality of the 'religious fury'. He added that it might have been either 'reality or imposture' but conceded that it was 'impossible to see the transports of rage and madness exhibited in a more striking manner' or to have before one's eyes 'a man more calculated

to inspire terror'.[41] Poison ingestion produced theatrical convulsions—real or fake—and while these were clearly spectacular for observers in the East, their narrative recuperations in the medical literature on the dancing disease made them more spectacular still, examples of a transhistorical epidemic that could seize readers themselves unawares.

This additive trope, suggesting the possibility of a near infinite number of further studies, provided the illusion of universality. Yet pathologists saw in the reiterations and repetitions of choreomania a sign of continuous change, indeed a type of *surrogation* or reperformance, by which choreomania always became itself—or something slightly different—again. Choreomania was, in its proliferating centres, mobile. Challenging the idea that diseases were biologically fixed, the French pathologist and historian Charles Anglada (1809–1878) argued that new diseases often appeared just as ancient ones became extinct. Some diseases underwent resurgences but often transformed as they did so.[42] Choreomanias appeared to be as old as human history, or older—animal, geological—and as the particular purview of the time and place at which they arose.

'SICILY IMPLIES ASIA AND AFRICA': LIVING RUINS AT EUROPE'S EDGE

In this sense, 'choreomania' emerged in the interstices between literature and medicine, performance and ethnography, as their imaginary empty middle, the chasm out of which global scientific modernity arose. But globalism was not homogenization; rather, it constituted myriad pockets and nodes, zones, and gulfs. No writer has been more credited with inventing a planetary scale of comparative literature than Goethe; yet even his analyses of *Weltliteratur* (world literature) suggest differential relations.[43]

---

geographical chart, antiquities, plants, animals & c. Drawn on the spot, under the author's inspection. Translated from the French by Henry Hunter, D. D., 3 vols., vol. 2 (London: John Stockdale, 1799), 38–43.

39. In Sonnini, *Travels in Upper and Lower Egypt*, 38–39.

40. Babington, translator's note, in Hecker, *Epidemics of the Middle Ages*, 121n4. See Sonnini, *Travels in Upper and Lower Egypt*, vol. 2, 40.

41. Babington, translator's note, in Hecker, *Epidemics of the Middle Ages*, 121n4. See Sonnini, *Travels in Upper and Lower Egypt*, vol. 2, 41.

42. Charles Anglada, *Étude sur les maladies éteintes et les maladies nouvelles, pour server à l'histoire des évolutions séculaires de la pathologie* (Paris: J.-B. Baillière, 1869). Anglada argued that demonomania, lycanthropy, spectropathy, choreomania or St. Vitus's dance (*danse de Saint-Guy*), tarantism, and convulsive theomania were not epidemics, as Hecker had thought, but neuroses originating in mental processes and propagated by what he called the instinct of imitation; they did not present real anatomical alterations among those affected, however intense the mental aberrations and sensorimotor troubles (50).

43. See e.g. David Damrosch, *What Is World Literature?* (Princeton, NJ: Princeton University Press, 2003).

In writing of his travels through southern Italy in the second half of the eighteenth century, Goethe wrote that for him, 'Sicily implies Asia and Africa'.[44] The Italian South, as performance ethnographer Jerri Daboo among others has pointed out, was widely imagined as a land of exotic rustics, an Oriental backwater more closely associated with the '"dark lands" of the Indies' than with Western Europe. It was a 'territory of passage', between east and west, north and south, yet in its relative isolation it bore a greater relationship to India than to northern Italy, according to Jesuit authorities who in the sixteenth century sent their missionaries there first to train for positions further east.[45] Jutting out into the Mediterranean at the southernmost tip of Europe, southern Italy bordered Africa to the south and the southern Balkans to the east. The Orientalist fantasy of the southern Italian peasant as a dark African or Asiatic other was counterbalanced only by the equally pervasive image of southern Italy as a land basking in classical antiquity. Southern Italy and Greece, for cultivated northerners, stood not only for Africa but also for all that was ancient. The ruins at Pompeii and Herculaneum were being excavated throughout the nineteenth century after their rediscovery in 1748, and travellers wishing to gain a taste of the exotic past looked to Europe's southerly backyard for an experience of ancient times.

In this antiquarian and archaeological fever, European visitors similarly 'discovered' the dance of the tarantella as living human remains conjuring Dionysian bacchanals. As Daboo has suggested, travellers such as Goethe and Henry Swinburne (1743–1803) found in the free movement of women dancing to tambourines a form of excess and eroticism that recalled to them ancient Maenads.[46] The past had seemingly stopped in these arid lands, and antiquity,

with some prompting, came into view. Writing *Travels in the Two Sicilies, by Henry Swinburne, esq., in the years 1777, 1778, 1789, and 1780* (1790), Swinburne described his experience, like Sonnini, commissioning a performance of the tarantella for his own edification. Finding no peasants presently engaging in this ancient practice, he located a *tarantata*—a woman who had been bitten by a tarantula—and bid her 'act the part'.[47] She complied and, accompanied by a 'great many musicians' summoned for the purposes, offered what she could of the ritual—performing it, he was assured by 'all present . . . to perfection'—until Swinburne finally terminated the event, judging it distasteful:

> At first she lolled stupidly on a chair, while the instruments were playing some dull music. They touched, at length, the chord supposed to vibrate to her heart, and up she sprang with a most hideous yell, staggered about the room like a drunken person, holding a handkerchief in both hands, raising them alternately, and moving in very true time. As the music grew brisker, her motions quickened, and she skipped about with great vigour and variety of steps, every now and then shrieking very loud. The scene was far from pleasant; and, at my desire, an end was put to it before the woman was tired.[48]

This woman's performance of the tarantella— 'stupid' and 'dull'—was far removed from the fantasy he had of it. For Swinburne, the tarantella revealed the crude remains of 'heathenish rites' and, more gloriously, Dionysian ecstasies. Tarantella dancers were in his view 'exact copies of the ancient priestesses of Bacchus' whose 'orgies' provided 'so darling an amusement' to worshippers. The rites of Dionysus, Swinburne

---

44. Johann Wolfgang von Goethe, *Italian Journey (1786–1788)*, trans. Elizabeth Meyer and W. H. Auden (London: Collins, 1962), 212; cited in Daboo, *Ritual, Rapture and Remorse*, 20.

45. Daboo, *Ritual, Rapture and Remorse*, 15, 20. On the Jesuit missionaries' imaginary of the region as an 'Italian India', see esp. Daboo, *Ritual, Rapture and Remorse*, 19–24; and de Martino, *La terra del rimorso*, 22–24. See also Jane Schneider, ed., *Italy's 'Southern Question': Orientalism in One Country* (Oxford: Berg, 1998). Daboo notes that the image of southern Italy as gateway to the past still holds. Conducting ethnographic research on the revival of tarantella music and dance practices, particularly with the Notte della Taranta festival held in the region since 1998, now attracting hundreds of thousands of visitors, she spoke to a man from Bologna (in the north) who admitted that 'he loved coming to Salento to experience the ancient past, the traditional life that was no longer present in the industrial North, but which he could hear in the music of the *pizzica*, now captured on his [MP3] player' (*Ritual, Rapture and Remorse*, 232).

46. Daboo, *Ritual, Rapture and Remorse*, 32.

47. Henry Swinburne, *Travels in the Two Sicilies, by Henry Swinburne, esq., in the years 1777, 1778, 1789, and 1780*, 2nd ed., 4 vols., vol. 2 (London: J. Nichols for T. Cadell and P. Elmsly, 1790), 304–305. See also Daboo, *Ritual, Rapture and Remorse*, 152–154.

48. Swinburne, *Travels in the Two Sicilies*, vol. 2, 305.

wrote, though 'memory of [their] ancient name and institution' had been 'effaced' after 'the introduction of Christianity [had] abolished all public exhibitions of these heathenish rites', were recuperated into the southern Italian tarantella and translated into the worship of St. Paul, who by the early modern period had become widely adopted as the *tarantati*'s Christian saint.[49] But Swinburne's fantasy and the practices he encountered failed to mesh. Peasants seemed to be poor copies of the ancient past; even when bidden, they seemed not to be able to remember the ancient history he thought their primitive bodies and minds so perfectly preserved.

The exalted image of the ancient dance of the *tarantati* carefully cultivated by foreigners poorly matched the reality of tarantella practices on the ground. Southern Italian peasants, Swinburne thought, performed bacchanalian remains: they beat the tambourine and sang in the Phrygian musical mode familiar from Near Eastern music, hands waving or clapping overhead, appearing to visitors such as himself to step right out of literary and pictorial representations of the ancient Greco-Roman world, yet they fell short of the ancient majesty of their Dionysian forebears—or of the ancient Greeks' fastidious northern European imitators. The southern Italian peasants' rituals seemed enigmatically to arise out of the past, preserving and performing antiquity, while disappointing the modern traveller anxious to catch a glimpse of what he thought he knew.

By Swinburne's account the Neapolitan tarantella, 'a low dance, consisting of turns on the heel, much footing, and snapping of the fingers', provided a 'holiday-diversion' for young women who, without knowing it, he contended, mimicked the 'ancestral' 'pictures of Herculaneum'.[50] Yet the tarantella also participated at times in actual physiological disease, he surmised, and had not entirely left behind those traces. Swinburne saw two types of dances: for the most part the dances were, he wrote, religious and spiritual holdovers from ancient Greece, elegant and refined. But in rare cases they still revealed a grotesque and rather pedestrian form of nervous disorder, which resembled but could not be equated with the religious rites of ancient Greece. 'If at any time these dancers are really

and involuntarily affected [by the spider's poison]', Swinburne remarked, 'I can suppose it to be nothing more than an attack upon their nerves, a species of St. Vitus's dance'.[51] St. Vitus's dance, in this usage, denoted chorea, later Sydenham's chorea (and eventually Huntington's chorea), terms ascribed to a range of spasmodic neurological conditions, as I have shown. When it appeared as 'nothing more' than this nervous disease, the tarantella bore little historiographic or artistic merit in Swinburne's mind; it was an 'attack upon the nerves', the mechanical result of animal toxicity, involuntary and fitful. It did not reveal any special insight into the ancient past, he thought. But those cases were exceptional; and for the most part, Swinburne remarked, the tarantella offered a special sort of knowledge about the moving past.

It may be that some women and men did suffer from chorea. But this neurological disorder is relatively rare, and Swinburne's desire to find in the tarantella a key to ancient history suggests a colonial drive to plumb history by way of contemporary bodies. These bodies, he, like his contemporaries, believed, resided more closely to the past by virtue of their residence at the imagined hinterlands of modern industrialized space. Peasants in the south of Italy were seen to be doubly removed from northern European visitors—by their class and their geography. As such, they appeared to observers to possess a special capacity to perform naturally and artlessly what northern Europeans reperformed by scholarly design. Reconstruction of ancient dances through the careful imitation of pictorial evidence from vase paintings and ethnographic narratives enabled some scholars, hobbyists, and artists to create imaginary versions of tarantellas or other 'ethnographic' dances. The figure of the tarantella, moving from southern Italy north, was by the nineteenth century becoming a crucible for phantasmatic imaginings of exotic alterity.

Dancers took note. The Austrian ballerina Fanny Elssler (1810–1884) famously rendered a lithe and graceful tarantella for the stage in *La Tarentule* [The Tarantula] (1839), a ballet pantomime set in the exotic province of Calabria. In this story, a young man is bitten by a tarantula and attended by a dirty old charlatan,

49. Swinburne, *Travels in the Two Sicilies*, vol. 2, 306–307.

50. Swinburne, *Travels in the Two Sicilies*, vol. 1, 94–95. Even the women's hairdos reproduced those 'seen on the Greek and Roman coins' (95).

51. Swinburne, *Travels in the Two Sicilies*, vol. 2, 306–307.

Omeopatico (Homeopath), who promises to cure him in exchange for the hand of the young man's fiancée. Horrified, she feigns being bitten by a tarantula herself and in imitation of her lover performs a convulsive dance. Faking death at the end of her performance, she is then swept away by friends and relatives, soon to be reunited with her fiancé.[52] The themes of lovesickness, deceit, peasant life, and feverish pain, treated lightly on the operatic stage, conjugate high romance and comedic misunderstanding with the spectacularity of convulsive disorders. Elssler's portrayal inspired Irish-born, self-styled 'Spanish' dancer Lola Montez (1821–1861) to render her own version of a tarantella-like dance in her gleefully erotic performance, *Spider Dance* (1855), in which she notoriously lifted her skirt above her head to reveal that she was wearing nothing underneath. Both works articulated the tarantella as a dance of seduction and femininity and, in Montez's case, dangerous sexuality and taboo. The tarantella on- and offstage projected a host of fantasies about the sexual life of 'savages' onto the Italian South, also crystallizing the imagined connection between exotic dance, antiquity, and nervous disease.

ORIENTALIST FANTASIES: TABLEAUX AND *ATTITUDES*

Swinburne's graphic imagination of the orgiastic Greco-Roman world derived from his encounter with classical literature and fanciful reconstructions popular among northern Europeans in the late eighteenth century. Some of these reconstructions were choreographed theatrical events, performed not onstage but in everyday life. Clad in a Grecian robe, Lady Emma Hamilton (1765–1815), wife of the British ambassador to Naples, Sir William Hamilton (1731–1803) and an experienced actress and hostess, presented visitors to their Neapolitan villa with what she called *attitudes* mimicking—like Charcot's hysteroepileptic maenads—Greek vase paintings, statues, and frescoes. She was depicted as a bacchante by the French rococo painter Louise Élisabeth Vigée

Le Brun (1755–1842) (fig. 7.1) and as a *tarantata* by the English portrait painter George Romney (1734–1802) before returning to England to teach her version of the tarantella to young women of the upper classes.[53] Lady Hamilton's endeavour to mimic Grecian *attitudes* suggests a contrapuntal movement transforming the tarantella just as these imitations sought to grasp it. Her exercises represented at once a northern European performance of antiquity transplanted onto a modern Neapolitan context and the artistic and scientific research processes by which this mimicry enabled the fantasy of greater access to an 'other'—portrayed as one's own special colonial heritage and bequest.

Literary and pictorial representations reinforced the image Europeans had of the ancient, Oriental tarantella and its proximity to the Bacchic past. In the novel *Corinne, ou l'Italie* (1807) by Madame de Staël (1766–1817), the heroine dances a tarantella in a ballroom in Naples, suggesting by her 'ritual steps' and 'sensual' movements the 'power exercised by the temple dancing girls over the Indian [sic] imagination'.[54] The 'charming tableaux' that her 'graceful' poses suggested would not be familiar only to De Staël's readers, who might experience a frisson implied in the comparison of Corinne's moves to those of voluptuous harem girls. The tableaux were also familiar to Corinne herself, who in her educated, free-spirited, and modern way 'knew so well all the poses depicted by the ancient painters and sculptors that, with a slight movement of the arms, placing her tambourine now above her head, now in front of her with one hand while the other ran along the bells with incredible skill, she brought to mind the dancing girls of Herculaneum and aroused, one after another, a host of new ideas for drawing and painting'.[55] Corinne embodied the modern woman's discovery of classical antiquity and her ability simultaneously to capture and to transcend the magic of ancient and modern art—sculpture, drawing, and painting—in her sensual moves. In Corinne, the power of imitation met an implicit prior knowledge of these forms in her erotic dance, underscoring her intellectual and carnal knowledge of antiquity and the East.

---

52. *La Tarentule, ballet pantomime en deux actes. Par M. Coralli. Musique de M. Casimir Gide* (Paris: Chez Jonas, Libraire de l'opéra, 1839).

53. Daboo, *Ritual, Rapture and Remorse*, 32–34.

54. Germaine de Staël (Madame de Staël), *Corinne, or, Italy*, trans. and ed. Sylvia Raphael (Oxford: Oxford University Press, 1998), 90–91. Daboo, *Ritual, Rapture and Remorse*, 35–36.

55. De Staël, *Corinne*, 90–91.

FIGURE 7.1   Portrait of Emma, Lady Hamilton as a Bacchante, by Louise Élisabeth Vigée Le Brun, c. 1790.

Tarantellas throughout the nineteenth and early twentieth centuries were purported to serve, paradoxically, both as a means by which women could know the past and as a window onto an ultimately unknowably ancient other. Tarantellas, more than any other form of choreomania, epitomized to their medical observers female knowledge and feminine deceit at once: animal automatisms and the careful ruse of the woman (as well as the colonial person) craftily ensnaring observers in her elaborate play. Wrapped into a medical discourse on hysteria, tarantellas corresponded to what Diamond describes as a 'modernist hunger for "primitive" experience'[56] and to what she notes were the 'accusations of fakery' that accompany hysteria of all sorts.[57] In Diamond's terms, 'hysteria marks the eruption of the lower, the animal', the dangerously sexual and, as such, the 'inexplicable'.[58] Hysteria, as a characteristic disorder most dramatically manifest among those understood to be intensely, even pathologically attuned to the ancient world through travel, imagination, or their own culture—implicitly tied to the geocultural territory associated with it—suggested a form of alterity that could be organized and described but, significantly, revealed resistance to the sort of knowing Said construes as characteristic of Orientalist structures of implicit power. The tarantella, widely understood in medicine and travel literature as a 'hysterical' form of dancing disease, presented to its observers a hermeneutic impasse, ultimately a performance of that which resisted scientific knowledge and thus

56. Diamond, *Unmaking Mimesis*, 39.
57. Diamond, *Unmaking Mimesis*, 9. See also Lüdtke, *Dances with Spiders*, 42, 56.
58. Diamond, *Unmaking Mimesis*, 9.

compelled observers to collection and comparison. Dancing diseases—like the Italian South, which played host to them—served as a litmus test, an imagined border, against which the fantasy of reason struck before tumbling into what (typically northern) Europeans perceived as childlike, animal irrationality: a force that was vaguely 'African', bodily, fitful, uncontrolled, and feminine in the ostensibly seductive impossibility of its being known.

As Said has argued of the long nineteenth century's Orientalist discourse, the imaginative distinction between 'our land' and 'barbarian land' 'does not require that the barbarians acknowledge the distinction'.[59] On the contrary, 'modern and primitive societies seem . . . to derive a sense of their identities negatively':[60] societies are defined primarily in terms of what they are *not* or, far more powerfully, what they *imagine* themselves not to be. More than this, Said notes, degrees of distance and proximity determine our sense of ourselves; and these too can be imaginary, fictitious. Our 'imaginative geography and history', Said writes, help us to 'intensify' our own sense of ourselves 'by dramatizing the distance and difference between what is close to it and what is far away'.[61] Sometimes, dramas depict tensions between imagined or felt senses of proximity and distance, sameness and alterity, kinship and foreignness, as in the many Attic tragedies that portray Oriental others: most prominently Dionysus, the emphatically Asiatic god whose excesses epitomized what may have been experienced as real threats from the ecstatic religions and mystery cults of Asia Minor and the Levant that were introduced into Athens during the Peloponnesian War.[62] Translated into nineteenth-century medical culture, southern Italy's status as a gateway to Africa excited and worried observers who were projecting nearly unknowable antiquity onto it.

A DOLL'S HOUSE: WORMHOLES ONTO MODERNITY

Nora, in Ibsen's play *A Doll's House*, performs a symbolically curative dance at a hinge moment in her narrative, as she is poised finally to leave her husband, Torvald. Ibsen, like Goethe and Swinburne, was aware of the myth surrounding the tarantella. Travelling through southern Italy while preparing this landmark play, Ibsen found in the dance of the tarantella a wormhole to the past which might catalyse an alternative reality for his modern heroine. In her sexually charged dance of seduction, Nora reveals what we may understand, following Daboo's analysis of the tarantella, after ethnomusicologist Paolo Toschi, as a *pizzica de core* (also known as a *pizzica pizzica*), a *pizzica* of the heart; but Nora also symbolically purges herself of Torvald's poison in what may be construed as a *pizzica tarantata*, a term used to denote the tarantella as a dance of possession and healing.[63]

For Torvald, Nora's dance was not nearly symbolic enough. She danced just 'a trifle too [realistically]' for his taste; her tarantella was 'a little more so than was, strictly speaking, artistically necessary'. His patronizing language fires her up further. Where he saw a 'wild and excitable' and 'childlike' temperament, signalling a discomfiting 'transformation' yet to come, she finds recourse to an ancient and foreign tradition, which she signals with her Italian shawl.[64] Though

59. Said, *Orientalism*, 54.

60. Said, *Orientalism*, 54.

61. Said, *Orientalism*, 55.

62. Said, *Orientalism*, 56.

63. On *pizzica de core* and *pizzica tarantata* see Daboo, *Ritual, Rapture and Remorse*, 24–29. Daboo notes that both originated in Taranto, in southern Italy. She also, after Toschi, notes a third *pizzica*, the *pizzica scherma*, typically performed by men and resembling a martial art representing a sword fight. According to de Martino, whose landmark study on the tarantella brought together a neuropsychiatrist, a psychologist, a cultural anthropologist, and an ethnomusicologist, in *La terra del rimorso* (and accompanying documentary film), harsh socioeconomic realities in the Italian south accounted for much of the persistence of the tarantella in the area. De Martino and his team noted histories of young women as well as men—particularly those working in the fields, more likely to be stung because of their economic precarity (their tendency to work long hours in the summer heat)—suffering from anxiety and depression, exacerbated by the real effects of socioeconomic stress and, resulting from this stress, difficulty maintaining self-esteem and securing love. In de Martino's view, the tarantella transformed from a ritual performance into a symbolic one, serving effectively in the twentieth century as a social salve, with the music and dance enfolding sufferers—of real and symbolic spider bites—back into a supportive community. See de Martino, *La terra del rimorso*, 53–54.

64. Henrik Ibsen, *A Doll's House*, in *A Doll's House and Other Plays*, trans. Peter Watts (London: Penguin Books, 1965), 202, 205, 210–213.

Nora is, Torvald says, his 'little Capri girl' . . . his 'capricious little Capri girl',[65] she understands that her world is lurching forward without him. It can do so, paradoxically, because she finds a way out of the inertia and alienation of her present condition by counterposing it with an alternative temporality (and geography)—in Burt's terms, with an uncannily alien other, facilitating the arrival of another modernity. The West finds in its Orientalizing vision of the primitive other not only its own biocultural prehistory, which it imagines it has surpassed, but a means for achieving self-determination by reconnecting to a supposedly purer state.

This suggests a reading of Ibsen's work away from notions of modernism as radical break with the past. Ibsen's plays are harbingers of modernism—in this case, modern feminism. But the tarantella scene shows this modernism dramatized by a contrapuntal movement 'backwards', connected to ancient and faraway modes of being erupting in a decisive moment of recursion. Modernity, in this regard, moves forward and looks backward—as well as around—just as it seeks points of convergence between parts of the globe and points in history, 'connecting dots' on what Roach calls the 'geohistorical matrix'.[66]

EXUBERANT COMPARATIVISM: THE *TIGRETIER*, MEDICAL GEOGRAPHY, AND COLONIAL TRAVEL

The tarantella was imagined in medical literature as transhistorical yet tethered to the land out of which it arose. It was conceived as a disease of southern Italy and the African South, a colourful (often coloured) variation on a broader dancing condition, choreomania. The grounds for comparison were tenuous, often based on anecdotal evidence. The following section turns to a dance understood by Hecker to be reminiscent of the tarantella, even identical to it, in his 'order of things', his choreomania taxonomy. Although he eventually disavowed the connection, the

ground for transposing early modern Italy onto the African continent was laid with his work, providing the basis for a further set of comparisons linking feminine and colonial duplicity and deceit. In the 1865 edition of his work on the dancing mania, much of the discussion of a so-called dancing mania in Abyssinia—the *tigretier*—disappeared, replaced with a cursory remark by the French physician Alfred Courbon (1829–1895). Courbon, in his 1861 *Observations topographiques et médicales recueillies dans un voyage à l'isthme de Suez etc.* [Medical and Topographical Observations Collected during a Voyage to the Isthmus of Suez etc.], denied the existence of the *tigretier* altogether, discussing instead what he called 'superstitious practices used in Abyssinia with the goal of treating diseases indistinctly, and often employed profitably through the work of deceit [ruse]'.[67] Courbon boasted that he had performed many investigations into this putative disease—the same described by Pearce thirty years prior, reprised by Hecker—and discovered, he surmised, that it did not exist. 'Everything that Pearce said of it is a fable, and most of the circumstances that he supposed, such as the bands of musicians and cold baths, are not even realizable in Abyssinia'.[68] His pronouncement, however offhanded, seems to have convinced Hecker and Hirsch to pull discussion of the *tigretier* out of Hecker's study. Yet Pearce's narrative had, both in Hecker's work and Babington's Orientalizing English translation, invited other writers I will discuss in the following pages to bring further comparisons to bear on dance-like diseases— and disease-like dances—from various parts of the world. Pearce's tale of Oriental Corybantes in Abyssinia offered anecdotal evidence that Bacchic manias were alive and well in the present day. Dancers apparently mimicking the gestures of their ancient and medieval forebears in a ritual in which sufferers were bedecked with borrowed jewels in the cathartic performance of a public dance provided ethnographic evidence for comparative medical history: Europe's past was to be found in its supposed African backyard. The truth-value of the *tigretier* was insignificant in this respect. Its story revealed the image of

---

65. Ibsen, *A Doll's House*, 213.

66. Roach, *Cities of the Dead*, xi.

67. Alfred Courbon, *Observations topographiques et médicales recueillies dans un voyage à l'isthme de Suez, sur le littoral de la mer Rouge et en Abyssinie* (Paris: Imprimerie Rignoux, 1861), 39.

68. Courbon, *Observations topographiques*, 39; quoted in Hecker, *Die Grossen Volkskrankheiten*, 123.

Africa mimicking, reproducing, and preserving an ancient and medieval Europe. Yet with these mimicries came accusations of doubling and, more grievously, deception.

The *tigretier*, Hecker noted, bore an indubitable resemblance to the late medieval and early modern tarantella, providing him—via Pearce's travel narrative—with vivid evidence for his comparative study of the dancing disease. Anecdotal information, drawn up in scenes that could be collated and compared, provided the illusion of scientific universality. Diagnosis took shape through anecdotal accumulation. Even when cases were eventually dismissed, like the *tigretier*, the traces their narratives left in the discursive journeys of the dancing disease made of choreomania an increasingly global complaint. Evidence through travel narratives also made the dancing disease all the more patently transhistorical, transcultural, and urgently contemporary. 'Comparison is the mother of observation', Hecker wrote, 'and may elucidate one phenomenon by another'—in particular 'the past by that which still exists'.[69] Social and political conditions in medieval Germany and early modern Italy, he argued, 'operate on the Abyssinians of the present day' in similar ways, so that 'in regard to superstition', for example, 'the conditions of the Abyssinians of modern times is . . . a mirror of the condition of the European nations in the middle ages'.[70] In Tigray province (what is now northern Ethiopia, bordering Eritrea and Sudan), where the Abyssinian 'dancing mania' was supposed to be most widespread, two occurrences 'completely in accord' with those of the European Middle Ages were observed: a type of Christian flagellation and belief in zoomorphism, 'which presents a lively image of the lycanthropy of the middle ages'.[71] These analogies enabled Hecker to offer further generalizations about choreomania, although his objects of analysis were only nebulously similar: the Abyssinian *tigretier* resembled the tarantella and St. Vitus's dance only inasmuch as its 'victims' showed a spontaneous urge to dance.[72]

They also showed signs of lethargy and listlessness, as in the tarantella, and executed their movements to music provided by hired hands.

Hecker used a number of sources to compile his narrative account, drawing particularly from Pearce's freshly published autobiography and travelogue. Pearce had introduced the strange tale of his wife's affliction by likening it to events depicted in biblical scripture. 'There is . . . a holy water at the church Oun Arvel', he wrote, 'which is greatly esteemed for the cure of persons afflicted with evil spirits'.[73] Yet he was aware that his readers might find his description unbelievable: 'This is a very wonderful disorder', he noted, 'which I cannot pass over in silence, though the reader may think it fabulous and ridiculous; yet we have accounts of something of the same kind in the New Testament, which the priests and learned men of Abyssinia believe to be the same complaint'.[74] Although many dances are mentioned in the Old and New Testaments, including Aaron's sister's dance after the passage through the Red Sea, David's dance before the Ark, and Judith's triumphant dance after the defeat of Holofernes, what mattered to Pearce was the convergence of modern-day Africa with the ancient Judeo-Christian past, granting credence, he thought, to this otherwise outlandish tale. But it did not excuse the tale—or events represented by it. On the contrary, the comparison only highlighted the supposedly ancient status of the Africans, who met Europeans such as himself, he thought, in the performance of a now uncannily reliveable past. And though Pearce characterized this dance as 'wonderful', 'fabulous', and 'ridiculous', he also, like Swinburne when he encountered the tarantella, thought it unseemly.

Pearce's description revealed an affliction cured by the public performance of a dance that relieved the dancers of their dispiritedness. He first experienced its effects on a female acquaintance, presumably white and European like himself, and then on his equally white wife—further proof, as far as he was concerned, that this was

---

69. Hecker, *Epidemics of the Middle Ages*, 127.

70. Hecker, *Epidemics of the Middle Ages*, 127.

71. Hecker, *Epidemics of the Middle Ages*, 127. On the history and geography of the Tigray (then frequently referred to as the 'Tigré') region in the early part of the nineteenth century, see George Long, ed., *The Penny Cyclopaedia of the Society for the Diffusion of Useful Knowledge*, 27 vols., vol. 1, A–Andes (London: Charles Knight, 1833), 52–58, 54–57.

72. See Hecker, *Epidemics of the Middle Ages*, 125.

73. Pearce, *The Life and Adventures of Nathaniel Pearce*, vol. 1, 290.

74. Pearce, *The Life and Adventures of Nathaniel Pearce*, vol. 1, 290. For a discussion of early Judeo-Christian dances in biblical literature, in the Old and New Testaments, see e.g. Backman, *Religious Dances*, esp. 9–38.

not just a local superstition confined to darker races but a potentially universal disorder and an ancient type of disease. 'This complaint', more widespread in women than in men, he noted, 'is called *tigretier*'. It 'seizes the body as if with a violent fever, and from that turns to a lingering sickness, which reduces the patients to skeletons, and often kills them, if the relations cannot procure the proper remedy'.[75] The remedy, he added, consists of the victim's relations joining together to defray the expense of a cure by calling upon a doctor who reads the Gospel of John and drenches the patient in cold water daily for seven days, although this unfortunately often resulted in the patient's death. If this approach was not effective, the family hired a band of trumpeters, drummers, and fifers and bought liquor. 'Then all the young men and women of the place assemble at the patient's house', he wrote, 'to perform' an 'extraordinary ceremony',[76] one of which he attended, not without some apprehension.

The display of 'wild'[77] behaviour on the part of the gaunt and sickly young woman he observed at first surprised and appalled him, although he acknowledged the effects of the cure on her. She had been lying for three months in a 'lingering state',[78] her speech reduced to unintelligible stuttering, 'seized with acute agony, and a flood of tears'[79] if a book or a priest were brought before her. She did not refuse Pearce's medicines, though he noted that they had no effect. When his neighbour, whose wife this was, decided finally to 'employ the usual remedy',[80] a band of musicians was arranged and silver ornaments were borrowed from neighbours. Pearce sat near her as she lay, at first, very still; but within two minutes of the music's start, she began to move very slightly, eventually sitting up and then standing, as if the rhythm of the music revived her. Pearce described the event's progression from her initial state of lethargy to her concluding leaps and bounds in a dramaturgical arc that made the whole affair a captivating theatre of emotional recovery. The liveliness of his description in a scenario in which he stages himself as a slightly sceptical but duly observing character offers one of the clearest choreographic accounts

of a so-called dancing mania, suggesting an overall rather controlled and even subdued affair, with little of the involuntary tremors, contractions, or paralyses characterizing the choreas and other neuromotor disorders that were continually likened to these cultural practices. But Pearce emphasized bodily disjointedness, excessive gesture, and (disdainfully) the appearance of egregious uncontrol. He wrote:

> The evening that the band began to play, I seated myself close by her side as she lay upon the couch, and about two minutes after the trumpets had begun to sound, I observed her shoulders begin to move, and soon afterwards her head and breast, and in less than a quarter of an hour she sat upon her couch. The wild look she had, though sometimes she smiled, made me draw off to a greater distance, being almost alarmed to see one nearly a skeleton move with such strength; her head, neck, shoulders, hands, and feet, all made a strong motion to the sound of the music, and in this manner she went on by degrees, until she stood up on her legs upon the floor. Afterwards she began to dance, and at times to jump about, and at last, as the music and noise of the singers increased, she often sprang three feet from the ground. When the music slackened, she would appear quite out of temper, but when it became louder, she would smile and be delighted.[81]

This account describes a woman stimulated by the sound of the music, progressing from a head, neck, shoulder, and chest nodding or shrugging motion to motion in the hands and feet, as she went from a lying to a sitting and eventually a standing position, soon dancing and springing around the space. He remarks that eventually the young woman's strength overpowered the musicians', so that they could not keep up with her and had to rest while she continued to dance and bound about the room, more and more stimulated when the music intensified.

75. Hecker, *Epidemics of the Middle Ages*, 124.
76. Hecker, *Epidemics of the Middle Ages*, 124.
77. Hecker, *Epidemics of the Middle Ages*, 125.
78. Pearce, *The Life and Adventures of Nathaniel Pearce*, vol. 1, 292; Hecker, *Epidemics of the Middle Ages*, 125.
79. Pearce, *The Life and Adventures of Nathaniel Pearce*, vol. 1, 291; Hecker, *Epidemics of the Middle Ages*, 125.
80. Pearce, *The Life and Adventures of Nathaniel Pearce*, vol. 1, 292; Hecker, *Epidemics of the Middle Ages*, 125
81. Pearce, *The Life and Adventures of Nathaniel Pearce*, vol. 1, 292; Hecker, *Epidemics of the Middle Ages*, 125.

If the home remedy was not sufficient, a third level of cure would take place the next day involving the whole town. In this third stage, the woman was again loaded with silver jewellery and stripped it while she danced; the pieces were returned to their owners by a helper. These performative loans we may surmise offered a symbolic means for family members and friends to demonstrate that they were caring for the afflicted person through a public show of support. She wore their jewels, gaining social and emotional recognition from the performance of material provision, before returning them, in a gesture of thanks. It seemed to work. But for Pearce, who was dumbfounded, it was also mildly insane. He describes the dance as an outlandish charade, a 'strange disorder',[82] in which the dancer displayed the 'maddest postures imaginable':

> Next day, according to the custom in the cure of this disorder, she was taken into the market-place, where several jars of *maize* or *tsug* were set in order by the relations, to give drink to the musicians and dancers. When the crowd had assembled and the music was ready, she was brought forth and began to dance and throw herself into the maddest postures imaginable, and in this manner she kept on the whole day. Towards evening she began to let fall her silver ornaments from her neck, arms, and legs, one at a time, so that in the course of three hours she was stripped of every article. A relation continually kept going after her as she danced, to pick up the ornaments, and afterwards delivered them to the owners from whom they were borrowed.[83]

The performance culminated in a sprint, after which the woman fell to the ground in a state of exhaustion, finally to recover her name and be rebaptized, 'proof' that she was cured.[84] The expenditure of energy seems to have enabled her recovery, revitalizing her through the music, dancing, running, and performative demonstration of social and kinship support.

But not all so-called victims or patients were responsive. Pearce wrote: 'some are taken in this manner to the market-place for many days before they can be cured, and it sometimes happens that they cannot be cured at all'.[85] Were they suffering from a different sort of fatigue, not receptive to these practices? What sort of fatigue was this? In Pearce's editor's terms, this was mostly a 'sham' put on by the Abyssinian ladies, who were 'fond of decking themselves out with trinkets and finery of all sorts', the 'lady's degree of importance' being 'weighed by the value and number of the ornaments and attendants, furnished by her relatives and friends'.[86] Like soldiers who shammed anomalous disorders and like schoolboys, these ladies were, this editor argued, '*malingerers*', not suffering from actual disease.[87] But as with the tarantella, the supportive spectatorship and dancing does seem to have relieved real states of boredom and depression; the dance was not a disease but on the contrary arguably its cure. As Khanna argues, reprising Fanon's analyses of colonial melancholy, 'faking' illness was a frequent accusation levied against North Africans believed to be pretending exhaustion in order to 'swindle' their way to a warm hospital bed.[88] But as Khanna and Fanon rightly note, colonial conditions often resulted in real states of alienation and depression that colonial employers and doctors dismissed out of hand. The tarantella, like the *tigretier*, was in part a way socially to counteract the nefarious effects of such alienation. As a sort of therapy emphasizing music, dancing, and social support, the practice of dancing to music seemed to viewers to be absurd, beside the point. It ran counter to a more broadly scientistic notion of disease that emphasized altered behaviours taken as signs, proof, of a disorderly state curable only through discipline or drugs. For Pearce, the listlessness and dancing were one dancing disease, governed by sham; but for the women whose stories he reported, the dancing seems to have provided real reprieve.

82. Pearce, *The Life and Adventures of Nathaniel Pearce*, vol. 1, 294; Hecker, *Epidemics of the Middle Ages*, 126.
83. Pearce, *The Life and Adventures of Nathaniel Pearce*, vol. 1, 293; Hecker, *Epidemics of the Middle Ages*, 125–126.
84. Pearce, *The Life and Adventures of Nathaniel Pearce*, vol. 1, 294; Hecker, *Epidemics of the Middle Ages*, 126.
85. Pearce, *The Life and Adventures of Nathaniel Pearce*, vol. 1, 294; Hecker, *Epidemics of the Middle Ages*, 126.
86. Pearce, *The Life and Adventures of Nathaniel Pearce*, vol. 1, 294–295.
87. Pearce, *The Life and Adventures of Nathaniel Pearce*, vol. 1, 295.
88. Khanna, *Dark Continents*, 176.

Pearce's wife, seized with the same affliction as the woman he had earlier observed, seems to have been struck by a not dissimilar sort of discomfort and caused him some embarrassment. She had, like this other woman, been listless and unhappy; he had, he admits, tried to whip her, thinking, he further admits, that it might help. She only fainted, and his attendants, hearing about her condition, called for some music, which he had been denying them for a while. That, Pearce was forced to observe, 'soon revived her'.[89] She underwent the same ceremony as the woman he had previously described, and although the cure took slightly longer in his wife's case, it was ultimately efficacious. 'One day I went privately, with a companion', Pearce wrote, 'to see my wife dance, and kept a short distance, as I was ashamed to go near the crowd. On looking steadfastly upon her, while dancing or jumping, more like a deer than a human being, I said that it certainly was not my wife; at which my companion burst into a fit of laughter, from which he could scarcely refrain all the way home'. Pearce added: 'men are sometimes afflicted with this dreadful disorder, but not frequently'.[90] Pearce's wife may have been bored, lonely, and depressed in a colonial outpost where her primary companion was a man who thought little of whipping her. The *tigretier* offered a temporary theatre of re-collectivization, repositioning her at the centre of another social circle and another concept of distress. The *tigretier* reconfigured her condition as *shared*, suggesting that her despondency merited routine public attention and care. So we have to imagine in the whoosh of her dance's shadow.

COLONIAL HYSTERIA: MANIA, DEPRESSION, AND FEMININE REVOLT

In the Tunisian postcolonial writer Albert Memmi's terms, the colonial subject's drama is to be never quite aligned with oneself.[91] At the cusp of revolt, the subordinated subject identifies with the oppressor to the point of an uncanny

doubling—uncanny because it is never entire, never consummated. The subject remains split, even while, in Memmi's analysis, the colonizers eventually project themselves onto the figures of the colonized, needing the colonized's subaltern status to assert their own economic, social, and political superiority, and their own seemingly illustrious work ethic, deployed in supposed contrast to the purported laziness of the colonized people. In this double portrait of two mutually dependent and monstrous beings, the colonial relation emerges as a grotesque mimicry, a farce that fails to reconcile colonial subjecthood with a perpetually alienating and alien reality in which both parties are continually displaced, reterritorialized, and never quite at home. Colonial melancholy in this respect acknowledges the affective and performative rift that such displacement continually produces, resulting in what Memmi and Fanon describe as the colonized person's eventual 'neurosis', treated—to disastrous effect—in psychiatric hospitals that fail to help colonized people for what is never properly diagnosed as perfectly justified rage.

In Khanna's analysis, women found themselves even more caught in the crossfire between psychiatric and psychoanalytic analyses of the 'life of savages' and 'dark continents' of colonial and psychoanalytic myth.[92] Imagined to be as enigmatic and unwieldy as the African continent as a whole, women presented colonial medical writers with the figure of a ticking bomb waiting to explode in a hysterical attack, just as women's attempts to conform to oppressive structures fatigued them to the point of overwrought submission and bursts of acting out—singing, dancing, shouting, crying—that were branded as buffoonish and sick.

Political conditions sit at the heart of the so-called dancing disease. This does not mean that Pearce's wife's dance or Nora's signalled direct political action. The *tigretier*, like the tarantella, appears in tightly controlled performances taking place within codified bounds, but these enabled participants to shift their places in a wider political ecology. The dances represented the controlled eruption of jubilant, socially

---

89. Pearce, *The Life and Adventures of Nathaniel Pearce*, vol. 1, 295–296; Hecker, *Epidemics of the Middle Ages*, 126.

90. Pearce, *The Life and Adventures of Nathaniel Pearce*, vol. 1, 296; Hecker, *Epidemics of the Middle Ages*, 126–127.

91. See Albert Memmi, *Portrait du colonisé, précédé du Portrait du colonisateur et d'une préface de Jean-Paul Sartre suivi de Les Canadiens français sont-ils des colonisés*, ed. revised and corrected by the author (Montréal: Les éditions l'étincelle, 1972), 125; Albert Memmi, *La dépendance: Esquisse pour un portrait du dépendant* (Paris: Gallimard, 1979). Bhabha, *The Location of Culture*, 122–123. See also Richard C. Keller, *Colonial Madness: Psychiatry in French North Africa* (Chicago: University of Chicago Press, 2007).

92. Khanna, *Dark Continents*.

sanctioned corporeality following states of inertia and despair. Although these dances were cast
as a dancing disease, the anger and depression
of 'choreomania' represented the normal consequences of abnormal conditions and the relief
that came from the performative recollectivization of social life.

SHAKERS AND
FAKERS: THE AFRICAN
'TARANTELLA'

In spite of repeated narrative evidence that tarantellas in many cases helped those who were
bitten by poisonous spiders or were otherwise
engaging in social dances symbolically representing such injuries, what marked modern analyses
was a decisive emphasis on the shamming widely
believed to have been at the heart of the dancing 'disease'. So while Baglivi influentially argued
that some dancers—especially women—took
advantage of the tradition to have a good time
(chapter 3 here), later authors set this feint at
the heart of their readings. In his article on the
'African Tarantula or Dancing Mania', in *Eastern
Anthropologist* (1952–1953), the South African
anthropologist and British senior district officer
in Nigeria, M. D. W. Jeffreys (1890–1975),
argued that the Italian tarantella was 'feigned
for commercial gain'.[93] His argument, borrowed
from an account by the British zoologist Sir Ray
Lankester (1847–1929), drew on Lankester's
claim that the dancing was staged. No one suffered from spider bites, Lankester wrote in 1914.
The tarantella was put on for the sake of credu-
lous travellers only:

> The whole story of the 'Tarantula' x x x [*sic*]
> is now discredited. It was believed that the
> bite of this spider caused a peculiar sleepi-
> ness and also painful symptoms in men and
> women, only to be cured by music, which
> set the bitten one dancing. The . . . whole
> thing was an elaborate imposture on the
> part of the Tarantese peasants who, for
> a fee paid by a credulous traveller, would

be bitten, simulate apparent collapse,
and then pretend to be restored by music
and the violent dancing of the 'tarantella'
which they declared they felt compelled to
perform.[94]

Lankester's belief that there really was no tarantella—or none derived from a real impulse to
dance or from any actual spider's bite—folded a
vehemently anti-theatrical prejudice into older
accounts of this Apulian cure. So while we may
surmise that peasants in some cases were very
plausibly taking Lankester for a ride or, as in
the case of the hapless woman Swinburne convinced to act out a tarantella for him, respond-
ing to the pressure to perform with a reasonable
sense that this show would provide a financial
opportunity for them, the exchange itself was
seen as a sickness characterized, among others, by a tendency to sham. These travellers
sought out a theatre of antiquity but balked
when they found any theatre at all. They wanted
naive acts, not creative opportunism. Lankester
took his accusations further. 'That there was no
connection with this frenzied dancing and the
bite of this spider', he added, 'could have been
deduced from the fact that the habitat of this
spider is widely spread and as a consequence has
been in contact with the human race for countless years'. Only in Apulia, Lankester wrote,
are humans bitten by this spider compelled to
dance. They must, therefore, he concluded, have
been shamming.[95]

Lankester's anti-theatrical and choreophobic prejudice, recuperated in Jeffreys's travel
narrative, shifted the discussion on tarantellas from scientific interest in toxicity, convulsions, and contagion to a social scientific stance
foregrounding incredulity: this was now to be
understood as mere tourist theatre. At the same
time, the story offered grounds for further comparison, as an account of a disorder that indicated colonial duplicity: the colonial peasant's
supposed pathological propensity to cheat.
Once an indication of pathological spontaneity,
the dancing disease now signalled its opposite:
lies. Jeffreys found further evidence for this

---

93. M. D. W. Jeffreys, 'African Tarantula or Dancing Mania', *Eastern Anthropologist* 6.2 (1952–1953): 98–105, 98.

94. Cited in Jeffreys, 'African Tarantula', 98.

95. Jeffreys, 'African Tarantula', 98. Transcultural psychiatrists in the late twentieth century have convincingly argued that
similar conditions taking place in different environments can yield quite different symptoms. To dismiss the venomous etiology
of the tarantella on the grounds that the same practice was not found elsewhere, suggesting that a few hundred years and thousands of southern Italians must have been lying about their urge to dance and counterfeiting their movements, underestimates the
complexity of the tarantella. See e.g. British epidemiologists Donaldson et al., 'The Dancing Plague'. They argue that the seasonal

in Nigeria. There, he saw a species of tarantula used for divination in events involving frenzied dances but noted hastily that 'there is no connection between the two' (tarantism in Italy and this Nigerian practice).[96] His insistence on the apparent analogy, and his equally emphatic insistence on their irreconcilable difference, perpetuated—while seemingly underplaying—the exuberant comparativism in place a century before. Jeffreys's use of the qualifier 'Now although' to open his comparative trope, suggested that he was indebted to the comparative mode of intellection popular among medical geographers and colonial physicians who travelled through these parts before him but was also exercising resistance to that mode in order to claim the singularity of the Nigerian case and thus a new sort of specialist knowledge.

He opened his essay with an account of the African tarantula's supposed Italian counterpart: both phenomena, he argued, involved gyration, frenzy, dancing, trances, and epileptic (or, in some cases, epileptiform) fits. Yet both were feigned, artificial, theatrical exercises put on for the sole purpose of beguiling naive travellers—presumably Western ethnographers such as himself. This paranoid, but possibly not altogether incorrect, account, proffered, like Pearce's, at arm's length, took anxiously into account the uncomfortable colonial relation in which Jeffreys appears as an interloper and possibly a fraud. Here, he stages himself at the receiving end of a con game in which he is not quite deceived: almost, but not quite. The hermeneutic scenario places him—just—above the Nigerian, whose tarantella he believes he can see through, thanks to the analyses of British officers who travelled before him.

The comparison placed his find in a treasure chest of colonial comparatives, enabling him to gain power over these subjects not only in his knowledge of the event's purported duplicity but also in his capacity to collect and compare this case to others. Jeffreys borrowed heavily from, in addition to Lankester's writing, British government archives, including a 1938 Annual Report on the Bamenda Division by the district officer, Mr. Swabey, whose description of the Nigerian 'tarantella', or Makka, Jeffreys quoted at length:

'The Makka movement [in Nigeria] originated in the neighbouring area of Mambilla in the Gashaka district of the Northern Provinces. It manifested itself in a *frenzied dance* in which most of the population, men and women joined. The dancers would *gyrate* in a *frenzy* to the drum, waving their arms like a windmill. They would then begin to *shake as in an epileptic fit*: their eyes began to stare *as in a trance* and then some would *fall to the ground*, apparently senseless'.[97]

Just as Jeffreys employs a comparative structure to frame his tale, so too similes serve Swabey to connect behaviours performed by Nigerians to a language used in medical literature and popular culture to describe similar events. The epileptic fit, the frenzy, and the trance, as well as motion resembling a windmill, painted a poetic portrait of familiar but incomprehensible behaviours accessible only through the medium of comparison afforded the learned colonial man. In the four sentences reproduced here, four qualifiers remove the activity from its geographic location, compared with structures that might be recognized by Jeffreys's readers: 'like', 'as', 'apparently', and the subjunctive ('would fall') portray the event—distant in place if not time—while explaining that the Nigerians engaged in such a performance only for commercial gain, *like the Apulians*, with whom readers were presumed already to be familiar. The Nigerian dancers, Jeffreys noted, 'would be pelted by the onlookers with *anini* (nickle tenths of a penny)'. He glossed: 'The reason for so doing was obscure but the money was apparently collected by a member of the society and subsequently spent on drink. Anyone who fell down in such a trance was admitted a member of the society'.[98] He had difficulty penetrating this society, making the elucidation of such a practice challenging—but all the more vital for his attempt to write at the

---

recurrence of tarantellas may be more than simply perpetuated by tradition or symbolism: a population of large venomous spiders thrives in the area due to its hot, dry climate and deforestation; more important, the venom's presence in the victims' bodies could account for its reactivation during periods of excessive heat, compelling them to engage in the curative dancing that Baglivi prominently described (202).

96. Jeffreys, 'African Tarantula', 98.

97. Jeffreys, 'African Tarantula', 98.

98. Jeffreys, 'African Tarantula', 98.

limits of scientific knowledge, which Britain's imperial reach appeared to facilitate.

Scientific knowledge was enabled by and was enabling the further collection of case histories, trophies for the colonial traveller and the emerging disciplines he endeavoured to cultivate—in this case, social anthropology, deriving from comparative medicine, drawing the contours of a relatively spurious psychology of feint abstracted from colonial cultural history. 'The immediate purpose of the society', Jeffreys noted, 'was difficult to discover as the people were very reticent but it appears that *Makka* would purge the country of witches, cure all illnesses, increase the yield of the farms and even raise the dead from the grave. In the village of Mbem', he added, 'a boy of about 12 years of age, who had fallen in the dance became a medium and interpreted the orders of *Makka* and these the people obeyed. The people would dance sometimes for three days on end and during this period all farm work and other activities ceased. Bands of people went about crying that now they had a new God'.[99]

Jeffreys explained that the function of these sorts of dances—everywhere in the world—was to achieve the 'physical catharsis of nervous tension by dancing'.[100] With this statement, he was effectively entering the social scientific 'order' of the dancing disease into the discursive realm of psychoanalysis and sexology: dancing, linked to sex, as its public sublimation, operated as a sign of the subterranean rumblings of primitive life within civilized bodies unable to contain their own animal forces. Dance, in this view, was an expression of disease, the eruption of automatic impulses into social space: dance in general—and excessive dances in particular (lasting three days, or involving visions and falls)—signalled the pathologically unspent energy of sex. This functionalist view of cultural life positioned 'dance' at the heart of society and politics, as the direct expression of their disorderly underside. Following Foucault's line of thinking on biopolitics and governance, by which discourse on sex makes otherwise unremarkable sexual activity into an object of scientific analysis and control,

I submit that dance comes to represent the sign of a nation's biosocial underside: disorderly dancing signals that the nation is, under the surface, uncontrolled. Dance is thereby attractive and titillating to all those attempting to read and to diagnose cultures comparatively; it is subject to scientific fascination and vicarious pleasure, as well as to nominal reprimand.

Comparative analyses implicitly linked African and American expressions of sexuality, suggesting that both were equally disordered and similarly manifested as an excessive propensity to dance—dancing in both cases was a symptom of sexual abstention. Comparing Uyo dancing in Calabar province in southeastern Nigeria to American Shakers, Jeffreys argued, revealed a 'great emphasis . . . laid on "sin,"' usually 'carnal or sexual sin', present in both contexts, provoking a similar use of dancing to achieve 'catharsis'. Physiologists know, he added, that 'if such repressions occur the nervous and muscular tension rises, rises until there is some form of catharsis, and violent exercise, such as prolonged dancing will discharge the pent up nervous and muscular energy and lower the threshold of the excitability of the psyche'.[101] The denunciation of marriage among Shakers, like the introduction of the Christian God and emphasis on abstention in Nigeria, forced the redirection of energetic flows into this sort of dance.[102] The simple biological 'fact' of 'an overaccumulation of sex hormones in the system', explained in the 1930s by the army physician and sexologist F. A. E. Crew (1886–1973), Jeffreys noted, accounted for the similarity of frenzies in various parts of the world where extreme religiosity had altered the course of people's regular source of physical release.[103] Repressed sexuality, resulting in grotesque deceit, was in his view at the heart of the tarantella and its Sub-Saharan relations. Once again, the dancing disease served as a litmus test for knowing—and in doing so colonizing—an almost unreachable state of history and biology imagined to reside, in a cruder and more observable form, elsewhere. Sex erupted in dance; or so the complex node linking the 'dancing disease' to

---

99. Jeffreys, 'African Tarantula', 98–99.

100. 'It is clear that all the manifestations, including those of the European Shakers, spring from common causes: discontent with present conditions, repressions, then sublimation of the psyche by the claim to a new revelation of God and religion, followed by a repudiation of the old, and finally a physical catharsis of nervous tension by dancing'. Jeffreys, 'African Tarantula', 104.

101. Jeffreys, 'African Tarantula', 104.

102. Jeffreys, 'African Tarantula', 103.

103. Cited in Jeffreys, 'African Tarantula', 104.

colonial depression and unrest suggests. Dance, it seemed, had no life of its own; dancing energetically, in the nineteenth- and twentieth-century discourse on choreomania, described only pathological waste. But this waste, this surplus, was vital, ethnographers seemed to suggest, for helping to explain why revolts and revolutions occurred; why women and men acted out.

As a way to draw out yet simultaneously to explain and to neutralize the alterity of cultural practices involving shaking, dancing, seizures, and songs, at a time when modern Europe was becoming, on the surface, ever more suave, torque-like, discourse on the dancing disease created an order of disorder, a trope that could be transplanted onto all sorts of foreign terrain. Yet as stories of the dancing disease travelled, picking up muck and dust along the way, getting battered, seeing different air and landscapes, their writers becoming malarial or conversant in various fields, the concept shifted, becoming more political.

In the next chapter, I turn to another history of writing on African dancing and movement disorders teetering between medical condition and shamanistic practice, political upheaval and theatrical deceit. With the *imanenjana* in Madagascar, observed by colonial physicians from the 1860s well into the early twentieth century, and the Brazilian revolt among disenfranchised *sertões*, geographic *movement*, enabled by colonial medicine, provoked a translatio between medical and cultural discourses that pitted the 'dancing disease', choreomania, awkwardly in these fields' shifting middle. Fieldwork performed by Charcot's students in particular enabled a translatio between neurological observation and political diagnosis, wrapping instances of social insurgency into the sprawling language of epidemic unrest.

8

Ecstasy-Belonging in Madagascar and Brazil

'New' national, international, or global emergences create an unsettling sense of transition, as if history is at a turning point; and it is in such *incubational* moments . . . that we experience the palimpsestical imprints of past, present, and future in peculiarly contemporary figures of time and meaning.

—Homi K. Bhabha, 'Framing Fanon' (2004)

Being-outside, and yet belonging: this is the topological structure of the state of exception.

—Giorgio Agamben, *State of Exception* (2005)

Politics are not located directly 'in' dance, but in the way dance manages to occupy (cultural) space.

—Mark Franko, 'Dance and the Political: States of Exception' (2006)

PERIPHERIES, LIMITS, AND BORDERLANDS: DANCE AT THE EDGE

The discourse on choreomania became increasingly political. This chapter offers thick description of two case studies at the peripheries of Europe's colonial empire, both marked by legacies traced back to Hecker's writing as well as to Charcot's clinic in Paris, the latter a clearinghouse for research internationally in the nineteenth century: here, we discover cases in Madagascar and Brazil, saturated with the travelling culture of medical research that characterized colonial modernity. After the antiquarian version of choreomania articulated in Hecker's writing and Charcot's comparative tableaux, choreomania in colonial medical circles, drawing from these archival repertoires, came to appear darker, more dangerous, and urgently contemporary: it was now described as a disorder of present nations uprising. This chapter traces this symbolic darkening and historical quickening to argue that with case studies in Madagascar and Brazil, colonial and missionary physicians became acutely aware of choreomania's political *effect* (and potential *effectiveness*). The dancing disease was not just a crowd condition, an oceanic mob, or a slightly irritating but not particularly dangerous feminine or colonial form of deceit; choreomania now signalled an epidemic case of anti-European revolt.

At stake, then, is the nineteenth-century language of choreomania harnessed by medical writers to describe social bodies performing public acts of political resistance. Choreomaniacs were increasingly described as the social underclass, restless and uncontained. They agitated their limbs and circulated throughout the land; yet their movements were not, some observers thought, entirely willed, even though these gestures may have been stimulated by a spirit of contestation. As such, the discomfiting contagiousness of these dark bodies' 'contagious moves', to reprise a phrase employed by Barbara

Browning to describe the supposedly epidemic spread of blackness in postcolonial music and dance, was countermanded, in colonial medical writing, by a discourse on involuntary motion.[1] Emphasis on involuntary movements, hallucinations, and 'possession' by ancestral spirits made the dancers seem less threatening because they were supposed to be suffering from automatic forms of neuromotor or psychiatric disease rather than the arguably more worrisome effects of political willpower. But the background of political contestation did not go unnoticed, and physicians in Madagascar, grappling with the coextensive appearance of spasmodic gestures and collective revolt, called this combination, after the European literature, 'choreomania'. Similarly in Brazil, I show at the end of this chapter, the disenfranchised *sertões* of northeastern Bahia gathered in self-administered colonies to extract themselves from a corrupt body politic and forge an alternative community against the logic of the nation state but were crushed in the process. They, too, like the Malagasy rebels, were branded 'choreomaniacs'. In both cases, social and political movements characterized by collective expressions of hope and discontentment suggest scenes of upheaval that reconstitute choreomania's archival repertoire along anti-colonial lines. In this chapter, choreomania becomes the modern scientific articulation of a convulsive body politic attempting to wrest itself from state rule.

ECSTASY-BELONGING: STATES OF EXCEPTION AND MONARCHICAL RULE

I borrow Agamben's concept of 'ecstasy-belonging' to articulate this concatenation of possession—significantly, *re*possession—and revolt. According to Agamben, ecstasy-belonging is normally reserved for a monarch, who sits simultaneously outside of and within a community.[2] As Franko points out, the monarch typically performs a 'state of exception' in that he (or she) takes it as his (or her) prerogative to decide how his (or her) political representation occurs, including aesthetically.[3] In reappropriating the

'state of exception' for themselves, 'choreomaniacs' instate a prior order of political rule and its political choreography. They perform their political representation beyond the current state embodied in the sovereign: in Madagascar, their ecstasy-belonging reinstates the monarch's ancestors, in a choreographic journey of iconographic recuperation that retraces ancient pathways and theatricalizes the older order's return. 'Choreomania' thus shifts politics in the capital by returning to an order prior to that of the current monarch, showing that that order never disappeared; it has always continued to ghost the present. The so-called choreomaniacs enacted thus a choreopolitical act of restitution, a performance of their own (re)institution of state power conjuring the spectre of a suprahistorical and supramonarchical figure. Although the 'people' are not strictly autonomous, nor is the regime democratic—this is not a representative rule of law—power lies among those who participate in the possibility of a collective return to a status quo ante, one that can (herein lies its power) be called on to disrupt and realign state politics at any time. The rule of law is in this sense *representational*: as Taussig suggests of the 'magic of the state', *possession* belongs to those who '[mediate] the spirit of the state with the body of the people'. 'Death', Taussig argues, 'accentuates the imaginative possibilities given in the shadow-play in the state of the whole; it provides the lurch of reality into the unknown' that characterizes 'magical transformation from figure to figure of speech'.[4] Reinstitution of a prior rule of law—which never disappeared—sets 'death' (symbolic or real) at the heart of state politics, constituted as the theatrical representation of a right and rite of return. In Madagascar, 'roots' and 'routes' (in Clifford and Gilroy's terms) are conjugated with 'rights' and 'rites' to perform the slippages, the 'magical transformations' 'from figure to figure of speech', making politics disease; but also, as I show further, making invisible spirits into forms that *seize* power where it hurts: in the nation's arteries, its throughways, going straight to the heart (the capital). The metaphor of the body politic, treated in previous chapters, comes further into focus as the body's 'spirit'—the ancestral forces

---

1. Barbara Browning, *Infectious Rhythm: Metaphors of Contagion and the Spread of African Culture* (New York: Routledge, 1998).
2. Giorgio Agamben, *State of Exception*, trans. Kevin Attell (Chicago: University of Chicago Press, 2005), 35.
3. Mark Franko, 'Dance and the Political: States of Exception', *Dance Research Journal* 38.1/2 (2006): 3–18, 11–12.
4. Michael Taussig, *The Magic of the State* (London: Routledge, 1997), 103.

haunting secular power in the nation state—comes to be perceived as ill, the illness manifest in the apparently senselessly flailing limbs of the nation's subjects.

Similarly in Brazil, a prior rule of law was called on by the *sertões*, who saw the present state of political rule as corrupt. In doing so, the Brazilian rebels instantiated a state of law outside the temporal order of the nation's state and so performed their own return to a prior rule *ecstatically*: by standing *outside*, and representing themselves. Unlike the Malagasy, however, they enacted their state of collective ecstasy far outside the site of state power in the capital, while calling on it negatively (by virtue of their withdrawal) to be dissolved. Their claim to justice was constituted not in a representational politics by which they would instate a new figure of authority (by recourse to the old) but by extracting themselves from the centre and so refusing exogenous rule, thus denouncing and suspending its legitimacy. Choreomanias, as states of exception in Madagascar and Brazil, suggest forms of government that replace regimes of state power with prior orders of *self*-governance. These orders *appear* in the paradoxically 'shapeless'—misshapen, disfigured—*shape* of disorder: a disorder of heightened gathering, a collective occupation of common space.

Choreopolitically, 'choreomanias' in Madagascar and Brazil thus mobilize states of ecstasy-belonging in the shape of a 'disorder' that in effect reinstates a prior rule of law: that of the more ancient past and that of the land, which is felt to underpin—literally to contain or to house—it. The *land* in these 'choreomanias' thus becomes a site of return, symbolically holding up (and holding) the demonstrators' claims to another political priority. In this sense, as the epigraph to this chapter by Bhabha—conjuring Walter Benjamin (1892–1940)—attests, 'choreomanias' articulate a messianic 'now-time' in which past, present, and future collide. 'Now-time', or *Jetztzeit* for Benjamin, is a messianic time of becoming, a palimpsestical conjuration of the past in a present moment calling forth a new future. Visible in the interstices of colonial correspondence, government and missionary archives, medical journals and ethnographic compendia—all the machinery of circulation that Said notes enables concepts like Orientalism and, I add,

'choreomania' to travel and grow—this 'now-time' *appears* on the medico-historical stage in the formless form of fitful movements. These are bodies gathering together, exercising what I call a politico-aesthetic (or choreopolitical) state of *commotion*.

OF CHOREAS AND CRUSADES: MIGRATING DISORDERS AND DISORDERS OF MIGRATION

The choreomaniacs' *commotion* occurred not only among bodies moving in space but also among bodies moving through space, bodies travelling together. In this regard, choreomania was constituted as a disorder of migration. Thus, although Muecke has recently argued that we can class the *ramanenjana*—perhaps 'anachronistically', he submits—as 'demonstrators',[5] medical writers in the nineteenth century emphasizing the *ramanenjana*'s stiff, spontaneous gestures and their tendency to gather suggests a discourse on epidemic disease cutting geopolitically across anthropological and medical lines. This view articulates choreomania choreographically, I submit, as a disorder not only of politics but of *commotion*—of movement-together, in a *movemented* nineteenth century, when movement and movements were thought (and written) in the same breath as movement disease. Thus the specifically anti-Western agitation of the *ramanenjana* situates them as revolutionary agents operating within (and acting on) a distinctly biopolitical sphere, ecstatically. Conversely, the theatre of political ecstasy-belonging they enact enables power to be instituted again and again in the theatricalized return to a higher rule of law—not a state of exception in this case so much as a state of return—one that refuses the monarch's individual exception.

Medical analyses in the second half of the nineteenth century wrapped political protest into the sphere of the dancing disease, cast as a disease of movement, travel, and social unrest. The Malagasy revolution of 1863 was a popular contestatory movement that aimed—and ultimately succeeded—at unseating the widely unpopular pro-European king Radama II (1829–1863). This movement was performed by

---

5. Muecke, 'Choreomanias', 8.

individuals known as *ramanenjana*—meaning 'to be made stiff' or 'to stiffen'[6]—widely reported to be proceeding from town to town, jerking and twisting their bodies in convulsive dancing cortèges accompanying the spirits of dead royalty; the 1863 movement as a whole was known as *imanenjana*.[7] This chapter shows a genealogical link posited between the *imanenjana* and previous cases of the 'dancing disease'. Colonial medical literature described these demonstrators alongside St. Vitus's dancers and other paradigmatic sufferers of 'choreomania'. But here, choreomania became for the first time distinctly current and contemporarily African, suggesting the common face of an epidemic dancing 'disease' welling up to haunt and displace Europe from within its colonies. This went beyond the *tigretier* described in the previous chapter, seen to be quaintly individual and symbolically ornamental to everyday life; here, whole groups gather to effect political change. Other differences make the *ramanenjana* significant in the discursive history of the 'dancing disease'. Dancers were described now for the first time distinctly in terms likening their movements to spirit possession (specifically possession by ancestors); and they were described as suffering from a particular neuromotor disorder like—but not exactly the same as—epidemic chorea, attributed by one physician to nervous paludism or the malaria endemic in the region. Debate raged; for the most part, physicians on the ground, Malagasy and Europeans alike, agreed that the *imanenjana* was a collective pathology of motion and emotion, exacerbated by sociocultural conditions, and had precedents among dance manias around the world. Nearly all agreed that anti-European sentiment spurred it on.

What united the choreomaniacs was that they moved at the same time, though not necessarily, as Browning suggests of African polyrhythms, in synchrony. Their movements *together* were movements that emphatically joined them in space, making simultaneous their individual disfigurations. For the French military physician and later anthropologist J. C. M. Boudin, the *ramanenjana* were primarily interesting for their comparative potential, specifically the fact that they moved and, in doing so, proved, he rightly noted, the existence of a tendency towards movement universal among people. Boudin argued that the *imanenjana* and movements like it revealed a worldwide tendency among humans to engage in motion, including travel. This motion affected individual limbs and significantly displaced whole groups of people across geographic expanses. Boudin argued that the *imanenjana* constituted one among many cases of choreomania suggesting, as he put it, a 'mysterious and irresistible urge [or need] for travel [displacement] and movement' ('mystérieux et irrésistible besoin de déplacement et de mouvement') common to all times, among all people. In 'Chorées épidémiques de Madagascar' [Epidemic Choreas of Madagascar], published in the *Bulletin de la Société d'Anthropologie de Paris* [Bulletin of the Anthropological Society of Paris] (1865), Boudin offered the usual catalogue of choreomanias, adding a few case studies from recent ethnographic literature, including the *imanenjana*, which he submitted was like St. Vitus's dance, the tarantella, the Convulsionaries of Saint-Médard, the *tigretier*, and the convulsions of the 'Morzine'—a group of women who were widely thought to have been possessed by demons in Haute-Savoie in the 1850s and 1860s and were diagnosed with epidemic hystero-demonopathy.

For Boudin, all disorders of motion revealed a mixture of geographic and historical effects, performing bodily transformation and transfer. Enumerating a range of case studies, he recognized that real scientific comparison between them was impossible without further study. Yet the enumeration suggested an order of things in which individual, like collective, motion tended towards or derived from disease. According to this reverse logic, all movement had the potential to *appear* as a movement disorder; because motion was a universal source of disease, it was thus, Boudin's analysis went, commonly human. He wrote:

One can observe—in various eras, at intervals usually so great as to make scientific comparisons [rapprochement] between

---

6. See for example James Sibree, member of the London Missionary Society, quoted in Maurice Bloch, *Placing the Dead: Tombs, Ancestral Villages, and Kinship Organization in Madagascar* (London: Seminar Press, 1971), 21–24. Also quoted in Muecke, 'Choreomanias', 6–7.

7. The term *imanenjana* refers to the event, whereas *ramanenjana* refers to the people engaged in it. I am grateful to anthropologist Lesley Sharp for this distinction. Most of the medical literature on 'choreomania' in Madagascar employs *ramanenjana* to describe the people and the event indiscriminately. Where possible, I have chosen to maintain the distinction.

the phenomena difficult—humankind seized with a mysterious and irresistible urge for travel [déplacement] and movement, an urge that in Antiquity resulted in the great migrations; in the Middle Ages, in the children's crusades and the great epidemics of chorea, from the dancing frenzy along the Rhine (the Germans' *Tanzwuth*) and the *Tarantism* in Apulia during the fourteenth and fifteenth centuries, to the *Convulsions* at the Saint-Médard cemetery, the *Tigretier* in Abyssinia, the modern convulsions of the Morzine and, finally, the current epidemic, known as *Ramanenjana*, which in 1863 struck a great part of the people of Madagascar.[8]

So whereas Boudin listed migrations and crusades alongside epidemic dance frenzies, he also highlighted the 'mysterious and irresistible' quality of all movement, a trait that, I argue, the discourse on choreomanias suggests they all share. Mysteriousness—near inexplicability—when collaged into scenes *appears* (theatrically) as if knowable. Seemingly strange tendencies become recognizable scenes, discursive zones of intensity. Following Foucault's analysis of the discourse on madness as a nearly indistinguishable set of events putatively brought by science from darkness into light, choreomanias *appear* in a chiaroscuro as that which—gossip has it—can be seen 'again and again' if you squint. And what this squinting reveals is people moving—generally, a lot, and in disorderly, nearly shapeless, fashion.

As with all the cases I have described, attempts at definition were always superseded by recourse to the list. Boudin, indebted to Hecker's paradigmatic collection of case studies, appears to prove 'choreomania' by recourse to the familiar set of examples. Yet in drawing also from new medical anthropologies of Africa and South America, Boudin extends Hecker's repertoire, making choreomania even more contemporary and apparently universal. Boudin opens with an account of the *ramanenjana* derived from reports published in the *Annales de la propagation de la foi* [Annals of the Propagation of the Faith] and the *Moniteur universel* [Universal Monitor], and goes on to list a West African practice whose description

he borrows from French physician Alfred Maury's (1817–1892) crosscultural *La magie et l'astrologie dans l'antiquité et au moyen âge ou étude sur les superstitions païennes* [Magic and Astrology in Antiquity and the Middle Ages or Study of Pagan Superstitions] (1860); early travel literature on the Dahomey (present-day Benin), whose dances Boudin summarily compares to Jurupari Indian dances in the Amazon reported by the naturalist and explorer Alfred Russel Wallace (1823–1913) in his *Travels on the Amazon and Rio Negro, with an account of the native tribes, and observations on the climate, geology, and natural history of the Amazon Valley* (1853); voodoo rites; and a host of further practices characterized by dramatic gestures, convulsions, falls, visions, and trance states. This alliance of choreas and crusades radically cuts across 'dance', disease, and politics, including what are typically considered movement disorders today as well as the political grievances associated with mass migration. For Boudin, all movement reveals choreography and suggests what Franko has called the interpenetration of dance and (geocultural) politics.[9]

'Choreomania' in Madagascar, then, reveals a nineteenth-century habit of mind according to which movement of all sorts is *of a sort*; yet, as I've shown, scientific collectionism appropriates this movement and the fantasies (the hallucinations and visions) thought to underpin (literally to move) it, displacing the arguably more productive entanglement of bodies in circulatory systems, systems that have the potential to *mobilize* contingencies in the sense that Martin, like Franko, argues constitutes dance's political potential. Choreomanias, then, signal a different order of political protest: that directed at the temporal order of the state—a 'now' time understood as secular and mundane, the exercise of geopolitical jurisdiction over the land. Choreomaniacs replace this temporal power with an order of power that signals a concept of belonging understood to precede and to supersede it. The power politics at play thus suggest a discursive process of *translatio* from a politico-spiritual to a scientific realm by which ecstasy-belonging, what I further describe as 'repossession' and utopian longing, become medicalized, even as writers witnessing scenes of upheaval recognize the 'purely' (though never

---

8. Boudin, 'Chorées épidémiques de Madagascar', 441; cited in Andrianjafy, *La Ramanenjana à Madagascar*, 13.

9. See esp. Franko, 'Dance and the Political', 14–15.

the 'merely') political force of these movements. Physicians and missionaries see the dancers' *commotion* as political (politically motivated) but never as political movement: it becomes epidemic contagion spurred on by high affect and shared sentiment; but the bodies are emptied of political will, seen as excess and deficiency, in effect as the prime movers of epidemic disease but not as deliberately active agents.

DAVIDSON'S PROXIMITY: POWER POLITICS IN THE CAPITAL

Andrew Davidson, writing two years after Boudin in the *Edinburgh Medical Review*, brought medical discussion of the *imanenjana* squarely onto colonial terrain. Stationed as a missionary physician in Madagascar to tend to an epidemic of smallpox, soon appointed court physician, and a recipient of the medal of the Order of Radama on account of his successful treatment of the king's son, Davidson was situated at the heart of the nation's power politics. Unlike most physicians writing about the 'dancing disease', he witnessed events he described as choreomania firsthand. This led him to politicize Hecker's historiographic and biophilosophical 'armchair' stance and bring Boudin's relatively benign crosscultural analysis into sharper national focus.[10] For Davidson, choreomania was a distinctly anti-colonial disease. In 'Choreomania: An Historical Sketch, with Some Account of an Epidemic Observed in Madagascar' (1867), he argued that it was thus of immediate practical concern to British authorities, who might wish to quell similar upheavals elsewhere. 'It would be foreign to the design of this paper', he wrote, 'to enter into any of the interesting psychological questions which suggest themselves in connexion with this subject; such as, the nature of the changes on the nervous centres, the primary cause of such changes, and the organic lesions resulting therefrom; inquiries such as these must be of deep interest to the physician, the philosopher, and the divine'.[11] But because choreomania spread among like-minded people, 'this disease is of special practical interest to the magistrate and medical jurist'. 'Such an epidemic may occur again in India or other countries where British interests may be deeply involved',[12] he cautioned, arguing for the missionary medical remit to speak to political power. Davidson's plea to administrators to take note appears to have gone relatively unheeded: authorities in London expressed some interest in the 'revolution' but not its psychophysical traits.[13] Only at the colonial frontlines did physicians such as Davidson see the shape that anti-colonial revolt could take: in this case, a dance-like 'epidemic' of circulation.

At the cusp of the outbreak of 1863, Davidson was prepared. London Missionary Society archives suggest that he had just requested, in a letter dated 4 May 1862, that the totality of all previously published Sydenham Society volumes be sent to him and had thus encountered Babington's translation of Hecker's writing.[14] Merely a few months later, Davidson experienced what he saw as a version of the same phenomenon. Assigning, like Hecker, a biomedical source to the dances, Davidson argued that they were, however, particularly nefarious on colonial soil. Because the dancing 'was associated with national prejudices, religious and political', it was especially liable, he argued, to contagion. Anti-colonial prejudices 'afforded, as it were, the condition, or one of the conditions, of [the dancing's] epidemic manifestation. These formed the bond of sympathetic union among the affected',[15] he argued, disturbing the ganglia at the base of the brain and the individual's motor centres, provoking disinhibited and uncoordinated locomotion.[16]

10. Andrew Davidson, 'Foreign Correspondence', *Medical Times and Gazette*, 3 January 1863.

11. Davidson, 'Choreomania', 136.

12. Davidson, 'Choreomania', 136.

13. Arthur Johnson, Foreign Secretary of the London Missionary Society, to Andrew Davidson, 27 July 1863, Africa, Southern Outgoing Letters, box 10, 1862–1865, Council for World Mission/London Missionary Society Archive, 1764–1977 (CWM/LMS), School of Oriental and African Studies Library, University of London.

14. In a letter dated 4 May 1862 addressed to the members of the London Missionary Society in England, Davidson asked for the *Medical Times* and the *Gazette* from 7 January 1863 to be sent to him, as well as the *Publications of the Sydenham Society* from 1862 and 1863, 'so far as published and in future as they appear'. Andrew Davidson, to the London Missionary Society, 4 May 1862, Madagascar, Incoming Correspondence, box 6, 1859–1863, CWM/LMS.

15. Davidson, 'Choreomania', 134.

16. Davidson, 'Choreomania', 133–134.

Choreomania was thus caused by strong emotion which translated into disorderly movement, including 'physical derangement' and sometimes death. Defining choreomania, with Hecker, as a 'psycho-physical disease' and an 'excited state', Davidson further summarized its traits locally. Choreomaniacs were characterized by a feverish demeanour, stiffness in the neck, and pain in the back and limbs.[17] They were also characterized by strong sentiments regarding specific colours and objects (in the Middle Ages, red; in Madagascar, the missionaries' black, pigs, and hats), shaking, frothing, falling, and, to varying degrees, social or political unrest. All choreomaniacs showed an uncontrollable impulse to dance, morbid love of music, speech impediments, and 'moral mania' primarily affecting young women and men of an 'excitable' temperament more liable to suffer from hysterical conditions—though the disease, he noted, by no means spared others. Choreomania was thus especially common among the 'superstitious' classes, unable or unwilling to curb their natural (animal) impulses.

Further comparing the *ramanenjana* to children, Davidson argued that choreomaniacs were 'capricious',[18] not only because they moved spontaneously together but because this tendency suggested a sort of pathological contagion that upright Europeans did not, in his view, share. The Malagasy 'infection', Davidson argued, was in particular reminiscent of the child pilgrimage at Erfurt in mid-July 1237 that involved over a thousand children (a case Hecker had outlined). These children 'assembled', Davidson wrote, '*as if by instinctive impulse, without preconcertion,* and unknown to their parents'.[19] Comparing the Malagasy demonstrators to these children, Davidson foregrounded the choreomaniacs' similar 'bond of sympathy', which could be explained by the climate of 'general excitement' characterizing all cases of choreomania. Public sentiment in the Middle Ages had been directed against priests, who had failed to offset the plague; similarly in Madagascar, the 'public mind was in a state of general excitement' due to the rapid emergence of a 'pretty strong anti-Christian, anti-European party . . . opposed to progress

and change'.[20] Christians were, he argued, thus 'exempt[ed]' from contagion, since their 'sympathies were rather *with* those changes, political and social, which disturbed the masses'; he and his peers were thus safely 'beyond the reach of the current'. Superior education, 'mental and moral', and a 'firm conviction that the whole affair was a demoniacal possession of their heathen countrymen' enabled Christians to view the events 'as outsiders, with the interest of observers', and 'without the fear which, in such a malady, is one of the means of its propagation'.[21]

To become epidemic, Davidson argued, choreomania had to 'seize some popular idea or superstition, at once so *firmly* believed as to lay hold of the heart of the people, and so *generally* as to afford scope for the operation of pathological sympathy'.[22] This slightly reconfigures Browning's notion of 'infectious rhythm', what she defines as an African brand of polyrhythmic percussive movement and music 'that has allowed for the characterization of diasporic culture as a chaotic or uncontrolled force which can only be countered by military or police violence',[23] and, I hasten to add, medicalization. So where Browning emphasizes contagious rhythm, Davidson attributes the viral spread of music and dancing to individuals' heightened capacity for sympathy and strong emotional and intellectual bond. Contagion was not just visceral or rhythmic but sociopolitical and ideological. Browning's analysis suggests that contemporary AIDS discourse has saturated images of contagious infection among often African and homosexual men through figures of biologically determined moral degeneracy. But virulence as a mode of intergenerational—and intercontinental—translation had roots in colonial medical practice that underscored dance and the performance of high affect long before.

Davidson presented a dramatic scenario of the events he witnessed firsthand, underscoring political insurgency as a viral act of sympathetic union. The *ramanenjana* flowed into the capital in droves in February and March 1863, proceeding from the southernmost tip of the island, the Bara region, where they had first begun

---

17. Davidson, 'Choreomania', 132.
18. Davidson, 'Choreomania', 133, 136.
19. Davidson, 'Choreomania', 131n1.
20. Davidson, 'Choreomania', 133–134.
21. Davidson, 'Choreomania', 131–132.
22. Davidson, 'Choreomania', 134.
23. Browning, *Infectious Rhythm*, 7.

congregating, to the Betsileo region inland. The movement spread from the periphery to the centre of the island, though Davidson also witnessed dancers congregating 'wonderful[ly]' in the remotest parts of the island, 'near solitary cottages'.[24] In these remote locations, the dancing was almost idyllic; but in the capital it assumed more disquieting tones, as the intensity of congregation coupled with the dancers' strange demeanour overpowered city dwellers, in his view. Everywhere they went the *ramanenjana* were accompanied by musicians and bystanders. They shook and frothed, performing various acts of mimicry. In particular they were recognized for swinging their heads from side to side and moving their hands up and down. According to Davidson, the 'attack' or crisis particular to the *ramanenjana* proceeded according to a distinct dramaturgy. They first suffered a pain in the chest and severe restlessness and then ran energetically towards any music they could hear, uttered deep sighs, with their gaze absent, and after dancing for some time, fell to the ground; as in narratives of the medieval dances, they exhausted musicians in the process.

The medico-political dramaturgy Davidson proffered extended to the *ramanenjana*'s places of encounter and contestation. Not entirely unlike St. Vitus's dancers, Davidson noted, the *ramanenjana* gathered in large numbers at symbolic sites; their words were largely unintelligible to observers. Props helped their collective performance of disaffection. The *ramanenjana* 'were fond of carrying about with them sugar-canes', he remarked. 'They held them in their hands, or carried them over the shoulder while they danced', sometimes balancing water bottles on their heads in a precarious show of acrobatism. All this took place in the open air, at a 'sacred stone' eight feet high and twelve feet in diameter 'in a plain below the city, where many of the kings of Madagascar have been crowned'. They 'danced there for hours on end, and concluded by placing the sugarcane, as a sort of offering, upon the stone'.[25] The Vatomasina, as this site was known, was chief among sacred sites in Madagascar and thus a natural rallying place for rebels to gather in their ecstatic enactment of sovereignty. Meeting in large numbers at night, the *ramanenjana* claimed intercourse with their ancestors, from whom they sought succour.[26] The dances lasted for many days, in the countryside as well as in Ambohimanga, the former capital turned Madagascar's sacred city, similarly a natural nexus of activity during the rebellion of 1863.

En route between sacred sites, and while they sang, danced, and trembled, the *ramanenjana* shouted threats and curses to the accompaniment of hand clapping, drums, or whatever other musical instruments were available. They were rumoured thus to be not only accompanied by but also still communicating with the dead (*ambiroa*), especially the former monarchs Andrianampoinimerina (1745–1810), Radama I (1810–1828), and the formidable Ranavalona I, 'The Cruel' (1828–1861), whose luggage was rumoured to have been entrusted to them by lesser members of the spirit world. Goaded on thus by spirit helpers, the *ramanenjana* endeavoured to carry Ranavalona's belongings from the land of the dead, Ambondrombé, to the capital,

24. The affliction, Davidson wrote, 'spread rapidly, as by a sort of infection, even to the most remote villages in the central province or *Imerina*, so that, having occasion to visit a distant part of the country in company with an Englishman, we found even in remote hamlets, and, more wonderful still, near solitary cottages, the sound of music, indicating that the mania had spread even there'. Davidson, 'Choreomania', 131. Further contemporary accounts appear in 'Missions de Madagascar', in *Annales de la propagation de la foi. Recueil périodique des lettres des évêques et des missionnaires des missions des deux mondes, et de tous les documents relatifs aux missions et à l'œuvre de la propagation de la foi*, vol. 35 (Lyon, 1863), 82–88; and 'Les Ramanenjanas, étrangleurs de Radama II, roi de Madagascar', in *Le Moniteur universel: Journal officiel de l'Empire Français*, no. 188, 7 July 1863, 937–938. According to the CWM/LMS board minutes for 1862–1865, James Sibree sailed for Madagascar on 24 August 1863, arriving in Antananarivo on 13 October, so would have missed the height of the uprising; he provides a second-hand account that rehearses Davidson's perspective in James Sibree, 'Appendix F. The Imanènjana, or Dancing Mania', in *Madagascar and Its People. Notes of a Four Years' Residence. With a Sketch of the History, Position, and Prospects of Mission Work amongst the Malagasy* (London: Religious Tract Society, 1870), 561–565. See also George A. Shaw, *Madagascar and France: With Some Account of the Island, Its People, Its Resources and Development* (London: Religious Tract Society, 1885); 'La chorémanie de Madagascar: Ramanenjana', *Journal Officiel de Madagascar et dépendances* (Tananarive), 29 August 1903: 9942–9943; Victorin Malzac, *Histoire du Royaume Hova, depuis ses origines jusqu'à sa fin* (Tananarive: Imprimerie Catholique, 1930); Hubert Deschamps, *Histoire de Madagascar* (Paris: Éditions Berger-Levrault, 1960). On Davidson's missionary work with smallpox, see A. Dandouau and G.-S. Chapus, *Histoire des Populations de Madagascar* (Paris: Larose, 1952), 207.

25. Davidson, 'Choreomania', 133. Besides sugar canes, they also placed fruit and branches on the sacred stone. See Émile Appolis, 'Une épidémie de Ramanenjana à Madagascar (1863–1864)', *Annales de l'Université de Madagascar* 3 (1964): 59–63, 61; reprinted in Charles Ranaivo, ed., *Ramanenjana* (Tananarive, Annales de l'Université de Madagascar, 1934–1964).

26. Davidson, 'Choreomania', 133.

where she would help them depose her puppet son.[27] Ghostly keys, swords, soap, chairs, chests, mattresses, and silver cutlery were all mimetically relayed from town to town, equipping dancers with a symbolic arsenal connecting them to the dead.[28]

By 12 March 1863, news of the commotion seized the capital; dancers followed, reaching Antananarivo by March 26. Along the way, those who had lagged behind were being chastised by helper spirits; they twisted and cried, writhing, as if being beaten. Many dancers' eyes were sunken in, rolled back, or bloodshot, further earning them the designation *ramenabe* ('all-red').[29] By the time the *ramanenjana* had congregated on the streets of Antananarivo, accompanied by ever-increasing scores of onlookers, the capital was in a state of heightened agitation. According to the Malagasy historian Émile Appolis (1903–1980), even some soldiers became affected by the 'dancing disease', throwing down their weapons and contorting their bodies; officers and one general were reported to have joined in the dance.[30]

In Davidson's eyes, the *ramanenjana*'s contortions constituted a textbook case of the dancing disease. But closer analysis of the *imanenjana*, as Muecke has argued, suggests this can be read in biopolitical terms as a collective revolt.[31] It can also further be read as a 'choreography of protest' (in Foster's terms) and choreopolitics (in Lepecki's). Bodies not only twisted and convulsed; they congregated in a way that suggested concerted action. The *ramanenjana* were '[creating] interference', to borrow Foster's term, from pacifist Gene Sharp.[32] They were implementing a regime of the 'not yet' that Lepecki argues constitutes choreopolitics, a bodily movement aiming towards a better state of affairs: more freedom conceived as the exercise of a potential for transformation.[33]

Paradoxically, the *ramanenjana*, like their medical observers, performed this interference by a movement of recursion, calling back to the past. Medical observers did this by calling on their own set of spirits—those of medical precedent, operating as props to buttress present theorization. But theory, like political conditions, moved along with these acts of recursion. In Madagascar, choreomania did not only denote a biohistorical upheaval seizing individuals' limbs as if they were caught in a gust of wind or a ferocious torrent. This was no longer the quaint tremor of the limbs observed, even admired, among medical subjects beatifically recalling bacchanals but a collective upheaval that signalled regime change. The stakes were higher than ever, and visitors, including Davidson, found themselves in the thick of a revolt in which they were directly implicated as associates of the loathed king.

REBELLION HOSTED BY THE SPIRITS OF THE PAST: THE DANCERS DEPOSE A PUPPET MONARCH

Traditional Malagasy law held that an unpopular monarch should be unseated. Radama II was thus ripe for being deposed; the *ramanenjana* merely reconfigured traditional practices to fit the colonial culture in the capital. The European presence had long been disputed on the Great Island. During the rule of Radama I, government sympathy towards missionaries had meant state protection, resulting in large-scale printing and translations of the New Testament and a rash of baptisms. Ranavalona I then instituted a sharp turn against the Christian church, eliminating nearly all European presence.[34] She was a notoriously powerful queen who dressed in Parisian fashions but maintained deep spiritual ties to

---

27. See Appolis, 'Une épidémie de Ramanenjana à Madagascar', 60. See also Bloch, *Placing the Dead*, esp. 22–35 and 125–222; Muecke, 'Choreomanias'; Muecke, *Contingency in Madagascar* (Bristol: Intellect Books, 2012), 38–42; Françoise Raison, 'Les Ramanenjana', *Lumière* (Tananarive), 13 August 1972.

28. In Raison, 'Les Ramanenjana', n.p.

29. 'Ra-menabe' also designates what Dr. Tsimahafotsy Randriamaro described as a collective hallucination, in which those possessed see a deep, vivid red colour that sends them frenetically on fugues and peregrinations through the northeast of the country. Tsimahafotsy Randriamaro, 'Le Ramanenjana à Madagascar', *Revue médicale de Madagascar* 1 (1959): 2–10, 4.

30. Appolis, 'Une épidémie de Ramanenjana à Madagascar', 61.

31. Muecke, 'Choreomanias', 7.

32. Foster borrows this phrase from pacifist Gene Sharp to describe non-violent protest. Foster, 'Choreographies of Protest', 395.

33. Lepecki, 'Choreopolice and Choreopolitics', 13–27.

34. Madagascar began undergoing major changes when colonial powers took hold of the administration of public affairs on the Great Island a few decades prior. The island's geographic location en route to the Cape of Good Hope had made of Madagascar an important strategic site for a variety of European interests: before the Suez Canal was opened in 1869, Madagascar was considered

traditional Malagasy practice and to the old Merina pantheon.[35] When her son Radama II acceded to the throne, he immediately reversed her anti-European policies, replacing her counsellors with his *menamaso* friends: the *menamaso* were pro-European, often Christian Merina nobility who broadly adopted European ways. Radama II was allying himself closely with British and French interests, offering them missionary and economic protection in exchange for material favours.[36]

This turned the Malagasy people against him. Within two years of his accession to the throne, Radama II's policies resulted in the near obliteration of Malagasy sovereignty on the island. Mutual courtship between the king and the colonial powers had intensified Christianization, angering the old nobility and the shaman class. More grievously, Radama II was widely considered to have sold the island to Europe, going against long-standing sentiment in Madagascar against foreign ownership of Malagasy land. All land was traditionally supposed to belong to the sovereign and remain under his or her sole jurisdiction. Yet Radama II offered the French Lambert Company possession of all rights over Malagasy territory between latitudes 12 and 16 degrees south, provoking local opposition so strong that a concession was soon made for the government to pay the Lambert Company $240,000 to rescind the claim. But the damage

was done. The Caldwell Charter, which Radama II signed on 23 August 1862 with the English, similarly granted substantial freedom of commerce and land seizure to the British, as well as full rights to product exportation and mine exploitation, returning only 10 percent of their profit to the state.[37] This surprised even the missionaries. Reverend William Ellis (1794–1872), a close associate of the king, remarked on the dizzying rate of Christianization, suggesting that there were now seven thousand Christians in Madagascar out of a total population in the capital of forty thousand (with 4 million on the whole island). Ellis attributed the 'remarkable spread' of Christianity to the king's 'favourable' policies and strong support for missionaries and traders. Davidson, who counted four thousand Christians on the island in a letter of 2 May 1862, similarly boasted of the strong presence of Christianity in his dispensary.[38] But this turn towards Europe was also seen as disruptive and taboo by many Malagasy. Hats, swine, and the missionaries' prized colour—black—were all unwelcome and were derided by the *ramanenjana* when they took to the streets.

The *ramanenjana* directed their discontentment against Europeans and against the king, who had let these foreigners in. When the revolt spread and hundreds of *ramanenjana* gathered around the Vatomasina to sing and dance in praise of his deceased mother, Radama II was ostensibly

a highly lucrative African possession. Its situation on Britain's commercial highway to India and China and its importance as a naval station for a Pacific squadron in case of war were not lost on journalists commenting on the events of 1863. In an article published on 11 July 1863 in the *Illustrated London News*, shortly after news of the *imanenjana* broke, writers noted that Franco-British rivalry for control of Madagascar had exacerbated political tensions, making this into an outright 'revolution'. 'The Revolution in Madagascar', *Illustrated London News*, 11 July 1863, vol. 63, no. 1212. See Sonia E. Howe, *The Drama of Madagascar* (London: Methuen, 1938), vii.

35. Howe, *The Drama of Madagascar*, 173–174. On Ranavalona I's anti-European policies, see also Dandouau and Chapus, *Histoire des Populations de Madagascar*, 189–193. Among other laws instituted during her reign, Dandouau and Chapus note a ban instituted 1 March 1835 against association with European work and religion; forced self-denunciations and retractions for anyone converted to Christianity, on penalty of capital punishment; as well as a 13 May 1845 law forcing Europeans to conform to Malagasy laws on the same footing as locals, thus subjecting them to corvées (forced labour), etc.

36. Radama II gained a bad reputation for collecting gifts from European authorities eager to win him over in exchange for trading rights and protection of their economic and missionary presence. In a letter to the directors of the London Missionary Society dated 12 August 1862, the king's deputy Ra Hanrika wrote thanks for gifts sent to Radama II via Ellis, including a bound English Bible, a portrait of the king in oils, a copy of Ellis's *History of Madagascar*, a large pair of globes mounted on a mahogany tripod, a royal foils atlas, and a figured velvet table cover. Ra Hanrika to directors of the London Missionary Society, 12 August 1862, CWM/LMS, Madagascar Incoming Correspondence, box 6, 1859–1863.

37. See George A. Shaw, *Madagascar and France*, 86; Deschamps, *Histoire de Madagascar*, 173–175. Madagascar's history in the following decades continued to be checkered: it became a French protectorate in 1890 and was under military control of the French by 1895–1896, when the Merina monarchy was formally abolished. It gained full independence only in 1960, although the Malagasy Republic was proclaimed in 1958 and reforms were introduced in 1956. All this took place after Madagascar had passed back into the hands of the British during World War II for one year and after a bloody uprising in 1947 that resulted in the death of eighty thousand Malagasy.

38. Claiming the importance of his clinic for Britain's mission, Davidson remarked that 'more heathen hear of the gospel . . . [there] than in the churches'. Andrew Davidson to directors of the London Missionary Society, 2 May 1862, CWM/LMS, Madagascar Incoming Correspondence, box 6, 1859–1863.

delighted, not indicating any suspicion that their turn towards her might concomitantly indicate a rejection of his rule.[39] In private, Radama II stated excitedly to Ellis that 'the spirits of his ancestors were coming from the north in the most formidable array, even with muskets and cannon'. Although Ellis expressed some scepticism as to the propitiousness or even truth of the affair, 'the king laughed and changed the subject'.[40] Camille de la Vaissière (1836–1887), a French missionary also close to the king at the time, noted that he seemed to be delighted that such an extraordinary event was taking place during his reign, as if it were a sign of its felicity rather than an omen of its impending conclusion.[41] For the British missionary Robert Toy, Radama II had implicitly encouraged the revolt through routine mismanagement leading to outright anarchy.[42]

The king seemed to be pandering to Catholics and Protestants, French and British, but feared the wrath of his subjects as well and pandered to them too. Although '[listening] with the most profound attention to the truths of the gospel', Radama II would, no sooner than a priest was out of sight, turn to his 'favourites' and perform the sermon 'in pantomime', to their 'delight'.[43] He decreed on 24 April 1863 that all Europeans should take off their hats before the frenzied ramanenjana, who reacted violently to the sight of these hated imports; a fine of 5 pounds was imposed on anyone who failed to comply. 'Of course we did no such thing', wrote Davidson, 'and at last the English were exempted from this proclamation'.[44] Ellis remarked that encounters with the ramanenjana were vexing for Christian officials, who continued to wear their hats, such that some had to duck down side streets 'rather than meet one of these vagrant dancers'.[45] Yet by 1 May the king himself was going around the capital without a hat, offering another mixed signal to the Malagasy and Europeans alike.[46]

Overall the 'revolution' of 1863, by which the king was deposed, was relatively pacific. Twenty thousand people stormed the capital in the week leading up to his removal, many having come from far away. But though the king had few troops in his service at the time and was, significantly, murdered in a skirmish, reportedly only about fifteen other people died, mostly menamaso members of his pro-European inner circle.[47] The ramanenjana had successfully brought about regime change in a dramatic but overall peaceful demonstration—a seizure of power noted by Europeans for its convulsive, literally seizure-like form. The ramanenjana twisted their bodies and in performing this deformation of the 'body politic' reinstated a rule

39. Described in Appolis, 'Une épidémie de Ramanenjana à Madagascar', 61, who cites a letter from P. Finaz to P. Jouen. See Raison, 'Les Ramanenjana'.

40. In Howe, The Drama of Madagascar, 228.

41. Le P. de la Vaissière, Histoire de Madagascar, ses habitants et ses missionnaires, 2 vols., vol. 1 (Paris: Librairie Victor Lecoffre, 1884), 393.

42. Toy wrote: 'While professing to despise the whole affair, everything [the King] . . . has done since its appearance has been to encourage it'. Robert Toy to directors of the London Missionary Society, CWM/LMS, Madagascar Incoming Correspondence, box 6, 1859–1863.

43. Writing to the directors of the London Missionary Society on 4 May 1862, Davidson noted that the king's leniency was leading to trouble. He complained of Radama II's 'foolishness', 'weakness', 'outrageous immorality', and high susceptibility to flattery, which was 'disgusting [even] the native officers'. Andrew Davidson to directors of the London Missionary Society, 4 May 1862, CWM/LMS, Madagascar Incoming Correspondence, box 6, 1859–1863. See also Deschamps, Histoire de Madagascar, 173–175. Everyone seemed implicated in the political machinations. Ellis noticed that the dancers, carrying offerings to Radama II from the 'land of the dead', flattered the king's vanity. 'The rumours of the voices and visions . . . seemed to be gaining increasing influence over [the king]. It was stated that his mother, the late queen, had appeared to some of these persons, and had said that she was disturbed and offended by the increase of the praying in Imerina, which she did not allow, and also at the swine being permitted to pollute the city. The bearers of the reports also carried presents to the king, which they said they had been directed by the spirits of his ancestors to bring'. William Ellis, Madagascar Revisited. Describing the Events of a New Reign and the Revolution Which Followed (London: John Murray, 1867), 265–266. Yet Ellis himself, Davidson argued, was being plotted against by the 'idol worshippers' because of his apparent intimacy with the king. With 'gifts' of 'death stones, fragments from graves, porcupine quills, herbs, reptiles, and others not easily named', they were conspiring to kill Ellis, though they failed ultimately to do so. Andrew Davidson to directors of the London Missionary Society, 4 May 1862, CWM/LMS, Madagascar Incoming Correspondence, box 6, 1859–1863. One theory suggested that Ellis killed Radama II himself by strangling him with a silk scarf in retribution for the king's supposed preference for the French. See Gabriel Gravier, Madagascar: Les Malgaches, Origines de la colonisation française, la conquête (Paris: Charles Delagrave, Libraire-Éditeur, 1904), 494–495.

44. Andrew Davidson to directors of the London Missionary Society, 4 May 1862, CWM/LMS, Madagascar Incoming Correspondence, box 6, 1859–1863. See Howe, 229.

45. Ellis, Madagascar Revisited, 267.

46. Appolis, 'Une épidémie de Ramanenjana à Madagascar', 61–62.

47. P. Adrien Boudou, Le Meurtre de Radama II, documents et discussion (Tananarive: Imprimerie Moderne de L'Emyrne, Pitot de la Beaujardière, 1938), 56.

sovereign to them, in which the monarch was a representation, not a state of exception; the state of exception was theirs to claim. The king's wife, Queen Rabodo, crowned under the ancestral name Rasoherina (1814–1868), was now set on the throne, along with the prime minister (ousted a year later), and, ruling with an iron fist, as had Ranavalona I, implemented anti-foreign policies isolating Madagascar from the West again.[48] A few more skirmishes were reported the following year at around the same time, and again the year after, but they were quickly subdued. These, too, like the upheaval of 1863, were described by observers as 'dancing manias'.[49] A further outbreak was reported in the Betsileo region in the 1910s, again to counter colonial incursions, but it, too, was suppressed.[50]

Yet the 'dancing disease', as it came to be known by observers, had come to form an integral part of anti-European practices curbing political power, particularly aimed against foreign intrusion. The 'dancing'—the choreography of this event of deposition—was now part of a broader history of choreopolitical practices that visitors to Madagascar described in the medical language of 'crisis': acts of bodily transformation that signalled a complex mode of acting out not easily assimilated to dance or disease, politics, religion, or spirituality.

THE POSSESSION OF THE DISPOSSESSED: TROUBLING CHRISTIANITY

Gatherings in the provinces like those reported by Davidson suggested a choreopolitics of appearance that, when conjugated with political grievance, resulted in the king's removal from the throne. But a host of smaller-scale practices were noted far beyond the skirmish in the capital. Bodily and spiritual exercises calling up the spirits of the dead were conjugated with the language of pathological sympathy, making these ghostly demarcations *appear* in the light of comparative medical science. Reverend Marc Finaz (1815–1880), a Jesuit missionary stationed in Madagascar, like Davidson, described the *ramanenjana*'s uprising as a 'crisis' and the participants as 'patients', though, also like Davidson, he does not appear to have attempted to cure (or to exorcise) any.[51] Instead, he seems baffled by the events, emphasizing the *ramanenjana*'s overwrought mental states and apparent lack of control as well as his own inability quite to know how to explain them. The *ramanenjana*'s exercises were characterized by physical transformations and altered states of mind, manifest for the most part, he noted, as dancing but also as a whole host of extraordinary activities and abilities. The reification of these theatres of crisis into choreomania reveals a fraught relationship in Western scientific writing between reality and appearance—in effect with the very *effect* that 'reality' was supposed to have on what *appears*. Bodies performing unusual feats of transformation seemed to be explicable only by recourse to the invisible action of the imagination. So, too, the unaccountability of these instances of acting out suggested a disease that could only have for its *effect* a corporeal transformation produced more or less by 'nothing'. In other words, medical language took these scenes fetishistically as signs of 'nothing' acting mysteriously on the body; it was that 'nothing' which—when it spread—became reified; made, in Taussig's terms, into disease, where nothing but contagion itself was spreading.[52]

---

48. See Robert Toy to directors of the London Missionary Society, dated 30 June 1864 and 31 May 1865, and R. G. Hartley to directors of the London Missionary Society, 29 May 1865. Hartley notes that a 'distrust of foreigners is deeply rooted in the hearts of the people'. For Toy, there was a 'growing hostility both to Christianity and to foreigners on the part of many in authority'. CWM/LMS, Madagascar Incoming Correspondence, box 7, 1864–1866. See also Raison, 'Les Ramanenjana'.

49. As the British missionary R. G. Hartley wrote from Antananarivo on 29 May 1865: 'The dancing mania which preceded the disturbances of 1863 has reappeared—this may portend nothing, it may however be the forerunner partly cause and partly consequence, of an excitement the results of which it is impossible to foresee', as in 1863. 'It has not yet appeared in the town and strict orders against it have been issued by the Queen'. Yet, 'it still . . . keeps breaking out though not', Hartley added, 'as yet to any alarming extent'. R. G. Hartley, Antananarivo, to directors of the London Missionary Society, 29 May 1865, CWM/LMS, Madagascar Incoming Correspondence, box 7, 1864–1866.

50. Pierre Boiteu, *Contribution à l'Histoire de la nation malgache* (Paris: Éditions Sociales, 1958), 138n.

51. 'The crisis is first evident by virtue of a violent pain in the head', Finaz wrote; 'blood flows to the upper limbs, the pulse is sharp and irregular'. Then, 'the patient goes from a state of extreme agitation to one of total prostration. He is seized by sudden frights, his words and gestures are broken; he seems, given his gait, to be half-drunk, his eyes are glazed, and fix on nothing around him, as if he were totally unconscious of the visible world and preoccupied only with the invisible world with which he claims to be communicating'; cited in Appolis, 'Une épidémie de Ramanenjana à Madagascar', 61. See Malzac, *Histoire du Royaume Hova*, 346.

52. On disease as reification, see esp. Taussig, *The Nervous System*, 83–109.

The state of the *ramanenjana* was in every sense a state of exception: it transformed participants' bodies beyond recognition, granting them unusual knowledge, and overturned social hierarchies in order to maintain an ancestral rule of law, ecstatically. The *ramanenjana*'s ability to communicate with the dead astonished Finaz. 'I have even heard of children only twelve or thirteen years old', he wrote, 'describe in the minutest detail traits, gaits, clothes of people they claim to see before their very eyes, and the elderly unanimously recognize one of these children's ancestors, or family slaves dead twenty or thirty years before the young visionaries were born'. What's more, the *ramanenjana* performed virtuosic feats in these states of possession or ecstasy-belonging: 'men who are not normally swimmers can suddenly swim, during these crises', Finaz wrote, 'though they lose this skill as soon as they have returned to a state of health'. Normal physiological functions were likewise supplanted by extraordinary abilities, often dancing, including in the most physically unlikely and socially taboo spaces. 'The *Ramanenjana* can be seen dancing with as much ease on a pointed rooftop as on any mat', Finaz wrote, and added: 'others carry jugs of water on their heads, dancing, wiggling around, bending in every which way without letting a single drop of water fall. They walk barefoot on prickly nopal [a type of cactus] and euphorbia [a plant with a poisonous sap] without their feet showing any scratches. They express no fear and no fatigue: girls, otherwise frail and fearful, go in the middle of the night to dance on their family graves (a terrible sacrilege in the eyes of the Malagasy), and stay there dancing on the tombstones until dawn'.[53] Everything suggested a choreopolitical upheaval of everyday life. The dancers succeeded in overcoming fear and emotional limitations, fatigue and physical stress.[54] In this sense, they were 'possessed' by some greater willpower granting them an extraordinary transcendence of the everyday; they experienced the *ecstatic* dissolution of their

present time with a performative communion reaching back to ancestors to bond together through shared memories of the dead—their way to actualize a better future. For the *ramanenjana*, a host of taboos had been broken by the king's squandering of Malagasy land. Entering into altered physical and emotional states enabled men and women, girls and boys, to enact another rule of law, mobilizing the individual and social body through a performance of 'sickness' (ancestor possession)—in effect mobilizing all the technologies of self by which, Taussig writes, a host of lived realities are reconfigured, as much as they may also be reappropriated and rewritten through the 'fabulation of reality' performed by doctors imputing to them a whole other range of reality and falsity principles.[55] The discourse on 'choreomania' rewrote the *imanenjana* as epidemic sickness, harmful to its hosts and almost equally to bystanders. In effect, the spectre of the consequences appeared, positing illness in the *future anterior*.

Malagasy possession practices, including the *tromba*, the *vazimba*, the *sampy*, the Salamanga, and the Fitampoha, were all mapped by observers such as Finaz onto a Christian model of religious enthusiasm that derided intense gesture and disorderly congregation and suggested instead a Christian model of gestural unobtrusiveness that saturated Western concepts of health and disease. Spiritual belief alone, rather than movement, should in this Christian-inflected worldview relieve aches and pains, anxiety, or spirit possession. Religion and spirituality had to be suave, quiet, still, torque-like; intense corporeal expression was misguided at best or diseased. For the British missionary J. A. (John Alden) Houlder, writing not long after the revolt of 1863, the Salamanga tribe constituted a form of 'native shakers' who were deluded, he thought, in their attempts to use music and movement to drive a 'sickness' 'out of their bodies'. They hopped up and down to the sound of drums, oblivious to his injunctions.[56]

---

53. Cited in Appolis, 'Une épidémie de Ramanenjana à Madagascar', 61. See Malzac, *Histoire du Royaume Hova*, 346.

54. In Appolis, 'Une épidémie de Ramanenjana à Madagascar', 346.

55. See esp. Taussig, *The Nervous System*, 86.

56. He wrote: 'On arrival we heard the beating of a drum, and a great noise of shouting and clapping hands. Looking in at the door of the house from whence it all came, I saw that the place was full of people, all crowded round three of their number . . . dancing up and down, hoping thereby to drive the sickness out of their bodies. They had been at it quite a long time with no indication of success. This was the custom called 'Sàlamànga', which was almost universally followed before the introduction of Christianity . . . . What with the foul air in the close place, and the long continued violence of their enforced exertion, perspiration was pouring from every part of the poor creatures' bodies, and they were ready to drop from exhaustion. Happily I succeeded in inducing these native shakers to desist for a time from their attempted cure, telling them it could do no good, and that if they went to the missionary at the nearest station he would probably be able to relieve their sufferings. But the people did not settle

Like Davidson and Finaz, Houlder was in the margins of a scene that refused modernity as he conceived it, while his colonizer's status as *fady* (taboo), *hasina* (supernaturally powerful), *vazaha* (alien to the island), and *vahiny* (alien to the clan) exacerbated the intensity of the spiritual conflict he witnessed.[57]

But for him, as for other European spectators, at once characters in the biopolitical drama of possession and standing warily on its sidelines, the shaking was intelligible inasmuch as it could be subject to comparative speculation that cross-referenced local events with scenes from the European past. Yet the events themselves were hybrid, recuperating Christian iconography to suggest the sort of 'circulatory system' that Gilroy alludes to in regard to the Black Atlantic and that we may apply to colonial bodies and practices more broadly at this time. Jesus, widely considered among Malagasy the 'royal ancestor' of the Christians, was believed to perform his own annual return on 5 April, at the end of the Christian Holy Week (Easter). This coincided with the height of the dancing 'epidemic',[58] which can thus be understood to have staged an iconic battle between Christian and Merina deities. The dancing enacted a culture war.

In this sense ghosted with the spectre of political uprisings, choreomania epitomized the modern colonial condition: 'pathological' movement was described among the disenfranchised and lower classes. Colonial physicians moved around the world yet appeared in these accounts to be individually 'still', torque-like, not possessed by unnecessary shaking or congregating. Yet when men and women in situations of political dispossession moved their bodies and circulated throughout the land against the grain of administrative power, this came to be described as an epidemic disease of disorderly locomotion. 'Choreomania' came in colonial medicine to describe a disorder of the inappositely moving underclasses.

CIRCULATORY SYSTEMS AND *GEO*-CHOREOPOLITICS

The 'possessed' performance of dispossession suggests an order of dance cutting across cultural, geographic, and aesthetico-political lines. Following Franko, I argue that, choreopolitically, movement (and dance) enacts a relationship between choreographic procedures and mass movements, including administrative procedures and protest.[59] Dance and popular movements are thus also public acts of choreopolitical mobilization. Dance, Franko writes, 'may perform protest, a direct and local way of upsetting a power balance'.[60] Thus 'epidemic choreas' are instances of state power becoming publically imbalanced or, as in Madagascar, becoming balanced *again*. In the process of disembalancing and rebalancing politics in the capital, the 'disorder' of dance becomes apparent *as disorder* (in effect as disease)—and concomitantly now of choreography. This is significant not only for the history of dance—as of the scientific and the political (in Franko's sense, inasmuch as dance and the political co-constitute one another 'intradisciplinarily')[61]—but also for the broader work of writing history: a history that is in effect always *of motion*, of the way power shifts and moves so that ways of seeing disorder (including 'disorderly' bodies) emerge. This zone of indeterminacy—these processes of translatio—displace 'choreomania' onto new zones of intensity and indigeneity—articulating new choreopolitics—representing the interplay of sameness and difference that characterizes the 'palimpsestical imprints of past, present and future' that are constitutive, in Bhabha's terms, of political emergence and change.[62]

'Choreomanias', then—their discursive history—help us rearticulate 'dance' in relationship to the performance of state politics, specifically as the politics of prior orders of

---

down very quietly, and, ever and anon, we heard the noise of the drumming and shouting'. J. A. Houlder, *Among the Malagasy: An Unconventional Record of Missionary Experience* (London: James Clarke, 1912), 79.

57. On the notion of *fady*, see esp. Arnold van Gennep, *Tabou et Totémisme à Madagascar: Étude descriptive et théorique* (Paris: Ernest Leroux, Éditeur, 1904). On foreigners' mixed status, see esp. 40.

58. Raison, 'Les Ramanenjana'.

59. Franko, 'Dance and the Political', 8.

60. Franko, 'Dance and the Political', 6.

61. Franko, 'Dance and the Political', 15.

62. Homi K. Bhabha, 'Foreword: Framing Fanon by Homi K. Bhabha', in Frantz Fanon, *The Wretched of the Earth*, trans. Richard Philcox (New York: Grove Press, 2004), vii–xli, xvi.

history *reappearing* as formlessness in the present. Thus this discursive history (this genealogy) of choreomanias in Madagascar and Brazil also helps us reconfigure the ways we understand movement figured in cultural theories, as a discursive force primarily allied with 'normally' moving bodies. Movement, theorized by Bhabha, Clifford, Gilroy, Roach, and others, typically describes the transcultural movement (or displacement) and attendant intermixture—the intercultural encounters—between bodies across geographies and historical eras.[63] These include all sorts of bodies but generally foreground ones that are black or white, mestizo or hybrid: bodies marked by race but not necessarily by intracorporeal states of disruptive motion. Interestingly, Boudin's entanglement of inter- and intracorporeal movement, furthered in Davidson, Finaz, and others' narratives, suggests a slightly different set of concerns, one I propose we use to supplement cultural theories of circulation. With Boudin, movement corresponds to the choreographic notion of bodies moving in space, whether they are shaking (in place) or travelling (across space). His alliance of choreas and crusades sets the choreographic at the heart of a concept of human nature (and history), offering a twist on the 'travelling culture' or 'circulatory system' that Clifford, Gilroy, and Roach put forward. For Gilroy, following Clifford, concepts of travel and circulation help to explain the perpetual re-hybridization of black, mestizo, and European bodies and ideas in transatlantic trade, highlighting the journeys that intellectuals, colonials, and slaves alike underwent, cross-pollinating one another's narratives and cultural practices (music, carnival, etc.).[64] Conversely, Boudin's emphasis on the relative singularity of cultures—in spite of their apparently universal tendencies to move—suggests a 'circulatory system' founded in crosscultural comparison but not yet an intermixture that was material and bodily, conceptual and narrative. Yet, for Boudin, another cross-section of movement occurs, affiliating bodies and spaces. With Boudin, bodies move across, with, and through but also in place. This perspective forecasts the dual emphasis on 'roots' and 'routes' that Clifford and Gilroy highlight and that characterizes the *ramanenjana*'s circulation through Madagascar; and it forecasts Clifford's notion of movement designating the fact of 'people going places'.[65] But Boudin's emphasis on people 'going places' coming to be ordered in a medico-anthropological taxonomy alongside twisting and jerking, hallucinating and dancing, suggests choreographic disorder signalling an aesthetico-political state of exception, a choreography of repossession. 'Politics', Franko writes, 'are not located directly 'in' dance, but in the way dance manages to occupy (cultural) space'.[66] With Boudin, the dancing disease is a state of exception intra- and intercorporeally.

The 'circulatory systems' in place in the nineteenth century by which men and women from the colonies went to Europe to study, returned with European ideas, and rewrote them at home, contrapuntally informed by local case histories, suggest continuous processes of rearticulation—the retheorization of movement and bodiliness—not only in the periphery of the colonial empires, but in the circulating literature that they produced. In this sense, following Gilroy and Bhabha, I submit that choreomanias reveal a rhizomorphic and palimpsestical literature according to which circulating histories are continually rewritten in an emergent, scientific global modernity that thinks about the ways bodies move *ecstatically*.

---

63. See for example Bhabha, *Location of Culture*; Clifford, *Routes*; Gilroy, *The Black Atlantic*; Roach, *Cities of the Dead*; also Taylor, *The Archive and the Repertoire*.

64. Gilroy articulates the concept of the transatlantic 'circulatory system', among others, in *The Black Atlantic* (88). See also Roach's adoption of this notion in *Cities of the Dead* (esp. 5), though Roach emphasizes 'circum-Atlantic cultural exchange' (5). For Gilroy's recuperation of Clifford's notion of 'travelling cultures', see e.g. Gilroy, *The Black Atlantic*, 17.

65. Clifford, *Routes*, 2.

66. Franko, 'Dance and the Political', 5. 'Cultural' space with the *ramanenjana* suggests something more than political or state aesthetics shaping new forms of national identification or monarchical rule: the *ramanenjana* perform a transversal occupation and *inhabitation* of space as their ancestral inheritance and bequest. Dance is what (politically) occupies cultural space inasmuch as this occupation brings about the continuation of politics tied indigenously to sacred sites. The same is true for the *sertões*, who claimed a nearly natural order of politics antedating the nation state; for the *sertões*, however, remaining *in place* allowed them to escape the vortex of power in the capital and so reconstitute themselves along other (ex-centric) lines.

TROMBA, BILO, RAMANENJANA: POSSESSION IN MADAGASCAR AS 'MÉMOIRE COLLECTIVE'

The *ramanenjana* were making political history through a performative recourse to the dead. Meanwhile Davidson, Boudin, Finaz, Houlder, and others tapped into another sort of ancestor worship to grace their own discursive ends. Colonial writers' efforts to link the *imanenjana* with earlier forms of choreomania mapped contemporary possession practices and political unrest onto one another as an epidemic dancing disease. Yet the complex of possession practices the *ramanenjana* participated in suggests choreographic precedent, a variation designed to oust foreigners from Malagasy land. A range of pre-existing practices underpinned the *ramanenjana*'s movements when they took to the streets. Henry Rusillon (1872–1938) argued that the 1863 *imanenjana* was grounded in the *tromba*, a traditional Malagasy possession practice. His thesis partially rehearsed Davidson's account, reproduced in an 1889 issue of the *Antananarivo Annual*, and was supplemented by writings by the missionary Antoine Abinal (1829–1887), de la Vaissière's *Vingt ans à Madagascar* (1885), and other eyewitness accounts. Rusillon described the *tromba* as a convulsive, gesticulatory, performative 'malady', a type of possession like St. Vitus's dance and the tarantella, noting, like Boudin, however, that further study should be pursued before more comparisons could accurately be made.[67] But comparisons offered the allure of transcultural diagnosis buttressed with historical hindsight, and for Rusillon the *tromba* of the Sakalave and the *bilo* of the Betsileo region spread, like the *imanenjana* and

other choreomanias, like a 'plague'. The *imanenjana*, just like the *bilo* and *tromba*, was in effect a type of choreomania and a routine possession practice in Madagascar, he argued: all described 'a nervous disease that affects everyone, men and women, young and old, but especially the young'. Significantly, Rusillon outlines a dramaturgy different from other accounts: those who suffered, he wrote, 'claim that their head aches, they leave their homes suddenly, go wandering, sometimes naked, by the hills and valleys, usually near the tombs. They are agitated, shaking their limbs and their whole bodies nervously'; he adds that they also have 'their hands sometimes held behind their backs as if they were tied up, then releasing them suddenly, they cry, through all of this, haltingly, "Hiaka, hiaka"': a cry of defiance and victory.[68] This suggests that the *ramanenjana* were engaging in a rehearsal for liberation, a performative *pre-enactment* of colonial oppression's undoing. They theatricalized their liberation in the symbolic gesture of clasping and releasing their hands behind their backs.[69] This slightly reconfigures Franko's discussion of the 'rehearsal' of monarchical power according to Foucault and philosopher Louis Marin (1931–1992): as Franko pointedly notes, Foucault's analysis of monarchical power rests on the *presentation* of power as suffering, in a spectacle of pain that constitutes the king's ritual biosuperiority again and again, whereas for Marin, the king's power lies in representation. The king in Marin's view becomes powerful by virtue of theatricalization, specifically in courtly ballets. The king is in effect symbolically powerful, and his power rests on this symbolism. The king in this regard transcends the super-powerful body able to withstand pain that Foucault's analysis highlights, becoming instead abstracted from earthly reality.[70] In the *ramanenjana*'s case,

---

67. Rusillon, who had left France in 1897 to engage in missionary work with the Société des Missions évangéliques de Paris in the Mahéréza district, was writing a few decades after the event. See Henry Rusillon, *Un Culte Dynastique avec évocation des morts chez les Sakalaves de Madagascar: Le 'Tromba'* (Paris: Librairie Alphonse Picard et Fils, 1912), 24, 8–9. Rusillon writes 1278 and 1274 in regard to St. Vitus's dance, but he is more likely referring to episodes of dancing reported in the 1370s in the aftermath of the Black Death. On Rusillon's life and work in Madagascar, see J. F. Siordet's biography, compiled from Rusillon's correspondence with the directors of the Société des Missions, *Henry Rusillon: Missionnaire à Madagascar (1872–1938)*, vol. 1, *Le Pionnier (1872–1913)* (Paris: Société des Missions Évangéliques, 1940).

68. Rusillon, *Un Culte Dynastique*, 13–14. Rusillon's pioneering work on the *tromba* influenced generations of writers in his wake. Raymond Decary, *Mœurs et Coutumes des Malgaches, avec cent un dessins de l'auteur*, describes the *tromba* in terms of 'affections choréiformes' ('choreiform affections') and the 1863 *imanenjana* as a 'chorémanie vraie ou manie de la danse' ('real choreomania or dancing mania') and a 'grande folie collective' ('great collective madness'). Raymond Decary, *Mœurs et Coutumes des Malgaches, avec cent un dessins de l'auteur* (Paris: Payot, 1951), 225–231.

69. On slavery and the *ramanenjana*, see esp. Raison, 'Les Ramanenjana'.

70. Mark Franko, 'Figural Inversions of Louis XIV's Dancing Body', in Franko and Richards, eds., *Acting on the Past*, 35–51, 44–46.

rehearsal posits a form of recuperation of power; a power that was temporarily lost, poorly handled by the monarch serving as its guardian. The *ramanenjana* in this case rehearse their *reprise* of power, their 'rehearsal' as a 'taking back'; in the French, a *prise de pouvoir* is literally a taking or seizing of power, and in this case the *ramanenjana* perform the seizure, fittingly, in a seizure-like way—though I would venture to say that the homonym offers a tenuous relationship at best. With this seizure, in effect a re-seizure, a 'reprise de pouvoir', the ritual performance is not so much symbolic as affective and structural: the *ramanenjana* take back what has always been theirs, a power moreover grounded not in supra-corporeal abilities (though as I showed earlier, they exercised extraordinary corporeal feats) but in evoking genealogical precedence, grounded in the earth, where the dead lie. The rehearsal for liberation the *ramanenjana* perform enacts a shared heritage and future in the 'now' time of distributed monarchical power, wherein the monarch is powerful only through the body politic that acquiesces to him. Power is being made to be powerful; this requires a body politic that gives, and has the power to take back, from a monarch, power that lies neither in images nor in spectacle but in the subjective relation.

The relationship of the *imanenjana*—as a rehearsal for wide-scale emancipation foregrounding ancestral returns—to other possession practices bears further noting. The *tromba*, still practiced in Madagascar, fêtes the spirits of dead royalty. The term *tromba* refers at once to those possessed by the royalty and to a state of possession involving collective gatherings, drumming, dancing, states of inebriation, and a spirit of excitement and anticipation. The *bilo* emphasizes deliverance from spirit possession, but not deceased royalty.[71] Sacred sites and ritual practices in the *imanenjana,* as in the *tromba* and *bilo,* antedated colonial rule, presenting

spaces and choreographic models for exerting control over the present through a collective, performative appeal to the past, in effect a way of enacting a geocultural choreography of protest: ancestors and ancestral sites would guide and support those wishing to drive foreigners and their acolytes out. In anthropologist Gillian Feeley-Harnik's analysis, 'the dead, as interpreted by the living, were the ultimate vehicle of sanction used in regulating complex economic and political relations'.[72] Following Roach, the living 'perform themselves' 'in the presence of others' (including the dead) by enacting what they believe they have been and what they consider that they are not. In this way, identity formation and power politics are always relational, always in Roach's terms *surrogative*: the new take on a mantle of the old which they travesty and translate. The productive relation between an imagined (or felt) prior self and a future becoming enables productive surrogation in the 'now', where protest (for example) theatricalizes a process of coming-to-be-again, even if this enactment of a return is partly fiction or fantasy. Actually, as Roach points out, mythic origins circulate, transformed (what I call translatio'd) along the way.[73]

Although Davidson noted the dancers' proximity to tombs, Rusillon thought he had not gone far enough in highlighting the centrality of these relations to the *imanenjana* as a whole: the *tromba*, like the *bilo*, required dancers to be possessed by the dead.[74] Following Taussig's concept of Western science as reifying social relations, making implicit associations (and their disorders) into 'things'—which can then be ordered, cured, and most of all phantasmatically described or redescribed as objectively reconstituted[75]— I argue that the *imanenjana*, like the *tromba*, emerges as a practice of political and social rebecoming in Madagascar, through *ecstatic* representation, grounded in a claim to the land. Proximity

71. See Paul Ottino, 'Le Tromba (Madagascar)', *L'homme* 5.1 (1965): 84–93, 84–85; Lesley A. Sharp, 'Playboy Princely Spirits of Madagascar: Possession as Youthful Commentary and Social Critique', *Anthropological Quarterly* 68.2 (1995): 75–88; Lesley A. Sharp, *The Possessed and the Dispossessed: Spirits, Identity and Power in a Madagascar Migrant Town* (Berkeley: University of California Press, 1996); Michael Lambek, 'The Sakalava Poiesis of History: Realizing the Past through Spirit Possession in Madagascar', *American Ethnologist* 25.2 (1998): 106–127. On memory, ancestry, and possession in Madagascar, see also esp. Karen Middleton, ed., *Ancestors, Power and History in Madagascar* (Leiden: Brill, 1999); Raymond Decary, *La mort et les coutumes funéraires à Madagascar* (Paris: G. P. Maisonneuve et Larose, 1962); J. F. Barré, *Pouvoir des Vivants, langages des morts* (Paris: François Maspero, 1977); Gillian Feeley-Harnik, 'The Political Economy of Death: Communication and Change in Malagasy Colonial History', *American Ethnologist* 11.1 (1984): 1–19; Jennifer Cole, 'The Work of Memory in Madagascar', *American Ethnologist* 25.4 (1998): 610–633.

72. Feeley-Harnik, 'The Political Economy of Death', 12.

73. Roach, *Cities of the Dead*, 5.

74. Rusillon, *Un Culte Dynastique*, 24–25.

75. See esp. Taussig, *Nervous System*, 83.

to the dead, residing in it, enabled this performative movement of recursion.

In anthropologist Lesley Sharp's analysis, following anthropologist Renato Rosaldo, the *tromba* as a possession ritual enables the exercise of a *mémoire collective* (collective memory) and thus the public performance of social commentary, enabling the concerted reparation of political and social lapses.[76] This is important particularly as regards the *imanenjana* as a practice that sought to oust foreigners from indigenously owned and indeed 'possessed' land. Likewise distrust of migrant and foreign presence on Malagasy soil still, Sharp points out, characterizes much Sakalava sentiment; wanderers and beggars, for instance, are treated with suspicion as *vahiny* (foreigners, guests).[77] Colonial Europeans were unwanted foreigners and, with the help of ancestral spirits, had to be removed. Hostile Europeans saw the Malagasy rebels as reincarnations of their own supposed medieval selves, while the Malagasy conjured their dead to oust the Europeans and their adherents.

The *ramanenjana*'s practices came into the choreomania repertoire as a disorder of heightened, pathological sympathy. But disease, Taussig insists, must necessarily be understood in 'synthetic' terms.[78] Disease is mutual, relational; it happens between two or more bodies or between a body and its environment, its ecology. 'Disease', Taussig writes in *The Nervous System* (1992), appears in the chasm between bodies and the worlds that surround, describe, and inscribe them. Disease is not independent but contingent, constituted by social contexts and described as such through particular discursive lenses. Events described as 'disease' are spurred on, provoked, and determined by a range of ecosophical factors: discontentment, excitement, pain, hope, and political unrest all make bodies *appear* as disorderly on a public stage. Here, the close proximity between twisting bodies and expressions of political commiseration served as grounds for a fantasy of contamination, as political intensities were expressed—and translated into—the choreopolitical movements of a collective revolt. The

'continuous coming-into-being of the state', Taussig further suggests (of a fictional Latin American country), 'rested on the continuous passing away of the body of the Liberator into the body of the people, and this constant passing-away itself depended on a capacity not merely to continuously resurrect his image, but to be possessed by his spirit by virtue of that image'.[79] The nation becomes itself through the theatricalized *appearance* of a ruler, instantiated as the people ecstatically become possessed—thus making *appear* a national body politic. The 'people' continually reconstitutes itself in the ruler's seemingly stable image, an image that becomes the nation's representation, even performance. The monarchical (or otherwise stately) body is abstracted and, in the Malagasy case, singularly suggests a whole (here anti-European) politics that antedates and supersedes the present. It performs future anteriority, a coming-to-be that is ghosted (palimpsestically) by the past.

As a variation on older themes involving the return of the dead, convulsions, agitation, dancing, and singing, the *imanenjana*, like other possession practices, though more intensely political than some in its effects, recuperated extant Malagasy practices in an effort to confront and outplay the icons of the West. Meanwhile, the comparative medical language of the dancing disease offered eyewitnesses, such as Davidson, a means of exegesis that biologized and so, too, implicitly neutralized the show of self-determination demonstrated in this political revolt. What we find is a medical theatre in which the doctor-observer, physician, and priest diagnosed a range of attitudes from the standpoint of what Taussig calls a 'doctor's model of illness',[80] by which illness is reified as a narrative and set of scenes, including political disaffection but eluding politics in any discussion of a cure. Notable, in fact, along with the choreomania diagnosis, is the extent to which physicians and priests withheld intervention; virtually none of the literature suggests an attempt at therapeutic resolution, though across the spectrum of 'fields' engaging in the discursive concatenation of 'dance manias' into a 'thing', medical language

76. Sharp, 'Playboy Princely Spirits', 76. See Renato Rosaldo, *Ilongot Headhunting 1883–1974: A Study in Society and History* (Stanford, CA: Stanford University Press, 1980); Lambek, 'The Sakalava Poiesis of History'.

77. Lesley A. Sharp, 'Wayward Pastoral Ghosts and Regional Xenophobia in a Northern Madagascar Town', *Africa: Journal of the International African Institute* 71.1 (2001): 38–81.

78. Taussig, *The Nervous System*, 83–109.

79. Taussig, *The Magic of the State*, 101–102.

80. Taussig, *The Nervous System*, 106.

prevails: patients, fevers, crises, and so on.[81] In the next section, a Malagasy physician offers one of the most medicalized versions of the *imanenjana*, situating his reading in conversation with French theories of chorea, epidemic chorea, and hysteroepilepsy but offering a local twist to the events emphasizing malaria and lies.

THE SHAMANS' DECEIT: ANDRIANJAFY'S REREADING

Dr. Andrianjafy, a Malagasy physician and neurology student at the Université de Montpellier in France in the 1890s, furthered European theories of epidemic chorea with a case study from Madagascar, extending the scope of the choreomania diagnosis and further medicalizing previous analyses, simultaneously reinscribing the *imanenjana* into a European discourse on nervous pathology and movement disorders and offering a more central role in the 'disease' to sociocultural and micro-political factors. Paradoxically, perhaps, Andrianjafy's status as a Malagasy national did not make him more sympathetic to the revolt; instead he occluded state politics almost entirely, signalling his effort to distance himself from current narratives and showing that the European physicians were most keenly invested in the politics of the dancing disease as directed against the (Europhilic) state.

Andrianjafy's concern was the first to engage with local ecologies. He argued in his M.D. thesis, *Le Ramanenjana à Madagascar (Choréomanie d'origine palustre)* [The Ramanenjana in Madagascar (Choreomania of Paludal Origin)] (1902) that the *ramanenjana* who took to the streets in 1863 actually suffered from a type of chorea major (choreomania) different from that known to European doctors, including St. Vitus's dance—still the paradigmatic case to which all other choreomanias were referred—insofar as the Malagasy type was not caused by hysteria, as Davidson and others held, but, Andrianjafy

maintained, by a subtype of epidemic paludism (malaria). This was, he argued, a form of malaria common in the rainy season known locally as *mena vary aloha*, or rice harvest.[82]

Andrianjafy remarked that this sort of malaria was largely unknown to European medical doctors and was poorly understood by European missionary physicians, who tended to reside in the coastal regions of Madagascar near the capital, where it rarely occurred. But Andrianjafy, whose father had been a physician, had observed such cases firsthand, and Andrianjafy now applied his European-trained knowledge to argue that European efforts to draw parallels between choreomanias had misconstrued the disease and underestimated the variety of disease categories on the ground. For Andrianjafy, different nations may play host to similar diseases, but local geographies, cultures, and customs shape these, producing distinct subtypes.[83] Nervous paludism in Madagascar, in particular, Andrianjafy argued, could be attributed to shamanic influence in the coastal regions, which had significantly motivated the course and evolution of the *imanenjana*, without, however, causing it outright. While briefly acknowledging the context of political rebellion in which the *ramanenjana* moved, Andrianjafy maintained that the possessed dancers' role in the eruption was attributable primarily to the backstage work of shamans, or *mpisikidy*. As in Charcot's clinic, Andrianjafy might have noted, it was the doctors—here, spiritual doctors—who prompted and orchestrated the course of the attacks. Dancers were stripped of their agency; they were merely pawns in a larger political game.

Andrianjafy's diagnosis echoed Davidson's but, drawing from Charcot's emphasis on hysterical acting out, complicated existing portraits of the dancing disease.[84] With Andrianjafy's account, we see that 'choreomania' in Madagascar referred symptomatically to political unrest, but also described convulsive malaria and, Andrianjafy pointedly notes, malarial symptoms (convulsions, bloodshot eyes, etc.) involuntarily or voluntarily feigned by

---

81. See also Muecke on medical language ('patients', 'praecordia', or epigastrum) saturating the first eyewitness accounts, which emphasized, he argues, a social body in distress—what he calls the 'collective singular'. Muecke, 'Choreomanias', 7.

82. Andrianjafy, *Le Ramanenjana à Madagascar*. For a more recent Malagasy medical account of the *ramanenjana*, see Randriamaro, 'Le Ramanenjana à Madagascar'.

83. 'Si chaque pays présente des maladies semblables, une foule de circonstances relatives aux mœurs et aux coutumes des habitants donnent un cachet particulier aux formes les plus banales de la maladie, le paludisme de l'espèce'. Andrianjafy, *Le Ramanenjana à Madagascar*, 14.

84. Andrianjafy's analysis reprises tropes familiar from Davidson's writing. The *ramanenjana* first complained of malaise, stiffness in the neck and chest, and pain in the spine and limbs. They usually experienced weight and pain in the epigastral region, and a

'patients' for various reasons: primarily because they wanted to escape working or because they accidentally or purposefully imitated those who did genuinely suffer from malaria. In this sense, Andrianjafy reprised Charcot's argument according to which 'hysteroepilepsy' referred to the voluntary or involuntary feigning of an epileptiform seizure; and Andrianjafy's taxonomy borrowed from later approaches to choreomania, applied primarily to the tarantella, according to which individuals suffering from the so-called dancing disease were feigning their symptoms for social or economic gain.

Andrianjafy thus organized his reading of choreomania in Madagascar into four categories, according to which there were : (1) the true *ramanenjana* ('ramanenjana "d'emblée"'; true spontaneous *ramanenjana*), who were simply malarial; (2) true *ramanenjana* by imitation, among victims of nervous malaria (true mimetic *ramanenjana*); this condition also had a malarial origin, but patients' symptoms were further stoked and manipulated by opportunist shamans; (3) *ramanenjana* by imitation among non-malarial victims of neurosis, such as children in hospitals, where real cases of chorea were rampant (*ramanenjana* by suggestion); and (4) *ramanenjana* among slaves who did not want to work during the rice harvest (*ramanenjana* by simulation). Andrianjafy argued that in true cases of *imanenjana*, fever was symptomatic, revealing a nervous disorder resulting in the patient's rhythmic agitation of the shoulders,

arms, fingers, and toes and the swinging of the head from side to side, although the attendant dancing to music these patients performed was, he insisted, choreographed by the *mpisikidy*. 'I have often observed patients suffering from simple convulsions or choreic affections', he wrote, 'that were invited, and even forced, by their family members, to perform rhythmic dance motions in order to satisfy the malevolent spirits said to love the music and dance'.[85] This strong social pressure to dance when confronted with nervous symptoms resulted in the over-inflation of the numbers of actual sufferers of choreomania in the so-called epidemic of 1863, in his view. Although some patients genuinely suffered from neuromotor disorders, others simply rode the wave of local revolt, coupled with a common curative practice according to which any combination of neurological or neuropsychiatric disturbances might be assuaged by a theatre of movement and sound bound to the old political hierarchy—that of the shaman class.

Andrianjafy's account is in many respects compelling. Although he seems too readily to dismiss real political protest as mere theatre, his portrait of patients being compelled to dance to ward off spirits (in effect pandering to the power politics of extended families and shamans) accords with standard accounts of nervous disorders explained by recourse to cultures of witchcraft. Indeed, Andrianjafy deftly reads the subtle politics at play in these instances of orchestrated acting out. Noting

---

sensation of burning, tearing, or bilious vomiting. Their pulse accelerated, then weakened, and their temperatures rose to 38 or 39 degrees Centigrade. After this feverish stage, they were moist and sweaty, their eyes red and their gaze blank. They would then start to rotate their heads—the true sign of the *ramanenjana*. This usually lasted one or two days. Then, the *ramanenjana* were seized with nervous agitation and 'great excitement'. From that point, at the slightest indication of music or sound, they lost control, ran to the source of the music they heard, and started to dance, usually for hours, at a 'vertiginous' speed. They would swing their heads from side to side, rhythmically, and wave their hands up and down with equally rhythmic regularity. The dancers never joined in the singing but emitted periodic sighs that showed that they were suffering. They were dazed, and their whole physiognomy took on an indefinable expression of loss and disorientation ('égarement'), as if they were strangers to their surroundings. They would, moreover, regulate the rhythm of the dancing to the music, which was always played as fast as possible; the dance thus often degenerated into mere foot-stomping. The patients danced thus, Andrianjafy argued, to the great astonishment of those present, as if they were possessed by some wayward spirit ('esprit malin'), with an almost supernatural endurance, exhausting the musicians until finally dropping to the ground 'as if dead'. See Andrianjafy, *Le Ramanenjana à Madagascar*, 14–15.

85. Andrianjafy, *Le Ramanenjana à Madagascar*, 33. Andrianjafy's description offers some information as regards the use of music in the 'cure'. 'Patients', he noted, usually relapsed after a few days, sometimes two or three times, always at the slightest sound of music or at the slightest provocation, in spite of a usual period of 'convalescence'. They were usually spurred on by drums, though other instruments, such as the *valiha* (a kind of guitar), and *lokango-voatavo* (a type of violin), also helped provoke the curative fervour. When those in attendance could not find any instruments, they clapped and sang rhythmic songs, such as: '*Oay lahy e! Oay lahy! / 'r' izy 'r' izy / Andriananahary lahy / 'r' izy 'r' izy.*' 'Masinà hiany, Veloma hiany / There he is! There he is! / He is there! He is there! / Andriananahary (spirit of the sickness) / He is there! He is there! / Bless him! May god be with him!' Andrianjafy argued that the *mpisikidy* thus considered the musicians to be the means of the cure—literally, the agents ('agents curateurs')—while they themselves acted as masters of ceremonies, accompanying the 'victims' to sites bordered by sacred stones, enjoining them to dance for hours while they divined the proper remedy. *Mpanoady* (charmers) and some family members also took part in cortèges leading to Ambohimanga, further testimony to the *mpisikidies*' stakes in the revolt. See Andrianjafy, *Le Ramanenjana à Madagascar*, 36.

strong kinaesthetic similarities between the *ramanenjana* and other choreics he studied at the Université de Montpellier in 1894, Andrianjafy nevertheless argued that hysteria was an epiphenomenon only, not a primary cause or symptom of the disease.[86] Instead, the Malagasy choreomania was influenced by superstitious belief in and fear of sorcery. While wealthier urban citizens might show some choreic symptoms, including tics or other dyskinesias, and consult physicians, poorer residents of the countryside, who had recourse only to the *mpisikidy*, were subject to the whole ceremonial theatre of music and dance that the shamans imposed and that exacerbated, he argued, their malarial condition.[87] In this regard, the *imanenjana* was a corrupt type of choreomania, whose spread should be attributed to the pernicious influence of the *mpisikidy*. It could thus be eliminated with proper enlightenment and progress, he noted, and the eradication of mosquitoes, whose negative effect on the victims' physical and mental states produced conditions ripe for the shamans' picking. This explanation suggests, reasonably, that environmental conditions exacerbated routine disorders of the nervous system but does not sufficiently account for the sociopolitical context of the 1863 revolt outlined above.

Taussig points out that concepts of disease often arise out of the reification of a subtle range of interrelated emotions and events, reduced to the biological and the singular. The therapeutic process, Taussig submits, thus requires 'an archaeology of the implicit' so that 'social relations . . . mapped into diseases' may be 'brought to light' and 'de-reified', '[liberating] the potential for dealing with antagonistic contradictions and breaking the chains of oppression'.[88] This suggests that counter-diagnosing medical claims to 'disease' involves peeling away what may be described as such from a complex of social and political relations, so that these in turn may be revealed. In the case of the Malagasy 'dancing disease', Andrianjafy claims to be revealing a political cast of shamans scheming to get peasants on their side, using the peasants' naivety,

trust, and potentially real malarial states (as well as their duplicity or laziness) for political gain. The peasants, we may surmise, may also have gained politically from this alliance, whether they performed their choreic roles entirely wilfully or not. The *imanenjana* then served as a means for the *mpisikidies* to reach out to village people to disrupt politics in the capital, and village people, in turn, may have willingly complied. The representational politics the dancers performed where ghosted not only by dead monarchs but also by a subtle hierarchy of power brokers acting in the present.

The *imanenjana*, then, constitutes a complex of events, some malarial, some political. But the reification of this complex into a 'disease' reveals not only a mixture of implicit social relations but also a process of discursive abstraction that is beholden to outside conversations and aims. In this case, Andrianjafy's reading (not unlike Davidson's) reaches over to Europe to integrate this case study into a conversation going on over there. This gesture of abstraction seeks to wrap these events into a discourse on epidemic hysteria, in effect globalizing a scientific conversation and so consolidating a further class of shamans—here, physicians—orchestrating the discussion on the 'dancing disease'. Although they were not orchestrating events on the ground, Davidson, Andrianjafy, and others were wrapping the *ramanenjana*'s practices into a conversation that made this complex politico-medical theatre—this discursive choreopolitics—into a diagnostic one; and that made, by this gesture of abstraction, a transnational class of professionals reading events for one another *ecstatically*, outside the body, in a sense to serve another sort of transnational state. Andrianjafy appears to be tethered to a conversation that serves his own professional ends. The Malagasy disease became an occasion for him to differ slightly, on expert grounds, with master neurologists in France. Just as physicians and missionaries read the political events of 1863 as taking place between shamanic ritual, neurological disorder, and 'psycho-physical' epidemic, the 'disorder' seems to have constituted a mixture of routine

---

86. Andrianjafy in particular followed clinical lectures by Professor Joseph Grasset (1849–1918), a student of Charcot and pioneer neuropsychiatrist as well as ardent enthusiast of occultist and spiritualist philosophies. Grasset may plausibly have been especially galvanized by Andrianjafy's efforts to tie contemporary neurology to spiritual practices in Madagascar. On Grasset's occultism and study with Charcot, see Martin Bock, 'The Power of Suggestion: Conrad, Professor Grasset, and French Medical Occultism', *Conradiana* 39.2 (2007): 97–112.

87. Andrianjafy, *Le Ramanenjana à Madagascar*, 36.

88. Taussig, *The Nervous System*, 93.

instances of malaria and political protest. More patently, the discourse surrounding the putative dancing disease suggests an empty middle, a criss-crossing of incompatible agendas and territorialities, and so the construction of a field of knowledge revealing first and foremost the desires and fears, anxieties and prejudices, that new (largely Western) scientific knowledge articulated: a distrust of jagged gesture, protesting crowds, and the concatenation of these things into a medicalized figure of unrest.

The dancers meanwhile suffered; but not, for the most part, from neurological or psychiatric disease. As in previous cases of so-called choreomania, some participants in the revolution of 1863 and in ritual curing ceremonies may have been choreic; many seem, in Andrianjafy's account, to have been seasonally malarial. But many protestors also performatively sought solace in a past time that would usher forth a new—extra-colonial—future. Colonialism was the disease, but 'choreomania' its increasingly global diagnosis.

While the medical study of political revolution, charismatic shamanism, and nervous disease prompted Boudin, Andrianjafy, and Davidson to cast the *ramanenjana* as choreomaniacs— malarial and hysterical—the next section suggests the recuperation of chorea and collective political revolt into psycholegal medicine in Brazil. This section thus draws the study of choreomania out to the Brazilian borderlands. Two quite distinct case studies appear in the Brazilian literature on choreomania, each as radically different as any case on the 'choreomania'

spectrum. One describes sightings of relatively benign psychomotor disorders in Itapagipe, in northern Brazil, which the Brazilian neurologist Dr. José Dantas de Souza Leite (1859–1925), who earned his doctorate at the Salpêtrière under Charcot, attributed to a resurgence of choreomania.[89] The other, more arresting case was supposed to have occurred epidemically among the disenfranchised *sertões* or backland peasants of Bahia, which the legal psychiatrist and anthropologist Dr. Raimundo Nina-Rodrigues (1862–1906), also well acquainted with Charcot's work and current sociological theories propounded, among others, by Le Bon, attributed to messianic psychopathology.[90] In Brazil, 'choreomania' referred not only to intensely kinematic revolt but, with this new literature, also to widespread insanity: collective delusion and social ferment. Choreomania, now described by physicians and social scientists in psycholegal terms as the disorder of a deluded, dismissible minority, also came to be a disorder of the distinctly lowest classes. In Nina-Rodrigues's view, the *sertões* were mad to follow their messianic leader to spiritual and political redemption: choreomania, in this case, no longer signified strange bodily gestures revealing antiquity or biological automatisms, or even the event of revolt, but a mass outbreak of irrational behaviour far removed to the most remote parts of the country. Unlike the dancers in Madagascar, the *sertões* did not appear directly to threaten central powers in the capital, although they irritated the principles and structures of the modern nation state; however, as in Madagascar and previous cases of

89. Souza Leite offered a new set of case studies on epidemic chorea in *Études de pathologie nerveuse* [Studies in Nervous Pathology] (1889), describing cases of *astasia-abasia* (also *astasia abasia*) or Blocq's disease (a gait disorder involving the patient's inability to walk, referred to as *abasia*, or stand, referred to as *astasia*) and other choreiform affections. See José Dantas de Souza Leite, *Études de pathologie nerveuse* (Paris: G. Steinheil, Éditeur, 1889), esp. 'Réflexions à propos de certaines maladies nerveuses observées à Bahia (Brésil). Faits d'astasie et d'abasie (Blocq), c'est-à-dire de l'affection dénommée: Incoordination motrice pour la station et la marche (Charcot et Richer). Prétendue épidémie de chorée de Sydenham', 52–65. Paul Blocq (1860–1896) described *astasia-abasia* with reference to clinical descriptions by Charcot and others, noting that 'paralysis, fits, tremors, and bizarre behaviour could be associated with the syndrome'. Michael S. Okun and Peter J. Koehler, 'Paul Blocq and (Psychogenic) Astasia Abasia', *Movement Disorders* 22.10 (2007): 1373–1378, 1373. See Paul Blocq, 'Sur une affection caractérisée par de l'astasie et de l'abasie', *Archives de neurologie* 15 (1888): 24–51, 187–211; Paul Blocq, *Les troubles de la marche dans les maladies nerveuses* (Paris: Rueff et Cie., 1893); Paul Blocq, *Études sur les maladies nerveuses* (Paris: Rueff et Cie., 1894).

90. Nina-Rodrigues published a further account of epidemic occurrences in Bahia, first in the *Annales médico-psychologiques*, in an essay titled 'Épidémie de folie religieuse au Brésil' (1898) and more extensively in his posthumously collected essays on choreomania, *As Collectividades Anormaes* (1939). This included chapters on choreiform abasia epidemics in northern Brazil ('A Abasia Choreiforme Epidemica No Norte do Brasil') and epidemics of insanity ('A loucoura epidemica de Canudos') as well as, significantly, a lengthy appendix titled simply 'Choreomania'. Events Nina-Rodrigues characterized as indicative of choreomania, occurring in Brazil in the 1890s, were attributable, he argued, not to organic lesions but to the magnetic presence of an exalted spiritual leader, Antonio Conselheiro, whose religious delirium prompted thousands of disenfranchised peasants or *sertões* to follow him towards spiritual redemption in the 1893–1897 Canudos revolt. See Raimundo Nina-Rodrigues, *As Collectividades Anormaes* (Rio de Janeiro: Civilização Brasileira S.A., 1939); 'Épidémie de folie religieuse au Brésil', *Annales médico-psychologiques: Journal de l'aliénation mentale et de la médecine légale des aliénés* 8.7 (1898): 371–392; and *La folie des foules: Nouvelle contribution à l'étude des folies épidémiques au Brésil* (Paris: Fonds Lacassagne, 1901).

the 'dancing disease', this revolt mobilized the romantic image of a return to a past time that would catapult participants into a new future. This romantic figure was shared by participants and observers, as if nostalgia were at once the cause of the 'disease' and its method of diagnosis. As I will show in subsequent chapters, utopic aspirations would increasingly dominate the literature on choreomania in the late nineteenth and early twentieth centuries, indicating the increasing alignment of the choreomania discourse with decolonization movements in the mid-twentieth century.

BRAZILIAN BACKLANDS: CHOREA, CHOREOMANIA, AND THE CANUDOS REVOLT

A new legacy of Brazilian writing on the dancing disease amalgamated political uprisings, messianic leadership, and everyday choreic gesture on the politically ambiguous terrain of legal psychopathy, as the Brazilian liberation movement known as the Canudos revolt was recuperated into a psycholegal discourse on pathological crowds mixed with a neuroscientific discourse on unwieldy individual gesture. As a type of choreomania, Nina-Rodrigues argued, the Canudos revolt was like involuntary choreas readily observed in city streets.[91] But the choreotopology and choreopolitics of the large-scale Canudos movement—the intensity of the action instantiated by the *sertões'* self-removal from everyday state-governed life—warranted assigning the Canudos revolt a special place in the globally growing repertoire of epidemic psychiatry. Nina-Rodrigues's discursive medicalization drew from the clinical observation of tics and gaits as well as political events, just as he was articulating a new field of inquiry between psychiatry and social science. In this sense, the interdisciplinary emergence of the modern choreomania concept revealed an intertextual field describing the pathologization of irregular gestures and performative expressions of high affect worldwide, extending Franko's notion of the intradisciplinary alliance between politics and dance to a further intradisciplinary sphere. All sciences and arts pertaining to the movements of bodies become political in this deep archaeology, this genealogy of 'dance' or of dance studies—specifically, they become political inasmuch as these entangled fields articulate a representational politics (and a politics of representation) by which certain *forms* of motion and their *appearances* on a public and discursive stage suggest the figuration of norms and their displacement. Movement becomes scientific, wrapped into particular genealogies of discourse; but it also fritters and spreads, circulates and shifts, across disciplinary arenas to become choreopolitical in a different sense.

Bodies do not just upset power balances by showing ideologies at play, 'performing protest'; they also upset power balances by rehearsing a *conjunctural* sphere that is disjunctive. The politics of and in 'dance' are not just contained in what Franko terms the coincidence of political becoming or ideology, nation and state formation, with aesthetic forms (modes of moving onstage first and foremost)[92] but also show the aporias between bodies moving and regimes of observation, 'scopic regimes'. A scopic regime, in film theorist Christian Metz's terms, signals the

---

91. The choreic episode in Itapagipe, in northern Brazil, had been reported to Nina-Rodrigues by a Brazilian physician trained in Paris, Dr. Affonso Saulnier de Pierrelevée (1830–1910). De Pierrelevée, Nina-Rodrigues reports, had noted that starting in 1856 and increasingly in the 1870s and 1880s an 'epidemic' of 'choreic affections' had appeared in the streets in northern Brazil. 'It is often possible these days', wrote De Pierrelevée, 'to encounter in the city's streets many patients whose singular gait draws the attention of all those who pass by'. Some, he wrote, drag their feet and behave as though they are suffering from paralysis of the legs; others appear to suffer from progressive muscular ataxy (the loss of full control of body movements). Others walk haltingly, irregularly, and even perform small jumps. All perform fantastic genuflexions, as if bearing the weight of their bodies with great difficulty. These choreiform movements were visible particularly in the upper part of the body, occasionally in the trunk, never when patients were sleeping or otherwise lying horizontal. De Pierrelevée noted that most of those afflicted were women suffering from anaemia but not fever; their breathing was irregular and after a few days degenerated into dyspnoea, a strong and difficult breathing, with palpitations in the heart area. It seems probable that this 'epidemic' amounted to a coincidental increase in the visibility (to him) of choreic disorders in the streets of Brazil in the period succeeding De Pierrelevée's encounter with chorea minor through his Parisian studies. Yet the notion of the epidemic was also appealing, and the strangeness of these physical demeanours—a theatre of urban tics and tragicomic gaits—suggestive to Nina-Rodrigues of more widespread social dysfunction. Nina-Rodrigues, *As Collectividades Anormaes*, 27–28.

92. On the 'conjunctural', see Franko, 'Dance and the Political', 4.

absence of the thing seen in the act of seeing;[93] what is seen is a phantasm, a projection caused by temporal delay (montage, collage). Between the act of conjuring another possible world, an ancestral spirit or a new politics, and the act of witnessing lies a chasm, and that is the choreo-political gulf that 'choreomania' inhabits. The temporal gulf is not just that of secular time, because often dancers and observers inhabited the same spaces, but an experience of time and temporality, an articulation of what is possible in terms of what came before, suggesting incompatible regimes of political becoming by which one form of visibility becomes another. One form of conjuration becomes an appearance—a ghost, a phantasm—transformed into the language of collective disease.

Choreomania thus *appears* at the threshold where politics *disappears* from the act of observation. Politics takes the shape of 'mere' dance or 'mere' theatre, as well as 'mere' disease: forms understood as containers of formlessness, as the representation of abstract gestures not designed to *go anywhere*, even if they may appear to perform acts of circulation. It is this appearance of gesturelessness—of the putative meaninglessness of the choreic gesture—that constitutes the relative violence of choreomania's biomedical articulation, as the ultimate neutralization of self-organized *commotion*.

According to Nina-Rodrigues, the self-styled messianic leader Antônio Conselheiro ('Anthony the Counselor') (1830–1897) led the rural *sertões* into 'epidemic madness' because he suffered from religious delirium. His delusions of grandeur—including his messianic belief in his role as the spiritual leader of the disenfranchised mestizo population of Bahia—triggered, in Nina-Rodrigues's account, a pathological uprising. Thousands of disenfranchised mestizos had followed Conselheiro in creating a spiritual community in the decade following the 1889 proclamation of the Brazilian state on the model of the European ones. By 1897, the peasants were violently suppressed in a series of bloody military actions that pitted a 'civilized', 'modern' nation state against the rural *sertões*.[94] Offering a timely politico-legal analysis of these occurrences on the fringes of the new nation's disciplinary regimes of state power, Nina-Rodrigues's article 'Épidémie de folie religieuse au Brésil' [Epidemic of Religious Insanity in Brazil] appeared in the 1898 volume of the Parisian journal of medical psychology and law *Annales médico-psychologiques*. Nina-Rodrigues argued that Conselheiro's 'psychosis' was shaped and catalysed by his environment: the 'sociological' factor contributing to the deployment of his psychotic state resulted in a magnetic force which he exerted on the people in whose midst he dwelled.[95]

The thousands of followers he accrued in the period following his arrival in the Brazilian *sertão* in 1876, and his rebaptism as Antônio Conselheiro, (relinquishing his birth name, Antônio Maciel), signalled, according to Nina-Rodrigues, the intensification of his delirium and the epidemic events it occasioned. Conselheiro's

---

93. See esp. Christian Metz, *The Imaginary Signifier: Psychoanalysis and the Cinema*, trans. Celia Britton, et al. (Bloomington: Indiana University Press, 1982).

94. See Robert M. Levine, 'Canudos in the National Context', *Americas* 48.2 (1991): 207–222, 207, and *Vale of Tears: Revisiting the Canudos Massacre in Northeastern Brazil, 1893–1897* (Berkeley, CA: University of California Press, 1992). See also Lori Madden, 'Evolution in the Interpretations of the Canudos Movement: An Evaluation of the Social Sciences', *Luso-Brazilian Review* 28.1 (1991): 59–75. The *Luso-Brazilian Review* published a special issue, 'The World out of Which Canudos Came', *Luso-Brazilian Review* 30.2 (1993), including these essays: Lori Madden, 'The Canudos War in History', 5–22; Gerald Michael Greenfield, 'Sertão and Sertanejo: An Interpretive Context for Canudos', 35–46; and Dain Borges, 'Salvador's 1890s: Paternalism and Its Discontents', 47–57. For a classic sociological study of the Canudos revolt in the context of other messianic movements in Brazil, see Maria Isaura Pereira De Queiroz, 'L'influence du Milieu Social Interne sur les mouvements messianiques brésiliens', *Archives de sociologie des religions* 5 (1958): 3–30. For a 'subaltern' interpretation of the Canudos revolt and Euclides da Cunha's 'national bible' *Os sertões* (1902), see Adriana M. C. Johnson, 'Subalternizing Canudos', *Modern Language Notes* 120.2 (2005): 355–382. Slavoj Žižek reads the Canudos 'outlaw community' as a 'utopian space'; Slavoj Žižek, 'From Politics to Biopolitics . . . and Back', *South Atlantic Quarterly* 103.2/3 (2004): 501–521, 511–512. See also Ernesto Laclau's discussion of the Canudos revolt in Judith Butler, Ernesto Laclau, and Slavoj Žižek, *Contingency, Hegemony, Universality: Contemporary Dialogues on the Left* (London: Verso, 2000), 82–83. Brazil has had its share of messianic movements, including the Tupí-Guaraní, first noted in the sixteenth century. See for example Alfred Metraux, 'Les Messies de l'Amérique du sud', *Archives de sociologie des religions* 5 (1957): 108–112; and Vittorio Lanternari, *The Religions of the Oppressed: A Study of Modern Messianic Cults*, trans. Lisa Sergio (New York: Knopf, 1963), 171–181. Patricia R. Pessar offers a discussion of a later millenarian episode in Brazil in the 1930s, in Patricia R. Pessar, *From Fanatics to Folk: Brazilian Millenarianism and Popular Culture* (Durham, NC: Duke University Press, 2004). Mario Vargas Llosa's novel *La guerra del fin del mundo* (Barcelona: Editorial Seix Barral, 1981), depicts the Canudos revolt in particularly harrowing terms.

95. Nina-Rodrigues, 'Épidémie'.

beatific approach to poverty and crime in that part of the country (he was often considered to be a saint and a Christ) eventually mounted into a climax of 'epidemic religious delirium'. The delirium evidenced by Conselheiro had found grounds, Nina-Rodrigues argued, in the psychology of the era and its environment, which were propitious for lighting a 'wildfire' of epidemic insanity ('du combustible pour alimenter l'incendie d'une véritable épidémie de folie').[96]

Nina-Rodrigues understood this event as a politicized brand of choreomania still genealogically linked to St. Vitus's dance and to Hecker's eccentric cast of ecstatics; but the disorder achieved new medico-legal proportions. In *As Collectividades Anormaes* [Abnormal Collectivities] (1939), particularly in his appendix on 'Choreomania', first published in the *Gazeta Medica da Bahía* (1883), Nina-Rodrigues likened the Canudos revolt to other choreomanias, including the tarantella, the *tigretier*, and the Convulsionaries of Saint-Médard, all examples that would have been familiar to his readers.[97] But Nina-Rodrigues's indebtedness to the growing literature on national cases of the 'dancing disease' also recast this condition in terms of individual psychopathology and the psychopathic imitation of a leader-god. This marked a departure from what would become the standard interpretation of the Canudos episode, according to which spiritual rebellion had led to revolt, cast in romantic nationalist terms.

In *Os Sertões* (1902), Euclides da Cunha (1866–1909), the Canudos revolt's most influential historian, offered a vivid eulogy of Brazil's 'backlands', whose 'extraordinary native sons' were rushing, he wrote, headlong towards 'extinction', precipitated by 'that implacable "motive force of history"' the 'inevitable crushing of weak races by the strong'.[98] The Canudos campaign waged by the Brazilian government was, for da Cunha, 'in the integral sense of the word a crime and, as such, to be denounced'.[99] A disaffected military officer turned civil and geological engineer and an ardent journalist at the time of the 1896–1897 Canudos campaign, da Cunha was well versed in European philosophy and literature, from Hegel to Humboldt. A self-styled 'romantic naturalist', he, like Rousseau contemplating his childhood village dance, highlighted the beauty of apparently spontaneous movement. Patriotism coloured every page of his work, with fervent depictions of the land and beatific descriptions of its inhabitants.[100] In his view, the Canudos revolt was an uprising from the land and, as such, a just, native, and natural upheaval waged against political wrongs. But with the Canudos revolt, the social and political marginality of the peasants and their off-centre uprising also threatened state power by virtue of the pull they seemingly held back to the earth, at the nation's edge. In da Cunha's analysis, the backland *sertões* were to be celebrated, revered, for their primitive naturalness, their essential purity.

Yet in this respect like Nina-Rodrigues, da Cunha also argued that their movement as a whole was pathological. This was because it was so seductive and infectious, it resulted in a 'backlands lawlessness' tantamount to disease. In da Cunha's terms, the revolt was, though natural and romantic, 'little more than symptomatic of a malady which, by no means confined to a corner of Bahía, was spreading to the capitals of the seabord'.[101] Da Cunha's ambivalence, ranging from passionate defence to tender caution, hardly sufficed to overturn far less genteel denigrations of the Canudos revolt waged by government forces.

Estimates suggest that fifteen to thirty-five thousand *sertões* were killed in the military campaign waged against Conselheiro's followers. This was the result of a government attempt to stamp out resistance to the new republican policies of assimilation and political unity and to a

96. Nina-Rodrigues, 'Épidémie', 381.

97. Nina-Rodrigues, *As Collectividades Anormaes*, 222. The appendix, 'Choreomania' (reproduced 219–231), was first published in *Gaseta Medica da Bahía*, ser. 2, 7.10 (April 1883). See also his introductory chapter, 'A Abasia choreiforme epidemica no norte do Brasil', presented to the Congresso Medico Brasileiro on 15 October 1890, which he opens by comparing the history of this affliction to the medieval choreomania (*As Collectividades Anormaes*, 23–48, 23).

98. Euclides da Cunha, *Rebellion in the Backlands*, trans. Samuel Putnam (Chicago: University of Chicago Press, 1944), xxix–xxx. Da Cunha's book is widely considered a classic of Brazilian historiography and model narrative of revolutionary uprising; for a discussion of its scientific and literary conjunction, see Raúl C. Goveira Fernandes, 'Euclides e a literatura: Comentérios sobre a "moldura" de Os Sertões', *Luso-Brazilian Review* 43.2 (2006): 45–62. Levine also provides a rich account of da Cunha's history in *Vale of Tears*, 17–22.

99. Da Cunha, *Rebellion in the Backlands*, xxx.

100. Da Cunha, *Rebellion in the Backlands*, 15.

101. Cited in Levine, *Vale of Tears*, 27.

new positivist regime touting 'order and progress' on its flag, mandated when a military coup overthrew the monarchy in 1889 and instituted the First Republic. The killings, justified through mediatized denunciations of Conselheiro's 'psychotic' pseudo-messianic presence, such as those put forward by Nina-Rodrigues, were further fuelled by government paranoia and a gross over-estimation of the *sertões*' power. As sociologist Maria Isaura Pereira De Queiroz argues, the *sertões* were illiterate and destitute Catholics without the resources for large-scale resistance to the military state beyond their collective withdrawal. Like many other millennialist movements, theirs sought a communal life of peace and brotherhood and articulated a sense of communal bonding before the hope of a new world. They looked forward to the arrival of a 'golden age' heralding the return of the Brazilian Empire, and the cessation of all crime and warfare and all requirement to work for material goods.[102]

Borrowing eschatological motifs from the state-sanctioned Christian religion but positing a temporal aporia, a messianic 'now-time' that suspended capital production and state control, the *sertões* presented a theatre of counter-mimicry with a twist. Their mimic game differed too radically from accepted conventions of messianic religion to warrant assimilation into the governing regime. Instead, as an atopic organization—staged in the nearly uninhabitable backlands—and an extra-temporal system on the 'other side' of 'historical progress', as Žižek maintains of the Canudos revolt, the *sertões* tripped up the choreography of difference that anti-colonial shows of mimicry normally occasioned.[103] Difference was conjugated with a motif of escape and extraction rather than excrescence; instead of performing an upheaval in the centre of the public sphere as the *ramanenjana* did, the *sertões* withdrew, disappeared. Their self-erasure from the body politic instantiated a magnetic black hole, a powerful force of messianic imagining that contravened the self-importance of the nation's capital. As such, the *sertões* and their leader had

to be eliminated, according to state policy, not because they threatened to invade the biopolitical centre, but because they weakened it by ignoring its rule.

Thus the Canudos revolt entered into the extended medical archive—the archival repertoire—of choreomania, now defined as psychosis, religious delirium, and epidemic delusion. This expanded definition mistranslated millennial expectation, making political unrest a disorder of mass misbelief. Brazilian studies of choreomania also continued to ally widespread social disorder with neurological jerks and tics. Choreas, as Brazilian neurologists saw it, were visible remains of large-scale movement disorders; more so still than in Europe, they appeared on city streets as signs—ciphers—of social distress, indicating that society was unwell. According to Souza Leite, a contemporary of Nina-Rodrigues who, like him, had studied with Charcot, diseases were universal; only different states of scientific knowledge determined the accuracy of their clinical description.[104] Like Andrianjafy translating neurological teachings from France back onto his native terrain, Souza Leite argued that individual body tremors in the streets of Bahia represented neuromotor disorders that were like those he had studied under Charcot and were not recognized as such by local inhabitants.

Observing men and women in June and July 1887 in the north of Brazil, Souza Leite suggested that the locally employed nomenclature was misguided: these rural occurrences, typically described as *caruára* (witchcraft, evil eye, torpor) and *treme-treme* (shaking, trembling), were actually neurological disorders. Indeed in many parts of the world, epilepsy, chorea, and other involuntary movements have been misattributed to witchcraft, ostracizing their sufferers. But Souza Leite's analysis is surprising: whereas physicians have typically named disorders traditionally thought to be caused by witchcraft in neurological or psychiatric terms, arguing that these were mechanical disorders and thus treatable, removing stigma (or replacing it with a stigma of another sort), Souza

---

102. Pereira De Queiroz, 'L'influence du Milieu Social', 10–12. On the government's misjudgment, see also Darién J. Davis, 'Review of *Guerra de Canudos* (1997 Film) by Sergio Rezende and *Passion and War in the Backlands of Canudos* (*Paxão e Guerra no Sertão de Canudos*) (1993 Film) by Antônio Olavo', *American Historical Review* 104.5 (1999): 1807–1809.

103. Žižek, 'From Politics to Biopolitics', 511–512.

104. Souza Leite, *Études de pathologie nerveuse*, 52. A number of theses on chorea minor (Sydenham's chorea) were published in Brazil in the following decades, including Normando Alonso, *Corea de Sydenham* (Buenos Aires: A. Guidi Buffarini, 1910), Tomás S. Molina, *Corea de Sydenham* (Buenos Aires: N. Marana, 1909), and Miguel Ochoa, *Consideraciones sobre algunas coreas* (Buenos Aires: A. Etcheparaborda, 1909).

Leite suggests that the events he observed were not individual instances of neuromotor or psychiatric dysfunction. While they might be mistaken for chorea minor (including Sydenham's chorea), he argued that they actually represented paradigmatic cases of chorea major, the 'real' chorea—choreomania, the dancing disease.[105]

Disorder in this case was not first of all individual but plural, collective; in the cases he observed—people shaking their bodies in the streets of northern Brazil—a collective dancing disorder was apparent among individuals, in fragmented form. The social body was broken: a previously collective form of disorderly corporeality now occurred individually, he submitted. This episode of choreomania represented not gestures spreading by imitation 'like wildfire' through an entire people but an underlying state of collective corporeal disjunction appearing sporadically in isolation. This radically reversed the view of choreomania prominent since Hecker's day, which suggested that choreomania appeared during times of crisis and spread; here, choreomania was already omnipresent, and the isolated cases observable in city streets were its publicly visible remains. In Souza Leite's analysis, as in Nina-Rodrigues's, choreomania was everywhere: in the North among individuals and in the South among crowds of peasant revolutionaries. Viewed through Charcot's students' chorea-tinted glasses, the world was full of choreomaniacs: people moving too awkwardly, too jerkily, too much, and in the wrong places. As with the *imanenjana* in Madagascar, Nina-Rodrigues and Souza Leite's descriptions of types of chorea referred as much to sociopolitical upheavals as to individual jerks and tics, diagnosed as neurological disease. When untreated, chorea provided a spectacle to passersby, just as leprosy had haunted streets and villages in the Middle Ages. But underlying this was a sort of 'madness' signalling collective revolt. This 'madness' was what was written against the grain of a disappearing centre, a black hole, the *appearance* of a nothingness cast as something which could be ordered and compared.

In this chapter, I have described how Charcot's students and acolytes travelled to Africa and South America, carrying his ideas about chorea and choreomania with them.

The extended spheres of influence of the Salpêtrière thus came to be felt as far away as Madagascar and Brazil. But this is not simply a case of Charcot's colleagues and collaborators taking his or Hecker's ideas with them wholesale. New processes of translation (translatio), repetition, and recuperation emerged as Malagasy and Brazilian neurologists rewrote European schools of thinking on hysteroepilepsy, chorea, and choreomania in para-colonial terms, often negotiating their own histories. Practical problems of shamanism, nationalism, and political uprisings took on a new urgency and political hue, as fitting, falling, and spasming bodies appearing in public space across the world seemed to confirm but also shifted the European discourse on the dancing disease. This chapter, then, has foregrounded peripheries in a whole different sense; not only the limits and peripheries of bodies flailing (arms, heads, eyes) but also the far reaches of European geographic space have come back to haunt the political centre. Colonial choreomanias thus represent reverse cases of possession: 'choreomaniacs" bodies are not just inhabited by the ghosts or spirits of ancestors but perform a sort of political spectrality, inasmuch as they enable ancient histories and other political realities theatrically to appear.

In the next chapter, dance manias nearly subside. Barely a textbook case of choreomania, with its jerks and twitches, the Ghost Dance among Native American Indians in the 1890s lends itself to discursive analysis because its first and most influential ethnographer likened it to the medieval St. Vitus's dance and other religious 'cults'. This tenuous genealogical link nevertheless highlights a persistent comparative thrust, positing a discursive relationship between instances of heightened collective activity and the performance of political gain. Imagined as a distant cousin of medieval European and biblical dances, the Ghost Dance, in James Mooney's estimation, importantly revealed the orgiastic European past on American soil: the Ghost Dance served as a window onto pre-industrial, antediluvian humanity. But the public mobilization of Native American bodies for political effect in the Ghost Dance also showcased a new sort of colonial violence: the violence of ethnocide and

105. 'Beaucoup de médecins croient que les individus atteints par l'épidémie de chorée sont des *choréiques vulgaires*, affectés de la *chorea minor*, maladie de Sydenham; et je ne sais pas s'ils ont songé à la *chorea major*, vraie chorée. Le peuple, se fondant sur une certaine apparence entre les mouvements des malades et une épizootie des gallinacés, nommée là-bas "caruára", appelle les choréiques *os caruára* ou encore *treme-treme*'. Souza Leite, *Études de pathologie nerveuse*, 64.

its enraged response. It shared choreomania's broadest symptomatic traits—collective corporeality revealing heightened states of emotion, rapidly proliferating spheres of influence, hallucinations and falls—but the Ghost Dance was also a pacific movement, a 'dancing disease', inasmuch as settlers and U.S. Indian agents (locally deployed government officials) termed this expenditure of energy flaunted by starving Indians as careless and perverse. The Ghost Dance in this final nineteenth-century formulation was termed pure excess, pure waste, with bodies shuffling against a backdrop of outright war, crushed in the cogs of advancing industrialization and the bureaucratic follies of a heightened capitalist age.

9

Ghost Dancing
Excess, Waste, and the American West

> A truly *military* society is a society of enterprise . . . whose end is given in the future, and excludes the madness of sacrifice.
>
> —Georges Bataille, *La part maudite* (1967)

THE GHOST DANCE may constitute the least clear 'case' of a 'dancing disease'. Neither a regular contender among medical encyclopedias and compendia that rehearse spurious but familiar connections between bacchanals, St. John's and St. Vitus's dances, the Convulsionaries of Saint-Médard, tarantellas, epilepsies, and choreas, among others (as well as a growing repertoire of 'choreomanias' overseas, as previous chapters show), nor subject to a properly medicalized literature on epidemic dancing or fitful gesture, the Ghost Dance among Sioux and other Native Americans in the late nineteenth century nevertheless shared with these other cases the language of a dancing 'craze' and, importantly for the discursive history I tell, a genealogical link traceable to Hecker's writing on St. Vitus's dance. Significantly, also, this chapter shows, the anthropological and government discourse on the Ghost Dance, which compared this native uprising to religious ecstasies, deployed, as with other so-called choreomanias, a language of excess, exaggeration, escalation, duplicity, barbarism, and insanity, as well as—to complicate things— natural, ecstatic connection with the earth and all things premodern. Ghost Dancing was at once volcanic and contagious; as such, it had to be curbed, many thought, at the cost of deadly military intervention. The Ghost Dance thus represents a genealogical offshoot in the rhizomatic story of the 'dancing disease', yet it significantly shows the extent to which the discursive politics of anti-colonial revolt hinge on the language of epidemic disorder—in this case, waged in the terms of cultural war.

As Jacqueline Shea Murphy has argued, colonialist policies against Native Americans in the 1880s revolved around antidance legislation that set dance—and, most powerfully, *ideas* about dance—at the heart of the U.S. government's attempts to annihilate Native culture and Native claims to indigenous land.[1]

---

1. Jacqueline Shea Murphy, *The People Have Never Stopped Dancing: Native American Modern Dance Histories* (Minneapolis: University of Minnesota Press, 2007), 32–34.

The government did so by assimilating Native American men, women, and children into white culture: 'attempts to "other" and subsequently erase Indians', Shea Murphy writes, depended on strategies that tapped into pre-existing myths about Indianness that were articulated in early European literature and iconography.[2] But dance, she argues, was the decisive borderline against which the difference between the Native and the white American was articulated, setting Natives on the side of dancing and white settlers on the side of *not* dancing. Dancing was described as a debauched, wasteful expenditure of time and energy; *not* dancing was in contrast pure, responsible, reasonable, and efficient in labour terms. Settlers who did *not* dance had plenty of energy left over to work. They were productive agents of economic power. Irresponsible Natives, by squandering their energy in all-night ceremonies, were seen as un-American and unpatriotic—stigmas that remain, though, as Shea Murphy reminds us, reprising Native American activist Leslie Marmon Silko from *Almanac of the Dead* (1991), 'the [Native American] people' actively and cunningly resisted government attempts to suppress their dancing; indeed, they 'never stopped dancing'.[3] In considering these anti-Native and antidance policies in light of the discursive history of the dancing disease, this chapter argues that government agents not only set Natives against whites in terms of a border between 'those who dance' and 'those who do not dance' but also, more ambivalently, imagined Natives as primitive ancestors of the whites, and attempted to eradicate dance as a way to eradicate their own ancient histories and thus enter full throttle into modernity.

Dance, as a practice 'indulged' in by Native Americans, became a contested measure of cultural difference and sameness, pitting modern settlers against a depraved but also familiar and childlike way of being that was no longer acceptable in the new, industrial, and industrious political and moral regime. But while religious puritanism had long ago set American settlers against many dance practices, telegrams, letters, and other official correspondence in the holdings of the National Archives and Records Administration further suggest that settlers also in fact danced. What set Native American dancing—and specifically Ghost Dances—apart, however, as that which provoked panic among settlers and U.S. Indian agents in the closing decades of the nineteenth century was its perceived excess. Native Americans not only danced, they danced too much, for too long; and, I also show, they were described in government correspondence and the popular press as dancing too jaggedly, too energetically, too disruptively. Their arms and knees jutted out at impossible angles; their faces contorted in anger and pain. According to these hyperbolic depictions, the dances spilled out of bounds, striking fear into the hearts of the Natives' self-avowedly quiet and industrious neighbours. The dancing was figured as a contagious and life-threatening expression of cultural defiance—threatening to the dancers and to those who lived near them. But whereas Europeans in Madagascar felt immune to the dancing mania, witnessing it mostly with some annoyance, settlers in the American West asked repeatedly for government intervention on their behalf. White settlers felt they were vulnerable, not so much because they might 'catch' the dancing but as stated targets in an environment openly hostile to them and to their government representatives—effectively to the American state. Yet most dancers were not openly hostile to the state, only to its failure to meet prior agreements. In this regard, the Ghost Dance was a reasonable affair and the government's counterattack rash and impulsive—precisely the qualities attributed to 'dance manias'.

Genealogically linked in early anthropology to St. Vitus's dance and other dancing manias, the Ghost Dance thus presents yet a new turn in the genealogy of the dancing disease: one in which the panicked circulation of news about the 'mania' resulted in real casualties, real repression, and the violent transposition of the dancers' ecstatic visions onto a canvas signalling real war. As a discursive zone of intensity in which concepts of history, antiquity, and alterity were played out, discussion surrounding the Ghost Dance thus epitomized a groundswell of debate on the *right* to dance and on various contingencies' rights to dispose of their energy and time as they saw fit. Native Americans, increasingly

---

2. Shea Murphy, *The People Have Never Stopped Dancing*, 54, see also esp. 29–52.

3. Leslie Marmon Silko, *Almanac of the Dead* (New York: Penguin, 1991); cited in Shea Murphy, *The People Have Never Stopped Dancing*, 1.

branded as unfit to dance or to circulate through-out the Plains as they wished, were ostracized from a regime touting, as in Brazil, order and progress. In the 'intradisciplinary' space of politics and dance, ideas about the Ghost Dance, then—ideas that were, as Shea Murphy suggests, conjured up for the most part by antidance critics who did not directly witness the dancing (which they perceived to be too 'heathenish' or evil to merit a direct encounter)[4]—articulate a correlative space in which dance and politics, anthropology and government policy, collide.

UNPRODUCTIVE EXPENDITURE: THE BIOPOLITICS OF 'WASTE'

Thus this chapter argues that negative ideas about the Ghost Dance rested on settler and government criticism of the dancers' apparent energetic excess and waste, in spite of the beatific and pastoral setting against which this 'waste' was supposedly performed. Just as in Africa and South America, dancers were considered primitive, *not yet* modern, participating in a system of value and exchange predicated not on energy conservation or material accumulation but on dilapidation. In this case, the Ghost Dance represents what Bataille has called 'unproductive expenditure', acts going against the logic of capital accumulation. Bataille sees 'unproductive expenditure', including non-reproductive sex, dancing, death rights, and potlatch as constitutive of an alternative economy derived from the collective employment of time or goods against (or ecstatically *beside*) bourgeois rationalism.[5] So, whereas 'capital' indexes the value of goods against an abstract common denominator always on the move, potlatch, dancing, and death rites emerge as indices mapped onto events that dramatically enact moments of exchange promising or concomitantly annulling debts rather than accumulating them with a view to the individual achievement of greatest power (or wealth) later. In this regard, death functions symbolically to actualize this alternative economy: the symbolic 'mini-deaths' performed by Ghost Dancers enact fissures in a current 'now-time' rent through with messianic promise. Time, then—its expenditure and direction—was at stake, as

Ghost Dancers asserted their own chronotopy in a landscape that was moving forward (without them). The spectre of ethnocide, thus, appears for the first time with the Ghost Dance, which performs a state of ecstasy-belonging, according to which the dancers claim back another form of sovereignty from the state of exception that the government calls forth.

Natives in the American West articulated a paradoxically *productive* practice of ecstatic sovereignty whereby calling on deceased ancestors in a collective *repossession* rite would help them, symbolically and through a renewed sense of self-worth, to repopulate tribes decimated by systematic government misrule. And they did so significantly by focusing inward—to the centre of a circle (and sets of circles), claiming sovereignty *here*. The Ghost Dance thus countermanded anthropologists' visions of Natives as natural resources, doubly ancestors of the whites and a people passing into the past, with the dancers' own claims that their ancestors would come back to oust the white colonial invaders. Modern historical time would be annihilated by a return to indigenous temporalities and modern space (significantly, plundered land) would be returned to the Natives, and to the Great Spirit.

AN 'INTENSITY OF CIRCULATIONS'

At the same time, structures of counter-mimesis came into play, as I will also show further in the ensuing chapters. Indian agents witnessing the dances discovered that they were not so different from white leisure practices. Ghost Dancers similarly recognized this similarity and invoked white settler rights by claiming their own right to enjoy the same. The whites and Natives were 'almost the same', in this formulation; not as different as they were uncannily proximous in space and in their corporeal exercises, if not in the uses to which they put them. Discourse surrounding the Ghost Dance by observers and participants, available for the first time (in the genealogy this book traces), suggested a zone of negotiation delimiting an imagined modernity from an equally imagined premodernity in emphatically use value terms. The choreography of this struggle for representation—articulated for the most

---

4. Shea Murphy, *The People Have Never Stopped Dancing*, 32–34.
5. Georges Bataille, *La part maudite, précédé de La notion de dépense* (Paris: Les Éditions de Minuit, 1967).

part in dramaturgies of *circulation*—gave shape to the fears and anxieties of the age: particularly concerning the acutely felt scarcity of resources and their (mis)distribution.

This chapter, then, like the previous and the next, highlights a choreography—and choreotopology—of circulation, what Foucault characterizes as a quintessentially 'modern' concern,[6] as dancers and messages about them moved through vast expanses of the American Plains, often accelerated by new technologies, including recently installed telegraph wires, which contributed to exacerbating fears of and rumours about the movement and intensified the speed with which (often faulty or exaggerated) news spread. The *mobilization* of ideas and resources in the Ghost Dance renders this a particularly intense case of 'choreomania', where, following Foucault, the 'intensity of circulations' makes, but also breaks, a movement which effectively appears through and against biopolitical power conceived in terms of capital.[7] This 'capital' is exercised in every sense as the site and mode whereby administration of 'productive' time and space occurs: the city where power is focused and the 'capitalizing' ideology by which this power works, notably through the exercise of subtle or not so subtle regulations administering resources towards an exogenously 'productive' end (an end often *not* given to those engaging in 'productive' labour). The Ghost Dance thus stages a battle between competing economies of circulation: on the one hand an economy emphasizing bands of dancers travelling between tribes to share information, gathering locally to pool energies and (human) resources (towards collective self-regeneration), and on the other long-range telegraphic wires and a detached military arsenal exercising controlled dispersion, aiming ideologically towards a cultivation of selfish individualism that ties individuals back into identification with the state and its system of biopolitical control.

'NOTHING IS NEW UNDER THE SUN': MOONEY'S DANCE BETWEEN BUREAUS AND TRIBES

Mooney, commissioned by the American Bureau of Ethnology to study the Cherokee tribe in Indian Territory in the fall of 1890, wrote the first decisive history of the Ghost Dance in the American Plains. His report, based on fieldwork conducted over a period of a few years and augmented by an examination of documentary material held by the Indian Office and the War Department of the United States, 'The Ghost-Dance Religion and the Sioux Outbreak of 1890', was published in 1896 (by the Government Printing Office) in the *Fourteenth Annual Report (Part 2) of the Bureau of Ethnology to the Smithsonian Institution, 1892–1893*.[8] His fieldwork extended from the Sioux to the Arapaho, the Cheyenne to the Comanche, and the Paiute to the Kiowa and the Caddo, and included records of songs, costumes, and local beliefs. His report also compared what he described as the Ghost Dance 'religion' to Hebrew, Christian, and 'Mohammedan' practices whose dances and stories offered him thematic and formal 'parallels'.[9]

Mooney described the 'convulsive ecstasy' practiced among Ranters, Quakers, and Fifth-Monarchy Men in particular as a deliberate insanity which, according to the 1877 history of Christian Nonconformism by Robert Barclay (1833–1876), had a 'singular power of producing a kind of sympathetic madness or temporary aberration of intellect'.[10] The *Schaff-Herzog Encyclopedia of Religious Knowledge*, translated from German in 1888 and informed by Hecker's work 'The Dancing Mania', offered Mooney further resources for comparing the Ghost Dance to other religious and spiritual movements, including the long history of choreomania.[11]

---

6. See Foucault, *Security, Territory, Population*, 29.

7. Foucault, *Security, Territory, Population*, 29.

8. James Mooney, *The Ghost-Dance Religion and Wounded Knee* (New York: Dover, 1973). This edition represents an unabridged publication of Mooney's original article 'The Ghost-Dance Religion and the Sioux Outbreak of 1890', in J. W. Powell, *Fourteenth Annual Report of the Bureau of Ethnology to the Smithsonian Institution, 1892–1893* (Washington, DC: Government Printing Office, 1896), 641–1136. On the Smithsonian's role in disseminating early American ethnographic writing, see esp. Curtis M. Hinsley Jr., *Savages and Scientists: The Smithsonian Institution and the Development of American Anthropology, 1846–1910* (Washington, DC: Smithsonian Institution Press, 1981).

9. Mooney, *The Ghost-Dance Religion*, 928–952.

10. Robert Barclay, *The Inner Life of the Religious Societies of the Commonwealth: Considered Principally with Reference to the Influence of Church Organization on the Spread of Christianity* (London: Hodder and Stoughton, 1877), 421; cited in Mooney, *The Ghost-Dance Religion*, 937.

11. See Schaff, ed., *A Religious Encyclopædia*, vol. 1, 602.

Convinced that 'nothing is new under the sun', Mooney argued that these outlandish practices had a common ancestry, describing a genealogy to which the modern West was inextricably linked. 'The systems of our highest modern civilizations', he wrote, 'have their counterparts among all the nations, and their chain of parallels stretches backwards link by link until we find their origin and interpretation in the customs and rites of our own barbarian ancestors, or of our still existing aboriginal tribes'.[12] Once again, as in previous cases of the 'dancing disease', the European past and indigenous present were conflated; linked by religious 'abnormalism'.

Implicit in Mooney's reflection was that the West, which viewed these abnormalisms, was immune from them. Following Canguilhem, pathology is implicitly that which is described as 'abnormal' in a given culture. Fittingly, the tendency towards a utopic desire for the collective return to a Golden Age that Mooney observed in cultures around the world comes to *appear* as pathological, just as Boudin's bemusement at the universality of 'movement' suggests the discursive appearance of an order of things (effectively an order of abnormalisms) that was choreographic. 'Disease' as the reification of abnormalism—what Taussig, as I showed in the previous chapter, further calls the concatenation of events into a singular thing abstracted out of the implicit relations or ecologies that produced it—signals noteworthy alterity: in effect the alterity of a (purportedly delusional) belief in what has become apparently invisible, including spirits or ghosts, or a lost Atlantis (a prior political or cultural state). The discursive *appearance* of this 'delusion' is the 'disorder' of choreomania, in effect the choreopolitical theatricalization of a fantasy that science would purportedly correct, if not by reasoning it out of its adherents then, as with the Ghost Dance, by the exercise of force.

Drawing further comparisons from newspaper articles, the Old and New Testaments, and travel narratives, such as *The Dervishes* (1868), by the secretary and dragoman of the American legation at Constantinople John P. Brown (1814–1872), Mooney noted that the field of enquiry into these 'abnormalisms' was vast: 'it would require a volume to treat of the various religious abnormalisms, based on hypnotism, trances, and the messiah idea, which have sprung up and flourished in different parts of our own country even within the last twenty years'.[13] Nonetheless, like Boudin, Mooney listed some of them, focusing on the beatific 'precedence' these examples suggested to the modern (Western) observer.

Mooney's language was tender and grandiose, intimating that he looked paternalistically on the people whose utopias he dutifully catalogued. 'What tribe or people has not had its golden age', he wrote, in the first chapter of his report, titled 'Paradise Lost',

> before Pandora's box was loosed, when women were nymphs and dryads and men were gods and heroes? And when the race lies crushed and groaning beneath an alien yoke, how natural is the dream of a redeemer, an Arthur, who shall return from exile or awake from some long sleep to drive out the usurper and win back for his people what they have lost . . . . The doctrines of the Hindu avatar, the Hebrew Messiah, the Christian millennium, and the Hesûnanin of the Indian Ghost dance are essentially the same, and have their origin in a hope and longing common to all humanity.[14]

His aim was to invite sympathy with the plight of Ghost Dancers by suggesting that they too were like modern whites—his implied readers. All cultures, he argued, had at the outset a prior state to which they sought longingly to return; some had merely surpassed this. Methodologically, Mooney's approach was to combine participant observation with study of 'precedents' to the Ghost Dance in other cultures. His work was intensive, allowing a degree of immersion not paralleled by other authors writing on the 'dancing disease'. Significantly, Mooney's account attempts least of any to ascribe a medical etiology to the events he witnessed first-hand, though he linked the Ghost Dance thematically and genealogically to St. Vitus's dance, completing a provisional translatio in the discursive history of choreomania from medical to anthropological discourse, instantiating a new regime of ethnographic veridiction. 'The field investigation occupied twenty-two months', Mooney noted, 'involving nearly 32,000 miles

12. Mooney, *The Ghost-Dance Religion*, 928.
13. Mooney, *The Ghost-Dance Religion*, 945.
14. Mooney, *The Ghost-Dance Religion*, 657.

of travel and more or less time spent with about twenty tribes'. What's more, and in contrast to other authors considered so far, Mooney danced, minutely recording the scenes he encountered in every detail: 'to obtain exact knowledge of the ceremony, the author also took part in the dance among the Arapaho and Cheyenne. He also carried a kodak and a tripod camera' and spent several months 'consulting manuscript documents and printed sources of information in the [Office of Indian Affairs and the War Department] . . . at Washington'. Personal correspondence with informed people across the country provided Mooney with additional source material, as did communication with two dozen or so 'Indian' informants and interpreters, including Standing Bear (1868–1939) and American Horse (1840–1908) of Pine Ridge, South Dakota; Black Coyote (d. 1890); Sitting Bull (1831–1890); and the Arapaho police of Darlington, Oklahoma.[15]

THE DUST UNSETTLES: ARCHIVES AND GHOSTS IN WASHINGTON

Mooney's novel approach to the Ghost Dance—involving fieldwork, historiography, and, significantly, participant observation—distinguished his treatment from the medical treatments of so-called dancing manias that circulated prior to his study. But his use of comparison between this and other dance-like uprisings, and the climate of political tension characterizing the Ghost Dance events, suggest that his work continued the comparative project of cataloguing dance frenzies, shifting the conversation provisionally onto ethnographic terrain. My own method has been to emphasize archival research, drawing in particular from records held in a collection named Special Case 188 in the materials of the National Archives and Records Administration at the Library of Congress—an unwieldy set of telegraphs, letters,

and files kept in a degraded condition, possibly suggesting wilful neglect of the material traces of one of the more devastating episodes in U.S. military history on Native land. On one occasion, as I suggested in the introduction, I found a trace of the choreography and got up to dance. But for the most part, records of the event are 'still', dusty, full of the sort of circulation proper to dust: 'dust', the verb, historian Carolyn Steedman writes, suggests taking away and sprinkling, as on a surface.[16] The movement of dust reveals a 'grand circularity, of nothing ever, ever going away',[17] so that the historian's work is that of 'finding things' in this dust; not just breathing bodies back to life metaphorically, in a great performance of ventriloquism or life resuscitation, but in the minutiae arrived at by combing through reams of otherwise useless statements conserved at times haphazardly by governments and administrators.[18] Yet this offered me what historian and anthropologist Ann Laura Stoler further describes as an 'ethno-*graphy*' of a different sort, emphasizing the discursive uncertainties and anxieties with regard to taxonomical and administrative procedures contained in these files; as well as the 'historical ontologies', in Hacking's terms, emerging in the interstices between what was written and what I could only surmise was left unsaid.[19] Like Stoler and Hacking I have been interested to consider the discursive (and ontological) systems characterizing new modes of seeing—scopic regimes—revealing ambivalence with regard to what may lie 'beneath' the faint *appearance* of dance frenzies in modern scientific and anthropological literature. Between the unwieldy bottom or underside and the surface taxonomy of choreomania emerges a discursive ontology (a way of understanding how language moves) of *clarification* performed by writers by recourse to a gesture of abstraction, according to which figures of uncontrol come to be (more or less) categorized. Indeed, following Stoler, it is this 'more or less' in the categorization that interests me. Dance manias were never

15. Mooney, *The Ghost-Dance Religion*, 654–655. Rani-Henrik Andersson points out that Mooney was not successful in all his requests for information; the Lakota Sioux in particular refused to talk to him directly about the dancing. Rani-Henrik Andersson, *The Lakota Ghost Dance of 1890* (Lincoln: University of Nebraska Press, 2008), xii. Subsequent comparisons of the Ghost Dance to other ecstatic religious movements by sociologists such as F. M. Davenport (1866–1956) failed similarly to allay fears about Ghost Dancing in the American Plains. In *Primitive Traits in Religious Revivals*, Davenport likened the Ghost Dance to other American religious movements among whites and non-whites, including the Indian Shakers (the 'red-skin Shakers of Puget Sound') and the 'white-skin Shakers of . . . the eastern states' (32).

16. Carolyn Steedman, *Dust* (Manchester: Manchester University Press, 2001), 160.

17. Steedman, *Dust*, 166.

18. Steedman, *Dust*, 10.

19. Emphasis mine. Stoler writes 'ethno-graphy'. See Ann Laura Stoler, *Along the Archival Grain: Epistemic Anxieties and Colonial Common Sense* (Princeton, NJ: Princeton University Press, 2009), 2; and Ian Hacking, *Historical Ontology* (Cambridge, MA: Harvard University Press, 2004).

entirely set into disciplinary systems but moved across disciplines and fields; they were always described as strange or obscure, eluding scientific, anthropological, or political finality and containment, even while dancers themselves were (as I will show) limited in their freedom to move. A *tendency towards* clarification thus takes place instead. The 'epistemic anxieties' Stoler describes plagued scientists perplexed by the heterogeneity of events and their undecipherability; their ultimate ungraspability. Dance manias were not objects one could hold, though many attempted to describe and to collage scenes in this form.

With the emergence of professional ethnography and anthropology and their institutionalization in the late nineteenth century, new approaches to collective ecstatic dances situated them in relationship to historical precedents and discursive genealogies of the dancing disease, as had medicine and colonial medicine before them, but also increasingly in a relationship to environments or milieus, the *oikonomies*—the systems of local governance—within and against which they emerged. With the Ghost Dance, transhistoricity gave way increasingly to comparative regionalism, so that the ethno-graphic traces left behind by writers reveal material as well as methodological changes taking place in the scientific world. Concern was now less theoretical and more applied, even prescriptive; ethnographers such as Mooney, coming into Native territory a few years after the Ghost Dance peaked, spoke to participants in an effort to offer the government—and wider anthropological profession—a clear view of narratives that had been anecdotally trickling in. Security rather than historiography was paramount, and the efficient government of U.S. territory the final aim. The antiquarian curiosity that had saturated previous discussions of choreomania receded to the sidelines, now merely framing a discourse aimed primarily at the efficient deployment of biopower grounded in specialist local knowledge.

DROMOGRAPHY AND THE BIOPOLITICS OF THE 'CAPITAL'

Thus the ethno-graphy emerging from the archives also gives rise to choreographic histories that trace the movements of texts and bodies across the American Plains, revealing the circulation of 'energies', for lack of a better word, that characterized them. Often, these were patent in the urgency of a scrawl—particularly by one inexperienced Indian agent, D. F. Royer, known as Lakota Kokipa-Koshkala (Young-Man-Afraid-of-Indians), whose panicked telegraphs to Washington suggested that on his agency (the Native territory he administered) the dancing was spiralling out of control. He requested military intervention, while other agents sat back, confident that the Ghost Dance was a mild and contained affair. But his alarm triggered requests for reports from Washington, DC, setting in motion a heightened sentiment that the United States was under attack from within its own margins.

As in the *imanenjana*, the nation's capital came to stand at the heart of the affair, but here it operated its power exogenously, in the regions where upheavals were taking place. What Foucault has described in his 1977–1978 lectures at the Collège de France, *Security, Territory, Population*, as the 'capitalization' of nations in the seventeenth and eighteenth centuries, when governments exercising biopower began systematically to flex muscles to control processes of life and death, as well as natural and biological resources (mountains, trees, the quality of the air) from a noble and aloof central location,[20] figured here as a centralizing power focused on Washington, DC. Washington was a place which was far removed from the locus of the Native American uprising but which controlled the spatialization of the territory by focusing activity back into and through this centralizing power. Thus the increasingly rapid circulation and crisscrossing of lines of communication between the regions and the capital exacerbated a sense of anxiety and uncertainty in the Plains, as settlers, agents, and Natives alike tried to figure out the extent and gravity of government neglect of Native populations—and potential intercession.

What these traces and partial scenarios reveal was a mood shift, an intense zone of change, in the history of the American West, showing anger and fear among Native Americans and settlers and competing concepts of land, agency, and space, as well as energetic and choreographic normalcy. Durkheim would describe the notion of anomie in the decade following the uprising,

---

20. See Foucault, *Security, Territory, Population*, esp. 27–38.

pinpointing a sense of lawlessness and root-lessness of life among 'moderns'; he described degeneration into a-regulation ('irréglementa-tion') and a 'sad spectacle' ('triste spectacle') attributable to the rapid speed of change in life everywhere, as modern economic modes of pro-duction alienated interpersonal relations and shifted concepts of energetic expenditure, recon-figuring social bonds.[21] This set the stage for what Virilio would later define as dromology, the science of speed and circulation that gave faster nations the upper hand: the rapidity of their movements and their ability quickly to mobilize opinion through mass media and other technol-ogies of communication gave them power over slower entities, whose speed of interchange, movements, and response times lagged.[22] In the case of the Ghost Dance, Native American rebels accordingly increased interpersonal contact in efforts to counteract government suppression of their basic living needs but did so at a differ-ent pace from that of their surroundings. The speed and expanse of Western Union's telegraph lines, introduced in the wake of the Civil War, overpowered the Natives' modes of circulation, mostly movement on foot or horseback. Yet the intensity of circulation and gathering among Ghost Dancers created a rhythmic and geocul-tural choreozone by which dancers found new routes towards ecstasy-belonging.

The drama of distance then constitutes a new spatial (and spatializing) turn in 'choreomania', as the sort of rumours and repetitions that char-acterized narratives of 'dancing manias' in the previous cases I have offered occurred for the most part at an intellectual distance; no action took place. Here, the biopolitical dromology operated against dancers whose movements were paradoxically too slow, though charac-terized as frenetic. The choreopolitics of their revolt conversely emphasized social solidarity and topology, or choreotopology: the gesture of gathering, closely and tangibly, *not* in the centre (the capital), nor in the furthest margins, like the Brazilian *sertões* (who sought to disappear entirely from the nation state), but within the Indian agencies where they resided, in order to

make their claims heard *where they were* and so to dance emphatically *in place*. The circulation they performed was instrumental to this ecstatic affirmation of *being-here*.

MENTAL GEOGNOSY: ANTHROPOLOGY, AND THE METAPHOR OF A LOST ATLANTIS

Native Americans were understood to be of the earth and thus to be plunderable, domesticable, like the earth. The new American worldview, based on Christian precepts, saw the natural world—in which were included 'Indians'—as its endowment. Anthropology aided in this task. For Mooney, anthropology was born out of an antiquarian impulse to 'see' forgotten antiquity and 'nature' in the struggles of the present. Metaphors of archaeology and myth, history, geology (or geognosy) and geography had already been influentially articulated by the American ethnologist Henry Rowe Schoolcraft (1793–1864) in his 1846 address to the New Confederacy of the Iroquois and to the non-Iroquois men of Rochester, New York—includ-ing the soon-to-be ethnographer, Lewis Henry Morgan (1818–1881)—he was urging to take up a pioneering role in the development of a new American 'tradition'. In this view, Natives were at once central to the new American way and prece-dent to it; they could thus logically be surpassed, as their 'impress' on the soil was supposedly in this exalted sense indelible. 'No people can bear a true nationality', he declared, 'which does not exfoliate, as it were, from its bosom, something that expresses the peculiarities of its own soil and climate'. America, he argued, had to extract its 'history' 'from the broad and deep quarries of its own mountains, foundation stones, and columns and capitals, which bear the impress of an indi-genous mental geognosy', effectively a science of rock formations and minerals equated more or less metaphorically with the indigenous mind, distinguishing America implicitly from urban, civilized Europe.[23] This discursive juxtaposition

---

21. Durkheim argues that the division of labour in modern economic life is often 'normal' but, 'like all biological facts', pre-sents 'pathological' forms. These occur where social solidarity gives way to its opposite and a chasm grows (between co-workers or between them and their employer); it is also exacerbated by the disintegration of family life and the replacement of 'communal' by 'adversarial' social and professional structures and activities. Durkheim, 'Préface de la seconde édition', in *De la division du travail social*, ii–iii, 343. On anomie, see also Durkheim, *Le suicide*, 264–311.

22. Paul Virilio, *Speed and Politics* (New York: Semiotext(e), 2006).

23. Cited in Hinsley, *Savages and Scientists*, 20.

of the indigenous, the intellectual, and the geological in the scientific deployment of local knowledge of terrains and territories heralded the new scientific culture of America with pomp, folding the 'indigenous' into American natural history. In the terms used by anthropologist Margaret Mead (1901–1978), Native Americans were symbolically ancestral and so were like the American settlers ('but not quite'): they too had been 'immigrants to the great empty continents of the New World where, like later European immigrants, they began a life without historical precedents. In the imagination of those who came from Europe, these earlier dwellers became a different kind of ancestor'.[24] Significantly, the difference was precisely the measure of contestation acted out in the Ghost Dance: a 'difference' suggesting that the Natives were *no longer* as different as they had once been and were thus subject, as I will show, *no longer* to a certain sort of exceptionalism by which they had been granted rations. They had to enter themselves headlong into modernity, and so become 'white' *right away*, if not by reason then by force.

Natives sought to counter this 'fictitious state of exception', what Agamben calls the construction of a scenario by which suspension of laws is meted out,[25] by returning to their own 'mental geognosy'—their own dwelling in and with the land—what I have elsewhere described as a dancing-place, a site embedded with genealogical and affective weight, through which kinship lines pass.[26] The Ghost Dance was a performance of and on a dancing-place, a site saturated with alternative historicities, in which affect-laden acts and messianic longings for a new future, saturated with relivings of the past, accumulated and were deployed, enabling a deep sense of collective self to emerge against state control.

Yet this concerted choreography of protest was unsettling for settlers unaccustomed to the lofty aspirations of ethnographic science and confused by the messianism that Natives displayed, a sort of religiosity at once too close to and too far from their own. Ultimately, the spectacle of an indigenous choreopolitics creolizing indigenous and Christian symbols of redemption and return catalysed the government to act: troops intervened on behalf of Indian agents who were worried about the spread of the dancing 'craze'. The massacre at Wounded Knee on 29 December 1890 resulted in the death of more than 300 Lakota Sioux by government fire, including some of the most prominent Ghost Dancers, and over 250 women and children.[27] Alarmist discourse surrounding the Ghost Dance emphasized the dancers' irrationalism, the sense that what they did to represent their claims was abnormal, wrong, and so negated the very claims put forward. One special agent, E. B. Reynolds, argued in a letter to the commissioner of Indian affairs in Washington, DC, T. J. Morgan, that the dancers did more than eschew economic rationality; they actively counteracted the government's costly attempt to 'wean' them from the 'customs of their ancestors'. Only military action, Reynolds surmised, might stop this, 'unless the cold weather accomplishes this end'.[28] The government in that regard viewed its role as tantamount to that of a natural force—doubled with the technological and military power that might supplement and surpass it.

Both sides of the spectral war operated cultural economies that occluded the other; likewise, both staged narratives rent through with antinomies, finally to produce a dialectics at a standstill, until the U.S. war machine eradicated its own imagined past in a wilful drive towards a 'productive', mechanistic future. This drive was governed by the supposed rational workings of capital and land distribution to the exclusion of freedom of movement and what Bataille in the epigraph to this chapter describes as the madness of sacrifice exercised among Natives—a prodigious irony, as Native Americans were 'sacrificed' in their turn by this machine of war.

24. Margaret Mead, 'Introduction', in Margaret Mead and Ruth L. Bunzel, eds., *The Golden Age of American Anthropology* (New York: Braziller, 1960), 1–12, 2.

25. See Agamben, *State of Exception*, 3–4.

26. In Kélina Gotman, 'The Dancing-Place: Towards a Geocultural and Geohistorical Theory of Performance Space', *Choreographic Practices* 3 (2012): 7–23.

27. Report by Major Whitside, to whom the Natives surrendered, as cited in Mooney, *The Ghost-Dance Religion*, 870. A useful, comprehensive history of the Wounded Knee massacre and events leading up to it is in William S. E. Coleman, *Voices of Wounded Knee* (Lincoln: University of Nebraska Press, 2000).

28. Special U.S. Indian Agent E. B. Reynolds, Pine Ridge Agency, SD, to T. J. Morgan, Commissioner of Indian Affairs, Washington, DC, 25 September 1890, The Ghost Dance, Special Case 188, Special Cases, Entry 102, Record Group 75, National Archives, Washington, DC (hereafter Ghost Dance, Special Case 188).

'THEY ARE EVERY YEAR CUTTING DOWN OUR RATIONS'

Widespread starvation had compelled Native Americans to gather in order to survive. Buffalo had been decimated over the course of the century leading up to the events, with increasing rapidity in the previous ten or twenty years. According to the American demographer Russell Thornton, the North American buffalo population had dwindled to eight hundred in 1895, down from twenty thousand ten years prior, and 1 million ten years before that; he estimates that before 1800, there may have been 40 million or more.[29] The Native American population itself had reached its lowest numbers in 1890, at around 228,000, down from 600,000 in 1800 and anywhere from 849,000 to a few million prior to the first European contact.[30] Census Bureau figures show that after this nadir in 1890, coinciding with the height of the Ghost Dance movement, buffalo and human populations began to rise again.[31] Thornton argues that the Ghost Dance was thus a 'revitalization movement' whose goal was nothing less than demographic regeneration.[32] Dancers lying on the ground in a trance state were imagining a new future and resisting the 'ethnocidal order'; they were visualizing a restoration of old ways and a renewed, sustainable livelihood.[33] Historian Jeffrey Ostler has argued that the Ghost Dance was an anti-colonial movement focused on accessing a spiritual power that would help Natives 'achieve revolutionary purposes', destroying the current world so as to replace it with a better one.[34] In Weston La Barre's terms, the Ghost Dance was the response of a 'traumatized' society to the stresses of acculturation.[35] For Roach, it was a 'rite of memory with spirit-world claims on the return of the ancestral dead'.[36] I suggest that the dancing and gathering produced a theatrical zone of intensity that meshed genealogies of corporeal, affective, and performance practice—what Roach further calls 'mnemonic reserves'[37]—with a heightened concept of futurity in a kinematic now-time of collective syncope (or suspension). The Ghost Dance movement and individual instances of Ghost Dancing served as a suspension of breath (literally, performed in the act of fainting) that interrupted cultural degeneration, starvation, and ethnocide, in which participants could imagine new forms of collective desire, grounded in a memory of the old. Trance-like states triggered real-world dreams allowing Ghost Dancers to step outside the present ecological and political devastation to create their own state of exception, ecstatically, one that would counter the demographic ruin exacerbated by the escalation of assimilationist policies in Washington, DC.

---

29. Russell Thornton, *We Shall Live Again: The 1870 and 1890 Ghost Dance Movements as Demographic Revitalization* (Cambridge: Cambridge University Press, 1986), 26–27.

30. Thornton, *We Shall Live Again*, 23; see also 20–45. Pierre Clastres (1934–1977) retorts that it is impossible to determine how many Native Americans lived on the American continent before the arrival of whites. Pierre Clastres, *La Société contre l'État: Recherches d'anthropologie politique* (Paris: Les Éditions de Minuit, 1974), 72. See Ann F. Ramenofsky, *Vectors of Death: The Archaeology of European Contact* (Albuquerque: University of New Mexico Press, 1987), and K. Dietz, 'Epidemics and Rumors: A Survey', *Journal of the Royal Statistical Society*, series A, 130 (1967): 505–528. A. L. Kroeber, in *Cultural and Natural Areas of Native North America* (Berkeley: University of California Press, 1963), and H. Dobyns, *Their Number Become Thinned: Native American Population Dynamics in Eastern North America* (Knoxville: University of Tennessee Press, 1983), provide low and high estimates, respectively, of the Native population at the time of the first sustained European contact in 1492, from Kroeber's 0.9 million to Dobyns's 18 million. See also Michael G. Davis, *Ecology, Sociopolitical Organization, and Cultural Change on the Southern Plains: A Critical Treatise in the Sociocultural Anthropology of Native North America* (Kirksville, MO: Thomas Jefferson University Press, 1996).

31. The 1980 census indicated a total Native American population of 1,361,869. Thornton, *We Shall Live Again*, 24.

32. Thornton, *We Shall Live Again*, xi.

33. Thornton, *We Shall Live Again*, xi. Disease had been running rampant at some Indian agencies. Indian agent James McLaughlin writes of 'the real causes of the late outbreak' and that 'in the autumn of 1888 measles broke out among the Indians and was epidemic at all the Sioux Agencies throughout the following winter. "Le Grippe" and "Whooping Cough" followed in the winter of 1889 & 90 and an unusual number of deaths resulted. The severe droughts rendered all efforts of agriculture a failure for the past three years and many of the Indians' stock cattle died of black leg'. James McLaughlin, Indian Agent, United States Indian Service, Standing Rock Agency, to Hon. T. J. Morgan, Commissioner of Indian Affairs, Washington, DC, 10 March 1891, Ghost Dance, Special Case 188.

34. Jeffrey Ostler, *The Plains Sioux and U.S. Colonialism from Lewis and Clark to Wounded Knee* (Cambridge: Cambridge University Press, 2004), esp. 243–263, 262.

35. Weston La Barre, *The Ghost Dance: Origins of Religion* (Garden City, NY: Doubleday, 1970), 44.

36. Roach, *Cities of the Dead*, 208.

37. Roach, *Cities of the Dead*, 25–26.

President Benjamin Harrison's (1833–1901) government had decreed the year before, in 1889, that 'Indians' were to lose their special status and right to cultural autonomy: 'First, the anomalous position heretofore occupied by the Indians in this country can no longer be maintained. Second, the logic of events demands the absorption of the Indians into our national life not as Indians but as American citizens. Third . . . the relations of the Indians to the government must rest solely upon the recognition of their individuality [i.e. as legal persons]. Fourth, the individual must conform to the white man's ways, peaceably if they will, forcibly if they must'.[38] On 10 February 1890, five reservations were established on roughly half of the former Great Sioux Reservation of South Dakota; the other half was sold to non-Natives 'at bargain prices', as anthropologist Alice Beck Kehoe notes.[39] Railroads were built through the reservations, and families had to live on individual allotments rather than in shared camps or villages as they had normally done. The Sioux had to support themselves with small-scale agriculture instead of hunting; farmers hired by the Bureau of Indian Affairs were deployed to instruct them in this new economy. Children were sent to boarding schools and made to speak English, subject to punishment if they failed to comply.

Yet these policies ran counter to a prior agreement, known as the Fort Laramie Treaty, reached between Sioux leaders and the government in 1868: a vote with approval by three-quarters of adult 'Indian' men was required to modify any arrangements to that treaty between the parties involved. The agreement had ceded the majority of the Sioux hunting lands to the government in exchange for the right in perpetuity to the Great Sioux Reservation. But the discovery of gold in the Black Hills portion of the reservation had prompted the government to rescind the agreement without a vote. In a letter to Washington, DC, dated 10 April 1891, Indian agent A. P. Dixon, of the Crow Creek and Lower Brule Consolidated Agency, retrospectively noted Congress's failure to 'make the appropriation, recommended

by the Indian Bureau, of $187,039.00 to compensate [the Indians] for the loss sustained in receiving less land per capita in their diminished Reservation than is received by the Indians occupying other diminished reservations. They are unable to comprehend clearly the distinction between Congress and the Government', he noted, 'and unable to recognize with satisfaction just why Congress should have a different opinion in regard to their claims, than that recommended by the Indian Commissioner, as promised them by the Sioux Commission'.[40] Arbitrary rule with respect to land—and land seizure—catapulted displaced Natives into the reasonable experience of spiritual anomie.

Rations were, moreover, cut to less than half—on account of the Natives' perceived laziness—causing many to suffer from starvation. Although food had earlier been provided on reservations in compensation for ceded land—until Native Americans could sustain themselves through farming—a semi-arid climate, heat, and drought in 1890 caused crops to fail that spring. The measles in 1889 and the grippe in 1890, as well as recurring bouts of whooping cough, weakened those already malnourished from crop failure.[41] Restrictions on travel meant that Natives could not seek other means of subsistence on adjacent territories as they had done in the past. This left most highly vulnerable to the crop failures and bad weather, conditions that were exacerbated by widespread negligence on the part of Indian agents: in July 1889, during the farming season, the Indians at Sioux Falls, South Dakota, were called to the local agency and kept there for a month by the Sioux Commission. Bishop W. H. Hare (1838–1909) noted that 'during their absence, their cattle broke into their fields and trod down, or ate up, their crops. The Indians reaped practically nothing'.[42] Commanding major General Nelson A. Miles (1839–1925) noted in a letter to the adjutant general of the United States Army in late January 1891 that the Natives 'claimed that they could not live on promises not fulfilled and half or two-thirds sufficient

38. Cited in Alice Beck Kehoe, *The Ghost Dance: Ethnohistory and Revitalization* (New York: Holt, Rinehart and Winston, 1989), 14.

39. Kehoe, *The Ghost Dance*, 14.

40. A. P. Dixon, Indian Agent, Crow Creek and Lower Brule Consolidated Agency, to Hon. Commissioner of Indian Affairs, 10 April 1891, Ghost Dance, Special Case 188.

41. Bishop W. H. Hare, Missionary District of South Dakota, Sioux Falls, SD, to Secretary of the Interior, 7 January 1891, Ghost Dance, Special Case 188. On debates among Indian agents regarding the role of hunger in the Ghost Dance, see also n45 here.

42. Bishop W. H. Hare, Missionary District of South Dakota, Sioux Falls, SD, to Secretary of the Interior, 7 January 1891, Ghost Dance, Special Case 188.

food. It is useless to suppose that they can support themselves when compelled to remain on their reservation where the crops have for the last year been a total failure'. He recommended that the government assure them of its good faith by carrying out the terms of the treaties.[43] But the government failed to respond; agreements were broken.

Sioux leaders who protested against these measures were branded as agitators.[44] Most tribal leaders simply wanted their provisions met: American Horse (1840–1908), Fast Thunder (b. c. 1839), Spotted Horse, Pretty Back, and Good Lance (b. c. 1846) remarked at a council held at Indian agent D. F. Royer's quarters at the Pine Ridge Agency in South Dakota that 'they are every year cutting down our rations and we do not get enough to keep us from suffering'. But Agent Royer dismissed the situation, explaining in his telegraphs to the commissioner of Indian affairs in Washington that 'some of the Indians were trying to account for this ghost dance craze by saying that the Government has not fulfilled the promises made'.[45]

The degree to which Natives at different agencies used the Ghost Dance as a platform for organizing varied. In the aftermath of the massacre at Wounded Knee, Natives at the Standing Rock, Cheyenne, and other neighbouring agencies began regularly to visit the graves of those killed in the skirmish, crying, howling, and working themselves into what one report described as a 'sad state of mind'.[46] But at Fort Sill, Oklahoma Territory, the attitudes were more placid. Lieutenant H. L. Scott (1853–1934) noted in the context of 'a small dance near the agency [that the whole excitement concerning the Messiah] was observed to be largely an affair for amusement for the young people'.[47] It was a new sort of dance, a new variation on older forms, and not, in this case, he argued, a program for venting anger or banding together to fight.

'MINI DEATHS': OF VISIONS AND SYNCOPES

Although doctrines differed, some aspects of the Ghost Dance were unvarying, particularly the shuffling sidestep to the left and dancers' falling to the ground in a state of exhaustion or syncope, described as a 'mini death'. These were not trances per se, one informant ventured, speaking to anthropologist Cora du Bois (1903–1991) in the 1940s: 'dancers might fall over in faint [sic]; revived by fanning with sagebrush twig. Was not a trance so far as informant knew; fainted simply from dancing too hard'.[48] Another participant,

43. Nelson A. Miles, Commanding Major General, Headquarters Division of Missouri, to Adjutant General of the U.S. Army, 27 January 1891, Ghost Dance, Special Case 188.

44. Kehoe, *The Ghost Dance*, 15–17.

45. D. F. Royer, Indian Agent, United States Indian Service, Office of Indian Agent, Pine Ridge Agency, SD, telegraph to R. V. Belt, Acting Commissioner of Indian Affairs, Washington, DC, 27 November 1890, Ghost Dance, Special Case 188. Bishop W. H. Hare, Missionary District of South Dakota, Sioux Falls, SD, to Secretary of the Interior, 7 January 1891, states that 'among the Pine Ridge Indians, at least, hunger has been an important element in the causes of discontent and insubordination'; Ghost Dance, Special Case 188. Indian Agent A. P. Dixon concurs: 'It is without doubt, that there existed, previous to the outbreak among the Indians, a feeling of dissatisfaction growing out of failure to receive regular and full rations, and the delay in shipment of Annuity clothing, owing to the dilatory manner with which the Indian Appropriation Bill was handled by Congress'; A. P. Dixon, Indian Agent at the Crow Creek and Lower Brule Consolidated Agency, to Hon. Commissioner of Indian Affairs, 10 April 1891, Ghost Dance, Special Case 188. Nelson A. Miles, writing to the adjutant general of the army, reports the same: 'They claimed that they could not live on promises not fulfilled and half or two-thirds sufficient food. It is useless to suppose that they can support themselves when compelled to remain on their reservation where the crops have for the last year been a total failure'. Nelson A. Miles, Headquarters Division of the Missouri, to Adjutant General of the U.S. Army, 27 January 1891, Ghost Dance, Special Case 188.

46. Penny, Acting Indian Agent, Pine Ridge Agency, SD, telegraph to Commissioner of Indian Affairs, Washington, DC, 8 April 1891, Ghost Dance, Special Case 188. Indian Agent George Wright said the same, adding that Indians from his reservation had gone to Pine Ridge for this purpose and that those visiting the graves were doubtless relatives from Cheyenne River. George Wright, Indian Agent, Rosebud Agency, SD, telegraph to Commissioner of Indian Affairs, 9 April 1891, Ghost Dance, Special Case 188. However, Indian agent Perain P. Palmer wrote to the commissioner to state that none of the Indians at Cheyenne River had visited Wounded Knee, as instructions had been given for all to remain at their homes, and that policemen were stationed at all the camps and were instructed to report any absences. He added that the Indians were generally 'well disposed' (and 'satisfied') and 'would remain loyal to the government'. Perain P. Palmer, Indian Agent, Cheyenne River Agency, to Hon. T. J. Morgan, Commissioner of Indian Affairs, Washington, DC, 10 April 1891, Ghost Dance, Special Case 188.

47. H. L. Scott, 1st Lieutenant, 7th Cavalry, Fort Sill, Oklahoma Territory, to Post Adjutant, Fort Sill, Oklahoma Territory, 30 January 1891, Ghost Dance, Special Case 188.

48. Cora Du Bois, 'The 1870 Ghost Dance', in *University of California Publications in Anthropological Records*, vol. 3, no. 1 (Berkeley: University of California Press, 1946), 1–152, 6. Ostler notes that 'after a while—an hour or two, sometimes less—some

who had escaped from school in 1890 with about fifty other children to participate in the Ghost Dance, told Sioux anthropologist Ella Deloria (1889–1971) that sheer exhaustion served to catalyse visions, producing an altered state of consciousness and dreams heightened by the intensity of the dance: 'Occasionally someone thoroughly exhausted and dizzy fell unconscious into the center and lay there "dead"', this participant recalled. 'After a while many lay about in that condition. They were now "dead" and seeing their dear ones. As each one came to, she, or he, slowly sat up and looked about, bewildered, and then began wailing inconsolably'.[49]

These exhausted visions reimagined life in the Plains, peopled by deceased ancestors, buffaloes, and a sense of joy and security past. According to Deloria's interlocutor, 'the visions varied at the start, but they ended the same way, like a chorus describing a great encampment of all the Dakotas who had ever died, where all were related and therefore understood each other, where the buffalo came eagerly to feed them, and there was no sorrow but only joy, where relatives thronged out with happy laughter to greet the newcomer . . . . Waking to the drab and wretched present after such a glowing vision, it was little wonder that they wailed as if their poor hearts would break in two with disillusionment'.[50] The visions were further provoked by fasting and were often preceded by running, moaning, and what Major Wirt Davis (1839–1914) called 'nervous prostration'.[51] Davis, who attended a dance at Boggy Creek in December 1890, described the event as a controlled and largely peaceful affair: a religious gathering, not a war-dance.[52]

The dancing area was carefully delineated, with sentinels prowling the outskirts, keeping dogs out (since they were said to break the spell of a trance and prevent visions), and making sure no fires were lit inside the ring. Wagons, buggies, and teepees were arranged around the outside,

with an abundance of foodstuffs that reminded him of 'old-fashioned Methodist or Baptist camp-meetings'.[53] Davis's detailed description of the dance, addressed to the assistant adjutant general of the War Department, merits reproducing at some length:

The Indians were dancing when we arrived and we were spectators until they stopped for dinner about 5 p.m. The dance was resumed about 6 p.m. and continued during the night and until 8 o'clock a.m. Usually the night dance begins about sunset and lasts until the Pleiades are in mid-heaven. I was present at the dance till 10 p.m., and also in the morning from 6:30 a.m. until 8 a.m., when it stopped. At one time 140 Indians—men, women and children—were in the ring dancing and singing the Messiah songs. The step in this dance is different from the step in the other Indian dances. The movement is to the left and is a glide with the left foot, followed by the right foot, and a bending of both knees, the right knee more bent than the left. There are at least six Messiah hymns of invocation and supplication. The Indians join hands, the fingers interlocked, dance in a circle while singing a Messiah hymn for fifteen or twenty minutes, then rest and again resume the dance. While resting they smoke and chat. When the 'power' seizes an Indian there ensues a swaying of the body, a spasmodic jerking of the muscles, he leaves the circle of dancers, moves wildly, sometimes running, around the interior of the circle, gesticulating, singing and moaning, and finally falls to the ground worn out from nervous prostration, exhaustion and dizziness. In this trance-like condition the Indians claim to have visions and, upon recovery,

of the dancers "became affected" (*ececa*) and "fainted" or "died" (*t'a*)'. Others '"went to the land of the spirits" (*wanagiyata ipi*)'. Ostler, *The Plains Sioux*, 258.

49. Cited in Ronald Niezen et al., *Spirit Wars: Native North American Religions in the Age of Nation Building* (Berkeley: University of California Press, 2000), 133. See Peter Nabokov, *Native American Testimony: A Chronicle of Indian-White Relations from Prophecy to the Present, 1492–1992* (New York: Penguin Books, 1992), 254–255.

50. In Niezen, *Spirit Wars*, 133.

51. Wirt Davis, Major, 5th Calvary, Inspector of Small Arms Practice, Headquarters Department of the Missouri, Office of the Inspector of Small Arms Practice, St. Louis, Missouri, to Assistant Adjutant General of the Department, 23 December 1890, Ghost Dance, Special Case 188.

52. Wirt Davis to Assistant Adjutant General of the Department, 23 December 1890, Ghost Dance, Special Case 188.

53. Davis writes: 'Jake, the chief of the Caddos, remarked that he had been to Methodist camp-meetings and that this meeting was similar to them in character and purpose'. Wirt Davis to Assistant Adjutant General of the Department, 23 December 1890, Ghost Dance, Special Case 188.

they go to their tepees and tell their relatives and friends what they have seen. At 9 o'clock p.m. I counted ten Indians, most of them women, lying on the ground and under the 'influence'. When the dance ended in the morning there were three lying on the ground, two of them were motionless and apparently insensible and the other, a Caddo woman, was moving her arms and exclaiming as it was interpreted to me by a Shawnee who spoke English: 'It is so—it is true'. When the dance stopped at 8 a.m., the dancers shook their blankets and quietly dispersed.[54]

For Davis, the dance was indebted to Christian iconography, deserving, as Lieutenant H. L. Scott had noted in a letter that eventually made its way to the secretary of war in Washington, the same protection afforded to all personal liberties and the freedom to engage in the pursuit of happiness.[55] These recommendations were not heeded, and although Davis stated plainly that Natives' anxieties had been exacerbated by conditions of want and were thus reasonable, noise coming from other quarters underlined the Natives' misery as fodder for unwarranted revolt.

WOVOKA: MAKING IT SNOW IN THE SUMMER, MAKING THE PEOPLE DANCE

Adherents of the Ghost Dance believed the spirits of dead Indians would come back to life and the earth would turn back into an Indian paradise. All whites would be cast out, and the Indians would live eternally. Many versions forecasted the abundant return of animals, fish, and other foodstuffs. Some merely predicted changes in the Natives' relations to whites. But as anthropologist A. L. Kroeber (1876–1960) has argued, the main thrust of the teachings was the return of the dead.[56]

Two movements were effectively described as Ghost Dances: a first, smaller movement, emerging in 1870, and then a resurgence of similar teachings in 1890, mobilizing a far greater contingency of dancer-agitators ('demonstrators') and resulting in the far greater escalation of power politics mentioned already. Unlike the *imanenjana*, the Ghost Dance operated a series of movements with multiple centres or poles, none directing dancers towards the capital, but circulating across the Plains, with doctrines and opinions that suggested a range of approaches to choreopolitical dissidence. Like the *imanenjana* and the Canudos revolt, the Ghost Dance was in large part initiated by a (self-styled) spiritual healer; but band leaders took a great part in the orchestration of the movement's choreography of protest, its ways of '[creating] interference', if only through a temporary suspension of 'productive' work time.[57] The 1870 Ghost Dance movement originated far from the Great Sioux Reservation of South Dakota, which would become the crucible of later events: further west, among the Northern Paiute or Paviotso of western Nevada on the Walker Lake reservation. The movement spread through the rest of Nevada, along the West Coast of the United States, and into Oregon and California.[58] It constituted a traditional Paviotso round dance—used for all special occasions—with a typical ring formation and shuffling sidestep to the left; men and

---

54. Wirt Davis to Assistant Adjutant General of the Department, 23 December 1890, Ghost Dance, Special Case 188.

55. H. L. Scott, 1st Lieutenant, 7th Cavalry, Fort Sill, [O]T, to the Post Adjutant at Fort Sill, IT [sic], 16 December 1890, Ghost Dance, Special Case 188. The letter was passed on to the assistant adjutant general in St. Louis, MO, and endorsed by W. Merritt, commanding brigadier general, who forwarded it to the adjutant general of the army. It was then submitted to the secretary of war by J. M. Schofield, commanding major general, and endorsed in Washington at army headquarters on 29 December 1890, not, however, succeeding in interrupting the rapid escalation towards military intervention; Ghost Dance, Special Case 188.

56. There were also variants in terms of how the dead would return. Sometimes it was said that a 'supreme ruler' was in charge of shuttling the spirits of the dead back to earth; or dead relatives would return from the south; or 'the dead would come from the east when the grass was about 8 inches high'. Other times it was said that the dead would return in armies from the rising sun, or they would return from their graves. In at least one instance, among the Natives in northern California, the 'dead would return . . . and would sweep the whites from the earth'. Thornton, *We Shall Live Again*, 3. See also Thornton, *We Shall Live Again*, 1–2, on the teachings and their spread.

57. Foster, 'Choreographies of Protest', 395.

58. See Thornton, *We Shall Live Again*, 1. See also Du Bois, 'The 1870 Ghost Dance'; Leslie Spier, 'The Ghost Dance of 1870 among the Klamath of Oregon', in *University of Washington Publications in Anthropology*, vol. 2, no. 2 (Seattle: University of Washington Press, 1927), 35–56; A. L. Kroeber, 'A Ghost-Dance in California', *Journal of American Folklore* 17 (1904): 32–35; and A.

women held hands, wearing ochre face paint. As the first Ghost Dance movement spread, local variations emerged.[59] Among these was the Earth Lodge cult, originating among the Wintun and Hill Patwin of northern California; rather than ushering in the return of the dead, it predicted the end of the world, a catastrophe that the participants would escape by taking cover in the subterranean houses they built. The Bole Maru in north-central California emphasized belief in the afterlife and a supreme being.[60]

The second Ghost Dance movement also began on the Walker Lake reservation, this time in January 1889, peaking in 1890 and continuing on well into the 1900s, gaining far more momentum and a wider spread than before.[61] The new practice of dancing in a circle while holding hands, taking care never to break the circle, which was typical in the first Ghost Dance, offered a departure from ring formations then familiar among most tribes. For the Sioux, dancing facing the centre and moving around the centre together, pausing at each of the four directions, or dancing into and away from a central tree, characterized the Sun Dance; but physical contact now enabled dancers to engage in direct corporeal communication. This allowed them 'to feel, holding on to the hand of your brother and sister', in the words of Sioux activist Mary Crow Dog (1954–2013), whose family conserved oral histories of the Ghost Dance, 'the rebirth of Indian unity, feel it with your flesh, through your skin'.[62]

The second Ghost Dance also more prominently heralded a vision of a new world. This was interpreted differently among different tribes and tribe members, according to local needs, dreams, aspirations, and relative willingness to adhere to the new white ways. As in previous cases, fiction—'lies'—sat at the heart of the Ghost Dance narrative, though with the Ghost Dance this was not the 'shamming' that observers construed as pathological but arguably fantastical narratives and playful tricks—white lies—that positively constituted (perhaps catalysed) a widely desired new world order. Wovoka, known as Jack Wilson (1856–1932), a Numu or Northern Paiute from western Nevada, had had a revelation on 1 January 1889 on the occasion of a solar eclipse. He believed that he was Jesus, and he became adept at evidencing his ability to control the weather and his invulnerability to bullets and other projectiles, a classic skill claimed by medicine men.[63] These claims he later repudiated, stating in an interview with General John Gibbon (1827–1896), commander of the Division of the Pacific in San Francisco, on 6 December 1890, that stories about his bullet-proof capabilities were only a joke.[64] Clark J. Guild (b. 1887), in his *Memories of My Work as a Lyon County Official, Nevada District Judge, and Nevada State Museum Founder* (1967), also notes that he knew Jack Wilson (Wovoka) personally and that Bill and Mack Wilson, sons of Wovoka's employer, had evidence of Wovoka's clever tricks: he had managed, for instance, to tie catfish to a string in an opening in a frozen river and claimed that the spirits helped him to fish, to the muted amazement of his Native audience.[65]

H. Gayton, 'The Ghost Dance of 1870 in South-Central California', *University of California Publications in American Archaeology and Ethnology* 28 (1930): 57–82.

59. Thornton, *We Shall Live Again*, 3–4.

60. See for example Du Bois, 'The 1870 Ghost Dance', 1–2.

61. On the military intervention leading up to and following the massacre at Wounded Knee, see Entry 2540, Division of the Missouri, 'Letters Sent by Headquarters in the Field, 1890–91', 1 vol.; and entry 2541, Division of the Missouri, 'Press Copies of Letters Sent by Headquarters in the field, 1890–91', 1 vol., in Record Group 393, Records of U.S. Army Continental Commands, 1821–1920, Part I, National Archives and Records Administration, Library of Congress.

62. Cited in Ostler, *The Plains Sioux*, 265.

63. Mooney describes Wovoka's 'great revelation' in *The Ghost-Dance Religion and Wounded Knee* (1896): 'On this occasion "the sun died" (was eclipsed) and [Wovoka] fell asleep in the daytime and was taken up to the other world. Here he saw God, with all the people who had died long ago engaged in their old-time sports and occupations, all happy and forever young. It was a pleasant land and full of game. After showing him all, God told him he must go back and tell his people they must be good and love one another, have no quarreling, and live in peace with the whites; that they must work, and not lie or steal; that they must put away all the old practices that savored of war; that if they faithfully obeyed his instructions they would at last be reunited with their friends in this other world, where there would be no more death or sickness or old age. He was then given the dance which he was commanded to bring back to his people. By performing this dance at intervals, for five consecutive days each time, they would secure this happiness to themselves and hasten the event. Finally God gave him control over the elements so that he could make it rain or snow or be dry at will, and appointed him his deputy to take charge of affairs in the west, while "Governor Harrison" would attend to matters in the east, and he, God, would look after the world above. [Wovoka] then returned to earth and began to preach as he was directed, convincing the people by exercising the wonderful powers that had been given to him'. Mooney, *The Ghost-Dance Religion*, 771–772.

64. Cited in Michael Hittman, *Wovoka and the Ghost Dance*, expanded ed. (Lincoln: University of Nebraska Press, 1990), 231–236, 235.

65. Cited in Hittman, *Wovoka and the Ghost Dance*, 307.

Further reports revealed that he tricked other Natives into believing in his powers, for example by having ice deposited up the river on a hot day, 'proving' to his audience that his prediction of snow and ice came true. His 'bulletproof vest' was made by giving Natives blank cartridges, shaking up some powder he had concealed in his shirt.[66] Mooney's report of his conversations with Wovoka confirmed Wovoka's denial of responsibility for claims to bulletproof 'ghost shirts' or to the dances involving 'hostility toward the whites'. But Wovoka did claim that his 'religion' was one of 'universal peace' and that while he was not Christ, the Son of God, he had received a message from God while in the spirit world, urging the Indians to dance the special Ghost Dance. He also 'genuinely', wrote Mooney, claimed some supernatural abilities, particularly in regard to rainmaking. Mooney was impressed by Wovoka's apparent assimilation of white ways: 'If appearances are in evidence, he is sincere in this [good will]', Mooney noted, 'for he was dressed in a good suit of white man's clothing, and works regularly on a ranch, although living in a wikiup'.[67] Wovoka's *appearance* as a white man ('almost . . . but not quite') sufficed to convince Mooney of the movement's relative legitimacy—at least as far as its (fiction-laden) origins were concerned.

In effect, the Ghost Dance brought about what Agamben characterizes, after early nineteenth-century French law, as a 'fictitious state of exception', one in which the sovereign decides whether a state of siege should be declared, this state serving conveniently as grounds for new laws, new measures, or an outright new world order to be instituted.[68] With the Ghost Dance, the fictitious state of exception—implicitly declared by the government arguably to institute far more radical anti-Native legislation than had previously been decreed, on the grounds of self-protection—was heightened by a complex of performative factors by which the Natives themselves performed a state of exception, *ecstatically*. Their ecstasy-belonging

effectively reclaimed the sovereign right to self-representation, performing heightened suspension of everyday life, a theatrical *coming-to-be* of a new state. The performance of this ecstasy-belonging and the dramaturgy and extended narratives (the fictions) accompanying its unfolding thus were varied, but Wovoka's initial teachings set the tone.

His revelation—described in a 'letter' he received from the spirit world—prescribed dancing for four nights and one day; taking a bath in the morning before going home, not telling the whites about this, but knowing that Jesus is on the ground, 'he just like cloud'. Also '[t]here will be no sickness and return to young [youth] again'. Dancers were 'not [to] refuse to work for white man' and 'not [to] make any trouble with them until you leave them'. 'I want you to make dance for six weeks', the letter said, 'eat and wash good clean yourselves'. Promise of the return of the Native ancestors was also stipulated: 'Every body is alive again, I dont know when they will [be] here, may be this fall or in spring'. Wovoka also promised rain and snow: 'I will give you a good cloud and give you chance to make you feel good. I give you a good spirit', he said, 'and give you all good paint'. But the tribes had to gather for this event: 'I want you people to come here again, want them in three months any trib[e]s of you from there'.[69] Wovoka's otherwise garbled message found a ready audience: he soon enjoyed substantial monetary rewards as he started to be revered as a messiah figure and was given gifts in exchange for the shirts and feathers he wore.[70] The message of hope he had delivered became intelligible as a cue to revolt in the suspended time of ecstasy-belonging that characterized an indigenous state of exception that was going to contravene the white world order.

News of Wovoka's miracles and revelation spread, and from the Smith and Mason valleys in Nevada his Ghost Dance doctrine reached Oregon and California. It then spread north, east, and south into Idaho, Montana, Utah, the Dakotas, Oklahoma Territory, Indian Territory, Missouri,

66. Cited in Hittman, *Wovoka and the Ghost Dance*, 308.

67. Cited in Hittman, *Wovoka and the Ghost Dance*, 237–244, 242–243.

68. See Agamben, *State of Exception*, 3–4.

69. 'The Messiah Letter'. Cheyenne and Arapaho versions cited in Mooney, *The Ghost-Dance Religion*, 780–781.

70. See especially 'The Dyer Tape', transcribed in Hittman, *Wovoka and the Ghost Dance*, 256–258, 257. C. S. Asbury, Special Indian Agent, Reno, Nevada, also stated in a letter to the commissioner of Indian affairs, Washington, DC, regarding 'Alleged activity of Jack Wilson, Wovoka, the Messiah': 'Jack is a mercenary fellow and it may be that his visits are purely for his own financial needs, as he is still able to collect considerable money from the Indians visited, for his work as a "big medicine man."' Asbury notes that Wovoka 'has been exceptionally free from the use of whiskey, opium, etc., and that his talks to the Indians . . . have been along the lines of temperance, morality and industry'; reproduced in Hittman, *Wovoka and the Ghost Dance*, 287–288, 287.

New Mexico, Arizona, and other states, eventually encompassing most of the central western United States.[71] The revelation evolved, but substantial portions of Wovoka's original vision remained, heralding the renovation and rejuvenation of the world through dance, song, and a rejection of aspects of white culture deemed destructive to Natives—alcohol in particular. Buffalo would roam free, all dead Indians would come back to life, disease would disappear, and food would be plentiful again. In Mooney's terms, this was a return to a status quo ante, a mythic past, Atlantis regained, laced with Abrahamic visions of Paradise. It also signalled the concerted orchestration of choreopolitical revolt.

In spite of its broad appeal, the doctrine was widely disputed. As Indian agent S. G. Fisher noted, 'scarcely any two tribes have the same ideas as to what they must do to bring about the desired result'.[72] Some tribes believed all whites would be destroyed, while others thought that whites and Indians would live together in this Paradise, or become one people. Captain Dick, a Paiute at Fort Bidwell in California, told an investigator that when 'Old Man' returned, all the Indians would climb up into the mountains to escape the flood that would kill the white people.[73] For Short Bull (1851–1935), the Messiah had already come to Earth, but white people had killed him.[74] For Porcupine (c. 1848–1929), the point was to stop fighting, not to project the death of all whites.[75] For Natives at the Standing Rock Agency, the dead would return to reinhabit the earth, which belonged to the Indians in the first place; they would also drive herds of buffalo and elegant wild horses, and the Great Spirit would see to it that white men were unable to make gunpowder and all attempts at such in the future would be a failure. Gunpowder now on hand would be useless against Indians; the Great Spirit had deserted the Indians for a long time but was with them now and against the whites. The Great Spirit would, moreover, 'cover the earth over with thirty feet of additional soil, well sodded and timbered, under which the whites [would] all be smothered, and any whites who escape[d] this great phenomenon [would] become small fishes in the rivers of the country'. But it was also true that in order to bring about this happy state of affairs, the Indians had to do their part and become organized.[76] According to a later variation, whites and Indians would have to die before the earth could be renewed—it was 'old and worn out'. The rivers were old, the mountains were all old, and 'there would have to be new ones'.[77]

As many variants emerged as there were areas of activity and sources of further doctrinal influence: the Mormons, in particular, were widely thought to have provided some aspects of their belief system to the Ghost Dance.[78] They believed, as Mooney noted, that the 'Indians' were descendants of the 'ten lost tribes', cherished 'as a part of their faith'; because Mormons believed that 'some of the lost Hebrew

71. Thornton, *We Shall Live Again*, 1. See his map of the geographic spread of the first and second Ghost Dances (2).

72. Cited in Gregory E. Smoak, *Ghost Dances and Identity: Prophetic Religion and American Indian Ethnogenesis in the Nineteenth Century* (Berkeley: University of California Press, 2006), 168.

73. In Smoak, *Ghost Dances and Identity*, 168.

74. Spier argues that the idea of a prophet 'dying' and returning to earth had been floating around for thirty years before the Ghost Dance doctrine emerged. Leslie Spier, *The Prophet Dance of the Northwest and Its Derivatives: The Source of the Ghost Dance*, General Series in Anthropology, no. 1 (Menasha, WI: George Banta, 1935), 23. He argues that the Ghost Dance was a kind of 'prophet dance' and that this genre had antecedents and variants throughout the Central Basin; in short, that Mooney's claim that it had emerged more or less out of nowhere was flawed (5). David F. Aberle adds that the Ghost Dance actually originated among the tribes of the Northwest, in the interior Plateau area: they had long believed in the imminent destruction and renewal of the world, the return of the dead, and the precipitation of these events through dance. David F. Aberle, 'The Prophet Dance and Reactions to White Contact', *Southwestern Journal of Anthropology* 15.1 (1959): 74–83.

75. Smoak, *Ghost Dances and Identity*, 168.

76. James McLaughlin, Indian Agent, Standing Rock Agency, to Hon. T. J. Morgan, Commissioner of Indian Affairs, Washington, DC, 17 October 1890, Ghost Dance, Special Case 188.

77. H. L. Scott, 1st Lieutenant, 7th Cavalry, Fort Sill, OT, to Post Adjutant, Fort Sill, OT, 3 January 1891, Ghost Dance, Special Case 188. Scott adds that 'this [information] was gotten from several different sources, but this whole subject is in a hazy and clouded condition, no two having exactly the same belief'.

78. See for example Garold D. Barney, *Mormons, Indians and the Ghost Dance Religion of 1890* (Lanham, MD: University Press of America, 1986); Thornton, *We Shall Live Again*, 5; Lanternari, *The Religions of the Oppressed*, 133–134; and Smoak, *Ghost Dances and Identity*, 167. The Mormons believed that the Indians should know that they were a Chosen People, remnants of one of the lost tribes, so that they could be redeemed and become white and happy; some appear to have participated in the Ghost Dancing (Barney, *Mormons*, esp. 3, 5–8). Wodziwob is also said to have encountered Mormons in 1870 and so coloured the Ghost Dance doctrine with Mormon eschatological beliefs (Lanternari, *The Religions of the Oppressed*, 133).

emigrants [were] still ice-bound in the frozen north. . . . When the news of this Indian revelation came to their ears, the Mormon priests accepted it as a prophecy of speedy fulfillment of their own traditions'.[79] A plethora of utopic spiritual movements were cropping up in the American West, allying messianic doctrines with ecstatic eschatological practices.[80] The Ghost Dance gained as many as a few thousand followers, though its proximity to other messianic movements in the American nineteenth and early twentieth centuries did not succeed in diminishing settler, agent, or government fears of Ghost Dance escalation or stem the movement's repression. Even as Ghost Dancers mixed Christian iconography with Native American dance and diplomatic practices, exchanging visits with one another, sharing information, they made what were ultimately modest and contained political demands.

CROSSED WIRES AND MEDIA MAYHEM

Yet the spread and transformation of Ghost Dance doctrine—and the amplification of fears on the part of Natives and government agents—provoked anxiety among settlers, which was exacerbated by various regimes of mobilization across the Plains. These included intertribal visits and councils; newspaper articles, which sensationalized the stories; and the increased circulation of misinformation between Indian agencies and the commissioner of Indian affairs. Indian agent James McLaughlin (1842–1923), in a letter dated 29 November 1890 to the commissioner, T. J. Morgan, complained of the 'wide spread reports

appearing in the newspapers which are greatly and criminally exaggerated, and in a majority of instances without any truth whatever in so far as this agency [Standing Rock] is concerned'. He added that these reports had 'caused an unnecessary alarm amongst settlers in the vicinity who have fled from their homes, panic stricken, to places of supposed safety, on false rumours that the Indians had broken out, the reports besides having this tendency to excite the Indians to hostility and disobedience of orders rather than to allay the excitement amongst them'.[81] In a second letter, dated 10 March 1891, McLaughlin complained again of the hasty escalation of violence provoked by injudicious reports: 'many absurd and sensational newspaper reports which alarmed frontier settlers and the public generally, causing additional troops to be sent into the Indian country and which with its active movements and the unlimited powers that were given the military in these operations alarmed the Indians very much and enabled the wily leaders to organize in better shape all the disaffected and more ignorant of the several bands of Sioux in what they were made to believe was common cause and their only safety'.[82] Indian agent Warren D. Robbins similarly wrote on 26 November 1890 that at the Nez Perce Agency, in Idaho, the only knowledge Natives there had of the 'craze' came from newspaper reports, as no emissaries had visited that agency.[83] News of the American troubles spread to London, as sensationalized versions of these events depicted crazed 'Indian' dancers in drawings appearing in, among others, the *Illustrated London News* (fig. 9.1). Natives were depicted brandishing tomahawks, with their feathers upright, their arms splayed, and their bodies hunched, in a crowd

79. Mooney, *The Ghost-Dance Religion*, 703.

80. See for example Robert S. Fogarty, *All Things New: American Communes and Utopian Movements, 1860–1914* (Lanham, MD: Lexington Books, 2003); James Matthew Morris and Andrea L. Kross, *Historical Dictionary of Utopianism* (Lanham, MD: Scarecrow Press, 2004); and J. Gordon Melton, *Encyclopedia of American Religions*, 5th ed. (Detroit: Gale, 1996).

81. James McLaughlin, Indian Agent, Standing Rock Agency, to Hon. T. J. Morgan, Commissioner of Indian Affairs, Washington, DC, 29 November 1890, Ghost Dance, Special Case 188. Andersson provides a useful analysis of press coverage of the Ghost Dance in *The Lakota Ghost Dance of 1890*, 192–250. Many newspapers, including the *New York Times* and the *Washington Post*, reported on the events without sending reporters directly to the scene; reporters who did go to the scene tended to gather in a small hotel at the Pine Ridge agency, many of them relatively inexperienced (192–193).

82. James McLaughlin, Indian Agent, Standing Rock Agency, to Hon. T. J. Morgan, Commissioner of Indian Affairs, Washington, DC, 10 March 1891, Ghost Dance, Special Case 188.

83. Warren D. Robbins, Indian Agent, Nez Perce Indian Agency, Idaho, to Hon. Geo. L. Shoup, Governor of the State of Idaho, 26 November 1890, Ghost Dance, Special Case 188. L. G. Moses similarly notes that 'dancing, peaceful Indians awaiting their divine redemption did not sell newspapers, so journalists surfeited the country with stories about Indians dancing themselves into frenzies as they awaited reinforcements from the risen dead'. L. G. Moses, '"The Father Tells Me So!" Wovoka: The Ghost Dance Prophet', *American Indian Quarterly* 9.3 (1985): 335–351, 342.

FIGURE 9.1 Ghost Dance of the Sioux Indians in North America (1891). From *Illustrated London News*, 3 January 1891, 15–16. Courtesy the Library of Congress, Prints and Photographs Division, LC-USZ62-52423.

dance that suggested bedlam. Sketches of the events on the other hand suggest a more subdued affair in some places; one drawing rendered from sketches made 'on the spot', reproduced in *Harper's Weekly* depicting a dance at Pine Ridge, South Dakota, in 1890 (fig. 9.2) shows physical closeness, relative intimacy, and upright postures; some women are wrapped in shawls, walking towards the observer, while another dancer faces skyward in profile. All leg and arm gestures are low to the ground and restrained. Meanwhile, the empty plains in the background suggest a relatively isolated affair, nothing conjuring the hyperkinetic crowd contagion of the sort imagined in the *Illustrated London News*. But dancers were angry, and placid stares hint at the spirit of defiance with which Natives were variously disputing the mounting economic deprivation against which the dancing took place.

'ONE BIG EAT, TO DIE LIKE MEN RATHER THAN LIKE STARVED RATS'

Dancing provided an occasion for distraction, bringing tribes together in a shared moment of ecstasy-belonging designed to counteract starvation and demoralization. Time and cattle were theirs to dispose of, and dancers performed this real and symbolic reappropriation on their home turf. So, whereas complaints against the Ghost Dancers emphasized their wastefulness and the supposed injury to the dancers' health that these events occasioned,[84] some settlers recognized the legitimacy and rationality of the whole affair. George A. Ferris, writing to the president and the secretary of war on 14 January 1891 in the name of the Dubuque Trades and Labor

---

84. H. L. Scott noted three objections raised against the dance being 'hurtful' to the dancers, as follows: '1) Because they leave their farms and stock to congregate for the purpose and their civilization is by so much retarded. 2) Because they kill their stock

FIGURE 9.2   The Ghost dance by the Ogallala [*sic*] Sioux at Pine Ridge Agency. Drawn by Frederic Remington, Pine Ridge, South Dakota (1890). From *Harper's Weekly,* 6 December 1890, 960–961. Courtesy the Library of Congress, Prints and Photographs Division, LC-USZ62-3726.

Congress in Iowa, argued that the 'Indians' were not wrong for 'wasting' their food and energy. In a relatively rare expression of solidarity with the Natives, he redirected the blame to the Interior Department, which drove the 'Indians', he said, on account of 'broken treaties extending through a period of over twenty years, and dishonest reduction in supply of rations . . . as a last resort into maddened rebellion, and to secure one "big eat", as Sitting Bull declared, "and die like men rather than like starved rats."' In Porcupine's terms, the Indians had to dance because if they didn't, they would 'get crazy and poor'; the apparently excessive expenditure of energy that the Ghost Dance required in effect reasonably offset their further demoralization. Ferris called on the president and the secretary of war to conduct, therefore, 'an immediate investigation of

the manifest wrongs, cruelties and long series of injustices in the stipulation of treaties and the reckless disregard afterwards of their provisions by government agents and post traders'.[85]

The only 'waste' was human, provoked by servility and starvation; the dance was a performative blow in the face of want that flaunted the vitality and dignity Natives were being denied. As I noted earlier, Bataille, writing forty years after these events, highlights wasteful expenditure as a vital contrast to pecuniary accumulation and capital gain. 'Humans . . . grant themselves the right to acquire, conserve, and consume rationally; but, they proscribe themselves 'unproductive expenditure' characteristic of so-called 'irrational', 'primitive' cultures ostensibly refusing to accumulate material goods. The idea of use-value is ubiquitous in modern life, Bataille

and eat it. And 3) The dance is injurious to their health'. H. L. Scott, 1st Lieutenant, 7th Cavalry, Fort Sill, [O]T, to Post Adjutant, Fort Sill, IT [*sic*], 16 December 1890, Ghost Dance, Special Case 188.

85. George A. Ferris, Office of the Corresponding Secretary of the Dubuque Trades and Labor Congress, Dubuque, Iowa, to Benjamin Harrison, President of the United States, and Secretary of War [Redfield Proctor (1831–1908)], Washington, DC, 14 January 1891, Ghost Dance, Special Case 188.

argues, but further submits that what may be considered 'useful' is often vague: if anything, utility might be measured in contrast to pleasure, so that excessive pleasure is considered irrational and 'pathological'. Activities that dissipate accumulated wealth run counter to generally held principles of usefulness in modern bourgeois capitalist society, always involving the acquisition and conservation of goods in a materialist paradigm.[86] Paradoxically, Natives 'wasting' their time and cattle had already been 'wasted' by a government that denied them the basic living conditions by which they could accumulate wealth or work 'productively' (in effect, on lands and according to schedules and methods now managed from the capital) if they so wished. The 'unproductive expenditure' of Native time in dancing was in effect, paradoxically, a luxury that should be afforded only the wealthiest, leisure classes—those who did not *need* to work. Natives were seen to be confusing class boundaries in a system designed to keep them on a par with (or just below) settlers who were barely earning their keep and were exemplary for the sweat and toil— the labour—they performed.

Bataille's notion then complements the 'nonproductive consumption of time' that the rising aristocratic class in the late nineteenth century in the United States boasted about, described by sociologist Thorstein Veblen (1857–1929) in *The Theory of the Leisure Class* (1899).[87] In Veblen's analysis, the upper classes prided themselves on unproductive labour, strictly opposed to the necessary, seemingly trivial (and emphatically corporeal), labour of most women and lower-class workers; the upper classes conserved and transmitted their wealth without breaking a sweat. Wealth was a marker of worth and its accumulation over generations a sign of superiority. The paradoxical expenditure, then, of the little wealth—conceived in terms of well-managed property and time—that Ghost Dancers had enabled them to *demonstrate* their rejection of a hypocritical system of value. Natives anyway had too little to eat; if they consumed the rest and

exhausted themselves in a seemingly brash act of energetic 'waste', they were thus also refusing the exogenous exercise of government biopower. Their 'value' system did not exclude the need for food or work but did refuse slavery to a system of rations that obstructed their autonomy and whose terms had been criminally neglected.

The terms of the Ghost Dance thus suggest outright cultural war. Government, settlers, and Indian agents employed a discourse of reprimand that stressed the excessive expenditure of time and energy required for participation in the Ghost Dance as a cause for its repression: it impeded the progress of civilization because it exhausted its participants too much to work. Whereas social dancing for leisure was acceptable when engaged in with moderation, the Ghost Dance, which Native Americans performed well into the night, often multiple times weekly, was said to go too far. A. P. Dixon, writing from Crow Creek and Lower Brule Consolidated Agency, South Dakota, on 18 December 1891 told the commissioner of Indian affairs that social gatherings were normally acceptable but the fatigue this Ghost Dancing caused was not: 'I am aware of nothing wrong in social gatherings among Indians, where dancing is participated in to a moderate degree, but the nature of Indians, as I observe it, is such as to crave variety and excess, and as a consequence, if allowed to dance at all, they dance excessively, the same persons oftentimes two nights in each week, continued until late at night, greatly to the expense of their physical endurance, and necessarily to the neglect of any work which they may have to do on the following day, owing to their fatigued condition'.[88] Not only did the dances exhaust participants, but Dixon saw 'no benefit to them growing out of the practice' and 'no good reason why the dances should not be absolutely prohibited, except', as he added, 'that the Indians would naturally argue that such an order would be a discrimination between their customs and the tolerated practices of the whites, to the abridgment of their personal liberty and freedom of action'.[89]

---

86. Georges Bataille, 'La notion de dépense', in Bataille, *La part maudite*, 23–45, esp. 25–38. One may counter that today excessive (materially useless) expenditure is the norm, even in an economic depression arguably worse than that of the 1930s during which Bataille wrote. Cultures of debt in fact require middle-class citizens to spend more than they earn instead of saving or accumulating parsimoniously, as Bataille argued of the bourgeoisie.

87. In John Frow, 'Invidious Distinction: Waste, Difference, and Classy Stuff', in Gay Hawkins and Stephen Muecke, eds., *Culture and Waste: The Creation and Destruction of Value* (Oxford: Rowan and Littlefield, 2003), 25–38, 27.

88. A. P. Dixon, Indian Agent, United States Indian Service, Crow Creek and Lower Brule Consolidated Agency, SD, to Hon. T. J. Morgan, Commissioner of Indian Affairs, Washington, DC, 18 December 1891, Ghost Dance, Special Case 188.

89. A. P. Dixon, Indian Agent, United States Indian Service, Crow Creek and Lower Brule Consolidated Agency, SD, to Hon. T. J. Morgan, Commissioner of Indian Affairs, Washington, DC, 18 December 1891, Ghost Dance, Special Case 188.

This paternalistic attitude was widespread. As settlers heard rumours of the Ghost Dance and began to witness such dances in their own areas, speculation as to the cause of the discontentment intensified; meanwhile, factions formed and opinions splintered among Natives and whites. 'Friendly Indians', well-disposed towards the government authorities and church missions, castigated the dances, suggesting that Natives should be further assimilated into the new Protestant paradigm. One such 'friendly Indian' told an Indian agent at the Yankton Agency, South Dakota, that the true cause of all the trouble was 'idleness': 'give these people work so that they can earn a livelihood and you will soon hear no more of Indian scares'.[90]

Indian agent John H. Waugh (1853–1894) offered a different approach. He wrote to the commissioner of Indian affairs on 29 June 1891 from Devils Lake Agency, North Dakota arguing that the dances were a reasonable form of leisure, providing respite from work, and were not a cause for alarm. On the contrary, when exercised with moderation, they offered Natives a harmless distraction and an incentive to work. They were damaging in extreme cases but tolerable in a 'milder form'; and he pointed out that although many white settlers at Indian agencies did work hard—as did many Natives—they, too, indulged in all kinds of amusements 'without any damage being done them morally or otherwise'.[91]

Nevertheless, efforts to acculturate Natives to the new settler mentality were articulated with force. At the 1896 Lake Mohonk Conference, Merrill E. Gates (1848–1922), a member of the Board of Indian Commissioners, stated that reformers' efforts should emphasize converting Indians to a culture of 'selfishness' and a quest for material wealth:

To bring him out of savagery into citizenship we must make the Indian more intelligently selfish . . . . We need to awaken in him wants. In his dull savagery he must be touched by the wings of the divine angel of discontent. Then he begins to look forward, to reach out. The desire for property of his own may become an intense education force. The wish for a home of his own awakens him to new efforts. Discontent with the teepee and the starving rations of the Indian camp in winter is needed to get the Indian out of his blanket and into trousers—and trousers with a pocket in them, and with a pocket that aches to be filled with dollars.[92]

Starvation, in this view, would prompt Natives to convert to a monetary regime, instructing them in the pursuit of a different sort of happiness: isolation and labour leading to financial reward. Wovoka had served as a model, in spite of his ambivalent status at the helm of the affair; he was reputed to have had good will towards the whites and demonstrated an 'industrious', 'moral', and 'temperate' attitude.[93] Quanah Parker (1845–1911), chief of the Comanche, was similarly commended for his 'progressiveness', defined by material affluence; he had four hundred cattle, many horses, a good farm, and lived in a house that cost $3,000, as Major Wirt Davis pointed out when forwarding a compliant letter by Parker to the authorities in Washington.[94] Prosperity was a sure marker of a Native's disposition towards whites and his investment in cooperating with the government and the culture of industry.

Natives who failed to accumulate wealth in the terms recognized by the engineers of the

90. E. M. Fortes [?], Indian Agent, Yankton Agency, 9 December 1890, Ghost Dance, Special Case 188.

91. Waugh wrote: 'Briefly stated my policy from the very first has been to forbid, discountenance and frown down upon dancing of any and all kinds. I have however incurred a great deal of opposition for my cause and after investigating the various kinds of dancing I have concluded that in defense to the often repeated request of some of our best old people who are non progressive anyway, I would relent to the extent of permitting dancing to some extent of the milder forms, provided such a course does not meet with your disapproval. I think that by the judicious use of a wise discretion to permit the mild forms of dancing would act as an incentive to those people to labor and encourage them to do their work well and in season, as they seem to feel as though they should be permitted some form of social enjoyment at stated times and festivals, pointing out the many innocent forms of amusements the white people indulge in without any damage being done them morally or otherwise'. John H. Waugh, Indian Agent, Devils Lake Agency, to Commissioner of Indian Affairs, Washington, DC, 29 June 1891, Ghost Dance, Special Case 188.

92. Cited in Susan E. Goff, 'The Ghost Dance Religion among the Plains Indians: A Religious Response to the Crisis of Forced Acculturation and Christianization', M.Div. thesis (Union Theological Seminary, 1980), 24–25.

93. See n70 here.

94. Wirt Davis, Major, 5th Cavalry, Inspector of Small Arms Practice, Headquarters Department of the Missouri, Office of the Inspector of Small Arms Practice, St. Louis, Missouri, covering letter to the Assistant Adjutant General of the [War] Department, 23 December 1890, to an enclosed letter from Quanah Parker, Chief of the Comanches, Cooper Creek, IT, to Editor Gazette, 7 December 1890, Ghost Dance, Special Case 188.

American way were 'unfriendly', weeds in a new field of dreams symbolically deemed otherwise ready for mass cultivation. Attempts by the government, Indian agents, and settlers to acculturate Natives to the new dollar economy pushed an agenda of self-control fed by want. Commanding Brigadier General W. Merritt (1836–1910) argued that 'under the influence of military discipline, regular habits, good food and clothing, together with the stimulus of earning a sum of money every month, their interests would become strongly identified with those of the Government, and the tendency would be of a civilizing and educational character'.[95] McLaughlin similarly claimed that 'civilization was steadily advancing among the Indians' but that 'this advancement was stubbornly opposed by the old time chiefs and medicine men, who, on account of the new ways and better order of things, were steadily losing their power . . . . This class of Indians', he added, who were 'clinging tenaciously to the old Indian life encouraged by their non-progressive followers were those', moreover, 'who strenuously opposed the ratification of the act of March 2nd, 1889 [ceding Sioux territory to Congress]'.[96]

Disaffection was not equally distributed. The Navajo, in the Southwest, enjoyed a successful trade economy and little desire to reject aspects of white culture; they depended on it for their prosperity.[97] A chief at White Earth, Minnesota, who was sympathetic to the Indian agents' cause co-signed a letter with his fellow tribesman Rev. Joseph Wakazoo (d. 1910) claiming that oxen, ploughs, wagons, and farms were going to waste or being misused while Natives were visiting different bands, as far as one hundred miles away, to dance. The chief and the reverend sought the government's intervention for this 'trouble in the Indian country arising from this dancing' and the 'hating of the Christian religion':

But this I tell you Hon. Commissioner that I am greatly ashamed seeing yokes of oxen with their yokes on collected [sic] where the heathen dance is going on. Was that what the oxen were given for? Again the plows that were given is that what they were issued for to be piled in a heap at the gambling place? Again the wagons which were given, were they given for the Indians to go visiting distant Bands? . . . When I look back at the Indian farms here they seem to me like farms from which the owners had moved, all grown up with weeds—not planted this year, all through this dancing. And those very Indians when I see them a few years ago the men all had good coats on that was when they listened to the missionaries. Now they look ragged and miserable. And the women then had good clothes[;] now through the dancing they are a sorry sight.[98]

Though performed to counteract demoralization, the 'Indian dances' were denounced as producing it: they were 'demoralizing in all their influences', according to another pastor. 'They are a hindrance to the cause of education, to church work, and to civilization in any direction. They keep the people poor', he complained. 'Though already so poor that they can hardly keep soul and body together, owing in great measure to [the] failure of [the] crops, they will give a cow or a pony, or go in[to] debt to make a feast for the dancers'. People were leaving their corn and potatoes unhoed, he said, and 'the boys from the schools are out at night, to look on, if not to participate in these dances'.[99]

Hewitt has argued that 'dance is a process of work that produces no work or artifact as residue'.[100] Dance instead is imagined in the aesthetic ideology of modernism as 'pure energy', pure expenditure, uncannily paralleling a 'capitalist

95. W. Merritt, Brigadier General Commanding, Headquarters Department of the Missouri, St. Louis, MO, to Adjutant General, U.S. Army, Washington, DC, 21 January 1891, Ghost Dance, Special Case 188.

96. James McLaughlin, Indian Agent, Standing Rock Agency, to Hon. T. J. Morgan, Commissioner of Indian Affairs, Washington, DC, 10 March 1891, Ghost Dance, Special Case 188.

97. On the Navajo, see for example Thornton, *We Shall Live Again*, 14; Kehoe, *The Ghost Dance*, 103, 110; Lanternari, *The Religions of the Oppressed*, 155.

98. Rev. Joseph Wakazoo, White Earth, MN, to Hon. Commissioner of Indian Affairs, Washington, DC, 17 July 1891, Ghost Dance, Special Case 188.

99. Chas. R. Crawford, Pastor of Good Will Church, W. K. Morris, Superintendent of the Mission School, and M. N. Adams, Missionary of the [illegible] Agency, SD, to Hon. T. J. Morgan, Commissioner of Indian Affairs, Washington, DC, 21 June 1890, Ghost Dance, Special Case 188.

100. Hewitt, *Social Choreography*, 25.

fantasy of pure profit, pure production'.[101] Dance is Janus-headed, at once expenditure and return, pure and immaterial, productive and wasteful, as it generates no *thing*, only experience, affect, relation, and moment. Dance appears as the live encounter and the fantasy of evanescence as well as the frisson of energetic surplus taking shape in an instant before disappearing, becoming memory. In this respect, dance signals the phantasmatization of life showing itself spectacularly before impending death. A dancing disease is arguably, then, the imagined excessiveness of life, its unproductive, luxurious expendability shown dramatically in a moment heralding the dancer's end. In this regard, choreomania, articulated in the Ghost Dance, represents the modern fantasy of a body—and a body politic—consummating itself in the ultimate act of energetic expenditure: a dance whose collective purpose is to go nowhere.

The Ghost Dances, I have argued, stage the biopolitics and choreopolitics of death; they occur where death is lurking because of systematic starvation, and they take place as a vivid sign of its refusal. Jean Baudrillard (1929–2007) argues that death appears frightening in modern capitalism because it represents the end point of capital accumulation and thus also of all productive expenditure. It is thus arguably tantamount to any dilapidation of energy, including in dance—whose excess becomes a modern capitalist disease. Death, like excessive dancing, offers one of the only ways out of a materialist regime of perpetual energetic and material accumulation. Symbolic death, such as in dreams and visions, temporarily interrupts the putatively forward march of time that is characteristic of a modern capitalist paradigm: symbolic death stages the escape from a life of accumulation and the (fictitious) material want that fuels it.[102] The Ghost Dance in this regard appears as a movement where the pathology of 'dance' potentially disappears with its dancers; the extenuation of the 'disease' comes with their extenuation. A regime of excessive dancing was what had to pass, according to this logic, into the past. Not surprisingly, dancers refusing this apparently natural course were branded fanatical.

'FANATICISM': BANDING IN TROUBLED TIMES

Rev. C. J. Cook, an English-speaking Native and missionary at the Pine Ridge Reservation, wrote to the commissioner of Indian affairs on 8 September 1890 to let him know that the situation at his agency was degenerating into 'fanaticism'. 'There is growing unrest among the Indians because of want of provisions, lack of beef, etc.', he wrote. 'This spirit of unrest has assumed shape through the wild fanaticism of the "ghost dance"'. Cook added that it would not take long before the situation resulted in open conflict. The Indian agent on his reservation had told him that morning that he had gone 'to see with his own eyes the dance' and corroborated this sentiment: 'He declared he has never seen anything so crazy and likely to, sooner or later, bring about a genuine trouble. Three Sundays ago there came near being a regular fight between them and the police. They pointed guns at each other. . . . The Agent, thinks the matter has gone beyond control. . . . [He] is now writing for instructions, advice, and the authority to call in the troops and severly [*sic*] punish the ring leaders. This means, I think, trouble'.[103] The same thing was happening in reservations across the American Plains. Indian agent Perain P. Palmer wrote to the commissioner of Indian affairs on 11 October 1890, from Cheyenne River Agency, South Dakota, stating that 'a number of Indians living along the Cheyenne River and known as Bigfoot's band are becoming very much excited about the coming of the Messiah'. His police had been 'unable to prevent them from holding what they call Ghost dances[.] These Indians are becoming very hostile to the police', he added. 'Some of the police have resigned'. He also pointed out that 'the Christian Indians are all quiet and well behaved'.[104] In a letter dated 25 October 1890 he wrote: 'many cattle have been reported to have been killed by the Indians'.[105] In a letter from Standing Rock Agency, 17 October 1890, McLaughlin warned the commissioner that the situation was escalating. The 'infection'

101. Hewitt, *Social Choreography*, 26.

102. Jean Baudrillard, *L'échange symbolique et la mort* (Paris: Éditions Gallimard, 1976), 225–226.

103. Rev. C. J. Cook, Pine Ridge Reserve, to Commissioner of Indian Affairs, Washington, DC, 8 September 1890, Ghost Dance, Special Case 188.

104. Perain P. Palmer, Cheyenne River Agency, SD, to Hon. T. J. Morgan, Commissioner of Indian Affairs, Washington, DC, 11 October 1890, Ghost Dance, Special Case 188.

105. Perain P. Palmer, Cheyenne River Agency, SD, to Hon. T. J. Morgan, Commissioner of Indian Affairs, Washington, DC, 25 October 1890, Ghost Dance, Special Case 188.

was terrible, he explained. It had come to be so 'promiscuous' that it now involved some Natives formerly considered to be 'progressive' and 'more intelligent'. 'Many of our very best Indians appear "dazed" and undecided when talking about [the Ghost Dance]'.[106]

Royer wired the commissioner on 13 November 1890 from the Pine Ridge Reservation to complain frantically that the 'condition of affairs' was going from bad to worse and required urgent attention: 'Yesterday in attempting to arrest an Indian for violation of regulations the offender drew a butcher knife on the police and in less than two minutes he was reinforced by two hundred ghost dancers all armed and ready to fight. Consequently the arrest was not made . . . . The police force are overpowered and disheartened. We have no protection and are at the mercy of these Crazy Dancers'.[107] Property had to be protected, and the settlers in at least one county, Eastern Mead, South Dakota, petitioned the commissioner for military support.[108]

WAR

What had its roots in the familiar 'Dreamer' or prophet beliefs in the return of the dead and the coming of a new age quickly devolved into open warfare, with the clash of civilizations—or, to borrow cultural theorist Arjun Appudurai's terms, a new 'civilization of clashes'[109]—as its most unprepossessing ambition. 'I have today directed the Secretary of War to assume a military responsibility for the suppression of any threatened outbreak', wrote President Harrison to the secretary of the Interior on 13 November

1890. 'In the meantime, I suggest that you advise your Agents to separate the well disposed from the ill disposed Indians; and . . . avoid forcing any issue that will result in an outbreak, until suitable military preparations can be made'.[110] The situation had quickly degenerated into an open contest, as settlers' fears continued to mount. Natives were seen arming themselves 'to the teeth', stocking up on guns and ammunition, making 'mysterious circles around their heads indicating that there [would] be some scalping done', riding their horses in a circle, a custom denoting war, 'killing cattle, breaking into houses, and stealing hay or destroying property that 'generally [belonged] to friendly Indians'.[111] James A. Cooper, from the Pine Ridge Agency, wrote to the acting commissioner and the commissioner of Indian affairs on 24 November and again via telegraph with Agent Royer on 28 November 1890, noting that a meeting had been called by the mayor of the city of Mandan on 17 November, which three-quarters of the adult male population of Mandan and surrounding areas had attended. A committee was set up to petition the president to attend to the danger they felt in regard to the Natives: 'Settlers by the score come to town and tell of Indians armed to the teeth . . . . [The Indians] assume menacing attitudes, tap their guns ominously and show their scalping knives . . . . Cavalry is what is needed to be of use in times of Indian uprising', Cooper remarked, 'and to inspire confidence on the part of the settlers', whose property was being destroyed.[112]

The government, concerned that these settlers did not feel 'comfortable' in these regions, ordered the deployment of troops.[113] Agent

106. James McLaughlin, Indian Agent, Standing Rock Agency, to Hon. T. J. Morgan, Commissioner of Indian Affairs, Washington, DC, 17 October 1890, Ghost Dance, Special Case 188.

107. D. F. Royer, Pine Ridge Reservation, telegraph to Commissioner of Indian Affairs, 13 November 1890, Ghost Dance, Special Case 188.

108. Pierre Lapointe, Chairman, and Robert Calovkson, Secretary, and signed by the elders of the Presbyterian Church, Yankton Agency, SD, to Commissioner of Indian Affairs, Washington, DC, 5 December 1895, Ghost Dance, Special Case 188.

109. Arjun Appudurai, *Fear of Small Numbers: An Essay on the Geography of Anger* (Durham, NC: Duke University Press, 2006).

110. Benjamin Harrison, Executive Mansion, Washington, to Hon. Secretary of the Interior, 13 November 1890, Ghost Dance, Special Case 188.

111. James A. Cooper, Pine Ridge Agency, to Acting Commissioner and Commissioner of Indian Affairs, Washington, DC, 24 November 1890, and James A. Cooper and D. F. Royer, telegraph to Acting Commissioner and Commissioner of Indian Affairs, Washington, DC, 28 November 1890, Ghost Dance, Special Case 188.

112. James A. Cooper, Pine Ridge Agency, to Acting Commissioner and Commissioner of Indian Affairs, Washington, DC, 24 November 1890, and James A. Cooper and D. F. Royer, telegraph to Acting Commissioner and Commissioner of Indian Affairs, Washington, DC, 28 November 1890, Ghost Dance, Special Case 188.

113. J. Fitzgerald wrote to the commissioner of Indian affairs: 'Owing to the Indian scare, as they are liable to break out any time, the settlers are all coming in town and the country is depopulating very fast and unless some action is taken to make the Indians give up their arms and fire people who sell them, this country is ruined. It is a sad sight to see women and

Royer asked for one thousand soldiers to be deployed to 'settle this dancing',[114] against six or seven hundred Natives en route to the Pine Ridge Agency to meet with local tribe members. Three thousand soldiers were eventually deployed by mid-November of that year, and more than three hundred Lakota Sioux were killed by government fire in the massacre at Wounded Knee on 29 December, marking a turning point in the conflict between Native Americans and American whites. This was a bitter zone of intensity, a devastating whirl of acceleration, against the grain of pacific efforts that were attempted among most parties involved at that point: Mooney suggests in his analysis that the 'butchery was the work of infuriated soldiers' shooting blindly against Natives who had 'come in good faith . . . to surrender and be at peace', according to official and unofficial correspondence, files, and conversation with parties on both sides.[115] The cost of the outbreak in one month was estimated at $1.2 million[116] (over $30 million today[117]), a financial—and human—sacrifice far greater than the provision of rations might have entailed.

In the end, only a small subset of the population was implicated in the more belligerent aspect of the Ghost Dance movement. While Royer complained bitterly that 'business [was] to a certain extent demoralized on account of the Indians not knowing what is to be done' and 'both the friendly [Indians] and the unfriendly' 'of course feel anxious',[118] so that 'all industry of course ceases',[119] most Natives, on many reservations, neither partook in nor condoned the Ghost Dance.[120]

Although described as a frenzy, the Ghost Dance was not nearly as excited, jagged, and erratic as its detractors made out, nor was it spontaneous; yet it suggested to Mooney a genealogical kinship with the dancing movements that contested death and depression, moral and physical desolation, and conditions of persecution that he saw in religious ecstasies everywhere. The universalizing sweep that his discursive gesture performed flattened Native American time while drawing attention to real material and political conditions of desperation, connecting this to other movements in aesthetic and narrative terms. His sympathy linked these dances to those of the dervishes and to the trances, dreams, and catalepsy of Jacob, who is told in a dream by God himself of the 'future greatness of the Jewish nation'.[121] Leaving aside American claims to exceptionalism formulated in the early part of the nineteenth century against the threat of European invasion, and furthered again after World War II, this Abrahamic vision suggested a pan-continental unity founded in ecstasies calling forth better worlds. This was not a wasteful expenditure but affective politics proposing a theatre of resistance on contested ground; the only waste was positive, affirming the expenditure of time and energy to create temporary zones of autonomy.[122]

CONTESTED LANDS AND NEW BEGINNINGS

The Ghost Dance has been described as a religion, a cult, a frenzy, and a war against whites

children in groups having no place to sleep leaving comfortable homes and their stock behind. People will not come here again unless they are confident [there] will be no more fear'. J. Fitzgerald, Valentino, NE, to Commissioner of Indian Affairs, 25 November 1890, Ghost Dance, Special Case 188.

114. D. F. Royer, Indian Agent, United States Indian Service, Office of Indian Agent, Pine Ridge Agency, SD, telegraph to R. V. Belt, Acting Commissioner of Indian Affairs, Washington, DC, 27 November 1890, Ghost Dance, Special Case 188.

115. Mooney, *The Ghost-Dance Religion*, 870.

116. Mooney, *The Ghost-Dance Religion*, 843.

117. This calculation is based on an estimated average 2.60% inflation calculated over the period between 1890–2016, based on the United States Department of Labor's Bureau of Labor Statistics annual Consumer Price Index. I am grateful to Andrew Potter for advice on this measure. See https://www.bls.gov/cpi.

118. D. F. Royer, Indian Agent, United States Indian Service, Office of Indian Agent, Pine Ridge Agency, SD, telegraph to R. V. Belt, Acting Commissioner of Indian Affairs, Washington, DC, 27 November 1890, Ghost Dance, Special Case 188.

119. J. A. Gilfillan, White Earth Reservation, MN, to Hon. Commissioner of Indian Affairs, Washington, DC, 11 December 1894, Ghost Dance, Special Case 188.

120. J. A. Gilfillan, White Earth Reservation, MN, to Hon. Commissioner of Indian Affairs, Washington, DC, 11 December 1894, Ghost Dance, Special Case 188.

121. Mooney, *The Ghost-Dance Religion*, 928.

122. I borrow the term from Hakim Bey, *T.A.Z.: The Temporary Autonomous Zone, Ontological Anarchy, Poetic Terrorism*, 2nd ed. (Brooklyn: Autonomedia, 2003).

and cast as a revitalization and a messianic movement fraught with contradictions and inconsistencies. Mooney wrote: '[Wovoka] has been denounced as an impostor, ridiculed as a lunatic, laughed at as a pretended Christ, while by Indians he is revered as a direct messenger from the other world, and among many of the remote tribes he is believed to be omniscient, to speak all languages, and to be invisible to a white man'.[123] Paradoxically, the fictitious state of exception he offered intensified a collective process of identity recovery during a time of violent political fissures. The 'ultimate message' of the Ghost Dance movement, in historian Gregory Smoak's terms, was 'one of Indian unity and identity', although in the aftermath of the Wounded Knee massacre, he adds, it became a 'metaphor for the desperate and illusory attempt of a people to recover the unrecoverable'.[124]

Yet attempts at recovery and recuperative reperformance in the succeeding hundred years redrew mnemonic reserves associated with the dance and attendant ethnocide. In December 1986, descendants of the Sioux massacred at Wounded Knee undertook a commemorative journey to trace Big Foot and the other Lakotas' path from their camp on the Cheyenne River to the Wounded Knee site, inaugurating the Si Tanka Wokiksuye (Big Foot Memorial Ride), and repeating this journey in December every year until the centennial of the massacre, 29 December 1990, when as many as 350 people joined. A ceremony performed at the mass grave at Wounded Knee re-enacted the event in reverse, as participants 'released the spirits of those who had died at Wounded Knee and wiped away their own tears', creating a new ceremony, the Wiping Away of Tears Ceremony,[125] rehearsing part of the original Wounded Knee journey but incorporating the spirits of the dead and their descendants and, significantly, omitting the Indian police and Indian agents who had fired the shots. This performative recreation allowed participants to reappropriate the history of the Wounded Knee massacre by returning to a dancing-place in an act of theatrical repetition that reconfigured the happening, featuring a new cast of characters performing—by their sole presence—the lapse between this and the historical event. The differential offered a sense of hope. Arvol Looking Horse described it as a symbol of the 'rebirth of our nation after 100 years of mourning'.[126] The massacre was not forgotten, but intensely remembered, re-inscribed into the force of a new gathering; here the Ghost Dance lingers as a choreopolitical moment that serves as a zone of intensity, a rupture, a syncope, opening out onto a dream space that 'queers' historical time, in Schneider's terms,[127] performing a protest that folds injury 'then' into a still fractured 'now', redrawing the genealogical map to host the spectres of future rebirths. Performatively, the Ghost Dance memorial ride serves not only as a slanted window onto past historical time but a gaze towards a dream of a radically altered future.

In the next chapter I turn to the South Pacific, where indigenous practices layered with European biblical symbols reveal a creolization process in a complex interplay of sameness and difference characterizing the struggle for anti-colonial liberation. I argue that anthropological literature in the second half of the twentieth century, romanticizing millennialist and eschatological movements among anti-colonial subjects, stretches the fantasies of the dancing disease further still, to draw anti-colonial frenzies into beatific scenes of natural political emergence. The colonial other is in this view still Europe and America's special legacy and bequest, but is also a beacon for Europe and America to look to as they articulate their own imagined liberation from the 'modern' world they have constructed. In this view, crises in the West—what Foucault has called the anxieties of the second half of the twentieth century about the possibility of upholding an Enlightenment standard of rationality—dramatized a clash between new advances in scientific research and the devastating effects

---

123. Mooney, *The Ghost-Dance Religion*, 766.

124. Smoak, *Ghost Dances and Identity*, 2, 191, 205.

125. Ostler, *The Plains Sioux*, 368.

126. Cited in Ostler, *The Plains Sioux*, 368. On memorialization and the Wounded Knee massacre, see also David W. Grua, *Surviving Wounded Knee: The Lakotas and the Politics of Memory* (New York: Oxford University Press, 2016).

127. Schneider, *Performing Remains*, 169–186.

of the two world wars, the failure of eighteenth-century revolutionary principles to deliver the kind of humanist idealism revolutionary writers had sought, and the disintegration of European legitimacy regarding its hold on the colonial world.[128] The discursive history of twentieth-century writing on the dancing disease thus reveals a further translatio: from a pathologizing to a eulogizing mode, heralding a new romance with the collective, the primitive, the 'native', and the 'Dionysian', and ambivalently celebrating new series of movements seeking to wrest participants free from colonial strangleholds.

128. As Foucault wrote, 'at the end of the colonial era, people began to ask the West what rights its culture, its science, its social organization and finally its rationality itself could have to laying claim to a universal validity'. Michel Foucault, 'Introduction', in Canguilhem, *The Normal and the Pathological*, 7–24, 12.

10

'The Gift of Seeing Resemblances'
Cargo Cults in the Antipodes

The monstrous double is also to be found wherever we encounter an 'I' and an 'Other' caught up in a constant interchange of differences.

— René Girard, *Violence and the Sacred* (1972)

In other words, the messianic sign is the sign of the mimetic.

— Michael Taussig, *Mimesis and Alterity* (1993)

WHEN THE *Beagle* landed in the Tierra del Fuego in 1832 and Charles Darwin's crew touched dry land, their first encounter with the Fuegians involved what appeared to be a spontaneous game of 'monkey see, monkey do': the travellers, squinting and making what Darwin (1809–1882) called 'monkey like faces', were met with identical gestures and 'still more hideous grimaces' among their Fuegian hosts.[1] Darwin reported that the Fuegians imitated his crew members' words almost exactly; and when 'a song was struck up' and his men started to dance, he 'thought [the Fuegians] would have fallen down with astonishment'. But the Fuegians 'immediately began themselves to waltz with one of the officers'. By evening, Darwin noted, 'we parted very good friends; which I think was fortunate, for the dancing & "sky-larking" had occasionally bordered on a trial of strength'.[2]

This sort of encounter, what Pratt describes as occurring in a 'contact zone', a 'social [space] where disparate cultures meet, clash, and grapple with each other, often in asymmetrical relations of domination and subordination',[3] involved a

---

1. Charles Darwin, *Beagle Diary*, ed. Richard Darwin Keynes (Cambridge: Cambridge University Press, 1988), 124. See also Inga Clendinnen, *Dancing with Strangers: Europeans and Australians at First Contact* (Cambridge: Cambridge University Press, 2005), 6–7. Darwin offers a slightly different account of the scene a few years later: the phrase 'monkey like' does not appear, nor does the spontaneous outbreak of dancing on the part of the Fuegians assembled; instead, Darwin notes, slightly more soberly, that 'one of the young men, when asked, had no objection to a little waltzing'. Charles Darwin, *Narrative of the Surveying Voyages of his Majesty's Ships Adventure and Beagle, between the years 1826 and 1836, describing their examination of the southern shores of South America, and the Beagle's circumnavigation of the globe*, 3 vols., vol. 3 (London: Henry Colburn, 1839), 229. Earlier in the same account, Darwin compares the 'party' assembled on their arrival as 'the most curious and interesting spectacle I had ever beheld': it 'altogether closely resembled the devils which come on the stage in such plays as [Carl Maria von Weber's 1821 opera] Der Freischutz' (228). See also Darwin, *Beagle Diary*, 122.
2. Darwin, *Beagle Diary*, 124–125.
3. Pratt, *Imperial Eyes*, 7.

performative dancing game and ostensive relation of play. It was a way for the British men to gain currency with their hosts and for their hosts to negotiate—assimilate, repeat, rehearse—this exogenous presence on their own land. The game may also have been amusing. It offered both parties a boisterous platform for communication through mockery and self-mockery.

Though Darwin's crew quickly abandoned the game of 'dancing & "sky-larking"' to penetrate further into the Fuegian land they had come to explore, his initial surprise at, and appreciation for, the Fuegians' 'laughable & interesting' capacity for imitation suggests a disinterested empathy founded in the shared performance of a mimetic relation: these Fuegians showed that they could dance.[4] Not only could they dance, they could waltz. There was hope for social and political relations eventually to flourish and evolve.

Reading this primal scene of colonial and ethnographic contact in *Mimesis and Alterity* (1993), Taussig suggests that the question '*why* looking at the savage is interesting' to Darwin's captain, Robert Fitz Roy (1805–1865), is answered thus: 'such looking is in itself a form of theorizing society and historical process'.[5] In particular, according to Fitz Roy, Taussig reports, 'the British were once like the Fuegians'; second, 'there is something absorbing in observing people displaying childlike ignorance'; and third, the Fuegians appeared to display a 'healthy, independent state of ignorance'.[6] While the first two observations receive substantial attention in the preceding chapters, in scenes depicting, to their observers' eyes, the observers' own imagined childlike past to themselves, the third merits further pause. Colonial others—and their purported historical counterparts, observed by physicians, medical historians, and ethnographers in the pages of history books—do not just display beatific innocence and a monkey-like capacity for imitation, or a dark and dangerous unhealthiness, chaotic and primal in a different sense, but also, more ambivalently, a form of independence that complicates the relation of precedence this fantasy sets up.

Colonial scenes such as this one reveal a nineteenth-century image of the 'dancing & "sky-larking"' past that links childlike naivety to animal and feminine states, what I have been describing as another form of Orientalism: sexually charged, Dionysian and crazed, a dancing body gone awry, re-emerging from the past to haunt the present. Such scenes also reveal a measure of difference to which Europeans obliquely aspire, and which they seek (violently if they must) to possess. 'Imitation', then, does not just suggest passage between two or more bodies. Imitation is also a space of circulation and of aggregate configurations that bewilder observers by their apparent incoherence. The interest in reading these scenes, then, is not just, as Fitz Roy suggested, beatifically to observe the past or to wonder at depictions of childlike innocence and a purportedly healthy state of uncontaminated nature, but to articulate inarticulacy—in other words, to write science. The phantasm of primeval dance appears as the amorphous other that modern science employs to imagine itself against. Through this looking glass emerges a distorted body, diffracted many times, a proliferation of uncontrollable instances of locomotion ricocheting back to the imagined beginnings of historical time.

Watching scientific men watching scenes of dance suggests a proliferation of contact zones and the theorization of a self, moved by these phantasms. In this chapter, I turn to the southern antipodes, to the Oceanic world. Melanesia and Polynesia become the sites (and sights) within which the discursive history of the dancing disease moves once more, as cargo cults quintessentially perform the modern fantasy of capitalist longing projected onto Pacific Islanders believed ecstatically to await the dead—and the spectre of material goods—in airplanes, boats, and rafts. But as this chapter argues, cargo cults also reperform the fantasy of ancient ecstatic practices recombined with European—specifically Christian—figures of awaiting and redemption. In this view, the spasmodic, agitated, restless theatre of returns that cargo cults in Papua New Guinea and New Zealand enact suggests a dancing disease in whiteface, a mimic game of waiting for the end of colonialism to come. In René Girard's (1923–2015) terms, the 'monstrous double' that emerges in an interplay of desires (and distrust) throws performer and witness into a hermeneutic conundrum, as the game of

---

4. Darwin, *Beagle Diary*, 125.

5. Michael Taussig, *Mimesis and Alterity: A Particular History of the Senses* (London: Routledge, 1993), 75.

6. Taussig, *Mimesis and Alterity*, 76.

alterity is trumped. Playing at the other is, in a perverse way, also becoming the other; the drag act belies a desirous, mimetic thrust that complicates any narrative of difference and liberation.

Yet, as the chapter further argues, European anthropologists folded the cargo cult and other millennialist narratives into a discourse on anti-colonial liberation worldwide, as if once again the colonial other were serving as a pure disciple of movement, including revolutionary movement, premodern and anti-industrial, signalling everything ancient, pre-linguistic, and organic in the long history of a corrupted and alienated West. Before moving to the cargo cults, the chapter considers the history of millennialist expectation in Jamaica, as an example of mimetic doubling that produces, in Taussig's terms, a 'two-layered' body.[7]

MAGIC AND MIMESIS: A HISTORY OF DOUBLINGS IN THE 'CONTACT ZONE'

Taussig has suggested that for Benjamin, primitivism and alterity are twin terms describing the 'mimetic faculty', what Benjamin called the ancient and magical 'gift of seeing resemblances'. This gift, according to Benjamin, was 'nothing other than a rudiment of the powerful compulsion in former times to become and behave like something else'.[8] The mimetic faculty, Taussig writes, is a remnant of the sort of primitive magic—described by pioneer anthropologist James Frazer (1854–1941) in *The Golden Bough* (1890)—that produces sympathetic acts of contagion, as when an object doubles what it is meant to represent or what it touches: a figurine standing in for a person it resembles (in the case of sympathetic magic), for example, or a nail clipping or strand of hair standing in for the person to whom it belonged (in the case of contagious magic). Seen as contaminating forces by virtue of their formal similarity or tactile proximity, the figurine and the nail clipping enact a sort of desirous thrust, in Girard's terms: the object desires its other, moves towards it,

overwhelms it. But this desire has to be reciprocal: in being contaminated, one is vulnerable to the power of the object because one is drawn to that which one resembles, and to that which has once been close by. Mimesis is 'two-layered': it implicates 'sentience and copying', feeling or desire and form.[9]

Contact produces a discursive zone of intensity in which the encounter compels theorization; proximity enacts a shudder of recognition that calls the subject (back) to himself or herself. The monstrosity this entails, as parties engaged in a game of mimetic doubling contemplate one another's alterity and sameness, produces a 'copy that is not a copy', in Taussig's terms, a copy with difference: a copy that copies right back, but while doing so opens a theatrical space of variation.[10] Yet, as Taussig implies, the choreography involved in this mimetic theatre also suggests a coded interplay of differences separating colonizer and colonized camps according to rules well known and cunningly manipulated by both. A white colonial ethnographer such as Malinowski, dressed in white colonial drag, poses with dark-skinned Trobriand islanders in a scene Taussig reads as deftly, subtly self-mocking.[11] The men hold suspiciously phallic gourds, and while Malinowski is wearing the expected white costume of the colonial anthropologist, he is elsewhere shown at work in little more than colourful long pants. The scene is posed, and we are left to assume that the islanders, too, were in on the conventions and comedy of this colonial theatre. So while the Fuegians danced Darwin's crew members' dance expertly, in Darwin's account, the crew also counter-imitated the Fuegians, who in turn counter-imitated them right back. This recursive loop, frustrating the closure of mimesis, sits at the heart of this chapter, which showcases anti-colonial dances and liberation movements in the South Seas counter-imitating European dress and Christian iconography in a play of 'primitive' revolt that recuperates, playfully perverts, and mistranslates symbols of whiteness. These movements perform translatios from the periphery to the centre of anti-colonial agitation, and from the symbols of

---

7. Taussig, *Mimesis and Alterity*, 80.

8. Walter Benjamin, 'On the Mimetic Faculty', in *Reflections*, ed. Peter Demetz, trans. E. Jephcott (New York: Harcourt Brace Jovanovich, 1979), 333. Taussig, *Mimesis and Alterity*, 33.

9. Taussig, *Mimesis and Alterity*, 80.

10. Taussig, *Mimesis and Alterity*, 115–128.

11. Michael Taussig, 'The Instrument of Ethnographic Observation', in *What Color Is the Sacred?* (Chicago: University of Chicago Press, 2009), 119–129.

power to those of its excessive imitation—and occasionally ambiguous subversion.

THE SIGN OF HISTORY: EX-CENTRICITY AND TEMPORAL LAG

I draw from Bhabha's theory of culture to articulate this mimetic slippage. Following Foucault, Bhabha suggests that 'history' cannot be found in a search for origins and grand narratives but in 'petits récits, imperceptible events, signs apparently *without* meaning and value—empty and excentric'. Bhabha writes:

> The sign of history does not consist in an essence of the event itself, nor exclusively in the *immediate consciousness* of its agents and actors, but in its form as a *spectacle*; spectacle that signifies *because of* the distanciation and displacement between the event and those who are its spectators. The indeterminacy of modernity, where the struggle of translation takes place, is not simply around the idea of progress or truth. Modernity, I suggest, is about the historical construction of a specific position of historical enunciation and address. It privileges those who 'bear witness', those who are 'subjected', or in the Fanonian sense . . . historically displaced. It gives them a representative position through the spatial distance, or the *time-lag* between the Great Event and its circulation as a historical sign of the 'people' or an 'epoch', that constitutes the memory and the moral of the event *as a narrative*, a disposition to cultural communality, a form of social and psychic identification. The discursive address of modernity— its structure of authority—decentres the Great Event, and speaks from that moment of 'imperceptibility', the supplementary space 'outside' or uncannily beside (*abseits*).[12]

In Bhabha's view, modernity is construed as that which is seen—in other words, as a theatre of witnessing and observation dramatizing the imagined spatial or temporal 'lag' between those doing the seeing and those who are seen.

The history of modernity is choreographic: it performs a continual set of micro displacements which reveal 'the supplementary space "outside" or uncannily beside' them: the geographic and geocultural space—(often colonial) territories— *into which* narratives (and bodies) continually move, and *from which* their spectacular aspect makes 'history' become *apparent*. What Bhabha calls 'excentric' signs (those occurring within these margins) further displace the apparent coherence of colonized as well as colonizer selves, which come to be theorized always at a remove and always *on the move*.

Such encounters can be described as 'uncanny', further following Burt, for whom the 'alien' body of modernity is 'uncanny': it is not quite at home (where home denotes a place of residence and returns), though it attempts to return 'there'. Subjects writing—theorizing— themselves are confronted with shifting spaces of imagined priority and futurity, in other words shifting genealogies, as they seek to recover what they find is already gone. The places to which they return reveal themselves never to have been quite *there* as imagined, but to be *here*, in a space of 'uncanny' encounter. I began this book with a genealogy of the decentred texts proliferating out of Hecker's essay 'The Dancing Mania', showing how colonial travel and Orientalist additions moved choreomania across disciplinary sites, in series of translatios by which the concept morphed, just as the world within and with which it moved did too. Here, following Bhabha, I argue the 'supplementary space "outside" or uncannily beside' the paradigmatic dancing manias—from the European Middle Ages, the Italian South, the French Revolutionary era, nineteenth-century religious awakenings, revolutionary Madagascar, and, at a stretch, the American Plains—present an even greater proliferation of spectacular events of history, medicine, and disorderly corporeality than the earliest choreomanias allowed, stretching the Dionysian undercurrent to its colonial edges. This cacophony of cases only very loosely linked to St. Vitus's dance emerges on the historical scene to trouble the contours of this 'strange affliction'. As cases move further from the often repeated core, the consistency and coherence of the disorder dissolves. No longer construed in medical and anthropological literature as core cases of the historical, medieval choreomania,

---

12. Bhabha, *The Location of Culture*, 348–349.

these events are nonetheless ghosted by the literature on the dancing disease that by now suffuses colonial medical and anthropological imaginaries implicitly.

BLACK CHRISTS: PERFORMATIVE MISCEGENATION IN JAMAICA

Before moving to the Melanesian and Polynesian cases, it is worth pausing on a prior, recurring figure of doubling and miscegenation that saturates the nineteenth- and twentieth-century imaginaries of colonial seepage, excess, and waste, as well as recuperation and what I call translatio. The figure of a Black Jesus—a Black Christ or messiah—is as old and widespread as it is contentious. The most revered religious icon in the Latin American world, the Black Christ of Esquipulas, in Guatemala, boasts Nordic features but is carved out of a dark, black wood. It is white and black, a sixteenth-century figurine that embodies indigenous colour and conqueror forms. But this perversion of Christianity's ostensibly white mission, this Christianity in the negative, also represents an indigenous subjectivity all the more natural-seeming (to white or mestizo observers) as its distance from an implicitly more or less white Christian core paradoxically renders the latter all the more apparently universal. Because the Black Christ is doubled racially, it is all the more allegorical: of this world and outside it. The black native becomes paradigmatically Christian; yet because of this surfeit of allegory, it also comes to represent doubleness *in excess* and, as such, appears 'abnormal' to many observers.[13]

Even in the most radical messianic movements—such as that among the Ras Tafaris in Jamaica in the 1930s, where a strict anti-white doctrine separated black followers from the rest of society in the belief that Haile Selassie (1892–1975) (emperor of Ethiopia, claimed to be a living god and a descendant of David) would deliver blacks from exile—separatism was played out through a hybrid set of cultural symbols. The Ras Tafaris claimed to be a lost tribe of Israel, enslaved to whites in a modern-day Babylon; they refused to interact with whites or with blacks who worked for whites. The movement, which echoed the 'Great Revival' of the 1860s in Jamaica, folded Judeo-Christian scripture into a narrative system and set of practices that became counter-mimetically Christian and pan-African, involving dancing, spirit seizure, flagellation, trances, confessions, and dreams. For Christian missionaries observing this part European, part African practice, the remainder, the 'abnormal' portion of the scenes they saw, was choreographic: bodies apparently running amok, disturbing a narrative throughline they thought they otherwise knew.

The 'Great Revival', described by at least one missionary as a widespread 'frenzy'[14] that ran through Jamaica at the same time as the uprising in Madagascar I described in chapter 8, similarly posits narrative creolization. To colonial observers, the simultaneous recuperation and rejection of Western biblical narratives meant a confusing spectacle of partial alterity. Rather than merely reach towards whiteness (and arrive at it, in Bhabha's iconic formulation, 'almost', 'but not quite'),[15] colonial subjects ran with Christian narratives, it seemed, excessively, performing them *too* earnestly, and corporeally. They did not just displace the Great Event (or 'canonical "centre"') but produced what Bhabha calls the 'enigma of authority',[16] redrawing the corporeal contours of Christianity.

Corporeal virtuosity was particularly noted of millennialist events but was treated by colonial ethnographers and missionaries with suspicion, as if the excess of fast-paced gestures, and the sudden onset of talents not previously displayed by revivalists, signalled the intercession of demonic powers. Both sides of the mimic game saw suprahuman, unnatural influence in the other. William Tyson, of the Wesleyan

13. The history of part-black, part-white messiahs in Africa is voluminous. On the Bashilele belief, which became widespread throughout the Congo in the 1930s, in the arrival of a part-black, part-white Man who would perform a host of miracles, including raising the dead, see e.g. Lanternari, *The Religions of the Oppressed*, 10.

14. William Tyson, Brown's Town, to General Secretaries of the Missionary Society, 23 April 1861, Wesleyan Methodist Missionary Society, Correspondence, Jamaica, in MMS/West Indies/Correspondence/FBN 49, 1858–1865, Methodist Missionary Society archive, School of Oriental and African Studies Library, University of London.

15. Bhabha, *The Location of Culture*, 122.

16. Bhabha, *The Location of Culture*: xi.

Methodist Missionary Society in Brown's Town, Jamaica, suggested in a letter to the society's general secretaries dated 23 April 1861 that a demonic influence was at play in the Great Revival, perverting the Christian message into a practice characterized by extraordinary feats of prowess: 'Some persons have been so affected, and have acted in such a *frantic* manner, and seem singly without any intention to deceive, as it had one to suspect a satanic influence: Beating themselves, tearing off and into shreds their garments, foaming and howling, running fiercely about, rushing up trees and balancing themselves in a most marvelous manner upon slender branches, performing desperate leaps; [illegible] at wood or eating grass; becoming dumb also, and having their physical strength ultimately prostrated'.[17] The doubling of alterities went further. Jesus himself multiplied. Tyson added that an informant 'who had taken part in services in which such cases have occurred . . . and who himself professed to have been converted during the revival' revealed that two forces (or spirits) were at play. One was the spirit of Jesus, 'a meek and quiet spirit, who convinces of sin, fills with sorrow and distress, but soon brings his subjects to find peace and joy in believing'. The other was a 'violent spirit which when it seizes hold of the people, they become frantic and scarcely know what they do'. Tyson remarked that his informant was unwilling to say whether he thought the second spirit was a good or a bad one; but, for Tyson, 'those who have been led astray by such fanaticism, or who have been guilty of great extravagances, have been after all comparatively few'. These wayward few also served to remind the Methodist missionary society of what God intended: continued efforts to civilize and to convert. In particular, opposition to all 'excessive' physical practices causing locals to become 'frantic' had to be subdued; this was the work of the first, demonic spirit. Evidently, Jesus, the 'meek' spirit, did not dance, run, howl, rush up trees, or lie prostrate.[18] Proper Christianity, in this view, was an unvarying and stationary practice, opposed to the excessive gesturality

and hypercorporeality of the demonic brand of Christianity that the Jamaican revivalists counter-imitated back to the missionaries.

Demonism was quintessentially a mirror distortion: in this case, colonial reproduction with difference, what Taussig describes as the 'ac/dc' interplay of mimesis and alterity, producing an 'artful combination', a 'combinatorial perplexity', a 'magnificent excessiveness over and beyond the fact that mimesis implies alterity as its flip-side'.[19] The devil's genius was to appear just like the original, but excessively so with respect to the original. Again following Taussig, this relationship of alterity and excess is complicated by the fact that between mimesis and alterity lies perpetual oscillation, so that 'it is far from easy to say who is the imitator and who is imitated, which is copy and which is original'.[20]

The collapsing of acts and corporealities between an endogenous and exogenous Christianity revealed Christian revivalists outdoing missionaries in their zeal, their belief, but also perhaps most spectacularly in their choreographic exercises. As an anti-colonial movement, with assimilationist undertones, this brand of revivalism went beyond white Christian religion by absorbing it so intensely as to make it virtually disappear to itself. The revivalist movement performed indigeneity as a recorporealization, a making-natural of colonial culture. This perplexed missionaries, who thought they were bringing culture to an uncultured place. The excessive quality and sweep of revivalists' imitations rendered them not only pathological but ecosophical in colonial discourse: excessive gestures appeared to arise spontaneously, involuntarily, out of native soil. According to a letter in the Wesleyan Methodist Missionary Society archives from Savannah-la-Mar, Jamaica, signed T. Raspass and dated 6 May 1861, the Jamaican revival approximated a hurricane sweeping over the island.[21] But the movement had been brewing for some time. The roots of this eschatological culture may have dated back to the American Revolutionary period, when several hundred United Empire Loyalists left for Jamaica, taking

17. William Tyson, Brown's Town, to General Secretaries of the Missionary Society, 23 April 1861, Wesleyan Methodist Missionary Society, Correspondence, Jamaica, FBN 49, 1858–1865.

18. William Tyson, Brown's Town, to General Secretaries of the Missionary Society, 23 April 1861, Wesleyan Methodist Missionary Society, Correspondence, Jamaica, FBN 49, 1858–1865.

19. Taussig, *Mimesis and Alterity*, 192.

20. Taussig, *Mimesis and Alterity*, 78.

21. T. Raspass, Savannah-la-mar, to Rev and dear Sirs, 6 May 1861, Wesleyan Methodist Missionary Society, Correspondence, Jamaica, FBN 49, 1858–1865.

their converted slaves with them. These 'unofficial missionaries' spread Christianity throughout the island, so that by the 1830s, the conversion of those who came to be known as Native Baptists had gained solid ground.[22] What these native Christians then catalysed was a mixture of part-indigenous, part-imported religion that clashed with official missionary teachings: in particular, the unorthodox use of drumming and shell-blowing, dancing, and spirit-seizure, miscegenated another Christianity, to white Europeans' eyes, so European missionaries could not quite claim to implant a pure, untouched Christianity entirely into new ground. Christianity was now wildly, jaggedly corporeal, just as it had been among the revivalists in Kentucky whose jerks and other hypercorporeal exercises I discussed in chapter 5. Only here, the native back-translation of heightened corporeality and virtuosity in religious practice rendered the adoption of Christian icons and words suspect: rather than appear to be simply very zealous, native Jamaicans seemed to be exceeding the bounds of religion and entering into uncomfortable pre- and potentially post-Christian terrain.

Messianic iconography concentrated in the figure of Jesus and the Hebrew narrative of a return to an ancient homeland, mixed with intense corporeal practices and ideas about different sorts of transformation and spirituality, so that running, dancing, howling, and spirit possession, considered taboo by the Western colonials, effected a translatio between local 'heathenism' and 'hereticism' and current biblical canon. What's more, these hybrid cultures, oscillating between mimesis and alterity, posited a choreography of difference in which Western colonial writers and native Jamaicans ended up articulating their own senses of difference (and eventually sameness) to one another as well as to themselves. Whereas the missionaries desired their teachings to be assimilated—even revered (certainly unquestioned)—the Jamaicans' recuperation and transformation of these practices enacted a counter-desire to consume what had

been brought to the island with the initial aim to conquer and subdue. From an ecosophical perspective, Caribbean bodies transformed hostile environments by adopting, assimilating, and excessively incorporating their signs: these (partly) colonized bodies performed a theatrical anthropophagy, consuming the narratives, signs, and symbols of their hosts the better to expel them in the end; yet in the process, they also became in part that which they consumed, handing back the colonizer's language, costume, and props.

Meanwhile, the consummation of one brand of Christianity, its excessive expenditure (even exhaustion) in the form of counter-mimetic perversions, yielded what the British social anthropologist Peter Worsley (1924–2013)—who influentially introduced the term 'third world' into English anthropology—called 'heart-searchings' on the part of the West.[23] The West's image had not been reflected back to itself in quite the narcissistic way it had imagined: colonial subjects were reappropriating Euro-Christian iconography, practices, and beliefs but challenging and *dragging* them into another spatio-temporal 'lag'—another (Jamaican) space 'uncannily beside' Europe. With this, the very image of a Western genealogy nestled in the infant backwaters of colonial geographies had to be reassessed.

CARGO CULTS IN MELANESIA: THE PAPUAN 'VAILALA MADNESS'

As Edward B. Tylor (1832–1917), one of the founders of British anthropology, noted, anthropology was a 'reformer's science'. It was construed as a politically progressive field, allowing 'the great modern nations to understand themselves, to weigh in a just balance their own merits and defects, and even in some measure forecast . . . the possibilities of the future'.[24] Anthropology was at the outset conceived as a

22. George Eaton Simpson, 'Jamaican Revivalist Cults', *Social and Economic Studies* 5.4 (1956): 321–442, 334.

23. Peter Worsley, *The Trumpet Shall Sound: A Study of 'Cargo' Cults in Melanesia*, 2nd ed. (New York: Schocken Books, 1968), 261. See also Peter Worsley, *The Third World* (Chicago: University of Chicago Press, 1964). In a contemporary review of Worsley's book, anthropologist Sidney W. Mintz noted that the term 'Tiers Monde' (third world) had been introduced into French sociology by Alfred Sauvy (1898–1990) nearly a decade earlier; the term had roots in the French Revolutionary notion of the 'Tiers état' (or third estate). See Sidney W. Mintz, 'Other: *The Third World*, by Peter Worsley', *American Anthropologist* 68.5 (1966): 1320–1326, 1321.

24. Cited in Henrika Kuklick, ed., *A New History of Anthropology* (Malden, MA: Blackwell, 2008), 58. See also Henrika Kuklick, 'Islands in the Pacific: Darwinian Biogeography and British Anthropology', *American Ethnologist* 23.3 (1996): 11–38.

natural science, at once politically engaged and unshakably scientifically objective, proceeding according to the new nineteenth-century scientific methods which construed science as a mode, a field, and a practice. At the same time, anthropology emerged from medical history and colonial medicine as a modern science fundamentally concerned with alternative temporalities. Anthropology hovered at the cusp of scientific atemporality between future and past, in a full, messianic present rent through with shards of primitivism, antiquity, animality, and lofty ideas about civilization. Soon, anthropology would become the field within which anti-colonial sentiment was most passionately deliberated, as this originally colonial medical science folded back onto itself to reveal people rising up around the world, shaking off foreign rule. But the new romantic thrust of twentieth-century anthropology was just as rent through with primitivist fantasies as its earlier incarnations, which had gazed dubiously at the beatitude of primitive savagery. As a site within which twentieth-century incarnations of the 'dance mania' took root, early to mid-twentieth century anthropology, still laced with medical debate, returned to the eschatological and millennialist scenes of medieval St. Vitus's dancers and the revolutionary uprisings, frenzies, and upheavals of the eighteenth- and nineteenth-century movements discussed in previous chapters but revealed a new borderland between ancient and 'modern' corporeality.

With the increasing prominence of fieldwork, mimetic gesticulations and collective dreams of better futures showed alien—inscrutable—bodies becoming ever more present and ever closer to the anthropologist's fantasy of a Lost Atlantis. Colonial men and women performed theatres of colonial hauntings that thrust figures of antiquity and archaicity up to their observers' faces. Colonial bodies were not just moving jaggedly, revealing states of heightened ('abnormal', pathological) excitement in the pages of medical books or on theatricalized hospital stages; their gestures became increasingly political. According to anthropological observers, men and women contorting their bodies and waving props and flags were engaging in discursive practices which, viewed in a Western light, could bring all men and women new forms of sovereignty. The West was implicated in a collective futurity that included the 'third world' paradoxically at the bottom and at the helm of a new boat.

Cargo cults were foremost among (anti-) colonial movements that enacted futurity while drawing on indigenous forms of belief and cultural practice. Steeped in a 'desirous' belief in the Europeans' power to bestow material wealth on the world (and thus also on the movement's followers), these movements, like the Ghost Dance, also sought the radical elimination of Europeans and their replacement with the ancestral dead. Although cargo cults have received substantial attention from anthropology, history, and religious and area studies in a rich body of literature articulating a complex entanglement of discourses, they have received considerably less attention in theatre, dance, and performance studies. Yet, as Dorothy Billings has argued, the politics of performance in at least one such cargo cult mined a rich history of ironic play that was misread by baffled Australians as inexplicable fantasy.[25] The late twentieth-century 'Johnson cult', based on the figure of Lyndon B. Johnson (1908–1973), whom Papuans in New Hanover claimed to vote for in an effort to have American power and wealth replace the local Australian government, performed a politics of resistance while appearing naively to misunderstand local structures of governmental authority. Simultaneously, as anthropologists, including Bronwen Douglas, have pointed out, recent anthropological interest in the so-called 'politics of tradition' has increasingly recognized the place of Christianity in Papuan belief, particularly in the latter part of the twentieth century.[26]

The 'Vailala Madness' in Papua New Guinea was paradigmatic among cargo cults, recuperated by twentieth-century anthropologists such as Worsley and the Italian historian of religions Vittorio Lanternari (1918–2010) as representative of the 'primitive' world rising up out of colonial oppression. Described by Lindstrom as the originary cargo cult in mid- to late twentieth-century social scientific discourse, the Vailala Madness became, as he points out, nearly equivalent to the broader term 'cargo cult', increasingly employed to designate any sort of 'unpredictable and inexplicable' 'eruption'.[27] According to the German missionary

---

25. Dorothy K. Billings, *Cargo Cult as Theater: Political Performance in the Pacific* (Oxford: Lexington Books, 2002).

26. Bronwen Douglas, 'From Invisible Christians to Gothic Theater: The Romance of the Millennial in Melanesian Anthropology', *Current Anthropology* 42.5 (2001): 615–650.

27. Lindstrom, *Cargo Cult*, 24.

The Gift of Seeing Resemblances' • 259

Georg Höltker (1895–1976), this included religious madness, ecstatic dreams of redemption, and the coming of a prosperous golden age.[28] According to later incarnations of the cargo cult dream, any wealth arriving on native shores from strange rafts, planes, or other vehicles signalled a 'cargo cult', a term that was eventually used to designate dubiously capitalist longings among native colonial subjects.[29]

Peaking in around 1919–1920, the Vailala Madness staged a return to a status quo ante by Papuans frustrated with changing social conditions under the colonial regime.[30] But the cult ambivalently mixed Christian eschatology and anti-European sentiment with roots in older practices forecasting the ancestral return of dead Papuans in rafts. The cult of Mansren (an apocryphal old man whose name meant ruler or lord) emerged in 1857 and, like the Ghost Dance discussed in the previous chapter, promised the renewal of heaven and earth. Mansren's reputed self-imposed exile in the Netherlands and impending return to New Guinea via Germany or Japan produced riotous outbreaks of ecstatic preparation, including the performance of special dances and songs: hundreds of people engaged in ecstatic singing and dancing, anticipating the arrival of Mansren and the return of the dead in boats.[31] It seems plausible that these were variations on the Papuan longhouse or mask dances employed for all major ceremonial occasions at the time. As Worsley has pointed out, the Vailala 'cult' swelled up and died down with the ebb and flow of colonial and Allied activity during World Wars I and II. Colonization by the Dutch and the arrival in the 1940s of the Japanese set into motion a dramatic performance of cultural revival, fuelled by cultural ambivalence and a projected return to old ways.[32]

Yet the Vailala movement constituted far less straightforwardly an anti-colonial revolt than some of the later anthropological literature suggests. According to the British missionary E. P. Jones, in a communication with the London Missionary Society dated 4 February 1920, Papuans performed a double movement, absorbing and rejecting 'Europe', which they cast as futurity and ancestry, a force at once exogenous and indigenous to themselves. The double movement literally expressed itself as 'vertigo': 'there seems to have been a sort of vision and then as they say their heads went round and round I suppose a sort of vertigo [sic]', Jones wrote, 'but the strange thing is that all seem to indicate in different ways that a new era was imminent from their ancestors'. A few years prior, at Toaripi, Jones was 'credited with being one of their returned ancestors'. But the confusion between European and native genealogies in Jones's view was patent: while the Papuans were heralding a return of their ancestors in rafts and other vehicles, they also claimed that they would be 'turned into Europeans with European dress implements food and even language, and also religion'. This Europhilia (and Christophilia) was so great, he noted, that 'they have flocked into the services everywhere and they are keen to possess books[;] they have bought me out of local stocks of books and I have had to write for the remainder of the edition of the New Testament'. Jones added, cautiously, that 'there are many ways of looking at this movement', including as a form of indige-nous ancestor worship laced with Christian ideas about redemption. 'The people of the Oil Field

---

28. In Lindstrom, *Cargo Cult*, 21–22.

29. Lindstrom deconstructs the myth of the cargo cultish desire for refrigerators, among other Western goods, in Lindstrom, 'Cargo Cult in the Third Millennium'.

30. Worsley, *The Trumpet Shall Sound*, 90. See also esp. 70–93. F. E. Williams, government anthropologist of Papua from 1922 to his death in 1943, offers a first-hand account in F. E. Williams, *The Vailala Madness and the Destruction of Native Ceremonies in the Gulf Division*, Territory of Papua, Anthrop. Report no. 4 (Port Moresby, 1923), and F. E. Williams, 'The Vailala Madness in Retrospect', in Evans-Pritchard, Firth, Malinowski, and Schapera, eds., *Essays Presented to C. G. Seligman*, 369–379. Williams notes that several alternative terms are used to describe the 'Vailala Madness', including 'The Gulf *Kavakava*', i.e., the 'Gulf Madness'; the 'Orokolo *kavakava*', in reference to the village of Orokol, which, paradoxically, 'is practically the one coastal village in the Gulf Division that has remained immune'; 'Head-he-go-round', the 'usual Pidgin-English expression'; '*Kwarana giroa*', or '*kwarana aika*', and '*Haro heraripi*', regional variants; '*Iki havere*' ('belly-don't-know'), a term used in coastal villages throughout the Gulf Division; and '*Abo abo*', meaning 'giddy' or 'crazy', terms used to the west in the Purari Delta. See Williams, *The Vailala Madness*, 2–3. See also Weston La Barre, 'Materials for a History of Studies of Crisis Cults: A Bibliographic Essay', *Current Anthropology* 12.1 (1971): 3–44. On cargo cults and 'indigenous millenarianism', see also esp. Holger Jebens, 'Signs of the Second Coming: On Eschatological Expectation and Disappointment in Highland and Seaboard Papua New Guinea', *Ethnohistory* 47.1 (2000): 171–204; R. Firth, 'The Theory of "Cargo" Cults: A Note on Tikopia', *Man* (1955): 130–132; R. M. Berndt, 'A Cargo Movement in the Eastern Central Highlands of New Guinea', *Oceania* 23.1 (1952): 40–65.

31. On the Mansren cult, see e.g. Worsley, *The Trumpet Shall Sound*, 126–139.

32. See Worsley, *The Trumpet Shall Sound*, 136–145.

near by thought it a political rising because some wild spirits talked of their ancestral spirits driving out those whites who were here trading but this is very rare'. Jones preferred to describe the phenomenon as a 'religious revival not in a usual evangelical sense though there is that in it in a small degree'. Overall, the district was 'aflame', and he required of the London Missionary Society six more men 'to meet the calls'.[33]

Europeans emerged as if out of a phantasmatic future conceived by Papuans as occurring in an alternative space (across the ocean, via rafts); but Europeans simultaneously had to be annihilated, as the far more ancient ancestors of the Papuans would come back again to take their place. The movement was short-lived. B. T. Butcher (b. 1877), also of the London Missionary Society, noted in his report for the year 1920 that 'the semi religious movement that was noticed last year has largely died away'. In a letter dated 1 January 1921 Jones added that the 'sort of mass movement which was partly christian partly heathen' which he had written about before was still present, but few incidents were now to be reported. Although Papuans seemed to have gained in religious zeal—one man was 'seized with violent agitation[,] his body shook as with ague and for a moment was unconscious'—the excitement was 'settling down'. Jones 'was able to soothe [this man] and [he] went home somewhat calmer'.[34]

The Australian-born British government anthropologist and ethnographer F. E. Williams (1893–1943), who provides the only substantial first-hand account of the Vailala Madness, often still cited as the most authoritative in anthropological literature, wrote an official report on the cult of the self-styled 'Jesus Christ Men', which was published as Territory of Papua Anthropology Report No. 4, 'The Vailala Madness and the Destruction of Native Ceremonies in the Gulf Division' (1923). In it, he recognizes the deep crisis colonialism had provoked among native Papuan islanders, suggesting that this so-called epidemic madness had run its course.

It was 'now more than twelve years since a movement known as the Vailala Madness began in the Gulf Division of Papua', he wrote. By the time of his writing, the madness had '[begun] to die its lingering death, and by now it [was] no more than a memory'. The Vailala Madness had, however, originally 'spread with the speed of an epidemic', meeting with 'high enthusiasm' among natives, who described it as 'hot'. Jerking motions of the head from side to side and leg and arm muscle twitches earned the Vailala episode designation as a modern-day 'St. Vitus' dance' by one eyewitness, the acting resident magistrate of the Gulf Division, G. H. Murray, in his annual report of 1919–1920.[35]

Expectations of miracles and 'miraculous happenings' had engendered what Williams called a 'mass hysteria', as 'great numbers were affected by a kind of *giddiness*; they lost or abandoned control of their limbs and reeled about the villages, one man involuntarily following the example of another until almost the whole population of a village might be affected at the same moment'. This frenetic and highly contagious condition, known as *haro heraripe*, that is, 'one's head is turning around' (or, in pidgin English, 'Head-he-go-round Men') occurred, Williams argued, involuntarily among the 'masses', who were imitating the leaders ('bosses'). The leaders, he argued, were 'affecting' this condition 'for their purposes'.[36] As in previous cases of so-called choreomania, bodily loss of control and choreographies of mass imitation, coupled with a theatre of manipulation and deceit, earned this episode designation as epidemic hysteria. The involuntary aspect of the event prompted Williams to use the term 'Automaniac', denoting the '*self-induced* condition of nervous or mental derangement'.[37] As with other cases of agitated social movements I turn to later in this chapter, the imitation of an excited leader was nearly sufficient to provoke gestural agitation among crowds. Similarly, what Agamben describes as the catastrophic disintegration of gesture in chorea (chapter 3 here) characterized the apparently impulsive 'automaniacal'

---

33. Report from E. P. Jones, British missionary, to London Missionary Society, 4 February 1920, CWM/LMS, Papua Reports, box 3, 1915–1926.

34. Report from E. P. Jones, British missionary, to the London Missionary Society, 1 January 1921, CWM/LMS, Papua Reports, box 3, 1915–1926.

35. See 'Reports by G. H. Murray, Acting Resident Magistrate, Gulf Division, re the Vailala Madness', in app. A of Williams, *The Vailala Madness*, 65–70.

36. Williams, 'The Vailala Madness in Retrospect', 369–370. Emphasis mine. See also Williams, *The Vailala Madness*, esp. 9–14.

37. Williams, *The Vailala Madness*, 4–5. Emphasis mine.

movement of men whose heads, according to Williams, 'turned around'. Here, however, gesture did not disintegrate into incoherence; specific terms and objects emerged out of the fray to signal a colonial encounter whose performance of giddy desire suggested an attempt to assimilate the exogenous culture of the foreign invaders with a ceremonial structure inherited from precolonial days.

Papuans denied themselves their old customs just as they assimilated colonial sounds: a mixture of pidgin German ('Djaman'), abolition of personal ornamentation, feathers, and other objects representing the old customs and ceremonies, and prophecies foretelling the return of the dead, often in the form of white men (as Williams noted, 'some Europeans were actually welcomed as the ghosts of Papuans') suggested profound cultural ambivalence and an attempt performatively to account for changes going on more broadly on Papuan shores. The preparation of food, with tables laid, down to the knives, forks, and decorations, staged the triumphant return of the ancestors, who would be nourished with the technological paraphernalia of the whites. Williams noted that the 'bosses', who had sole access to the *ahea uvi* (hot houses) where the spirits were supposed to return, must have profited from these lavish displays 'long after the masses had ceased to show any nervous or physical symptoms'.[38]

For Williams, the leaders were not all (or not originally all) feigning; ecstatic seizures and visions, which had preceded the 'Madness', and belief by Williams's informants that the early days had been characterized by actual miracles continued to grant the period between 1919 and 1921 the mark of a new 'golden age' connected mimetically with the old. Rapid change and the miscegenation of new beliefs—from mistranslations and reinterpretations of objects such as the Anglo-Persian Oil Company's wireless device, turned into a device for receiving messages of deliverance through a flagpole[39]—meshed nostalgia and fascination with European language and dress, symbols and technology. As Williams wrote in his report on the Vailala Madness, poles had made their way into the Papuan cosmogony in a variety of ways:

'the flag pole appears to have been instituted by the London Missionary Society a good many years ago. The villagers were given flags, and might hoist them on any signal occasion: but particularly, as I understand, on Sunday . . . . Now, however, it has certainly been adopted by the Vailala Madness as one of its cult-objects'.[40] One of the flagpole's main functions was to 'receive messages from the dead through its agency'. Singing 'vigorously' at the foot of these poles helped to catalyse the arrival of the message; the message, then, having come down the flagpole and into the ground, 'went up into the belly of the leader, and thence into and out of his mouth'.[41]

These scenes of recuperation constitute what Agamben calls the 'experience of language as such, in its pure self-reference':[42] language (like gesture) signals not just the communication of a message but the communication of the communicability of the message. Communicability—the 'sentient' or tactile aspect of 'copying' language—takes precedence over the semantic content of any message deployed. Within the act of displacing language at its threshold (at the edge of the sea or at the tip of a pole) was a series of encounters that dissolved the distinctness of (foreign) language. Messages, which came 'from the sea "like the wind,"' mixed Christian biblical references with sounds from the English language (among others) for an audience of Papuans who may have been familiar with neither. At Arihava, in April 1922, Williams noted a man 'delivering an exhortation from the platform of an *eravo* [long house]. Dancing and singing was going on near at hand and his voice was almost drowned, but numbers of people were gathered about the platform; watching and listening. He spoke at the top of his voice, and very rapidly: the language, I am told, was English, and was not understood by the people present. The only phrases intelligible to me were "*Ihova*" [Jehovah] (with frequent pointing to the sky); "Me wantum *kaikai*" [cake] and "He all right"'.[43] Other terms used included 'Heave 'em up' and 'Come on boy'. Williams added: 'the speaker was highly excited, striking himself continually on the chest. Throughout the performance his right leg trembled violently as if quite uncontrolled'.

38. Williams, 'The Vailala Madness in Retrospect', 369–371.
39. Williams, 'The Vailala Madness in Retrospect', 377.
40. Williams, *The Vailala Madness*, 23.
41. Williams, *The Vailala Madness*, 24.
42. Giorgio Agamben, *Infancy and History: On the Destruction of Experience*, trans. Liz Heron (London: Verso, 2007), 6.
43. Williams, *The Vailala Madness*, 6.

Another man, who took his place on the platform, seemed quite to 'lack inspiration'. Although his leg trembled, it did so 'without the same appearance of spontaneity'.[44] In the theatre of mimetic doublings that this event performs, spontaneity (or the 'appearance of spontaneity') holds currency as an indicator of the event's proximity to desire for the other within the context of a synthetic ceremony. For the colonial medical and anthropological observer, these events signalled a theatre of *intelligibilization*, where the otherwise opaque Papuan body and sounds were rent through with shards of whiteness and gestures indicating assimilation of and proximity to a new cast of seemingly magical, potent white things (cake, sky, Jehovah).

W. M. Strong (d. 1946), government anthropologist and chief medical officer at Port Moresby, argued in his introduction to Williams's official report that this 'Madness' could be interpreted from a number of standpoints, including notably as a reaction to what Williams noted was the unfortunate 'suppression of ceremonies, games, dances, and the like', which '[robbed] the natives of that zest of life which is derived from social enjoyments' and '[led] to ugly social abnormalities'.[45] The 'all work and no play' policy colonialists favoured was, [Williams] argued, 'less profitable for primitive man than for civilized savages'. Significantly, this Protestant work ethic kept Papuans from enjoying what for them amounted to a healthy balance between work and play: 'those who, genuinely anxious to improve the native's condition . . . argue that for him work is the prime essential' fail to realize that 'energy denied its proper outlet will break loose at some unexpected point'. In Williams's terms, 'repression leads to abnormality; . . . it is not improbable', he ventured, 'that in the Vailala Madness the voluntary suppression of the ceremonies contributes something towards the repulsive and ridiculous behaviour of its victims'. As he put it: 'The ceremonies—to say nothing of their artistic and emotional value—are *healthy* [emphasis in original] social activities . . . evolved or accepted and modified in perfect accordance with the character and desires of the people. So long as they are allowed to follow one another regularly the feelings of the people will pursue their natural course of rising, culmination and subsidence: this is the anabolism and katabolism of collective feeling'.[46] This organic metaphor posited collective life as being organized according to metabolic relations, composed of organic build-up (anabolism) and subsequent expenditure or release (catabolism). In this view, dances and other ceremonies were as necessary and healthy as they were organic. So, too, their suppression, in Williams's view, caused more trouble than it resolved. Interference into the natural course of humans' energetic expenditure provoked outbreaks, hysterias: as he argued, 'hold down or stifle these purely natural activities [i.e., ceremonies], and you may have to deal with an objective case of collective hysteria'. Williams's further comparison of the 'stifling' of Papuans' natural social activities to the early Neapolitans stuffing the Vesuvius with concrete to try to stave off its 'intermittent puffs', thus catalysing the volcanic eruption of 79 CE, further set his interpretation of the 'Vailala Madness' into alignment with an organic metaphor describing primitive and natural revolt.[47] The volcano and the Papuans were equally subject to cataclysmic eruption.

In Strong's terms, 'those who regard [the Papuan native] as a *labour machine* will say that the Madness only shows that the native is better working where such Madness could be prevented by the method referred to' by Mr. Williams, *i.e.*, tolerating the Papuans' enjoyment of the '*healthy*' exercise of their ceremonies. Others, however, Strong wrote, enumerating ways of considering this phenomenon, 'will argue that the Madness shows the necessity of suppressing all native culture—forgetting that the Madness is merely a strange and ill-assorted mixture of both native and European culture. To the medical man', he added, 'the account will be of interest as an account of crowd psychology verging on to the pathological'. And 'to those who are interested in comparative religion the account will be of interest as a present-day example of the beginnings of a creed and ritual'. Strong added that this was similar to the early days of 'Mahommedanism', where a 'psychological atmosphere' of ecstatic preparation resembled that of the Papuans today. Finally, 'to those concerned with the administration of Papua, [Williams's] report will be of interest as an example of the difficulty of foretelling how European influence and teaching will affect the Papuan native. The interest of the

44. Williams, *The Vailala Madness*, 6.
45. Williams, *The Vailala Madness*, 56.
46. Williams, *The Vailala Madness*, 57.
47. Williams, *The Vailala Madness*, 56 57.

account to the pure ethnographer is so great that it hardly needs pointing out'.[48]

The Vailala Madness offered a palimpsestical view of native life and European influence: it was at once impenetrable, confusing, rich, complex, and obscure—so puzzling that it could be interpreted from nearly any angle. Indeed, 'reading' and translating the Vailala Madness into metaphorical and pragmatic terms, linking it to more familiar tropes, became the colonial ethnographer and administrator's greatest challenge and accomplishment. At once false proof that games had to continue to be suppressed, insight into pathological instances of crowd psychology and early religion, and a window onto the life of so-called ethnological people, the Vailala Madness served as a crucible for the hermeneutic challenges of colonial rule. The conjunction of functions this report presented to the physician, the sociologist, the ethnographer, and the scholar of religions—as well as the generally concerned person, whose interest in Papuan labour and health was gestured towards without further qualification—offered the report reader (in this case initially members of the London Missionary Society) an ambivalent picture of the effects of the introduction of the Christian religion and European technologies into the 'native culture' of the Gulf Division.

Hermeneutic challenges and the constant negotiation of legibility, translation, and counter-mimicry were endemic. Confusion over the performance of 'making Christmas', as Papuans sometimes described the erection of platforms and flagpoles and the endeavour of 'making merry [such as] at an ordinary dance', suggested slippages between Christian and native Papuan concepts of pleasure and duty, and the Papuans' adoption and theatrical redeployment of European objects and affects.[49]

Colonial power requires a double articulation by which to explain the double standard that posits freedom and rational enlightenment as universal principles only partially attainable in the colonies. Colonial people are cast as almost free, almost rational; and, as the Papuan case suggests, almost able to conform to a Protestant ethics of 'all work and no play'. But they fail entirely to subscribe to this, in the colonialist's view, and this is where the 'madness' appears to

emerge. The European articulation of this difference rests on the Papuans' imagined status as natural beings whose metabolisms require energetic outlets (in Strong's terms) yet whose partial imitation of Western language and ceremonies suggests a culture never quite able to catch up to the West. Papuans were at once at least as natural as their Western counterparts, inasmuch as they also required a balance between festivity and labour (they are not 'labour machines'), and locked out of modern temporalities by virtue of their imitative excess. They imitated the West, but they also imitated one another imitating the West, in an excessive exercise of counter-imitation that led to collective 'madness'. As a site for negotiating the West's encounter with colonial assimilation and mis-assimilation, the Vailala Madness suggests a disciplinary articulation between medical anthropology, positing biological universalism, and an incipient discourse on culture and cultural difference.

For Worsley, increasing contact and communication (or miscommunication) between colonial and colonized peoples produced a sort of midcentury anthropology-sociology complex—or crisis—which extended by the 1960s to the emergence of anthropological and sociological studies of Hollywood, mental hospitals, and Australian aborigines and Bushmen; the objects of study characteristic of these two fields had meshed, though methods now differed. Anthropologists were less sure than ever of their status as privileged viewers, able to survey their subjects from a safe, generally geocultural, distance; at the same time, distinctions between 'backward'- and 'forward'-tending nations persisted. 'This overlapping of fields and interchange of techniques', Worsley wrote, 'is part of a process of ever-growing interaction between backward and advanced peoples, of the breakdown of colonial societies, their absorption into wider politics and the growth of new national entities. It has been a process', he added, 'marked' for social scientists 'by *heart-searchings* about the inadequacy of anti-evolutionary, particularly functionalist, anthropological theories formulated on the basis of the study of "untouched" primitive societies and which later proved to be inadequate when applied to the phenomena of "culture contact"'.[50] The process of surveying the

---

48. W. M. Strong, 'Introduction', in Williams, *The Vailala Madness*, ix–xiii, ix.

49. 'Reports by G. H. Murray, Acting Resident Magistrate, Gulf Division, re the Vailala Madness', 65–70, 66.

50. Worsley, *The Trumpet Shall Sound*, 261–262. Emphasis mine.

land and its inhabitants had to confront the two-way vector of cultural exchange that characterized mimetic (and counter-mimetic) encounters between peoples.

This contact zone suggests a site for the articulation of 'dance' between medicine and colonial anthropology, between theatre and political history, and between performance and 'culture'. To the extent that Papuan 'head-he-go-round-men' engaged in corporeal recuperations of white ceremonial choreographies, enunciating white (German, British) words ('heave 'em up', etc.) and recombining colonial props (flags, poles, cutlery) with extant ceremonies (long tables, etc.), the performative doubling of past and future in a messianic 'now-time' of expectation reveals a zone of intensity, in which colonial medical and anthropological readings of native performance rearticulated the West's concept of its own difference (its theorization of its self) right back. As a site for the negotiation of sameness and difference, the Vailala Madness instantiated a theatre of making-similar, in which counter-mimicry rendered white gestures and speech jagged and mad. The dance of counter-imitation showed that native Papuans were not, as in Bhabha's formulation of the colonial condition, 'almost the same [as whites], but not quite'[51] but rather the converse: almost entirely different, but not quite.

CARGO CULTS IN POLYNESIA: THE MILLENNIAL 'CULT' OF THE HAUHAU

A second cargo cult, revealing an almost mirror image of the Papuan Vailala Madness, brings these relations of counter-mimicry and performance further to light. Similarly staging a theatre of millennial expectation and choreographic recuperation, as well as jagged gesturalities, seeming linguistic unintelligibility, and the performance of fragmentary eloquence against a backdrop of apparent incohesion, the Maoris' Hauhau movement, like the so-called Vailala Madness, emerged in the second half of the nineteenth century. Like the Vailala Madness, it was theorized by colonial medical anthropologists in the first decades of the twentieth century as an instance of primitive beatitude and natural upheaval: at once a disease and a locally specific cultural happening in part attributable to human (particularly colonial) intercession. Alternately known as the Pai Marire movement, meaning 'the good and the peaceful', the Hauhau movement emerged in 1864 as an alternative to Christian religion under British colonial rule. As with the Vailala Madness, it borrowed from Christianity yet anticipated the swift disappearance of Europeans from Maori land.

Te-Ua (d. 1866), a Maori leader, had converted to Anglicanism under the British and, claiming converse with the angel Gabriel, who he said taught him the symbols and rituals of a new religion based on the Book of Revelation, laid the ground for a set of practices that recombined Maori props and practices and Christian eschatological beliefs.[52] In Te-Ua's version, men and women were to enjoy free sexual commerce with one another, and all Europeans were to be driven back to the sea, from whence they came, with the help of angels conjured by the utterance of the word 'Hau!'[53] With all the Europeans gone, adepts would learn European sciences and arts, as well as the English language, effortlessly, with the help of Hauhau priests and angels. A central pole, or *niu*, traditionally used for divination in Maori practice, now served as the focal point

51. Bhabha, *The Location of Culture*, 122.

52. See Lanternari, *The Religions of the Oppressed*, 248–259. See also R. W. Winks, 'The Doctrine of Hauhauism', *Journal of the Polynesian Society* 62.3 (1953): 199–236; W. Greenwood, 'The Upraised Hand, or the Spiritual Significance of the Rise of the Ringatu Faith', *Journal of the Polynesian Society* 51.1 (1942): 1–81; Paul Clark, 'Hauhau': *The Pai Marire Search for Maori Identity* (Auckland: University of Auckland Press, 1975); S. Barton Babbage, *Hauhauism: An Episode in the Maori Wars, 1863–1866* (Wellington, New Zealand: A. H. & A. W. Reed, 1937); James Cowan, *The New Zealand Wars: A History of the Maori Campaigns and the Pioneering Period*, 2 vols., vol. 2, *The Hauhau Wars, 1864–72* (New York: AMS Press, 1969); James O. Gump, 'The Imperialism of Cultural Assimilation: Sir George Grey's Encounter with the Maori and the Xhosa, 1845–1868', *Journal of World History* 9.1 (1998): 89–106, 101–103; and Kenelm Burridge, *New Heaven, New Earth: A Study of Millenarian Activities* (New York: Schocken Books, 1969), 15–22. James Belich, in *The Victorian Interpretation of Racial Conflict: The Maori, the British, and the New Zealand Wars* (Montreal: McGill-Queen's University Press, 1989), notes that the movement may not have arisen from despair at defeat in war and that 'just how revolutionary an ideological change the new religions represented remains open to question . . . . Similar cults had emerged before the [Maori] wars, and early Maori Christianity itself can arguably be understood as a syncretic religion, even an adjustment cult' (204).

53. For a discussion of the term 'Hau', alternately denoting power, wind, breath, and life force, see Burridge, *New Heaven, New Earth*, 17.

around which special dances and songs called *karakia* and *waiata* were to be performed, using a mixture of words borrowed from Hebrew, English, German, Greek, and Italian. Lanternari, in *The Religions of the Oppressed*, noted that rhythmic dancing among the Hauhau was carried to a 'fever pitch' as adepts 'fell prey' to 'collective seizures' and 'trances'.[54]

The *niu* ceremony, performed to generate a state of ecstasy among participants, blended British political and religious iconography, recuperated into Maori practice. Colourful banners, with crosses similar to those of the British flag and the mission banners, hung from the top of the *niu*. Te-Ua's belief that he was the new Moses (and the Maoris the new chosen people of God, descended from the tribes of Judah) and that New Zealand was the New Canaan transposed the Christian and British onto the Maori world and the biblical Sermon on the Mount onto the Maori *niu*, from which the divine message was to descend. This practice continued in relatively full force until 1886, when Te-Ua surrendered to British officers, who were alarmed at anti-British riots that had broken out among some adherents. The movement continued in fits and starts until about 1892. Although Te-Ua's doctrine was pacific, emphasizing virtuousness, righteousness, and eventual reunion with the dead, some of the Hauhaus' belligerence towards the military and missionaries had caused alarm. British soldiers, in an early battle, had been taken by surprise, decapitated, smoked, and paraded around the village. A missionary who had until then lived relatively quietly among the Maori was crucified, and his eyes were swallowed whole.[55] Interpretations abounded, but most generally accepted was that the Hauhaus were rebelling against colonial incursions on their land; in one Hauhau's words: 'Bishop [Williams], many years ago we received the faith from you. Now we return it to you, for there has been found a new and precious thing by which we shall keep our land'.[56] Another Hauhau was reported to have said: 'These men, these missionaries, were

always telling us, "Lay up for yourselves treasure in heaven". And so, while we were looking up to heaven, our land was snatched away from beneath our feet'.[57]

For Kenelm Burridge, a British anthropologist whose *New Heaven New Earth: A Study of Millenarian Activities* (1969) is still one of the most frequently cited works on millennialism today, land seizure was central to the emergence of the Hauhau movement in Polynesia. The relation of the land to the ancestors (who were believed to lie inside it), its function of providing sustenance, and its role in warfare and other sources of power or prestige (*mana*), made the land symbolically and pragmatically a focal point for Maori life. Understandably, its usurpation by the British was cause for revolt.[58] In conjunction with the Christian-inflected personality cult of Te-Ua, the Hauhau had emerged out of an earlier, land-based movement, the King movement: a flood of British and other Europeans arriving in New Zealand in the 1850s had prompted the formation of a 'pan-tribal anti-land-selling league', as historian James Gump writes in his account of nineteenth-century Maori conflicts.[59] Fighting over land tenure peaked in the 1860s in what were known as the Maori wars, at first rallying new tribes to the King movement and eventually morphing into the broader, more dramatic Hauhau (Pai Marire) movement. The theatricalization of the conflict over the land—and the bloodiness of the conflict—earned the Hauhau movement a bleak place in the annals of official Maori history. Historian Paul Clark describes the Hauhau as having been vilified in travel guides and school history, which pitted the 'mad' Hauhau against the forces of law and order. Clark's succinct account of the process captures its narrative line: 'On 2 March 1865 New Zealand history gained its first martyr and New Zealand historiography her first madmen'. The reiteration of the tragedy of the missionary assassination had become common knowledge, as had the Hauhaus' belief that they were impervious to bullets: 'words like fanaticism,

---

54. In Lanternari, *The Religions of the Oppressed*, 251.

55. In Burridge, *New Heaven, New Earth*, 18.

56. Cited in Burridge, *New Heaven, New Earth*, 19.

57. In Burridge, *New Heaven, New Earth*, 19.

58. Burridge, *New Heaven, New Earth*, 19–20.

59. Gump, 'The Imperialism of Cultural Assimilation', 102. See also M. P. K. Sorrenson, 'The Maori King Movement, 1858–1885', in Robert Chapman and Keith Sinclair, eds., *Studies of a Small Democracy: Essays in Honour of Willis Airey* (Auckland: University of Auckland Press, 1963), 33–55. Clark notes that although settlement had developed in the 1840s, a New Zealand population census in 1858 indicated that the European settlers outnumbered the Maoris ('Hauhau', 1).

reversion, and barbarism [abounded]' 'in the education of New Zealanders, and in popular and scholarly writing'.[60] This officialization of the conflict had the added benefit of a thrilling depiction of natives gone amok; they were not just savage, they were clinically mad.

But they were also typically eulogized, less for their madness than for the ancient warrior culture their practices conjured up in the minds of their ethnographer dramaturges. What Clark describes is a narrativization process that powerfully dramatizes the war between the 'brutal' Maoris and the British. Now classic works published by the New Zealand writer and publicity officer James Cowan (1870–1943) in 1922 and by S. Barton Babbage (1916–2012) in 1937 riled up their readers with fantasies of a warrior culture as terrifying as it was powerfully subdued. Cowan prefaces his study with grandiloquent terms, describing 'desperation', a 'long racial conflict', 'many a day spent . . . on the fern-grown site of some fortification or on some battle-ground, in gathering from the veteran bush fighters of two races the stories of the past', and 'stirring tales . . . drilled into the memory of the native of the old type by unvarying repetition in the tribal home'. The mixture of romantic adulation and paternalism was best expressed in his invocation of 'the generation of men now fast passing away'. The 'young Maori's mind', he reported, 'has been transformed by books and colleges, and he has lost the marvellous memorializing powers of his forefathers'.[61] In this adulating and romantic view, Maoris had been a natural people, close to the earth; European learning had corrupted them. And the Maoris' own war against the Europeans had destroyed what little primitive spirit they once had.

Cowan was not immune to the use of comparison in describing the 'friendly mist which befogged a foe', one of the central beliefs of the Hauhau, denoting their supposed ability to hide themselves from their enemies by uttering a spell, the *huna*, which provoked a fog. He wrote: 'we read of very much the same kind of supernatural mist in the "Iliad."'[62] This comment is dropped into his account like an afterthought, an aside; yet it connects these 'holy warriors' with the Grecian past, simultaneously removing their story in time while bringing it closer to his readers' assumed areas of knowledge and points of reference. The analogy is casual, and similar analogies are sparse; yet their effect, to elicit his readers' sympathy, as well as admiration or awe, for these tragic heroes captures the pathos of Cowan's narrative in a classical turn of rhetoric foregrounding pity mixed with edification.

Babbage similarly condoned the Hauhau for their political resistance, understandable, he argued, given the 'land . . . issue': 'it is no wonder that there was a reversion to the old primitive policy' and 'not strange that religious enthusiasm was invoked in the political struggle. Under strain and stress there is frequently a tendency to turn towards the supernatural. Hauhauism provided a fresh battle cry, promising them deliverance from their degradation'. However, he added, 'at times it was almost the form of madness, and psychologically was a kind of group neurosis'.[63] Freud's *Totem and Taboo* (1913) had twenty years before likened the 'psychic life of savages' to 'neurotics'. Inquiry into savages' 'stages of development' and 'legends, myths and fairy tales' offered modern Europeans a wormhole into their own pre-conscious past.[64] Similarly, for Babbage, the history of these savages offered a literature that looked deeply into the workings of the human mind in a child-like state, where mimesis governs all relations between nature, its symbols, and the self.

The *niu*, Moses, Te-Ua, and their government, as well as their postwar historiographers, showed forth a battle over an autochthonous claim to territory, obliquely expressed through the dramatic creolization of biblical, European, and Maori objects, practices, and beliefs. This geocultural drama staged what cultural geographer Joël Bonnemaison (1940–1997) has described as the 'circulation/iconology dialectic' by which icons transform as they move. This dialectic, often epitomized in objects and narratives, troubles the standard opposition of 'opening vs.

60. Clark, 'Hauhau', vii.

61. Cowan, *The New Zealand Wars*, v.

62. Cowan, *The New Zealand Wars*, 9.

63. Babbage, *Hauhauism*, 71. The term 'group neurosis' to describe the Hauhau was perhaps first used by the moral psychologist and professor of anthropology I. L. G. Sutherland (1897–1952), in *The Maori Situation* (Wellington, NZ: Harry H. Tombs, 1935), 31.

64. Sigmund Freud, *Totem and Taboo*, trans. A. A. Brill (New York: Vintage Books, 1946), 3.

closing, universalism vs. localism, cosmopolitanism vs. isolation'.[65] Genealogies shifted on new terrain, in a translatio from West to South and, in disciplinary terms, from missionary religion to historiography. Genealogically and choreographically, the Maori movement conjugated icons and spaces mimetically to displace the (Western) fantasy of scientific universalism in the particularities of counter-mimetic acts.

ROMANTIC RECUPERATION: MODERN ANTHROPOLOGY'S PHANTASMATIC BACKYARD

The romantic recuperation of millennialist movements such as the Papuan Vailala Madness and the Maori Hauhau into twentieth-century literature on anti-colonial revolution belies the fact that these early movements were also composed of strong measures of colonial mimesis and iconographic recombination. In the ambivalent exercises of counter-imitation that natives performed, Europeans encountered something slightly different from what they thought natives represented as supposedly barbarian ancestors of the whites: not pure experience, as Agamben suggests of the West's notion of the state of 'infancy' allegedly resting at the dawn of civilization, prior to language and gesture, but an ambiguous show of iconographic, linguistic, and narrative recuperation by which the colonial saw himself mirrored back in a disconcertingly distorted form.[66] This show of counter-mimesis could not, the colonial thought, represent the West's infancy, though natives came to be increasingly imagined as a key to its future. Similarly, natives recuperated European tropes as a way to empower themselves, not through separatism but through wilful assimilation and back-translation. Back-translation implies the movement or transfer (the translatio) *back into* one language of the words or phrases exported from it into another in an act of translation. Expressions like 'Heave 'em up' and 'Me wantum kaikai' or performances such as 'making Christmas' adopted colonial expressions, defamiliarizing them through repronunciation, and reperforming them within a context of indigenous recollectivization that pushed the colonial to the margins of the event. The event, meanwhile, became apparent as (virtually) unintelligible to observers who thought (nominally) that they knew what they were bringing to the 'savage', namely civilization, (European) language, religion, and everyday articles such as cutlery and dress.

The doubling of mimesis is nearly comical in its parallelism: the colonial West and the colonized South were equally finding in the alien body of the other a representation of their own past and their (soon to be liberated) future. These nativist movements' assimilation into twentieth-century anthropological agendas that pitted a now corrupt, decadent West against the supposed purity of the savage other thus fails to take the heterogeneous mixture of practices, the constant de- and reterritorializations, the back-translations, into account. Indeed, the Papuan and Maori mixtures of 'heathen' and 'Christian' religiosity do not, on closer scrutiny, immediately reveal the kind of uncompromising upheaval that anthropologists such as E. W. P. Chinnery (1887–1972) and A. C. Haddon (1855–1940) described in their landmark essay 'Five New Religious Cults in British New Guinea', published in *Hibbert Journal* (1917). For Chinnery and Haddon, 'social unrest' and the emergence of new forms of religion, especially when accompanied by the emergence of a heroic leader, occurred in civilizations 'at all stages'. The present 'fervor' that they noted in New Guinea constituted a paradigmatic form of religious renewal in the face of colonization.[67]

Instead, new waves of writing on decolonization movements remained tethered to old tropes. Jagged movements, rolling eyes, and apparently epidemic hysteria—now signalling a 'good' pure

65. Joël Bonnemaison, *Culture and Space: Conceiving a New Cultural Geography*, ed. Chantal Blanc-Pamard et al., trans. Josée Pénot-Demetry (London: Tauris, 2005), 43.

66. Agamben, *Infancy and History*.

67. 'An awakening of religious activity is a frequent characteristic of periods of social unrest. The weakening or disruption of the old social order may stimulate new and often bizarre ideals, and these may give rise to religious movements that strive to sanction social and political aspirations. Communities that feel themselves oppressed anticipate the emergence of a hero who will restore their prosperity and prestige. And when the people are imbued with religious fervor the expected hero will be regarded as a Messiah. Phenomena of this kind are well known in history, and are not unknown at the present day among all peoples in all stages of civilization'. E. W. P. Chinnery and A. C. Haddon, 'Five New Religious Cults in British New Guinea', *Hibbert Journal* 15.3 (1917): 448–63, 455; cited in Burridge, *New Heaven, New Earth*, 3–4.

primitivism—all characterized the uprisings and revolts taking the colonial world by storm, as told in the new literature on crosscultural anthropology. In Lanternari's grandiloquent terms, 'the *cry for freedom* rising from the throats of the oppressed peoples is fraught with lessons for us to learn . . . . These new worlds, so very different from ours, are now experiencing a crisis; but their impact upon the West has thrown our civilization into shock, initiating an era of travail which can be fruitful for all mankind if it leads to a broader humanism than the world has ever before known'.[68] His study *Movimenti religiosi di libertà e di salvezza dei popoli oppressi* [The Religions of the Oppressed: A Study of Modern Messianic Cults] (1960)—a title suggesting compassion, romantic allegiance, and a paternalistic sort of emotionality, gesturing towards a unified world connecting 'ethnological', 'primitive civilizations' with 'modern', 'Western' ones[69]—claimed inspiration from the oppressed. 'Today', he wrote, 'as we watch the so-called savage or backward peoples [cosiddetti 'incolti' o 'selvaggi'] come to the fore and take their place on the world stage, it becomes the cultural, political, and moral duty of those who belong to the so-called cultured and elite civilization [civiltà cosiddetta 'colta' ed 'eletta'] to recognize the call to freedom and liberation rising from the mouths of thousands of prophets who speak from the jungles of the Congo, from the remote islands of Melanesia'.[70]

Not only were oppressed people, in Africa and the South Pacific, rising up against the oppressive conditions in which they lived—serving the modern historian with a romantic model to emulate—they were also worthy of the historian's interest insofar as they were in a sense part of an extended 'family'. As with the Native Americans discussed in the last chapter, these African and Oceanic people, Lanternari wrote, '[revealed] characteristics found in ancient or in prehistoric cultures . . . [at] the roots of our present Western civilization'. The myth of primitive ancestry, as ancient as new world 'discoveries' themselves, prompted, in this context, a new

genealogy, hinging on the projected reversal of the oppressor-oppressed relation: the West was now to heed the third world, which it articulated as its forgotten but passionate, forward-thinking, colonial cousin. 'This call' for freedom, Lanternari intoned, 'demands an answer from the Western world'.[71] At the time of the 1963 preface to the English edition of Lanternari's work, three years of anti-colonial struggles had brought the purpose of this kind of study to even greater light: crowds of people in the French and Belgian Congo, in Upper Volta, Sierra Leone, Ivory Coast, Tanganyika, and other parts of Africa had 'shaken off the yoke of colonial rule'.[72] The religious tenor of these liberationist movements was not lost on Lanternari, who saw in the future emancipation of the world's people and concomitant 'erasure' of all 'evil' an ancient eschatological trope fundamental to the very institution as well as the progress of civilization. 'The problem of the relationship between history and eschatology', he wrote, and the 'contradictory, yet indissoluble, bond between current reality and future goals . . . [which] lies at the root of almost every major human experience' was a question that had not yet 'been solved even for the West'.[73] But the West was ready to learn from its colonial peers.

Lanternari underscored the political tenor of this collective brand of excitement, recuperating 'nativist' movements into a global rhetoric of revolt. For Lanternari, 'the birth of these movements can only be understood in the light of historical conditions relating to the colonial experiences and to the striving of subject peoples to become emancipated'.[74] For Worsley, writing in 1968 at the peak of the counter-cultural movement of the 1960s, 'the cults . . . express social and moral solidarity and independence in a highly charged emotional situation resulting from the overthrow or questioning of ancient ethical values'.[75] Social historian George Rosen (1910–1977), also writing in 1968 in *Madness in Society*, similarly argued that 'movements [that] derived from the clash

68. Lanternari, *The Religions of the Oppressed*, viii.

69. Lanternari, *The Religions of the Oppressed*, vi–vii.

70. Lanternari, *The Religions of the Oppressed*, vii; and Vittorio Lanternari, *Movimenti religiosi di libertà e di salvezza dei popoli oppressi* (Milan: Feltrinelli, 1960), 10.

71. Lanternari, *The Religions of the Oppressed*, vii.

72. Lanternari, *The Religions of the Oppressed*, xi.

73. Lanternari, *The Religions of the Oppressed*, xii.

74. Lanternari, *The Religions of the Oppressed*, v.

75. Worsley, *The Trumpet Shall Sound*, 248.

of peoples and cultures, particularly in colonial settings . . . occur within emotionally charged and explosive situations . . . where there is dissatisfaction with existing conditions'.[76] Eric Hobsbawm (1917–2012), in *Primitive Rebels* (1965), emphasized the 'revolutionary' rhetoric of 'hope' in 'a complete and radical change in the world which will be reflected in the millennium'—a 'hope', he added, 'not confined to primitivism'.[77] For the Oxford sociologist of religions Bryan R. Wilson (1926–2004), millennialist movements were politically motivated, if not 'revolutionist'. In *Magic and the Millennium* (1973), Wilson argued that 'millennialism represents . . . .a vision of a different social order'.[78] So, too, historian Michael Adas, in *Prophets of Rebellion: Millenarian Protest Movements against the European Colonial Order* (1979), argued that 'millenarian protest movements' and 'prophetic rebellion' from Java and New Zealand to East-Central India, German East Africa (Tanzania), and British Burma, offered a comparative history of 'social protest'.[79] But the recuperation of the Vailala and other messianic 'cults' into a modern social scientific discourse on revolutionary liberation and political emancipation side-stepped the extent to which these movements were also staged in strong iconographically and narratologically assimilationist terms. Whereas they called on 'mnemonic reserves' and native genealogies, mixing native with Christian iconography, they rarely translated into concerted political action in the first instance. Trances and ecstatic visions suggested a performative withdrawal from the colonial situation, a messianic temporality seeking future liberation from the past yet also paradoxically becoming European, becoming 'white', without whites or Europeans around.

The rise of anthropology as a discursive platform for discussing, analysing, and interpreting societies across the world, often in the service of government administration, prompted the relative extinction of the choreomania diagnosis as a strictly medical disease. No longer visible as a purely (or a merely) biomedical entity, choreomania—and allied choreiform activities, including trance and possession, psychotropic and ecstatic states—came to be subsumed under the general banner of culture. These were not abnormal (i.e., pathological) activities but objects of fascination with the other (primitive, pre-modern, non-Western), of nostalgia, and, eventually, of a romantic annexation to the broader contestatory movement of the 1960s and 1970s. As the nineteenth-century medicalization of corporeal upheavals moved increasingly into the realm of cultural discourse, what McCarren calls medicine and dance's twin capacities for discovering 'new realities for the body' resulted in a new politicization of body culture. Writers entrenched in anthropological discourses on otherness wove romantic longings for the primeval past into a scientific discourse on social and political protest. So the genealogy—the choreography—of the dancing disease took a new turn. Narratives of alterity and the creolization of European and colonial iconographies prompted early twentieth-century ethnographic writing to extend the discursive project of mapping political uprisings onto social and corporeal terrain, folding a new wave of theatrical revolts into old fantasies of primitive frenzy. These new scenes described an era of sociopolitical change, genealogically linked to the old but tending towards an imagined common futurity rooted discursively in everything ancient, pre-linguistic, and organic in the long history of a (self-styled) corrupted and alienated West. In the next chapter, popular culture rooted in black and Latin dance moves erupts in a show of collective and convulsive gestures on the American dance scene, gathered once more into the medical discourse on the dancing disease. Psychoanalytic theory, indebted to primitivist fantasies of the 'savage' and yet simultaneously childlike body, articulates a vision of America colonized by sexually charged spontaneity. Choreic, jagged moves in the popular dance scene become all the more contentious and simultaneously mimicked as they tap into fantasies of unruly, spirited dancing ascribed to foreigners and to the underclasses—at the same time unraveling a language of desire and of longing for free movement.

---

76. Rosen, *Madness*, 221–223.

77. Eric J. Hobsbawm, *Primitive Rebels: Studies in Archaic Forms of Social Movement in the 19th and 20th Centuries* (New York: Norton, 1965), 57.

78. Bryan R. Wilson, *Magic and the Millennium: A Sociological Study of Religious Movements of Protest among Tribal and Third-World Peoples* (New York and Evanston: Harper & Row, 1973), 6.

79. Michael Adas, *Prophets of Rebellion: Millenarian Protest Movements against the European Colonial Order* (Chapel Hill: University of North Carolina Press, 1979).

11

Monstrous Grace
Blackness and the New Dance 'Crazes'

Nowadays we dance morning, noon and night. What is more, we are unconsciously, while we dance, warring . . . against fat, against sickness, and against nervous troubles. For we are exercising. We are making ourselves lithe and slim and healthy, and these are things that all the reformers in the world could not do for us.

—Irene Castle, *Modern Dancing* (1914)

Everybody, almost the whole world, is dancing the new dances.

—A. A. Brill, 'The Psychopathology of the New Dances' (1914)

We are only too tempted to view as happy a people that makes us happy when we view it, because of the poetic or aesthetic emotion that its spectacle provides us.

—Michel Leiris, 'L'ethnographe devant le colonialisme' (1950)

PRIMITIVISM AND THE SAVAGE IDEAL

Writing in 1950, surrealist anthropologist Michel Leiris (1901–1990) cautioned his readers about the 'poetic and aesthetic emotion' that the spectacle of a faraway people provided to sentimental observers.[1] Colonialism, he argued, reflected a fantasy of indigenous wholesomeness and primitive integrity that exalted anthropologists, who were stimulated by the thoughts of revolts and revolutions emanating from the subjects of their research. But ethnographers and anthropologists had to fight battles on their home turf first.[2] Civil liberties, equality among the sexes, and other pressing political needs had to be addressed in Europe as well as in the colonies. It was not sufficient to gape at colonial subjects rising up on native soil. The nostalgic proximity between European and colonial peoples that Leiris noted, and the theatrical relation that he recognized between European academics and colonial subjects, revealed a philosophical rift. As this and the previous chapter argue, the spectacle of historical crisis spawned an ambivalent body of writing marked by the rise of scientific ideas about cultural difference. This was what Claude Lévi-Strauss (1908–2009), in a 1952 study commissioned by the newly formed UNESCO, called the illusion of monstrosity: in lieu of the 'natural phenomenon' that the idea of cultural diversity might imply, ethnographers were producing a scandal of difference founded on the utter alterity of the 'savage', the 'other', those who are not 'from here' ('de chez nous').[3]

---

1. Michel Leiris, 'L'ethnographe devant le colonialisme', in *Cinq études d'ethnologie* (Paris: Denoël/Gonthier, 1969), 83–122, 88, 112.
2. Leiris, 'L'ethnographe devant le colonialisme', 88, 112.
3. Claude Lévi-Strauss, *Race et histoire* (Paris: Denoël, 1987), 19.

Although it was gaining a new flavour of political urgency at the dawn of the 1960s social movements, this primitivist fantasy was not new. The idea of the collective, ancient, dancing other—at once savage, fascinating, and undisciplined—ran through the history of nineteenth- and twentieth-century intellectual culture. Increasingly, as this chapter shows, the fantasy of the primitive dancing 'other' was racialized—specifically, made black—and the tension over this other's proximity to 'rational' European man was intensified. No longer only a denizen of the Grecian past or the Oriental colony, the frenzied dancing body was increasingly now understood as indigenous to a new black modernity. In Burt's terms, the 'alien' body of modernity was primitive, feminine, disruptive, and energetic; it was also a body (and place) to which one (imaginatively) returned, as to a dark and ultimately unrecoverable womb. Further paradigmatic of what Girard calls the 'monstrous double'—as I showed in the previous chapter, an encounter between 'an "I" and an "Other" caught up in a constant interchange of differences'— the 'alien' body of modernity took other bodily forms into itself to become its own (m)other.[4] In becoming 'possessed',[5] in vulturizing and ventriloquizing other corporealities, modern subjects imagined themselves double: at once that which they came from (a fantasy awkwardly conjugated for some with post-Darwinian discomfort at the notion of a common African heritage) and that which they went towards (as I showed in the previous chapter, the shared promise of a new 'third world'); that which they ingested, mimicked, and recorporealized and that which they spit back out, cleaned up, and transformed—performing what Gilroy calls a 'politics of transfiguration', by which oppressors and oppressed continuously undercut one another with cultural and countercultural reappropriations.[6] Modernity emerged contrapuntally to a phantasmatic 'past' that had,

according to this ac/dc logic, to be outgrown, superseded (*again and again*).

This was epitomized in the 'African' contribution to modernity of Josephine Baker, what bell hooks describes as Baker's 'lived contradiction': the projection of an Africanist fantasy concocted out of Baker's African-American heritage for Europeans telling her what black dance should or should not be.[7] As Burt notes, Baker's moves, by her own account, were likened to St. Vitus's dance. In the *Revue Nègre*, she wrote: 'One of the critics compared our movements to St Vitus's Dance. "What kind of dance is that?" I asked. "It's a nervous disorder that makes you tremble all over." "That's not a sickness," I retorted. "It's the way we act in church back home." "Here in France, God likes us to kneel quietly." Why didn't God demand the same behaviour in France as in Harlem? It would make things so much easier'.[8] What Baker saw as normal corporeality 'back home' in Harlem was understood as a sickness in Europe, a nervous disorder hardly distinguishable from Baker's brand of black dance.

Burt argues that the language of 'dislocation, disruption and frenzy' used by critics to describe Baker's performances 'might otherwise have summed up the social experiences of metropolitan modernity'.[9] Baker performed freedom from nineteenth-century bourgeois culture, summing up at once a modernist thrust towards social, scientific, and technological progress, Burt points out, and a white European desire to commune with the racial other.[10] For McCarren, modern responses to Baker's ambivalent blackness were symptomatic of a wider trend according to which African and African-American dance signalled the 'potential to represent madness'.[11] The link between neurological, psychiatric, and African figures of disorder was tight. Citing satirist Georges Thenon (known as 'Rip') in his preface to the 1927 collection of lithographs *Le Tumulte noir* [Black Tumult], by

---

4. René Girard, *Violence and the Sacred*, trans. Patrick Gregory (Baltimore: Johns Hopkins University Press, 1977), 164.

5. Girard, *Violence and the Sacred*, 165.

6. Gilroy, *The Black Atlantic*, 37.

7. Burt, *Alien Bodies*, 70. Jayna Brown compellingly argues that Baker remained throughout her career a 'mediating figure between the nations and races', ostensibly (at least performatively) loyal to De Gaulle but also 'multi-dispositioned', representative of primitivism—the '[timeless] savage'—in a context of French negrophilia but also more sprawlingly of Haitian, Tunisian, and Vietnamese colonial regimes and the 'infinitely metropolitan' sophisticate. Jayna Brown, *Babylon Girls: Black Women Performers and the Shaping of the Modern* (Durham, NC: Duke University Press, 2008), 252–254.

8. Josephine Baker and Joseph Bouillon, *Josephine* (London: W. H. Allen, 1978), 53; cited in Burt, *Alien Bodies*, 69. See also McCarren, *Dancing Machines*, 175.

9. Burt, *Alien Bodies*, 81.

10. Burt, *Alien Bodies*, 81.

11. McCarren, *Dancing Machines*, 178.

illustrator Paul Colin (1892–1985), McCarren makes note of the fashion for black—African as well as African-American—dances that were imagined in the early twentieth century as physical and mental illnesses: what 'Rip' teasingly called the 'Charlestonesque epidemic' was also a 'Charentonesque epidemic', an epidemic of physical contortions and alienation worthy of the psychiatric hospital Charenton.[12] 'Negropathy' and 'Negromania' were similarly, for 'Rip', direct conduits to the madhouse.[13] Jayna Brown, drawing from *The Key to Uncle Tom's Cabin* (1853), by Harriet Beecher Stowe (1811–1896), further underscores the science of phrenology in 'proving' that blacks were Oriental: not only was the 'Negro temperament' 'vivid' and fanciful, continually possessed by the workings of the imagination, but black, 'like oriental[,] nations'—in Stowe's terms, 'the Hebrew of old and the Oriental nations of the present'— 'incline much toward outward expression, violent gesticulations, and agitating movements of the body'.[14]

McCarren argues that conjugated with this primitivist fantasy was a fascination for all things machinic: cinema, together with ever more rapid industrialization and technologization, heralded a new choreographic vocabulary of tics and jerks, what would later become the popping and krumping, slow-motion effects, robot imitations, and corporeal fragmentation of hip-hop, or what I further call an *alterkinetic* aesthetics that favours the skip, the hop, the glide, and the rotation in equal measure, and smooth as well as striated rhythms. In this chapter, black and Latin American moves, described as characterizing a primitivist and machinic, hyper-angular modernity, reached a new peak as popular and medical discourses surrounding a deluge of new dance 'crazes' persisted in calling them sick, '[symptomatic] of an epidemic of contagion', as dance critic André Levinson (1887–1933) put it.[15] Yet, as discussions of sex bubbled up in neuroscientific, psychiatric, and psychological literature, in the wake of Freud's writings

after his studies with Charcot and his own flirtations with primitivist art and myth, a new surge of opinions regarding the (social and sexual, and the emphatically *re*productive) healthiness of the new dances also signalled a discursive turn.

The 'tumescence' characteristic of the 'new dances' represented a healthy outlet for sexual energy, in the opinion of at least one clinical neurologist and psychiatrist, Dr. A. A. Brill (1874–1948), who was close to Freud at the time. But just as the discourse on sex required tasteful and discreet framing and perpetual qualification, so, too, debates regarding the pathological (or healthy) character of the 'new dances' centred on quantity as well as quality. Too much dancing was problematic; so too angular, flailing, overly theatrical motions (imitating animals, for example), and overt performances of sexual attraction were taboo in much of the European and American popular press, which parroted for the most part the new social sciences.

The fragmentary discourse on the new dances was one in which the entire social apparatus was at stake. 'Reading' the fashion for new dances was reading a social choreography in which a broad range of choreographic aesthetics came into play: some apparently symptomatic of epilepsy and hysteria, others apparently indicative of low social class or foreign status. Ambivalence regarding the healthiness of the 'new dances' and the dance 'craze' was thus ambivalence regarding the way health should look. As this chapter argues, beauty—nearly always construed as the expression of good health and moral rectitude—had at once to be natural and artificial, effortless and crafted. 'Grace' was intentional, cultivated; it differentiated itself from automatic, animal moves. To dance with elegance and grace was to rewrite the body as a body of civilization and modernity. But, I argue in this chapter, the spectre of primitivism continued to haunt lithe, 'modern' figures of beauty, as their precondition and triumphant countersign. The 'modernity' of modern social dancing—most prominently, the tango—was widely imagined to rise out of a disorderly past:

12. McCarren, *Dancing Machines*, 175.

13. McCarren, *Dancing Machines*, 175.

14. Brown, *Babylon Girls*, 78. See Harriet Beecher Stowe, *A Key to Uncle Tom's Cabin: Presenting the Original Facts and Documents upon Which the Story Is Founded, Together with Corroborative Statements Verifying the Truth of the Work* (Boston: John P. Jewett & Co., 1858), 27. Stowe further writes that the 'negro race' is 'peculiarly susceptible and impressible' and particularly 'extravagant' in religious meetings: 'They will laugh, weep, embrace each other convulsively, and sometimes become entirely paralyzed and cataleptic', in contrast to the 'cool, logical and practical' 'Anglo-Saxon race' (27–28). Blacks are defined not only in terms of effusive gesture (significantly, as I have shown throughout this book, like another class of 'Orientals', Jews) but also by excessively rapid changes between such seemingly 'peculiar' states, so that convulsions lead to catalepsy.

15. Cited in McCarren, *Dancing Machines*, 175.

a fiction conserved and massaged to prove modern society's upward trajectory. Through dance, modernity emerged contrapuntally, as a symbol of ascent and disentanglement.

Baker's moves, although 'read' as African, primitive, and machinic, excited the early twentieth-century imagination inasmuch as they eluded full legibility, frustrating the closure of representation. They appeared to many contemporary writers uncanny: familiar and yet foreign, animal and automatic, mechanical and biological. Yet they were highly stylized, careful, deliberate, crafted, artful, and as such potentially repeatable—in short, choreographic. As an emphatically choreographic form of what may otherwise look like a sort of nervous disease, St. Vitus's dance (still imagined, in Baker's retelling, as a spontaneous and unrepeatable disorder), Baker's jagged gestures and aesthetic incongruities signalled a performative 'return of the repressed', a term Freud coined around this time to describe the re-emergence of ancient traumas theatricalized in the modern body and mind. By standing in for what was old and diseased and simultaneously for what was fresh and new, Baker appeared on the modern stage as a powerful cipher for the articulation of white and black Europe and America's fraught relationships to their imagined pasts. Her 'banana skirt' was nearly parodic of African savagery, yet her grace and choreographic precision were reminiscent to some of the Russian ballet. Indeed, nearly coincident with a new wave of enthusiasm over stylized 'black' moves was a trend in ancient Greek 'maenad' dances inspired by vase paintings popularized by, among others, the classical scholar Jane Harrison (1850–1928) following her archaeological excavations, as well as the flowing tunics and 'natural' movement of Isadora Duncan (1877–1927)—arguably the most famous of early twentieth-century maenads, for whom dancing was a 'Dionysian ecstasy', an enabler of disindividuation, feminine communion, and cathartic collapse.[16] Influenced by Duncan's romantic brand of Dionysianism and free, 'natural' movement, Vaslav Nijinsky (1889–1950), further spurred on by the visionary impresario Sergei Diaghilev (1872–1929), brought his own brand of primitive, titillating, feline sexuality and godlike prowess to the concert hall stage. Soon, as the British popular writer Samuel Beach Chester (b. 1880) wrote, everyone was clad in Russian exotica and attempting balletic—as well as tango and other dance—feats.[17]

Dionysianism merged with colonial exoticism, bringing black and Oriental moves to western Europe via the American South and Russian East. In Khanna's terms, psychoanalysis was a colonial discipline, drawing from national and colonial archaeology and anthropology to imagine 'the unconscious, the evolutionary trajectory of human civilization, and the origins of repression'.[18] After Darwin, many whites tried to but could not shake the image of a shared African ancestry, an image that confounded travellers active in the everyday business of colonial administration and ethnographic research. Yet many 'moderns' in Europe and America—white and black—aspired to a world of greater racial harmony, even transcendence, reaching imaginatively towards an ever more stylized Africa. The aesthetic passage to modernity was forked: African, Greek, and European at the same time; and aesthetically jagged, rapturous, and smooth. The 'alien' body of a mixed-race modernity discovered exciting angularities in African masks and in Baker's Charleston but recuperated these into a still fraught discourse on disorder, unreason, and the dancing 'craze'.

BLACKNESS AND GESTURAL MODERNITY

'Blackness' is highly disputed terrain, though consistent in concepts of blackness and the recent history of blacks is what Gilroy has called a position 'in but not necessarily of the modern, western world'.[19] Modernity in this view is

16. Isadora Duncan, *My Life* (New York: Norton, 2013), 131; cited in Mark Franko, *Dancing Modernism/Performing Politics* (Bloomington: Indiana University Press, 1995), 17. See also Fiona Macintosh, 'Dancing Maenads in Early Twentieth-Century Britain', in Fiona Macintosh, ed., *The Ancient Dancer in the Modern World: Responses to Greek and Roman Dance* (Oxford: Oxford University Press, 2010), 188–208. On the relationship between Duncan, Nijinsky, and ragtime, see also Susan Manning, *Ecstasy and the Demon: The Dances of Mary Wigman* (Minneapolis: University of Minnesota Press, 2006), xxiii.

17. Samuel Beach Chester, *Secrets of the Tango: Its History and How to Dance It. Fully Illustrated with Photographs and Diagrams* (London: T. Werner Laurie, [1914]), 55.

18. Khanna, *Dark Continents*, 26.

19. Gilroy, *The Black Atlantic*, 29.

Western, and though it is composed of black (and brown) men and women, these men and women are marginalized, contained within but cast to the side of an inexorably white centre, in spite of the constant traffic between white and black subjects in what Gilroy terms the intellectual, social, and cultural heritage of the Black Atlantic. For Thomas DeFrantz, blackness can be articulated in aesthetic terms—significantly, a broadly white experience of the illegibility of these terms. Black movements performed on the concert hall stage in the first half of the twentieth century were 'untidy and dangerous to some white viewers because their aesthetic imperatives were largely inscrutable'.[20] Black dance epitomized an obscure, 'antimodern' aesthetics, what DeFrantz characterizes as 'downward-directed energy, insistent rhythmicity, angularity of line, percussive rupture of underlying flow, individualism within a group dynamic, and access to a dynamic "flash of the spirit" that confirms simultaneously temporal presence and ubiquitous spirituality'.[21]

Blackness and Theban, Dionysian Orientalism served as twin phantasms underpinning scientific concepts of modernity, which do not so much sideline black and Oriental others but set them at the heart of the modern enterprise, just where it becomes unhinged from the imagined illegibility and obscurity of the past. According to this reading, modernity appears as articulation, intelligibilization; but, significantly, it requires a fantasy of the unintelligible against which to set this process of bringing to light. Disorderly dance becomes the object of intelligibilization against which modernity sets itself. Rather than suggesting a triumphalist scientism that simply makes light out of the dark, this view argues that intelligibilization is a constant process of negotiation, a constant interplay of sameness and difference, a politics of transculturation and transfiguration. This is not only a 'white' problem but a problem of modernity as that which discursively and performatively sets itself in a mimetic relationship to the putatively obscure past. This 'modernity' construes disorderly figures of alterity to see itself as like but fundamentally different from its own distortions. Aesthetic 'modernity' cannot do without its twisting, 'Charentonesque' others.

Choreomanias, while not equivalent to 'black dance' in the sense DeFrantz suggests, shared many characteristics with it: a purportedly 'antimodern' aesthetics, angularity, and insistent rhythmicity. But the choreomanias diverge from this in being even more phantasmatically alien than black dance. The choreomanias, while black, inasmuch as they are imagined as pre- and antimodern, are also characterized, I have shown, by their irregular rhythmicity and disorganized movement, rather than the steady persistence of what DeFrantz characterizes as a deep, 'downward-directed' percussive beat. The choreomanias, by and large, suggested 'upward' movement, a slightly 'hysterical' tendency towards hallucination, as well as the sort of collective Dionysianism that Brazilian artist Hélio Oiticica (1937–1980) describes as dissolving the 'I'.[22] Rather than demonstrating 'individualism within a group dynamic', individuals prey to the dancing disease disappeared into groups and collectivities, pathologically losing their individuality in a putatively animal return to a pre-civilized, pre-historical, orgiastic (and now increasingly black) state of being. But before being rewritten as sexually productive (reproductive), the blackness of the modern choreomanias had to be discursively purged of the hypersexuality typically attributed to black dance. These dancers were now black yet white, signalling the transfiguration of a 'downward' aesthetic upward.

The paradox of this animal-yet-antique condition beset the discourse on nineteenth-century dancing manias I have described thus far. But with the advent of new animal-like and jagged dances in the twentieth century, a new set of paradoxes emerged. Jazz, tango, and the social dances known as 'animal dances' erupted onto the popular and social dancing scene to trouble medical interpretations of the dancing disease. Recast as a popular and social plague emphasizing youth culture and the contamination of black (as well as occasionally Latin) moves among primarily white people, the dancing 'disease' now signalled a racially marked hyper-locomotion and extreme gregariousness but also a 'healthy' tendency in the white middle classes towards physical sport.

---

20. Thomas F. DeFrantz, *Dancing Revelations: Alvin Ailey's Embodiment of African American Culture* (Oxford: Oxford University Press, 2004), 20.

21. DeFrantz, *Dancing Revelations*, 21.

22. Hélio Oiticica, 'Dance in My Experience (Diary Entries//1965–66)', in Lepecki, ed., *Dance*, 52.

THE JAZZ ERA: THE CAKEWALK AND THE EPILEPTIFORM BLACK

Ragtime and then jazz took Europe and America by storm in the first decades of the twentieth century. For Leiris, this represented an intoxicating youth culture light years away from the stuffy formalism of the previous generation. Jazz was animal and nocturnal. In *L'âge d'homme* [Manhood] (1939), his experimental auto-ethnographic novel, Leiris wrote of an early 1920s Parisian world of all-night jazz clubs suffused with tropical heat, orgiastic abandonment, frenzy, possession, and a feeling of religious communion derived from dancing; eroticism; his first substantial encounter with Negroes; and what he called a broadly pervasive yet naive wonderment at the apparent comforts of modern progress as well as the new rhythms that promised a world that was accepting of his and his peers' awakening sexual desires.[23] This culture of fête and jazz was primitive and modern; it was of the moment, and it was exotic. The fête Leiris described in Paris was characterized by dancing, drinking, and relative rhythmic novelty but also uncertainty with respect to modern life and to a pervasive proselytizing culture celebrating modern civilization and war. America was emerging as a military and cultural power, and the Harlem Renaissance, then at its apogee in the 1920s, was rippling over to France. Leiris and his friends wore tapered trousers and pointy shoes 'to look American', he wrote; they jiggled their shoulders in an attempt to do the '*shimmy*'.[24] But 'modernity' was ambivalent: what was new to them was also what they experienced as primitive, in contrast to a different discourse on modernity that was coming out of the World War I trenches and the reconstruction of the West. That modernity was machinic, cold, and anonymous without ecstasy. It smelled of death rather than life. It was steeped in an old European world attempting to grapple with ruin by moving blindly forward without looking back.

New dances from the American South made their way to fashionable Parisian night clubs.

The bunny hop, the grizzly bear, and soon the Charleston followed in the steps of the parodic 1900s and 1910s cakewalk, bringing a whole new generation of black moves to a Europe giddy with exhaustion from World War I. Whereas the cakewalk, based on ragtime sounds, and according to legend originally performed on southern plantations (for a cake provided by the plantation's master), mimicked white Americans' haughty postures and upright stance, animal dances showcased unabashed copulation. The Bunny Hug, as Nadine George-Graves writes, simulated fornicating rabbits, 'with rapid hopping, shaking, grinding, and wiggling'.[25] The grizzly bear imitated a dancing bear, with clumsy, heavy steps performed on the toes, the body swaying from side to side, and the couple flopped over onto one another, their arms dangling over each other's shoulders. Every once in a while, someone would yell out 'It's a Bear!' and dancers might raise their arms, mimicking a clawing motion. The turkey trot similarly engaged a couple's bent arms waving like turkey wings, while the couple were facing, the man holding the woman at the waist. Again, the man and woman might perform small hops, as the man moved behind the woman with sexual innuendo. Other animal dances included the kangaroo hop, the eagle rock, the horse trot, the kangaroo dip, the chicken scratch, the crab step, the herringbone twist, and the lame duck, while a range of non-animal dances showcased characters and places from the American South, including, most famously, by the 1920s, the Charleston.[26]

Yet, as Gordon has pointed out of the cakewalk, the translation—what I have called the translatio—from 'Negro' to white moves was never simple or unidirectional. White music hall performers rechoreographed cakewalk dances for a spectatorship already accustomed to the epileptic performances that had emerged out of Charcot's clinic and made their way onto Parisian cabaret stages. Epileptic gestures—performed as exaggerated jerkiness, postural inversions, and grimaces—merged on music hall stages with the 'new' black moves, seen as contorted, comical, and grotesque. As Gordon notes, the cakewalk evolved towards an epileptic exhibition;

---

23. Michel Leiris, *L'âge d'homme, précédé de La littérature considérée comme une tauromachie* (Paris: Éditions Gallimard, 1939), 159–160.

24. Leiris, *L'âge d'homme*, 162.

25. Nadine George-Graves, '"Just Like Being at the Zoo": Primitivity and Ragtime Dance', in Julie Malnig, ed., *Ballroom, Boogie, Shimmy Sham, Shake: A Social and Popular Dance Reader* (Urbana: University of Illinois Press, 2009), 55–71, 61.

26. George-Graves, '"Just Like Being at the Zoo,"' 61–63.

black gestures were 'reworked and denatured' by music hall artists according to French audience expectations cultivated in universal expositions, human zoos, and the racial classification of Africans as subhuman in the popular press.[27] As cabaret singer and belle époque actress Yvette Guilbert (1865–1944) noted, black music had 'unhinged' French families, who pivoted or teetered off their axes—they were 'désaxés', off balance; 'déhanchés', swinging their hips; they waddled ('[ils] se dandinent'). What Guilbert called the 'African virus' had possessed them like an epidemic of chicken pox.[28] Gordon further notes Levinson's chastisement of 'Negro dance' as a 'black virus upon European civilization' that spread through dance halls; for Levinson, this 'virus' was '[symptomatic] of an epidemic contagion of society which should concern the pathologist'.[29]

As Browning has argued, black and Latin rhythms have quintessentially worried white European and American moralists threatened by the apparently uncontrollable, uncontainable quality that they express.[30] Black music in particular was thought to exercise its 'voodoo' on upright (white) citizens vulnerable to contagion and the spectre of death. Yet the extent to which this threat was recuperated and transformed by European culture and society in the early decades of the twentieth century suggests that black culture from the African colonies and the American South—reaching Chicago and Harlem—was also imagined according to myths of alterity and antiquity founded in a fantasy of a primitive Grecian past mingling with the mechanical gestures of neurological disease. Civilization and culture, animal rhythms and childlike irrationality, were two sides of one coin in the medical (and moral) discourse, and though moralists and pathologists alike were concerned with the apparently 'viral' spread of blackness on European soil, this 'virus' immediately recombined with new strands of jagged gesturality on the ground, further to confound aesthetic delineations. As a photo advertisement for a vaudeville spoof on the Charleston shows (fig. 11.1), the recuperation of black moves by exaggeratedly sick, thin, ungainly, distorted white bodies made these into quintessentially white pathologies: dancers dressed in everyday business attire, a trouser leg half pulled up, eyes bugged out, heavily rimmed in dark paint to suggest fatigue bordering on psychopathological alienation, suggested that whites could not keep up with blacks. The whites are self-mocking, suggesting the recuperation of and possibly imagined ascendancy over an invasion of black moves. The dancers present a caricature of the Charleston, performed most famously by Baker at the Folies Bergère. Significantly, their counter-mimetic performance of her choreography misfires. In a widely reproduced image, Baker poses with her knees pointing outward in perfectly opposing triangles to form a diamond shape, her arms crossed in front of her at right angles in a perfect X (fig. 11.2). Thus, in making jagged what is otherwise a perfectly symmetrical (and in this sense classical) pose, these vaudeville dancers also caricature the discourse according to which the new popular dances are sick, viral, epidemic—pathologies of (white and black) culture and motion.

Offering what I describe as an alterkinetic aesthetic, this comedic spoof on the Charleston and its popularly chastising response recuperates the discursive theatre of disorder in a performative re-enactment according to which racialized gesture and neuromotor disease are positively recombined. White middle-class workers in this version suffer both from a culture of overwork and from the putative exhaustion of too much play. They become 'crazy' by dancing too much, and the jagged, angular quality of the new moves gives rise to comedic impotence: they are *not* suave; not seductive. The black dances have become white in this image, and in becoming white, they are made awkward and ridiculous: not elegant as in Baker's performance. The only

27. Rae Beth Gordon, 'Les rythmes contagieux d'une danse noire: Le cake-walk', *Intermédialités* 16 (2010): 57–81, 68. The literature on primitivism and négritude in the Parisian cultural and artistic avant-garde is vast. See also Petrine Archer-Straw, *Negrophilia: Avant-garde Paris and Black Culture in the 1920s* (London: Thames and Hudson, 2000); William Rubin, ed., *'Primitivism' in Twentieth-Century Art: Affinity of the Tribal and the Modern*, 2 vols. (New York: Museum of Modern Art, 1984); Carole Sweeney, *From Fetish to Subject: Race, Modernism, and Primitivism, 1919–1935* (Westport, CT: Praeger, 2004).

28. Yvette Guilbert, *Une heure de musique avec Yvette Guilbert* (Paris: Éditions Cosmopolites, 1930), 11; cited in Gordon, 'Les rythmes contagieux', 79.

29. André Levinson, 'The Negro Dance: Under European Eyes', *Theatre Arts Monthly* 11.4 (1927): 282–293, 282; cited in Gordon, 'Les rythmes contagieux', 79.

30. Browning, *Infectious Rhythm.*

FIGURE 11.1 'Charleston posed by Ted Rogers, Jien Saergent and Viola Worden who are appearing with great success in vaudeville'. The photo appears alongside an article by Curtis Mitchell, 'Why Dorothy Dances Jazz Steps: Fred Stone, American Comedian, Tells Why He Trained His Daughter in Eccentric Rather Than Classical Dancing'. Originally in *Dance Magazine*, March 1926, 28–29. Courtesy the Jerome Robbins Dance Division, The New York Public Library for the Performing Arts, Astor, Lennox and Tilden Foundations.

way to dance these 'new' dances (for whites) is through the self-mocking operation of counter-mimesis, by which the dances are branded as ultimately inaccessible (because too black), yet through transfiguration, they are recuperated into the semiotic system of another genre: the familiar white hysteric. According to this redistribution of the aesthetic politics of jagged dance, colonial hysteria discussed in earlier chapters gave way to a white brand of hysteria that was contrapuntally articulated against the grain of black animal dances whose sexual play, when purged, left little more than a ghoulish body.

TANGO TEAS: 'GRACEFUL' RECREATION

Meanwhile, tango was increasingly described in the first decades of the twentieth century as a new epidemic dance 'craze', rippling through well-heeled society in Paris and New York, where the institution of tango teas, or *thés dansants* brought a distinctly African-inflected Latin American exoticism to the social dance circuit. Peaking in the spring of 1914, 'when the modern dance-craze was reaching its maddest exuberance', in one dance master's terms,

FIGURE 11.2   Postcard of Josephine Baker performing the Charleston at the Folies-Bergère, 1926. Photo by Stanislaus Julian Walery.

an explosion of self-educational guides to dancing emerged, instructing aspiring dancers in the proper steps and etiquette.[31] From Samuel Beach Chester's *Secrets of the Tango: Its History and How to Dance It* (c. 1914) to *Maurice's Art of Dancing: an autobiographical sketch with complete descriptions of modern dances and full illustrations showing the various steps and positions* (1915), by the Belgian-American dance master Maurice

Mouvet (1889–1927), and *Modern Dancing* (1914), by the upright American duo Irene (1893–1969) and Vernon Castle (1887–1918), tango and social dance guides on the model of the old Victorian dance manuals covered everything from the easier 'hesitation' waltz to the Brazilian *maxixe*, a 'guitar-like', even more sinuous cousin of the tango, in Chester's terms.[32] The aesthetic figure of the 'torque' that Schwartz has

---

31. Maurice Mouvet, *Maurice's Art of Dancing: An Autobiographical Sketch with Complete Descriptions of Modern Dances and Full Illustrations Showing the Various Steps and Positions* (New York: Schirmer, [1915]), 72.

32. Chester, *Secrets of the Tango*, 20.

put forward—describing a nineteenth- and early twentieth-century predilection for torsion or unwinding as of a coil—was reaching a peak with the sinuous tango, and although the recently explosive *Le Sacre du printemps* had just hit Paris in late May 1913 with its violently percussive beats and insistently syncopated rhythms, tango promised a smoother but no less titillating groove, inspired, Chester noted, by the 'furore' the Russian dancers had provoked.[33]

Paradoxically, tango, though a 'dance mania', inasmuch as it 'spread more universally than any dance since the world began',[34] in Chester's hyperbolic language, promised to return the world to a state of litheness and grace. The polka, which had made its way to Britain from bohemian central Europe, had started 'the jerky craze', in Chester's admonishing view, that continued in the cakewalk and the rough-and-tumble animal dances of the ragtime era—the grizzly bear and the turkey trot—but tango now promised to return dancers to healthy, elegant refinement.[35] Citing the physical culturist A. Wallace Jones, Chester noted that the tango 'gives exceptionally beneficial physical results'.[36] Sociability, exercise, and improved posture, aiding digestion, respiration, and circulation, were among the fabulous paybacks the tango promised.[37]

Writing from London, Chester applauded the joie de vivre that tango dancing revealed among his otherwise glum co-nationals. Healthiness countermanded otherwise unsavoury aspects of the dance, and although distinctly Parisian in its undertones and exotically Latin American and gypsy in its perpetually mythologized roots, the tango could be recuperated into an English economy of good posture and good grace. Everywhere it went, the tango seemed to conserve a dangerous exoticism and yet mould itself to local norms. In spite of the risqué sensuousness of the dance, in which men and women were enlaced more closely than ever before, the tango was articulated as a new, free, sophisticated practice whose benefits to health and well-being countermanded any morally deleterious effects on dancers not otherwise accustomed to winding their arms around one another morning, noon, and night.

The tango had travelled. Although perhaps an extreme example of the international mobility of the dance teacher, Mouvet represented a brand of roving expert who picked dance styles up where he went, developed his own, and became increasingly sought out as a performer and instructor at once. Winding his way through Paris, London, Vienna, Budapest, Monte Carlo, and New York, Mouvet danced before royalty and ambassadors, gaining and losing dance partners along the way. He noted that the waltz, which had swept through Vienna and Paris before making its way to the United States, was replaced stateside with an effervescence of new styles, 'as if by some wave of religious mania the entire country became obsessed with the dance-desire'.[38] He attributed this 'frenzy' to the 'twentieth century's restless yearning for novelty',[39] just as he recognized that this facile passion for fads might be superseded by careful mastery of a few standard and versatile steps. In Chester's terms, the tango had overshadowed all other dances and pastimes; in its 'engulfing, cataclysmic proposition it is far ahead of polo or yachting; its soft tentacles extend in all directions, squeezing vitality into the bondage of pleasure'. It was not exceptional only for its exoticism, as it displaced other exotic acts. Rather, tango was global: 'The War Dance of the Red Indian, the Highland Fling, the Irish Jig—all are interred. Arabian dances have been lost in the Arabian Nights. The merely Monmartre [sic] efforts at the Moulin Rouge are forgotten. Fabulous fancies of the imagination are easily eclipsed in one mighty, overwhelming reality, the Tango of to-day. Whether it is the *Tango Argentin* or the

---

33. Chester, *Secrets of the Tango*, 55.

34. Chester, *Secrets of the Tango*, 42.

35. 'So far as dancing is concerned, [the tango] is a revolution. It is an extraordinary change—an absolute volte-face from the jerky dances which have ruled the ball-rooms for the past few years. These dances—the one-step, the two-step, and variations of their kind, pleasantly known as the Bunny-Hug, the Grizzly-Bear and the Turkey-Trot—emphatically did not make for grace. The Tango, on the other hand, is a particularly graceful dance . . . . The Polka is to blame for a lot. It really started the jerky craze, from which we have never really recovered. The Tango will tend to check this and make us more graceful again'. Chester, *Secrets of the Tango*, 47–48.

36. Cited in Chester, *Secrets of the Tango*, 47.

37. Cited in Chester, *Secrets of the Tango*, 47–48.

38. Mouvet, *Maurice's Art of Dancing*, 69.

39. Mouvet, *Maurice's Art of Dancing*, 70.

Tango Londinien, it is the Tango all the same!'[40] Tango styles varied, but the tango 'engulfed' everyone 'the same'.

Ballroom and tango classes and salons mushroomed across Europe and America in the first decades of the twentieth century. Tango teas emerged in the 1910s to allow women and men to dance not only in the evening but in the afternoon, and soon in the morning, too. Chester notes a newspaper article exclaiming at the ubiquity of tango, now danceable 'at Every Meal!': 'After Tango Teas, Tango Dinners and Tango Suppers—Tango Breakfasts'. 'Not, of course', Chester hastens to add, 'couples who prance round the breakfast table at one's home, but eleven o'clock affairs at one of the West End *cafés*. Such is the latest development of the latest craze. So profitable have Tango experts found the "boom", that every day more experts are coming to London from all parts of the world. When the lucky dancers are not dancing, the majority of them are teaching ambitious learners'.[41]

Widely seen, as cultural historian Lewis Erenberg has pointed out in his now classic account of fin-de-siècle American popular dance culture, as an occasion for married and unmarried women to rub shoulders with insalubrious migrants, often under the cover of an expedition to go shopping, tango teas also offered a relatively above-ground retort to the supposedly grimy and crime-ridden culture of the still more dubious cabaret.[42] But cabarets, too, underwent a transformation during this period. All-day dancing emerged in tandem with a culture of all-night entertainment during which patrons were increasingly invited to join in the show. In Erenberg's account, a booming world of night-time performances had transformed New York nightlife in the period between 1912 and 1916, with lavish halls boasting dining tables spilling out onto dance floors, out of which the new ballroom stars emerged—most prominently, Irene and Vernon Castle. Initially, dancers offered stand-alone performances; later they mingled with patrons, and soon restaurantgoers themselves built up an appetite to learn the same steps they saw. Although this suggested

a sophisticated society of Broadway glitter, Erenberg points out the 'childlike' pleasures of play that these events occasioned. The 'Midnight Frolic' at the Ziegfeld Follies invited patrons to wear silly hats and blow noisemakers, 'recreating' the 'prerational and emotionally expressive period of childhood' when the world was all 'excitement' and 'careless fun'.[43]

In Erenberg's analysis, the dance 'craze' was a return to childhood and an opportunity to break down the long-standing cultural hold of the Protestant work ethic over the middle classes, who found that they could let go inasmuch as they trespassed onto exotic cultural terrain. The argument is familiar. In Lepecki's terms, it rehearses 'a familiar theme in critical race studies: that of the animation of whiteness's melancholic nature . . . by energizing, contagious, black "soul power". The animation of whiteness by black soul and black motions', Lepecki writes, 'participates entirely . . . of narratives that equate dance with the uncanny infusion of life in the corpse'.[44] Equating 'this "soul power", this surge of motion in the apathetic European body that infects and suspends the endemic melancholia of whiteness every time it witnesses the spectacle of uncanny motions', from the slave plantation to the postcolonial dance hall, with 'the primal fantasy underlying . . . colonialist exploitation', Lepecki suggests that Western dancing is 'fantastically conceived' as the uncanny animation of inert corporeal matter.[45] Awkwardly residing outside the body, in the act of spiritual infusion of vitality into the mechanical (white) body from an exogenous (generally foreign or racially other)—spiritually potent—source, 'dance' becomes, in the Western imagination, ontologically prior to a ghostly body—a body that is already (almost) dead. Resonant with DeFrantz's suggestion that black dance is spiritually charged in the white Western imagination, this model of dance also rehearses an Aristotelian version of conception whereby femininity provides the matter or body and masculinity the spirit or soul in a new being: here, blackness, this time titillatingly masculine and hypersexed, animates a limp white body that nevertheless resists total transformation into

40. Chester, *Secrets of the Tango*, 10.
41. Chester, *Secrets of the Tango*, 49.
42. Lewis A. Erenberg, *Steppin' Out: New York Nightlife and the Transformation of American Culture, 1890–1930* (Chicago: University of Chicago Press, 1984), 79.
43. Erenberg, *Steppin' Out*, 127–128.
44. Lepecki, *Exhausting Dance*, 109.
45. Lepecki, *Exhausting Dance*, 109.

the imaginary hypersexed blackness and spirituality of the black body-spirit. The white body borrows, dances, but only so far. In the miscegenation of the new Euro-American moves out of African and African-American dance cultures, a part-white, part-black corporeality emerges on the modern stage constantly to negotiate a process of monstrous doubling, counter-mimicry, and creolization, what Édouard Glissant calls a relational poetics, a nostalgic *métissage* constantly displacing itself.[46]

The popular recuperation of so-called alien (largely black) moves by primarily white middle-class bodies in the first decades of the twentieth century also resulted in these moves' re-indigenization, their 'whitening'. The contamination went both ways. In Chester's terms, tango was international: it 'encircles the globe . . . [increasing] like a snowball, accumulating steps as it moves along';[47] but it lost some of its supposedly primitive danger in becoming global, civilized. Though rousingly 'originating in "the wilds"', tango became tamer, 'highly complex and even delicate', Chester wrote, 'by passing through many phases of worldly life'. Paris in particular served as a cultural crucible at this time in the English imaginary, at once reaching over to colonial Africa and vaguely accessible to the upright English West.[48] Everything exotic and mad, it seemed to the English, passed through Paris.

Yet the exact location of tango's origins was unclear: alternately attributed to ancient Pyrrhic war dances among the Greeks, to the chica—what Chester called an 'unpleasant' South American dance said to have originated from the 'negroes'—or to the slightly more (to him) palatable Spanish tango, which had reputedly travelled back to Europe from Latin America, tango was undeniably other, temporally and geographically.[49] The haziness of its origins only added to its mystique. Indeed, tango gained its modernity—it became a paradigmatically and paradoxically 'modern' dance—inasmuch as it figuratively reached back to and simultaneously transcended a supposedly uncouth state of natural abandon.

The colonialist and classist overtones in Chester's account are clear: with the Briton, Chester wrote, 'the fate of the Tango is in safe keeping. He took it up when it had a questionable reputation, and already that reputation is vanishing like a thin mist swept from a mountain-top by the morning sun'.[50] Tango, in becoming English, gained the articulacy only an upright, educated Henry Higgins could grant an Eliza Doolittle pulled up from out of the gutter.

Like the contemporaneous cakewalk and later the Charleston, tango dances were rooted in underground cultures, which they exoticized and rewrote: with the tango, working-class, often foreign, choreographies came to the 'surface' of polite society and—transfigured—almost as quickly disappeared from view. Only a few years before the tango burst onto the international social dance scene in the early 1910s, the notoriously violent 'Apache' dance, borrowed from stylized gang fighting among the Parisian underclass and the fiction of Native American warrior culture after which it was named, made its way to the genteel salons of Paris and New York. In the case of the Apache, it was literally drawn from the underground taverns of Paris. Mouvet, its greatest exponent and popularizer, characterized the event as a true 'sensation'.[51] The Apache was a 'peculiarly vicious and savage dance', he wrote, full of 'primitive savage grace'; but carefully mastered, it could be rehearsed with all the outward form of the emotion and none of the actual brutality.[52] In 1909 Mouvet had been taken by a fellow dancer at the Moulin Rouge, Max Dearly (1874–1943), to the underworld of the Paris Halles, 'down a flight of dark, evil-smelling stairs, badly lighted and grewsome'.[53] There, in the notorious Caveau des Innocents, they witnessed a 'filthy',

---

46. Glissant describes a relational poetics founded in colonial encounters shaping complex subjectivities more than any national myth of origin might. Such encounters provide moments of mutuality in which parties are never quite equal but co-produce instances of identification (and disidentification), yielding mobile subjects: subjects always in a state of transition and change. Édouard Glissant, *Le discours antillais* (Paris: Gallimard, 1997), esp. 419–431.

47. Chester, *Secrets of the Tango*, 14.

48. Chester, *Secrets of the Tango*, 13.

49. Chester, *Secrets of the Tango*, 57.

50. Chester, *Secrets of the Tango*, 61.

51. Mouvet, *Maurice's Art of Dancing*, 29–30.

52. Mouvet, *Maurice's Art of Dancing*, 28.

53. Mouvet, *Maurice's Art of Dancing*, 26.

'rough' world, full of Apaches—the underworld 'gunm[e]n of Paris'—playing poker, with their 'girls'. A 'rickety' piano with stained keys, played by a 'villainously ugly little hunchback', whose 'deformity took on a grotesque menace' in this light, accompanied the dance they had come to see and soon take, like a pair of colonial travellers or wayward modern-day Orpheuses, back up to the Parisian glitterati.[54]

The dance, performed to a *valse Chaloupée*, the 'waltz of the Apache', began with a slap across the mouth, delivered by the Apache with nonchalance to a young woman, 'his girl', who consented to carrying out the dance with him. At its conclusion, she lay limp on the floor, and the Apache returned to his gaming. Mouvet and Dearly learned the steps from the Apaches, thrilled at the 'sensation' it would create all over Paris. When Mouvet, after six weeks of practice, took his version of the dance to the Café de Paris with his partner, Leona, both had practiced mimicking the 'terrible gestures' of the Apaches. Mouvet dropped his jaw in the same 'grimly vicious reproduction of brutality that had crept into [the Apache's] face' when Mouvet had witnessed the dance first-hand; so, too, Leona 'trained her features to something between abject fear and devotion'.[55] The performance had its effect, and 'for a little while', Mouvet wrote, 'I *was* an Apache, more ruthless, more savage, more violent, more fearless than any of them. The sensation astonished even myself. I had never known such excitement in that café before'.[56] Handsomely paid back for

their labour and the 'intense nervous strain' the performance had provoked in them, Mouvet and his partner—together with this 'new' dance—became, as he put it not too modestly, the talk of *tout Paris*.[57] Soon, Mouvet and his partner were invited to Biarritz to dance before King Edward VII (1841–1910), one of numerous monarchs to enjoy the frisson that such a stylized performance of lawlessness and violence could provoke. The tango, which was brought to Paris, according to Mouvet, in one of many apocryphal stories of its emergence, by some South American dancers who found their way to the Café de Paris, would soon follow.

The new dances, including the Apache and ever proliferating variations on the tango, were rough, brazen, and sinuous but also 'alluring', 'insinuating', and 'subtle',[58] and though performed with great control, evoked a world inaccessible to most audiences and performers. Inevitably, apologists and detractors vied for the last word. In a vitriolic rebuke by the evangelist preacher Mordecai Ham (1877–1961), the new dances were 'satanic'. Quoting a speech Dr. Frank Richardson gave to the Medical Association of New Jersey, Ham argued that the dances were 'impure, contaminating and deadly'.[59] Dr. S. Grover Burnett of Kansas City, former president of the medical school of the University of Missouri, also quoted by Ham, claimed that 'one-tenth of the insane of this country have lost their minds on account of troubles which may commonly be traced to modern dances'.[60] Insanity, death, sexual gratification, and lost

---

54. Mouvet, *Maurice's Art of Dancing*, 27.

55. Mouvet, *Maurice's Art of Dancing*, 29.

56. Mouvet, *Maurice's Art of Dancing*, 30.

57. Mouvet, *Maurice's Art of Dancing*, 30.

58. Mouvet, *Maurice's Art of Dancing*, 33.

59. Mordecai Franklin Ham, *Light on the Dance: The Modern Dance; A Historical and Analytical Treatment of the Subject; Religious, Social, Hygienic, Industrial Aspects As Viewed by the Pulpit, the Press, Medical Authorities, Municipal Authorities, Social Workers, Etc.*, 2nd rev. ed. (n.p., [1916]), 25. The language of satanism appears throughout. See e.g. 41. Ham, who argues that there can be no Christian who is also a dancer, further suggests that 'the Greek word *komo* or *komos* translated "rioting" in Romans 13:13 and "revellings" in Gallatians 5:21, and "revellings" in I Peter 4:3 meant dancing in the original': dancing was not only 'lascivious' and 'wanton', it was, moreover, an incitement to revolt (17). Ham drew extensively from medical and other 'authorities' and was not unique in his reprobation at the time. See e.g. Beryl and Associates, eds., *Immorality of Modern Dances* (New York: Everitt and Francis and S. F. McLean, 1904), who attribute a lust for bodily contact to round and square dances, arguing that modern square dances contain 'a great deal of the indelicate French dance of the eighteenth century, called the "Branle", consisting of several persons joining hands, leaping in circles and keeping each other in continual motion', as well as the 'immodest Spanish "Pavane", in which the performers look maliciously at each other, strutting like peacocks, fluttering, fondling, cooing and wooing, approaching and retreating and imitating something in the animal kingdom, until at last . . . both parties rush like maniacs to the wild close embrace . . . . To some extent they imitate the lecherous Satyrs and the deliriously lustful Bacchantes, whom history describes as frolicsome and addicted to various shameful kinds of sensual enjoyment'. The modern dances were thus animal and foreign, as well as dissolutely and madly Dionysian. Beryl and Associates, *Immorality of Modern Dances*, 37–38.

60. Ham, *Light on the Dance*, 27.

worker productivity were among the social ills that beset all those who danced without 'putting daylight' between them. What's more, according to the Swedish-American psychologist Hans Huldricksen, further quoted by Ham, 'shameless extravagance, voluptuous dances and unbridaled [sic] luxury and profligacy' gave rise to nothing less than 'The War Disease', the most alarming alleged result of these 'extravagant entertainments'.[61]

Like the Ghost Dance among the Plains Indians, 'reckless luxury', epitomized by English costume balls at Covent Garden, was said to threaten destabilization of the moral order, leading to social dissolution and death.[62] Although these carefully hand-picked examples served to authorize Ham's own rancorous preaching, they reflected widespread currents of malaise circulating concomitantly with the otherwise buoyant spirit of play and loosening of social mores that was rippling through 1910s and 1920s Europe and America.

The language of reprobation was rising to the same heights of hyperbolic distortion as earlier portrayals of dance manias. According to a *Sun* editorial, the new 'dances are a reversion to the grossest practices of savage man'; they were 'based on the primitive motive of orgies enjoyed by the aboriginal inhabitants of every uncivilized land'.[63] So-called 'tango pirates'—lower-class men who seduced higher-class women at tango teas—were barbarous and decadent, egregiously predatory, and, paradoxically, effeminate in their predilection for round-the-clock dancing.[64]

Admonitions against the threat to young girls were paramount. But women and girls (and effeminate men) were not the only ones who enjoyed the new dance regime. As a *McClure's* story, 'Dance-Mad Billy' (1915), makes clear, women were sometimes the last to let down their guard and get dancing. Once they did, sometimes with their partners in life and sometimes with partners acquired on the dance floor,

they found that they could network, socialize, and exercise all at once. Dancing, for wives as for husbands, boosted creative inspiration and productivity and reinjected married life as well as work with joie de vivre.[65]

The so-called new dance craze fit every moral agenda, simultaneously boosting energy, sapping energy, consolidating relationships, and dissolving relationships. As Wagner has pointed out, critics cited rising numbers of divorces during this period, attributing the breakdown of society to the uncontrollable dancing fad (as well as to feminine emancipation).[66] The harshest indictments emerging out of the ensuing decades suggested that the ebullience of the Roaring Twenties, leading to the dramatic Wall Street crash of October 1929, could be traced back to flapper culture and the rage for loose clothes, defiance of corsets, and too-close but also too angular and gangly dance styles. Simultaneously, a culture of wholesomeness emerged, rearticulating the vivacity of modern dancing in terms of social health. Not only were individuals and couples benefiting; social mores at large would be cleaned up with correct posture, controlled socializing, and, according to the new discourse on wholesomeness, a proper channelling of spontaneous, childlike energies into respectable and graceful corporeal forms.

THE CASTLES: HEALTHY DANCING FOR THE WHITE MIDDLE CLASSES

Irene and Vernon Castle were at the forefront of this trend. Establishing a thriving business of social dance lessons targeted at young women and men who would not otherwise venture out into lower-class dancing establishments, the Castles argued that dancing was healthy, proper, and good. In their terms, 'dancing, properly executed, is neither vulgar nor immodest, but, on

---

61. In Ham, *Light on the Dance*, 35.

62. In Ham, *Light on the Dance*, 35–36.

63. 'The Revolt of Decency', *New York Sun*, cited in *Literary Digest*, 9 April 1913, 894. Erenberg, *Steppin' Out*, 81. On 19 July 1913 an article titled 'Carnality in Song, Dance, and Dress' quotes Cora Harris, writing in the Philadelphia *Saturday Evening Post*, who—'purely analytic in her method'—'says that the turkey trot is "a form of amusement designed for primitive people by primitive people before they discovered the danger of being too natural"'. For Harris, this previously 'religious' expression was now 'the universal titter of femininity', 'transient' and '[hysterical]'. She predicted it would be 'gone before the end of the year'. In *Literary Digest* 19 July 1913, 101–102, 102.

64. See Erenberg, *Steppin' Out*, 83–85.

65. Mary Stewart Cutting, 'Dance-Mad Billy', *McClure's* 45 (September 1915): 22–43.

66. Wagner, *Adversaries of Dance*, esp. 202, 237–291.

the contrary, the personification of refinement, grace, and modesty. Our aim', they wrote,

'is to uplift dancing, purify it, and place it before the public in its proper light. When this has been done, we feel convinced that no objection can possibly be urged against it on the grounds of impropriety, but rather that social reformers will join with the medical profession in the view that dancing is not only a rejuvenator of good health and spirits, but a means of preserving youth, prolonging life, and acquiring grace, elegance, and beauty'.[67]

Modern dance was healthy and good because it was graceful; it worked in the service of beauty and youth, offering 'clean fun' and 'healthy relaxation' 'to offset the hard work of the day'.[68] The Castles' short instructional handbook concluded with a brief article, 'Dance and Health', by Dr. J. Ralph Jacoby, who argued that dance, as the 'practice of joyousness', also developed the 'power of control': properly exercised, the body could become strong and house a strong will.[69] This Grecian virtue, also highlighted by the Castles' dance school superintendent, Mrs. Elisabeth Marbury (1856–1933), in her introduction to the handbook, suggested that the 'grace and beauty and classic rhythm' of modern dancing descended from ancient Oriental (specifically Theban) tomb dances, which came to the West via Rome. For Marbury, modern America traced its lineage back to Thebes, paradoxically to Dionysus, the wily Theban god. But what made these dances modern was their transcendence of this ancient heritage. They were modern because they heralded from the Dionysian East and because they purified, regularized, and updated these ancient sepulchral rites. Their modernity was, implicit in Marbury's terms, contrapuntal.

It was also smooth. There was no 'hopping' in the Castles' modern dancing, no 'contortions of the body', no 'flouncing of the elbows', 'twisting of the arms', no 'fantastic dips', Marbury wrote.[70] It did not matter much that these contortions, dips, and 'hoppings' referred primarily to black and black-inspired moves: the bunny hop, the grizzly bear, the turkey trot, many of which playfully imitated animal gaits (and which, as Brown notes, Irene Castle learned from the black dancer and former chorus line member at the Harlem Darktown Follies, Ethel Williams).[71] The tango, likewise lifted out of its purportedly dark and dirty Argentinian heritage—became heir of the 'stately' minuet. In the Castles' version, 'there is in it no strenuous clasping of partners, no hideous gyrations of the limbs, no abnormal twisting, no vicious angles'. Instead, 'the Castle Tango is courtly and artistic', Marbury stressed.[72] All 'folk' roots were at once mentioned and cast aside; modern dancing was emphatically that which elevated itself out of the imagined primeval muck of ancient times, darker races, and lower classes. Modernity in her view was healthful, hearty, and adroit; significantly, it was also defined in contrast to a version of the past fantasized as twisting, gyrating, and irregular, as well as Oriental and unrefined. 'Shuffles and twists and wriggles and jumps are no longer words to be used in connection with dancing', the Castles wrote.[73] Dancing should not be done in a 'romping spirit', with the whole body, but with the feet primarily, while the upper body remained erect. The Castles' tango was a stately and slow dance, 'simple, and not full of jerky and complicated steps'.[74]

Yet in order to highlight this triumphant overcoming of the old uncouth dances, the new dances had also spectrally to encompass these as their implied negatives: their black, Latin, lower-class, and immigrant origins, which appeared almost *sous rature*, under erasure, carefully

---

67. Mr. & Mrs. Vernon Castle, *Modern Dancing* (New York: Harper and Brothers, 1914), 17.

68. Elisabeth Marbury, 'Introduction', in Castle, *Modern Dancing*, 19–29, 24–27.

69. J. Ralph Jacoby, 'Dance and Health', in Castle, *Modern Dancing*, 173–176, 175–176.

70. Marbury, 'Introduction', 19–20.

71. Brown, *Babylon Girls*, 157, 164, 171. Brown further notes that the Castles hired James Reese Europe and his Society Orchestra to play at private dance functions they hosted, after which 'high society would hire only black musicians'; yet black dancers, whose moves white dance professionals assimilated—as novelties—into their own acts, increasingly worked, 'with a few exceptions', 'behind the scenes, informally and unrecognized' (170–172; see also 210–216).

72. Marbury, 'Introduction', 20.

73. Castle, *Modern Dancing*, 39

74. Castle, *Modern Dancing*, 86.

recuperated into a clean, white body culture. As the Castles write in 'Castle House Suggestions for Correct Dancing':

> *Do not wriggle the shoulders.*
> *Do not shake the hips.*
> *Do not twist the body.*
> *Do not flounce the elbows.*
> *Do not pump the arms.*
> *Do not hop—glide instead.*
> *Avoid low, fantastic, and acrobatic dips.*
> *Stand far enough away from each other to allow free movement of the body in order to dance gracefully and comfortably. . . .*
> *Drop the Turkey Trot, the Grizzly Bear, the Bunny Hug, etc. These dances are ugly, ungraceful, and out of fashion.*[75]

The Castles' instructions are composed almost entirely of negatives. Aspiring dancers wanting to learn the Castle House style of dancing—the 'correct' style—are enjoined to drop all the playful, recognizably black, elements of the ragtime-era animal dances coming out of the plantation South. The 'correct' style, in the Castles' influential view, is emphatically smooth: dancers glide rather than hop. They succeed in diverting attention away from their bodies and the potential for sexual arousal arising from these bodies' proximity to one another, presenting instead a polite style of dancing as prescriptive as it is controlled. The Darwinian language of upward motion and civilized progress out of ungainliness, animality, and downward stooping suffuses the text the Castles propose. Blackness is spectral in their high-society steps: in Brown's terms, subject to 'erasure'. 'The black subject', Brown writes, 'is evacuated, removed'. Paradoxically, this process of removal was effected by way of 'absorption': white Americans did not try to become black but to 'absorb' 'the slave body', 'its power', and thus to 'affirm its servitude'.[76] The process of making black bodies invisible *still, yet again*, enabled a further transfiguration of blackness by which American whiteness *appeared* through ever evolving operations of 'willful misrecognition'.[77] As in other cases I have described in this book, the fiction of a savage underbelly underpins the

language of modern dance in a popular discourse on bodily modernity. Modern dancing erects itself phantasmatically out of the supposedly disorganized, irregularly choreographed past, which it conjugates with a new, efficient bodily futurity.

For Bergson, a concept that encompasses its opposite is always richer and more complex than any other: chaos implies order, which it distorts; non-being implies being; the possible implies the real.[78] Modernity likewise implies savagery, antiquity, irregularity, and an ancient type of motion that underlies but is opposite to the proper expression of good health. In other words, modernity is underpinned by a fantastical corporeal disorder, a dancing disease which it is modernity's supposed burden to purge, albeit with as much zeal as was apparently displayed in the disorder in the first place. Again the operation of counter-mimicry is arresting. Not only is the 'mania' for modern dancing virus-like, zealously purging and amending an older, more pernicious dancing disease, but these older and newer manias are suspiciously similar in tone. The dancing the Castles and their acolytes promoted was in their view natural, childlike, and purportedly universal. A good rag, they wrote, compelled one to move. Movement was the expression of a healthy body and a sound mind, even a disposition towards pleasure. 'If we bar dancing from the world', Marbury wrote, 'we bar one of the supreme human expressions of happiness and exultation. The tiny child skips for joy and prances to the music of the hand organ long before it knows the difference between happiness and sorrow. In time of festival in many countries dancing is the keynote of the gathering'.[79] Learning to dance was to share in a universal culture of happiness yet to distance oneself from the very expressions of joy that seemed to result in sexually charged, ebullient, and ungainly body postures elsewhere.

Irene Vernon famously became an icon of the New Woman, carefree and healthy but polished. She posited dance as a beauty aid, a slimming device, an elixir of youth; a natural and easy way to maintain naturally rosy cheeks without cosmetic aid. She reformed fashions and hairstyles, favouring softer corsets, more comfortable shoes, and a close crop—the famous

---

75. Castle, *Modern Dancing*, 177.
76. Brown, *Babylon Girls*, 174.
77. Brown, *Babylon Girls*, 174.
78. Gilles Deleuze, *Le bergsonisme* (Paris: Presses Universitaires de France, 2011), 6.
79. Marbury, 'Introduction', 21.

twenties bob. At the same time, her celebration of the vigorous, healthy and 'youthful spirit' at times hazardously approached the fascistic body culture that National Socialists hailed less than two decades later. Wholesomeness, in her view, a 'contagious' and a 'hilarious' force, exuded unmitigated pride in youthful bodies, epitomizing the rugged, can-do spirit of the West.[80] Clean, vigorous dancing girls and boys were signs of moral overcoming and spiritual as well as physical advantage, corporeal trophies in a bright new world that believed it rose resolutely up out of the imagined vulgarity of African-American slavery and cultural overdependence on a decadent European past.

HEALTHY TUMESCENCE: FREUD, BRILL, AND SEXUAL TABOO

The borderline against which an ancient and chaotic sort of dancing could be fixed moved constantly. As I have shown, 'bad', irregular dancing happened in the elusive past, and elsewhere; it was also what cropped up in the present as the spontaneous expression of archaic disorderly ways. In that respect, it was properly modern, but only inasmuch as it revealed modern stresses, modern modes of acting out according to more primitive corporeal forms. Accordingly, the first decades of the twentieth century saw an explosion of writing on dance 'crazes'. Virtually every decade of the twentieth century had its own craze, from the cakewalk and the Charleston to the Lindy hop, the grizzly bear, the bunny hug, and the swing to the twist, the mambo, disco, and eventually raves. What remained constant was the language of contagion and moral outrage at the animal, primitive, ugly, and always too fast tempo of the new moves, as well as their situation at the frontiers of white civilized society, often in black or Latin quarters and among the supposedly degenerate youth. But running through the pathologizing refrain of these public admonitions was a contrary trend, extolling the virtues of dancing for individual and social—often sexual—health. No longer just a strange and wonderful excrescence from historical antiquity, with odd appearances

among exotic peoples in the present day, dance manias in the first half of the twentieth century came to be described as squarely contemporary affairs tapping into what came increasingly to be understood as humans' healthy primal urges to move, to dance, and to shake.

Dancing frequently or at length and with abandon, in this respect, was described in morally ambivalent terms. It was healthy inasmuch as it was an expression of the fundamental workings of the human mechanism (the impulse to move and mate through sexualized attraction rituals); and it was suspect inasmuch as those engaging in such disinhibited dancing were evidently failing to suppress their basic animal urges. Freud early on set the stage for this ambivalent moral stance, following his studies with Charcot at the Salpêtrière in the 1880s and his continued exploration of hysterical symptoms in his private practice. Unlike Charcot, Freud saw hysterical gesticulations and delusional beliefs as caused by suppressed sexuality, often provoked by early childhood trauma. Although Charcot found the seat of hysteria in the patient's autonomous nervous system, for Freud hysteria was ultimately the product of psychological trauma located in the patient's mind: the patient's mental rather than physiological apparatus. It could frequently be cured, he found, by talking.

His comparison in *Totem and Taboo* between what he described as the neurotic life of children and that of savages further anchored spontaneous, apparently meaningless gesture into a primitivist discourse aligned with the world of art. Pablo Picasso (1881–1973), Georges Braque (1882–1963), and other contemporaries of Freud had discovered in the masks of colonial Africa a new aesthetic regime founded in jagged angularity, one that sat comfortably with the hypothesis that primitive men and women held the key to childlike discoordination and uncensored motor impulses. This primitivist aesthetic, which Burt describes as constitutive of modern art and choreography, depended upon what Martha Graham (1894–1991) would later describe as a means of retrieving 'ancestral footsteps', 'cultures from the past'.[81]

With the rise in aesthetic enthusiasm for Dionysianism among the Cambridge Ritualists, a small group of classical scholars eager to reinstitute Dionysus as the god of

---

80. Castle, *Modern Dancing*, 164.
81. Martha Graham, *Blood Memory: An Autobiography* (London: Scepter Books, 1991), 13; cited in Burt, *Alien Bodies*, 162.

ecstatic pleasure, Freud's brand of primitivism joined early comparative anthropology, neurology, colonial medicine, archaeology, and classics in founding new lines of thought around primitive sexuality. Heavily indebted, like the Cambridge Ritualists, to Greek tragedy in his iconic rewriting of the Oedipus myth, Freud read widely and pilfered from the new fields, borrowing as much from early comparative ritualism as he gave to the new psychological method. Active at Oxford as well as Cambridge at the turn of the twentieth century, the Ritualists—most prominently Harrison and Gilbert Murray (1866–1957)—believed that Greek tragedy originated in a magical, primitive, prehistoric fertility rite that celebrated the death and rebirth of Dionysus. Working on the heels of early comparative anthropology, particularly the pioneering work of E. B. Tylor in *Primitive Culture* (1871) and Frazer in *The Golden Bough*, the Ritualists saw productive comparisons between the primitive life of savages and ancient Greece. Similarly influenced by Tylor and Frazer's work, Freud reprised their comparative enthusiasm and reach to the past in compiling his iconic study of infantile recurrence and totemic primitivism.

Though in parts barely more than an extended paraphrase of Frazer's writing, *Totem and Taboo* lays the groundwork for a renewed brand of scientific thinking about the past: antiquity, in Freud's analysis, was little more than the primal seat of modernity's traumatic wound. Incest taboos in particular could be found among 'savages', neurotics, and children, suggesting that the similarity between these groups differentiated them generally from 'civilized' man. More important, the repression of incest and other highly sexualized taboos gave way to complex cases of individual distress and widespread societal disorder. With his recuperation of ancient Greek anthropological culture into his analysis of 'savage' life, Freud rearticulated the discourse on primitive corporeality as hinging on interior processes and inarticulate pasts. The primitive within us was, for Freud, axiomatic; so, too, our capacity to display primitive behaviour was, in turn, fundamental. At our core, for Freud, we were still pre-linguistic and infantile; we only covered this up more or less well with 'civilization'; fittingly,

outrageous and superstitious behaviours were still pervasive in human culture.

This was not necessarily a bad thing. Freud's English translator, Brill, a clinical psychiatrist and neurologist at Columbia University in New York, argued that 'dance manias' were healthy affairs. In an article published in the *New York Medical Journal*, 'The Psychopathology of the New Dances' (1914), Brill suggested that 'the present dancing mania' was decidedly an 'epidemic' affair, a 'psychic epidemic' well known to psychiatrists familiar with such phenomena as the folie à deux. More to the point, the 'present dancing epidemic' was 'not new to history. For centuries dancing manias broke out in different countries', Brill wrote, 'and although they were not as widespread as the present one, they aroused as much, if not more, attention'.[82] Comparing the present mania to the familiar assortment of paradigmatic cases, Brill noted that dancing epidemics had broken out in Aachen in 1374 and Strasbourg in 1518—and had been cured through popular appeal to St. Vitus. Like religious crusades, they were violent enthusiasms highly transmissible from person to person. The present epidemic in contrast was not religious, Brill wrote, but was virtually global: it 'spread like wildfire over the whole civilized world'. 'Everybody', Brill wrote, 'almost the whole world, is dancing the new dances'.[83]

Brill decided to witness the dances himself. What he found surprised him. Whereas he agreed with friends and patients that the dances were 'wild and emotional', he also noted that they 'offered more muscular exertion, more contact, and more motion' than the old dances—particularly the waltz—and therefore, as he put it, 'more opportunity for tumescence'. The dances quite literally provoked people to be aroused and to copulate. As he put it, the new dances, like the old ones, satisfied a fundamental sexual need: they were 'manifestly erotic' and thus provided an opportunity for 'emotional discharge' and 'gratification'. But why were these new dances more popular than the old styles? Brill decided boldly to distribute a questionnaire to 'a few hundred enthusiastic dancers', approached by his friends and patients, who would ask them whether they had 'ever become sexually excited while dancing the new dances' or 'while watching

82. A. A. Brill, 'The Psychopathology of the New Dances', *New York Medical Journal* 99.17 (1914): 834–837, 834.
83. Brill, 'The Psychopathology of the New Dances', 834.

the new dances'. He also asked whether they had ever experienced the same feelings while dancing or watching the old dances.[84] The answers, once again, surprised him. After a few months, he had collected responses from 342 people, including 119 women and 223 men. Of these, he noted, only fourteen men and eight women admitted to having become sexually excited while dancing the new dances; sixteen men and nine women admitted that they had become sexually excited while watching the new dances; and eleven men and six women suggested that they had become sexually excited while dancing or watching the old dances. He further noted that 'the sixteen men and nine women who gave an affirmative answer to the second question, included also those men and women who gave the same answers to the first and third questions'; thus, only a pool of twenty-five persons in total answered yes to any question. The conclusion, he thought, was patent: a very small minority of men and women were sexually aroused by the new dances (or, at least, admitted to this arousal); and, what's more, there was no difference to speak of, he concluded, between the new and the old styles. Nearly half of the men and all of the women who had responded in the affirmative were known to him, moreover, and displayed, he thought, a 'hyperesthetic sexuality'. Riding in an automobile, bicycling, or horseback riding all produced sexual excitement in these people; a small majority of the women, moreover, had for various reasons been deprived of normal sexual contact and were thus plausibly more prone to sexual arousal. More interestingly, watching dance was at least as sexually arousing as dancing. 'The onlookers', Brill suggested, 'furnished the greatest percentage of those who experienced somatic sexual feelings'. As the majority of those who objected to the dances had never danced themselves but only witnessed the dancing, he concluded that observers who became vexed suffered an excess of sexual feeling that was 'immediately repressed', resulting in 'a strong outburst of indignation'.[85]

Brill's conclusion was to condone the dances as healthy and good. Motion was as necessary to adults as it was to children, who relished rocking, swaying, flying, and shaking games. And 'motion pleasure', a form of 'autoerotic sexual manifestation', was at the basis of dancing, enabling the normal gratification of the sexual instinct and providing the more pleasure and gratified love the more contact and muscular exertion the new dances afforded.[86] Brill's summary analysis enabled him to interpret the recent 'psychic epidemic' as a result of 'mental and emotional repressions', following Freud's theory of neurotic and psychotic abnormality. The medieval 'dancing epidemics', thus, were naturally, in Brill's view, caused by 'the tyranny of the feudal system and the church, which for a long time kept the people in an oppressed and wretched state, allowing them no outlet for their emotions'. 'The present dancing epidemic', Brill argued, was 'due to similar causes'. Puritanical prudery and Anglo-Saxon hypocrisy had led to widespread sexual repression, which the new dances assuaged. Particularly in America, where prudery was most acute, stifling women, who were subject to a debilitating double standard, the new dances could do what the suffragette movement also did for women in England: offer a 'safety valve for repressed tension'.[87]

Though Brill, by his own admission, did not dance himself,[88] his benignly patronizing support for the popular dance movement in the mid-1910s ignited slightly amused hyperbolic accounts in the popular press. An article published in the *New York Times* on 26 April 1914 reprised his article, as well as recent writing by the neurologist Gustave F. Boehme (1860–1949) of the West Side German Dispensary and Hospital. Boehme was researching 'tango-foot', a condition born from too much tango dancing, resulting in a new brand of occupational disorder, after bursitis or 'housemaid's knee', 'miner's elbow', and 'weaver's bottom'. This new disorder was extended to 'the devotees of Terpsichore' who complained of pain in the front of the foot accompanied by a slightly rheumatoid stiffness or bruising, resulting in a slight limp. Boehme recognized the requirement for great flexibility of the ankle in the new dances,

84. Brill, 'The Psychopathology of the New Dances', 835.
85. Brill, 'The Psychopathology of the New Dances', 836.
86. Brill, 'The Psychopathology of the New Dances', 836.
87. Brill, 'The Psychopathology of the New Dances', 837.
88. Brill, 'The Psychopathology of the New Dances', 837.

particularly the tango but also the tango-like Brazilian *maxixe* and the hesitation waltz, all of which involved repeated extension, flexion, and adduction of the foot. The best cure, in Boehme's opinion, was to cease dancing altogether, limit walking, and engage in baking bread or other foodstuffs for a few days: this would reduce the swelling and restore the ankle and foot tendons to their proper state.[89]

Women were caught in the crossfire of the new dance craze and its medical—as well as moral—adjudication. In Brill's analysis, women were more repressed, tenser, and therefore more galvanized (as well as relieved) by the dancing. Yet Boehme thought they should never have left home. Domestic duties were not compatible with the new dance craze, which provoked dancers to stay out longer hours and dance more frequently, and with greater energy and vigour, than in previous times. Debate about the healthiness of dancing raged. As the Castles pointed out in their handbook, a number of new medical opinions suggested, against the moralizing reprobations of the day, that the new dancing offered a healthy form of exercise. What's more, dancers drank less, the Castles pointed out, and moved their bodies 'instead of becoming torpid around a card-table'.[90] For the neuropsychiatrist Dr. Charles L. Dana (1852–1935), whose *Text-Book of Nervous Diseases and Psychiatry* (1915) the Castles quoted for support, 'dancing, including gymnastic dancing and folk dancing, under proper conditions and limitations, is one of the best exercises for persons of all ages. It is especially adapted to the temperament, physique, and dress of women'.[91] The concept of 'excess' was highly equivocal: excess lay largely in the eyes of the beholder. Dancers themselves, except in the case of a hurt foot, never in my readings sought out medical help. At most, their obsessiveness sparked political or domestic crises (and occasionally resolutions), described in magazines and the popular press. But the figure of the dancing disease that was of interest to medical professionals and, increasingly, to popular opinion suggested a vital surplus upending social life.

ANAESTHESIS: DANCE MARATHONS AND THE LIMITS OF SENSE

After tango, jazz, the Charleston, and animal dances suffused urban dancing life in the 1910s and 1920s, the spectacle of vital energy—its expenditure and depletion—fuelled another dancing 'craze', the so-called 'dance marathons', at the turn of the 1930s (fig. 11.3). But whereas the proliferation of 'new dances' that was characteristic of the first two decades of the twentieth century had seemed to threaten (and enhance) conjugal life, to upend and simultaneously to fashion ambiguous forms of racial segregation and intermixture, the dance marathons appeared spectacularly to be going nowhere; to showcase excess eviscerating itself. Dance marathons suspended the regularity of the work week entirely, while hinging on a performance of round-the-clock work doubling as entertainment. Marathoners danced—often, merely shuffled—for days, weeks, even months at a time in exchange for food or shelter. Rather than dancing excessively fast, they danced excessively *long*; and paradoxically became experts in *not* feeling: they anaesthetized themselves not only to calluses and boils but to the hunger and rootlessness of the Great Depression, hoping in the meantime by their endurance to become noticed and famed. Yet, judging by newspaper coverage from the period, most noticed in dance marathons were the dancers' lopsided, drooping bodies, anaesthetic in another sense: they were exhausted, subsisting at the other limits of (monstrous) exuberance and grace. The spectacle they offered observers was of near lifelessness: they performed a depleted passage into 'bare life'.

'Dance marathons have been but one type of a wave of fatigue contests which has rolled across the country in the last four or five years',[92] wrote sociologist James T. Farrell (1904–1979) in an article titled 'The Dance Marathons' (1931). Influenced by Thorstein Veblen at the University of Chicago, Farrell saw dance marathons as stupid lower-class entertainments, products of

---

89. 'Calls Dance Mania Psychic Epidemic: Participants Less Violent Than Centuries Ago, Says Dr. Brill. Here's Tango-Foot Also. But You Can Get That (If You Want It) by Running a Sewing Machine, Says Dr. Boehme', *New York Times*, 26 April 1914, 36.

90. Castle, *Modern Dancing*, 33.

91. Cited in Castle, *Modern Dancing*, 33–34.

92. James T. Farrell, 'The Dance Marathons', *MELUS* 18.1 (1993): 133–143, 133. See also Ellen Skerrett, 'James T. Farrell's "The Dance Marathons"', *MELUS* 18.1 (1993): 127–131.

FIGURE 11.3 Advertisement for a dance marathon. From Lawrence Mathews, Photographic Scrapbooks: Dance Marathons, c. 1930–1939. Courtesy the Jerome Robbins Dance Division, The New York Public Library for the Performing Arts, Astor, Lennox and Tilden Foundations.

the new organization of leisure that thrived on the 'release of responsibility', novelty, and cheap celebrity. The dance marathons, unlike the medieval flagellant movement, to which he compared them, were 'psychopathic' and 'subnormal' events, deprived of what he saw as the rich spiritual context of the Middle Ages. Dance marathons, Farrell argued, sprang up in the chaotic, anarchic, spiritually void environment of a crassly materialistic modernity in which poor people sought a 'moral holiday' from workday obligations. They also sought monetary rewards and renown which they thought would enable them to forget their misery in the novel glare of the public spotlight.

Dance marathons in depression-era Europe and America galvanized hundreds and eventually thousands of participants who danced relentlessly for days, weeks, and even months at a time. As Carol Martin has written, dance marathons were 'endurance entertainments', the latest in a craze for competitions and world records that was unleashed after the inauguration of the first modern Olympic Games in 1896.[93] They also harked back to novelty happenings from the late nineteenth century, including a 'continuous' medicine show described in the Houdini collection at the Library of Congress: according to Martin, participants walked continuously around the perimeter of a seated arena, performing special feats on the hour for prizes.[94] Marathons could take any number of forms: one man pushed a peanut up a hill with his nose continuously for thirty days, winning a $500 bet; others held hands, drank milk, ate eggs, chewed gum, sat at length atop flagpoles, walked, or

93. Carol Martin, *Dance Marathons: Performing American Culture of the 1920s and 1930s* (Jackson: University Press of Mississippi, 1994), xvi–xviii.

94. Martin, *Dance Marathons*, xvii.

FIGURE 11.4   A dance marathon. From Lawrence Mathews, *Photographic Scrapbooks: Dance Marathons*, c. 1930–1939, courtesy Jerome Robbins Dance Division, The New York Public Library for the Performing Arts, Astor, Lennox and Tilden Foundations.

danced continuously for ever longer periods of time.[95] After starting in Britain and then moving to Europe and America, dance marathons gained increasingly hyperbolic media attention, pitting one nation against another, one competitor against another, and soon enough, humans against time and life itself. With dance marathons, the story of choreomania appears temporarily to arrive at an exhausted halt, as dancers, folded into a public discourse on health and cinematic theatricality, tended increasingly towards the apparent aim of barely moving and *not-feeling*.

Yet they danced a lot, and in that they appeared 'lunatic', according to mildly lampooning coverage in the *Sunday Mirror Magazine*.[96] The craze was relatively subdued. Photographic archives of marathoners held at the New York Public Library for the Performing Arts show couples barely moving in the last stages of a competition, during which they may have slept for only a few minutes every hour for months at a

time. They brushed their teeth, ate, groomed themselves, and used the facilities during carefully circumscribed breaks, even while 'dancing'. By the end, some are not shuffling their feet at all anymore but barely swaying. Dancers take turns holding their partners limp in their arms, slumped over, half delirious, occasionally falling to the ground before being scooped back up by hired attendants. The task was to keep moving at all costs. This was not dancing as much as remaining approximately upright, at the limits of motion, even passively so.

At first, marathons involved acts of dancing prowess, and as the events came to be increasingly commercialized and managed by magnetic impresarios, venues capitalized on—even created—famous dancing couples to provide entertainments for curious onlookers. Some marathoners became semi-professional, moving from one marathon to the next in search of their own brand of theatrical gold, perfecting comic feats for critical acclaim and cash showers. As

95. Martin, *Dance Marathons*, 5–6.

96. 'Pictures That Tell a Story—and Tell It Better Than Words. Our Latest Lunacies', *Sunday Mirror Magazine*, 8 October 1933, 2.

Martin has pointed out, marathons inevitably made up a portion of heightened theatricality, mixing 'real life' exhaustion and the performance of real pain with a choreographed theatrical frame complete with time clocks, staged dramas (including fake and occasionally real weddings), and familiar—often good or bad—characters, as in professional wrestling.[97] But whereas Martin argues that marathons eventually lost their audiences because essentially nothing happened for days at a time during these events and the novelty eventually wore thin, I argue that the marathons' continued appeal and lingering status in the popular imagination was also this catabolic fall into nothingness.

What I call *anaesthesis* pits the ungainly, tired, and 'ugly' against an aesthetic regime centred on heightened affect, sense, and feeling, as well as beauty and elegance. In dance marathons, dancers hardly moved; occasionally, they collapsed. The beaten-down, exhausted fall, signifying defeat in contest, signalled breakdown without release. There was no breakthrough, no shift that produced a new sensation, a new realm of possibilities. Whereas choreomanias were characterized in medical and anthropological literature by their jerky, inelegant, erratic, and spontaneous, almost animal motion, dance marathons, paradoxically, in their sluggish but determined shows of endurance, demonstrated an excess of will, a surplus of voluntary motion, extreme dancing at the final frontier of men's and women's ability to endure physical and mental pain through continuous dance. Dance marathons were a new sort of mania in this configuration: they tapped into a discourse on poor health in opposition to work—nurses' and doctors' stations were regular features of the dance halls, and ice blocks were regularly used to numb swollen limbs—but also capitalized on the performance of extreme banality, and participants' and spectators' extreme endurance of this banality, cloaked in a spirit of incessant eventfulness and fun.

Marathoners performed the ultimate theatre of work and simultaneously the ultimate public performance of economic failure: though a very small minority were professional dancers and many others hoped to gain a dime from cash prizes (or at least be sheltered and fed), dance marathoners also fundamentally showcased the collective passing of time (fig. 11.4). Dance, in this context, hovering at the limit of choreographed motion, showcased the final limits of endurance, performing anaesthetic prowess, an ability to surpass even the extreme sensation of continuous dancing. Dancers affected the jerky movements, contortions, flappings, and twists of black and black-inspired popular dances, to arrive at a completely limp state of bare motion doubling as the ultimate spectacle of willpower, sacrifice, and capacity to thrive in the face of adversity and want. Dance marathoners epitomized gestureless motion: motion without purpose or end, except inasmuch as winning a dance marathon signalled the ability to be the last couple standing, 'still'. Time was the marathoners' greatest enemy but also what they dramatically triumphed against. Time, increasingly, was the yardstick against which new manias were publicly measured: for dancers' excessive endurance more than the supposed monstrosity of their contortions. So, too, in fighting a gruelling race against time, dances were abstracted from theatrical gesture: the performance of unending motion was dramatic enough.

'THE "JITTERBUG" AGE'

By the end of World War II, America and the rest of the world had lifted itself from this torpor and found a new dance 'craze' to call its own; but, as with the medically inflected popular literature on dance manias I have discussed in this book, the 'craze' highlighted gestureless motion. The 1940s, fittingly, were dubbed the 'jitterbug' age—directionless, purposeless, nearsighted, materialistic, and gadget-happy—by Reverend Dr. Christopher J. McCombe, speaking from his pulpit on the Upper West Side of New York.[98] A court ruling some four years later suggested that the jitterbug dance was 'crazy' and that those engaging in it became 'crazy': 'The word "bug" is defined among other meanings as "a crazy person, scheme or idea"', the court ruled. 'The word "jitters" means "extreme nervousness"'.[99] The combination was toxic, setting one

---

97. Martin, *Dance Marathons*. See also Carol Martin, 'Reality Dance: American Dance Marathons', in Malnig, ed., *Ballroom, Boogie, Shimmy Sham, Shake*, 93–108.

98. 'Present Is Scored as "Jitterbug" Age: McCombe Holds We Have Lost Direction and Are Bound to Immediate Interests', *New York Times*, 21 October 1940, 12.

99. 'Court Rules Jitterbug Is All Word Implies, Jitter for "Nervous" and Bug for "Crazy"', *New York Times*, 3 May 1944, 21.

unwitting participant into a tizzy after she was 'sent into a spin by a "jive-maddened marine"' and sustained unspecified injuries.[100] More worrisome in East Germany, the jitterbug (or *Swing heini*) was said, by Communist authorities keen to keep America's swing music at bay, to 'rape' 'German culture' and '[prostitute] Germany's musical heritage' with its 'wild convulsions'. 'Jazz addicts' in Soviet-occupied Germany were cautioned to 'work off their surplus energy on rubble piles' rather than succumb to this 'Marshall Plan export' designed to 'deaden the minds of the masses' with its saxophone doodling and trumpet blares.[101] The post–World War II world was edgy, skittish. Burt notes that for Katherine Dunham, the jitterbug relieved tension rather than building tension, as the 'fascistic' mass dances of the 1930s purported to do.[102]

When Elvis Presley (1935–1977) burst onto the American cultural scene in the 1950s with his black moves and childlike pouty lips, swinging his hips and hooking his knees inward like a rag doll, he fused all of the racial and sexual ambivalence of the preceding decades in a torrent of energy that provoked its own mania. Psychiatric and psychoanalytic literature, bleeding into the popular press, once again weighed in with injunctions against this contagious behaviour spilling out of bounds.[103] Youth culture and the new spirit of contestation appeared to be ever more dramatically out of hand. Rock 'n' roll, jagged and fast, in its turn donned the mantle of the 'dancing disease'.

'THE RAVING FRENZY OF THE HIGHWAYS': CHOREA IN THE AGE OF ROCK 'N' ROLL

Joost A. M. Meerloo (1903–1976), physician and psychiatrist at Columbia University, read the energetic outpouring of the 1950s and 1960s as yet another incarnation of the dancing

disease—a disease now so modern that it could be found in the very spirit of car culture, youth culture, and of course rock 'n' roll. So, whereas the literature on rock 'n' roll is vast, far too much so to treat adequately here, the persistence of the imagined genealogy and discourse of choreomania it represents compels a cursory glance. For Meerloo, dance manias, which have surfaced, he argued, from prehistory to the present, constitute an expression of mass anger, impotence, and frustration, a raging desire to return to the womb and anaesthetize oneself to society through rhythmic pulsations similar to what a mother uses when rocking her child to sleep. Dance maniacs are trapped, for Meerloo, in their childlike impulses, are sexually and socially unfulfilled: it is never possible, he pointedly notes, to return to the womb. An account he provides of a jukebox scene in which some disenfranchised youth hit up against the alienating violence of 'modernity' encapsulates virtually all the paradoxes and prejudices of the discourse on choreomania I have presented thus far, from the language of primitive and childlike animality to dancers' nearly incoherent shrieking and writhing; epileptiform 'seizures'; uncontrollable and spontaneous outbursts; convulsions; ambivalently white and black cultural roots; pantomimic motion, 'regressive' and 'automatic' at once, tribal and ecstatic, aimless, and apparently drunken; and the final anaesthetization of all sensation (and sense) in an exhausted collapse. The description bears quoting at length. In a chapter titled 'Syncopated Rapture', in *Dance Craze and Sacred Dance* (1961), Meerloo writes:

Once I witnessed a spontaneous outburst of Rock 'n' Roll in a small town. Here, in a combination of drugstore and diner, a juke box sent forth a seductive rhythm supported by a whining set of sounds. From the very first note the young people near the small bar became untamable. They started to dance; no, that is hardly the right word. A frenzied rhythmic seizure

---

100. 'Court Rules Jitterbug Is All Word Implies'.

101. 'Reds Advise Germans of Jitterbug Dangers', *New York Times*, 11 August 1949, 26.

102. Burt, *Alien Bodies*, 190–191.

103. The full explosion of 'Elvis mania' tends to be dated to 1956. See e.g. Joel Williamson, *Elvis Presley: A Southern Life* (New York: Oxford University Press, 2015), 41–42. Williamson notes that the language of mania and contagion extended particularly to teenage girls, widely described as 'hysterical', even '[psychotically] ill'. Williamson, *Elvis Presley*, 44. Shayla Thiel-Stern discusses the gendered aspect of popular music- and dance-induced 'moral panic' in Shayla Thiel-Stern, *From the Dance Hall to Facebook: Teen Girls, Mass Media, and Moral Panic in the United States 1905–2010* (Boston: University of Massachusetts Press, 2014), attributing popular disdain for such enthusiasm to sexism aimed particularly at younger (adolescent) women. For a recent journalistic account of the link between medieval 'dance manias', Franz Liszt mania, Beatlemania, and countless

took possession of them: they yelled and shouted and rocked themselves more and more into a rhythmic trance until it had gone far beyond all the accepted versions of human dancing.

Before the music had started, the place had been the usual, rather dull meeting place . . . . Then the juke box fills the awkward silence with primitive melodramatic noise. Suddenly, as if by magic, the quivering rhythm gets hold of the teenagers and lures them from their high perches at the counter. The music brings to life an age-old inner complaint, a nagging melody. It is the crying and hopeless sorrow of deprived and frustrated mankind, aroused by all the pouting and self-pity we feel for ourselves. The forgotten and rejected baby in us awakens and pants for new satisfaction, for new rocking and endearment. Negro-blues and cowboy song and jazzy rhythm are united in a seductive rocking and blubbering. There is squealing and whimpering, whining and yelping, writhing, rocking and rolling, aroused by a tortuous rhythmic monotony. The stepped up tempo and beat may go over into the madness of oblivion and selfdestruction [sic].

From now on the youngsters forget their boring civilization, and the infant and prehistoric man in them comes to life. A wild pantomime is displayed, resembling the rhythm of tribal utterances and the convulsive outcry of revivals. This is neither music nor plain, unadulterated sex, as some authors claim, but merely suggestive rhythm, a common return to the Nirvanic dance. The music is full of baby sounds. The dance means being energized by one's own body rhythms and by the desperate ecstasy that wants to cast off control. True, it is also an outburst of sexual rhythm of the pelvis without real erotic fulfilment, and with an aimless shaking of the hips. It is the exalted trance of a dream without reality; it is an outlet, an act of common frustration without joyful rapture.

This glamorous show of ecstatic abandon covers up an empty feeling of something lacking deep inside them. It is the incoherent expression of living in a seemingly love-lorn world. It is sleep-dancing and mass-hypnotism, a collective trance. It is boredom and frustration concentrated into a rhythmic trance of the body, while the mind is benumbed. Awareness is gone, personality is gone, shame is gone. In the rocking trance man is like drunk—dance drunk. He may attack, he may foam with rage, he may yell, he may destroy, he may use some vulgar movements that are usually taboo—civilized restraint is gone. Such regressive rhythm can give the illusion of life as a passive rolling on, as a self-revolving automatic movement of whirling sensation. It can make people whine constantly because they do not want to step out of their lullabye into reality and responsibility. But this very craze can help the dancers to overcome frustrations and to give them the vitalizing regression that makes them more tolerant to the world afterwards.[104]

In Meerloo's account, rock 'n' roll dons all the characteristics of choreomania: crazes that erupt in a collective, organic return to primeval substance without form; to motion without choreography. As with the romantic recuperations of choreomania that I discussed in the previous chapters, and as in Leiris's account, this experience of formlessness paradoxically enabled the fantasy of a new world order to emerge, in contrast to the stark, machinic rhythms of modernity and the childlike, nearly animal power underlying them. The sexual rhythmicity without sexual reproduction was excessive but presented the possibility of a translation or transfiguration: from sheer anger and energy to revolt. Yet, in spite of its revolutionary potential, all this energy was redirected to economic ends and the money-making frenzy of contemporary American capitalism. 'Swept on by a tremendous money-making potential of those who make the musical records', Meerloo wrote, rock 'n' roll 'demonstrated the violent mayhem long

---

other popular 'manias', 'frenzies', and 'madnesses', including for the far more recent boy band One Direction, see e.g. Dorian Lynskey, 'Beatlemania: The "Screamers" and Other Tales of Fandom', *Guardian*, 29 September 2013. http://www.theguardian.com/music/2013/sep/29/beatlemania-screamers-fandom-teenagers-hysteria, accessed 12 March 2016.

104. Joost A. M. Meerloo, *Dance Craze and Sacred Dance* (London: Peter Owen, 1962), 32–34.

repressed everywhere on earth' transformed into capitalist greed.[105]

In the new age, '[ancient] chorea has become the raving frenzy of the highways'.[106] St. Vitus's dance was now a mad choreography of fast and slow lanes, a four-wheeled rage displaced onto automobiles and aeroplanes.[107] McCarren describes the modern rhythmicity and choreography of cars and machines in *Dancing Machines: Choreography in the Age of Mechanical Reproduction* (2003), concomitant to what Sloterdijk has called 'infinite mobilization', the ceaseless roar of movement for movement's sake in the hyperindustrial age. This movement for movement's sake further corresponds to what I have called, after Agamben, 'meaningless gesture', a 'pure' choreography denoting the tautological relationship chorea holds to dance: as movement deprived of ulterior purpose, movement performed without end. This book has described the pathologization of such movement surging up seemingly without rhythm or structure. I have argued that the pathologization of such apparently excessive and uncontrolled movement—tics, jerks, swaying, hopping, running, prostration, shaking, and falls—constitutes an ideological underbelly in the long history of a transnationally mobile scientific modernity, a prejudice still rampant in contemporary approaches to crowd control and to the rapid popping and krumping of hip-hop, breakdance, and other historically black forms of popular dance and music culture.

RAVES, BURNING MAN: CAPITAL RECUPERATION

As this chapter itself moves rapidly forward in time to the late twentieth and early twenty-first centuries, we see that the remnants of the 'choreomania' prejudice are strong. The awkward concatenation of speed culture with the figure of the primitive beatitude of the horde morphed in the 1990s into a new Dionysian paradigm. Rave parties—in which thousands of revellers gathered to drop MDMA (methylenedioxymethamphetamine, aka Ecstasy) and dance for days or weeks to machinically fast-paced electronic music—were transforming into (typically non-orgiastic) bacchanalia that re-romanticized counter-cultural movements and their imagined antecedents in the Grecian past.[108] This return to the Dionysian myth of collective manias, partially divested of colonial undertones, recast them in the guise of a new millennialist enthusiasm recuperating premodern antiquity into the postmodern. New romantic interest in the primitive and the enthusiastic embrace of technology made rave parties at once classically ecstatic and hyper-modern: electronic beats spun by all-night DJs graced outdoor dance parties in a back-to-nature—yet technophilic—setting. Large fuzzy pants, water bottles, and tiny backpacks stocking energy bars, MDMA, 'speed', and other methamphetamines, as well as other rave-party paraphernalia, turned rave culture into a movement of international and, soon, international commercial proportions. The Berlin Love Parade, which mobilized millions of dancers beginning in 1989, four months before the Berlin Wall fell, and was intended to be a party whose spirit was 'healing' through music and dance, also became an instrument of capital gain. McFit, a European fitness club, poured 1,000,000 euros into the party, which was expected to attract at least 750,000 people in 2006.[109] In 2010, the Love Parade came to a close, after twenty-one dancers died and over five hundred more were injured in a crush.[110]

The epic Burning Man events have similarly offered modern-day partygoers (and world

---

105. Meerloo, *Dance Craze*, 32–34.

106. Joost A. M. Meerloo, *Delusion and Mass-Delusion* (New York: Nervous and Mental Disease Monographs, 1949), 75.

107. Meerloo, *Dance Craze*, 30.

108. See François Gauthier and Guy Ménard, eds., *Technoritualités: Religiosité rave* (Montreal: Université du Québec à Montréal, 2001); Graham St John, ed., *Rave Culture and Religion* (New York: Routledge, 2004); Marie-Claude Vaudrin, *La musique techno, ou, Le retour de Dionysos: Je rave, tu raves, nous rêvons* (Paris: L'Harmattan, 2004); and Andy Brown, *Rave: The Spiritual Dimension* (Hampshire: Kaos, 1994). On the politics of raves as counter-culture, see also Michel Gaillot, Jean-Luc Nancy, and Michel Maffesoli, *Multiple Meaning: Techno, an Artistic and Political Laboratory of the Present*, trans. Warren Niesluchowski (Paris: Éditions Dis voir, 1999); and Lionel Bourg, *La liesse populaire en France: 'Rave' et lutte de classes, le néo-populisme à l'œuvre, brèves considérations à propos des mouvements de foule du 12 juillet 1998* (Saussines: Cadex, 1998). On dance prohibitions, raves, and the New York City cabaret laws, see Tara McCall, *This Is Not a Rave: In the Shadow of a Subculture* (New York: Thunder's Mouth Press, 2001).

109. A. J. Goldman, 'Berliners Will Again Be Dancing in the Streets', *New York Times*, 15 July 2006.

110. See 'Berlin Love Parade: In Brief', http://www.berlinloveparade.com, last accessed 21 June 2017.

love seekers) a 'neo-pagan' dancing place since 1986. Tens of thousands of celebrants flock every year to this week-long festival to enjoy the 'immediate experience' of 'contact' with the 'natural world'.[111] Similarly, in the last ten or twenty years, a surge of renewed interest in the tarantella as a dying cultural form has shifted anthropological discourse into the sphere of cultural heritage, casting this as local tradition to preserve and emotionally to reconnect with. The surge in popularity of tarantella culture among younger generations has yielded an explosion of festivals, concerts, and recordings throughout the Italian south. The Notte della Taranta (Night of the Taranta), held every August in Puglia, has brought a mass-scale culture of international pop stardom to revivals of the tarantella, with performances for audiences of up to four hundred thousand people eager to cultivate a sense of historical continuity in the region, boosting local revenue through national and international tourism. Hip-hop and techno remixes of traditional tarantella tunes are widely available on street corners and YouTube, updating the trend with an urban beat, further boosting local revenue and cultural pride. But this particularism—seeing the tarantella as quintessentially southern Italian—also recuperates and nearly eliminates a complicated medico-historical node, taming and repackaging it into a bundle of local cultural practices. The translatio from a medical to an anthropological and now a 'heritage' discourse moves the tarantella, with its cast of discursive others, out of one scene of observation and into another, revealing—staging—yet another transfiguration of the 'past'.

The coda that follows moves to my own field of observation and final reflections on modernity and the Bacchic choir: what I conceive as the deep configuration of crowd politics as a politics of border control, stemming tides of migration and 'spill'. Simultaneously, the boisterous, unwieldy transformation of bodies—their public *appearance* and occupation of space—*figures* a productively contestatory disorder.

---

111. The 10 Principles of Burning Man, http://www.burningman.org/culture/philosophical-center/10-principles, accessed 14 March 2016. See also Brian Doherty, *This Is Burning Man: The Rise of the New American Underground* (Dallas: BenBella Books, 2006); Lee Gilmore and Mark van Proyen, eds., *AfterBurn: Reflections on Burning Man* (Albuquerque: University of New Mexico Press, 2005); and Jessica Bruder et al., *Burning Book: A Visual History of Burning Man* (New York: Simon Spotlight Entertainment, 2007).

Coda

Moving Fields, Modernity, and the Bacchic Chorus

> Anxiety links us to the memory of the past while we struggle to choose a path through the ambiguous history of the present.
>
> —Homi K. Bhabha, *The Location of Culture* (1994)

> I'm working with a notion of comparative knowledge produced through an *itinerary*, always marked by a 'way in', a history of locations and a location of histories.
>
> —James Clifford, *Routes* (1997)

AT THE conclusion to *Les mots et les choses: Une archéologie des science humaines* [The Order of Things: An Archaeology of the Human Sciences] (1966), Foucault argues that 'man' is a relatively recent invention—and, more so, that 'man' has only recently (at most in Europe since the sixteenth century) figured at the centre of a web of social and human sciences, an object of scientific and social scientific analysis and biopower. In her recent reading of Foucault's lectures on biopolitics, Wendy Brown further notes that Foucault by and large avoids discussion of the demos, the plural body, the organized grouping of the individuals that make up a democratic 'society'.[1] This book does not quite deal with the organized group but with another sort of plural body conspicuously absent from Foucault's analysis of biopower; another account of the scientific and social scientific language—the historical epistemology (or discursive history)—of 'man'.

With choreomania, the demos is in disarray. The discursive black hole Foucault describes as 'madness' emerges as a discursive zone of articulation around which scientific knowledge *about* chaotically moving bodies organizes itself. This book offers another way of doing—and writing—biohistory, as a history of (moving) bodies *disorganized* in scientific discourse, collaged and transposed onto one another through the very literary operations of comparison and anecdote. These movements, occurring in scenes, *petits récits*, and minor displacements, nevertheless present tidal shifts: what Foucault, after Canguilhem, called conceptual *displacements* and *transformations*,[2] which I have further described in terms of the geopolitical, trans-discursive movements of translatio.

This alternative history of 'man', at the heart of a demos in disarray, reveals choreopolitics at the core of a complex interplay of modern

---

1. See Brown, *Undoing the Demos*, esp. 85–87.
2. Foucault, *L'archéologie du savoir*, 11.

imaginings. But the demos (or its dishevelled other half, choreomania) does not become constituted any more decisively than does 'man'. Rather, 'man', like his shaking, plural conceptual counterparts, at closer scrutiny melts right back into the seascape Foucault alludes to at the conclusion of *The Order Of Things*: 'man', Foucault writes, just as he was conjured into being in recent centuries, might just as soon become 'erased, like a face drawn in sand at the edge of the sea', dissolving back into the plural and heteromorphic formations he emerged from.[3] Yet if 'man' in Foucault's analysis is a sand drawing, at the limit of the sea, liable at any moment to be washed away again into the discursive vastness of scientific thinking before 'he' (and arguably she) was imagined, written, drawn, then the Dionysian throng emerges as the oceanic fiction at the limit of which this 'man' emerges. I have argued that 'man', in broadly 'modern' Europe—by which I mean a Europe and its colonies constantly preoccupied with looking back over their shoulders at an ever-receding past—conceived himself *in relation to* the nearly intangible figure of the organic mob, the movement of pre-individuated bodies, cast, as I have argued, as a rumbling horde. I have further argued that this horde was frequently imagined as feminine (though not always female) and dark, obscure (often black), animal, and childlike, in Khanna's terms, after Freud, a 'dark continent' of ultimately indescribable—yet paradoxically *again and again* described—alterity. This horde appears as the phantasmatic negative against which a fiction of scientific lucidity (and cultural universality) arose, in the nineteenth and twentieth centuries, paradoxically, *anecdotally*.

The fiction and fantasy of the unthinking horde is not new but emerges with force in the nineteenth century, morphing and passing across discursive terrains through the twentieth, and arguably still subtly in force today. In his 12 November 1965 diary entry 'Dance in My Experience', Oiticica describes the '"Dionysian" dance' as one that is 'born out of the interior rhythm of the collective, [and] exteriorizes itself as a characteristic of popular groupings, nations, etc'.[4] Contrary to the '[excessive] intellectualization' of ballet and 'opposed to organized choreography', the '"Dionysian" dance' for Oiticica thrives on improvisation. Improvisation allows 'immersion into rhythm [to take] place', yielding 'a flux where the intellect remains obscured by an internal mythical force that operates at an individual and collective level'. The flux is so strong, Oiticica writes, that the distinction between the individual and the collective vanishes.[5] The quotation marks around 'Dionysian' are significant. By his own admission, Oiticica is not talking about the literal Dionysian dance—the ecstasies and rituals of bacchantic men and women dramatized by Euripides in the fifth century BCE and decried by Plato a few decades later; though arguably even those accounts were fantastical conjurings. Oiticica does not purport to offer a historical reconstruction or reperformance of Greek events. But he has a strong felt sense of the Dionysian and what it means to him and to his readers: a rhythmic, pulsating force that calls up nations and in which the experience of individuality dissolves.

DROMOGRAPHY: DANCE AND THE SPEED OF CHANGE

This coda brings the discursive history of choreomania back to a consideration of 'discipline', to argue finally that the choreopolitical dimension of the dancing crowd as a constitutive force of social and discursive government poses the question of borders and border policing. In this sense, conjuration of the 'discipline' of dance—and discursive disciplinarization of dancing bodies recounted in this book—reveals an ambivalent disciplinary move on my part, at once claiming 'choreomania' in or as a history of ideas about 'dance' and performance and refusing such a neat disciplinary alignment. The borders of fields are always in motion, I have argued with Martin, subject to performative re-enactments and displacements, even while institutions and markets (and governments) find it far more efficacious, Foucault decisively showed, to keep knowledge and bodies aligned.

A recent news story serves as a case in point. A few Israeli soldiers briefly joined in a dance

---

3. Foucault, *The Order of Things*, 422. This remark is especially premonitory, given the recent surge of writing on the 'posthuman', new materialisms, and other scientific and philosophical paradigms seeking to undo the supposed unity (and hegemony over all other aspects of the natural world) of 'man'.

4. Oiticica, 'Dance in My Experience', 52.

5. Oiticica, 'Dance in My Experience', 52.

with some Palestinian wedding revellers in Hebron. This temporary shared social space resulted in the Israelis' dismissal from service on the grounds of reckless 'exposure to unnecessary danger',[6] and the viral spread of their disciplinarization on social media. The Israeli Defense Forces chiefs' message was clear: these soldiers should have stayed apart, actors in a theatre of war, performing, without flinching, their role as guardians of a state of emergency without release. Engaging in this communal dance ripped the fabric of opposition and impasse; a symbolic hole was torn through the wall separating the two camps. The soldiers' reprimand was staged for the Israeli public and for the world at large. Yet YouTube uploads suggest a proliferation of moments of play rippling through the fabric of military deadlock: soldiers breaking out in a playfully choreographed dance while patrolling eerily quiet streets, or in one case leading a group of Palestinian children in an impromptu game of mimicry to the 1970s disco tune 'Hands Up, Baby Hands Up', perverting the usual policing choreography requiring the weaker party to put their hands up in a gesture not of play but of surrender. These moments of *common dance* subvert a political fabric that allows only tightly choreographed moments of crossover and no moments of improvised breaks.[7]

The irony in the Israeli case is patent: the soldier leading the 1970s disco dance still holds a machine gun strapped to his back, and he and the children are separated by an electric fence. He is standing on a tall concrete block many feet higher than they are. Perhaps he covertly mocks their willingness to join in a game in which he has them put their hands up. But they all wave their arms right and left, up and down, doing the wave, bobbing their knees, and bouncing around; the children seem to be enjoying themselves, as does the soldier, and for a moment the encounter suggests a different sort of relation, predicated not on martial discipline but on the loose play of imitation. Projected to a deferred audience via YouTube, the dance shows

a moment of respite and rapprochement framed by the absurd arsenal of military technology.

Moments of shared intensity shift the performance of power balance and provisionally its experience, emerging as excrescences in the fabric of everyday life that serve to contest the status quo, to mark time, and to join people temporarily in crowd formations that spill out into public space and transform private homes. Some of the cases this book has described have been more dance-like; others might not have been recognized as such by those engaging in them. The figure of dance as an aesthetic formation privileging movement encompasses forms that might elsewhere be described as sport, ritual, or, in cases here, movement disorders and epidemic disease. But uniting these, I have shown, was a discursive genealogy that linked modern notions of energetic efficiency and somatic normativity with social movements erupting worldwide. I have traced the journey of these corporeal and discursive formations with the aim to show not only how barely choreographed moments have marked various eras but also how these were grouped together under the banner term 'choreomania' at a time when shifts in energetic expenditure and the reorganization of disciplines brought new ways of seeing to light.

THE MOVEMENT OF THOUGHT

The concept of choreomania, I have shown, is hardly distinguishable from the events it seeks to designate: events linked to disorders of the nervous system and to altered states of consciousness as well as to crowd contact and apparently simple village fêtes. Multi-stranded and polydisciplinary, the trajectory of choreomania thus shows how concepts move and fields emerge and transform with them. Following Canguilhem and Foucault, I have argued that the history of a concept is not ultimately the history of its progressive refinement or its increasingly rational, enlightened, or abstract formulation;

---

6. Seth Freedman, 'Israel Should Praise Their Dancing IDF Soldiers, Not Condemn Them', *Guardian*, 29 August 2013, http://www.theguardian.com/commentisfree/2013/aug/29/israel-gangnam-idf-soldiers, accessed 9 September 2013.

7. It would merit another study of its own to think about the 'break' with Fred Moten: discussing the 'blackness' of improvisation, Moten writes in a chapter titled 'The Sentimental Avant-Garde' (playfully disrupting the language of military strategy that the term 'avant-garde' normally implies) of 'a kind of lyricism of the surplus—invagination, rupture, collision, augmentation'. He further writes: 'Such blackness is only in that it exceeds itself; it bears the groundedness of an uncontainable outside. It's an erotics of the cut, submerged in the broken, breaking space-time of an improvisation'. See Fred Moten, *In the Break: The Aesthetics of the Black Radical Tradition* (Minneapolis: University of Minnesota Press, 2003), 26.

rather, it is the history—the story—of its passage through various fields of elaboration and validation ('champs de constitution et de validité') and the successive language rules ('règles d'usage') through which it operates.[8] The history of a concept tells the story of the theoretical worlds, contexts, and homes (*oikoi*) through which it is formed, repeated, expanded, and eventually reified.

Yet I have also shown that choreomania was never entirely reified; it has remained plastic and malleable, slippery and abstruse. The concept itself mimicked its object, moving as rapidly and raggedly as that to which it ostensibly referred. Although concepts of every sort do so, choreomania has had a peculiar life, at once marginal and all-pervasive, emerging in its early modern form with Paracelsus, reaching a peak in the mid- to late-nineteenth century, and petering out in the early days of the twentieth century, although cognate ideas existed long before, describing bacchanals, most glaringly, and other benign forms of religious heresy; and others continued to emerge in different forms long after. Arguably, literature on the twist, the mambo, raves, flash mobs, big dances, and even the viral spread of the Harlem shake or Psy's 'Gangnam Style' borrows from the lexical field particular to choreomania, though its medical mantle has largely been shed. Only the figure of the virus maintains a link to the modern language of contagion; curiously, the long history of medical literature on dance manias has been largely occluded.[9]

THE PERSISTENCE OF VISION

Yet in medical literature and the popular press, dance manias continue to crop up as holdovers of some lost, more superstitious, and more irrational time that in this view is still curiously, dramatically with us: conversion hysterias, mass hysterias, and especially mass psychogenic illnesses are often referred back to older events, including, paradigmatically, St. Vitus's dance. Not only does this view continue to pathologize a broad range of complex social phenomena, but the strangeness and apparent illegibility of 'dance manias' continues to grant them a special status as medical and historical curiosities.[10] Recent psychiatric literature, particularly in the field of transcultural psychiatry, links epidemic dancing to other forms of 'culture-bound syndromes' such as *koro*, or testicle-shrinkage anxiety, *latah*, and *amok*, describing these as culturally specific forms of medical (often hysterical) disease.[11] Historians have continued to link

8. '*Déplacements* et *transformations* des concepts: les analyses de G. Canguilhem peuvent servir de modèles; elles montrent que l'histoire d'un concept n'est pas, en tout et pour tout, celle de son affinement progressif, de sa rationalité continûment croissante, de son gradient d'abstraction, mais celle de ses divers champs de constitution et de validité, celle de ses règles successives d'usage, des milieux théoriques multiples où s'est poursuivie et achevée son élaboration'. Foucault, *L'archéologie du savoir*, 11.

9. See e.g. Harmony Bench, 'Screendance 2.0: Social Dance-Media', *Participations* 7.2 (2010), http://www.participations.org/Volume%207/Issue%202/special/bench.htm, accessed 21 September 2013. Susan Leigh Foster, in 'Movement's Contagion: The Kinesthetic Impact of Performance', points to early physiological studies of kinaesthesia and proprioception (termed the 'sixth sense') and to John Martin's 1930s comment that dance affects viewers contagiously; but these are concepts of contagion or mimicry operating between dancer and viewer rather than within a group, threatening to spread to a larger one. See Susan Leigh Foster, 'Movement's Contagion: The Kinesthetic Impact of Performance', in Tracy Davis, ed., *The Cambridge Companion to Performance Studies* (New York: Cambridge University Press, 2009), 46–59.

10. See for example 'Dancing Mania (St. John's Dance, St. Vitus's Dance, Tarantism)', in George Childs Kohn, ed., *Encyclopedia of Plague and Pestilence: From Ancient Times to the Present*, rev. ed. (New York: Facts on File, 2001), 75–76, 75. Roderick E. McGrew, in his entry 'Dancing Mania. Tarantism', in *Encyclopedia of Medical History* (New York: McGraw-Hill, 1985), calls the 'dancing mania' a 'well-defined, ritualistic behavior pattern' and an 'outbreak of hysteria' (83). Thierry Grandmougin, Catherine Bourdet, and Jean-Marc Gurrachaga argue that the medical history of chorea began with a strange plague ('étrange fléau') along the Rhine characterized by a desperate and irrepressible urge to dance, pronounced suggestibility, and epidemic propagation. Thierry Grandmougin, Catherine Bourdet, and Jean-Marc Gurrachaga, 'De la danse de Saint Guy à la chorée de Huntington: Rappels sur l'émergence d'un concept medical', *M/S médecine/sciences* 13 (1997): 850–854, 850. More recently still, Thiago Cardoso Vale and Francisco Cardoso rehearse the well-worn story that original descriptions of chorea (the movement disorder) date back to the medieval epidemic 'dancing mania'. Thiago Cardoso Vale and Francisco Cardoso, 'Chorea: A Journey through History', *Tremor and Other Hyperkinetic Movements* 5 (2015), doi: 10.7916/D8WM1C98, accessed 12 May 2016.

11. See Wen-Shing Tseng, 'Epidemic Mental Disorders', in *Handbook of Cultural Psychiatry* (San Diego: Academic Press, 2001), 265–290. Tseng argues that epidemic mental disorders can be traced to the dancing epidemics of the 1300s–1600s; he links these to the possessions of Loudun, witchcraft trials, and H. G. Wells's *War of the Worlds* before connecting them in turn to *koro* in Singapore, Thailand, Southern China, and India, as well as to a nervous twitching epidemic among high school girls in 1939 in Baltimore and a range of other anxiety and panic attacks and collective delusions. See also Wen-Shing Tseng, *Clinician's Guide to Cultural Psychiatry* (Honolulu: University of Hawaii School of Medicine, 2003). On *koro* see esp. Pow Meng Yap's original 'Koro—A Culture-Bound Depersonalization Syndrome', *British Journal of Psychiatry* 111.470 (1965): 43–50.

'dancing manias' to collective hysterias obliquely rehearsed in amateur scientific and medical historiography, bemoaning the inexplicable, 'strange' quality of the dances as if they were exceptionally peculiar and remained forever locked out of contemporary modes of understanding. In Rosen's terms, dancing manias were 'bizarre' phenomena redolent of a faraway past, explicable if anything only by reference to the ill-defined notion of 'stress'.[12] Historian John Waller upped the ante and called these 'deadly dance[s]' 'terrifyingly bizarre' and 'extraordinary' reminders of the 'ineffable strangeness of the human brain'.[13]

Arguably dance manias were rarely bizarre, though they were described at great length as such. Indeed, a range of dance-like events appeared on the scene of modern thought as instances of a broader pathological condition, a disorder of erratic, excess motion. Baffling by the sheer breadth of phenomena supposedly encompassing it, the discursive history of 'choreomania' unravels a cross-disciplinary language of pathological contagion that suggests persistent discomfort among writers with the imagined incursion of an unwieldy past into the present. Modernity, in this view, wrestles with the spectre of childlike, exuberant spontaneity, a myth that is cultivated and repeated. By projecting this myth onto colonial people and political underclasses, scientific modernity wraps itself in a figurative counterpoint: a straight, white, pure, and virtually motionless being, aseptic and ascetic at once. Not even modern architecture's straight edges—epitomizing functional, anti-baroque aesthetics—were ever so clean. They, too, like the triumphalist scientism they represented, are always haunted by the phantasm of a dirty and uncontainable past that might at any point come back to unhinge them.

PLURAL AND POLYMORPHIC HYSTERIAS

Thus the discursive history of choreomania has maintained a strong link to medicine and neurology, movement disorders and psychiatric epidemiology. Transposed onto contemporary medical frames, the notion of choreomania gels into the figure of collective hysteria awkwardly mapped onto the medical history of movement disorders, including various forms of dyskinesia, a general term used to describe the irregular and unpredictable motion of people's limbs. Patients suffering from these are subject to concomitant voyeurism and ostracization, as well as inaccurate and confusing diagnostic representations, as a recent article in the *New England Journal of Medicine* underlines.[14] But chorea major, choreomania, continues to enjoy a minor, parallel life in the annals of neurological history. Classed as a disease, it is still routinely defined as a strange

---

12. Rosen, in *Madness in Society*, describes dancing manias as 'one of the more bizarre episodes in the history of medieval Europe' (196). John Waller, who popularized a sensationalizing history of the 1518 dancing 'epidemic' in *A Time to Dance, a Time to Die: The Extraordinary Story of the Dancing Plague of 1518* (Cambridge: Icon Books, 2008), wrote that this was 'one of the strangest epidemics in recorded history'. Waller, 'In a Spin', 117. In 'Falling Down', *Guardian*, 18 September 2008, his article on an outbreak of fainting in a school in Tanzania, Waller also wrote that for doctors studying this and related phenomena (he cites a laughing epidemic in villages west of Lake Victoria in 1962) 'the events were reminiscent of a far stranger and darker phenomenon: the dancing plague' and goes on to note that it was 'perhaps the most bizarre of all mass hysterias'; http://www.guardian.co.uk/science/2008/sep/18/psychology, accessed 6 September 2012. See also John Waller, 'A Forgotten Plague: Making Sense of Dancing Mania', *Lancet* 373.9664 (2009): 624–625. Backman described the fourteenth-century dances as reaching a 'terrifying intensity' (*Religious Dances*, 190). In a slightly less hyperbolic vein, Midelfort argues that one of the major problems in dealing with early modern histories of madness is 'the possibility, even the likelihood, that [they] experienced certain disorders that no longer occur. In cases like the dancing mania, we encounter strange diseases that do not fit into modern diagnostic categories very well' (*A History of Madness*, 25). In *Exorcism and Enlightenment: Johann Joseph Gassner and the Demons of Eighteenth-Century Germany* (New Haven: Yale University Press, 2005), Midelfort notes that we still do not know what St. Vitus's dance was. Jean Fogo Russell argued that the ravages of modern war and dictatorships provoked contemporary forms of emotionally charged phenomena, 'hysterical' as in the Middle Ages but taking place in music clubs and jazz festivals. Russell, 'Dancing Mania', 191. Robert E. Bartholomew, who has written countless books, articles, and opinion pieces on the dancing mania 'myth', has opted for a mass psychogenic illness hypothesis, arguing that there never was any such thing as a dancing mania any more than there have been UFO landings or witchcraft. See for example Robert E. Bartholomew, *Exotic Deviance: Medicalizing Cultural Idioms from Strangeness to Illness* (Boulder, CO: University Press of Colorado, 2000); and Robert E. Bartholomew, *Little Green Men, Meowing Nuns and Head-Hunting Panics: A Study of Mass Psychogenic Illness and Social Delusion* (Jefferson, NC: McFarland, 2001).

13. Waller, 'In a Spin', 117, 121.

14. Maria Stamelou et al., 'Movement Disorders on YouTube—Caveat Spectator', *New England Journal of Medicine* 365.12 (2011): 1160–1161.

chapter in epidemic pathology, neurology, and, alternatively, epidemic and social psychiatry. Considered as a mass psychogenic illness, epidemic chorea fits all too snugly into a contemporary taxonomy of hysterias that Showalter has suggested are 'flooding' the contemporary media landscape, 'infecting', in her terms, countries and cultures all over the world.[15] In Micale's view, the hysterical diagnosis disappeared after having reached a heyday in Charcot's time, both as a clinical malady and cultural metaphor.[16] But the cultural imaginary of the hysteric is still strong, serving as a marker for all forms of acting out.

So were the 'choreomaniacs' hysterical? I have argued that the history of ideas about choreomania sits alongside that of the so-called great nineteenth-century hysterias, of the Blanches, the Augustines, and the Anna O.s of Charcot's and Freud's clinics. But choreomanias occupy a space of collective motility that is more akin to collective ecstasy or enthusiasm, classed as hyperkinetic activity not always mapped onto neurological (or psychosocial) terrain. The history of their neurological description is significant, and Charcot's sphere of influence ensured the global spread of the choreomania concept; yet the particular mixture of motile and mental disorders—and plural formations within which 'choreomanias' occurred—suggests that their discursive 'field' occupied a different space, proper to moving groups.

In this regard, the hyperkinesis that characterized nineteenth-century views of choreomania put political uprisings and jerky physical disorders in the same light, seeing all hyperactive locomotion as part of a new world order that rehearses the old, but faster; and, significantly, more erratically. The lack of control described among choreomaniacs marked them against the orderly workings of political society and the normal functioning of biological mechanisms in the figure of a collective body politic that squirmed and threw tantrums at the dawning of a bleaker day, refusing to conform; and refusing to sit still.

This acceleration and intensification suggests a restlessness in the modern age that is different from the neurasthenic or hysterical behaviours of women (and men) too sexually repressed to

navigate a Victorian society asking them to control desire by denying it. Early formulations of hysteria suggested a non-sexual etiology, pitting childishness against corporeal control and intellectual reserve. I have argued that this culture of control has fed a modern narrative describing regimented activity and especially work, resulting not so much in the disciplining or policing of individuals and social groups that Foucault describes as in the self-propelled—and mutually reinforced—hyperactivity of an industrial society that is divorced, paradoxically, from the pleasure of non-material expenditure (expenditure of time and energy) that its wealth could occasion. This hyperactivity leads to action exercised without recourse to an affective or corporeal practice of joy, except inasmuch as the latter contributes to a perpetual increase in material gain. Rest, as such, and conviviality become valuable only inasmuch as they feed heightened output.

Yet surely we do not dance or congregate so as to work more efficiently later but engage in moments of effervescence so as to perform a present rift in the fabric of everyday life that is more vital than productivity measures or performance indicators allow. This is play not as reward but as good. Choreomania, in this view, recuperated as a term positively to denote communality, offers a moment of exuberance and a temporary joining together that can play a vital part in reinscribing our body politics with sweat, touch, dreams, and occasional collective jolts.

MOVEMENT, MODERNITY, AND THE CHORUS

As a history of modernity, then, the story of choreomania breaks with notions of the machinic new, suggesting a corporeal history obsessed with returns to the past, the primitive, and the Dionysian. Martin Puchner has argued that the history of modernity is founded in the myth of novelty and a revolutionary rupture with the past;[17] so, too, Lefebvre argues that modernism is the 'cult of innovation for innovation's sake, innovation as fetish', a trend that becomes fully fledged at the end of the nineteenth century.[18]

15. Elaine Showalter, *Hystories: Hysterical Epidemics and Modern Culture* (New York: Picador, 1997), 5–6.

16. See esp. Micale, *Approaching Hysteria*, and Mark S. Micale, 'On the "Disappearance" of Hysteria: A Study in the Clinical Deconstruction of a Diagnosis', *Isis* 84.3 (1993): 496–526.

17. See Martin Puchner, *Poetry of the Revolution: Marx, Manifestos, and the Avant-Garde* (Princeton, NJ: Princeton University Press, 2006).

18. Lefebvre, *Introduction to Modernity*, 169.

At the same time, modernity is theorized in every era, from the seventeenth-century *querelle des anciens et modernes* (quarrel of the ancients and moderns) to Rousseau's diatribes against modern music as opposed to what he saw as primitive, natural, primeval sounds.[19] Yet I have shown that modernity—even as myth of the new—never took place except in relation to fantasies of return; on the contrary, productive conjunctions between history and historicity, the classical and the avant-garde, the Edenic and the apocalyptic, the primitive and the civilized, offer a scene of writing wherein the perennial Bacchic chorus—the collective legend of the choir[20]—finds a discursive habitus peopled by the figures of the past. Modernity in this regard is not rupture but relation. It is ghosted, haunted, by primitive scenes against which it sets itself and which constitute its fiction of sameness and difference: modernity seeks to situate itself on a continuum with other worlds—geographic and historical—while folding new forms of collectivity into prototypes putatively dug up from the past. Modernity is anxious to wrest itself from its inheritance and just as anxious to find grounding in it; this dual pull creates a kinetic moment, in which movement itself is at stake, and the relative velocities connecting past and present, here and elsewhere, produce intensities that converge on choreic and choreographic tropes, striking slightly different chords in every new era according to these differential relations.

The dancing chorus, as a crowd that represents the public sphere connected to ancient ways of moving and rioting, judging and imagining, serves, in the story I have told, as a trope and crucible, through which may be viewed the advances and strains of modernity from the mid-nineteenth to the mid-twentieth century, a time of intense intellectual and kinaesthetic convergences. No longer heroes in a tragic drama in which the chorus stands in judgment to one side, modern men and women find themselves swept up—or risking being swept up—in a tidal wave of bodies and thoughts that constitutes a social corpus which requires the cohesion of the choir while denying itself such comfort and familiarity; the 'choreomaniacal' body is chaotic, jumbled. It is not cohesive. As such, it stands as a signature for all forms of collective motility against the supposed rationality and efficiency of industrialization.

SCIENTIFIC ROUTES

My emphasis on the scientific routes of exchange must be taken to include in 'science' the cultural, anthropological, and performative vectors of thought and scenes of writing that 'science'—through the bodies of scientists observing, recording, and staying dutifully out of the way of dancers—managed (culturally) to produce. In effect, choreomania was written as a transcultural literature by a cast of medical men who were increasingly watching bodies up close and were, in tandem with or in proximity to but not in exactly the same way as the administrative powers deploying them overseas, concerned with performative uprisings as symptoms of biopolitical disorder. Choreomania, then, emerges as a conceptual node articulating an approach to disorder that does not exactly map onto today's medical, political, social, or dance histories but reveals an underlying cross-pollination across these spheres. With choreomania, we see a history of thinking moving, and a history of the way thinking in motion about movement was configured at a time of intense change: where *displacement* itself became a subject of scientific *détournement* or deviation, what I further call translatio.

The problem is not confined to the age of empire; on the contrary, the circulation of bodies that intensified with colonialism continues in today's migration patterns. White-collar workers tend to be considered proactively and productively to move, to circulate; lower classes moving across borders, or in unsanctioned spaces, continue to be described (in spite of stark economic imperative) as unproductive, excessive, unnecessary, contagious, and thus nearly unstoppable: a condition, understood nearly in terms of epidemic disease, that requires more than laws—state violence—to stem. *Appearance* in public space, then, is at stake. Most prominently, *appearance into* public space comes to

---

19. Lefebvre, *Introduction to Modernity*, 168–169.

20. Rancière gestures towards a space of thinking about the choreographic and political potential of the choir—a term he uses ambiguously to denote what I would describe as the frame and form of action performed by what he calls a new humanity ('le chœur en acte des hommes nouveaux')—as well as a Symbolist figuration of a 'collective legend' ('figuration symboliste de la légende collective'), in Jacques Rancière, *Le partage du sensible: Esthétique et politique* (Paris: La Fabrique-éditions, 2000), 15–25, 22.

be contested in the terms of a dancing disease, a term implying (all too) heightened mobility. Yet moving bodies—what I have also described ('perhaps anachronistically'), with Muecke, as *demonstrators*—sought to assert their due; in the case of the *ramanenjana* (chapter 8), they obtained it.

There are two kinds of circulation, then: the circulation of bodies across lands (according to choreopolitical processes of *displacement* and travel) and the circulation of ideas, their re-indigenization and discursive translatio; neither mapped exactly onto the other, and in this *mis*-mapping, the fantasy of choreomania *appears*. Concept formation (in Taussig's terms, the magical work of making ideas *appear* as 'things', and making things and events concomitantly *appear* as singular 'ideas') is never smooth, nor are diagnoses and definitions more airtight than the choreopolitical worlds they attempt (often haphazardly) to describe. Rather concepts, often made up of diagnoses, *form* and unform, and in this (largely aesthetic) operation, whole literatures emerge. Scenes appear to offer dramaturgical consistency—they seem patently to 'stick'—and so become 'scenarios' (in Taylor's terms), which then underpin disease and conceptual categories, as their narrative 'proof'.

This process of reification—what I further describe, with Stimson, as a gesture of abstraction—constitutes, Taussig argues, the process of diagnosing 'disease' in a Western (largely colonial) paradigm in which the empirical sciences take it as their task to decode the borderline between appearance and essence, duplicity and truth. Spirit possession, spiritual agency, and other seemingly abnormal feats of bodily transformation or unaccountable effects on the material world belie, according to the Western scientific (empirical) worldview, Taussig reminds us, an actual basis in reality that fantasies regarding spirit belief occlude.[21] Western science is dedicated to uncovering what it construes as lies. In this respect, 'choreomania' signals the fantasy of a particular lie that Western and Western-trained scientists seek to reveal: the 'lie' according to which bodies in disrepair are actually subject to the nefarious workings of an overactive imagination, not real material conditions. This reveals a subterranean

world of fantasy, dreams, and ambitions whose slips and trips it is the physician's special task to decipher. In colonial outposts, postures unfamiliar to Western-trained scientists *appear* as disorderly inasmuch as the source of their movements could not always be grasped except through comparison. The spectacle of these bodies' contortions constituted a 'disease', abstracted and mapped onto *appearances* similarly observed or read about elsewhere. In this way, 'choreomania' was construed as a set of apparently similar appearances, and the task of diagnosing it as that of comparing them to one another.

AGON: DANCE AND THE SCENE OF WRITING

These scenes of disarray were patently difficult to write; medical writers struggled with them, and very few choreographic descriptions of 'choreomaniacal' dances exist: they state only that men and women shook, frothed, fell, and raved. Yet these dances, as a counterpart to increasingly upright and orderly dances such as the sanitized waltz or minuet, encompassed everything primitive, dangerous, weird, or unsavoury that the imagined past and the figured other had to offer. Rancière notes in *Le partage du sensible: esthétique et politique* [The Politics of Aesthetics] (2000) that opposed to the Bacchic dancing Plato decried was a healthier and more politically desirable form of collectivity representing the authentic expression of a community in motion:[22] the chorus served as an orderly polis, a form of social life—and a symbolic political formation—removed from the world of the bacchanals and the theatre, both of which Plato had wanted outlawed. These contradictory motions, embracing the chorus (and military choreography) while rejecting poetry and theatre, situated Plato at the vanguard of generations of writers puzzling over history's repetitions and returns, as Dionysian mysteries and their rumoured lookalikes cropped up again and again, occasioning sightings in various parts of the world.

The chorus was a form whose figure could be incorporated into the political realm, as a representation of social order and public opinion, unlike bacchanals, which fell just outside the realm of orderly citizenry; they were too messy,

---

21. See esp. Taussig, *Mimesis and Alterity*, 127, 176–177.
22. Rancière, *Le partage du sensible*, 15–16.

dark, confusing, and obscure properly to write or to fit into a clean kinaesthetic taxonomy. Dances that appear erratic and disrupt a smooth, facile bodily integrity worry viewers who are seeking explanations whispered from the wings. So, too, dancers possessed by the figures of the past—haunted by ancestors, moved by otherworldly presences—do not 'read'; they do not offer clarity of form or language. So the messy dances, the bacchanals and the choreomanias, fell together into the black hole of Dionysian ecstasy, not quite choruses and not quite mobs or crowd formations either. They were written in terms of what one may understand as anti-aesthetic properties, including incoherence and primitive archaicity, yet they were complicated, mobile, and always, to reappropriate Bhabha's iconic phrase once more, 'not quite' art.[23]

Choreomania, then, as a form of movement and form of thinking which flits back and forth between disorder and disease, joy, pleasure and rapture, revolt, and restlessness and agitation, appears on the scene of modernity as a chorus in disrepair, a social body that configures itself around a new aesthetics and a new politics linked in their aspirations to a myth of the old. As I have shown throughout this book, modernity is haunted, whether through the fantasies of antiquarian enthusiasts believing that they are stumbling upon contemporary incarnations of historic phenomena or through dancers conjuring up the dead. This is not so much a *hauntology* in the sense Derrida describes—figures of thought hovering between presence and absence, existence and non-existence[24]—but a distinct imaginary peopled by *revenants*, those who return, to bolster and support, and to serve as guarantors of, a new world order. By coming back, these *revenants* underpin the present and so, too, the future, to make it less anomic, less lonely. Figured as corporeal and affective memories, they people a world stripped of its coordinates, counterbalancing the speed of change, the dromology of everyday life, anchoring it in a sense of home and an affective and corporeal history.

These figures of the past are conjured—called up—discursively and corporeally: medieval dancers, bacchantes, the ghosts of dead monarchs in Madagascar and of Native American Indians in the Plains, appear out of pages as if to constitute a new order of things *pell-mell*; yet this is an order of things that returns. In choreographic terms, it turns again: it performs yet another volte-face. This theatre of returns performs a double movement, at once looking forward and reaching back in a quickstep that finds balance only where it teeters just at the limit of an intellectual abyss. Every time, movement conjured up from the past plays against corporeal and affective abstraction and alienation in the present: offering the illusion (and experience) of a 'canny' moment, homey, opposed to the uncanny whirl of modernity.

SPATIAL PRACTICE, MOVING FIELDS

Rest, then, is the anti-story in this story; and modernity in this regard is a breathless, restless moment. It is defined by edginess, agitation, and erratic gestures, as well as distrust of spontaneity, collectivity, and lack of control. So the choreozones in this book cluster concepts and practices and their relational velocity, their rate of change. This is a dancing history that moves in a tragic frame, an eternal return, a past that is always renewing its relation to the past (to its historicity), in what Rancière calls the aesthetic regime of the arts: a regime that does not 'oppose ancient and modern' but posits contrasting regimes of historicity.[25] The present is always a return to past structures; it defines itself by the differential increment that separates it from a portion of the past and, as such, it is always relational. The present looks backwards and in so doing configures a new relationship to what it sees, and to its mode of looking.

I submit that Rancière's model describes not only an aesthetic regime but more broadly a manner of conceiving politics, economics, and social life in the present that undoes narratives of linear progress, as well as archaeology and genealogy. Instead of layers of history, historical accidents or fortuities, the discursive choreographer uncovers constantly renegotiated relations, played out as networks, imaginings, recuperations, and interactions: movements of thought. Each era, in the view I propose, is

---

23. Bhabha, *The Location of Culture*, 122.

24. In Jacques Derrida, *Spectres de Marx* (Paris: Galilée, 1993).

25. 'Le régime esthétique des arts n'oppose pas l'ancien et le moderne. Il oppose plus profondément deux régimes d'historicité'. Rancière, *Le partage du sensible*, 35.

traversed through with particular figments of the past to which it returns, fantasizing about them in distinct ways; the total cluster, the zone of intensity, that makes up this set of relations constitutes that moment's epistemic and kinaesthetic force, its ways of moving and seeing, determining what dialogues it engages in, and what conversations or puzzles it chooses to rehabilitate and to rewrite, and how.

Discursive practices shifted and moved intensely in the story I have told, stimulating the emergence or crystallization of modern disciplines not so much as hegemonic forces of knowing but as mobile entities, clusters of concept-events, crisscrossing one another, cross-pollinating with and pilfering from their neighbours as they found new fields in which to grow before moving on—shifting ground—again. The history of fields thus has also been at stake in this book, as ways of seeing and performing relationships to history and dance morphed in the latter part of the nineteenth and early twentieth centuries. Going out 'in the field', as a space saturated with particular modes of seeing, doing, moving, and being, provoked occasions for discursive and interpersonal relations different from those acquired at home. Fieldwork in this regard constitutes its own methods of choreography: its own ways of organizing bodies in space. In Clifford's terms, the field conjures 'an act of physically *going out* into a *cleared space of work*'; it is an 'embodied spatial practice', one whose border is unstable, constantly remapped—discursively—and corporeally negotiated.[26] The process of disciplining a field may begin in the early days of its institutional life, but it is constantly reworked through institutional practices and individual bodily histories. Displacement and travel, journeys and rifts, rather than belonging, move these fields along.

In the same way, performance itself, like dance, emerges as a mobile entity, an object and methodology situated between moving and doing, showing and writing—one that lurches, skips, rattles, and starts. It presents the figure of a comedic body, messy and corporeal, not so much striving to achieve (to *perform*) in an economy of productive makings but falling and dreaming, hopping, lifting, jiving, and joining hands in a motion focused in towards a group; like a jester, it creates a break and an opening

in the rhythm of everyday life, gesturing at bodily failure. Performance in this view moves, speeds up and slows down; it is not a *theatron*, a seeing-place, but morphs and splits, obfuscating, triumphant, and puckish. Like Dionysus, it laughs, contorts itself, and changes shape. This creature is all action and all transformation, non-teleological and undisciplined. It is also all kinesis, though it can morph into figures of order and control or chaos and spontaneity, only to slip out again to rebecome pure velocity, pure fête, a temporary zone of intensity, a carnival and an uprising, disorder and insurgency. This is not the figure of the pure dissident or rebel so much as the figure of change: the performance as concept-event dances, like Zarathustra—another one of this figure's masks—philosophizing on the tombs of its ancestors and shifting gears already before it can be pinned down. Performance as motility forces us to reconsider the industrial and capitalistic connotations of the field that Jon McKenzie has highlighted,[27] preferring instead a model within which raucousness and play present protean intellectual and corporeal formations.

MEANINGLESS GESTURE

Concomitant with this haunting by the past and roguish disposition is another trait the 'choreomanias' share: the appearance of meaninglessness. The pathologization of individual and collective movements as 'choreomania' brings with it their de-semiotization, their descent into semiotic darkness. Dance manias, in medical literature, have no overarching narratives; these are not representational performances. Barring a few exceptions noted throughout this book, dancers imitate one another—putatively pathologically—without the intention to represent specific objects or events. In medical literature, dance manias 'mean' only highly contagious, generally erratic whole-body gesture. The discourse on choreomania thus is a discourse on gestural futility and, in a certain sense, pure gesture, gesture that has no purpose, not even to reproduce itself. This is resonant with what, Hewitt has noted, corresponds to a Kantian aesthetic of 'purposiveness without purpose': for Hewitt, dance in the nineteenth century becomes an 'aesthetic practice that responds to

---

26. Clifford, *Routes*, 53–54.
27. Jon McKenzie, *Perform or Else: From Discipline to Performance* (London: Routledge, 2001).

the "loss of gesture" or "destruction of experience"' that Agamben describes of chorea. Reprising Agamben's analysis of choreic gesture from de la Tourette's nineteenth-century neurological writing, as well as from the essay 'La théorie de la démarche' [The Theory of Gait] (1833) by Honoré de Balzac (1799–1850), Hewitt notes that dance, as a sort of pure choreic stuttering, fails as gesture 'through an inability either to begin or to complete the gesture'. Dance in this sense 'figures a linguistic play that neglects the work of semiotic closure'.[28] Choreic gesture, Hewitt argues, is for Agamben 'movement "independent of any motor purpose"'.[29] In 'Notes on Gesture', Agamben argues that 'if dance is gesture, it is so . . . because it is nothing more than the endurance and the exhibition of the media character of corporeal movements. *The gesture is the exhibition of a mediality: it is the process of making a means visible as such*'.[30] Dance 'opens the ethical dimension' for human beings,[31] Agamben writes; it is that which signals the possibility of communication, of reaching-towards; though dance may 'sign' nothing in itself. Dance as gesture in Agamben's view is the 'communication of a communicability', it communicates—and it aestheticizes—the very possibility of communication, and therefore arguably of ethics and politics.[32]

In other words, chorea in the nineteenth century signals the dissolution of dance as a meaningful site for articulating community: chorea, as meaningless gesture, signals communication's undoing. This is not to suggest that the idea of chorea is tantamount to its historical reality; that somehow there is an excess of chorea in nineteenth-century modernity, and therefore the social body is in disarray. But following

Agamben's analysis, chorea as a figure of thought helps articulate an experience of modernity as that which moves without going anywhere or meaning anything. Chorea signals modern rootlessness and anomie, a loss of social laws. Liberated from the requirement to 'mean', that is, to articulate the way language does, chorea becomes bodily movement shorn of history and linguistic symbolism. It does not come from or reach towards another world; it is its own meaningless world. It becomes 'merely' aesthetic, just as it loses its potential for politics. Chorea, in this view, is non-teleological and non-purposive, non-signifying and non-representative: it cannot become 'democratic', as it represents the event of modernity's disarticulation. I have shown throughout this book that choreomania as a figure of thought does something very similar, though slightly different: whereas chorea signals meaningless gesture, choreomania is the dizzying epidemic eruption of meaningless gesture and bodily dislocation reproducing itself, and therefore the terrifying power of the headless crowd. This crowd is not just frightening on account of its seeming lack of control; it is frightening (to some observers) inasmuch as it moves jerkily and spontaneously, without signifying anything except its own intensity. Choreomania becomes a figure for thinking large-scale gesture that has apparently no semiotic value except to reproduce itself.

The nineteenth century thus represents the dissolution of meaningful gesture and the descent of politics into chorea. Chorea becomes the fantastical litmus test against which the nineteenth century measures its capacity for gesture, meaning, and sense. The purported illegibility of choreic gesture—its open, unfinished, ostensibly

---

28. Hewitt, *Social Choreography*, 82–83. See Agamben, 'Notes on Gesture', in Agamben, *Means without End*.

29. Hewitt, *Social Choreography*, 83.

30. Agamben, 'Notes on Gesture', in Agamben, *Means without End*, 58. I slightly prefer the translation given by Liz Heron, in this instance: 'If dance is gesture, this is . . . because it is nothing but the physical tolerance of bodily movements and the display of their mediating nature. *Gesture is the display of mediation, the making visible of a means as such*'. Agamben, 'Notes on Gesture', in Agamben, *Infancy and History*, 147–156, 155. Hewitt is also working with this translation, which renders slightly more ambiguous the 'mediality' of gesture in relation to media technologies—film and photography in particular, which Agamben goes on to discuss next—opening a slightly wider aperture of meaning to include bodily movement and dance, as sites or events (as gestures, in his terms) of mediation, that is, of relation or translation, of *movement-towards*, movement that is always in between one point, one place, and the next. Agamben's original posits 'mediality' (or 'mediation') as 'medialità', which perhaps more strongly than the English has the connotation of in-between-ness (the medium as middle) and passage, movement, or travel: 'Se la danza è gesto, è perché essa non è invece altro che la sopportazione e l'establizio del carattere mediale dei movimenti corporei. Il gesto è l'esibizione di una medialità, il render visible un mezzo come tale. Esso fa apparire l'essere-in-un-medio dell'uomo, e, in questo modo, apre per lui la dimensione etica . . . . Il gesto è, in questo senso, comunicazione di una comunicabilità'. Giorgio Agamben, 'Note sul gesto', in Giorgio Agamben, *Mezzi senza fine: Note sulla politica* (Turin: Bollati Boringhieri, 1996), 45–53, 51–52.

31. Agamben, 'Notes on Gesture', in Agamben, *Means without End*, 58.

32. Agamben, 'Notes on Gesture', in Agamben, *Means without End*, 59.

purposeless stature—signals a loss of social code and the end of communicating with others in a shared ethical, political (and aesthetic) sphere. 'Chorea' becomes anaesthetic: not just ugly and inelegant or unrefined, but shapeless. When 'choreomanias' appeared in heightened political contexts—wars, uprisings, rebellions—their medical interest and the urgency of their analysis as public maladies became ever more acute. In those cases, the appearance of meaninglessness was trumped by the intensity with which movement and gesture showed the tendency to spread. In these cases, the contagiousness of such seemingly meaningless gesture was worrisome above all: it signalled the rapid proliferation of irrational behaviours and thus the extensive influence of the mobile and gesturing yet apparently inarticulate and directionless horde.

AFFECTIVE AGGREGATES, PUBLIC SPHERES

This collective agitation amounted to a class of kinaesthetically expressed affective profligacies that oscillated between joy and grief, showing unchecked movement in the public sphere and taking national and international intensities to new peaks of exhibitionist fervour. In Athanasiou's and Butler's analyses of political uprisings in Greece, Egypt, Syria, and elsewhere, however, exhibitionism constitutes social politics, in a positive affective space of affirmation.[33] Crowds perform mutual vulnerability and states of being-with one another in public space that signals, by the presence (and *presencing*) of these bodies, the political value of an otherwise barely intelligible corporeal subjectivity. These are bodies that are not making juridical demands other than asserting a right to live, to take place, and to express passion and emotion in the aggregate. That in itself is a demand that claims movement and affect as political goods not superior to or different from individual agency but operating in a mutual force field, predicated on individual responsibility and liberty just as it asserts a common right to be together, to appear together, to expose the publicness of the public sphere—the *polis*—for what it is: a common area in which

bodies circulate, rest, and occupy space. These bodies perform a collective 'thereness' that refuses to go away but obdurately resists the tyranny of material precariousness, insisting that life flows through passionate, sensitive, and enraged aggregates of people that embody and enact the everydayness and banality of bare life.

This is not a state of exception but a state of ordinariness making itself present: it is a bare crowd, bodies acting out, moving, moved, shifted and shifting, refusing to perform except inasmuch as they are making themselves known in a capital economy that denies them the essential demands of sentient life. These are lives instead that laugh and love, hurt and cry, fear and dance, as well as work: lives too full, too exuberant, too emotive, perhaps too sentimentally feminine and primitive, in Athanasiou's terms, to withstand the dehumanizing effects of contemporary corporate capitalism.[34] This does not mean that they are not capable of ruthless judgment and legal indictment: on the contrary, these are bodies speaking a discourse of exclusion by creating performative acts of inclusion and empathy against the grain. They are not just imitating one another mindlessly, childishly, but drawing strength from one another by their co-presence in a public sphere that becomes—and is shown to have always been—theirs to inhabit. These individuals, banding together in public, revolting against the obliteration of warmth and affect in a social, economic, and political regime that instrumentalizes bodies and minds to the point of annihilation—literally killing or provoking some citizens to political suicide[35]—speak by showing supportive plurality and so refusing alienation.

I have shown that the grounds for this acting out were set at least as far back as the mid-nineteenth century, in an industrial context in which collective bodies rising up and showing their penchant for performative play were folded into a discourse on affective exaggeration. The result was a discursive temperance or abstemiousness that sought to quell passions, redirecting flows into the workforce. This was a workforce that one might imagine too brittle—too inelastic—to adopt organized systems of capital accumulation without the respite offered

---

33. Butler and Athanasiou, *Dispossession*.

34. Butler and Athanasiou, *Dispossession*, 177.

35. See e.g. David Stuckler and Sanjay Basu, *The Body Economic: Why Austerity Kills. Recessions, Budget Battles, and the Politics of Life and Death* (New York: Basic Books, 2013).

by unsanctioned leisure: unchoreographed social fêtes, cabaret crowds, and popular demonstrations. Crowds, discursively and politically abstracted from the corporeal desires and kinaesthetic bonds that hold them together in public space, lose the vitality that makes states into nations and aggregates into meaningful, passionate, and emotionally vibrant social groups. The nation becomes an empty shell, until these bodies can reclaim public space and reinvest the group, the locality, or the square with the spirit of animation that the political system—any political system—might be meant, in the final analysis, to protect.

FORWARD/BACK

I have suggested the 'archival repertoire' as a term to designate the ever-moving, plastic quality of the paper trail that makes up the material stuff within which choreomania, the dancing disease, took shape. But, fittingly, the archival repertoire extends into a living, present act. I have deliberately echoed here Schneider's title from her afterword to *Performing Remains: Art and War in Times of Theatrical Reenactment* (2011), 'And back—Afterword', in order to underscore the perpetual acts of repetition and rehearsal that we perform in writing all the time, the community of citation, sometimes more explicit, sometimes more implicit, that make up every act of writing and every encounter. *Performing Remains* argues that theatre and performance are always taking place again; but also, significantly, that they are therefore never entirely dead or alive. Theatre, as that which uncannily doubles life, hovers in a space of repetition performed always with a measure of difference, a hop—step that never falls in the same place and always attempts to move forward but does so inevitably by looking back, behind its shoulder, at what is always already gone.

In disappearing, constantly, and in appearing, constantly, theatre, dance, and performance *perform* renewal and ghostly returns, returns that are ghostly before they have even had a chance to purport to die; in this half-living, half-dying state, traditions, canons, and concepts are formed. I had a chance to 'reperform' Meige's archival return to Echternach, following in June 2011 the steps—or my imagination of the steps—he took over a hundred

years before. Meige, as I showed in chapter 6, sought to see, in context, a live example of the hysteroepileptic convulsions that he knew from Charcot's clinical lectures took place, in a town that purportedly still rehearsed a processional festival that fêted the dancing disease. He found only a shell of this supposedly once vibrant tradition: a policed, choreographed theatre of civic pride, recapitulating *again and again* a history that had already by then entirely forgotten its predecessors. In attempting to return to this site to see the Echternach dancing procession for myself a few years ago, I found that the blare of the brass horns and the monotony of the repetitious steps—traditionally, five steps forward, four steps back; five steps forward, three steps back; or three steps forward, two steps back (the most traditional number, according to the tourist literature provided to pilgrims)[36]—assaulted my senses and, in the end, dulled my desire compliantly to perform. I had agreed to attend 'in a spirit of pilgrimage', as tourist literature and event organizers prompted. But my pilgrimage was to an archival source; not even that, it was to the spectral reperformance of an archival site once undertaken by a French physician now long dead. What had I sought to find? What had he sought to find in returning to this site?

Fieldwork for a historian of dance—and, even more evanescently, for a historian of ideas about dance—provides a strange conundrum: at once chasing after shadows and perpetually mired in words, we must nevertheless convince ourselves that there are places—books, towns, events—through which we might access other ways of seeing the world, ways that might unravel our own understandings about the past and its chimeras, as well as about our own presents. Of course this notion of the past recedes as we find ourselves consistently confronted with our own stubborn presence, our own *presentness* and the infuriatingly tenacious way in which this constant being in the present moves along forward in time with us. We are always only ever in the present moment. So what have I been able to say of the past? What have I been able to imagine? I have shown that presents, whenever they may be, are always suffused with a particular colour and tone of imagining their own relationship to a past. In this regard, history is always already theatrical: it imagines itself ghosted by something

---

36. A detailed account of this debate can be found on the pilgrimage's website, http://www.willibrord.lu/rubrique4/Dancing-procession/historical-aspects, accessed 12 November 2012.

that came before, and which it rehearses again, with difference. It is the measure of 'difference' that makes every present what it is: a version of the past cast in this or that particular flavour or style of new garb, this or that particular rendition of the medieval, the Dionysian, the Roman, or what have you. I have argued that 'modernity'—a particular facet of modernity, a clustering of 'modern' self-imaginings—appears to have been haunted throughout the nineteenth and early twentieth centuries by a version of the past conceived as erratic, fitful, and collective. Yet, uncannily, this past was also present, elsewhere. It emerged spectrally, mysteriously, in colonial places, in faraway lands; it even re-emerged in the present day among lower or 'superstitious' classes. Modernity, then, was—and is, arguably—a force of difference and alienation, inasmuch as it separates and alienates itself from what it sees as having come prior. As a performative trope, this version of modernity posits the new as stuffed to the gills with the old, unable to shake its heritage but prancing about in a shiny new costume that suggests (to itself) that it has.

Like the pilgrims' steps at Echternach, this book has felt at times—most times—like a dance over lost and invisible bones, three steps forward, two steps back. I hope, if anything, to have suggested that diagonal steps, tumbles, strutting, shaking, ticking, and swooning are all also fruitful ways of moving, and that syncopated beats and irregular rhythms might constitute an alterkinetic aesthetics, a way of seeing 'beautiful' movements as those which may also be erratic, unpredictable, chaotic, and yes, dis-eased. Performance maker Jess Thom, who styles herself 'Touretteshero', boasts as her motto: 'Changing the world one tic at a time'. She bursts into apparently nonsensical language bits constantly ('biscuit', 'hedgehog'), has seizures, speaks highly articulately in conversation, and smiles infectiously in equal measure, exuberant and confident in the knowledge that her involuntary movements and speech acts are creative outbursts—what she calls a creative language machine—inaccessible to 'neurotypical' people.[37]

Chorea, epilepsy, and other neurological disorders are complex fantasies imbricated in centuries of imaginative associations, putative precedents, and horizontal affiliations. I have shown that the history of what may now be construed as movement disorders has by and large typically been associated in scientific and popular literature with uncomfortable political uprisings, intense group sentiment, and expressions of emotion, including ebullience, anger, and grief, as well as a highly racialized notion of colonial mimicry and pantomimic theatre. But by this token, the same disorders can also be seen positively as outbursts and outpourings, rehearsals for other possible worlds, other ways of seeing the strictures of social choreography in everyday life, and other ways of imagining our relationships to our presents and our pasts. In this view, choreomania, the dancing disease, in all its plural manifestations, is also arguably a choreographic cataclysm in the history of human progress, a set or series of very varied disturbances in the rhythmic order of 'black', 'white', 'Latin', and so many other intermixed strands of popular music and social dancing; also a figure of thought infiltrating innumerable disciplines, a modern fiction that is simultaneously antimodern, irregular, fleeting, and evanescent but intuitive and enduring. And it is none of those things. Like any chimera, or any ghost, choreomania hovers spectrally over (and under) the modern imagination, reflecting our worries and anxieties back to us in an elusive, distorted, and constantly changing form. I began this book by suggesting that it told the story of a fantasy: a complex, morphing, travelling idea about the dancing disease as it moved through modern scientific and social scientific literature. Like any fantasy, and any concept, it is also a reality, ineluctably in the world, affecting (and affected by) real lives. In pulling this fantasy apart at the seams—without ever being able to 'catch' the ghost—I hope to have provided the groundwork for rearticulating other fantasies and concepts, in which uncontrollable, spasmodic, sporadic, and apparently inexplicable kinaesthetic acts are welcome as symptoms of a diverse body politic, as diverse as it is new and old.

As the Echternach dancing procession evolved in the first half of the twentieth century, the increasing regularity of the steps suggested that earlier convulsions had come to be choreographed into a tightly knit social performance of religious cohesion—a far cry from the heterodox

---

37. Andy Horwitz in conversation with Jess Thom (Touretteshero) and Hassan Mahamdallie, 'Talking/Making/Taking Part: a festival of theatre and discussion', Oval House, London, 22–23 November 2015; see also Jess Thom, *Welcome to Biscuitland: A Year in the Life of Touretteshero* (London: Souvenir Press, 2012).

FIGURE C.1 Echternach dancing procession, 14 June 2011. Photo by the author.

gatherings and claims to miraculous intervention of the preceding centuries. When I attended, a friendly francophone local explained to me that the Germans hopped forward, while the francophones hopped to the side, a very subtle distinction I only started to make out by the end of our round; and indeed, this myth—which he was keen to present to me—belied the fact that to my left, a friendly, quiet German man seemed to hop the same way as everyone else. We all respected a pattern which I noted in my diary as 'Left hop right hop left hop right hop left hop right hop . . .', in rows of five, neatly kept in place throughout by little white handkerchiefs which we held between us.

In the organizer Pierre Kauthen's account, a slightly more sophisticated choreography had come to be meticulously observed by Boy Scouts and civilians, who were effectively brought into line by municipal authorities keen to preserve a common national heritage with as little boisterous disturbance as possible.[38] Stipulations that dancers should proceed four or five abreast[39] seem also to have passed out of favour in the interwar period, most plausibly because it was too difficult to find space for performance in the street, given

the new mass appeal of the event. Streets were crowded with cars, and now that journalists were converging upon the site, while radios blared and police officers kept everyone in check, there was little room for the kind of chaos that the procession had previously been known to engender.[40]

The new, politicized dancing procession excluded the truly ill, beggars, and other potentially disruptive people, turning the event into a parade for the glory of the modern nation and the wealth of the tourist and leisure industry.[41] Guy, my French informant, and the parish priest I happened upon the next day, Father Théophile Walin, both assured me that there was no more talk of movement disorders and hardly any memory that this had ever played a part in the procession. Father Walin knew of one woman who had suffered from some condition, which he could not exactly recall, and who had asked her son to hop in her stead. This had alleviated her suffering, he informed me. But he knew of no other cases. Now, the young people, he said, dance as an expression of joy, and to 'pray with the feet'.[42]

This was a crowd formation offering a picture of motor efficiency and the orderly display of

---

38. Kauthen, 'La procession dansante', 257–258.

39. Krack, 'Relicts of Dancing Mania', 2169.

40. See Kauthen, 'La procession dansante', 256. On the culture of musicianship in the dancing procession at Echternach, see 258–259.

41. See Kauthen, 'La procession dansante', 262.

42. Personal communication with Father Théophile Walin, 15 June 2011.

FIGURE C.2   Echternach dancing procession, 14 June 2011. Photo by the author.

FIGURE C.3   Echternach dancing procession, 14 June 2011. Photo by the author.

healthy persons to one another, for one another. This theatre of normalcy had gradually supplanted a far unsteadier public procession, in which all sorts of 'disorder' were at play. Today, nine thousand dancers and three thousand spectators gather to rehearse an event that has long since refantasized the fiction of a medieval tradition. When I attended, like Meige, I looked obliquely for signs of movement disorders, noting a first aid van parked outside the basilica on the evening before. Older spectators lined the parade in wheelchairs, surely gladdened at this expression of coordinated—if subdued—motion (fig. C.1).

Others watched from in front of a fairground, reminding me of the ghostly quality of this event as entertainment (fig. C.2): not a mania but a form of intensity, an enthusiasm, enacting the orderly and the haphazard, the methodical and the disciplined, as well as the spirit of fête; in an event that partook, for all of its solemn overtones, of both (fig. C.3). It was a repetition of something that had served as a sort of yearly frenetic activity, crystallized through the centuries, transformed after a couple of world wars, whose imprint on the local walls was still patent, as Guy pointed out, gesturing towards bullet holes. Yet through this rehearsal of an idea about the past, the event spoke only of the present: the present as something, precisely, that returns. Something that is relational, a reminder of other presents; something that one can look forward to, by remembering that it has always or almost always occurred in more or less this way. It had outgrown its status as a dancing disease, but this procession, linked through a chain of associations with St. Vitus's dance, the Convulsionaries of Saint-Médard, and Charcot's clinic, presented the modern tourist-participant and reperformer (myself) with a sort of nostalgia for or phantasm of what may never have actually existed.

These leaps at and around tombs, either for a cure or, in this case, nothing better than a collective day out in the nearby town, gestured towards a performance of history for the pleasure and joy of it—for the common, joint experience of repetition. A theatre of repetition performed as if always anew; or, one might add, always moving, hopping if not hobbling along, in a circle around the basilica. Here, the theatre of returns did not attempt a strict movement backwards; it did not try to capture what was ostensibly gone, archived, long dead. It continued, forward and back, forward and back, reconfiguring the historicity of the event in the ecstasy of progressive amnesia.

Bibliography

Aberle, David F., 'Arctic Hysteria and Latah in Malaysia', *New York Academy of Sciences* 14 (1952): 291–297.

Aberle, David F., 'The Prophet Dance and Reactions to White Contact', *Southwestern Journal of Anthropology* 15.1 (1959): 74–83.

Aberth, John, *The Black Death: The Great Mortality of 1348–1350: A Brief History with Documents* (New York: Bedford St. Martin's, 2005).

Aberth, John, *From the Brink of the Apocalypse: Confronting Famine, War, Plague, and Death in the Later Middle Ages*, 2nd ed. (New York: Routledge, 2010).

Adas, Michael, *Prophets of Rebellion: Millenarian Protest Movements against the European Colonial Order* (Chapel Hill: University of North Carolina Press, 1979).

Agamben, Giorgio, *Infancy and History: On the Destruction of Experience*, trans. Liz Heron (London: Verso, 2007).

Agamben, Giorgio, *Mezzi senza fine: Note sulla politica* (Turin: Bollati Boringhieri, 1996).

Agamben, Giorgio, 'Movement', in André Lepecki, ed., Dance (Cambridge, MA: MIT Press, 2012), 142–144.

Agamben, Giorgio, 'Notes on Gesture', in Giorgio Agamben, *Means without End: Notes on Politics*, trans. Vincenzo Binetti and Cesare Casarino (Minneapolis: University of Minnesota Press, 2000), 48–59.

Agamben, Giorgio, *The Signature of All Things: On Method*, trans. Luca D'Isanto with Kevin Attell (New York: Zone Books, 2009).

Agamben, Giorgio, *State of Exception*, trans. Kevin Attell (Chicago: University of Chicago Press, 2005).

Aisenberg, Andrew Robert, *Contagion: Disease, Government, and the 'Social Question' in Nineteenth-Century France* (Stanford, CA: Stanford University Press, 1999).

Aitken, William, *The Science and Practice of Medicine*, 2 vols., vol. 1 (London: Charles Griffin and Company, 1864).

Alberti, Samuel J. M. M., *Morbid Curiosities: Medical Museums in Nineteenth-Century Britain* (Oxford: Oxford University Press, 2011).

Alexandro, Alexander ab, *Genialum dierum* (Paris: Riogny, 1539).

Alliez, Éric, 'Présentation: Tarde et le problème de la constitution', in Gabriel Tarde, *Monadologie et sociologie*, ed. Éric Alliez (Le Plessis-Robinson: Institut synthélabo pour le progrès de la connaissance, 1999), 9–32.

Alonso, Normando, *Corea de Sydenham* (Buenos Aires: A. Guidi Buffarini, 1910).

Andermann, F., and E. Andermann, 'Hyperekplexia and Other Disorders of Startle: Differential Diagnosis with Epilepsy', in Peter W. Kaplan and Robert S. Fisher, eds., *Imitators of Epilepsy*, 2nd ed. (New York: Demos Medical, 2005), 185–190.

Andermann, F., and E. Andermann, 'Startle Disorders of Man: Hyperekplexia, Jumping and Startle Epilepsy', *Brain & Development* 10.4 (1988): 213–222.

Anderson, Benedict, *Imagined Communities: Reflections on the Origin and Spread of Nationalism*, rev. ed. (London: Verso, 2006).

Anderson, Warwick, *Colonial Pathologies: American Tropical Medicine, Race, and Hygiene in the Philippines* (Durham, NC: Duke University Press, 2006).

Andersson, Rani-Henrik, *The Lakota Ghost Dance of 1890* (Lincoln: University of Nebraska Press, 2008).

Andree, John, *Cases of the Epilepsy, Hysteric fits, and St. Vitus Dance, with the Process of Cure: Interpreted with Practical Observations . . .* (London: W. Meadows and J. Clarke, 1746).

Andrianjafy, *La Ramanenjana à Madagascar (Chorémanie d'origine palustre)* (Montpellier: Imprimerie Delord-Boehm et Martial, 1902).

Anglada, Charles, *Étude sur les maladies éteintes et les maladies nouvelles, pour server à l'histoire des évolutions séculaires de la pathologie* (Paris: J.-B. Baillière, 1869).

Annales de la propagation de la foi. Recueil périodique des lettres des évêques et des missionnaires des missions des deux mondes, et de tous les documents relatifs aux missions et à l'œuvre de la propagation de la foi, vol. 35 (Lyon, 1863).

Anon., *A Walk in Shetland by Two Eccentrics* (Edinburgh: Stillies, Brothers; and Aberdeen: Lewis Smith, 1831).

Appolis, Émile, 'Une épidémie de Ramanenjana à Madagascar (1863–1864)', *Annales de l'Université de Madagascar* 3 (1964): 59–63.

Appudurai, Arjun, *Fear of Small Numbers: An Essay on the Geography of Anger* (Durham, NC: Duke University Press, 2006).

Apter, Emily, *The Translation Zone: A New Comparative Literature* (Princeton, NJ: Princeton University Press, 2006).

Arac, Jonathan, ed., *After Foucault: Humanistic Knowledge, Postmodern Challenges* (New Brunswick, NJ: Rutgers University Press, 1991).

Aragon, Louis, and André Breton, *La Révolution surréaliste: Collection complète* (Paris: Jean-Michel Place, 1991).

Archer-Straw, Petrine, *Negrophilia: Avant-garde Paris and Black Culture in the 1920s* (London: Thames and Hudson, 2000).

Ardoynis, Santes de, *De venenis* (Venice: Bernardinus Rizus, 1492).

Arendt, Hannah, *On Violence* (San Diego: Harcourt, Brace, 1970).

Arendt, Hannah, *Was ist Politik? Fragmente aus dem Nachlass* (Munich: Piper, 1993).

Arkin, Lisa C., and Marian Smith, 'National Dance in the Romantic Ballet', in Lynn Garafola, ed., *Rethinking the Sylph: New Perspectives on the Romantic Ballet* (Middletown, CT: Wesleyan University Press, 1997), 11–68.

Asad, Talal, ed., *Anthropology and the Colonial Encounter* (Amherst, NY: Prometheus Books, 1995).

Ashley, Kathleen, 'Introduction: The Moving Subjects of Processional Performance', in Kathleen Ashley and Wim Hüsken, eds., *Moving Subjects: Processional Performance in the Middle Ages and the Renaissance* (Amsterdam: Rodopi, 2001), 7–34.

Attwell, H., 'The Echternach Whitsuntide Dancers', *Notes and Queries* 7.9 (1890): 381–382.

Aubert, Geneviève, 'Charcot Revisited: The Case of Bruegel's Chorea', *Archives of Neurology* 62 (2005): 155–161.

Axenfeld, Alexandre, *Des névroses* (Paris: Germer Baillière Libraire-Éditeur, 1864).

Babbage, S. Barton, *Hauhauism: An Episode in the Maori Wars, 1863–1866* (Wellington, New Zealand: A. H. & A. W. Reed, 1937).

Babonneix, Léon, *Les chorées: Avec 34 figures dans le texte* (Paris: Ernest Flammarion, 1924).

Bacha, Eugène, ed., *Chronique Liégeoise de 1402* (Brussels: Librairie Kiessling, 1900).

Backman, E. Louis, *Religious Dances in the Christian Church and in Popular Medicine*, trans. E. Classen (London: Allen and Unwin, 1952).

Baglivi, Giorgio, *The practice of physick, reduc'd to the ancient way of observations containing a just parallel between the wisdom and experience of the ancients, and the hypothesis's of modern physicians . . . Together with several new and curious dissertations; particularly of the tarantula and the nature of its poison: of the use and abuse of blistering plasters: of epidemical apoplexies, &c. . . . , 2nd ed.*

(London: D. Midwinter, B. Lintot, G. Strahan, J. Round, W. Taylor, J. Osborn and J. Clark, 1723).

Baillière, J.-B., *Histoire de nos relations avec l'académie de médecine, 1827–1871. Lettre addressée à MM. les membres de l'Académie pour servir de complément au Bulletin de l'Académie de médecine . . .* (Paris, J.-B. Baillière, 1872).

Baker, Josephine, and Joseph Bouillon, *Josephine* (London: W. H. Allen, 1978).

Bakhtin, Mikhail, *Rabelais and His World*, trans. Hélène Iswolsky (Bloomington: Indiana University Press, 1984).

Baldwin, Peter, *Contagion and the State in Europe, 1830–1930* (Cambridge: Cambridge University Press, 1999).

Barclay, Robert, *The Inner Life of the Religious Societies of the Commonwealth: Considered Principally with Reference to the Influence of Church Organization on the Spread of Christianity* (London: Hodder and Stoughton, 1877).

Barré, J. F., *Pouvoir des Vivants, langages des morts* (Paris: François Maspero, 1977).

Bartholomew, Robert E., *Exotic Deviance: Medicalizing Cultural Idioms from Strangeness to Illness* (Boulder: University Press of Colorado, 2000).

Bartholomew, Robert E., *Little Green Men, Meowing Nuns and Head-Hunting Panics: A Study of Mass Psychogenic Illness and Social Delusion* (Jefferson, NC: McFarland, 2001).

Bartosik-Vélez, Elise, 'Translatio Imperii: Virgil and Peter Martyr's Columbus', *Comparative Literature Studies* 46.4 (2009): 559–588.

Baruch, Bernard M., 'Foreword', in Charles Mackay, *Extraordinary Popular Delusions and the Madness of Crowds* (London: L. C. Page, 1932).

Bashford, Alison, and Claire Hooker, eds., *Contagion: Historical and Cultural Studies* (London: Routledge, 2001).

Baslet, Gaston, Ashok Seshadri, Adriana Bermeo-Ovalle, Ken Willment, and Lorna Myers, 'Psychogenic Non-Epileptic Seizures: An Updated Primer', *Psychosomatics* 57.1 (2016): 1–17.

Bataille, Georges, *La part maudite, précédé de La notion de dépense* (Paris: Les Éditions de Minuit, 1967).

Batson, Glenna, with Margaret Wilson, *Body and Mind in Motion: Dance and Neuroscience in Conversation* (Bristol: Intellect Books, 2014).

Baudrillard, Jean, *L'échange symbolique et la mort* (Paris: Éditions Gallimard, 1976).

Beard, G., 'Experiments with the Jumpers of Maine', *Popular Science Monthly* 18 (1880): 170–178.

Beard, G., 'Remarks upon Jumpers or Jumping Frenchmen', *Journal of Nervous and Mental Disease* 5 (1878): 623–640.

Beckmann, Johann Christoff, *Gründliche Fürstellung etlicher in Hn. D. Joh. Christ. Beckmanns . . . neu ausgegangener Historia des Fürstenthums Anhalt befindlicher fürnemlich wieder das Hochfürstl*, ed. Christian Knaut (Halle Im Magdeburg: zufinden in Rengerischer Bucchandlung, 1710).

Beer, Gillian, *Darwin's Plots: Evolutionary Narrative in Darwin, George Eliot and Nineteenth-Century Fiction*, 3rd ed. (Cambridge: Cambridge University Press, 2009).

Bégin, Louis Jacques, *Dictionnaire des termes de médecine, chirurgie, art vétérinaire, pharmacie, histoire naturelle, botanique, physique, chimie, etc.* (Paris: Baillière, Crevot, Béchet, 1823).

Beizer, Janet, *Ventriloquized Bodies: Narratives of Hysteria in Nineteenth-Century France* (Ithaca, NY: Cornell University Press, 1994).

Beka, Johannes de, *Canonicus Ultrajectinus* (Utrecht, 1643).

Beka, Johannes de, *La Traduction Française de la Chronographia Johannis de Beka*, ed. Willem Noomen (The Hague: Uitgeverij Excelsior, 1954).

Belich, James, *The Victorian Interpretation of Racial Conflict: The Maori, the British, and the New Zealand Wars* (Montreal: McGill-Queen's University Press, 1989).

Bell, Dean Phillip, *Jews in the Early Modern World* (Lanham, MD: Rowman and Littlefield, 2008).

Benbadis, Selim R., and W. Allen Hauser, 'An Estimate of the Prevalence of Psychogenic Non-Epileptic Seizures', *Seizure: European Journal of Epilepsy* 9.4 (2000): 280–281.

Bench, Harmony, 'Screendance 2.0: Social Dance-Media', *Participations* 7.2 (2010), http://www.participations.org/Volume%207/Issue%202/special/bench.htm. Accessed 21 September 2013.

Benjamin, Walter, *Reflections*, ed. Peter Demetz, trans. E. Jephcott (New York: Harcourt Brace Jovanovich, 1979).

Ben-Shalom, Ram, 'Medieval Jewry in Christendom', in Martin Goodman, Jeremy Cohen, and David Sorkin, eds., *The Oxford Handbook of Jewish Studies* (Oxford: Oxford University Press, 2002), 153–192.

Benson, Michael, *Predictions of Fire* (New York: Kinetikon Pictures, 1996).

Bergson, Henri, *L'évolution créatrice* (Paris: Presses Universitaires de France, 2001).

Bergson, Henri, *Le rire: Essai sur la signification du comique* (Paris: PUF Quadrige, 1999).

'Berlin Love Parade: In Brief', http://www.berlinloveparade.com. Last accessed 21 June 2017.

Bernadac, Christian, and Sylvain Fourcassié, eds., *Les possédés de Chaillot* (Paris: Jean-Claude Lattès, 1983).

Berndt, R. M., 'A Cargo Movement in the Eastern Central Highlands of New Guinea', *Oceania*, 23.1 (1952): 40–65.

Berthoz, Alain, *The Brain's Sense of Movement*, trans. Giselle Weiss (Cambridge, MA: Harvard University Press, 2000).

Beryl and Associates, eds., *Immorality of Modern Dances* (New York: Everitt and Francis Co. and S. F. McLean and Co., 1904).

Bey, Hakim, *T.A.Z.: The Temporary Autonomous Zone, Ontological Anarchy, Poetic Terrorism*. 2nd ed. (Brooklyn: Autonomedia, 2003).

Bhabha, Homi K., 'Foreword: Framing Fanon by Homi K. Bhabha', in Frantz Fanon, *The Wretched of the Earth*, trans. Richard Philcox (New York: Grove Press, 2004), vii–xli.

Bhabha, Homi K., *The Location of Culture* (London: Routlege, 1994).

Billings, Dorothy K., *Cargo Cult as Theater: Political Performance in the Pacific* (Oxford: Lexington Books, 2002).

Blaagaard, Bolette B., 'Workings of Whiteness: Interview with Vron Ware', *Social Identities* 17.1 (2011): 153–161.

Bläsing, Bettina, Martin Puttke, and Thomas Schack, eds., *The Neurocognition of Dance: Mind, Movement and Motor Skills* (Hove, East Sussex: Psychology Press, 2010).

Bloch, Maurice, *Placing the Dead: Tombs, Ancestral Villages, and Kinship Organization in Madagascar* (London: Seminar Press, 1971).

Blocq, Paul, *Études sur les maladies nerveuses* (Paris: Rueff et Cie., 1894).

Blocq, Paul, 'Sur une affection caractérisée par de l'astasie et de l'abasie', *Archives de neurologie* 15 (1888): 24–51 and 187–211.

Blocq, Paul, *Les troubles de la marche dans les maladies nerveuses* (Paris: Rueff et Cie., 1893).

Bock, Martin, 'The Power of Suggestion: Conrad, Professor Grasset, and French Medical Occultism', *Conradiana* 39.2 (2007): 97–112.

Bodin, Jean, *De la démonomanie des sorciers* (Paris: Jacques du Puys Libraire Juré, 1580).

Böhme, Franz M., 'Tanzwut im Mittelalter', in Franz M. Böhme, *Geschichte des Tanzes in Deutschland*, 2 vols., vol. 1 (Leipzig: Druck und Verlag von Breitkopf & Härtel, 1886), 40–44.

Boissier Sauvages de la Croix, François, *Nosologie méthodique, ou distribution des maladies en classes, en genres, et en espèces, suivant l'esprit de Sydenham, & la méthode des botanistes . . .*, 10 vols., vol. 2 (Lyon: Chez Jean-Marie Bruyset, Imprimeur-Libraire, 1772).

Boiteu, Pierre, *Contribution à l'Histoire de la nation malgache* (Paris: Éditions Sociales, 1958).

Bonnemaison, Joël, *Culture and Space: Conceiving a New Cultural Geography*, ed. Chantal Blanc-Pamard et al., trans. Josée Pénot-Demetry (London: I. B. Tauris, 2005).

Booth, C. C., 'Medical Communication: The Old and the New. The Development of Medical Journals in Britain', *British Medical Journal* 285 (1982): 105–108.

Borch, Christian, *The Politics of Crowds: An Alternative History of Sociology* (Cambridge: Cambridge University Press, 2013).

Borges, Dain, 'Salvador's 1890s: Paternalism and Its Discontents', *Luso-Brazilian Review* 30.2 (1993): 47–57.

Boruchoff, David A., 'New Spain, New England, and the New Jerusalem: The "Translation" of Empire, Faith and Learning (*Translatio Imperii, Fidei ac Scientiae*) in the Colonial Missionary Project', *Early American Literature* 43.1 (2008): 5–34.

Boudin, J. C. M., 'Sur les Chorées épidémiques de Madagascar, d'Italie et d'Abyssinie', *Bulletin de la Société d'Anthropologie de Paris* 6 (1865): 441–454.

Boudou, P. Adrien, *Le Meurtre de Radama II, documents et discussion* (Tananarive: Imprimerie Moderne de L'Emyrne, Pitot de la Beaujardière, 1938).

Bougeant, Guillaume-Hyacinthe, *Les Quakres françois ou les nouveaux trembleurs. Comédie* (Utrecht: H. Khyrks le Jeune, 1732).

Bougeant, Guillaume-Hyacinthe, *Le saint déniché ou la banqueroute des marchands de miracles. Comédie* (La Haye: Pierre Oiseau, à la Cycongne, 1732).

Bouillaud, J., 'Chorée', in G. Andral et al., *Dictionnaire de médecine et de chirurgie pratiques*, 15 vols., vol. 5 (Paris: Gabon, Méquignon-Marvis, J.-B. Baillière, Crochard, 1829–1836), 262–272.

Bourg, Lionel, *La liesse populaire en France: 'rave' et lutte de classes, le néo-populisme à l'œuvre, brèves considérations à propos des mouvements de foule du 12 juillet 1998* (Saussines: Cadex, 1998).

Bourneville, Désiré-Magloire, and Paul Regnard, *Iconographie photographique de la Salpêtrière (Service de M. Charcot)*, 3 vols., vol. 1 (Paris: Aux bureaux du Progrès Médical, 1876–1880).

Bouteille, Étienne-Michel, *Traité de la chorée, ou, Danse de St. Guy* (Paris: Vincard, 1810).

Braziel, Jana Evans, and Kathleen LeBesco, 'Performing Excess', *Women & Performance: A Journal of Feminist Theory* 15.2 (2005): 9–13.

Bricheteau, Félix, 'Relation d'une épidémie de chorée observée à l'Hôpital Necker', *Archives générales de médecine* 1 (1863): 433–447, 532–549.

Briggs, Charles F., *The Body Broken: Medieval Europe 1300–1520* (London: Routledge, 2011).

Bright, Richard, *Reports of Medical Cases, Selected with a View to Illustrating Symptoms and Cures of Diseases by Reference to Morbid Anatomy* (London: Longman, 1831).

Brill, A. A., 'The Psychopathology of the New Dances', *New York Medical Journal followed by the . . .* 99.17 (1914): 834–837.

Brodkin, Karen, *How Jews Became White Folks and What That Says About Race in America* (New Brunswick, NJ: Rutgers University Press, 1998).

Brown, Andy, *Rave: The Spiritual Dimension* (Hampshire: Kaos, 1994).

Brown, Jayna, *Babylon Girls: Black Women Performers and the Shaping of the Modern* (Durham, NC: Duke University Press, 2008).

Brown, Wendy, *Undoing the Demos: Neoliberalism's Stealth Revolution* (Brooklyn: Zone Books, 2015).

Browning, Barbara, *Infectious Rhythm: Metaphors of Contagion and the Spread of African Culture* (New York: Routledge, 1998).

Bruder, Jessica, et al., *Burning Book: A Visual History of Burning Man* (New York: Simon Spotlight Entertainment, 2007).

Buckley, Ann, and Cynthia J. Cyrus, eds., *Music, Dance and Society: Medieval and Renaissance Studies in Memory of Ingrid G. Brainard* (Kalamazoo: Medieval Institute Publications, 2011).

Burridge, Kenelm, *New Heaven, New Earth: A Study of Millenarian Activities* (New York: Schocken Books, 1969).

Burt, Ramsay, *Alien Bodies: Representations of Modernity, 'Race' and Nation in Early Modern Dance* (London: Routledge, 1998).

Burton, Robert, *The Anatomy of Melancholy*, ed. Floyd Dell and Paul Jordan-Smith (New York: Tudor, 1927).

Butler, Alban, *Butler's Lives of the Saints*, rev. Kathleen Jones, ed. Paul Burns, 12 vols., vol. 6 (Collegeville, MN: Liturgical Press, 1997).

Butler, Judith, and Athena Athanasiou, *Dispossession: The Performative in the Political* (Cambridge: Polity Press, 2013).

Butler, Judith, Ernesto Laclau, and Slavoj Žižek, *Contingency, Hegemony, Universality: Contemporary Dialogues on the Left* (London: Verso, 2000).

Caldwell, Janice McLarren, *Literature and Medicine in Nineteenth-Century Britain: From Mary Shelley to George Eliot* (Cambridge: Cambridge University Press, 2008).

'Calls Dance Mania Psychic Epidemic: Participants Less Violent Than Centuries Ago, Says Dr. Brill. Here's Tango-Foot Also. But You Can Get That (If You Want It) by Running a Sewing Machine, Says Dr. Boehme', *New York Times*, 26 April 1914, 36.

Calmeil, Louis-Florentin, *De la folie, considérée sous le point de vue pathologique, philosophique, historique et judiciaire, depuis la renaissance des sciences en Europe jusqu'au dix-neuvième siècle; description des grandes épidémies de délire, simple ou compliqué, qui ont atteint les Populations d'autrefois et régné dans les Monastères. Exposé des condamnations auxquelles la folie méconnue a souvent donné lieu*, 2 vols. (Paris: J.-B. Baillière, 1845).

Canetti, Elias, *Crowds and Power*, trans. Carol Stewart (New York: Continuum, 1962).

Canguilhem, Georges, *The Normal and the Pathological, with an Introduction by Michel Foucault*, trans. Carolyn R. Fawcett with Robert S. Cohen (New York: Zone Books, 1991).

Cantor, Geoffrey, et al., *Science in the Nineteenth-Century Periodical: Reading the Magazine of Nature* (Cambridge: Cambridge University Press, 2004).

'Carnality in Song, Dance, and Dress', *Literary Digest* 19 July 1913, 101–102.

Cartwright, Peter, *Autobiography of Peter Cartwright* (New York: Abingdon Press, 1956).

Castle, Mr. & Mrs. Vernon, *Modern Dancing* (New York: Harper, 1914).

Catton, James, *The History and Description of the Shetland Islands; With an Account of the Manners, Customs, Circumstances, Superstitions and Religion of the Inhabitants* (Wainfleet: P. I. Tuxford, 1838).

Cauchie, Alfred, and Alphonse van Hove, eds., *Documents sur la principauté de Liège (1230–1532)*, 2 vols., vol. 1 (Brussels: M. Weissenbruch, 1908).

Certeau, Michel de, *La possession de Loudun* (Paris: Éditions Gallimard, 1990).

Champion, Pierre, *La Galerie des Rois* (Paris: Bernard Grasset, 1934).

Chapeauville, Jean, et al., *Contribution à l'historiographie liégeoise*, ed. René Hoven (Brussels: Classe des lettres, Académie royale de Belgique, 2004).

Chapman, John V., 'Forgotten Giant: Pierre Gardel', *Dance Research* 5.1 (1987): 3–20.

Charcot, Jean-Martin, *Clinical Lectures on Diseases of the Nervous System*, ed. with an introduction by Ruth Harris, trans. Thomas Savill (London: Tavistock/Routledge, 1991).

Charcot, Jean-Martin, *Œuvres complètes*, ed. Désiré Magloire Bourneville et al., 9 vols. (Paris: Bureaux du progrès médical, 1886–1890).

Charcot, Jean-Martin, *Œuvres complètes: 1, Leçons sur les maladies du système nerveux*, ed. Désiré Magloire Bourneville, 1 vol. (Paris: Bureaux du progrès médical, 1892).

Charcot, Jean-Martin, and Paul Richer, *Les démoniaques dans l'art* (Paris: A. Delahaye et E. Lecrosnier, 1887).

Charcot, Jean-Martin, and Paul Richer, *Les difformes et les malades dans l'art, avec 87 figures intercalées dans le texte* (Paris: Lecrosnier et Babé, 1889).

Chester, Samuel Beach, *Secrets of the Tango: Its History and How to Dance It. Fully Illustrated with Photographs and Diagrams* (London: T. Werner Laurie, [1914]).

Chinnery, E. W. P., and A. C. Haddon, 'Five New Religious Cults in British New Guinea', *Hibbert Journal* 15.3 (1917): 448–463.

Christensen, Allan Conrad, *Nineteenth-Century Narratives of Contagion: 'Our Feverish Contact'* (London: Routledge, 2005).

Cixous, Hélène, and Catherine Clément, *La Jeune Née* (Paris: Éditions 10/18, 1975).

Clark, Paul, *'Hauhau': The Pai Marire Search for Maori Identity* (Auckland: University of Auckland Press, 1975).

Clastres, Pierre, *La Société contre l'État: Recherches d'anthropologie politique* (Paris: Les Éditions de Minuit, 1974).

Clendinnen, Inga, *Dancing with Strangers: Europeans and Australians at First Contact* (Cambridge: Cambridge University Press, 2005).

Cleveland, Catherine C., *The Great Revival in the West, 1797–1805* (Chicago: University of Chicago Press, 1916).

Clifford, James, *Routes: Travel and Translation in the Late Twentieth Century* (Cambridge, MA: Harvard University Press, 1997).

C. O'C. E., 'The Leaping Procession at Echternach', *Irish Jesuit Province* 14.155 (May 1886): 257–260.

Cochart, Dominique, 'Les foules et la commune, analyse des premiers écrits de psychologie des foules', *Recherches de psychologie sociale* 4 (1982): 49–60.

Cohn, Samuel K., Jr., 'The Black Death and the Burning of Jews', *Past & Present* 196 (2007): 3–36.

Cohn, Samuel K., Jr., *The Black Death Transformed: Disease and Culture in Early Renaissance Europe* (London: Arnold, 2003).

Cohn, Samuel K., Jr., *Cultures of Plague: Medical Thinking at the End of the Renaissance* (Oxford: Oxford University Press, 2010).

Cohn, Samuel K., Jr., ed. and trans., *Popular Protest in Late Medieval Europe: Italy, France and Flanders* (Manchester: Manchester University Press, 2004).

Cole, Jennifer, 'The Work of Memory in Madagascar', *American Ethnologist* 25.4 (1998): 610–633.

Coleman, William S. E., *Voices of Wounded Knee* (Lincoln: University of Nebraska Press, 2000).

Collini, Stefan, 'Introduction', in C. P. Snow, *The Two Cultures, with Introduction by Stefan Collini* (Cambridge: Cambridge University Press, 1998).

Cornish, James, 'Remarkable Effects of Fanaticism on the Inhabitants of Several Towns in Cornwall', *London Medical and Physical Journal* 31 (1814): 373–379.

Cortet, Eugène, *Essai sur les fêtes religieuses et les traditions populaires qui s'y rattachent* (Paris: Ernest Thorin, 1867).

The Council for World Mission/London Missionary Society Archive, 1764–1977, School of Oriental and African Studies Library, University of London.

Courbon, Alfred, *Observations topographiques et médicales recueillies dans un voyage à l'isthme de Suez, sur le littoral de la mer Rouge et en Abyssinie* (Paris: Imprimerie Rignoux, 1861).

'Court Rules Jitterbug Is All Word Implies, Jitter for "Nervous" and Bug for "Crazy"', *New York Times*, 3 May 1944, 21.

Cowan, James, *The New Zealand Wars: A History of the Maori Campaigns and the Pioneering Period*, 2 vols., vol. 2, *The Hauhau Wars, 1864–1872* (New York: AMS Press, 1969).

Cubitt, Sean, 'Anecdotal Evidence', *NECSUS: European Journal of Media Studies* 2.1 (2013): 5–18.

Curtius, Ernst Robert, *European Literature and the Latin Middle Ages*, trans. Willard R. Trask (Princeton, NJ: Princeton University Press, 1991).

Cutting, Mary Stewart, 'Dance-Mad Billy', *McClure's* 45 (September 1915): 22–43.

Daboo, Jerri, *Ritual, Rapture and Remorse: A Study of Tarantism and Pizzica in Salento* (Bern: Peter Lang, 2010).

da Cunha, Euclides, *Rebellion in the Backlands*, trans. Samuel Putnam (Chicago: University of Chicago Press, 1944).

Dames, Nicholas, *The Physiology of the Novel: Reading, Neural Science, and the Form of Victorian Fiction* (New York: Oxford University Press, 2007).

Damrosch, David, *What Is World Literature?* (Princeton, NJ: Princeton University Press, 2003).

'A Dancing Epidemic', *Chambers's Journal of Popular Literature, Science and Arts* 20.1040 (1883): 760–762.

'The Dancing Mania', *Penny Magazine of the Society for the Diffusion of Useful Knowledge* 8.488 (1839): 439–440.

Dandouau, A., and G.-S. Chapus, *Histoire des Populations de Madagascar* (Paris: Larose, 1952).

Darwin, Charles, *Beagle Diary*, ed. Richard Darwin Keynes (Cambridge: Cambridge University Press, 1988).

Darwin, Charles, *Narrative of the Surveying Voyages of his Majesty's Ships Adventure and Beagle, between the years 1826 and 1836, describing their examination of the southern shores of South America, and the Beagle's circumnavigation of the globe*, 3 vols., vol. 3 (London: Henry Colburn, 1839).

Darwin, Charles, *On the Origin of Species. Or the Preservation of Favoured Races in the Struggle for Life* (London: John Murray, 1859).

Davenport, F. M., *Primitive Traits in Religious Revivals: A Study in Mental and Social Evolution* (New York: Macmillan, 1905).

Davidson, Andrew, 'Choreomania: An Historical Sketch, with Some Account of an Epidemic Observed in Madagascar', *Edinburgh Medical Journal* 13.2 (1867): 124–136.

Davidson, Andrew, 'Foreign Correspondence', *Medical Times and Gazette*, 3 January 1863.

Davidson, Hilary, 'Sex and Sin: The Magic of Red Shoes', in Peter McNeil and Giorgio Riello, eds., *Shoes: A History from Sandals to Sneakers* (London: Bloomsbury, 2006), 272–289.

Davis, Darién J., 'Review of *Guerra de Canudos* (1997 Film) by Sergio Rezende and *Passion and War in the Backlands of Canudos* (*Paxão e Guerra no Sertão de Canudos*) (1993 Film) by Antônio Olavo', *American Historical Review* 104.5 (1999): 1807–1809.

Davis, Michael G., *Ecology, Sociopolitical Organization, and Cultural Change on the Southern Plains: A Critical Treatise in the Sociocultural Anthropology of Native North America* (Kirksville, MO: Thomas Jefferson University Press, 1996).

Dawson, Gowan, *Darwin, Literature and Victorian Respectability* (Cambridge: Cambridge University Press, 2010).

Deaux, George, *The Black Death 1347* (New York: Weybright and Talley, 1969).

Debus, Allen G., *The Chemical Philosophy: Paracelsian Science and Medicine in the Sixteenth and Seventeenth Centuries*, 2 vols. (Mineola, NY: Dover, 2002).

Decary, Raymond, *Mœurs et Coutumes des Malgaches, avec cent un dessins de l'auteur* (Paris: Payot, 1951).

Decary, Raymond, *La mort et les coutumes funéraires à Madagascar* (Paris: G. P. Maisonneuve et Larose, 1962).

De Costa, Caroline, 'St Anthony's Fire and Living Ligatures: A Short History of Ergometrine', *Lancet* 359 (2002): 1768–1770.

DeFrantz, Thomas F., *Dancing Revelations: Alvin Ailey's Embodiment of African American Culture* (Oxford: Oxford University Press, 2004).

Delaney, John J., *Dictionary of Saints* (Garden City, NJ: Doubleday, 1980).

Deleuze, Gilles, *Le bergsonisme* (Paris: Presses Universitaires de France, 2011).

Deleuze, Gilles, *Différence et répétition* (Paris: Presses Universitaires de France, 1968).

Deleuze, Gilles, *Foucault* (Paris: Les éditions de minuit, 2004).

Deleuze, Gilles, *Francis Bacon: The Logic of Sensation*, trans. Daniel W. Smith (Minneapolis: University of Minnesota Press, 2003).

Deleuze, Gilles, and Félix Guattari, *Capitalisme et schizophrénie 2: Mille plateaux* (Paris: Les Éditions de Minuit, 1980).

Deleuze, Gilles, and Félix Guattari, *Qu'est-ce que la philosophie?* (Paris: Les éditions de minuit, 1991).

Deleuze, Gilles, and Félix Guattari, *What Is Philosophy?*, trans. Hugh Tomlinson and Graham Burchell (London: Verso, 1994).

Del Giudice, Luisa, and Nancy van Deusen, *Performing Ecstasies: Music, Dance and Ritual in the Mediterranean* (Ottawa: Institute of Medieval Music, 2005).

De Martino, Ernesto, *The Land of Remorse: A Study of Southern Italian Tarantism*, ed. and trans. Dorothy Louise Zinn (London: Free Association Books, 2005).

De Martino, Ernesto, *La terra del rimorso: Contributo a una storia religiosa del Sud* (Milan: Il Saggiatore, 1961).

Derrida, Jacques, *Of Grammatology*, trans. Gayatri Chakravorty Spivak (Baltimore: John Hopkins University Press, 1998).

Derrida, Jacques, *Spectres de Marx* (Paris: Galilée, 1993).

Deschamps, Hubert, *Histoire de Madagascar* (Paris, Éditions Berger-Levrault, 1960).

Despine, Prosper, *De la contagion morale; faits démontrant son existence, son explication scientifique; du danger que présente pour la moralité et la sécurité publiques la relation des crimes données par les journaux* (Marseille: E. Camoin, 1870).

Devereux, Georges, *Essais d'ethnopsychiatrie générale* (Paris: Gallimard, 1970).

Diamond, Elin, *Unmaking Mimesis: Essays on Feminism and Gender* (New York: Routledge, 1997).

Diderot, Denis, and Jean le Rond d'Alembert, eds., *L'Encyclopédie ou Dictionnaire raisonné des sciences, des arts et des métiers*, 3rd ed., 28 vols., vol. 9 (Geneva: Chez Jean-Léonard Pellet, 1779).

Didi-Huberman, Georges, *Invention of Hysteria: Charcot and the Photographic Iconography of the Salpêtrière*, trans. Alisa Hartz (Cambridge, MA: MIT Press, 2003).

Dietz, K., 'Epidemics and Rumors: A Survey', *Journal of the Royal Statistical Society*, series A, 130 (1967): 505–528.

Dissertation sur les miracles, Et en particulier sur ceux qui ont été operés au Tombeau de Mr. de Pâris, en l'Eglise de S. Medard de Paris, avec la Relation & les preuves de celui qui s'est fait le 3e Novembre 1730 en la personne d'Anne le Franc de la Paroisse de S. Barthelemy (Paris, 1731).

Dobson, R. B., ed., *The Peasants' Revolt of 1381*, 2nd ed. (London: Macmillan, 1983).

Dobyns, H., *Their Number Become Thinned: Native American Population Dynamics in Eastern North America* (Knoxville: University of Tennessee Press, 1983).

Doherty, Brian, *This Is Burning Man: The Rise of the New American Underground* (Dallas: BenBella Books, 2006).

Donaldson, L. J., J. Cavanagh, and J. Rankin, 'The Dancing Plague: A Public Health Conundrum', *Public Health* 111 (1997): 201–204.

Douglas, Bronwen, 'From Invisible Christians to Gothic Theater: The Romance of the Millennial in Melanesian Anthropology', *Current Anthropology* 42.5 (2001): 615–650.

'Dr Madden's "Phantasmata,"' *Chambers's Journal of Popular Literature, Science and Arts* 237 (1858): 34–37.

Du Bois, Cora, 'The 1870 Ghost Dance', in *University of California Publications in Anthropological Records*, vol. 3, no. 1 (Berkeley: University of California Press, 1946), 1–152.

Du Camp, Maxime, *Les Convulsions de Paris*, 4 vols., vol. 1 (Paris: Librairie Hachette, 1878–1880).

Du Camp, Maxime, *Paris: Ses organes, ses fonctions et sa vie dans la seconde moitié de XIXe siècle*, 6 vols., vol. 4 (Paris: Hachette, 1873).

Dufour, Valentin, *Recherches sur la Dance Macabre peinte en 1425 au Cimetière des Innocents* [sic] (Paris: Bureaux du Bibliophile Français, 1873).

Duncan, Isadora, *My Life* (New York: Norton, 2013).

Durkheim, Émile, *De la division du travail social*, 8th ed. (Paris: Presses Universitaires de France, 1967).

Durkheim, Émile, *Le suicide: Étude de sociologie* (Paris: Presses Universitaires de France, 2002).

Eadie, Mervyn J., 'Convulsive Ergotism: Epidemics of Serotonin Syndrome?', *Lancet Neurology* 2.7 (2003): 429–434.

Edmondston, Eliza, *Sketches and Tales of the Shetland Islands* (Edinburgh: Sutherland & Knox; and London: Simpkin, Marshall & Co., 1856).

Eftychiadis, A. C., and T. S. N. Chen, 'Historical Note: Saint Vitus and His Dance', *Journal of Neurology, Neurosurgery and Psychiatry* 70 (2001): 14.

Ehrenreich, Barbara, *Dancing in the Streets: A History of Collective Joy* (London: Granta, 2007).

Elias, Norbert, *The Civilizing Process: Sociogenetic and Psychogenetic Investigations*, ed. E. Dunning, J. Goudsblom, and S. Mennell, trans. E. Jephcott (Oxford: Blackwell, 2000).

Ellis, William, *Madagascar Revisited. Describing the Events of a New Reign and the Revolution Which Followed* (London: John Murray, 1867).

'Endemic and Epidemic Diseases', *Penny Magazine for the Diffusion of Useful Knowledge* 10.605 (1841): 346–348.

Enders, Jody, 'The Spectacle of the Scaffolding: Rape and the Violent Foundations of Medieval Theatre Studies', *Theatre Journal* 56.2 (2004): 163–181.

Engelhardt, Molly, *Dancing out of Line: Ballrooms, Ballets, and Mobility in Victorian Fiction and Culture* (Athens: Ohio University Press, 2009).

Entry 2540, Division of the Missouri, 'Letters Sent by Headquarters in the Field, 1890–91', 1 vol.; and entry 2541, Division of the Missouri, 'Press Copies of Letters Sent by Headquarters in the field, 1890–91', 1 vol. Record Group 393, Records of U.S. Army Continental Commands, 1821–1920, Part I. National Archives and Records Administration, Library of Congress.

'Epidemics, Past and Present—Their Origin and Distribution', *Scottish Review* 4.13 (1865): 593–604.

Erenberg, Lewis A., *Steppin' Out: New York Nightlife and the Transformation of American Culture, 1890–1930* (Chicago: University of Chicago Press, 1984).

Esquirol, Étienne, *Des maladies mentales considérées sous le rapport médical, hygiénique et médico-légal*, 2 vols., vol. 1 (Paris: J.-B. Baillière, 1838).

Eustace, Frances, with Pamela M. King, 'Dances of the Living and the Dead: A Study of *Danse Macabre* Imagery within the Context of Late-Medieval Dance Culture', in Sophie Oosterwijk and Stefanie Knöll, eds., *Mixed Metaphors: The Danse Macabre in Medieval and Early Modern Europe* (Newcastle upon Tyne: Cambridge Scholars, 2011), 43–71.

Evans, F. W., *Shakers: Compendium of the Origin, History, Principles, Rules and Regulations, Government, and Doctrines of the United Society of Believers in Christ's Second Appearing: With*

*Biographies of Ann Lee, William Lee, Jas. Whittaker,
J. Hocknell, J. Meacham, and Lucy Wright*
(New York: D. Appleton and Company, 1859).

Evans, John, *A Sketch of the Denominations of the
Christian World; to which is prefixed an outline of
Atheism, Deism, Theophilanthropism, Judaism,
and Mahometanism: With a chronological table
of the leading events of the ecclesiastical history,
from the birth of Christ to the present time*,
13th ed. (London: B. and R. Crosby and Co.
Stationers, 1814).

Farmer, David Hugh, *The Oxford Dictionary of
Saints*, 5th ed. (Oxford: Oxford University
Press, 2003).

Farrell, James T., 'The Dance Marathons', *MELUS*
18.1 (1993): 133–143.

Feeley-Harnik, Gillian, 'The Political Economy of
Death: Communication and Change in Malagasy
Colonial History', *American Ethnologist* 11.1
(1984): 1–19.

Félice, Philippe de, *L'enchantement des danses et la
magie du verbe: Essai sur quelques formes inférieures
de la vie mystique* (Paris: Albin Michel, 1957).

Félice, Philippe de, *Foules en délire, extases
collectives: Essai sur quelques formes inférieures de
la mystique* (Paris: Éditions Albin Michel, 1947).

Fernandes, Raúl C. Goveira, 'Euclides e a
literatura: Comentérios sobre a "moldura" de Os
Sertões', *Luso-Brazilian Review* 43.2 (2006): 45–62.

Firth, R., 'The Theory of "Cargo" Cults: A Note on
Tikopia', *Man* (1955): 130–132.

Fogarty, Robert S., *All Things New: American
Communes and Utopian Movements, 1860–1914*
(Lanham, MD: Lexington Books, 2003).

Foster, Susan Leigh, 'Choreographies of Protest',
Theatre Journal 55.3 (2003): 395–412.

Foster, Susan Leigh, *Choreographing
Empathy: Kinesthesia in Performance*
(London: Routledge, 2011).

Foster, Susan Leigh, 'Movement's Contagion: The
Kinesthetic Impact of Performance', in
Tracy Davis, ed., *The Cambridge Companion to
Performance Studies* (New York: Cambridge
University Press, 2009), 46–59.

Foster, Susan Leigh, *Reading Dancing: Bodies
and Subjects in Contemporary American Dance*
(Berkeley: University of California Press, 1986).

Foster, Susan Leigh, 'Textual Evidances', in Ellen
W. Goellner and Jacqueline Shea Murphy, eds.,
*Bodies of the Text: Dance as Theory, Literature as
Dance* (New Brunswick, NJ: Rutgers University
Press, 1995), 231–246.

Foucault, Michel, *Les Anormaux* (Paris: Éditions du
Seuil/Gallimard, 1999).

Foucault, Michel, *L'archéologie du savoir*
(Paris: Éditions Gallimard, 1969).

Foucault, Michel, *Dits et écrits 1954–1988*,
ed. Daniel Defert and François Ewald
with Jacques Lagrange, 2 vols., vol. 1
(Paris: Gallimard, 2001).

Foucault, Michel, *Folie et déraison. Histoire de la folie
à l'âge classique* (Paris: Plon, 1961).

Foucault, Michel, *Folie et déraison. Histoire de la folie
à l'âge classique* (Paris: Plon, 1964).

Foucault, Michel, *Histoire de la folie à l'âge classique*
(Paris: Éditions Gallimard, 1972).

Foucault, Michel, *Histoire de la sexualité*, vol. 1
(Paris: Éditions Gallimard, 1976).

Foucault, Michel, *History of Madness*, ed. Jean
Khalfa, trans. John Murphy and Jean Khalfa
(London: Routledge, 2006).

Foucault, Michel, *Madness and Civilization: A History
of Insanity in the Age of Reason*, trans. Richard
Howard (New York: Pantheon, 1965).

Foucault, Michel, *Madness and Civilization: A History
of Insanity in the Age of Reason*, trans. Richard
Howard (London: Tavistock, 1967).

Foucault, Michel, *Madness and Civilization: A History
of Insanity in the Age of Reason*, trans. Richard
Howard (London: Routledge, 1989).

Foucault, Michel, *Les mots et les choses: Une
archéologie des sciences humaines* (Paris: Éditions
Gallimard, 1966).

Foucault, Michel, *Naissance de la biopolitique: Cours
au Collège de France 1978–1979* (Paris: Éditions
du Seuil/Gallimard, 2004).

Foucault, Michel, 'Nietzsche, Genealogy, History',
in James D. Faubion, ed., *Aesthetics, Method,
and Epistemology: Essential Works of Foucault
1954–1984*, trans. Robert Hurley, 3 vols., vol. 2
(New York: New Press, 1998), 369–391.

Foucault, Michel, *The Order of Things: An Archaeology
of the Human Sciences*, trans. Alan Sheridan
(London: Routledge Classics, 2002).

Foucault, Michel, *Le pouvoir psychiatrique: Cours au
Collège de France, 1973–1974* (Paris: Éditions du
Seuil/Gallimard, 2003).

Foucault, Michel, *Security, Territory,
Population: Lectures at the Collège de France
1977–1978*, ed. Arnold I. Davidson, trans.
Graham Burchell (London: Palgrave
Macmillan, 2007).

Foucault, Michel, *Surveiller et punir: Naissance de la
Prison* (Paris: Éditions Gallimard, 1975).

Foucault, Michel, 'What Is an Author?', trans. Josué
V. Harari, in Paul Rabinow, ed., *The Foucault
Reader* (New York: Pantheon Books, 1984),
101–120.

Foucault, Michel, ed., *Moi, Pierre Rivière, ayant égorgé ma mère, ma sœur et mon frère . . . Un cas de parricide au XIXe siècle* (Paris: Gallimard, 1973).

Fournial, Henri, *Essai sur la psychologie des foules. Considérations médico-judiciaires sur les responsabilités collectives* (Lyon: A. Storck; and Paris: G. Masson, 1899).

Fournier, A., 'Vieilles coutumes, usages et traditions populaires des Vosges provenant des cultes antiques et particulièrement de celui du soleil', *Bulletin de la Société philomatique vosgienne* 16 (1890–1891): 137–205.

Franko, Mark, 'Dance and the Political: States of Exception', *Dance Research Journal* 38.1/2 (2006): 3–18.

Franko, Mark, 'Dance and the Political: States of Exception', in Susanne Franco and Marina Nordera, eds., *Dance Discourses: Keywords in Dance Research* (London: Routledge, 2007), 11–28.

Franko, Mark, *Dance as Text: Ideologies of the Baroque Body*, rev. ed. (Oxford: Oxford University Press, 2015).

Franko, Mark, *Dancing Modernism/Performing Politics* (Bloomington: Indiana University Press, 1995)

Franko, Mark, 'Figural Inversions of Louis XIV's Dancing Body', in Mark Franko and Annette Richards, eds., *Acting on the Past: Historical Performance across the Disciplines* (Hanover, NH: Wesleyan University Press, 2000), 35–51.

Franko, Mark, 'Mimique', in Carrie Noland and Sally Ann Ness, eds., *Migrations of Gesture* (Minneapolis: University of Minnesota Press, 2008), 241–258.

Franko, Mark, *The Work of Dance: Labor, Movement, and Identity in the 1930s* (Middletown, CT: Wesleyan University Press, 2002).

Franko, Mark, and Annette Richards, 'Actualizing Absence: The Pastness of Performance', in Mark Franko and Annette Richards, eds., *Acting on the Past: Historical Performance across the Disciplines* (Hanover, NH: Wesleyan University Press, 2000), 1–9.

Frédéricq, Paul, 'De secten der geeselaars en der dansers in de Nederlanden tijdens de 14de eeuw', in *Mémoires de l'académie royale des sciences des lettres et des beaux-arts de Belgique*, vol. 53 (Brussels: Hayez, October 1895–June 1898), 1–62.

Freedman, Seth, 'Israel Should Praise Their Dancing IDF Soldiers, Not Condemn Them', *Guardian*, 29 August 2013, http://www.theguardian.com/commentisfree/2013/aug/29/israel-gangnam-idf-soldiers. Accessed 9 September 2013.

Freud, Sigmund, *Civilization and Its Discontents*, ed. and trans. James Strachey (New York: Norton, 1989).

Freud, Sigmund, *Group Psychology and the Analysis of the Ego*, ed. and trans. James Strachey (New York: Norton, 1959).

Freud, Sigmund, *Totem and Taboo*, trans. A. A. Brill (New York: Vintage Books, 1946).

Frow, John, 'Invidious Distinction: Waste, Difference, and Classy Stuff', in Gay Hawkins and Stephen Muecke, eds., *Culture and Waste: The Creation and Destruction of Value* (Oxford: Rowan and Littlefield, 2003), 25–38.

Futcher, Thomas B., *An Account of the Dancing Mania of Europe and of Epidemic Convulsions in Kentucky* (Baltimore, 1905).

Gagnol, L'abbé, *Le jansénisme convulsionnaire et l'affaire de la planchette*, d'après les archives de la Bastille (Paris: Librairie générale catholique, 1911).

Gaidoz, H., 'Le Grand-Duché de Luxembourg', *Nouvelle Revue* 66 (1890): 800–817.

Gaillot, Michel, Jean-Luc Nancy, and Michel Maffesoli, *Multiple Meaning: Techno, an Artistic and Political Laboratory of the Present*, trans. Warren Niesluchowski (Paris: Éditions Dis voir, 1999).

Gardel, Pierre, *La dansomanie, folie-pantomime, en deux actes.* (Paris: De l'Imprimerie de Ballard, 1800).

Garrett, Clarke, *Origins of the Shakers: From the Old World to the New World* (Baltimore: Johns Hopkins University Press, 1998).

Gauthier, François, and Guy Ménard, eds., *Technoritualités: Religiosité rave* (Montréal: Université du Québec à Montréal, 2001).

Gayton, A. H., 'The Ghost Dance of 1870 in South-Central California', *University of California Publications in American Archaeology and Ethnology* 28 (1930): 57–82.

'General Considerations on Epidemic Diseases', *Chambers's Edinburgh Journal* 296 (1849): 132–136.

George-Graves, Nadine, ' "Just Like Being at the Zoo": Primitivity and Ragtime Dance', in Julie Malnig, ed., *Ballroom, Boogie, Shimmy Sham, Shake: A Social and Popular Dance Reader* (Urbana: University of Illinois Press, 2009), 55–71.

The Ghost Dance, Record Group 75, Entry 102, Special Cases, Special Case 188, National Archives, Washington, DC.

Gilman, Sander L., 'The Image of the Hysteric', in Sander L. Gilman, Helen King, Roy Porter, G. S. Rousseau, and Elaine Showalter, *Hysteria beyond Freud* (Berkeley: University of California Press, 1993), 345–436.

Gilman, Sander L., *Seeing the Insane: A Cultural History of Madness and Art in the Western World* (New York: Wiley, 1982).

Gilman, Sander L., Helen King, Roy Porter, G. S. Rousseau, and Elaine Showalter, *Hysteria beyond Freud* (Berkeley: University of California Press, 1993).

Gilmore, Lee, and Mark van Proyen, eds., *AfterBurn: Reflections on Burning Man* (Albuquerque: University of New Mexico Press, 2005).

Gilroy, Paul, *The Black Atlantic: Modernity and Double Consciousness* (London: Verso, 1993).

Gingras, Yves, 'Naming without Necessity: On the Genealogy and Uses of the Label "Historical Epistemology,"' *CIRST—Note de recherche 2010-01* (January 2010), http://www.chss.uqam. ca/Portals/0/docs/articles/2010-01.pdf. Last accessed 7 June 2017.

Girard, René, *Violence and the Sacred*, trans. Patrick Gregory (Baltimore: Johns Hopkins University Press, 1977).

Glissant, Édouard, *Le discours antillais* (Paris: Gallimard, 1997).

Goethe, Johann Wolfgang von, *Italian Journey (1786–1788)*, trans. Elizabeth Meyer and W. H. Auden (London: Collins, 1962).

Goetz, Christopher G., 'Shakespeare in Charcot's Neurologic Teaching', *Archives of Neurology* 45.8 (1988): 920–921.

Goetz, Christopher G., 'Visual Art in the Neurologic Career of Jean-Martin Charcot', *Archives of Neurology* 48.4 (1991): 421–425.

Goetz, Christopher G., Michel Bonduelle, and Toby Gelfand, *Charcot: Constructing Neurology* (New York: Oxford University Press, 1995).

Goff, Susan E., 'The Ghost Dance Religion among the Plains Indians: A Religious Response to the Crisis of Forced Acculturation and Christianization', M.Div. thesis (Union Theological Seminary, 1980).

Goldman, A. J., 'Berliners Will Again Be Dancing in the Streets', *New York Times*, 15 July 2006.

Goldstein, Jan, 'The Uses of Male Hysteria: Medical and Literary Discourse in Nineteenth-Century France', *Representations* 34 (1991): 134–165.

Gordon, Colin, 'Histoire de la folie: An Unknown book by Michel Foucault', in Arthur Still and Irving Velody, eds., *Rewriting the History of Madness: Studies in Foucault's 'Histoire de la folie'* (London: Routledge, 1992), 19–42.

Gordon, Colin, 'Rewriting the History of Misreading', in Arthur Still and Irving Velody, eds., *Rewriting the History of Madness: Studies in Foucault's 'Histoire de la folie'* (London: Routledge, 1992), 167–184.

Gordon, Rae Beth, *Dances with Darwin, 1875–1910: Vernacular Modernity in France* (Farnham: Ashgate, 2009).

Gordon, Rae Beth, 'Les rythmes contagieux d'une danse noire: Le cake-walk', *Intermédialités* 16 (2010): 57–81.

Gordon, Rae Beth, *Why the French Love Jerry Lewis: From Cabaret to Early Cinema* (Stanford, CA: Stanford University Press, 2001).

Gotman, Kélina, 'Chorea Minor, Chorea Major, Choreomania: Entangled Medical and Colonial Histories', in Johannes Birringer and Josephine Fenger, eds., *Tanz und WahnSinn/Dance and ChoreoMania* (Leipzig: Henschel Verlag, 2011), 83–97.

Gotman, Kélina, 'The Dancing-Place: Towards a Geocultural and Geohistorical Theory of Performance Space', *Choreographic Practices* 3 (2012): 7–23.

Gotman, Kélina, 'Epilepsy, Chorea and Involuntary Movements Onstage: The Aesthetics and Politics of Alterkinetic Dance', *About Performance* 11 (2011): 159–183.

Gotman, Kélina, 'The Neural Metaphor', in Melissa Littlefield and Janelle Johnson, eds., *The Neuroscientific Turn: Transdisciplinarity in the Age of the Brain* (Ann Arbor: University of Michigan Press, 2012), 71–86.

Gotman, Kélina, 'Translatio', *Performance Research* 21.5 (2016): 17–20.

Gougaud, L., 'La danse dans les églises', *Revue d'Histoire Ecclésiastique* 15 (1914): 5–22, 229–245.

Gowers, W., *Epilepsy and Other Chronic Convulsive Disorders: Their Causes, Symptoms and Treatment* (London: J. A. Churchill, 1881).

Graham, Martha, *Blood Memory: An Autobiography* (London: Scepter Books, 1991).

Grandmougin, Thierry, Catherine Bourdet, and Jean-Marc Gurrachaga, 'De la danse de Saint Guy à la chorée de Huntington: Rappels sur l'émergence d'un concept medical', *M/S médecine/sciences* 13 (1997): 850–854.

Gravier, Gabriel, *Madagascar: Les Malgaches, Origines de la colonisation française, la conquête* (Paris: Charles Delagrave, Libraire-Éditeur, 1904).

Green, Calvin, and Seth Youngs Wells, *Summary view of the Millennial Church or United Society of Believers, Commonly Called Shakers. Comprising the Rise, Progress and Practical Order of the Society. Together with the General Principles of Their Faith and Testimony*, 2nd ed. (Albany, NY: C. Van Benthuysen, 1848).

Greenfield, Gerald Michael, 'Sertão and Sertanejo: An Interpretive Context for Canudos', *Luso-Brazilian Review* 30.2 (1993): 35–46.

Greenwood, W., 'The Upraised Hand, or the Spiritual Significance of the Rise of the Ringatu Faith', *Journal of the Polynesian Society* 51.1 (1942): 1–81.

Grua, David W., *Surviving Wounded Knee: The Lakotas and the Politics of Memory* (New York: Oxford University Press, 2016).

Guattari, Félix, *The Three Ecologies*, trans. Ian Pindar and Paul Sutton (London: Continuum, 2008).

Guilbert, Yvette, *Une heure de musique avec Yvette Guilbert* (Paris: Éditions Cosmopolites, 1930).

Gump, James O., 'The Imperialism of Cultural Assimilation: Sir George Grey's Encounter with the Maori and the Xhosa, 1845–1868', *Journal of World History* 9.1 (1998): 89–106.

Hacking, Ian, 'Déraison', *History of the Human Sciences* 24.4 (2011): 13–23.

Hacking, Ian, *Historical Ontology* (Cambridge, MA: Harvard University Press, 2004).

Hacking, Ian, *Rewriting the Soul: Multiple Personality and the Sciences of Memory* (Princeton, NJ: Princeton University Press, 1995).

Haddon, Alfred C., 'Appreciation', in E. E. Evans-Pritchard, Raymond Firth, Bronisław Malinowski, and Isaac Schapera, eds., *Essays Presented to C. G. Seligman* (London: K. Paul, Trench, Tübner, 1934), 1–4.

Haddon, Alfred C., *History of Anthropology* (London: Watts, 1910).

Haddon, Alfred C., ed., *Reports of the Cambridge Anthropological Expedition to Torres Straits* (Cambridge: Cambridge University Press, 1901).

Ham, Mordecai Franklin, *Light on the Dance: The Modern Dance; A Historical and Analytical Treatment of the Subject; Religious, Social, Hygienic, Industrial Aspects As Viewed by the Pulpit, the Press, Medical Authorities, Municipal Authorities, Social Workers, Etc.*, 2nd rev. ed. (n.p., [1916]).

Hammond, William A., 'Miryachit: A Newly Discovered Disease of the Nervous System and Its Analogues', *British Medical Journal* 1.1216 (1884): 758–759.

Hardison, J., 'Are the Jumping Frenchmen of Maine Goosey?', *Journal of the American Medical Association* 244 (1980): 70.

Hardt, Michael, and Antonio Negri, *Multitude: War and Democracy in the Age of Empire* (London: Penguin, 2004).

Harris, John, *Lexicon technicum: or, an universal English dictionary of arts and sciences: explaining not only the terms of art, but the arts themselves*, 2 vols., vol. 1 (London: D. Brown, et al., 1704).

Harris, Joseph, 'The Early History of European Ballads—The Legend of the Kolbigk Dance or Chorea-Famosa, Its Social Origins, Oral Tradition, and Historical Credibility. German by E. E. Metzner, 1972', *Speculum: A Journal of Medieval Studies* 50.3 (1975): 522–525.

Harris, Max, *Sacred Folly: A New History of the Feast of Fools* (Ithaca, NY: Cornell University Press, 2011).

Harris, Ruth, *Lourdes: Body and Spirit in the Secular Age* (New York: Viking, 1999).

Haynes, Kenneth, *English Literature and Ancient Languages* (Oxford: Oxford University Press, 2003).

Hecker, J. F. C., *The Black Death, and The Dancing Mania*, ed. Henry Morley, trans. B. G. Babington (London: Cassell & Company, 1888).

Hecker, J. F. C., *De danswoede, eene volksziekte der Middeleeuwen, in de Nederlanden, Duitschland en Italië, volgens het hoogduitsch door G. J. Pool* (Amsterdam: Sülpke, 1833).

Hecker, J. F. C., *La Danzimania, malattia poplare nel medio-evo*, trans. Valentino Fassetta (Firenze: Ricordi, 1838).

Hecker, J. F. C., *Die Grossen Volkskrankheiten des mittelalters: Historisch-pathologische Untersuchungen*, ed. August Hirsch (Berlin: Verlag von Th. Chr. Fr. Enslin, 1865).

Hecker, J. F. C., *The Epidemics of the Middle Ages*, trans. B. G. Babington (London: Sherwood, Gilbert and Piper, 1835).

Hecker, J. F. C., *The Epidemics of the Middle Ages*, trans. B. G. Babington (London: Trübner & Co., 1859).

Hecker, J. F. C., 'Mémoire sur la chorée épidémique du moyen âge', trans. Ferdinand Dubois, *Annales d'hygiène et de médecine légale* 12 (1834): 312–390.

Hecker, J. F. C., *Die Tanzwuth, eine Volkskrankheit im Mittelalter* (Berlin: T. C. F. Enslin, 1832).

Henrichs, Albert, 'The Last of the Detractors: Friedrich Nietzsche's Condemnation of Euripides', *Greek, Roman and Byzantine Studies* 27.4 (1986): 369–397.

Herlihy, David, *The Black Death and the Transformation of the West*, ed. and intro. Samuel K. Cohn, Jr. (Cambridge, MA: Harvard University Press, 1997).

Hermann, Elfriede, 'Dissolving the Self-Other Dichotomy in Western "Cargo Cult" Constructions', in Holger Jebens, ed., *Cargo, Cult, and Culture Critique* (Honolulu: University of Hawai'i Press, 2004), 36–58.

Hewitt, Andrew, *Social Choreography: Ideology as Performance in Dance and Everyday Movement* (Durham, NC: Duke University Press, 2005).

Hibbert, Samuel, *A description of the Shetland Islands, comprising an account of their geology, scenery, antiquities, and superstitions* (Edinburgh: A. Constable & Co., 1822).

Hinsley, Curtis M., Jr., *Savages and Scientists: The Smithsonian Institution and the Development of American Anthropology, 1846–1910* (Washington, DC: Smithsonian Institution Press, 1981).

Hirsch, August, *Handbook of Geographical and Historical Pathology*, trans. from 2nd German ed. by Charles Creighton, 3 vols., vol. 3 (London: New Sydenham Society, 1886).

Hittman, Michael, *Wovoka and the Ghost Dance*, expanded ed. (Lincoln: University of Nebraska Press, 1990).

Hobsbawm, Eric J., *Primitive Rebels: Studies in Archaic Forms of Social Movement in the 19th and 20th Centuries* (New York: Norton, 1965).

Holweck, F. G., *A Biographical Dictionary of the Saints, with a General Introduction on Hagiography* (Saint Louis: Herder, 1924).

Horden, Peregrine, ed., *Music as Medicine: The History of Music Therapy since Antiquity* (Aldershot, Hants: Ashgate, 2000).

Horrox, Rosemarie, ed. and trans., *The Black Death* (Manchester: Manchester University Press, 1994).

Horst, Gregor, *Observationum medicinalium singularium*, 4 vols. (Ulm: Typis Saurianis, 1628).

Houlder, J. A., *Among the Malagasy: An Unconventional Record of Missionary Experience* (London: Clarke, 1912).

Howard, R., and R. Ford, 'From the Jumping Frenchmen of Maine to Post-Traumatic Stress Disorder: The Startle Response in Neuropsychiatry', *Psychological Medicine* 22.3 (1992): 695–707.

Howe, Sonia E., *The Drama of Madagascar* (London: Methuen, 1938).

Hustvedt, Asti, *Medical Muses: Hysteria in Nineteenth-Century Paris* (London: Bloomsbury, 2012).

Huxley, Thomas Henry, *Science and Culture, and Other Essays* (New York: D. Appleton, 1882).

Ibsen, Henrik, *A Doll's House and Other Plays*, trans. Peter Watts (London: Penguin Books, 1965).

Ignatiev, Noel, *How the Irish Became White* (London: Routledge, 1995).

Jacoby, J. Ralph, 'Dance and Health', in Mr. & Mrs. Vernon Castle, *Modern Dancing* (New York: Harper, 1914), 173–176.

Janet, Pierre, *De l'angoisse à l'extase: Études sur les croyances et les sentiments*, 2 vols., vol. 2 (Paris: Félix Alcan, 1926–1927).

Jean des Preis (dit d'Outremeuse), *Ly Myeur des Histors, Chronique*, ed. Stanislas Bormans, 7 vols. (Brussels: F. Hayez, 1864–1887).

Jebens, Holger, ed., *Cargo, Cult, and Culture Critique* (Honolulu: University of Hawai'i Press, 2004).

Jebens, Holger, 'Signs of the Second Coming: On Eschatological Expectation and Disappointment in Highland and Seaboard Papua New Guinea', *Ethnohistory* 47.1 (2000): 171–204.

Jeffreys, M. D. W., 'African Tarantula or Dancing Mania', *Eastern Anthropologist* 6.2 (1952–1953): 98–105.

Johnson, Adriana M. C., 'Subalternizing Canudos', *Modern Language Notes* 120.2 (2005): 355–382.

Johnson, Charles A., *The Frontier Camp Meeting: Religion's Harvest Time* (Dallas: Southern Methodist University Press, 1955).

Johnstone, Hilda, ed., *Annales Gandenses: Annals of Ghent*, trans. Hilda Johnstone (London: Thomas Nelson, 1951).

Jones, Colin, and Roy Porter, eds., *Reassessing Foucault: Power, Medicine, and the Body* (London: Routledge, 1998).

Jonsson, Stefan, 'The Invention of the Masses: The Crowd in French Culture from the Revolution to the Commune', in Jeffrey T. Schnapp and Matthew Tiews, eds., *Crowds* (Stanford, CA: Stanford University Press, 2006), 47–75.

Jordan, Mark D., *Convulsing Bodies: Religion and Resistance in Foucault* (Stanford, CA: Stanford University Press, 2015).

Jordanova, Ludmilla, *Sexual Visions: Images of Gender in Science and Medicine between the Eighteenth and Twentieth Centuries* (Madison: University of Wisconsin Press, 1989).

Justice-Malloy, Rhona, 'Charcot and the Theatre of Hysteria', *Journal of Popular Culture* 28.4 (1995): 133–138.

Kahan, Michèle Bokobza, 'Ethos in Testimony: The Case of Carré de Montgeron, a Jansenist and a Convulsionary in the Century of Enlightenment', *Eighteenth-Century Studies* 43.4 (2010): 419–433.

Kaplan, Martha, *Neither Cargo nor Cult: Ritual Politics and the Colonial Imagination in Fiji* (Durham: Duke University Press, 1995).

Kastner, Georges, *La Danse des morts: Dissertations et recherches historiques, philosophiques, littéraires et musicales* (Paris: Brandus, 1852).

Kauthen, Pierre, 'La procession dansante dans la 1re moitié du 20e siècle', in G. Kiesel and J. Schroeder, eds., *Willibrord: Apostel der Niederlande Gründer der Abtei Echternach* (Luxembourg: Éditions de l'Imprimerie Saint-Paul, 1989), 251–263.

Kehoe, Alice Beck, *The Ghost Dance: Ethnohistory and Revitalization* (New York: Holt, Rinehart and Winston, 1989).

Keller, Richard C., *Colonial Madness: Psychiatry in French North Africa* (Chicago: University of Chicago Press, 2007).

Kelsen, H., 'The Conception of the State and Social Psychology with Special Reference to Freud's Group Theory', *International Journal of Psycho-Analysis* 5 (1924): 1–38.

Khanna, Ranjana, *Dark Continents: Psychoanalysis and Colonialism* (Durham, NC: Duke University Press, 2003).

Kierkegaard, Søren, *La répétition*, trans. Jacques Privat (Paris: Éditions Payot et Rrivages, 2003).

Kiesel, G. and J. Schroeder, eds., *Willibrord: Apostel der Niederlande Gründer der Abtei Echternach* (Luxembourg: Éditions de l'Imprimerie Saint-Paul, 1989).

King, Don W., et al., 'Convulsive Non-Epileptic Seizures', in A. James Rowan and John R. Gates, eds., *Non-Epileptic Seizures* (Boston: Butterworth-Heinemann, 1993), 31–37.

Kirmayer, L. J., and D. Groleau, 'Affective Disorders in Cultural Context', *Psychiatric Clinics of North America* 24.3 (2001): 465–478.

Knox, Ronald A., *Enthusiasm: A Chapter in the History of Religion, with Special Reference to the XVII and XVIII Centuries* (New York: Oxford University Press, 1950).

Kohn, George Childs, ed., *Encyclopedia of Plague and Pestilence: From Ancient Times to the Present*, rev. ed. (New York: Facts on File, 2001).

Kracauer, Siegfried, 'The Mass Ornament', in *The Mass Ornament: Weimer Essays*, ed. and trans. Thomas Y. Levin (Cambridge, MA: Harvard University Press, 1995), 75–86.

Krack, Paul, 'Relicts of Dancing Mania: The Dancing Procession of Echternach', *Neurology* 53.9 (1999): 2169–2172.

Kreiser, B. Robert, *Miracles, Convulsions, and Ecclesiastical Politics in Early Eighteenth-Century Paris* (Princeton, NJ: Princeton University Press, 1978).

Kristeva, Julia, *Étrangers à nous-mêmes* (Paris: Fayard, 1988).

Kroeber, A. L., *Cultural and Natural Areas of Native North America* (Berkeley: University of California Press, 1963).

Kroeber, A. L., 'A Ghost-Dance in California', *Journal of American Folklore* 17 (1904): 32–35.

Kronick, David A., 'Medical "Publishing Societies" in Eighteenth-Century Britain', *Bulletin of the Medical Library Association* 82.3 (1994): 277–282.

Kuklick, Henrika, 'The British Tradition', in Henrika Kuklick, ed., *A New History of Anthropology* (Malden, MA: Blackwell, 2008), 52–78.

Kuklick, Henrika, 'Islands in the Pacific: Darwinian Biogeography and British Anthropology', *American Ethnologist* 23.3 (1996): 11–38.

Kuklick, Henrika, ed., *A New History of Anthropology* (Malden, MA: Blackwell, 2008).

La Barre, Weston, *The Ghost Dance: Origins of Religion* (Garden City, NY: Doubleday, 1970).

La Barre, Weston, 'Materials for a History of Studies of Crisis Cults: A Bibliographic Essay', *Current Anthropology* 12.1 (1971): 3–44.

Laborde, J. V., *Les hommes et les actes de l'insurrection de Paris devant la psychologie morbide: Lettres à M. le docteur Moreau* (Paris: Baillière, 1872).

'La chorémanie de Madagascar: Ramanenjana', *Journal Officiel de Madagascar et dépendances* (Tananarive), 29 August 1903: 9942–9943.

LaCapra, Dominick, 'Foucault, History and Madness', in Arthur Still and Irving Velody, eds., *Rewriting the History of Madness: Studies in Foucault's 'Histoire de la folie'* (London: Routledge, 1992), 78–85.

Lacroix, P., *Vie militaire et religieuse au Moyen Age et à l'époque de la Renaissance* (Paris: Librairie Didot, 1873).

Lambek, Michael, 'The Sakalava Poiesis of History: Realizing the Past through Spirit Possession in Madagascar', *American Ethnologist* 25.2 (1998): 106–127.

Langhorne, John, *Letters on Religious Retirement, Melancholy, and Enthusiasm* (London: H. Payne and W. Cropley, 1762).

Langlois, Eustache-Hyacinthe, *Essai historique, philosophique et pittoresque sur les danses des morts*, 2 vols. (Rouen: Lebrument, 1851).

Lanternari, Vittorio, *Movimenti religiosi di libertà e di salvezza dei popoli oppressi* (Milan: Feltrinelli, 1960).

Lanternari, Vittorio, *The Religions of the Oppressed: A Study of Modern Messianic Cults*, trans. Lisa Sergio (New York: Knopf, 1963).

La Tarentule, ballet pantomime en deux actes. Par M. Coralli. Musique de M. Casimir Gide (Paris: Chez Jonas, Libraire de l'opéra, 1839).

la Tourette, Gilles de, 'Étude sur une affection nerveuse caractérisée par l'incoordination motrice accompagnée d'écholalie et de coprolalie', *Archives of Neurology* 9 (1884): 19–42, 158–200.

La Vaissière, Camille de, *Histoire de Madagascar, ses habitants et ses missionnaires*, 2 vols. vol. 1 (Paris: Librairie Victor Lecoffre, 1884).

Lavallene, Edouard, ed., *Histoire du Limbourg, suivie de celle des comtés de Daelhem et de Fauquemont, des Annales de l'Abbaye de Rolduc, par M. S. P. Ernst, curé d'Afden, ancien chanoine de Rolduc*, vol. 5 (Liège: Librairie de P. J. Collardin, 1840).

Le Bon, Gustave, *The Crowd: A Study of the Popular Mind* (London: Benn, 1920).

Le Bon, Gustave, *Psychologie des foules* (Paris: Félix Alcan, 1895).

Leclerc, Marie-Dominique, 'Réemplois, avatars, redécouverte', in Marie-Dominique Leclerc, Danielle Quérel, and Alain Robert, *Danser avec la mort: Les danses macabres dans les manuscrits et livres imprimés du XVe au XXe siècle* (Lyon: Musée de l'imprimerie, Lyon, 2004).

Le Goff, Jacques, *Medieval Civilization, 400–1500*, trans. Julia Barrow (London: Folio Society, 2011).

Le Muisit, Gilles, *Chronique et annales de Gilles le Muisit, abbé de Saint-Martin de Tournai (1272–1352)* (Paris: Librairie Renouard, 1906).

Lefebvre, Henri, *Introduction to Modernity: Twelve Preludes, September 1959–May 1961*, trans. John Moore (London: Verso, 1995).

Leiris, Michel, *L'âge d'homme, précédé de La littérature considérée comme une tauromachie* (Paris: Éditions Gallimard, 1939).

Leiris, Michel, *Cinq études d'ethnologie* (Paris: Denoël/Gonthier, 1969).

Lepecki, André, 'The Body as Archive: Will to Re-Enact and the Afterlives of Dances', *Dance Research Journal* 42.2 (2010): 28–48.

Lepecki, André, 'Choreopolice and Choreopolitics: Or, the Task of the Dancer', *TDR: The Drama Review* 57.4 [T220] (2013): 13–27.

Lepecki, André, *Exhausting Dance: Performance and the Politics of Movement* (London: Routledge, 2006).

Lettenhove, J. M. B. C. Kervyn de, *Histoire de Flandre, 1304–1384*, 6 vols., vol. 3 (Brussels: A. Vandale, 1847).

Lettenhove, J. M. B. C. Kervyn de, *Istore et Croniques de Flandres, d'après les textes de divers manuscrits*, 2 vols. (Brussels: F. Hayez and Commission Royale d'Histoire, 1879–1880).

Levine, Robert M., 'Canudos in the National Context', *Americas* 48.2 (1991): 207–222.

Levine, Robert M., *Vale of Tears: Revisiting the Canudos Massacre in Northeastern Brazil, 1893–1897* (Berkeley: University of California Press, 1992).

Levinson, André, 'The Negro Dance: Under European Eyes', *Theatre Arts Monthly* 11.4 (1927): 282–293.

Lévi-Strauss, Claude, *Race et histoire* (Paris: Denoël, 1987).

Liebscher, Hellmuth, 'Ein kartographischer Beitrag zur Geschichte der Tanzwut', M. D. diss. (Leipzig University, 1931).

Lindstrom, Lamont, 'Cargo Cult at the Third Millennium', in Holger Jebens, ed., *Cargo, Cult, and Culture Critique* (Honolulu: University of Hawai'i Press, 2004), 15–35.

Lindstrom, Lamont, *Cargo Cult: Strange Stories of Desire from Melanesia and Beyond* (Honolulu: University of Hawaii Press, 1993).

Littré, Émile, 'Des grandes épidémies', *Revue des Deux-Mondes*, 15 January 1836.

Littré, Émile, *Dictionnaire de la langue française*, 4 vols. (Paris: Hachette, 1873).

Littré, Émile, *Dictionnaire de médecine, de chirurgie, de pharmacie et de sciences qui s'y rattachent*, 21st ed., ed. Gilbert Augustin (Paris: J.-B. Baillière, 1905–1908).

Littré, Émile, 'Épidémies: La chorée, maladie épidémique du moyen âge (*Die Tanswuth* [sic], *eine volkskrankheit im mittelalter*), par le docteur Hecker, de Berlin, 1832', *Gazette médicale de Paris*, vol. 4, no. 2.1, 3 January 1833: 5–6.

Littré, Émile, *Médecine et médecins* (Paris: Didier, 1872).

Llosa, Mario Vargas, *La guerra del fin del mundo* (Barcelona: Editorial Seix Barral, 1981).

Long, George, ed., *The Penny Cyclopaedia of the Society for the Diffusion of Useful Knowledge*, 27 vols., vol. 1, *A–Andes* (London: Charles Knight, 1833).

Lucas, Prosper, *De l'imitation contagieuse, ou de la propagation sympathique des névroses et des monomanies* (Paris: Didot le Jeune, 1833).

Lüdtke, Karen, *Dances with Spiders: Crisis, Celebrity and Celebration in Southern Italy* (Oxford: Berghahn Books, 2009).

Luys, Jules Bernard, *Études de physiologie et de pathologie cérébrales* (Paris: Baillière, 1874).

Lynskey, Dorian, 'Beatlemania: The "Screamers" and Other Tales of Fandom', *Guardian*, 29 September 2013, http://www.theguardian.com/music/2013/sep/29/beatlemania-screamers-fandom-teenagers-hysteria. Accessed 12 March 2016.

Lyotard, Jean-François, *L'enthousiasme: La critique kantienne de l'histoire* (Paris: Éditions Galilée, 1986).

Macintosh, Fiona, 'Dancing Maenads in Early Twentieth-Century Britain', in Fiona Macintosh, ed., *The Ancient Dancer in the*

*Modern World: Responses to Greek and Roman
Dance* (Oxford: Oxford University Press, 2010),
188–208.

Madden, Lori, 'The Canudos War in History', *Luso-
Brazilian Review* 30.2 (1993): 5–22.

Madden, Lori, 'Evolution in the Interpretations
of the Canudos Movement: An Evaluation of
the Social Sciences', *Luso-Brazilian Review* 28.1
(1991): 59–75.

Maher, W. B., and B. Maher, 'The Ship of Fools;
Stultifera Navis or *Ignis Fatuus*?', *American
Psychologist* 37.7 (1982): 756–761.

Maire, Catherine-Laurence, *De la cause de Dieu à la
cause de la Nation: Le jansénisme au XVIIIe siècle*
(Paris: Éditions Gallimard, 1998).

Maire, Catherine-Laurence, ed., *Les
convulsionnaires de Saint-Médard: Miracles,
convulsions et prophéties à Paris au XVIIIe siècle*
(Paris: Gallimard/Julliard, 1985).

Malament, Barbara, ed., *After the Reformation. Essays
in Honor of J. H. Hexter* (Philadelphia: University
of Pennsylvania Press, 1980).

Malzac, Victorin, *Histoire du Royaume Hova, depuis
ses origines jusqu'à sa fin* (Tananarive: Imprimerie
Catholique, 1930).

Manco, Fabrizio, 'Bodied Experiences of
Madness: A *Tarantato*'s Perception', in
Johannes Birringer and Josephine Fenger, eds.,
Tanz und WahnSinn/Dance and ChoreoMania
(Leipzig: Henschel Verlag, 2011), 264–283.

Manning, Susan, *Ecstasy and the Demon: The Dances
of Mary Wigman* (Minneapolis: University of
Minnesota Press, 2006).

Marbury, Elisabeth, 'Introduction', in Mr.
& Mrs. Vernon Castle, *Modern Dancing*
(New York: Harper, 1914), 19–29.

Marey, Étienne-Jules, *Du mouvement dans les
fonctions de la vie. Leçons faites au Collège de
France* (Paris: Germer Baillière, 1868).

Martin, Alfred, 'Geschichte der Tanzkrankheit
in Deutschland', *Zeitschrift des Vereins für
Volkskunde* 24 (1914): 113–134, 225–239.

Martin, Carol, *Dance Marathons: Performing
American Culture of the 1920s and
1930s* (Jackson: University Press of
Mississippi, 1994).

Martin, Carol, 'Reality Dance: American Dance
Marathons', in Julie Malnig, ed., *Ballroom,
Boogie, Shimmy Sham, Shake: A Social and Popular
Dance Reader* (Urbana: University of Illinois
Press, 2009), 93–108.

Martin, Randy, *Critical Moves: Dance Studies
in Theory and Politics* (Durham, NC: Duke
University Press, 1998).

Marx, Karl, *Capital*, vol. 1, trans. Ben Fowkes
(London: Penguin Books, 1990).

Marx, Karl, *Grundrisse: Foundations of the Critique
of Political Economy*, trans. Martin Nicolaus
(London: Penguin, 1993).

Massey, J. M., and E. W. Massey, 'Ergot, the "Jerks",
and Revivals', *Clinical Neuropharmacology* 7.1
(1984): 99–105.

Mathieu, Pierre-François, *Histoire des miraculés
et des convulsionnaires de Saint-Médard*
(Paris: Didier et Cie, 1864).

Matthews, Lawrence, clippings scrapbook, Jerome
Robbins Dance Division, New York Public
Library for the Performing Arts.

Matthews, Lawrence, photographic scrapbook,
Jerome Robbins Dance Division, New York
Public Library for the Performing Arts.

Mattioli, Petrus Andreas, *Commentarii
secundo aucti, in libros sex pedacii dioscoridis*
(Venice: Valgrisiana, 1560).

McCall, Tara, *This Is Not a Rave: In the Shadow
of a Subculture* (New York: Thunder's Mouth
Press, 2001).

McCarren, Felicia, *Dance Pathologies: Performance,
Poetics, Medicine* (Stanford, CA: Stanford
University Press, 1998).

McCarren, Felicia, *Dancing Machines: Choreographies
of the Age of Mechanical Reproduction* (Stanford,
CA: Stanford University Press, 2003).

McCarren, Felicia, *French Moves: The Cultural
Politics of Le Hip Hop* (Oxford: Oxford University
Press, 2013).

McCarren, Felicia, 'The "Symptomatic Act" circa
1900: Hysteria, Hypnosis, Electricity, Dance',
Critical Inquiry 21.4 (Summer 1995): 748–774.

McConachie, Bruce, and F. Elizabeth Hart,
eds., *Performance and Cognition: Theatre
Studies and the Cognitive Turn* (Abingdon,
Oxon: Routledge, 2006).

McDougall, William, *The Group Mind, a Sketch
of the Principles of Collective Psychology,
with Some Attempt to Apply Them to the
Interpretation of National Life and Character*
(Cambridge: Cambridge University Press, 1920).

McGrew, Roderick E., *Encyclopedia of Medical History*
(New York: McGraw-Hill, 1985).

McKenzie, Jon, *Perform or Else: From Discipline to
Performance* (London: Routledge, 2001).

McMaster, J. B., *A History of the People of the
United States: From the Revolution to the Civil
War*, 8 vols., vol. 2 (New York: D. Appleton,
1883–1913).

Mead, Margaret, 'Introduction', in Margaret Mead
and Ruth L. Bunzel, eds., *The Golden Age of*

American Anthropology (New York: Braziller, 1960), 1–12.

Measuring Worth, http://www.measuringworth. com/uscompare/relativevalue.p hp. Accessed 2 March 2016.

Meerloo, Joost A. M., *Dance Craze and Sacred Dance* (London: Peter Owen, 1962).

Meerloo, Joost A. M., *Delusion and Mass-Delusion* (New York: Nervous and Mental Disease Monographs, 1949).

Megill, Allan, 'Foucault, Ambiguity and the Rhetoric of Historiography', in Arthur Still and Irving Velody, eds., *Rewriting the History of Madness: Studies in Foucault's 'Histoire de la folie'* (London: Routledge, 1992), 86–104.

Meige, Henri, 'La procession dansante d'Echternach', *Nouvelle iconographie de la Salpêtrière* 17 (1904): 248–264, 320–336.

Melton, J. Gordon, *Encyclopedia of American Religions*, 5th ed. (Detroit: Gale, 1996).

Memmi, Albert, *La dépendance: Esquisse pour un portrait du dépendant* (Paris: Gallimard, 1979).

Memmi, Albert, *Portrait du colonisé, précédé du Portrait du colonisateur et d'une préface de Jean-Paul Sartre suivi de Les Canadiens français sont-ils des colonisés*, éd. revue et corrigée par l'auteur (Montreal: Les éditions l'étincelle, 1972).

Menestrier, Claude François, *Des ballets anciens et modernes selon les règles du théâtre* (Paris: Chez René Guignard, 1682).

'Mental Epidemics', *Fraser's Magazine for Town and Country* 65.388 (April 1862): 490–505.

Mercurialis, Hieronymus, *De venenis et morbis venenosis tractatus locupletissimi* (Venice: Paulum Meietum, 1584).

Merryweather, Mary, *Experience of Factory Life, Being a Record of Fourteen Years' Work at Mr. Courtauld's Silk Mill at Halstead, in Essex*, 3rd ed. (London: E. Faithfull, 1862).

Metraux, Alfred, 'Les Messies de l'Amérique du sud', *Archives de sociologie des religions* 5 (1957): 108–112.

Metz, Christian, *The Imaginary Signifier: Psychoanalysis and the Cinema*, trans. Celia Britton et al. (Bloomington: Indiana University Press, 1982).

Meynell, G. G., *The Two Sydenham Societies: A History and Bibliography of the Medical Classics Published by the Sydenham Society and the New Sydenham Society (1844–1911)* (Acrise, Kent: Winterdown Books, 1985).

Mézeray, François Eudes de, *Abrégé chronologique de l'histoire de France*, vol. 3 (Amsterdam: Abraham Wolfgang, Prés de la Bourne, 1688).

Micale, Mark S., *Approaching Hysteria: Disease and Its Interpretation* (Princeton, NJ: Princeton University Press, 1995).

Micale, Mark S., 'Charcot and the Idea of Hysteria in the Male: Gender, Mental Science, and Medical Diagnosis in Late Nineteenth-Century France', *Medical History* 34.4 (1990): 363–411.

Micale, Mark S., 'Hysteria and Its Historiography: A Review of Past and Present Writings', *History of Science* 27 (1989): 223–261, 317–351.

Micale, Mark S., 'Hysteria and Its Historiography: Future Perspectives', *History of Psychiatry* 1 (1990): 33–124.

Micale, Mark S., *Hysterical Men: The Hidden History of Male Nervous Illness* (Cambridge, MA: Harvard University Press, 2008).

Micale, Mark S., 'On the "Disappearance" of Hysteria: A Study in the Clinical Deconstruction of a Diagnosis', *Isis* 84.3 (1993): 496–526.

Michelet, Jules, *Histoire de France* [1833–1841], 2nd rev. ed., 16 vols., vol. 4 (Paris: C. Marpon et E. Flammarion, 1879).

Middleton, Charles Theodore, *A new and complete system of geography. Containing a full, accurate, authentic and interesting account and description of Europe, Asia, Africa, and America . . .*, 2 vols., vol. 1 (London: J. Cooke, 1778–1779).

Middleton, Karen, ed., *Ancestors, Power and History in Madagascar* (Leiden: Brill, 1999).

Midelfort, H. C. Erik, *Exorcism and Enlightenment: Johann Joseph Gassner and the Demons of Eighteenth-Century Germany* (New Haven: Yale University Press, 2005).

Midelfort, H. C. Erik, *A History of Madness in Sixteenth-Century Germany* (Stanford, CA: Stanford University Press, 1999).

Midelfort, H. C. Erik, 'Madness and Civilization in Early Modern Europe: A Reappraisal of Michel Foucault', in Barbara Malament, ed., *After the Reformation: Essays in Honor of J. H. Hexter* (Philadelphia: University of Pennsylvania Press, 1980), 247–266.

Midelfort, H. C. Erik, 'Reading and Believing: On the Reappraisal of Michel Foucault', in Arthur Still and Irving Velody, eds., *Rewriting the History of Madness: Studies in Foucault's 'Histoire de la folie'* (London: Routledge, 1992), 105–109.

Minorita, Martinus (Martini Minoritae), 'Flores temporum, ab hermanno janvensi continuati usque ad Carolum IV. Imp.', in Jo. Georgio Eccardo (Johann George von Eckhart), *Corpus historicum medii aevi, sive Scriptores res in orbe universo, præcipue in Germania, a* temporibus maxime Caroli M. Imperatoris usque ad finem seculi post C. N. XV. gestas enarrantes aut illustrantes e variis codicibus manuscriptis (Lipsiæ: Apud Jo. Frid. Gleditscchii, B. Fil., 1723), 1551–1640.

Mintz, Sidney W., 'Other: *The Third World*, by Peter Worsley', *American Anthropologist* 68.5 (1966): 1320–1326.

Minutoli, Baroness von, *Recollections of Egypt, by the Baroness von Minutoli*, trans. S. L. H. (London: Treutell & Würtz, Treuttel, Jun. & Richter, 1827).

M'Nemar, Richard, *The Kentucky Revival, or, a short history of the late extraordinary outpouring of the spirit of God in the western states of America, agreeably to scripture promises and prophecies concerning the latter day: with a brief account of the entrance and progress of what the world call shakerism among the subjects of the late revival in Ohio and Kentucky. Presented to the true Zion traveler as a memorial of the wilderness journey* (New York: Edward O. Jenkins, 1846).

Molina, Tomás S., *Corea de Sydenham* (Buenos Aires: N. Marana, 1909).

Mollat, Michel, and Philippe Wolff, *The Popular Revolutions of the Late Middle Ages*, trans. A. L. Lytton-Sells (London: Allen and Unwin, 1973).

Montgeron, Louis-Basile Carré de, *La vérité des miracles opérés par l'intercession de M. de Paris, Démontrée contre M. l'Archevêque de Sens. Ouvrage dédié au Roy. Par M. de Montgeron, conseiller au parlement* (Utrecht: Libraires de la Compagnie, 1737).

Mooney, James, 'The Ghost-Dance Religion and the Sioux Outbreak of 1890', in J. W. Powell, *Fourteenth Annual Report of the Bureau of Ethnology to the Smithsonian Institution, 1892–93* (Washington, DC: Government Printing Office, 1896), 641–1136.

Mooney, James, *The Ghost-Dance Religion and Wounded Knee* (New York: Dover, 1973).

Moore, Gregory, *Nietzsche, Biology and Metaphor* (Cambridge: Cambridge University Press, 2004).

Morley, Henry, 'Introduction', in J. F. C. Hecker, *The Black Death, and The Dancing Mania*, ed. Henry Morley, trans. B. G. Babington (London: Cassell & Company, 1888), 5–8.

Morris, James Matthew, and Andrea L. Kross, *Historical Dictionary of Utopianism* (Lanham, MD: Scarecrow Press, 2004).

Moses, L. G., '"The Father Tells Me So!" Wovoka: The Ghost Dance Prophet', *American Indian Quarterly* 9.3 (1985): 335–351.

Moten, Fred, *In the Break: The Aesthetics of the Black Radical Tradition* (Minneapolis: University of Minnesota Press, 2003).

Mouvet, Maurice, *Maurice's Art of Dancing: An Autobiographical Sketch with Complete Descriptions of Modern Dances and Full Illustrations Showing the Various Steps and Positions* (New York: G. Schirmer, [1915]).

Muecke, Stephen, 'Choreomanias: Movements through Our Body', *Performance Research* 8.4 (2003): 6–10.

Muhry, Alfred, and Edward G. Davis, *Observations on the comparative state of medicine in France, England, and Germany, during a journey into these countries in the year 1835* (Philadelphia: A. Waldie, 1838).

Mullally, Robert, *The Carole: A Study of Medieval Dance* (Farnham: Ashgate, 2011).

Munby, A. N. L., *The History and Bibliography of Science in England*, Eighth Annual Zeitlin and Verbrugge Lecture in Bibliography (Berkeley: School of Librarianship, University of California, 1968).

Nabokov, Peter, *Native American Testimony: A Chronicle of Indian-White Relations from Prophecy to the Present, 1492–1992* (New York: Penguin Books, 1992).

Ness, Sally Ann, 'The Inscription of Gesture: Inward Migrations in Dance', in Carrie Noland and Sally Ann Ness, eds., *Migrations of Gesture* (Minneapolis: University of Minnesota Press, 2008), 1–30.

Neyen, A., 'De l'origine et du but véritable de la procession dansante d'Echternach', *Bulletin de l'Institut archéologique liégeois* 15 (1880): 223–297.

Nietzsche, Friedrich, *Beyond Good and Evil: Prelude to a Philosophy of the Future*, trans. Walter Kaufmann (New York: Vintage Books, 1989).

Nietzsche, Friedrich, *The Birth of Tragedy and Other Writings*, ed. Raymond Geuss and Ronald Speirs, trans. Ronald Speirs (Cambridge: Cambridge University Press, 1999).

Nietzsche, Friedrich, *Die Geburt der Tragödie aus dem Geiste der Musik* (Leipzig: Verlag von E. W. Fritzsch, 1872).

Nietzsche, Friedrich, *On the Genealogy of Morality*, ed. Keith Ansell-Pearson, trans. Carol Diethe (Cambridge: Cambridge University Press, 1994).

Nietzsche, Friedrich, 'On the Uses and Disadvantages of History for Life', in Friedrich Nietzsche, *Untimely Meditations*, ed. Daniel Breazeale, trans. R. J. Hollingdale (Cambridge: Cambridge University Press, 1997), 57–123.

Nietzsche, Friedrich, *Thus Spoke Zarathustra: A Book for All and None*, ed. Adrian Del Caro and Robert Pippin, trans. Adrian Del Caro (Cambridge: Cambridge University Press, 2006).

Nietzsche, Friedrich, 'Twilight of the Idols; or How to Philosophize with a Hammer', in *Twilight of the Idols and The Antichrist*, trans. R. J. Hollingdale (London: Penguin, 1990), 29–122.

Niezen, Ronald, et al., *Spirit Wars: Native North American Religions in the Age of Nation Building* (Berkeley: University of California Press, 2000).

Nina-Rodrigues, Raimundo, *As Collectividades Anormaes* (Rio de Janeiro: Civilização Brasileira S.A., 1939).

Nina-Rodrigues, Raimundo, 'Choreomania', *Gaseta Medica da Bahía*, series 2, 7.10, April 1883.

Nina-Rodrigues, Raimundo, 'Épidémie de folie religieuse au Brésil', *Annales médico-psychologiques: Journal de l'aliénation mentale et de la médecine légale des aliénés* 8.7 (1898): 371–392.

Nina-Rodrigues, Raimundo, *La folie des foules: Nouvelle contribution à l'étude des folies épidémiques au Brésil* (Paris: Fonds Lacassagne, 1901).

Noland, Carrie, and Sally Ann Ness, eds., *Migrations of Gesture* (Minneapolis: University of Minnesota Press, 2008).

Nutton, Vivian, 'The Seeds of Disease: An Explanation of Contagion and Infection from the Greeks to the Renaissance', *Medical History* 27 (1983): 1–34.

Ober, William B., 'The Sydenham Society (1843–1857): Rise and Fall', *Mount Sinai Journal of Medicine* 41.2 (1974): 294–305.

Ochoa, Miguel, *Consideraciones sobre algunas coreas* (Buenos Aires: A. Etchepareborda, 1909).

Oiticia, Hélio, 'Dance in My Experience (Diary Entries)//1965–66', in André Lepecki, ed., *Dance* (London: MIT Press, 2012), 52.

Okun, Michael S., and Peter J. Koehler, 'Paul Blocq and (Psychogenic) Astasia Abasia', *Movement Disorders* 22.10 (2007): 1373–1378.

'On Epidemic Delusions', *Scottish Review* 2.7 (1854): 193–208.

Oosterwijk, Sophie, 'Dance, Dialogue and Duality in the Medieval *Danse Macabre*', in Sophie Oosterwijk and Stefanie Knöll, eds., *Mixed Metaphors: The Danse Macabre in Medieval and Early Modern Europe* (Newcastle upon Tyne: Cambridge Scholars, 2011), 9–42.

Oosterwijk, Sophie, and Stefanie Knöll, eds., *Mixed Metaphors: The Danse Macabre in Medieval and Early Modern Europe* (Newcastle upon Tyne: Cambridge Scholars, 2011).

Osler, Sir William, *On Chorea and Choreiform Affections* (Philadelphia: P. Blakiston, Son & Co, 1894).

Osterreich, T. K., *Possession, Demoniacal and Other, among Primitive Races, in Antiquity, the Middle Ages, and Modern Times*, trans. D. Ibberson (New York: Richard R. Smith, 1930).

Ostler, Jeffrey, *The Plains Sioux and U.S. Colonialism from Lewis and Clark to Wounded Knee* (Cambridge: Cambridge University Press, 2004).

Otis, Laura, 'Introduction', in Laura Otis, ed., *Literature and Science in the Nineteenth Century: An Anthology* (Oxford: Oxford University Press, 2009), xvii–xxviii.

Otis, Laura, *Membranes: Metaphors of Invasion in Nineteenth-Century Literature, Science, and Politics* (Baltimore: Johns Hopkins University Press, 1999).

Ottino, Paul, 'Le Tromba (Madagascar)', *L'homme* 5.1 (1965): 84–93.

Pagel, Walter, *Paracelsus: An Introduction to Philosophical Medicine in the Era of the Renaissance*, 2nd rev. ed. (Basel: Karger, 1982).

Paracelsus, 'The Diseases That Deprive Man of His Reason, Such as St. Vitus' Dance, Falling Sickness, Melancholy, and Insanity, and Their Correct Treatment', trans. Gregory Zilboorg, in Paracelsus, *Four Treatises of Theophrastus von Hohenheim called Paracelsus*, ed. Henry E. Sigerist (Baltimore: Johns Hopkins University Press, 1996), 127–212.

Paracelsus, *Paracelsus (Theophrastus Bombastus von Hohenheim, 1493–1541): Essential Theoretical Writings*, ed. and trans. Andrew Weeks (Leiden: Brill, 2008).

Parfitt-Brown, Clare, 'The Problem of Popularity: The Cancan between the French and Digital Revolutions', in Sherrill Dodds and Susan C. Cook, eds., *Bodies of Sound: Studies across Popular Music and Dance* (Farnham: Ashgate, 2013), 9–24.

Park, R. H. R., and M. P. Park, 'Saint Vitus' Dance: Vital Misconceptions by Sydenham and Bruegel', *Journal of the Royal Society of Medicine* 83.8 (1990): 512–515.

Pearce, Nathaniel, *The Life and Adventures of Nathaniel Pearce, written by himself, during a residence in Abyssinia, from the year 1810 to 1819*, ed. J. J. Halls, Esq., 2 vols., vol. 1 (London: Henry Colburn and Richard Bentley, 1831).

Pearl, Jonathan L., 'Introduction', in Jean Bodin, *On the Demon-Mania of Witches*, trans. Randy A. Scott (Toronto: Centre for Reformation and Renaissance Studies, 1995).

Pearsall, Arlene Epp, 'Johannes Pauli and the Strasbourg Dancers', *Franciscan Studies* 52.1 (1992): 203–214.

Peignot, Gabriel, *Recherches historiques et littéraires sur les danses des morts et sur l'origine des cartes à jouer* (Dijon and Paris: Lagier, 1826).

Penny, H. G., and M. Bunzl, eds., *Worldly Provincialism: German Anthropology in the Age of Empire* (Ann Arbor: University of Michigan Press, 2003).

Perotti, Niccolò, *Cornucopiae latinae linguae* (Basle: J. Walder, 1536).

Pessar, Patricia R., *From Fanatics to Folk: Brazilian Millenarianism and Popular Culture* (Durham, NC: Duke University Press, 2004).

Petri de Herentals, Prioris Floreffiensis, *Vita Gregorii XI* (Paris, 1693).

'Pictures That Tell a Story—and Tell It Better Than Words. Our Latest Lunacies', *Sunday Mirror Magazine*, 8 October 1933.

Plato, *Laws*, trans. E. A. Taylor, in Plato, *The Collected Dialogues of Plato, Including the Letters*, ed. Edith Hamilton and Huntington Cairns (Princeton, NJ: Princeton University Press, 2002), 1225–1503.

Poovey, Mary, *Making a Social Body: British Cultural Formation, 1830–1864* (Chicago: University of Chicago Press, 1995).

Posnett, Hutcheson Macaulay, *Comparative Literature* (New York: Appleton, 1892).

Pratt, Mary Louise, *Imperial Eyes: Travel Writing and Transculturation*, 2nd ed. (London: Routledge, 2008).

'Present Is Scored as "Jitterbug" Age: McCombe Holds We Have Lost Direction and Are Bound to Immediate Interests', *New York Times*, 21 October 1940, 12.

Proudhon, Joseph, *Œuvres complètes de P.-J. Proudhon*, 26 vols., vol. 20 (Brussels: A. Lacroix, Verboeckhoven & cie., 1850–1871).

Proudhon, Joseph, *Philosophie du progrès: Programme* (Brussels: Alphonse Lebègue, 1853).

Proudhon, Joseph, *Philosophie du progrès, suivi de La justice poursuivie par l'église, nouvelle édition* (Brussels, 1868).

Puchner, Martin, *Poetry of the Revolution: Marx, Manifestos, and the Avant-Garde* (Princeton, NJ: Princeton University Press, 2006).

Pugh, Tison, and Angela Jane Weisl, *Medievalisms: Making the Past Present* (London: Routledge, 2013).

Queiroz, Maria Isaura Pereira de, 'L'influence du Milieu Social Interne sur les mouvements messianiques brésiliens', *Archives de sociologie des religions* 5 (1958): 3–30.

Rabinbach, Anson, *The Human Motor: Energy, Fatigue, and the Origins of Modernity* (Berkeley: University of California Press, 1992).

Radet, Jean-Baptiste, Pierre-Yvon Barré, and François-Georges Fouques Desfontaines, *Le procès du Fandango ou la fandangomanie,* *comédie-vaudeville, en un acte*, 2nd ed. (Paris: Fages, libraire du théatre du Vaudeville, 1810).

Radulphus de Rivo, *Decani Tongrensis, gesta pontificum Leodiensium ab anno tertio Engelberti a Marcka usque ad Joannem de Bavaria*, in Jean Chapeauville, ed., *Qui gesta Pontificum Tungrensium, Traiectensium, et Leodiensium*, 3 vols., vol. 3 (Leodii: Typis C. Ouvverx iunioris, 1612–1616).

Raison, Françoise, 'Les Ramanenjana', *Lumière* (Tananarive), 13 August 1972.

'Les Ramanenjanas, étrangleurs de Radama II, roi de Madagascar', in *Le Moniteur universel: Journal officiel de l'Empire Français*, no. 188, 7 July 1863, 937–938.

Ramenofsky, Ann F., *Vectors of Death: The Archaeology of European Contact* (Albuquerque: University of New Mexico Press, 1987).

Ranaivo, Charles, ed., *Ramanenjana* (Tananarive: Annales de l'Université de Madagascar, 1934–1964).

Rancière, Jacques, *Le partage du sensible: Esthétique et politique* (Paris: La Fabrique-éditions, 2000).

Rancière, Jacques, *Staging the People: The Proletarian and His Double*, trans. David Fernbach (London: Verso, 2011).

Randriamaro, Tsimahafotsy, 'Le Ramanenjana à Madagascar', *Revue médicale de Madagascar* 1 (1959): 2–10.

'Reds Advise Germans of Jitterbug Dangers', *New York Times*, 11 August 1949, 26.

Regnard, Paul, *Les maladies épidémiques de l'esprit: Sorcellerie, magnétisme, morphinisme, délire des grandeurs* (Paris: E. Plon, Nourrit et Cie, 1887).

Régnier, Christian, 'J.-B. Baillière (1797–1885), The Pioneering Publisher Who Promoted French Medicine throughout the World', *Medicographia* 27.1 (2005): 87–96.

Reich, Wilhelm, *The Mass Psychology of Fascism*, ed. Mary Higgins and Chester M. Raphael, trans. Vincent R. Carfagno (New York: Farrar, Strauss and Giroux, 1970).

'The Revolution in Madagascar', *Illustrated London News* 43.1212, 11 July 1863.

Reynolds, Dee, and Matthew Reason, eds., *Kinesthetic Empathy in Creative and Cultural Practices* (Bristol: Intellect Books, 2012).

Riché, Pierre, 'Danses profanes et religieuses dans le haut Moyen Age', in Robert Mandrou, ed., *Histoire sociale, sensibilités collectives et mentalités. Mélanges Robert Mandrou* (Paris: Presses Universitaires de France, 1985), 159–167.

Richer, Paul, *L'art et la médecine* (Paris: Gaultier, Magnier, et cie., 1903).

Richer, Paul, *Études sur l'hystéro-épilepsie, ou Grande Hystérie* (Paris: Adrien Delahaye et Émile Lecrosnier, 1881).

Roach, Joseph, *Cities of the Dead: Circum-Atlantic Performance* (New York: Columbia University Press, 1996).

Roach, Joseph, *The Player's Passion: Studies in the Science of Acting* (Ann Arbor: University of Michigan Press, 1993).

Robertson, Felix, *An Essay on Chorea Sancti Viti* (Philadelphia: Joseph Rakestraw, 1805).

Robinson, Douglas, *Translation and Empire: Postcolonial Theories Explained* (London: Routledge, 2014).

Rodríguez-García, Rosé María, 'The Regime of Translation in Miguel Antonio Caro's Colombia', *diacritics* 34.3 (2004): 143–175.

Roger, Henri, *Recherches cliniques sur la chorée, sur le rhumatisme et sur les maladies du cœur chez les enfants* (Paris: Asselin, 1866).

Rohmann, Gregor, 'The Invention of the Dancing Mania: Frankish Christianity, Platonic Cosmology and Bodily Expressions in Sacred Space', *Medieval History Journal* 12 (2009): 13–45.

Rohmann, Gregor, *Tanzwut: Kosmos, Kirche und Mensch in der Bedeutungsgeschichte eines mittelalterlichen Krankheitskonzepts* (Göttingen: Vandenhoeck and Ruprecht, 2012).

Rosaldo, Renato, *Ilongot Headhunting 1883–1974: A Study in Society and History* (Stanford, CA: Stanford University Press, 1980).

Rosen, George, *Madness in Society: Chapters in the Historical Sociology of Mental Illness* (London: Routledge & Kegan Paul, 1968).

Ross, E. A., *Social Psychology: An Outline and Source Book* (New York: Macmillan, 1908).

Ross, Janice, 'Illness as Danced Urban Ritual', in Mark Franko, ed., *Ritual and Event: Interdisciplinary Perspectives* (London: Routledge, 2007), 138–158.

Rouget, Gilbert, *Music and Trance: A Theory of the Relations between Music and Possession*, trans. and rev. Brunhilde Biebuyck in collaboration with the author (Chicago: University of Chicago Press, 1985).

Rousseau, Jean-Jacques, *Lettre à d'Alembert sur son article Genève*, ed. Micheal Launay (Paris: Garnier-Flammarion, 1967).

Rubin, Miri, *Gentile Tales: The Narrative Assault on Late Medieval Jews* (New Haven: Yale University Press, 1999).

Rubin, William, ed., *'Primitivism' in Twentieth-Century Art: Affinity of the Tribal and the Modern*, 2 vols. (New York: Museum of Modern Art, 1984).

Rusillon, Henry, *Un Culte Dynastique avec évocation des morts chez les Sakalaves de Madagascar. Le 'Tromba'* (Paris: Librairie Alphonse Picard et Fils, 1912).

Russell, Jean Fogo, 'Dancing Mania', in K. F. Russell, *Festschrift for Kenneth Fitzpatrick Russell; Proceedings of a Symposium Arranged by the Section of Medical History., A.M.A. (Victorian Branch)* (Carlton, Victoria: Queensberry Hill Press, 1978), 159–197.

Sahlin, Margit, *Étude sur la carole médiévale: L'origine du mot et ses rapports avec l'église* (Uppsala: Almqvist & Wiksells, 1940).

Said, Edward W., *Freud and the Non-European* (London: Verso, 2003).

Said, Edward W., 'Michel Foucault, 1926–1984', in Jonathan Arac, ed., *After Foucault: Humanistic Knowledge, Postmodern Challenges* (New Brunswick, NJ: Rutgers University Press, 1991), 1–11.

Said, Edward W., 'Opponents, Audiences, Constituencies and Community', in Hal Foster, ed., *The Anti-Aesthetic: Essays on Postmodern Culture* (Port Townsend, WA: Bay Press, 1983), 135–159.

Said, Edward W., *Orientalism* (New York: Vintage Books, 1994).

Said, Edward W., *Reflections on Exile and Other Essays* (Cambridge, MA: Harvard University Press, 2000).

Saint-Hilaire, M.-H., and J.-M. Saint-Hilaire, 'Jumping Frenchmen of Maine, Videotape Documentary', *Movement Disorders* 16.3 (2001): 530.

Saint-Hilaire, M.-H., and J.-M. Saint-Hilaire, 'The "Ragin' Cajuns", Videotape Documentary', *Movement Disorders* 16.3 (2001): 531–532.

Saint-Hilaire, M.-H., J.-M. Saint-Hilaire, and L. Granger, 'Jumping Frenchmen of Maine', *Neurology* 36 (1986): 1269–1271.

Schachter, Steven C. and W. Curt LaFrance, Jr., eds., *Gates and Rowan's Nonepileptic Seizures*, 3rd ed. (Cambridge: Cambridge University Press, 2010).

Schade, Sigrid, 'Charcot and the Spectacle of the Hysterical Body: The "Pathos Formula" as an Aesthetic Staging of Psychiatric Discourse: A Blind Spot in the Reception of Warburg', *Art History* 18.4 (1995): 499–517.

Schaff, Philip, ed., *A Religious Encyclopædia: Or Dictionary of Biblical, Historical, Doctrinal, and Practical Theology. Based on the Real-Encyklopädie of Herzog, Plitt and Hauck*, 3rd ed., 4 vols., vol. 1 (London: Funk and Wagnalls Company, 1891).

Schechter, David Chas., 'St. Vitus' Dance and Rheumatic Disease', *New York State Journal of Medicine* 75 (1975): 1091–1102.

Schenck von Grafenberg, Johannes, 'Praefatio ad lectorem', in *Observationes medicae de capite humano: hoc est, exempla capitis morborum, causarum, signorum, eventuum, curationum, ut singularia, sic abdita et monstrosa. Ex claris. medicorum, veterum simul & recentriorum scriptis* (Basel: Ex Officina Frobeniana, 1584).

Schnapp, Jeffrey T., 'Mob Porn', in Schnapp and Tiews, eds., *Crowds*' with 'in Jeffrey T. Schnapp and Matthew Tiews, eds., *Crowds* (Stanford, CA: Stanford University Press, 2006), 1–45.

Schnapp, Jeffrey T., and Matthew Tiews, eds., *Crowds* (Stanford, CA: Stanford University Press, 2006).

Schneider, Rebecca, *Performing Remains: Art and War in Times of Theatrical Reenactment* (London: Routledge, 2011).

Schroeder, J., Zur Frage frühmittelalterlicher Kulttänze am Grabe Willibrords in Echternach in G. Kiesel and J. Schroeder, eds., *Willibrord: Apostel der Niederlande, Gründer der Abtei Echternach* (Luxembourg: Editions Saint-Paul, 1989), 186–193.

Schwartz, Hillel, 'Torque: The New Kinaesthetic of the Twentieth Century', in Jonathan Crary and Sanford Kwinter, eds., *Zone 6: Incorporations* (Cambridge, MA: MIT Press, 1992), 71–127.

Sée, Germain, *De la chorée. Rapports du rhumatisme et des maladies du cœur avec les affections nerveuses convulsives* (Paris: Baillère, 1850).

Sergi, Giuseppe, 'Psicosi Epidemica', *Rivista di Filosofia Scientifica*, series 2a, 8 (1889): 151–172.

Sharp, Lesley A., 'Playboy Princely Spirits of Madagascar: Possession as Youthful Commentary and Social Critique', *Anthropological Quarterly* 68.2 (1995): 75–88.

Sharp, Lesley A., *The Possessed and the Dispossessed: Spirits, Identity and Power in a Madagascar Migrant Town* (Berkeley: University of California Press, 1996).

Sharp, Lesley A., 'Wayward Pastoral Ghosts and Regional Xenophobia in a Northern Madagascar Town', *Africa: Journal of the International African Institute* 71.1 (2001): 38–81.

Shaughnessy, Nicola, ed., *Affective Performance and Cognitive Science: Body, Brain and Being* (London: Bloomsbury Methuen, 2013).

Shaw, George A., *Madagascar and France: With Some Account of the Island, Its People, Its Resources and Development* (London: Religious Tract Society, 1885).

Shay, Anthony, *Choreophobia: Solo Improvised Dance in the Iranian World* (Costa Mesa, CA: Mazda, 1999).

Shea Murphy, Jacqueline, *The People Have Never Stopped Dancing: Native American Modern Dance Histories* (Minneapolis: University of Minnesota Press, 2007).

Shirokogoroff, Sergei M., *The Psychomental Complex of the Tungus* (London: Kegan Paul, 1935).

Showalter, Elaine, *The Female Malady: Women, Madness and English Culture, 1830–1980* (New York: Pantheon Books, 1986).

Showalter, Elaine, 'Hysteria, Feminism and Gender' in Sander L. Gilman, Helen King, Roy Porter, G. S. Rousseau, and Elaine Showalter, *Hysteria beyond Freud* (Berkeley: University of California Press, 1993), 286–335.

Showalter, Elaine, *Hystories: Hysterical Epidemics and Modern Culture* (New York: Columbia University Press, 1997).

Showalter, Elaine, *Sexual Anarchy: Gender and Culture at the Fin de Siècle,* new ed. (London: Virago Press, 1992).

Sibree, James, *Madagascar and Its People. Notes of a Four Years' Residence. With a Sketch of the History, Position, and Prospects of Mission Work amongst the Malagasy* (London: Religious Tract Society, 1870).

Sighele, Scipio, *La foule criminelle: Essai de psychologie collective*, 2nd ed., trans. Paul Vigny (Paris: Félix Alcan, 1901).

Silen, Karen, 'Elisabeth of Spalbeek: Dancing the Passion', in Lynn Brooks, ed., *Women's Work: Making Dance in Europe before 1800* (Madison: University of Wisconsin Press, 2007), 207–227.

Silko, Leslie Marmon, *Almanac of the Dead* (New York: Penguin, 1991).

Simons, Ronald C., *Boo! Culture, Experience, and the Startle Reflex* (Oxford: Oxford University Press, 1996).

Simons, Ronald C., 'The Resolution of the Latah Paradox', *Journal of Nervous and Mental Disease* 168.4 (1980): 195–206.

Simpson, George Eaton, 'Jamaican Revivalist Cults', *Social and Economic Studies* 5.4 (1956): 321–442.

Siordet, J. F., *Henry Rusillon: Missionnaire à Madagascar (1872–1938). I. Le Pionnier (1872–1913)* (Paris: Société des Missions Évangéliques, 1940).

Siraisi, Nancy G., *History, Medicine, and the Traditions of Renaissance Learning* (Ann Arbor: University of Michigan Press, 2007).

Siraisi, Nancy G., *Medieval and Renaissance Medicine: An Introduction to Knowledge and Practice* (Chicago: University of Chicago Press, 1990).

Skerrett, Ellen, 'James T. Farrell's "The Dance Marathons,"' *MELUS* 18.1 (1993): 127–131.

Sloterdijk, Peter, *La mobilisation infinie: Vers une critique de la cinétique politique*, trans. Hans Hildenbrand (Paris: Christian Bourgois, 2000).

Sloterdijk, Peter, 'Mobilization of the Planet from the Spirit of Self-Intensification', *TDR: The Drama Review* 50.4 [T192] (2006): 36–43.

Smoak, Gregory E., *Ghost Dances and Identity: Prophetic Religion and American Indian Ethnogenesis in the Nineteenth Century* (Berkeley: University of California Press, 2006).

Snow, C. P., *The Two Cultures, with Introduction by Stefan Collini* (Cambridge: Cambridge University Press, 1998).

Sonnini de Manoncourt, Charles-Nicolas-Sigisbert, *Travels in Upper and Lower Egypt, undertaken by order of the old government of France, by C. S. Sonnini, engineer in the French navy, and member of several scientific and literary societies. Illustrated with forty engravings; consisting of portraits, views, plans, a geographical chart, antiquities, plants, animals & c. Drawn on the spot, under the author's inspection. Translated from the French by Henry Hunter, D.D.*, 3 vols., vol. 2 (London: John Stockdale, 1799).

Sorrenson, M. P. K., 'The Maori King Movement, 1858–1885', in Robert Chapman and Keith Sinclair, eds., *Studies of a Small Democracy: Essays in Honour of Willis Airey* (Auckland: University of Auckland Press, 1963), 33–55.

Souza Leite, José Dantas de, *Études de pathologie nerveuse* (Paris: G. Steinheil, Éditeur, 1889).

Specklin, Daniel, *Les collectanées de Daniel Specklin, chronique strasbourgeoise du seizième siècle. Fragments recueillis par Rodolphe Reuss*, in L. Dacheux, ed., *Fragments des anciennes chroniques d'Alsace*, 4 vols., vol. 2 (Strasbourg: Librairie J. Noiriel, 1890).

Spier, Leslie, 'The Ghost Dance of 1870 among the Klamath of Oregon', in *University of Washington Publications in Anthropology*, vol. 2, no. 2 (Seattle: University of Washington Press, 1927), 35–56.

Spier, Leslie, *The Prophet Dance of the Northwest and Its Derivatives: The Source of the Ghost Dance*, General Series in Anthropology, no. 1 (Menasha, WI: George Banta, 1935).

Sprandel, Rolf, *Monumenta Germaniae historica, scriptores rerum Germanicarum*, new series, vol. 15, *Die Kölner Weltchronik 1273/88–1376*, Herausgegeben von Rolf Sprandel (Munich: Monumenta Germaniae Historica, 1991).

Staël, Germaine de (Madame de Staël), *Corinne, or, Italy*, trans. and ed. Sylvia Raphael (Oxford: Oxford University Press, 1998).

Stamelou, Maria, et al., 'Movement Disorders on YouTube—Caveat Spectator', *New England Journal of Medicine* 365.12 (2011): 1160–1161.

Steedman, Carolyn, *Dust* (Manchester: Manchester University Press, 2001).

Stenzel, Karl, ed., *Die Straßburger Chronik des elsässischen Humanisten Hieronymus Gebwiler* (Berlin, 1926).

Stevens, John, *Words and Music in the Middle Ages: Song, Narrative, Dance and Drama, 1050–1350* (Cambridge: Cambridge University Press, 1986).

Stiles, Anne, *Popular Fiction and Brain Science in the Late Nineteenth Century* (Cambridge: Cambridge University Press, 2012).

Still, Arthur, and Irving Velody, eds., *Rewriting the History of Madness: Studies in Foucault's 'Histoire de la folie'* (London: Routledge, 1992).

Stimson, Blake, 'Gesture and Abstraction', in Carrie Noland and Sally Ann Ness, eds., *Migrations of Gesture* (Minneapolis: University of Minnesota Press, 2008), 69–83.

St John, Graham, ed., *Rave Culture and Religion* (New York: Routledge, 2004).

Stoler, Ann Laura, *Along the Archival Grain: Epistemic Anxieties and Colonial Common Sense* (Princeton, NJ: Princeton University Press, 2009).

Stowe, Harriet Beecher, *A Key to Uncle Tom's Cabin: Presenting the Original Facts and Documents upon Which the Story Is Founded, Together with Corroborative Statements Verifying the Truth of the Work* (Boston: John P. Jewett & Co., 1858).

Strayer, Brian E., *Suffering Saints: Jansenists and Convulsionnaires in France, 1640–1799* (Eastbourne: Sussex Academic Press, 2008).

Stuckler, David, and Sanjay Basu, *The Body Economic: Why Austerity Kills. Recessions, Budget Battles, and the Politics of Life and Death* (New York: Basic Books, 2013).

Sutherland, I. L. G., *The Maori Situation* (Wellington, NZ: Harry H. Tombs, 1935).

Sutton, W. L., 'Report on the Medical Topography and the Epidemic Diseases of Kentucky', *Transactions of the American Medical Association* 11 (1858): 74–165.

Sweeney, Carole, *From Fetish to Subject: Race, Modernism, and Primitivism, 1919–1935* (Westport, CT: Prager, 2004).

Swinburne, Henry, *Travels in the Two Sicilies, by Henry Swinburne, esq., in the years 1777, 1778, 1789, and 1780*, 2nd ed., 4 vols., vol. 2 (London: J. Nichols for T. Cadell and P. Elmsly, 1790).

Sydenham, Thomas, *Processus integri in Morbis fere omnibus Curandis* (London, 1692).

Székely, György, 'Le mouvement des flagellants au 14e siècle, son caractère et ses causes', in Jacques Le Goff, ed., *Hérésies et sociétés dans l'Europe préindustrielle. 11e–18e siècles* (Paris: Mouton & Co., 1968): 229–241.

Taine, Hippolyte, *Les origines de la France contemporaine*, 6 vols., vol. 2 (Paris: Librairie Hachette, 1878).

Tarde, Gabriel, *Études pénales et sociales* (Lyon: A. Storck; and Paris: G. Masson, 1892).

Tarde, Gabriel, *Les lois de l'imitation*, ed. Bruno Karsenti (Paris: Éditions Kimé, 1993).

Tarde, Gabriel, *Monadologie et sociologie*, ed. Éric Alliez (Le Plessis-Robinson: Institut synthélabo pour le progrès de la connaissance, 1999).

Tarde, Gabriel, *L'opinion et la foule*, ed. Dominique Reynié (Paris: Presses Universitaires de France, 1989).

Taussig, Michael, *The Magic of the State* (London: Routledge, 1997).

Taussig, Michael, *Mimesis and Alterity: A Particular History of the Senses* (London: Routledge, 1993).

Taussig, Michael, *The Nervous System* (London: Routledge, 1992).

Taussig, Michael, *What Color Is the Sacred?* (Chicago: University of Chicago Press, 2009).

Taylor, Diana, *The Archive and the Repertoire: Performing Cultural Memory in the Americas* (Durham, NC: Duke University Press, 2003).

Taylor, Isaac, *Fanaticism* (London: Holdsworth and Ball, 1833).

Taylor, Isaac, *Natural History of Enthusiasm*, 4th ed. (London: Holdsworth and Ball, 1830).

Temkin, Oswei, *The Falling Sickness: A History of Epilepsy from the Greeks to the Beginnings of Modern Neurology*, 2nd rev. ed. (Baltimore: Johns Hopkins University Press, 1994).

The 10 Principles of Burning Man, http://www.burningman.org/culture/philosophical-center/10-principles. Accessed 14 March 2016.

Thiel-Stern, Shayla, *From the Dance Hall to Facebook: Teen Girls, Mass Media, and Moral Panic in the United States 1905–2010* (Boston: University of Massachusetts Press, 2014).

Thom, Jess, *Welcome to Biscuitland: A Year in the Life of Touretteshero* (London: Souvenir Press, 2012).

Thom, Jess, in conversation with Andy Horwitz and Hassan Mahamdallie, 'Talking/Making/Taking Part: a festival of theatre and discussion', Oval House, London, 22–23 November 2015.

Thorne, F. C., 'Startle Neurosis', *American Journal of Psychiatry* 101 (1944): 105–109.

Thornton, Russell, *We Shall Live Again: The 1870 and 1890 Ghost Dance Movements as Demographic Revitalization* (Cambridge: Cambridge University Press, 1986).

Tresch, M., *La chanson populaire luxembourgeoise* (Luxembourg: Victor Buck, 1929).

Trotter, Wilfred, *Instincts of the Herd in Peace and War* (London: T. Fisher Unwin, 1916).

Tseng, Wen-Shing, *Clinician's Guide to Cultural Psychiatry* (Honolulu: University of Hawaii School of Medicine, 2003).

Tseng, Wen-Shing, 'Epidemic Mental Disorders', in *Handbook of Cultural Psychiatry* (San Diego: Academic Press, 2001), 265–290.

Tweedie, Alexander, *A System of Practical Medicine* (Philadelphia: Lea & Blanchard, 1840).

Vale, Thiago Cardoso, and Francisco Cardoso, 'Chorea: A Journey through History', *Tremor and Other Hyperkinetic Movements* 5 (2015), doi: 10.7916/D8WM1C98. Accessed 12 May 2016.

van Gennep, Arnold, *Tabou et Totémisme à Madagascar: Étude descriptive et théorique* (Paris: Ernest Leroux, Éditeur, 1904).

van Ginneken, Jaap, *Crowds, Psychology, and Politics 1871–1899* (Cambridge: Cambridge University Press, 1992).

Vaudrin, Marie-Claude, *La musique techno, ou, Le retour de Dionysos: Je rave, tu raves, nous rêvons* (Paris: L'Harmattan, 2004).

Vidal, Daniel, *Miracles et convulsions jansénistes au XVIIIe siècle: Le mal et sa connaissance* (Paris: Presses Universitaires de France, 1987).

Vigouroux, Auguste, and Paul Juquelier, *La contagion mentale* (Paris: Octave Dion, Éditeur, 1905).

Vintimille du Luc, Charles-Gaspard-Guillaume de, *Mandement de Mgr l'archevêque de Paris au sujet d'un écrit qui a pour titre: Dissertation sur les miracles, et en particulier sur ceux qui ont été opérez au tombeau de M. de Paris en l'église de S. Médard de Paris; avec la Relation & les preuves de celui qui s'est fait le 3e Novembre 1730 en la personne d'Anne le Franc, de la Paroisse de S. Barthelemy* (Paris: Chez Pierre Simon, 1731).

Virchow, Rudolf, *Disease, Life, and Man: Selected Essays*, trans. Lelland J. Rather (Stanford, CA: Stanford University Press, 1958).

Virchow, Rudolf, *Die Einheitsbestrebungen in der wissenschaftlichen Medizin* (Berlin: G. Reimer, 1849).

Virilio, Paul, *Speed and Politics* (New York: Semiotext(e), 2006).

Vloberg, Maurice, *Les fêtes de France: Coutumes religieuses et populaires* (Grenoble: B. Arthaud, 1936).

Voltaire, *Dictionnaire philosophique portatif, Nouvelle Edition, revue, corrigée & augmentée de divers Articles par l'auteur* (London: J. B. H. Leclerc, 1765).

Wagner, Ann, *Adversaries of Dance: From the Puritans to the Present* (Urbana: University of Illinois Press, 1997).

Waller, John, 'Falling Down', *Guardian*, 18 September 2008, http://www.guardian.co.uk/science/2008/sep/18/psychology. Accessed 6 September 2012.

Waller, John, 'A Forgotten Plague: Making Sense of Dancing Mania', *Lancet* 373.9664 (2009): 624–625.

Waller, John, 'In a Spin: The Mysterious Dancing Epidemic of 1518', *Endeavour* 32.3 (2008): 117–121.

Waller, John, *A Time to Dance, a Time to Die: The Extraordinary Story of the Dancing Plague of 1518* (London: Icon Books, 2009).

Ware, Vron, *Beyond the Pale: White Women, Racism, and History* (London: Verso, 1992).

Watkins, Dom Basil, ed., *The Book of Saints: A Comprehensive Biographical Dictionary*, 7th ed. (New York: Continuum, 2002).

Watson, Thomas, *Lectures on the principles and practice of physic; delivered at King's College, London*, 2nd ed., 2 vols., vol. 1 (London: John W. Parker, West Strand, 1848).

Watt, Robert, 'Cases of periodical jactitation, or chorea', in *Medico-Chirurgical Transactions* 5 (1814): 1–23.

Webster, Charles, *Paracelsus: Medicine, Magic and Mission at the End of Time* (New Haven: Yale University Press, 2008).

Weeks, Andrew, *Paracelsus: Speculative Theory and the Crisis of the Early Reformation* (Albany, NY: State University of New York Press, 1997).

Wencker, Jean, 'La chronique strasbourgeoise de Jean Wencker', in L. Dacheux, *Les chroniques strasbourgeoises de Jacques Trausch et de Jean Wencker. Les annales de Sébastien Brant. Fragments recueillis par l'abbé Dacheux*, in *Fragments des anciennes chroniques strasbourgeoises*, 4 vols., vol. 3 (Strasbourg: Imprimerie Strasbourgeoise, 1892), 75–207.

Wencker, Jean, ed., 'Annales de Sébastien Brant. Suite et fin', in L. Dacheux, *Fragments des anciennes chroniques d'alsace*, 4 vols., vol. 3 (Strasbourg: Imprimerie Strasbourgeoise, 1901), 243–470.

Wesleyan Methodist Missionary Society, Correspondence, Jamaica, MMS/West Indies/Correspondence/FBN 49, 1858–1865, Methodist Missionary Society archive, School of Oriental and African Studies Library, University of London.

Wexler, Alice R., 'Chorea and Community in a Nineteenth-Century Town', *Bulletin of the History of Medicine* 76.3 (2002): 495–527.

White, T. Pilkington, 'The Cycling Epidemic', *Scottish Review* 29 (1897): 56–74.

Wicke, Ernst Conrad, *Versuch einer Monographie des grossen Veitstanzes und der unwillkürlichen Muskelbewegung, nebst Bermerkungen über den Taranteltanz und die Beriberi* (Leipzig: F. A. Brockhaus, 1844).

Wilkie, Fiona, *Performance, Transport and Mobility: Making Passage* (Houndmills, Basingstoke: Palgrave, 2015).

Williams, Drid, *Ten Lectures on Theories of the Dance* (Metuchen, NJ: Scarecrow Press, 1991).

Williams, F. E., *The Vailala Madness and the Destruction of Native Ceremonies in the Gulf Division*, Territory of Papua, Anthropology Report No. 4 (Port Moresby, Papua, 1923).

Williams, F. E., 'The Vailala Madness in Retrospect', in E. E. Evans-Pritchard, Raymond Firth, Bronisław Malinowski, and Isaac Schapera, eds., *Essays Presented to C. G. Seligman* (London: K. Paul, Trench, Tübner, 1934), 369–379.

Williamson, Joel, *Elvis Presley: A Southern Life* (New York: Oxford University Press, 2015).

'Willibrordus-Bauverein', http://www.willibrord.lu/rubrique4/Dancing-procession/historical-aspects. Accessed 12 November 2012.

Wilson, Bryan R., *Magic and the Millennium: A Sociological Study of Religious Movements of Protest among Tribal and Third-World Peoples* (New York: Harper and Row, 1973).

Wilson, Lindsay, *Women and Medicine in the French Enlightenment: The Debate over Maladies des Femmes* (Baltimore: Johns Hopkins University Press, 1993).

Winks, R. W., 'The Doctrine of Hauhauism', *Journal of the Polynesian Society* 62.3 (1953): 199–236.

Wiseman, Hannah, and Markus Reuber, 'New Insights into Psychogenic Non-Epileptic Seizures 2011–2014', *Seizure: European Journal of Epilepsy* 29 (2015): 69–80.

Witkowski, Ludwig, 'Einige Bemerkungen über den Veitstanz des Mitelalters und über psychische Infection', *Allgemeine Zeitschrift für Psychiatrie und Psychisch-Gerichtliche Medizin* 35 (1879): 591–598.

Wolfhagen, Ehlen von, *Die Limburger Chronik, Eingeleitet von Otto H. Brandt. Mit 17 Abbildungen und Anhang* (Jena: Eugen Diederichs, 1922).

Worsley, Peter, *The Third World* (Chicago: University of Chicago Press, 1964).

Worsley, Peter, *The Trumpet Shall Sound: A Study of 'Cargo' Cults in Melanesia*, 2nd ed. (New York: Schocken Books, 1968).

Worthen, William B., 'Antigone's Bones', *TDR: The Drama Review* 52.3 [T199] (2008): 10–33.

Wright, S., 'An Experimental Inquiry into the Physiological Action of Ergot of Rye', *Edinburgh Medical and Surgical Journal* 52 (1839): 293–334.

Wright, S., 'An Experimental Inquiry into the Physiological Action of Ergot of Rye', *Edinburgh Medical and Surgical Journal* 52 (1840): 1–35.

Yandell, David W., 'Epidemic Convulsions', *Brain* 4.3 (1881): 339–350.

Yap, Pow Meng, 'Koro—A Culture-Bound Depersonalization Syndrome', *British Journal of Psychiatry* 111.470 (1965): 43–50.

Young, Julian, *Friedrich Nietzsche: A Philosophical Biography* (Cambridge: Cambridge University Press, 2010).

Ziegler, Philip, *The Black Death* (London: Readers Union Collins, 1969).

Žižek, Slavoj, 'From Politics to Biopolitics . . . and Back', *South Atlantic Quarterly* 103.2/3 (2004): 501–521.

Žižek, Slavoj, *The Plague of Fantasies* (London: Verso, 1997).

Index

affect, 6–7, 10, 12–14, 29, 39, 59, 69, 76, 124, 131
    and contagious imitation, 34, 201–202
    and crowds, 120–121
    and effect, 94, 103
    and enthusiasm, 91–94, 103, 128
    and excess, 107–108, 120n36, 133
    histories of, 32
    and memory, 232–233, 306
    and nationalism, 89, 105, 107
    pathologized, 218
    and politics, 212, 249, 309
    theatricalized, 117, 156, 264
Africa, 88, 199–202
    and the 'African tarantella', 192–195
    and ancient Greece, 182, 277
    and European historicity, 187–188
    and femininity, 165
    and modernity, 9, 173, 272, 274
    and Orientalism, 5, 21, 25, 172–174, 186
    and racism, 277
    and southern Italy, 167, 171, 181–182, 186–187
    and stylization, 274, 287
    See also anti-colonialism; blackness: and black dance;
        'dark continent'; race
African-American, 287
    and dance, 9, 173, 272–273, 282
    See also blackness: and black dance
'again and again', 10, 146, 150, 160, 177, 198, 200, 211, 272,
    299, 305, 310
Agamben, Giorgio
    and gesture, 20, 70–71, 77, 261, 296, 308, 308n30
    and infancy, 268
    and movement, 16–17, 159
    See also ecstasy-belonging; language; paradigm; state of
        exception
aggregation, 17, 28, 65, 253, 309–310
    and social theory, 32, 113, 117–125, 136
AIDS, 202
alien, 106, 110, 209. See also foreigners/foreignness
alienation, 95, 173, 187, 254, 270, 309
    and colonial melancholy, 190–191
    and crowds, 120
    and modernity, 231, 294, 306, 311
    social in relation to mental, 108, 273, 277
    See also anomie
'alien body', 9–10, 173, 255, 259, 268, 272, 274, 282
'almost the same, but not quite', 176, 176n21, 193, 232, 239,
    256, 265, 306
alterkinetics. See aesthetics
American way, 231, 246
anaesthesis, 69, 113, 119, 290–293, 294, 309
anarchism, and anarchy, 29, 29–30n15, 104, 206
anatomy, 82, 143, 166–167, 181n42
    theatre, 32
ancestors, 306–307
    Africans as, of whites, 274
    bacchants as, of 'demoniacs' 143
    customs of, among Native Americans, 232
    Europeans as, of Papuans, 260
    and land, 266
    and myth of primitive, 269, 287
    Native Americans as, of whites, 225–226, 228, 232
    Papuans as, of Europeans, 268
    return of, with cargo cults, 260–262
    return of, with Ghost Dance, 226, 233, 236, 239, 259
    St. Vitus's dance, among modern Germany's, 80

tarantella as mimicking classical, 183
    See also possession
Anderson, Benedict, 107
Anderson, Warwick, 35, 39
Andrianjafy, Dr., 214–217, 221
anecdote, 3, 8–10, 20, 31, 39, 96, 140, 143, 177, 187–188,
    230, 298–299
animal dances, 273, 275–286
animality, 5, 9, 274–275, 294–295
    and crowds, 114–137
    and hysteria, 185
    and imitation, 33
    and modern dance, 286–287
    and Orientalism, 186, 253, 299
    and sex, 194, 276, 287
    and toxicity in serpent-dance, 181–183
    and vital spirits, 75–76, 81–83
anomie, 133, 230–231, 231n21, 234, 308
anthropology
    academic, and 'desire', 7, 250, 254, 258–260, 264,
        268–270, 271
    and cultural heritage, 297
    emergence of, 30, 72, 141, 161, 165–167, 166n89, 166n91,
        174–175, 194, 198–200, 210, 228, 230
    and government, 166, 224–226, 230, 260n30,
        261–264, 270
    and performance, 174
anti-colonialism, 21, 197, 201, 221–222, 257
    and anthropology, 259–260
    and decolonization movements, 250, 254, 268–269
    and the Ghost Dance, 12, 224, 233
anti-dance prejudice. See choreophobia; dance prohibitions
anti-Europeanism, 196, 199, 202, 205, 205n35, 207, 260. See
    also anti-colonialism
anti-modernity, 112–113, 174, 275, 311. See also modernity
antiquarianism, 20–21, 26, 30–39, 60, 65, 150, 165, 180, 182,
    196, 231, 306
antiquity, 7, 9–11, 54, 60, 217, 225, 288, 296
    accessible through travel, 182–184, 192
    and Grecian sentiment, 66–68
    re-emerging in modern medicine, 140–141, 145,
        165, 180n37
anti-theatricality, 20, 91, 101, 103, 192, 305. See also theatre;
    theatricality
anxiety, 132, 186n63, 198, 230, 241, 301, 301n11
anxiousness, 10, 54, 57, 61
    and modernity, 9, 174, 183, 193, 249, 263, 304
Apache (dance), 282–283
appearance, 14, 42–47, 55, 60, 60n94, 66, 69, 89, 90, 92, 222,
    228–229, 239
    medicine, defined as, 19–20, 213
    and politics, 113, 198–200, 207, 210, 218–219, 297, 304–305,
        307, 309
    of theatre, 101
Arabia, 174, 179, 280
Arabic, 37
arc de cercle. See attitudes passionnelles
archaeology, 32, 68, 165–166, 172, 182, 231, 274, 288
    as figure of speech, 141, 218, 306
    See also Foucault, Michel; Taussig, Michael
archaicity, 47, 52, 54, 60–61, 122, 134, 171, 259, 287, 306
'archival drag', 141, 146, 151, 164–165
archival repertoire, 6, 8, 16, 27, 55, 89, 123, 150–151, 161,
    164, 171, 196–197, 200, 213, 218, 221, 310
archival return, 161–165, 310–314
archival scene, 26

symbolic, 247, 288

See also Black Death (bubonic plague); Dance of death (*danse macabre*)

decolonization. *See* colonialism

DeFrantz, Thomas, 275, 281–282

Deleuze, Gilles, 2, 6, 29–30n15, 92

and Guattari, 4, 18, 124

delirium, 48, 62, 104, 106, 108, 110n75, 157, 283n59, 292

manic, 86

melancholic, 80, 175

religious, 131, 219–221

delusion, 15, 29, 48, 67, 80, 178, 217, 219, 221, 228, 301n11

demography, 48n35, 49, 51, 233

demons/demonism and demoniacal possession, 33, 50, 54–58, 60n94, 60n95, 72–77, 86, 142–143, 145–146, 155, 199, 202, 256–257

and *Les démoniaques dans l'art* [Demoniacs in Art], 95–96, 98–99, 99, 147, 148, 145–150, 154, 154, 160

and demonomania, 4, 73, 120, 178, 181n42

demonstration/demonstrator, 158, 190, 213

in political arena, 118, 120, 198, 206, 237, 244, 305, 310

scientific, 143

demoralization, 242–243, 246, 249

demos, 112, 113, 117, 123, 298–299

déplacement, 165–166, 199–200, 301n8

Derrida, Jacques, 6, 43n6, 306

desire, 7, 71, 91, 173, 176n21, 217, 253–254, 258, 262, 263, 270, 272, 276, 280, 294, 303, 310

collective, 228, 233

Diamond, Elin, 14, 139, 185

Diderot, Denis, and Jean le Rond d'Alembert, 36

Didi-Huberman, Georges, 14, 146

Dionysianism, 299

in Foucault's work, 66

informing classical scholarship, 287–288

informing modern and contemporary dance, 274–275, 285

informing crowd and psychoanalytic theory, 121

in Nietzsche's work, 66–69

performance in relation to, 307

understood as 'Eastern', 5, 171, 186

Dionysus. *See* bacchanals (Dionysian); Dionysianism

disability, 17–18, 135–136n119

discipline and disciplines, xiii–xiv, 1–4, 7, 10, 12–14, 16–18, 25n1, 27, 36, 39, 44, 72, 90, 92, 100, 105, 112–113, 118–119, 126, 129, 131, 139–140n2, 140, 142, 157, 166n91, 167, 174, 176, 190, 194, 209, 218–219, 226, 230, 246, 255, 264, 272, 299–300, 303, 307, 311, 313–314. *See also* aesthetics; Foucault, Michel

discourse, 1–22, 29, 39, 44–45, 71, 72, 73, 77, 84, 87, 89, 91, 112–114, 119, 123, 126, 134, 144, 149, 164, 167, 171–174, 176, 188, 200, 217–218, 222, 224–225, 226, 228–231, 249, 254–255, 273, 275–277, 297, 298–300, 303–310

and anthropology and ethnography, 228–229, 259, 264, 270, 297

and choreomania, as pre-discursive, 165, 294

colonial, 10, 257

on crowds, publics, and political association, 118, 123, 125

and dance, 195–198, 200, 208, 273–274, 277, 284, 286, 292–293

and disease, reification of, 213–214, 216, 228

on nation and pathology, 104–105, 107, 114–116

and ontology, 229

physiological, 134

and primitivism, 185–186, 287–288

and psychology and psychoanalysis, 122, 194

and scene, 91, 200

and theorization, 254

See also aesthetics; choreography; Foucault, Michel; genealogy; language; rhizome; topology; translation; zone of intensity

discursive history, xiv, 1, 1n1, 3, 5, 8, 25–28, 32, 39, 112–113, 115, 165, 172, 199, 209–210, 224–225, 228, 251, 253, 298–299, 302. *See also* discourse; method

discursivization, 3, 8–9, 114

disease

defined, 144, 207, 213, 216, 219, 228, 305

and retrospective diagnosis, 6

as universal or local, 214, 221

See also comparativism; cure; geography: medical; health

'disease of civilization', 92, 108

'disease of nations', 175

disorder, 3–4, 7, 12–13, 14–15, 16–18, 21, 26–27, 30, 33, 39–40, 44–45, 47, 54–55, 58, 63, 80, 82, 85–86, 89, 119, 128, 131n95, 144, 153, 171–172, 179, 188, 190–191, 194–195, 198–200, 209, 213, 222, 228, 255, 272–275, 277, 286, 304–305, 307, 311

See also movement disorder

dragging, gesture of, 136, 136n122. *See also* 'archival drag'

drama. *See* theatre

dramaturgy, 114, 189, 203, 211, 227, 239, 267, 305

and hysteroepilepsy, 99, 153, 156

dream, 68, 110, 163–164n75, 228, 233, 236, 238, 246–250, 256, 259–260, 295, 303, 305, 307

dromography, 230, 299

dromology (science of speed), 231, 306

drugs, 190. *See also* MDMA (ecstasy) (drug); speed (drug)

drums, 49, 79, 91, 158–159n62, 189, 193, 203, 208, 212, 215n85, 258

drunkenness, 75, 110, 149, 149n33

behaviour resembling, 182, 207n51, 294–295

'sleep-drunkenness', 135–136n19

Du Camp, Maxime, 116

Duncan, Isadora, 274

Dunham, Katherine, 9, 173, 294

Durkheim, Émile, 118, 124, 133, 230–231, 231n21

dust, 229

earth, 61, 77, 94, 211–212, 220, 224, 231, 237, 238n63, 240, 240n74, 260, 267, 295–296

Echternach Leaping (or Dancing) Procession, 50, 60–61n96, 87, 145–150, 161–165, 163, 310–314, 312, 313. *See also* dancing procession

ecology, 15, 17, 44, 49, 76–77, 82, 89, 96, 115, 122n51, 175, 214, 233

and disease, definition of, 213, 228

institutional, 25–26

political, 191

economy, 26, 29, 58, 107, 112, 113n4, 114, 119, 122–123, 126, 144, 186n63, 191, 205, 212, 215, 225–227, 231–232, 234, 242, 244n86, 246, 293, 295, 304, 309

ecosophy, 15, 17, 33, 36, 42, 44, 51, 71, 75–76, 213, 257–258

ecstasy-belonging, 19, 197, 198, 200–201, 208, 226, 231, 239, 242

education, 13, 18–19, 138, 179, 184, 202, 245–246, 266–267, 282

self-education guides, 279

See also school

effect, 94, 103–104, 196, 207

Egypt/Egyptians, 42, 79, 178–179, 180n37, 180–181, 309

ekphrasis, 140, 165

elegance, 91, 158–159n62, 183, 240, 273, 277, 285, 293

and inelegance, 47, 293, 309

See also aesthetics; grace; torque

emotion, 59n90, 82, 86, 99, 117, 120n36, 128n73, 162, 199, 202, 208, 216, 263, 269–270, 281, 311
　　and chorea, 158
　　collective/political, 110–111, 112, 121–123, 309–310
　　and convulsions, 133, 152
　　and emotional recovery, 189–190
　　heightened or extreme, 10, 29, 36, 39, 68, 87, 92, 107, 109, 110n75, 139, 149–150, 162
　　and imitation, 137
　　and outlet, 288–289
　　provoked by spectacle, 91–92, 95n17, 271
　　and religion, 79, 104, 130, 132
　　theatrical, 14, 35–36, 103, 282
　　See also aesthetics
empty middle, 119, 141, 181, 217
encounter, 52, 63, 91, 117, 127, 150, 162–163, 172–174, 176, 180, 183–184, 203, 206, 210, 218n91, 226, 229, 240n78, 247, 252, 254–255, 262, 264–265, 268, 272, 276, 282n46, 300, 310
encyclopedia, 28, 28–29n10, 31, 36
energy, 69, 90, 110, 117, 124, 194–195, 203, 225–226, 230, 246–247, 272, 284, 290, 294–295, 300
　　bars, 296
　　and blackness, 275, 281
　　in crowds, 110, 120–121
　　depletion or dilapidation, 78–79n37, 247
　　and fatigue, 134–135
　　and outlet, 264, 273
　　and surplus/excess, 29, 104, 107, 112, 247, 294
　　See also expenditure (energetic); waste
Enlightenment, 47, 179, 251
　　and anti-theatricality, 101
　　and colonialism, 264
　　and France, 96
　　and imanenjana, 216
　　and madness, 43, 65
　　and post-Enlightenment, 113
　　See also Rousseau, Jean-Jacques; spontaneity
entertainment, 15, 56, 60, 83, 94, 102–103, 104, 134, 135n114, 136, 135–136n119, 154–155, 281, 284, 290–292, 313
　　reading of events as providing, 179
enthusiasm, 303, 314
　　contagious or excessive, liable to incite disorder, 34, 61, 63, 89, 90, 95, 100–101, 104–107, 109, 111, 117, 126–130, 132–133, 162, 261, 288
　　and Dionysianism, 67, 69, 296
　　expressed as excessive affect and effect, 94, 103–104
　　philosophical and religious writing on, 91–92, 94
　　positively inviting political change, 267
　　possession cultures compared with religious, 208
　　religious, as salve for boredom, 135
　　St. Vitus's dance defined as, 80
　　sublime, 92
　　understood as a nervous condition, 143
　　See also 'too muchness'
epidemiology, 8, 14, 30–32, 33–34, 37, 44, 53–54, 56, 65, 126–127, 136, 140, 175, 302
epilepsy, 13, 53, 61n97, 67, 69, 71–77, 86, 88–89, 108–109n69, 125, 125n62, 132, 142, 144, 146–147, 149, 149n33, 149–150n35, 154, 154n46, 160, 162, 164, 193, 221, 311
'epidemic', 128–129
　　See also hysteroepilepsy; seizure
'epileptic singers', 15, 15n35, 159. See also hysteroepilepsy
epistemology, 1, 10, 20, 38, 39, 123, 230, 307
　　and 'epistemic anxieties', 230

historical, 1, 1n1, 298
erasure, 225, 269, 299
　　and blackness, 286
　　and self-erasure, 221
　　and sous rature (under erasure), 6–7, 285
ergotism (rye poisoning), 19, 53, 60n96, 88
eruption, 185, 259, 263
eschatology, 221, 240n78, 241, 257–260, 265, 269. See also messianism; utopianism
Esquirol, Étienne, 92, 105n55, 108, 178n28. See also psychiatry: and monomania
ethnography, 12, 161–162, 165, 167, 181, 182n45, 193, 222, 228, 230, 231–232, 253, 254, 263–264, 267, 270, 271
　　and auto-ethnography, 84n67, 276
　　and 'ethnographic' dances, 183, 187
　　and ethno-graphy, 229
　　See also anthropology
Europe/European, 5, 9–11, 20, 30, 31, 38, 42, 48–49, 51, 54, 57, 60, 66–68, 72–73, 87–88, 118, 127, 145, 162, 165, 167, 171–176, 178n28, 180n37, 181–184, 186–188, 194n100, 196–199, 202, 204–206, 209, 210, 213–214, 216, 219–222, 225, 228, 231–233, 249–251, 253–256, 258–268, 270, 271–274, 276–277, 280–282, 287, 291–292, 298–299
　　See also anti-European
evidence, 54, 71, 74n12, 140–141, 145, 146, 150, 183, 220, 238
　　and self-evidence, 35, 143
　　See also anecdote
exaggeration, 10, 27, 44, 54, 60, 89, 90–92, 102, 104–106, 120n36, 152n37, 224, 227, 241, 276–277, 309
excavation, 7, 26, 32, 41, 66, 105, 140, 160, 167, 172, 182, 274
excess, 6–8, 12, 15–16, 29, 39, 44–47, 60–61, 69, 79–80, 90–93, 104–109, 110n75, 112–115, 119, 155, 162, 167, 176n21, 186, 189, 194, 201, 224–226, 244, 247, 254–258, 264, 289–293, 295–296, 299, 308
　　locomotion, in cycling mania, 29
　　See also affect; enthusiasm; expenditure (energetic); gesture; psychiatry: and monomania; 'too muchness'
exhaustion, 112, 116, 156n52, 157, 190, 276, 277
　　dancing (or leaping, walking, etc.) until reaching, 33, 48, 52–53, 56, 62, 77–80, 85, 102, 130, 147–148n30, 158–159n62, 162, 178–179, 190, 208–209n56, 214–215n84, 235–236, 244, 290, 292–293, 294
　　of musicians, 203, 214–215n84
　　and work, 132–134, 244
exile, 11, 57, 228, 256, 260
expenditure (energetic), 127, 131, 190, 194, 231, 243–244, 247, 249, 263, 290, 300, 303. See also 'unproductive expenditure'; waste
experimental method, 18, 71–72, 137, 146, 276
　　and modernity, 10, 26
　　See also clinic/clinicalism; observation; Paracelsus (Theophrastus von Hohenheim)
exuberant comparativism. See comparativism
eyewitness, 47, 50, 53, 56, 78, 84, 128n73, 129–131, 154–155n47, 180, 211, 213, 261

'fabulation of reality', 208
factory, 132–133, 135
faking, 184
　　and convulsions, 101–103, 181
　　and hysteria, 185
　　and theatre, 91, 293
　　women, and colonial subjects, accused of, 83–84, 173–174, 190
falling, 9, 31, 69, 87, 96, 128n79, 131n96, 202, 222

and exhaustion, 80, 235
and falling sickness, 71, 76–77, 147n30, 149
Fanon, Frantz, 172, 190–191, 255
fantasy, 18–19, 20, 52, 60, 141, 228, 246–247, 253, 259, 295,
305–308, 311
and alterity/Orientalism, 5, 25, 41–42, 171–172,
182–186, 275
and antiquity/Dionysianism, 33, 41–42, 69, 150, 160–161,
171–172, 182–186, 299, 304
and hysteria, 139, 156
primitivist, 270, 271–273, 281
and refantasization, 313
of scientific universalism, 268
fascism, 16, 119, 137–138, 287, 294
fatigue, 134–135, 173, 190–191, 244, 277
absent among *ramanenjana*, 208
before dancing, 80
and 'fatigue contest', 290
See also colonial melancholy; exhaustion
fear
absent, among insurgents, 117–118, 208
associated with demonism and sorcery, 73–75, 216
and the Ghost Dance, 12, 225, 227, 241, 248, 248–249n113
performance of, in the *Apache*, 283
propagating contagion, 202
and St. John's dance, 56, 58
used to assuage religious zeal, 131
See also startle disorder
Félice, Philippe de, 19, 41, 49, 94n14, 114
femininity, 19, 55n69, 150, 272, 274, 281
choreomania characterized by, 6, 11, 19–20, 77, 94
and colonialism, 165, 174, 185–187
and effeminacy, 284
and excess, 91, 94, 106–107
and feminism/emancipation, 12, 139, 160–161n68,
187, 284
and hysteria or hysteroepilepsy, 14, 139, 160
and Orientalism, 5, 11, 171–172
and primitivism, 284n63, 309
and the social body/the crowd, 120, 120n36, 122n51, 125,
133–134
and taboo, 184
See also 'dark continent'; gender; 'too muchness'
festival/fête, 74n10, 104, 109–110, 138, 143, 150, 182n45,
212, 245n91, 276, 286, 297, 300, 302n12, 307, 310,
313–314
atmosphere, 131
medieval, popular and religious, 53, 58–63, 67, 78–80, 87
See also carnival; St. John's Day dances
fiction, 25–26, 45, 65, 94n14, 99, 122–123, 163–164, 177, 212,
213, 238–239, 273–274, 282, 286, 299, 304, 311, 313
and fictionalization, 9–10
field
academic/of knowledge, 3–7, 11–13, 18–20, 25n1, 27, 31,
38, 39, 72, 77, 89, 124, 127, 134, 136, 137, 140–143,
165–167, 174–177, 195, 213–214, 217, 218, 230,
258–259, 264, 288, 299–301, 303, 307
agricultural/geomorphic, 48, 50, 186n63, 234
expanded, 21
of observation, 141, 297
See also dance studies; discipline and disciplines;
performance studies; translatio
fieldwork, 21, 69, 105, 141, 161, 165–167, 171–172, 195,
227–229, 259, 307, 310
flagellants, 48, 50–52, 79, 291
flux, 16, 124, 299
footnotes, 26, 27, 39, 54, 91, 177–181. *See also* Babington, B. G.

foreigners/foreignness, 9–11, 37–38, 47–48, 52, 55–56, 60,
77, 107, 140, 171, 173, 177, 179, 183, 186, 195, 205,
259, 262, 270, 273–274, 281–282
and anti-foreignness, 207, 207n48, 211–213, 259
formlessness, 14, 36, 198, 209–210, 219, 295
Foster, Susan Leigh, 2–3, 13–14, 14n34, 15–16, 18n46, 42, 90,
204, 301n9. *See also* choreography
Foucault, Michel
and the 'abnormal', 5–6, 52, 64, 90, 105
and archaeology, 28, 39, 65, 177, 298
and 'author function', 26
and biohistory, 42
and biopower, 113, 116, 122, 298
and circulation, 227
and colonialism, 250–251, 251n128
and convulsions, 90, 94
and *déraison*, 41, 43n6, 43–44, 105
and discourse, 1, 1n1, 41–42, 44–45, 65–66, 113, 119, 141,
194, 200, 298–299
and 'docile bodies', 115
and ethnography, 167
and genealogy, xiv, 1–2, 11, 28, 41, 66
and governmentality, 6n8, 28, 113, 119, 121–122, 194,
211, 230
and heterotopia, 173
and the history of madness, 6n8, 41–46, 47n23, 52, 59,
64–66, 69, 92, 105–106, 141, 173, 200, 298
and institutions, 39, 41–42, 44, 116, 131, 299
and the Iranian revolution, 6n8, 112–113
and language, 41, 65, 65n111, 298, 300–301
and leprosy (plague), 51–52
and liberalism, 113n4, 119, 123
and 'man', 131, 298–299
and the 'Orient', 41
and religion, 95n18
and Tarde, 124n58
and topology, 2
and *véridiction* (veridiction), 27, 34, 228
and *vérité* (truth), 27, 34, 105n55
See also abstraction; aesthetics; biohistory; biopower;
Brown, Wendy; Canguilhem, Georges; concept; Franko,
Mark; genealogy; Jordan, Mark D.; Nietzsche, Friedrich;
'order of things'; police; Said, Edward W.; scene
Franko, Mark, 12–13, 13–14n34, 55n69, 65, 65n114, 197,
200, 209, 210, 210n66, 211, 218
Freeman, Elizabeth, and 'temporal drag', 141
French Revolution, 92, 104, 106, 108, 115–116, 122n51. *See
also* revolution
Freud, Sigmund, 19, 36
and crowds, 114, 121–122
and hysteria, 8, 100, 158, 287, 303
and primitivism, 44, 105, 161, 273, 274, 288
and *Totem and Taboo*, 267, 288
See also 'dark continent'
future anterior, 208, 213

gait, 207n51, 208, 217n89, 218, 285, 308
Gardel, Pierre, 104
genealogy, 1n1, 2–3, 6, 7, 10, 11–12, 15, 18–22, 28, 34, 36,
39–40, 42, 71, 80, 84, 87, 105, 114, 163, 165–167,
171–172, 199, 218, 220, 222, 224–226, 228, 230, 249,
250, 255, 258, 268, 269–270, 294, 300, 306
and ancestry, 212, 232, 260
metaphor of family, 89
and Nietzsche, 66–68
performance, 163–164n75, 233
See also Foucault, Michel

gender, 5n7, 49, 106, 160–161n68, 294–295n103. *See also* femininity; queerness; 'too muchness'
geo-choreopolitics, 22, 39, 209–210
geognosy. *See* mental geognosy
geography, 3–4, 20, 25, 135n115, 166–167, 179–180, 183, 186–187, 193, 199, 204–205n34, 209–210, 214, 222, 231, 255, 258, 267, 282, 304
　and expansion, 30
　and leisure, 179
　medical, 174–176, 176n15, 193
　See also geo-choreopolitics; translation
geopolitics. *See* politics
germs/germ theory, 30, 35, 137. *See also* contagion
gesture, 5–9, 29, 33–35, 69, 167, 190, 207n51, 222, 242, 306–309, 314
　and amplification, 44, 46
　and blackness, 21, 273n14, 274, 276–277, 287
　and choreography, 3, 17–18, 110–111, 114, 283, 296, 300
　and dance, 307–309, 308n30
　discursive, 39, 249
　and exaggeration and excess, 15–16, 20, 60, 60–61n96, 90–95, 104–105, 160, 189, 208, 256–257
　and gesturelessness, 219, 293
　and historicity, 145, 150–152, 156, 158–159, 160–161, 171, 187, 287
　and hysteroepilepsy, 139–146, 149–153, 156–163
　and imitation and contagion, 18–19, 21, 110–111, 116–117, 120, 126–129, 132–136
　and intelligibility/intelligibilization, 3, 8, 89, 103, 149–150, 153, 157–158, 160, 219, 261–265, 308–309
　irregular, 5, 14, 71, 86, 87, 119, 175
　and language, 262, 268
　and political resistance, 196–197, 211, 231, 259
　pure, 307
　'purposeless', and chorea, 20, 70–72, 77, 159, 307–308
　and theatricality, 98, 100–101, 114, 126–129, 140–141, 153, 156–157, 158–159, 187, 211, 252
　and writing, 17–18
　See also Agamben, Giorgio; torque
gesture of abstraction, 13–14, 36, 44–45, 65, 75, 161, 216, 229, 300–301, 305
ghosts, 61–62n99, 75, 204, 207, 262, 281, 306, 311
　and ghostliness, 313
　and Holy Ghost, 130
　and *revenants* 306
　See also ancestors; Ghost Dance; spirit
Ghost Dance, 12, 222–223, 224–250, 242, 243
　and 'waste', 12, 107, 223, 225, 226, 231, 243–244, 246–247, 249
ghosting (discursive), 197, 209, 213, 255–256, 304, 310–311
　performative, and politics, 216, 219, 222, 281, 310
gift, 205n36, 206n43, 239
　and 'gift of seeing resemblances', 254
Gilroy, Paul, 10, 20, 72, 167, 174, 209, 210, 272, 274–275
Giselle, 79n41, 107
Glissant, Édouard, 282, 282n46
globalism/globality, 14, 45, 177, 179, 188, 196, 216–218, 269, 280, 282, 288, 303
　and modernity, 3, 172–173, 181, 210
Goethe, Johann Wolfgang von, 62, 181, 200. *See also* comparativism
'going places', 210
Gordon, Rae Beth, 14–15, 134, 159–160, 276–277
government, 12, 94, 107, 116, 121–122, 123, 198, 204–205, 218, 220–221, 224–227, 230–249, 259, 299

archives, 193, 229
　and Orientalism, 172
　See also anthropology; Foucault, Michel
grace, 84n67, 110, 183, 184, 273, 274, 280, 284, 290
　and Irene and Vernon Castle, 284–286
　divine, 57
　savage, 9, 282
　and torque, 91, 114
Graham, Martha, 287
grave/gravesite, 83, 89, 94, 94n14, 161n69, 206n43, 208, 235, 235n46, 250. *See also* dead
Greece, 309
　ancient, 19, 33–34, 37, 42, 66–68, 72n3, 82n54, 116, 121, 143, 161, 176, 178n28, 183n50, 183–184, 267, 274, 282, 285, 288, 296, 299
　compared with Africa, 182, 277
　See also Africa; bacchanals (Dionysian); maenad; Orientalism
'group mind', 121
Guattari, Félix, 17
　and Deleuze, 4, 18, 124
　See also ecosophy

Hacking, Ian, 6, 43n6, 65, 143–144, 229
hallucination, 31, 47, 53, 76, 81, 88, 108n69, 109, 131, 139, 156–157, 160, 197, 200, 204n29, 210, 223, 275
Hamilton, Lady Emma, 184, *185*
Harlem shake, 301
haunting, 48, 60n95, 222, 306, 307
　and colonialism, 172, 199, 259
　and modernity, 9, 13, 15, 30, 171, 172, 197–198, 253, 273, 302, 304, 306, 311
　See also ghosts
hauntology, 306
health, 67, 176n15, 208, 263
　appearance of, childlike, 253
　concepts of, changing, 109, 144, 208, 292
　dancing (and 'ceremonies') good for, 263, 273, 275, 280, 284–290, 305
　debates on 'new' dances and, 290
　displayed, in dancing procession, 312–313
　individual mental, in crowd, 120
　poor, caused by dancing, 242, 242–243n84
　poor, prevented by dancing, 61, 64
　poor, restored by dancing, 82–83
　public, administration, 31, 35, 175
　recovery of, and miracles, 94
　sexual, 138, 273, 287
　and work, balanced (by dancing), 263–264, 293
　See also cure
Hebrew, 74n10, 266. *See also* Jews
Hecker, J. F. C., 8, 19–20, 25–40, 42–44, 47–48, 55–56, 61–62, 66, 68, 95–96, 115–116, 125n62, 132–133, 133n110, 142, 145–146, 153, 166, 175, 181n42, 187–188, 196, 200–202, 220, 222, 224, 227, 255
　and 'The Dancing Mania' (*Die Tanzwuth*), 8, 25, 28, 28n6, 38, 42, 55–56, 96, 145, 166, 175, 187, 227
　See also Babington, B. G.
Herder, Johann Gottfried von, 69, 166
heterotopia. *See* Foucault, Michel
Hewitt, Andrew, 17, 112, 117, 118–119, 125, 159, 246–247, 307–308
Hirsh, August, 28n6, 133–134, 136, 175–176, 187
history, 1–21, 25–27, 32, 60, 66, 71, 107–108, 112–116, 124, 141, 153, 161, 165–167, 173, 181, 196, 220–221, 231–232, 250, 253, 255, 266, 303–308, 310–311, 314

intelligibility, 3, 209, 239, 248, 262, 309
   and hysteria, 8
   and imitation, 125, 263
   and modernity, 9, 275
   social, of gesture, 8
   and unintelligibility, 5, 65, 172, 189, 203, 265, 268, 275
Iranian revolution. *See* Foucault, Michel
Islamic dance, 13
Islamic 'Orient', 116
Italian (language), 28, 73, 266
Italy, 49, 105, 116, 118, 120, 297
   and Africa, 182, 186–188, 193
   and ancient Greece, 183–184
   early modern, and dancing, 50n48, 109
   and 'Italian India', 182
   southern vs. northern, 174, 182–183
   See also tarantella, Italian

Jamaica, 256–258
jazz, 275, 276, 290, 294, 295, 302n12
Jeffreys, M. D. W., 192–194
'Jerks', 126–131, 136n122
'jerky craze' (in dance), 280, 280n35, 285
Jesus, 145, 209, 238, 239, 257, 258, 261
   and Black Jesus, 256
Jetztzeit. See 'now-time' (*Jetztzeit*)
Jews, 42, 50, 57, 119, 227, 228, 240–241, 258, 273, 273n14
   and Dreyfus affair, 123
   and Jewish dance, 53, 54, 60, 74, 227, 249
   See also Hebrew
jitterbug (dance), 293–294
Jordan, Mark D., 69, 94
Jordanova, Ludmilla, 139n1
journalism, 5, 204–205n34, 220, 241n83, 294n103, 312. *See also* hyperbole; media
jumping, 34, 56, 60n95, 77n30, 102, 164, 175, 189, 191, 218n91, 285
   and Charcot, 157, 158–159n62
   and Jumpers, 33, 134–135, 135–136n119
   and Leaping (or Dancing) Procession at Echternach, 87, 164
St. John's Day, 147, 149, 149n39

Kabbala, 75
Kant, Immanuel
   and 'purposiveness without purpose', 159, 307
   and sublime enthusiasm, 92–94
   See also aesthetics
Khanna, Ranjana, 172, 190, 191, 274, 299
Kierkegaard, Søren, 45
kinaesthetics, 7–8, 13, 17–18, 76, 134, 162, 215–216, 301n9, 304, 305–306, 309, 311
kinesis, 8, 16, 17, 45, 47, 72, 75, 77–78, 81, 94, 107, 109, 126, 127, 131, 135, 156, 217, 233, 304, 307
   and alterkinetics, 71, 175, 273, 277, 311
   and dyskinesia, 302
   and hyperkinesis, 10, 52, 70, 72, 303
knowledge, 1n1, 4–6, 8–9n20, 12, 27, 37, 39, 72, 140, 143–144, 179, 183–185, 193–194, 208, 217, 229, 241, 266–267, 298–299, 311
   and disciplinarization and institutions, 39, 42, 193–194, 299
   feminine, 184–185
   local, 127, 193–194, 229, 230–232
   medical, 37, 39, 85, 108, 143–144, 158, 175–176, 179, 214, 221
   and modernity, 9–10, 172
   and movement, 44–45, 298

and Orientalism, 25, 172, 184–185
   See also comparativism; discourse; epistemology; Foucault, Michel; genealogy; institutions; method; translatio
Kolbig (or Kölbigk) (dances), 61–62, 61–62n99, *63*, 88
Kuhn, Thomas, 39–40, 42

laboratory, 35. *See also* clinic/clinicalism
labour, 119, 205n35, 231n21, 283
   and labourers, 55, 79, 110, 128
   and labouring actions, 139, 159
   and 'labour machine', 263, 264
   and labour pains, 69
   and productivity, 20, 107, 126, 133–134, 225, 227, 244, 245
   See also worker
La dansomanie, 104, 106, 108–109
La fandangomanie, 106–107, 108–109
'lag'. *See* time: and *time-lag* (or temporal lag)
Lancet, 38, 88n86, 302n12
land, 198, 200, 205, 208, 212–213, 220, 224, 226, 230, 232, 234, 238n63, 244, 252–253, 264–265, 266–267, 305
Langlois, Eustache-Hyacinthe, 45n16, 53–54, 61n99
language, 1, 3, 4, 6–7, 8–9n20, 9, 11, 13–14, 16, 22, 29–30n15, 30, 35, 56, 71, 91, 100, 104, 114n6, 115–116, 125, 150, 157, 163–164n75, 171, 193, 195, 196, 207, 213–214, 214n81, 219, 224, 229, 258, 264, 270, 272, 283n59, 286–287, 294, 294–295n103, 298, 300n7, 301, 302, 306, 308
   English, foreign, and translation, 28, 28n6, 37, 93, 175, 250, 260, 262, 265, 268
   and gesture, 77, 139, 262, 268
   and social body, 123
   and style, 48, 61–62n99, 109, 121, 186, 228, 280, 284
   and Tourette's syndrome, 311
   See also Foucault, Michel
Lanternari, Vittorio, 240n78, 256n13, 259, 266, 269
La Tarentule, 183–184
laughter, 90, 101, 104, 120, 134, 135, 162, 191, 206, 236, 250, 253, 273n14, 307, 309
   and laughing epidemic, 302n12
   and laughing veins, 76
   See also comedy
law, 22, 29–30n15, 64, 204, 205n35, 304
   and lawlessness, and outlaws, 52, 133, 219n94, 220, 230–231, 283
   against public revelry, 50n48, 60–61, 64, 79, 94, 101, 109, 305
   rule of (in state politics), 197–198, 208, 266
   and witchcraft, 73n7
   See also anomie; psycholegal discourse; state of exception
laziness. *See* idleness
leaping, 47, 50, 53–56, 56n75, 58, 61–63, 63n106, 74, 85, 102–103, 111, 130–131, 149–150, 177–178, 189, 257, 283n59
   chorea (*chorée saltatoire*), 157–158, 158–159n62, 162
   procession, 161–165, 310–314
Le Bon, Gustave, 118, 120–121, 217
Lefebvre, Henri, 9, 303
Leibniz, Gottfried Wilhelm, 124
Leiris, Michel, 271, 276, 295
leisure, 107, 179, 226, 244, 290–291, 309–310, 312
Lepecki, André, 8–9n20, 10, 15–16, 118, 140, 204, 281
leprosy. *See* plague
Levinson, André, 273, 277
Lévi-Strauss, Claude, 271
liberalism. *See* Foucault, Michel
liberation, 110, 211–212, 250, 254, 269–270

Middle Ages, European, 31, 47–64, 73
  and body politic, 126n66
  and Christianity, 59–63
  and epidemics, 28n6, 38, 42
  fantasy of bacchanalian, 27, 40, 45, 66–69, 306
  and feeling of modernity, 60
  figure of, in modern science, 87, 96, 145, 160, 161–162, 164, 220n97
  'hysteria' in the, 302n12
  imagined to recur in colonies, 171, 180, 187–188, 202, 213
  and Jews, 57n79
  'madness' in the, 45–47, 52, 64–65
  and medicine, 60, 73
  modern dances compared with, 289, 291
  modern historiography and the imagination of the, 47, 52–55, 302n12, 311
  as paradigmatic era of dancing manias, 20, 33, 81, 84, 86, 89, 96, 172, 200, 222, 255, 259, 294–295n103, 301n10
  and performance culture, 52
  and tarantism, 82n54
  and torture spectacle, 94
  and 'tradition', 313
  See also Christianity; Foucault, Michel; Hecker, J. F. C.
Middleton, Charles Theodore, 179–180
Midelfort, H. C. Erik, 46n17, 80, 302n12
midsummer festivities, 61–62. See also St. John's Day dances
migration, 31, 62–63, 198–201, 297, 304
  of discourse, 26, 39, 167
  gestural, 13
military, 91, 135n114, 162, 166, 205n37, 219–221, 224, 227, 229–230, 232, 237n55, 241, 246, 248, 250, 266, 276, 300, 300n7, 305. See also police
mimesis, 204, 215, 254–255, 262–263, 267–268, 275
  and alterity, 176, 253–254, 257–258
  and animality, 82, 129–130
  automatic, 136–137
  and counter-mimesis, 226, 256, 258, 265, 268, 277–278
  and hysteroepilepsy, 149, 157–158
  and the 'mimetic faculty', 254
  psychic mimeticism, 134
  See also imitation; mimicry
mimicry, 11, 33, 67, 100, 134, 183–184, 187–188, 191, 203, 270, 272, 276, 283, 300, 301, 301n9
  colonial, 176n21, 253, 256, 311
  counter-mimicry, 221, 264–265, 282, 286
  and hysteroepilepsy, 152, 156–157
  and 'mimic' imitation, 125–126
  and pantomime, 136, 294, 311
  See also imitation; mimesis
miracles, 73, 93–95, 97–101, 103, 149, 154, 162, 180, 239, 256n13, 261–262, 311–312
mise en scène, 27, 152–154, 156–157, 160–161, 180
missionary, 182, 182n45, 202, 204–208, 208–209n56, 245–246, 256–258, 266–268
  Christianity, and fanaticism, 92
  physician, 196, 201, 203n24, 214
  See also London Missionary Society
'mnemonic reserves', 163, 163–164n75, 233, 250, 270
mobility, 4, 8, 18, 45, 103, 117–118, 120, 174, 181, 280, 282n46, 305–307, 309
  and automobiles, 289, 296
  and immobility, 120n38
  and 'mobiles', 117
  and social class, 110
mobility studies, 3, 17
mobilization, 2, 10n25, 12–13, 17, 90, 118, 123, 198, 200, 208–209, 222, 227, 231, 237, 241, 296

modernity, 2–4, 7–8, 18–19, 25–27, 31, 38, 44, 65, 69–70, 96, 113–114, 165, 171–174, 187, 208–210, 225–226, 232, 282, 285–286, 288, 291, 294–297
  and blackness, 272–276
  defined, 9–11, 255, 302–304, 306, 308, 311
  and hysteria and neurology, 15, 140, 159–160
  'medieval', 47, 53, 60
  and premodernity, 66, 150, 174, 226
  and the social body, 118–119, 122, 134
monadology, 124
monarch. See sovereign (monarch)
money, 30, 59n91, 193, 239n70, 245–246, 295
monomania. See psychiatry: and monomania
monstrosity
  and alterity, 252–254, 271, 272, 282
  revolution as an expression of, 115, 117
  science of, 166n89
Montgeron, Carré de, 96, 103
morality (and immorality), 5, 30, 53–54, 57, 62, 66, 80, 106–107, 179, 202, 206n43, 225, 239n70, 245, 255, 269, 273, 277, 287, 290–291
  and demoralization, 132, 242–243, 246, 249
  and moral contagion ('moral mania'), 120, 122, 202, 294–295n103
  and moral discipline, as remedy, 131
  and moral effects, of theatre and dance, 91, 280, 284, 287
  and moral impression, 86
  and 'moral physiognomy', 116
Morley, Henry, 31
Mormons, 240–241, 240n78
Moten, Fred, 300n7
Mouvet, Maurice, 279–280, 282–283
movement, xiv, 2–22, 25–27, 29–30n15, 29–30, 32, 34, 42, 44–45, 47, 53–55, 55n69, 60, 68, 72–73, 77, 78–79, 87, 89, 159, 161, 163, 163–164n75, 165–166, 173–175, 177, 195, 198–201, 204, 209–210, 218, 228, 229–232, 296, 298–300, 304–309, 308n30, 314
  and archival repertoire, 140–141, 150–151, 153
  choreic/dyskinetic, 69, 70–71, 74n9, 80–81, 85–86, 136, 136n122, 156–160, 311
  figurative, 100, 104
  and genealogy, 65n111, 66
  of the imagination, and limbs, 75–76
  and migration, 62–63, 167
  recovery of, 94
  slow and heavy, as cure, 73–74
  and social/public bodies, 110–111, 112–121, 123–133
  and transmission, 82, 109, 137
  See also contrapuntal; déplacement; mobilization; translatio
movement disorder, 4, 17, 70, 86–87, 142–143, 149, 164–165, 175, 195, 199–200, 214, 221, 300, 302, 311–313
Muecke, Stephen, 19, 198, 204, 214n81, 305
music, 11, 30, 33–34, 49–50, 79, 81–84, 109, 147, 147–148n30, 150, 158–159n62, 162, 164, 174, 182n45, 182–183, 186n63, 187–192, 202–203, 203n24, 208, 214–215n84, 215n85, 215–216, 277, 285n71, 286, 294–296, 302n12, 304. See also song/singing
Muybridge, Eadweard, 29

nakedness. See nudity
nation, 9–10, 14–15, 26, 29–30n15, 31, 93, 112, 113n4, 115–116, 119, 123, 137–138, 194, 196–198, 201, 210n66, 213–214, 217–221, 234, 250, 272n7, 282n46, 297, 299, 309–310, 312
  and anthropology, 258, 264
  and capitals/capitalization, 201, 221, 230–231

performance (*cont.*)

of crowds and aggregate bodies, 113–115, 119, 138, 221–222, 304, 304n20, 309

and doubling/transfiguration and indigeneity, 252–253, 258–259, 262–266, 268, 270, 272

and everyday life, 300, 303

and gender, 35, 91

and history/historicity and archival repertoire, 8, 11–13, 34, 97, 140–141, 145–156, 163, 182–183, 184, 187–188, 259, 274, 275, 310–314

and hysteria and hysteroepilepsy, 84n67, 97, 100, 139–141, 145–159

and labour and efficiency, 107, 122, 244, 290–293, 303, 307

and 'mad dog', 178n28

and memory, 212–213, 232–233, 250

and mockery, 56n72, 103, 106, 134, 135n114, 253

and nationalistic 'madness', 104–107

and Orientalism, 184–186, 187

pantomimic, 206

and peregrination, 117

of political resistance and protest, 16, 191–192, 196–199, 206–207, 209–210, 210n65, 211–213, 218–219, 221–222, 239, 242–243, 259

popular and religious, 50–54, 63, 67, 73–74, 79, 86, 90–92, 94–103, 110, 130–131, 162, 180–181, 186n63, 188–191, 192–193, 202–204, 276, 281, 290–293

and possession practices, 19, 207–209, 211–213, 215–217, 257

and race, 35, 256, 272, 274, 275–277

stage, 14–15, 104, 106–107, 184, 186–187, 275, 276–277, 283

See also reperformance

performance studies, 1, 3, 7, 12–13, 14, 17, 18n46, 72, 114, 134, 174, 259, 299

periphery, 9–10, 46, 52, 58, 63, 91, 167, 196, 203, 210, 222, 254–255

Petri de Herentals (Petrus de Herental), 50, 55–56

photograph, 4, 146, 292, 308n30

pilgrimage, 48, 50–51, 51n53, 62–63, 78, 145–150, 147, 161n69, 162, 164–165, 310–311. *See also* child pilgrimages

Pinel, Philippe, 38, 108, 125n62

plague, 17, 27, 54, 81

caused by dancing and loose morals, 55, 57

convulsive movements deriving from, 54

and dances as 'plague-like', 74

and 'dancing plague', 4, 31, 42, 51, 56–57, 78, 301n10, 302n12

histories of, 31–33

'of insurrection', 48

language of, 109, 116, 119, 126, 211

and leprosy, 51–52, 146

and persecution of Jews, 57n79

and 'plague dances' (*Pesttänze*), 50

and 'post-plague dances', 53, 63

See also Black Death (bubonic plague)

Plato, 46, 109, 140, 299, 305. *See also* bacchanals (Dionysian)

plot, 27, 35, 102, 104. *See also* narrative

poetry, 34–35, 305

and ethnographic emotion, 271

and hysteria as 'greatest poetic discovery', 15, 160

and neurology and poesis, 161

and relational poetics, 282, 282n46

poison, 80–83, 86, 180–181, 183, 192, 208

'social', 122

and *spiritus vitae*, 76

symbolic, 186

See also ergotism (rye poisoning)

police, 22, 101n38, 108, 110, 162, 202, 229, 235n46, 247–248, 250, 310, 312

Foucault and, state, 39, 105

See also choreography; military

politics, 7, 9, 12–13, 15–17, 19–22, 29–30n15, 29–31, 34, 36, 39, 71–72, 74–76, 90–96, 105–106, 110–111, 112–126, 131, 137–138, 174, 188, 191, 196–223, 224–226, 229–230, 241, 249–250, 253, 258–261, 264–267, 268n67, 269–270, 271–272, 290, 300, 303–312

and biopolitics, xiii, 19, 33, 35, 52, 65, 113, 116, 119, 122, 124, 194, 198, 204, 209, 226–227, 230–231, 247, 298, 304

border, 5, 297

and geopolitics, and geography, 3, 105, 180, 198, 200, 298

See also aesthetics (and politics); body politic; choreopolitics; ecstasy-belonging; occupation (of space); protest; state of exception

polka, 280, 280n35

Poovey, Mary, 126. *See also* social body

Posnett, Hutcheson Macaulay, 176

possession, 19, 53, 54–55, 60, 60n94, 73, 75, 79n41, 80, 84n67, 86, 94–95, 95n17, 99, 128–131, 142–143, 145–146, 180, 197, 199–200, 202, 204n29, 207–209, 211–214, 214–215n84, 222, 258, 270, 272, 276–277, 294–295, 301n11, 305–306

and dispossession, 84n67, 106, 209

of land, 213

and repossession, 174, 197, 210, 226

See also ecstasy-belonging

poverty/poor, 36, 51, 55, 78, 126, 126n66, 173, 216, 218–219, 243, 246, 291. *See also* class; money

Pratt, Mary Louise, 52, 165, 252. *See also* 'contact zone'

pre-enactment, 149, 211

Presley, Elvis, 294

primitivism, 7, 9, 15, 19, 42, 44, 68, 105, 131, 132n101, 134–135, 137, 194, 220, 225–226, 243, 251, 259, 263–265, 267, 268–270, 271–274, 276–277, 282, 284, 284n63, 287–288, 294–296, 303–306, 309

and crowds, 120–121

and discourse on madness, 65, 65n111

and hysteria, 185

and the mimetic faculty, 254

and Orientalism, 5, 11, 41, 186–187

See also aesthetics; ancestors; discourse; Freud, Sigmund

procession. *See* dancing procession

productivism, 126, 133, 134. *See also* Rabinbach, Anson; 'unproductive expenditure'

progress, 11, 28–31, 36, 42, 60, 71, 72n3, 96, 113, 116, 118, 176, 202, 216, 220–221, 226, 244–246, 248, 255, 269, 272, 276, 286, 300–301, 306, 311

and 'progressive' politics, 76, 124, 258

promiscuousness, 248

property, 244–245, 248

prophet, 74, 93, 100, 240n74, 269–270

protest, 21–22, 114–115, 198, 200, 209, 212, 215–218, 235, 250, 270

choreographies of, 15–16, 90, 114, 204, 212, 232, 237

Proudhon, Pierre-Joseph, 29–30, 29–30n15

psychiatry, 89, 90–93, 145n20

and chorea, 86–87

comparative, 175

early theories, and dancing, 53, 77, 84–85

epidemic, 218

and Foucault, 65, 105n55

and hospitals, 22, 67, 191, 273

and monomania, 45–46, 104–110

transcultural , 192–193n95, 301
  See also colonial melancholy; enthusiasm; Foucault, Michel
psychoanalysis, 121, 160–161n68, 194
  and colonialism, 172, 191, 270, 274
  and neurology, 161
  See also 'dark continent'; Freud, Sigmund; Khanna, Ranjana
psycholegal discourse, 217–219
psychopathy (psychopathology), 87, 117, 126, 277
  messianic, 217–220
  and modern social dancing, 288–291
public, 48, 96, 101–102, 123–124, 137, 159, 241, 285
  and 'general public' (readership), 28–29, 180
  and public 'joy', 91
  and public opinion, 102, 137, 202, 305
public health, 30–31, 175, 309
public security, 122, 230
public space, 2, 14–15, 22, [45], 51–52, 63, 71, 78, 90–92, 104–107, 110, 112–117, 179–180, 183, 213, 221–222, 293, 297, 300, 304–305, 309–310, 312–313
  and gender, 6, 90–91, 119, 133, 160, 190–191
  and race, 119
  See also space
publishing houses, 26, 37–38, 37n52, 175n11

queerness
  and gesture, 6
  and nationalism and religion, 92, 114
  and the social body, 119, 125
  and temporality, 250
  See also 'too muchness'
querelle des anciens et modernes, 304

Rabinbach, Anson, 126, 134–136
race, 5n7, 9, 15, 21, 119, 141, 166, 175, 210, 220, 228, 256, 267, 272, 272n7, 273n14, 274–278, 281–282, 285–287, 290, 294, 311. *See also* aesthetics; blackness; whiteness
Radulphus de Rivo, 57
ragtime, 274n16, 276, 280, 286
ramanenjana. See *imanenjana*
Rancière, Jacques, 110, 304n20, 305–306
rave, 22, 296
reading, 5, 13, 13–14n34, 16–17, 39, 59–60, 65, 95n17, 118, 140, 143–144, 149–150, 153, 160, 166, 174, 177, 179, 215–216, 253, 264–265, 273. *See also* choreography; writing
red (colour), 56, 202, 204n29. *See also* shoes
Red Shoes, The, 79n41, 107
re-enactment, 8–9n20, 141, 145–146, 167, 250, 277, 299. See also *pre*-enactment
Regnard, Paul, 96, 97n27, 99, 101n36, 143, 152, 155
rehearsal, 7, 13, 35, 103, 107, 163–164n75, 211–212, 218, 250, 253, 281–282, 303, 310–311, 313–314
Reich, Wilhelm, 137–138
religion, 69, 207–208, 232, 256–261, 263–269, 301, 311–312
  and antiquity, 183, 186
  and comparativism, 176, 227–228, 249, 263
  contested, in Ghost Dance, 236, 239, 246
  and ecstatic enthusiasm, 33–34, 91–92, 119, 126–138, 142–143, 162, 178–179, 180–181, 224, 273n14
  European, banned, 205n35
  and iconography, 146, 150–151, 157, 256
  and medical theory, 71, 73–75
  and medieval dances, 47–48, 51, 55–64, 79, 81, 111
  and political upheaval, 201
  and religiosity, in modern social dance, 276, 280, 284n63, 288

and 'religious delirium', 108–109, 108–109n69, 217n90, 219–221
  and puritanism, 194, 225
  and theatricality, 89, 90–92, 96, 100–104, 152–153
  See also Christianity; clergy; Convulsionaries of Saint-Médard; institutions; spirituality/spiritualism
reperformance, 8–9n20, 139–140, 152, 157, 172–174, 181, 183, 250, 253, 268, 299, 310, 314
repertoire, 7, 50, 163. *See also* archival repertoire
repossession. See possession
representation, 45n16, 99–100, 101, 105, 107, 118–119, 123, 140–141, 149–150, 153, 159, 167, 173, 183–184, 194, 197–198, 206–207, 211–213, 216, 218–219, 226, 232, 239, 254–256, 268, 272, 302, 307–308
  closure of, 89, 274
residue, 3, 16, 163–164n75, 165, 167, 246
restlessness, 10, 17, 58, 84–85, 111, 134, 157, 178n27, 196, 203, 253, 280, 303
  and rest, 306
revenants. See ghosts
revolution, 6n8, 15, 31, 46, 102–104, 110, 112–113, 115–116, 118, 137, 180, 195, 251, 254, 265n52, 295
  anti-colonial, romanticized, 268, 270, 271
  in Brazil, 222
  French (1789), 92, 96, 104, 106, 108, 115–116, 122n51, 161, 171, 258n23
  industrial, 30, 133, 135
  July revolution of 1830, 16, 110
  in Madagascar, 198, 201, 204–205n34, 206, 217
  Native American, 233
  Paris Commune (1871), 115–117
  and revolutions of 1848, 105, 110, 115
  and rupture with the past, 303
  tango as, 280n35
rhizome, 2–3, 10, 25, 39, 75–76, 165, 173, 210, 224
rhythm, 7, 69, 74, 77, 109, 118, 145n21, 189, 199, 202, 215, 214–215n84, 215n85, 266, 273, 275–280, 285, 294–296, 299, 307, 311
  and 'rhythmic hysteric chorea', 158, 158–159n62
Richer, Paul, 95–96, 98–99, 142–143, 145–150, 154, 160
ritual, 8–9n20, 18n46, 52, 57–58, 99, 129, 182–184, 186n63, 187, 211–213, 216–217, 263, 265, 287–288, 299–300, 301n10
Roach, Joseph, 14, 30, 35, 36, 187, 210, 210n64, 212, 233. *See also* 'mnemonic reserves'; surrogation
Robertson, Felix, 85, 127–129, 131, 132, 179
rock 'n' roll, 294–295
rolling, 96
  and rolling exercise, 130
  and rolling eyes, 98, 129
Roma (Gypsy), 57. *See also* Bohemia
roots, 42, 65n111, 74–76, 86, 100, 108, 173, 269, 280, 285
  and rootlessness, in modernity, 9, 173, 231, 290, 308
  and routes, 20, 197, 210
Rousseau, Jean-Jacques, 91–92, 117, 220, 304
routes, 5, 165, 304. *See also* roots
rumour, 19, 39, 89, 203, 206n43, 227, 231, 241, 245, 305
running, 52, 83, 130, 157, 177–178, 190, 236, 257–258, 296
Russia, 274, 280

sacred sites, 61–62n99, 62, 149, 203, 210n66, 212, 215n85
Sacre du printemps (Le), 280
sacrifice, 224, 232, 249, 293
Said, Edward W., 1, 4–7, 11, 25, 25n1, 32–33, 112–113, 171–176, 185–186. *See also* Orientalism
satanism, 10, 53, 55, 82, 142, 257, 283, 283n59. *See also* witchcraft

and healing, 237
and illness (*Geisteskranke*), 175
and spiritual movements, 241
and spiritual power, 233
and rapture or ecstasy, 19, 33–34, 128, 143
and redemption, communal, 217, 217n90, 219–220
spiritus vitae. See vital spirits (or *spiritus vitae*)
spontaneity, 5, 11, 13, 46, 66, 71, 84, 126, 128–129, 131, 161, 188, 257, 270, 287, 293–294, 302, 306–308
appearance of, 131, 192, 263
and *attitudes*, hysteroepileptic, 152, 161–162
compared with structured choreography, 16, 110, 274, 284
dangerous and animalistic, in crowds, 120–123
and gestural imitation, 33, 36, 133, 252
and 'mental contagion', 137
and 'natural' village dancing, 91–92, 220
and radical politics, 90, 103–104, 110, 112–113, 137
among *ramanenjana*, 202, 215
sport, 8–9n20, 238n63, 275, 300
and fitness club, 296
and sportiness, of Americans, 35
square dance, 283n59
startle disorder, 134–136, 135n114, 135–136n119
starvation. *See* hunger
state of exception, 196–198, 207–208, 210, 226, 232–233, 239, 250, 309
Steedman, Carolyn, 229
stiffness, 95, 198–199, 202, 214–215n84, 289
'stillness', 141
Stimson, Blake, 13, 305. *See also* gesture of abstraction
St. John's Day dances, 39, 43n5, 53, 54n66, 55–62, 73, 78, 85, 149n33, 149–150n35, 153–154
and Friedrich Nietzsche, 66–68
See also St. Vitus's dance
St. John's Day fire, 75
Stoler, Ann Laura, 229–230
Stowe, Harriet Beecher, 273, 273n14
Strasbourg dancing mania, 51, 77–80
stress, 135, 153, 186n63, 208, 233, 267, 287, 302
St. Vitus (patron saint), 72–73, 78, 162
St. Vitus's dance, 15
compared with witches' sabbath, 74
description of, as popular fête, 54, 54n66, 61, 178n27
to designate 'epidemic', 127, 127n69, 133
to designate individual movement disorder (often chorea), 74n9, 136, 183
familiarity of the name and narratives, 28n9, 107
imagery of, 146–151, *147, 148, 151*
medical description of, with Paracelsus, 10, 71–72, 74–77, 84
medical description of, various, early modern, 80–81
medical terminology ambiguous regarding, 4, 84–89, 133n110, 160
as paradigmatic of the 'dancing mania', 20, 26, 173, 177
and Strasbourg 'mania', 78–80
and translatio, from St. John to, 73
uncertainty as to nature or cause of, 301–302, 301n10, 302n12
used in analogy with other 'dances', 12, 95, 97n27, 143, 175, 178, 188, 199, 203, 211, 214, 220, 227–228, 261, 272, 288, 296
See also chorea; 'Jerks'; St. John's Day dances; Strasbourg dancing mania
style. *See* language
sublime enthusiasm. *See* enthusiasm
suggestion, 120, 137, 215
suicide, 108, 309. *See also* anomie

superstition, 288, 311
choreomaniacs as prone to, 47, 77, 86, 96, 177–178, 187–189, 202, 216, 301
monomanias and, 108
religious, opposed to experimental method, 10, 75
surrogation, 72, 172–173, 181, 212
sweating, 81–82, 179, 214–215n84, 244, 303
Sydenham, Thomas, 84–85, 87–89, 136, 158
Sydenham's chorea, 86. *See also* chorea; St. Vitus's dance
Sydenham Society, 28, 28n6, 37–38, 201
and New Sydenham Society, 38, 38–39n65, 175n11
sympathy, 34, 44, 50, 74–75, 104, 106–111, 123, 125, 125n62, 127–128, 131, 132–134, 136–138, 201–202, 204, 207, 213, 214, 227–228, 246, 249, 254, 267. *See also* imitation

taboo, 19, 184, 205, 208–209, 288, 295. *See also* Freud, Sigmund
Taine, Hippolyte, 115–116, 118
tango, 22, 273–275, 278–285, 289–290
Tanzwut, 60n95, 61–62n99, 78–79n37, 87, 200
tarantella, Italian
'dances' compared with, 95, 109–110, 187–194
and music therapy, 84n67, 186n63
and *Notte della Taranta*, 182n45, 297
Orientalized, as living gateway to antiquity, 172–174, 182–187
and representations onstage, 183–184, 186–187
and stress, 186n63
theorised in early modern medicine, 82–84
women and others as faking, 83–84, 185, 192–193
Tarde, Gabriel, 118, 120n38, 123–125, 133n109, 136
Taussig, Michael
and disease, 19, 207–208, 212–213, 216, 228, 305
and distraction and tactility, 39
and the 'magic of the state', 197, 213
and mimesis, 252–254, 257
Taylor, Diana, 8, 8–9n20, 27. *See also* archives; repertoire; scene: and scenario
technology, 30, 36, 176, 227, 231, 232, 262, 264, 272–273, 296, 300, 308n30
of self, 208
telegraph, 30, 176, 227, 229–231
temporality. *See* time
territory, 105, 110, 158, 165, 185, 205, 230–232, 234, 246, 255, 267
and reterritorialization (and deterritorialization), 191, 268
and territoriality, 217
and 'territory of passage', 182
theatre, 90, 91–92, 173, 191–193, 219, 253, 277, 311
ceremonial, 216
colonial, 254–255, 258–259, 263–265
and Convulsionaries of Saint-Médard, 89, 94, 95n21, 96, 99–103, 153–154
as duplicity, 84, 91
and hysteroepilepsy, 143, 145–146, 151–154, 156, 159–161
and (inter-)disciplinarity, 17–18, 18n46, 36, 265
language of, 30, 35, 66
medieval, 59
of observation, 95n17, 131, 263, 271
and performance, 307
of return, and repetition, 140, 146, 156, 197–198, 250, 306, 310, 313–314
theories of, and acting, 14, 35–36
of war, 300
See also anti-theatricality; appearance; scene; theatricality

witchcraft
  associated with tarantellas, 82
  belief in, 77
  and black magic, accusations of, 75
  colonial, narratives of, 194
  delusions, 29
  experimental medicine disproving theories of, 10, 71–72, 76
  to explain neurological disorder, 215, 221–222
  histories of, associated with dancing manias, 177–178
  and Jewish dances, 53, 74
  as precursor to hysteroepilepsy, 142, 155
  trials, 73, 301n11
  and witches' sabbath, 50, 73–74
  See also satanism
Witkowski, Ludwig, 175
worker, 2, 6, 35, 110, 120, 133–135, 160–161n68, 231n21, 244, 277, 283–284, 304
world literature, 34, 181
Worsley, Peter, 258–260, 264, 269
Worthen, William B., 8n20

writing, 2–3, 9, 11–12, 13, 18, 20, 30, 31, 35, 39, 54, 65–66, 119, 165, 172, 182, 207, 209, 255, 267, 298, 307, 310
  and handwriting, 8
  and scenes of writing, 304–306
  See also choreography

Yandell, David W., 128–131
youth, 109, 275, 276, 285–287, 294

Zarathustra, 307
zigzag, 4, 10, 141, 165, 172
  and gesture, 158–159n62
Žižek, Slavoj, 105–106, 221
zoanthropy, 178, 178n28
  and lycanthropy, 81, 178n28, 188
Zola, Émile, 123
zone of intensity, 2, 27, 30, 39, 46, 54, 63–65, 91, 110, 176–177, 200, 209, 225, 233, 249–250, 265, 307. *See also* choreozone